# THE ULTIMATE

# COSORI

# AIR FRYER

# COOKBOOK

# 1001

Vibrant, Fast and Easy Recipes Tailored
For The New COSORI Premium Air Fryer

**Diana H. Johansen**

# Table of Content

## Chapter 10 Desserts ............................ 134

## Chapter 11 Wraps and Sandwiches ... 146

## Chapter 12 Holiday Specials ...............152

## Chapter 13 Fast and Easy Everyday Favorites................................................157

## Chapter 14 Casseroles, Frittatas, and Quiches ................................................164

# MY STORY WITH THE COSORI AIR FRYER

The thought of a homemade meal cooked from scratch sounds lovely if only I had time! Who knew that it was possible to become so busy that one would forget to cook or simply be too exhausted to hover over pots that never seem to empty? The traditional lifestyle of cooking fresh foods—straight from the garden to the kitchen—seems like a fantasy in my fast-paced urban lifestyle; I know I am not the only one who feels this way. As many mothers enter the corporate environment and fill up 9-to-5 jobs, no one is left at home to prepare home-cooked meals that simmer for hours in a pot. Even for a foodie like myself, I find it nearly impossible to whip up delicious meals made from scratch while tending to my four children and answering a day's worth of emails in the evenings. For many years, I settled for unhealthy takeout meals that would appease the children and afford me the much needed time to work on other essential tasks. However, these quick and greasy takeout dinners were simply not sustainable in the long run for the health and well-being of my family. I knew that I had to find another convenient alternative that would meet all of my culinary and lifestyle needs.

Christmas came around, and guess what I received from my dear husband? An COSORI Air Fryer with a note, "This might be what you were looking for." I did not know what to expect as I unwrapped this elegant and professional kitchen gadget. The first time I used my COSORI Air Fryer was for a Sunday roast dinner. The Air Fryer assumed the role of kitchen chef, and this allowed me to take time out to read a book while the machine did all the work. This multifunctional appliance gave me the option of air frying, baking, roasting, broiling, reheating, dehydrating, and rotisserie cooking my food to make a fantastic dinner.

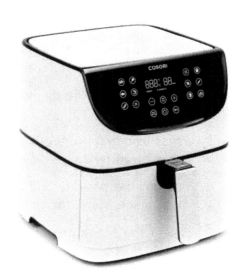

# Step by Step Guide to the COSORI Air Fryer

## After Unboxing

1. Remove all packaging from the air fryer, including any temporary stickers.

2. Place the air fryer on a stable, level, heat-resistant surface. Keep away from areas that can be damaged by steam (such as walls or cupboards).

3. Pull the handle to remove the baskets. Remove all plastic from the baskets.

4. Press the basket release button to separate the inner basket from the outer basket.

5. Wash both baskets thoroughly, using either a dishwasher or a non-abrasive sponge.

6. Wipe the inside and outside of the air fryer with a slightly moist cloth. Dry with a towel.

7. Put the baskets back inside the air fryer.

## Test Run

A test run will help you become familiar with your air fryer, make sure it's working correctly, and clean it of possible residues in the process.

1. Make sure the air fryer baskets are empty and plug in the air fryer.

2. Press Preheat. The display will show "400°F" and "5 MIN".

3. Press to begin preheating. When preheating is done, the air fryer will beep.

4. Pull out the baskets and let them cool for 5 minutes. Then place the empty baskets back in the air fryer.

5. Select the Steak preset. The display will show "400°F" and "6 MIN".

6. Press Temp/Time twice. The time will blink on the display. Press the - button once to change the time to 5 minutes.

7. Press to begin. When finished, the air fryer will beep.

8. Pull out the baskets. This time, let the baskets cool completely for 10–30 minutes.

## Basket Tips

- Only separate the baskets to clean or after cooking.

- The button guard protects the release button from being pressed accidentally. Slide the button guard forward to press the release button.

- Never press the release button while carrying the baskets.

- Only press the basket release button with the baskets resting on a counter, or any level, heat-resistant surface.

- The handle is attached to the inner basket, not the outer basket. When you press the release button, the outer basket will drop.

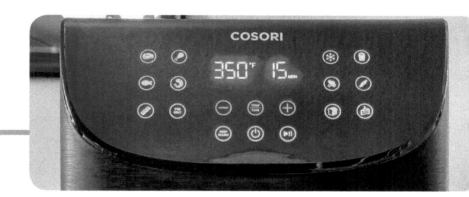

# USING YOUR AIR FRYER

## Preheating

We recommend preheating before placing food into the air fryer, unless your air fryer is already hot. Food will not cook thoroughly without preheating.

1. Plug in. Turn on the air fryer.

2. Press Preheat. The display will show "400°F" and "5 MIN".

3. Optionally, press the + or – buttons to change the temperature. The time will adjust automatically.

4. Press Start to begin preheating.

5. When preheating is done, the air fryer will beep 3 times. The display will show the set preheat temperature.

| Temperature Time |
| --- |
| **400°F / 204°C 5 minutes** |
| **390°F / 199°C 5 minutes** |
| **380°F / 193°C 5 minutes** |
| **370°F / 188°C 4 minutes** |
| **360°F / 182°C 4 minutes** |
| **350°F / 177°C 4 minutes** |
| **340°F / 171°C 4 minutes** |
| **330°F / 166°C and below 3 minutes** |

# AIR FRYING

1. Preheat your air fryer.

2. When your air fryer displays "READY", add food to the baskets.

3. Select a preset cooking program

**Note:** See Shaking Food.

4. Press SHAKE to add or remove a Shake Reminder during cooking.

5. Press to begin air frying.

6. When the Shake Reminder is turned on, it will appear halfway through cooking time. The air fryer will beep 5 times, and ((SHAKE)) will blink on the display.

a. Take the baskets out of the air fryer, being careful of hot steam. The air fryer will pause cooking automatically, and the display will turn off until the baskets are replaced.

b. Shake or flip the food. Be careful not to press the basket release button.

c. Put the baskets back into the air fryer.

7. Optionally, customize the temperature and time, and add a Shake Reminder. You can do this anytime during cooking.

a. Press Temp/Time to change temperature or time. The temperature or time will blink on the display.

b. Press the + or – buttons to change the temperature (170°–400°F / 77°–204°C) or time (1–60 minutes).

**Note:** Presets are programmed with an ideal time and temperature for cooking certain foods. You can also set a custom time and temperature without choosing a preset.

8. The air fryer will beep 3 times when finished.

**Note:**

- To rapidly increase or decrease time or temperature, press and hold the + or – buttons.

- If you do not press Temp/Time, then pressing + or – will automatically change temperature.

9. Optionally, press Keep Warm. Press the + or – buttons to change the time (1–60 minutes).

10. Take the baskets out of the air fryer, being careful of hot steam.

11. Remove the inner basket from the outer basket to serve food. When separating baskets:

a. Make sure the baskets are resting on a flat surface.

b. Watch for hot oil or fat collected in the outer basket. To avoid splashing, drain oil before replacing inner basket.

12. Allow to cool before cleaning.

# Preset Settings

Using a preset is the easiest way to air fry.

Presets are programmed with an ideal time and temperature for cooking certain foods.

- You can customize a preset's time (1–60 minutes), temperature (170°–400°F /77°–204°C), and Shake Reminder, unless noted.

To save a preset:

1. Choose a preset and adjust the time and temperature. Optionally, add or remove the Shake Reminder by pressing SHAKE.

2. Press and hold the preset icon until the air fryer beeps 1 time.

To reset a preset:

– Without making changes, press and hold both the preset icon and Temp/Time icon for

3. seconds until the air fryer beeps 1 time.

To reset all presets:

Press and hold both + and –for 3 seconds until the air fryer beeps 1 time.

# Precautions for using the COSORI Air Fryer

## General Safety Tips

- Do not immerse the air fryer housing or plug in water or liquid.

- Closely supervise children near your air fryer.

- Unplug when not in use, and before cleaning. Allow to cool before putting on or taking off parts.

- Do not use your air fryer if it is damaged, not working, or if the cord or plug is damaged.

## Contact Customer Support

- Do not use third-party replacement parts or accessories, as this may cause injuries.

- Do not use outdoors.

- Do not place the air fryer or any of its parts on a stove, near gas or electric burners, or in a heated oven.

- Be extremely cautious when moving your air fryer (or removing the baskets) if it contains hot oil or other hot liquids.

- Do not clean with metal scouring pads. Metal fragments can break off the pad and touch electrical parts, creating a risk of electric shock.

- Do not place anything on top of your air fryer.

**Do not store anything inside your air fryer.**

- Never use your air fryer without the baskets in place.

- Do not place oversized foods or metal utensils into your air fryer.

- Do not place paper, cardboard, non-heatresistant plastic, or similar materials, into your air fryer. You may use parchment paper or foil.

- Never put baking or parchment paper into the air fryer without food on top. Air circulation can cause paper to lift and touch heating coils.

- Always use heat-safe containers. Be extremely cautious if using containers that aren't metal or glass.

- Keep your air fryer away from flammable materials (curtains, tablecloths, etc). Use on a flat, stable, heat-resistant surface away from heat sources or liquids.

**While the COSORI Air Fryer is Working**

- An air fryer works with hot air only. Never fill the baskets with oil or fat.

- Never use your air fryer without the baskets in place.

- Do not place oversized foods or metal utensils into your air fryer.

- Do not place paper, cardboard, non-heatresistant plastic, or similar materials, into your air fryer. You may use parchment paper or foil.

- Never put baking or parchment paper into the air fryer without food on top. Air circulation can cause paper to lift and touch heating coils.

- Always use heat-safe containers. Be extremely cautious if using containers that aren't metal or glass.

- Keep your air fryer away from flammable materials (curtains, tablecloths, etc). Use on a flat, stable, heat-resistant surface away from heat sources or liquids.

- Immediately turn off and unplug your air fryer if you see dark smoke coming out. White smoke is normal, caused by heating fat or food splashing, but dark smoke means that food is burning or there is a circuit problem. Wait for smoke to clear before pulling the baskets out. If the cause was not burnt food, contact Customer Support

- Do not leave your air fryer unattended while in use.

# Chapter 1 Sauces, Dips, and Dressing

## Asian Flavor Hot Sauce

**Prep time: 5 minutes | Cook time: 0 minutes | Makes ½ cup**

⅓ cup low-fat mayonnaise
2 teaspoons rice vinegar

1 to 2 teaspoons hot sauce
1 teaspoon sesame oil

Stir together all the ingredients in a small bowl until well combined. Serve it with chicken or veggie stir-fry over rice. It can be refrigerated in an airtight container for up to 2 weeks.

## Cashew-Almond Milk Sauce

**Prep time: 15 minutes | Cook time: 5 minutes | Makes 3 cups**

¾ cup raw cashews
¼ cup boiling water
1 tablespoon olive oil
4 garlic cloves, minced
1½ cups unsweetened almond

milk
1 tablespoon arrowroot powder
1 teaspoon salt
1 tablespoon nutritional yeast
1¼ cups marinara sauce

Put the cashews in a heatproof bowl and add boiling water to cover. Let soak for 10 minutes. Drain the cashews and place them in a blender. Add ¼ cup boiling water and blend for 1 to 2 minutes or until creamy. Set aside. In a small saucepan, heat the olive oil over medium heat. Add the garlic and sauté for 2 minutes until golden. Whisk in the almond milk, arrowroot powder, and salt. Bring to a simmer. Continue to simmer, whisking frequently, for about 5 minutes or until the sauce thickens. Carefully transfer the hot almond milk mixture to the blender with the cashews. Blend for 30 seconds to combine, then add the nutritional yeast and marinara sauce. Blend for 1 minute or until creamy.

## Avocado Tahini Dressing

**Prep time: 5 minutes | Cook time: 0 minutes | Makes 12 tablespoons**

1 large avocado, pitted and peeled
½ cup water
2 tablespoons tahini
2 tablespoons freshly squeezed lemon juice
1 teaspoon dried basil

1 teaspoon white wine vinegar
1 garlic clove
¼ teaspoon pink Himalayan salt
¼ teaspoon freshly ground black pepper

Combine all the ingredients in a food processor and blend until smooth.

## Indian Garam Masala

**Prep time: 10 minutes | Cook time: 0 minutes | Makes: ¼ cup**

2 tablespoons coriander seeds
1 teaspoon cumin seeds
½ teaspoon whole black cloves
½ teaspoon cardamom seeds
2 dried bay leaves

3 dried red chiles; or ½ teaspoon cayenne pepper or red pepper flakes
1 (2-inch) piece cinnamon stick

In a clean coffee grinder or spice mill, combine all the spices and grind, shaking so all the seeds and bits get into the blades, until the mixture has the consistency of a moderately fine powder. Unplug the grinder and turn it upside down. (You want all the ground spices to collect in the lid so you can easily scoop them out without cutting yourself on the blades.) Store in an airtight container in a cool, dark place for up to 2 months.

## Dijon Balsamic Dressing

**Prep time: 5 minutes | Cook time: 0 minutes | Makes 1 cup**

2 tablespoons Dijon mustard
¼ cup balsamic vinegar

¾ cup olive oil

Put all ingredients in a jar with a tight-fitting lid. Put on the lid and shake vigorously until thoroughly combined. Refrigerate until ready to use and shake well before serving.

## Cashew Mayonnaise

**Prep time: 5 minutes | Cook time: 0 minutes | Makes 18 tablespoons**

1 cup cashews, soaked in hot water for at least 1 hour
¼ cup plus 3 tablespoons milk
1 tablespoon apple cider vinegar
1 tablespoon freshly squeezed

lemon juice
1 tablespoon Dijon mustard
1 tablespoon aquafaba
⅛ teaspoon pink Himalayan salt

In a food processor, combine all the ingredients and blend until creamy and smooth.

## Homemade Cashew Pesto

**Prep time: 10 minutes | Cook time: 0 minutes | Makes 1 cup**

¼ cup raw cashews
Juice of 1 lemon
2 garlic cloves
⅓ red onion (about 2 ounces / 56 g in total)

1 tablespoon olive oil
4 cups basil leaves, packed
1 cup wheatgrass
¼ cup water
¼ teaspoon salt

Put the cashews in a heatproof bowl and add boiling water to cover. Soak for 5 minutes and then drain. Put all ingredients in a blender and blend for 2 to 3 minutes or until fully combined.

## Ranch Cashew Dressing

**Prep time: 15 minutes | Cook time: 0 minutes | Serves 12**

1 cup cashews, soaked in warm water for at least 1 hour
½ cup water
2 tablespoons freshly squeezed lemon juice

1 tablespoon vinegar
1 teaspoon garlic powder
1 teaspoon onion powder
2 teaspoons dried dill

In a food processor, combine the cashews, water, lemon juice, vinegar, garlic powder, and onion powder. Blend until creamy and smooth. Add the dill and pulse a few times until combined.

## Sweet Mustard Sauce

**Prep time: 10 minutes | Cook time: 0 minutes | Makes about 1 cup**

½ cup raw honey or maple syrup
½ cup Dijon mustard

1 teaspoon toasted sesame oil
1 garlic clove, minced

Whisk together all the ingredients in a small bowl until smooth. Refrigerate to chill for at least 2 hours for best flavor. This sauce can be served as a dip for fresh vegetables or a spread for wraps and sandwiches. It's perfect for salads, grilled or roasted meats.

## Garlicky Cauliflower Alfredo Sauce

**Prep time: 2 minutes | Cook time: 0 minutes | Makes 4 cups**

2 tablespoons olive oil
6 garlic cloves, minced
3 cups unsweetened almond milk
1 (1-pound / 454-g) head cauliflower, cut into florets

1 teaspoon salt
¼ teaspoon freshly ground black pepper
Juice of 1 lemon
4 tablespoons nutritional yeast

In a medium saucepan, heat the olive oil over medium-high heat. Add the garlic and sauté for 1 minute or until fragrant. Add the almond milk, stir, and bring to a boil. Gently add the cauliflower. Stir in the salt and pepper and return to a boil. Continue cooking over medium-high heat for 5 minutes or until the cauliflower is soft. Stir frequently and reduce heat if needed to prevent the liquid from boiling over. Carefully transfer the cauliflower and cooking liquid to a food processor, using a slotted spoon to scoop out the larger pieces of cauliflower before pouring in the liquid. Add the lemon and nutritional yeast and blend for 1 to 2 minutes until smooth. Serve immediately.

## Fresh Cilantro Pesto

**Prep time: 10 minutes | Cook time: 0 minutes | Serves: 4**

1 cup fresh cilantro leaves
1 jalapeño
2 tablespoons vegetable oil
2 tablespoons fresh lemon juice

2 tablespoons minced fresh ginger
2 tablespoons minced garlic
1 teaspoon kosher salt

In a blender, combine the cilantro, jalapeño, vegetable oil, lemon juice, ginger, garlic, and salt. Blend until smooth.

## Balsamic-Mustard Vinaigrette

**Prep time: 5 minutes | Cook time: 0 minutes | Makes 12 tablespoons**

6 tablespoons water
4 tablespoons Dijon mustard
4 tablespoons balsamic vinegar
1 teaspoon maple syrup

½ teaspoon pink Himalayan salt
¼ teaspoon freshly ground black pepper

In a bowl, whisk together all the ingredients.

## Spicy Harissa Paste

**Prep time: 10 minutes | Cook time: 5 minutes | Makes: 1 cup**

½ cup olive oil
6 cloves garlic, minced
2 tablespoons smoked paprika
1 tablespoon ground coriander
1 tablespoon ground cumin

1 teaspoon ground caraway
1 teaspoon kosher salt
½ to 1 teaspoon cayenne pepper

In a medium microwave-safe bowl, combine all the ingredients. Microwave on high for 1 minute, stirring halfway through the cooking time. (You can also heat this on the stovetop until the oil is hot and bubbling. Or, if you must use your air fryer for everything, preheat air fryer to 350ºF (177ºC). When your air fryer displays "READY" (select the cooking preset, and make minor adjustments according to your desired doneness.) and choose a shake reminder. Cook in the air fryer at 350ºF (177ºC) for 5 to 6 minutes, or until the paste is heated through.) Cool completely. Store in an airtight container in the refrigerator for up to 1 month.

## Classic Remoulade

**Prep time: 5 minutes | Cook time: 0 minutes | Serves 4**

¾ cup mayonnaise
1 garlic clove, minced
2 tablespoons mustard
1 teaspoon horseradish

1 teaspoon Cajun seasoning
1 teaspoon dill pickle juice
½ teaspoon paprika
¼ teaspoon hot pepper sauce

Whisk together all the ingredients in a small bowl until completely mixed. It can be used as a delicious dip for a sandwich, burger spread or veggies, or you can serve it with chicken fingers for a dipping sauce.

## Korean Gochujang Sauce

**Prep time: 5 minutes | Cook time: 0 minutes | Makes: a scant ½ cup**

2 tablespoons gochujang (Korean red pepper paste)
1 tablespoon mayonnaise
1 tablespoon toasted sesame oil

1 tablespoon minced fresh ginger
1 tablespoon minced garlic
1 teaspoon agave nectar

In a small bowl, combine the gochujang, mayonnaise, sesame oil, ginger, garlic, and agave. Stir until well combined. Use immediately or store in the refrigerator, covered, for up to 3 days.

## Traditional Greek Tzatziki

**Prep time: 10 minutes | Cook time: 0 minutes | Makes: 2 cups**

1 large cucumber, peeled and grated
1 cup plain Greek yogurt
2 to 3 garlic cloves, minced
1 tablespoon tahini (sesame paste)

1 tablespoon fresh lemon juice
½ teaspoon kosher salt, or to taste
Chopped fresh parsley or dill, for garnish (optional)

In a medium bowl, combine the cucumber, yogurt, garlic, tahini, lemon juice, and salt. Stir until well combined. Cover and chill until ready to serve. Right before serving, sprinkle with chopped fresh parsley, if desired.

## Cashew-Dill Dip

**Prep time: 10 minutes | Cook time: 0 minutes | Makes 1 cup**

¾ cup cashews, soaked in water for at least 4 hours and drained
Juice and zest of 1 lemon
¼ cup water

2 tablespoons chopped fresh dill
¼ teaspoon salt, plus additional as needed

Blend the cashew, lemon juice and zest, and water in a blender until smooth and creamy. Fold in the dill and salt and blend again. Taste and add additional salt as needed. Transfer to the refrigerator to chill for at least 1 hour to blend the flavors. This dip perfectly goes with the crackers or tacos. It also can be used as a sauce for roasted vegetables or a sandwich spread.

## Caesar Salad Dressing

**Prep time: 5 minutes | Cook time: 0 minutes | Makes about ⅔ cup**

½ cup extra-virgin olive oil
1 teaspoon anchovy paste
2 tablespoons freshly squeezed lemon juice
¼ teaspoon kosher salt or ⅛

teaspoon fine salt
¼ teaspoon minced or pressed garlic
1 egg, beaten

Add all the ingredients to a tall, narrow container. Purée the mixture with an immersion blender until smooth. Use immediately.

## Ginger Teriyaki Sauce

**Prep time: 5 minutes | Cook time: 0 minutes | Serves 4**

¼ cup pineapple juice
¼ cup low-sodium soy sauce
2 tablespoons packed brown sugar
1 tablespoon arrowroot powder

or cornstarch
1 tablespoon grated fresh ginger
1 teaspoon garlic powder

Mix together all the ingredients in a small bowl and whisk to incorporate. Serve immediately, or transfer to an airtight container and refrigerate until ready to use.

## Lemony Kale and Almond Pesto

**Prep time: 15 minutes | Cook time: 0 minutes | Makes about 1 cup**

2 cups chopped kale leaves, rinsed well and stemmed
½ cup toasted almonds
2 garlic cloves
3 tablespoons extra-virgin olive oil
3 tablespoons freshly squeezed

lemon juice
2 teaspoons lemon zest
1 teaspoon salt
½ teaspoon freshly ground black pepper
¼ teaspoon red pepper flakes

Place all the ingredients in a food processor and pulse until smoothly puréed. It tastes great with the eggs, salads, soup, pasta, cracker, and sandwiches.

## Lemon Mustard Vinaigrette

**Prep time: 5 minutes | Cook time: 0 minutes | Makes about 6 tablespoons**

¼ cup extra-virgin olive oil
1 garlic clove, minced
2 tablespoons freshly squeezed lemon juice

1 teaspoon Dijon mustard
½ teaspoon raw honey
¼ teaspoon salt
¼ teaspoon dried basil

Place all the ingredients in a mason jar. Cover and shake vigorously until thoroughly mixed and well emulsified. Serve chilled.

## Peanut-Coconut Dressing

**Prep time: 5 minutes | Cook time: 0 minutes | Serves 8**

1 cup lite coconut milk
¼ cup freshly squeezed lime juice
¼ cup creamy peanut butter
2 tablespoons low-sodium soy

sauce or tamari
3 garlic cloves, minced
1 tablespoon grated fresh ginger

Place all the ingredients in a food processor or blender and process until completely mixed and smooth. It's delicious served over grilled chicken or tossed with noodles and green onions.

## Spiced Mushroom Apple Gravy

**Prep time: 5 minutes | Cook time: 10 minutes | Serves 4**

2 cups vegetable broth
½ cup finely chopped mushrooms
2 tablespoons whole wheat flour
1 tablespoon unsweetened applesauce

1 teaspoon onion powder
½ teaspoon dried thyme
¼ teaspoon dried rosemary
⅛ teaspoon pink Himalayan salt
Freshly ground black pepper, to taste

In a nonstick saucepan over medium-high heat, combine all the ingredients and mix well. Bring to a boil, stirring frequently, reduce the heat to low, and simmer, stirring constantly, until it thickens.

## Lime Peanut Sauce

**Prep time: 10 minutes | Cook time: 0 minutes | Serves: 4**

⅓ cup peanut butter
¼ cup hot water
2 tablespoons soy sauce
2 tablespoons rice vinegar

Juice of 1 lime
1 teaspoon minced fresh ginger
1 teaspoon minced garlic
1 teaspoon black pepper

In a blender container, combine the peanut butter, hot water, soy sauce, vinegar, lime juice, ginger, garlic, and pepper. Blend until smooth. Use immediately or store in an airtight container in the refrigerator for a week or more.

## Green Lentil Dip

**Prep time: 10 minutes | Cook time: 15 minutes | Makes 3 cups**

2½ cups water, divided
1 cup dried green or brown lentils, rinsed
⅓ cup tahini

1 garlic clove
½ teaspoon salt, plus additional as needed

Mix 2 cups of water and lentils in a medium pot and bring to a boil over high heat. Once it starts to boil, reduce the heat to low, and bring to a simmer for 15 minutes, or until the lentils are tender. If there is any water remaining in the pot, simply drain it off. Transfer the cooked lentils to a food processor, along with the remaining ingredients. Pulse until a hummus-like consistency is achieved. Taste and add additional salt as needed. It's tasty used as a sandwich spread, and you can also serve it over whole-wheat pita bread or crackers.

# Chapter 2 Breakfasts

## Bacon Omelet Bread Cups

Prep time: 5 minutes | Cook time: 8 minutes | Serves 4

4 crusty rolls
5 eggs, beaten
½ teaspoon thyme, dried

3 strips cooked bacon, chopped
2 tablespoons heavy cream
4 Gouda cheese thin slices

Preheat air fryer to 330ºF (166ºC). Cut the tops off the rolls and remove the inside with your fingers. Line the rolls with a slice of cheese and press down, so the cheese conforms to the inside of the roll. In a bowl, mix the eggs, heavy cream, bacon, and thyme. Stuff the rolls with the egg mixture. Lay them in the greased air fryer's basket when your air fryer displays "READY" (select the cooking preset, and make minor adjustments according to your desired doneness.) and choose a shake reminder. Bake for 8 to 10 minutes or until the eggs become puffy, and the roll shows a golden brown texture. Remove and serve immediately.

## Colby Cheese and Ham Egg Cups

Prep time: 5 minutes | Cook time: 8 minutes | Serves 6

4 eggs, beaten
1 tablespoon olive oil
½ cup Colby cheese, shredded
2¼ cups frozen hash browns,

thawed
1 cup smoked ham, chopped
½ teaspoon Cajun seasoning

Preheat air fryer to 360ºF (182ºC). Gather 12 silicone muffin cups and coat with olive oil. Whisk the eggs, hash browns, smoked ham, Colby cheese, and Cajun seasoning in a medium bowl and add a heaping spoonful into each muffin cup. Put the muffin cups in the fryer basket when your air fryer displays "READY" (select the cooking preset, and make minor adjustments according to your desired doneness.) and choose a shake reminder. And AirFry 8 to 10 minutes until golden brown and the center is set. Transfer to a wire rack to cool completely. Serve.

## Air-Fried All-in-One Toast

Prep time: 10 minutes | Cook time: 10 minutes | Serves 1

1 strip bacon, diced
1 slice 1-inch thick bread
1 egg

Salt and freshly ground black pepper, to taste
¼ cup grated Colby cheese

Preheat the air fryer to 400ºF (204ºC). Air fry the bacon for 3 minutes, shaking the basket once or twice while it cooks. Remove the bacon to a paper towel lined plate and set aside. Use a sharp paring knife to score a large circle in the middle of the slice of bread, cutting halfway through, but not all the way through to the cutting board. Press down on the circle in the center of the bread slice to create an indentation. Transfer the slice of bread, hole side up, to the air fryer basket. Crack the egg into the center of the bread, and season with salt and pepper. When your air fryer displays "READY" (select the cooking preset, and make minor adjustments according to your desired doneness.) and choose a shake reminder. Adjust the air fryer temperature to 380ºF (193ºC) and air fry for 5 minutes. Sprinkle the grated cheese around the edges of the bread, leaving the center of the yolk uncovered, and top with the cooked bacon. Press the cheese and bacon into the bread lightly to help anchor it to the bread and prevent it from blowing around in the air fryer. Air fry for one or two more minutes, just to melt the cheese and finish cooking the egg. Serve immediately.

## Mozzarella Prosciutto Bruschetta

Prep time: 5 minutes | Cook time: 4 minutes | Serves 2

½ cup tomatoes, finely chopped
3 ounces (85 g) Mozzarella cheese, grated
3 prosciutto slices, chopped

1 tablespoon olive oil
1 teaspoon dried basil
6 small French bread slices

Preheat air fryer to 350ºF (180ºC). When your air fryer displays "READY" (select the cooking preset, and make minor adjustments according to your desired doneness.) and choose a shake reminder. Add in the bread slices and toast for 3 minutes on AirFry mode. Remove and top the bread with tomatoes, prosciutto, and mozzarella cheese. Sprinkle basil all over and drizzle with olive oil. Return to the fryer and cook for 1 more minute, just to heat through. Serve warm.

## Sausage Frittata with Parmesan Cheese

Prep time: 10 minutes | Cook time: 13 minutes | Serves 2

1 sausage, chopped
Salt and black pepper, to taste
1 tablespoon parsley, chopped
4 eggs

1 tablespoon olive oil
4 cherry tomatoes, halved
2 tablespoons Parmesan cheese, shredded

Preheat air fryer to 360ºF (182ºC). When your air fryer displays "READY" (select the cooking preset, and make minor adjustments according to your desired doneness.) and choose a shake reminder. Place tomatoes and sausages in the air fryer's basket and cook for 5 minutes. Remove them to a bowl and mix in eggs, salt, parsley, Parmesan cheese, olive oil, and black pepper. Add the mixture to a greased baking pan and fit in the fryer. Bake for 8 minutes. Serve hot.

## Walnut and Apple Muffins

Prep time: 15 minutes | Cook time: 10 minutes | Makes 8 muffins

1 cup flour
⅓ cup sugar
1 teaspoon baking powder
¼ teaspoon baking soda
¼ teaspoon salt
1 teaspoon cinnamon
¼ teaspoon ginger
¼ teaspoon nutmeg
1 egg

2 tablespoons pancake syrup, plus 2 teaspoons
2 tablespoons melted butter, plus 2 teaspoons
¾ cup unsweetened applesauce
½ teaspoon vanilla extract
¼ cup chopped walnuts
¼ cup diced apple

Preheat the air fryer to 330ºF (166ºC). In a large bowl, stir together the flour, sugar, baking powder, baking soda, salt, cinnamon, ginger, and nutmeg. In a small bowl, beat egg until frothy. Add syrup, butter, applesauce, and vanilla and mix well. Pour egg mixture into dry ingredients and stir just until moistened. Gently stir in nuts and diced apple. Divide batter among 8 parchment paper-lined muffin cups. Put 4 muffin cups in air fryer basket when your air fryer displays "READY" (select the cooking preset, and make minor adjustments according to your desired doneness.) and choose a shake reminder. Bake for 10 minutes. Repeat with remaining 4 muffins or until toothpick inserted in center comes out clean. Serve warm.

## Ricotta Shrimp and Egg Muffins
**Prep time: 10 minutes | Cook time: 16 minutes | Serves 4**

4 eggs, beaten
2 tablespoons olive oil
½ small red bell pepper, finely diced
1 garlic clove, minced
4 ounces (113 g) shrimp,

cooked, chopped
4 teaspoons ricotta cheese, crumbled
1 teaspoon dry dill
Salt and black pepper, to taste

Preheat air fryer to 360ºF (182ºC). Warm the olive oil in a skillet over medium heat. Sauté the bell pepper and garlic until the pepper is soft, then add the shrimp. Season with dill, salt, and pepper and cook for about 5 minutes. Remove from the heat and mix in the eggs. Grease 4 ramekins with cooking spray. Divide the mixture between the ramekins. When your air fryer displays "READY" (select the cooking preset, and make minor adjustments according to your desired doneness.) and choose a shake reminder. Place them in the fryer and cook for 6 minutes. Remove and stir the mixture. Sprinkle with ricotta and return to the fryer. Cook for 5 minutes until the eggs are set, and the top is lightly browned. Let sit for 2 minutes, invert on a plate, while warm and serve.

## Hard-Boiled Eggs
**Prep time: 5 minutes | Cook time: 15 minutes | Serves 6**

6 eggs

Preheat air fryer to 250ºF (121ºC). Place the eggs in the air fryer basket. (You can put the eggs in an oven-safe bowl if you are worried about them rolling around and breaking.) When your air fryer displays "READY" (select the cooking preset, and make minor adjustments according to your desired doneness.) and choose a shake reminder. Set the temperature to 250ºF (121ºC). Set the timer and bake for 15 minutes (if you prefer a soft-boiled egg, reduce the cook time to 10 minutes). Meanwhile, fill a medium mixing bowl half full of ice water. Use tongs to remove the eggs from the air fryer basket, and transfer them to the ice water bath. Let the eggs sit for 5 minutes in the ice water. Peel and eat on the spot or refrigerate for up to 1 week.

## Granola Stuffed Apples
**Prep time: 5 minutes | Cook time: 20 minutes | Serves 4**

4 Granny Smith or other firm apples
1 cup granola
2 tablespoons light brown sugar

¾ teaspoon cinnamon
2 tablespoons unsalted butter, melted
1 cup water or apple juice

Working one apple at a time, cut a circle around the apple stem and scoop out the core, taking care not to cut all the way through to the bottom. (This should leave an empty cavity in the middle of the apple for the granola.) Repeat with the remaining apples. In a small bowl, combine the granola, brown sugar, and cinnamon. Pour the melted butter over the ingredients and stir with a fork. Divide the granola mixture among the apples, packing it tightly into the empty cavity. Place the apples in the cake pan insert for the air fryer. Pour the water or juice around the apples. When your air fryer displays "READY" (select the cooking preset, and make minor adjustments according to your desired doneness.) and choose a shake reminder. Bake at 350ºF (177ºC) for 20 minutes until the apples are soft all the way through. (If the granola begins to scorch before the apples are fully cooked, cover the top of the apples with a small piece of aluminum foil.) Serve warm with a dollop of crème fraîche or yogurt, if desired.

## Apple-Glazed Doughnut Holes
**Prep time: 15 minutes | Cook time: 6 minutes | Makes 10 mini doughnuts**

**For the Doughnut Holes:**
1½ cups all-purpose flour
2 tablespoons granulated sugar
2 teaspoons baking powder
1 teaspoon baking soda
½ teaspoon kosher salt
Pinch of freshly grated nutmeg
**For the Glaze:**
½ cup powdered sugar
2 tablespoons unsweetened applesauce

¼ cup plus 2 tablespoons buttermilk, chilled
2 tablespoons apple cider (hard or nonalcoholic), chilled
1 large egg, lightly beaten
Vegetable oil, for brushing

¼ teaspoon vanilla extract
Pinch of kosher salt

In a bowl, whisk together the flour, granulated sugar, baking powder, baking soda, salt, and nutmeg until smooth. Add the buttermilk, cider, and egg and stir with a small rubber spatula or spoon until the dough just comes together. Using a 1-ounce ice cream scoop or 2 tablespoons, scoop and drop 10 balls of dough into the air fryer basket, spaced evenly apart, and brush the tops lightly with oil. When your air fryer displays "READY" (select the cooking preset, and make minor adjustments according to your desired doneness.) and choose a shake reminder. Cook at 350ºF (177ºC) until the doughnut holes are golden brown and fluffy, about 6 minutes. Transfer the doughnut holes to a wire rack to cool completely. In a small bowl, stir together the powdered sugar, applesauce, vanilla, and salt until smooth. Dip the tops of the doughnuts holes in the glaze, then let stand until the glaze sets before serving. If you're impatient and want warm doughnuts, have the glaze ready to go while the doughnuts cook, then use the glaze as a dipping sauce for the warm doughnuts, fresh out of the air fryer.

## Kiwi-Pecan Muffins
**Prep time: 10 minutes | Cook time: 15 minutes | Serves 4**

1 cup flour
1 kiwi, mashed
¼ cup powdered sugar
1 teaspoon milk

1 tablespoon pecans, chopped
½ teaspoon baking powder
¼ cup oats
¼ cup butter, room temperature

Preheat air fryer to 350ºF (180ºC). Place the sugar, pecans, kiwi, and butter in a bowl and mix well. In another bowl, mix the flour, baking powder, and oats and stir well. Combine the two mixtures and stir in the milk. Pour the batter into a greased muffin tin that fits in the fryer. When your air fryer displays "READY" (select the cooking preset, and make minor adjustments according to your desired doneness.) and choose a shake reminder. Bake for 15 minutes. Remove to a wire rack and leave to cool for a few minutes before removing from the muffin tin. Enjoy!

## Honey Banana Pastry
**Prep time: 5 minutes | Cook time: 12 minutes | Serves 2**

3 bananas, sliced
3 tablespoons honey
2 puff pastry sheets, cut into

thin strips
1 cup fresh berries to serve

Preheat air fryer to 340ºF (171ºC). Place the banana slices into a greased baking dish. Cover with pastry strips and drizzle with honey. When your air fryer displays "READY" (select the cooking preset, and make minor adjustments according to your desired doneness.) and choose a shake reminder. Bake in the air fryer for 12 minutes until golden. Serve with berries.

## Eggs in Hole

**Prep time: 5 minutes | Cook time: 8 minutes | Serves 2**

2 bread slices
2 eggs

Salt and black pepper, to taste
2 tablespoons butter

Preheat air fryer to 360ºF (182ºC). Place a heatproof bowl in the fryer's basket and brush with butter. Make a hole in the middle of the bread slices with a bread knife and place on the heatproof bowl in 2 batches. Crack an egg into the center of each hole; season. When your air fryer displays "READY" (select the cooking preset, and make minor adjustments according to your desired doneness.) and choose a shake reminder. Bake in the air fryer for 4 minutes. Turn the bread with a spatula and cook for another 4 minutes. Serve warm.

## Parmesan Shirred Eggs

**Prep time: 10 minutes | Cook time: 14 minutes | Serves 2**

2 teaspoons butter
4 eggs
2 tablespoons heavy cream
4 slices ham
3 tablespoons Parmesan

cheese, grated
¼ teaspoon paprika
Salt and black pepper, to taste
2 teaspoons chopped chives

Preheat air fryer to 320ºF (160ºC). Arrange the ham slices on the bottom of a greased pie pan to cover it completely. Whisk one egg along with the heavy cream, salt, and pepper in a small bowl. Pour the mixture over the ham slices. Crack the other eggs on top and sprinkle with Parmesan cheese. When your air fryer displays "READY" (select the cooking preset, and make minor adjustments according to your desired doneness.) and choose a shake reminder. AirFry for 14 minutes. Garnish with paprika and fresh chives and serve.

## Italian Herb Bacon Hot Dogs

**Prep time: 5 minutes | Cook time: 15 minutes | Serves 4**

3 brazilian sausages, cut into 3 equal pieces
9 slices bacon

1 tablespoon Italian herbs
Salt and ground black pepper, to taste

Preheat the air fryer to 355ºF (179ºC). Take each slice of bacon and wrap around each piece of sausage. Sprinkle with Italian herbs, salt and pepper. When your air fryer displays "READY" (select the cooking preset, and make minor adjustments according to your desired doneness.) and choose a shake reminder. Air fry the sausages in the preheated air fryer for 15 minutes. Serve warm.

## Flax Seeds Porridge

**Prep time: 5 minutes | Cook time: 10 minutes | Serves 4**

1 cup steel-cut oats
1 tablespoon flax seeds
1 tablespoon peanut butter

1 tablespoon butter
1 cup milk
2 tablespoons honey

Preheat air fryer to 350ºF (180ºC). Combine all ingredients in an ovenproof bowl. Place the bowl in the air fryer when your air fryer displays "READY" (select the cooking preset, and make minor adjustments according to your desired doneness.) and choose a shake reminder. Bake for 10 minutes. Let cool for a few minutes before serving.

## Loaded Egg Bell Pepper Rings

**Prep time: 5 minutes | Cook time: 6 minutes | Serves 4**

4 eggs
1 bell pepper, cut into four ¾-inch rings

5 cherry tomatoes, halved
Salt and black pepper, to taste

Preheat air fryer to 360ºF (182ºC). Put the bell pepper rings in a greased baking pan and crack an egg into each one. Season with salt and pepper. Top with the halved cherry tomatoes. Put the pan into the air fryer when your air fryer displays "READY" (select the cooking preset, and make minor adjustments according to your desired doneness.) and choose a shake reminder. Air fry for 6 to 9 minutes, or until the eggs are have set. Serve and enjoy!

## German Pancake

**Prep time: 5 minutes | Cook time: 12 minutes | Serves 4**

3 eggs, beaten
2 tablespoons butter, melted
1 cup flour

2 tablespoons sugar, powdered
½ cup milk
1 cup fresh strawberries, sliced

Preheat air fryer to 330ºF (166ºC). In a bowl, mix flour, milk, and eggs until fully incorporated. Grease a baking pan that fits in your air fryer with the butter and pour in the mixture. Place the pan in the air fryer's basket when your air fryer displays "READY" (select the cooking preset, and make minor adjustments according to your desired doneness.) and choose a shake reminder. AirFry for 12 to 16 minutes until the pancake is fluffy and golden brown. Drizzle powdered sugar and arrange sliced strawberries on top to serve.

## Japanese Tofu Omelet

**Prep time: 10 minutes | Cook time: 8 minutes | Serves 1**

1 cup cubed tofu
3 whole eggs
Salt and black pepper, to taste
¼ teaspoon ground coriander
¼ teaspoon cumin

1 teaspoon soy sauce
1 tablespoon green onions, chopped
¼ onion, chopped

In a bowl, mix eggs, onion, soy sauce, coriander, cumin, black pepper, and salt. Add in cubed tofu and pour the mixture into a greased baking tray. Place in the air fryer when your air fryer displays "READY" (select the cooking preset, and make minor adjustments according to your desired doneness.) and choose a shake reminder. Bake for 8 minutes at 400ºF (205ºC). When ready, remove, and sprinkle with green onions to serve.

## Cottage Cheese-Kale Omelet

**Prep time: 5 minutes | Cook time: 10 minutes | Serves 2**

5 eggs
3 tablespoons cottage cheese, crumbled
1 cup kale, chopped
½ tablespoon fresh basil,

chopped
½ tablespoon fresh parsley, chopped
Salt and black pepper, to taste

Beat the eggs, salt, and pepper in a bowl. Stir in the rest of the ingredients. Pour the mixture into a greased baking pan and fit in the air fryer. When your air fryer displays "READY" (select the cooking preset, and make minor adjustments according to your desired doneness.) and choose a shake reminder. Bake for 10 minutes at 330ºF (166ºC) until slightly golden and set.

## Breaded Avocado Tempura

**Prep time: 5 minutes | Cook time: 8 minutes | Serves 4**

| | |
|---|---|
| ½ cup breadcrumbs | pitted, peeled, and sliced |
| ½ teaspoon salt 1 avocado, | ½ cup liquid from beans |

Preheat air fryer to 360ºF (182ºC). In a bowl, add the crumbs and salt and mix to combine. Sprinkle the avocado with the beans' liquid and then coat in the crumbs. Arrange the slices in one layer inside the fryer when your air fryer displays "READY" (select the cooking preset, and make minor adjustments according to your desired doneness.) and choose a shake reminder. AirFry for 8 to 10 minutes, shaking once or twice. Serve warm

## Macaroni and Cheese

**Prep time: 10 minutes | Cook time: 10 minutes | Serves 2**

| | |
|---|---|
| 1 cup cooked macaroni | to taste |
| 1 cup grated Cheddar cheese | 1 tablespoon grated Parmesan |
| ½ cup warm milk | cheese |
| Salt and ground black pepper, | |

Preheat the air fryer to 350ºF (177ºC). In a baking dish, mix all the ingredients, except for Parmesan. Put the dish inside the air fryer when your air fryer displays "READY" (select the cooking preset, and make minor adjustments according to your desired doneness.) and choose a shake reminder. Bake for 10 minutes. Add the Parmesan cheese on top and serve.

## Golden Croutons

**Prep time: 5 minutes | Cook time: 6 minutes | Serves 4**

| | |
|---|---|
| 2 cups bread cubes | Garlic salt and black pepper, to |
| 2 tablespoons butter, melted | taste |
| 1 teaspoon dried parsley | |

Mix the cubed bread with butter, parsley, garlic salt, and black pepper until well coated. Place in the fryer's basket when your air fryer displays "READY" (select the cooking preset, and make minor adjustments according to your desired doneness.) and choose a shake reminder. AirFry for 6 to 8 minutes at 380ºF (193ºC), shaking once until golden brown. Use in soups.

## Rosemary Tofu

**Prep time: 15 minutes | Cook time: 14 minutes | Serves 4**

| | |
|---|---|
| 1 (8-ounce / 227-g) package firm or extra-firm tofu | 1 teaspoon dried rosemary |
| 4 teaspoons tamari or shoyu | 1 teaspoon dried dill |
| 1 teaspoon onion granules | 2 teaspoons arrowroot (or cornstarch) |
| ½ teaspoon garlic granules | 2 teaspoons neutral-flavored oil |
| ½ teaspoon turmeric powder | (such as sunflower, safflower, |
| ¼ teaspoon freshly ground black pepper | or melted refined coconut) |
| 2 tablespoons nutritional yeast | Cooking oil spray (sunflower, safflower, or refined coconut) |

Cut the tofu into slices and press out the excess water. Cut the slices into ½-inch cubes and place in a bowl. Sprinkle with the tamari and toss gently to coat. Set aside for a few minutes. Toss the tofu again, then add the onion, garlic, turmeric, and pepper. Gently toss to thoroughly coat. Add the nutritional yeast, rosemary, dill, and arrowroot. Toss gently to coat. Finally, drizzle with the oil and toss one last time. Spray the air fryer basket with the oil. Place the tofu in the air fryer basket when your air fryer displays "READY" (select the cooking preset, and make minor adjustments according to your desired doneness.) and choose a shake reminder. Bake for 7 minutes. Remove, shake gently (so that the tofu cooks evenly), and cook for another 7 minutes, or until the tofu is crisp and browned.

## Blueberry-Almond Oat Bars

**Prep time: 10 minutes | Cook time: 10 minutes | Makes 12 bars**

| | |
|---|---|
| 2 cups rolled oats | 2 eggs, lightly beaten |
| ¼ cup ground almonds | ½ cup canola oil |
| ¼ cup sugar | ½ cup milk |
| 1 teaspoon baking powder | 1 teaspoon vanilla extract |
| ½ teaspoon ground cinnamon | 2 cups blueberries |

Spray a baking pan that fits in your air fryer with cooking spray. In a bowl, add oats, almonds, sugar, baking powder, and cinnamon and stir well. In another bowl, whisk eggs, canola oil, milk, and vanilla. Stir the wet ingredients gently into the oat mixture. Fold in the blueberries. Pour the mixture into the pan and place it in the fryer. When your air fryer displays "READY" (select the cooking preset, and make minor adjustments according to your desired doneness.) and choose a shake reminder. Cook for 10 minutes at 350ºF (180ºC). Let it cool on a wire rack. Cut into 12 bars.

## Meaty Mozzarella Omelet

**Prep time: 10 minutes | Cook time: 10 minutes | Serves 2**

| | |
|---|---|
| 1 beef sausage, chopped | 4 eggs |
| 4 slices prosciutto, chopped | 1 green onion, chopped |
| 3 ounces (85 g) salami, chopped | 1 tablespoon ketchup |
| 1 cup Mozzarella cheese, grated | 1 teaspoon fresh parsley, chopped |

Preheat air fryer to 350ºF (180ºC). Whisk the eggs with ketchup in a bowl. Stir in green onion, mozzarella, salami, and prosciutto. When your air fryer displays "READY" (select the cooking preset, and make minor adjustments according to your desired doneness.) and choose a shake reminder. AirFry the sausage in a greased baking tray in the fryer for 2 minutes. Slide-out and pour the egg mixture on top. Cook for another 8 minutes until golden. Serve sliced with parsley.

## Walnut Muffins with Apple Sauce

**Prep time: 15 minutes | Cook time: 20 minutes | Makes 8 muffins**

| | |
|---|---|
| 1 cup flour | 2 tablespoons melted butter, |
| ⅓ cup sugar | plus 2 teaspoons |
| 1 teaspoon baking powder | ¾ cup unsweetened |
| ¼ teaspoon baking soda | applesauce |
| ¼ teaspoon salt | ½ teaspoon vanilla extract |
| 1 teaspoon cinnamon | ¼ cup chopped walnuts |
| ¼ teaspoon ginger | ¼ cup diced apple |
| ¼ teaspoon nutmeg | 8 foil muffin cups, liners |
| 1 egg | removed and sprayed with |
| 2 tablespoons pancake syrup, plus 2 teaspoons | cooking spray |

Preheat air fryer to 330ºF (166ºC). In a large bowl, stir together flour, sugar, baking powder, baking soda, salt, cinnamon, ginger, and nutmeg. In a small bowl, beat egg until frothy. Add syrup, butter, applesauce, and vanilla and mix well. Pour egg mixture into dry ingredients and stir just until moistened. Gently stir in nuts and diced apple. Divide batter among the 8 muffin cups. Place 4 muffin cups in air fryer basket when your air fryer displays "READY" (select the cooking preset, and make minor adjustments according to your desired doneness.) and choose a shake reminder. Cook at 330ºF (166ºC) for 9 to 11 minutes. Repeat with remaining 4 muffins or until toothpick inserted in center comes out clean.

## Indian Masala Omelet

**Prep time: 10 minutes | Cook time: 10 minutes | Serves 1**

1 garlic clove, crushed
2 green onions
½ chili powder
½ teaspoon garam masala
2 eggs

1 tablespoon olive oil
1 tablespoon fresh cilantro, chopped
Salt and black pepper, to taste

Warm the olive oil in a skillet over medium. Add and sauté the spring onions and garlic for 2 minutes until softened. Sprinkle with chili powder, garam masala, salt, and pepper. Set aside. Preheat air fryer to 340°F (171°C). In a bowl, mix the eggs with salt and black pepper. Add in the masala mixture and stir well. Transfer to a greased baking that fits into your air fryer. When your air fryer displays "READY" (select the cooking preset, and make minor adjustments according to your desired doneness.) and choose a shake reminder. Bake in the fryer for 8 minutes until golden, flipping once. Scatter your omelet with cilantro and serve immediately.

## Herb Parmesan Bagel

**Prep time: 10 minutes | Cook time: 6 minutes | Serves 1**

1 tablespoon butter, softened
¼ teaspoon dried basil
¼ teaspoon dried parsley
¼ teaspoon garlic powder

1 tablespoon Parmesan cheese, grated
Salt and black pepper, to taste
1 bagel, halved

Preheat air fryer to 370°F (188°C). Place the bagel halves in the fryer when your air fryer displays "READY" (select the cooking preset, and make minor adjustments according to your desired doneness.) and choose a shake reminder. Toast for 3 minutes on AirFry mode. Mix butter, Parmesan cheese, garlic, basil, and parsley in a bowl. Season with salt and pepper. Spread the mixture onto the toasted bagel and return to the fryer to AirFry for 3 more minutes. Serve.

## Carrot and Golden Raisin Muffins

**Prep time: 10 minutes | Cook time: 12 minutes | Makes 8 muffins**

1½ cups whole-wheat pastry flour
1 teaspoon low-sodium baking powder
⅓ cup brown sugar
½ teaspoon ground cinnamon

1 egg
2 egg whites
⅔ cup almond milk
3 tablespoons safflower oil
½ cup finely shredded carrots
⅓ cup golden raisins, chopped

In a medium bowl, combine the flour, baking powder, brown sugar, and cinnamon, and mix well. In a small bowl, combine the egg, egg whites, almond milk, and oil and beat until combined. Stir the egg mixture into the dry ingredients just until combined. Don't overbeat; some lumps should be in the batter—that's just fine. Stir the shredded carrot and chopped raisins gently into the batter. Double up 16 foil muffin cups to make 8 cups. Put 4 of the cups into the air fryer and fill ¾ full with the batter. When your air fryer displays "READY" (select the cooking preset, and make minor adjustments according to your desired doneness.) and choose a shake reminder. Bake for 12 to 17 minutes or until the tops of the muffins spring back when lightly touched with your finger. Repeat with remaining muffin cups and the remaining batter. Cool the muffins on a wire rack for 10 minutes before serving.

## Buttery Brown Sugar-Pumpkin Donut Holes

**Prep time: 10 minutes | Cook time: 5 minutes | Makes 12 donut holes**

1 cup whole-wheat pastry flour, plus more as needed
3 tablespoons packed brown sugar
½ teaspoon ground cinnamon
1 teaspoon low-sodium baking powder
⅓ cup canned no-salt-added

pumpkin purée
3 tablespoons 2 percent milk, plus more as needed
2 tablespoons unsalted butter, melted
1 egg white
Powdered sugar (optional)

In a medium bowl, mix the pastry flour, brown sugar, cinnamon, and baking powder. In a small bowl, beat the pumpkin, milk, butter, and egg white until combined. Add the pumpkin mixture to the dry ingredients and mix until combined. You may need to add more flour or milk to form a soft dough. Divide the dough into 12 pieces. With floured hands, form each piece into a ball. Cut a piece of parchment paper or aluminum foil to fit inside the air fryer basket but about 1 inch smaller in diameter. Poke holes in the paper or foil and place it in the basket. Put 6 donut holes into the basket, leaving some space around each. When your air fryer displays "READY" (select the cooking preset, and make minor adjustments according to your desired doneness.) and choose a shake reminder. Air-fry for 5 to 7 minutes, or until the donut holes reach an internal temperature of 200°F (93°C) and are firm and light golden brown. Let cool for 5 minutes. Remove from the basket and roll in powdered sugar, if desired. Repeat with the remaining donut holes and serve.

## Brown Sugar-Mango Bread

**Prep time: 10 minutes | Cook time: 18 minutes | Serves 6**

½ cup butter, melted
1 egg, lightly beaten
½ cup brown sugar
1 teaspoon vanilla extract
3 ripe mangoes, mashed

1½ cups flour
1 teaspoon baking powder
½ teaspoon grated nutmeg
½ teaspoon ground cinnamon

Line a loaf tin with baking paper. In a bowl, whisk melted butter, egg, sugar, vanilla, and mangoes. Sift in flour, baking powder, nutmeg, and ground cinnamon and stir without overmixing. Pour the batter into the tin and place in the air fryer. When your air fryer displays "READY" (select the cooking preset, and make minor adjustments according to your desired doneness.) and choose a shake reminder. Bake for 18 to 20 minutes at 330°F (166°C). Let cool before slicing and serve.

## Air-Fried Crispy Bacon

**Prep time: 5 minutes | Cook time: 5 minutes | Serves 5**

10 slices bacon

Preheat air fryer to 400°F (204°C). Cut the bacon slices in half, so they will fit in the air fryer. Place the half-slices in the fryer basket in a single layer. (You may need to cook the bacon in more than one batch.) When your air fryer displays "READY" (select the cooking preset, and make minor adjustments according to your desired doneness.) and choose a shake reminder. Set the temperature to 400°F (204°C). Set the timer and fry for 5 minutes. Open the drawer and check the bacon. (The power of the fan may have caused the bacon to fly around during the cooking process. If so, use a fork or tongs to rearrange the slices.) Reset the timer and fry for 5 minutes more. When the time has elapsed, check the bacon again. If you like your bacon crispier, cook it for another 1 to 2 minutes.

## Chickpeas Donuts with Cinnamon

**Prep time: 10 minutes | Cook time: 10 minutes | Serves 6**

1 cup flour
¼ cup sugar
1 teaspoon baking powder
½ teaspoon salt
¼ teaspoon cinnamon

1 tablespoon coconut oil, melted
2 tablespoons aquafaba or liquid from canned chickpeas
¼ cup milk

Put the sugar, flour and baking powder in a bowl and combine. Mix in the salt and cinnamon. In a separate bowl, combine the aquafaba, milk and coconut oil. Slowly pour the dry ingredients into the wet ingredients and combine well to create a sticky dough. Refrigerate for at least an hour. Pre-heat your Air Fryer at 370°F (188°C). Using your hands, shape the dough into several small balls and place each one inside the fryer. When your air fryer displays "READY" (select the cooking preset, and make minor adjustments according to your desired doneness.) and choose a shake reminder. Cook for 10 minutes, refraining from shaking the basket as they cook. Lightly dust the balls with sugar and cinnamon and serve with a hot cup of coffee.

## Veggie Strata

**Prep time: 10 minutes | Cook time: 15 minutes | Serves 4**

8 large asparagus spears, trimmed and cut into 2-inch pieces
⅓ cup shredded carrot
½ cup chopped red bell pepper
2 slices low-sodium whole-

wheat bread, cut into ½-inch cubes
3 egg whites
1 egg
3 tablespoons 1 percent milk
½ teaspoon dried thyme

In a 6-by-2-inch pan, combine the asparagus, carrot, red bell pepper, and 1 tablespoon of water. Bake in the air fryer (select the cooking preset, and make minor adjustments according to your desired doneness.) and choose a shake reminder for 3 to 5 minutes, or until crisp-tender. Drain well. Add the bread cubes to the vegetables and gently toss. In a medium bowl, whisk the egg whites, egg, milk, and thyme until frothy. Pour the egg mixture into the pan. Bake for 11 to 15 minutes, or until the strata is slightly puffy and set and the top starts to brown. Serve.

## Cheddar Avocado Quesadillas

**Prep time: 10 minutes | Cook time: 11 minutes | Serves 4**

4 eggs
2 tablespoons skim milk
Salt and ground black pepper, to taste
Cooking spray
4 flour tortillas

4 tablespoons salsa
2 ounces (57 g) Cheddar cheese, grated
½ small avocado, peeled and thinly sliced

Preheat the air fryer to 270°F (132°C). Beat together the eggs, milk, salt, and pepper. Spray a baking pan lightly with cooking spray and add egg mixture. When your air fryer displays "READY" (select the cooking preset, and make minor adjustments according to your desired doneness.) and choose a shake reminder. Bake for 8 minutes, stirring every 1 to 2 minutes, until eggs are scrambled to the liking. Remove and set aside. Spray one side of each tortilla with cooking spray. Flip over. Divide eggs, salsa, cheese, and avocado among the tortillas, covering only half of each tortilla. Fold each tortilla in half and press down lightly. Increase the temperature of the air fryer to 390°F (199°C). Put 2 tortillas in air fryer basket and air fry for 3 minutes or until cheese melts and outside feels slightly crispy. Repeat with remaining two tortillas. Cut each cooked tortilla into halves. Serve warm.

## Banana and Chia Seeds Pudding

**Prep time: 5 minutes | Cook time: 0 minutes | Serves 1**

1 can full-fat coconut milk
1 medium- or small-sized banana, ripe

½ teaspoon cinnamon
1 teaspoon vanilla extract
¼ cup chia seeds

In a bowl, mash the banana until soft. Add the remaining ingredients and mix until incorporated. Cover and place in your refrigerator overnight. Serve!

## Cheesy Bacon and Broccoli Bread Pudding

**Prep time: 15 minutes | Cook time: 48 minutes | Serves 2 to 4**

½ pound (227 g) thick cut bacon, cut into ¼-inch pieces
3 cups brioche bread, cut into ½-inch cubes
2 tablespoons butter, melted
3 eggs
1 cup milk

½ teaspoon salt
Freshly ground black pepper, to taste
1 cup frozen broccoli florets, thawed and chopped
1½ cups grated Swiss cheese

Preheat the air fryer to 400°F (204°C). When your air fryer displays "READY" (select the cooking preset, and make minor adjustments according to your desired doneness.) and choose a shake reminder. Air fry the bacon for 8 minutes until crispy, shaking the basket a few times to help it air fry evenly. Remove the bacon and set it aside on a paper towel. Air fry the brioche bread cubes for 2 minutes to dry and toast lightly. Butter a cake pan. Combine all the remaining ingredients in a large bowl and toss well. Transfer the mixture to the buttered cake pan, cover with aluminum foil and refrigerate the bread pudding overnight, or for at least 8 hours. Remove the cake pan from the refrigerator an hour before you plan to bake and let it sit on the countertop to come to room temperature. Preheat the air fryer to 330°F (166°C). Transfer the covered cake pan to the basket of the air fryer, lowering the pan into the basket. Fold the ends of the aluminum foil over the top of the pan before returning the basket to the air fryer. Bake for 20 minutes. Remove the foil and air fry for an additional 20 minutes. If the top browns a little too much before the custard has set, simply return the foil to the pan. The bread pudding has cooked through when a skewer inserted into the center comes out clean. Serve warm.

## Mushroom Bread Boat Eggs

**Prep time: 10 minutes | Cook time: 13 minutes | Serves 4**

4 pistolette rolls
1 teaspoon butter
¼ cup diced fresh mushrooms
½ teaspoon dried onion flakes
4 eggs

½ teaspoon salt
¼ teaspoon dried dill weed
¼ teaspoon dried parsley
1 tablespoon milk

Preheat the air fryer to 390°F (199°C). Cut a rectangle in the top of each roll and scoop out center, leaving ½-inch shell on the sides and bottom. Place butter, mushrooms, and dried onion in air fryer baking pan and cook for 1 minute. Stir and cook 3 more minutes. In a medium bowl, beat together the eggs, salt, dill, parsley, and milk. Pour mixture into pan with mushrooms. When your air fryer displays "READY" (select the cooking preset, and make minor adjustments according to your desired doneness.) and choose a shake reminder. Cook at 390°F (199°C) for 2 minutes. Stir. Continue cooking for 3 or 4 minutes, stirring every minute, until eggs are scrambled to your liking. Remove baking pan from air fryer and fill rolls with scrambled egg mixture. Place filled rolls in air fryer basket and cook at 390°F (199°C) for 2 to 3 minutes or until rolls are lightly browned.

## Simple Bacon Eggs on the Go

**Prep time: 5 minutes | Cook time: 15 minutes | Serves 1**

2 eggs
4 ounces (113 g) bacon, cooked

Salt and ground black pepper, to taste

Preheat the air fryer to 400ºF (204ºC). Put liners in a regular cupcake tin. Crack an egg into each of the cups and add the bacon. Season with some pepper and salt. When your air fryer displays "READY" (select the cooking preset, and make minor adjustments according to your desired doneness.) and choose a shake reminder. Bake in the preheated air fryer for 15 minutes, or until the eggs are set. Serve warm.

## Sweet Banana Bread

**Prep time: 10 minutes | Cook time: 22 minutes | Makes 3 loaves**

3 ripe bananas, mashed
1 cup sugar
1 large egg
4 tablespoons (½ stick)

unsalted butter, melted
1½ cups all-purpose flour
1 teaspoon baking soda
1 teaspoon salt

Coat the insides of 3 mini loaf pans with cooking spray. In a large mixing bowl, mix the bananas and sugar. In a separate large mixing bowl, combine the egg, butter, flour, baking soda, and salt and mix well. Add the banana mixture to the egg and flour mixture. Mix well. Divide the batter evenly among the prepared pans. Preheat the air fryer to 310ºF (154ºC). Set the mini loaf pans into the air fryer basket. When your air fryer displays "READY" (select the cooking preset, and make minor adjustments according to your desired doneness.) and choose a shake reminder. Bake in the preheated air fryer for 22 minutes. Insert a toothpick into the center of each loaf; if it comes out clean, they are done. When the loaves are cooked through, remove the pans from the air fryer basket. Turn out the loaves onto a wire rack to cool. Serve warm.

## Cherry Tarts with Vanilla Frosting

**Prep time: 10 minutes | Cook time: 20 minutes | Serves 6**

**For the Tarts:**
2 refrigerated piecrusts
⅓ cup cherry preserves
**For the Frosting:**
½ cup vanilla yogurt
1 ounce (28 g) cream cheese

1 teaspoon cornstarch
Cooking oil

1 teaspoon stevia
Rainbow sprinkles, for garnish

Place the piecrusts on a flat surface. Using a knife or pizza cutter, cut each piecrust into 3 rectangles, for 6 total. (I discard the unused dough left from slicing the edges.) In a small bowl, combine the preserves and cornstarch. Mix well. Scoop 1 tablespoon of the preserves mixture onto the top half of each piece of piecrust. Fold the bottom of each piece up to close the tart. Using the back of a fork, press along the edges of each tart to seal. Spray the breakfast tarts with cooking oil and place them in the air fryer. I do not recommend stacking the breakfast tarts. They will stick together if stacked. You may need to prepare them in two batches. When your air fryer displays "READY" (select the cooking preset, and make minor adjustments according to your desired doneness.) and choose a shake reminder. Cook for 10 minutes. Allow the breakfast tarts to cool fully before removing from the air fryer. If necessary, repeat steps 5 and 6 for the remaining breakfast tarts. In a small bowl, combine the yogurt, cream cheese, and stevia. Mix well. Spread the breakfast tarts with frosting and top with sprinkles, and serve.

## Yellow Banana Churros with Oatmeal

**Prep time: 15 minutes | Cook time: 15 minutes | Serves 2**

**For the Churros:**
1 large yellow banana, peeled, cut in half lengthwise, then cut in half widthwise
2 tablespoons whole-wheat pastry flour
⅛ teaspoon sea salt
**For the Oatmeal:**
¾ cup rolled oats

2 teaspoons oil (sunflower or melted coconut)
1 teaspoon water
Cooking spray
1 tablespoon coconut sugar
½ teaspoon cinnamon

1½ cups water

Put the 4 banana pieces in a medium-size bowl and add the flour and salt. Stir gently. Add the oil and water. Stir gently until evenly mixed. You may need to press some coating onto the banana pieces. Spray the air fryer basket with the oil spray. Put the banana pieces in the air fryer basket when your air fryer displays "READY" (select the cooking preset, and make minor adjustments according to your desired doneness.) and choose a shake reminder. Air fry for 5 minutes. Remove, gently turn over, and air fry for another 5 minutes or until browned. In a medium bowl, add the coconut sugar and cinnamon and stir to combine. When the banana pieces are nicely browned, spray with the oil and place in the cinnamon-sugar bowl. Toss gently with a spatula to coat the banana pieces with the mixture. While the bananas are cooking, make the oatmeal. In a medium pot, bring the oats and water to a boil, then reduce to low heat. Simmer, stirring often, until all the water is absorbed, about 5 minutes. Put the oatmeal into two bowls. Top the oatmeal with the coated banana pieces and serve immediately.

## Yummy Donut Holes

**Prep time: 15 minutes | Cook time: 8 minutes | Makes 12 donut holes**

1 tablespoon ground flaxseed
1½ tablespoons water
¼ cup nondairy milk, unsweetened
2 tablespoons neutral-flavored oil (sunflower, safflower, or refined coconut)
1½ teaspoons vanilla
1½ cups whole-wheat pastry flour or all-purpose gluten-free

flour
¾ cup coconut sugar, divided
2½ teaspoons cinnamon, divided
½ teaspoon nutmeg
¼ teaspoon sea salt
¾ teaspoon baking powder
Cooking oil spray (refined coconut, sunflower, or safflower)

In a medium bowl, stir the flaxseed with the water and set aside for 5 minutes, or until gooey and thick. Add the milk, oil, and vanilla. Stir well and set this wet mixture aside. In a small bowl, combine the flour, ½ cup coconut sugar, ½ teaspoon cinnamon, nutmeg, salt, and baking powder. Stir very well. Add this mixture to the wet mixture and stir together—it will be stiff, so you'll need to knead it lightly, just until all of the ingredients are thoroughly combined. Spray the air fryer basket with oil. Pull off bits of the dough and roll into balls (about 1 inch in size each). Place in the basket, leaving room in between as they'll increase in size a smidge. (You'll need to work in batches, as you probably won't be able to cook all 12 at once.) Spray the tops with oil and fry for 6 minutes. Remove the pan, spray the donut holes with oil again, flip them over, and spray them with oil again. Fry them for 2 more minutes, or until golden-brown. During these last 2 minutes of frying, place the remaining 4 tablespoons coconut sugar and 2 teaspoons cinnamon in a bowl, and stir to combine. When the donut holes are done frying, remove them one at a time and coat them as follows: Spray with oil again and toss with the cinnamon-sugar mixture. Spray one last time, and coat with the cinnamon-sugar one last time. Enjoy fresh and warm if possible, as they're best that way.

## Barbecue Cheesy Chicken Flatbreads

**Prep time: 10 minutes | Cook time: 10 minutes | Serves 2 to 4**

2 cups chopped cooked chicken
¾ cup prepared barbecue sauce
2 prepared naan flatbreads
½ cup shredded smoked Gouda cheese

¾ cup shredded Mozzarella cheese
½ small red onion, halved and thinly sliced
2 tablespoons chopped fresh cilantro

Preheat the air fryer to 400ºF (204ºC). In a medium bowl, toss together the chicken and ¼ cup of the barbecue sauce. Spread half the remaining barbecue sauce on one of the flatbreads. Top with half the chicken and half each of the Gouda and Mozzarella cheeses. Sprinkle with half the red onion. Gently press the cheese and onions onto the chicken with your fingers. Carefully place one flatbread in the air-fryer basket. When your air fryer displays "READY" (select the cooking preset, and make minor adjustments according to your desired doneness.) and choose a shake reminder. Set the air fryer to 400ºF (204ºC) for 10 minutes, until the bread is browned around the edges and the cheese is bubbling and golden brown. If not, cook for 2 minutes more. Transfer the flatbread to a plate and repeat to cook the second flatbread. Sprinkle with the chopped cilantro before serving.

## Fresh Blueberry Muffins

**Prep time: 10 minutes | Cook time: 14 minutes | Serves 10**

⅔ cup all-purpose flour
1 teaspoon baking powder
2 tablespoons sugar
1 egg
2 teaspoons vanilla extract

⅓ cup low-fat milk
3 tablespoons unsalted butter, melted
¾ cup fresh blueberries

Preheat the air fryer to 320ºF (160ºC). In a medium mixing bowl, combine the flour, baking powder, sugar, egg, vanilla, milk, and melted butter and mix well. Fold in the blueberries. Coat the inside of an air fryer muffin tin with cooking spray. Fill each muffin cup about two-thirds full. Set the muffin tin into the air fryer basket. (You may need to cook the muffins in more than one batch.) When your air fryer displays "READY" (select the cooking preset, and make minor adjustments according to your desired doneness.) and choose a shake reminder. Set the temperature to 320ºF (160ºC). Set the timer and bake for 14 minutes. Insert a toothpick into the center of a muffin; if it comes out clean, they are done. If batter clings to the toothpick, cook the muffins for 2 minutes more and check again. When the muffins are cooked through, use silicone oven mitts to remove the muffin tin from the air fryer basket. Turn out the muffins onto a wire rack to cool slightly before serving.

## Cool Paprika Hash Browns

**Prep time: 5 minutes | Cook time: 20 minutes | Serves 4**

4 russet potatoes
1 teaspoon paprika
Salt, to taste

Pepper, to taste
Cooking oil

Peel the potatoes using a vegetable peeler. Using a cheese grater, shred the potatoes. If your grater has different-size holes, use the area of the tool with the largest holes. Place the shredded potatoes in a large bowl of cold water. Let sit for 5 minutes. Cold water helps remove excess starch from the potatoes. Stir to help dissolve the starch. Drain the potatoes and dry with paper towels or napkins. Make sure the potatoes are completely dry. Season the potatoes with the paprika and salt and pepper to taste. Spray the potatoes with cooking oil and transfer them to the air fryer. Cook for 20 minutes, shaking the basket every 5 minutes (a total of 4 times). Cool before serving.

## Speedy Buttermilk Biscuits

**Prep time: 5 minutes | Cook time: 5 minutes | Makes 12 biscuits**

2 cups all-purpose flour, plus more for dusting the work surface
1 tablespoon baking powder
¼ teaspoon baking soda
2 teaspoons sugar

1 teaspoon salt
6 tablespoons cold unsalted butter, cut into 1-tablespoon slices
¾ cup buttermilk

Preheat the air fryer to 360ºF (182ºC). Spray the air fryer basket with olive oil. In a large mixing bowl, combine the flour, baking powder, baking soda, sugar, and salt and mix well. Using a fork, cut in the butter until the mixture resembles coarse meal. Add the buttermilk and mix until smooth. Dust more flour on a clean work surface. Turn the dough out onto the work surface and roll it out until it is about ½ inch thick. Using a 2-inch biscuit cutter, cut out the biscuits. Put the uncooked biscuits in the greased air fryer basket in a single layer. When your air fryer displays "READY" (select the cooking preset, and make minor adjustments according to your desired doneness.) and choose a shake reminder. Bake for 5 minutes. Transfer the cooked biscuits from the air fryer to a platter. Cut the remaining biscuits. Bake the remaining biscuits. Serve warm.

## Canadian Bacon-Cheese Muffins

**Prep time: 5 minutes | Cook time: 8 minutes | Serves 4**

4 English muffins
8 slices Canadian bacon

4 slices cheese
Cooking oil

Split each English muffin. Assemble the breakfast sandwiches by layering 2 slices of Canadian bacon and 1 slice of cheese onto each English muffin bottom. Top with the other half of the English muffin. Place the sandwiches in the air fryer. Spray the top of each with cooking oil. When your air fryer displays "READY" (select the cooking preset, and make minor adjustments according to your desired doneness.) and choose a shake reminder. Cook for 4 minutes. Open the air fryer and flip the sandwiches. Cook for an additional 4 minutes. Cool before serving.

## Cheddar and Veggie Egg Cups

**Prep time: 10 minutes | Cook time: 19 minutes | Serves 2**

Vegetable oil, for greasing
2 large eggs
½ cup mixed diced vegetables, such as onions, bell peppers, mushrooms, tomatoes
½ cup shredded sharp Cheddar cheese

2 tablespoons half-and-half
1 tablespoon chopped fresh cilantro (or other fresh herb of your choice)
Kosher salt and black pepper, to taste

Preheat the air fryer to 400ºF (204ºC). Grease two 6-ounce ramekins with vegetable oil. In a medium bowl, whisk together the eggs, vegetables, ¼ cup of the cheese, the half-and-half, cilantro, and salt and pepper to taste. Divide the mixture between the prepared ramekins. Place the ramekins in the air-fryer basket. Set the air fryer to 300ºF (149ºC) for 15 minutes. Top the cups with the remaining ¼ cup cheese. When your air fryer displays "READY" (select the cooking preset, and make minor adjustments according to your desired doneness.) and choose a shake reminder. Set the air fryer to 400ºF (204ºC) and cook for 4 minutes, until the cheese on top is melted and lightly browned. Serve immediately, or store in an airtight container in the refrigerator up to a week.

## Bacon and Cheddar Cheese Muffins

**Prep time: 5 minutes | Cook time: 20 minutes | Serves 1**

1 medium egg
¼ cup heavy cream
1 slice cooked bacon (cured,

pan-fried, cooked)
1 ounce (28 g) Cheddar cheese
Salt and black pepper, to taste

Preheat your fryer to 350ºF (177ºC). In a bowl, mix the eggs with the cream, salt and pepper. Spread into muffin tins and fill the cups half full. Place 1 slice of bacon into each muffin hole and half ounce of cheese on top of each muffin. When your air fryer displays "READY" (select the cooking preset, and make minor adjustments according to your desired doneness.) and choose a shake reminder. Bake for around 15 to 20 minutes or until slightly browned. Add another ½ ounce of cheese onto each muffin and broil until the cheese is slightly browned. Serve!

## Ham and Cheddar Cheese Muffins

**Prep time: 10 minutes | Cook time: 12 minutes | Makes 8 muffins**

¾ cup yellow cornmeal
¼ cup flour
1½ teaspoons baking powder
¼ teaspoon salt
1 egg, beaten
2 tablespoons canola oil
½ cup milk

½ cup shredded sharp Cheddar cheese
½ cup diced ham
8 foil muffin cups, liners removed and sprayed with cooking spray

Preheat air fryer to 390ºF (199ºC). In a medium bowl, stir together the cornmeal, flour, baking powder, and salt. Add egg, oil, and milk to dry ingredients and mix well. Stir in shredded cheese and diced ham. Divide batter among the muffin cups. Place 4 filled muffin cups in air fryer basket when your air fryer displays "READY" (select the cooking preset, and make minor adjustments according to your desired doneness.) and choose a shake reminder. Bake for 5 minutes. Reduce temperature to 330ºF (166ºC) and bake for 1 to 2 minutes or until toothpick inserted in center of muffin comes out clean. Repeat steps 6 and 7 to cook remaining muffins.

## Chocolate and Almond Crescent Rolls

**Prep time: 5 minutes | Cook time: 8 minutes | Serves 4 to 6**

1 (8-ounce / 227-g) tube of crescent roll dough
⅔ cup semi-sweet or bittersweet chocolate chunks

1 egg white, lightly beaten
¼ cup sliced almonds
Powdered sugar, for dusting
Butter or oil

Pre-heat the air fryer to 350ºF (177ºC). Unwrap the crescent roll dough and separate it into triangles with the points facing away from you. Place a row of chocolate chunks along the bottom edge of the dough. (If you are using chips, make it a double row.) Roll the dough up around the chocolate and then place another row of chunks on the dough. Roll again and finish with one or two chocolate chunks. Be sure to leave the end free of chocolate so that it can adhere to the rest of the roll. Brush the tops of the crescent rolls with the lightly beaten egg white and sprinkle the almonds on top, pressing them into the crescent dough so they adhere. Brush the bottom of the air fryer basket with butter or oil and transfer the crescent rolls to the basket. When your air fryer displays "READY" (select the cooking preset, and make minor adjustments according to your desired doneness.) and choose a shake reminder. Air-fry at 350ºF (177ºC) for 8 minutes. Remove and let the crescent rolls cool before dusting with powdered sugar and serving.

## Baked Cinnamon Rolls

**Prep time: 5 minutes | Cook time: 12 minutes | Makes 8 cinnamon rolls**

1 can of cinnamon rolls

Preheat the air fryer to 340ºF (171ºC). Spray the air fryer basket with olive oil. Separate the canned cinnamon rolls and place them in the air fryer basket. When your air fryer displays "READY" (select the cooking preset, and make minor adjustments according to your desired doneness.) and choose a shake reminder. Set the temperature to 340ºF (171ºC). Set the timer and bake for 6 minutes. Using tongs, flip the cinnamon rolls. Reset the timer and bake for another 6 minutes. When the rolls are done cooking, use tongs to remove them from the air fryer. Transfer them to a platter and spread them with the icing that comes in the package.

## British Breakfast

**Prep time: 5 minutes | Cook time: 25 minutes | Serves 2**

1 cup potatoes, sliced and diced
2 cups beans in tomato sauce
2 eggs

1 tablespoon olive oil
1 sausage
Salt, to taste

Preheat the air fryer to 390ºF (199ºC) and allow to warm. Break the eggs onto a baking dish and sprinkle with salt. Lay the beans on the dish, next to the eggs. In a bowl, coat the potatoes with the olive oil. Sprinkle with salt. Transfer the bowl of potato slices to the air fryer when your air fryer displays "READY" (select the cooking preset, and make minor adjustments according to your desired doneness.) and choose a shake reminder. Bake for 10 minutes. Swap out the bowl of potatoes for the dish containing the eggs and beans. Bake for another 10 minutes. Cover the potatoes with parchment paper. Slice up the sausage and throw the slices on top of the beans and eggs. Bake for another 5 minutes. Serve with the potatoes.

## Cheddar Quesadillas

**Prep time: 10 minutes | Cook time: 18 minutes | Serves 4**

4 eggs
2 tablespoons skim milk
Salt and pepper, to taste
Oil for misting or cooking spray
4 flour tortillas

4 tablespoons salsa
2 ounces (57 g) Cheddar cheese, grated
½ small avocado, peeled and thinly sliced

Preheat air fryer to 270ºF (132ºC). Beat together eggs, milk, salt, and pepper. Spray a 6 x 6-inch air fryer baking pan lightly with cooking spray and add egg mixture. Cook 8 to 9 minutes, stirring every 1 to 2 minutes, until eggs are scrambled to your liking. Remove and set aside. Spray one side of each tortilla with oil or cooking spray. Flip over. Divide eggs, salsa, cheese, and avocado among the tortillas, covering only half of each tortilla. Fold each tortilla in half and press down lightly. Place 2 tortillas in air fryer basket when your air fryer displays "READY" (select the cooking preset, and make minor adjustments according to your desired doneness.) and choose a shake reminder. Cook at 390ºF (199ºC) for 3 minutes or until cheese melts and outside feels slightly crispy. Repeat with remaining two tortillas. Cut each cooked tortilla into halves or thirds.

## Cornflakes Toast Sticks with Maple Syrup

**Prep time: 10 minutes | Cook time: 6 minutes | Serves 4**

2 eggs
½ cup milk
⅛ teaspoon salt
½ teaspoon pure vanilla extract
¾ cup crushed cornflakes

6 slices sandwich bread, each slice cut into 4 strips
Maple syrup, for dipping
Cooking spray

Preheat the air fryer to 390ºF (199ºC). In a small bowl, beat together the eggs, milk, salt, and vanilla. Put crushed cornflakes on a plate or in a shallow dish. Dip bread strips in egg mixture, shake off excess, and roll in cornflake crumbs. Spray both sides of bread strips with oil. Put bread strips in air fryer basket in a single layer when your air fryer displays "READY" (select the cooking preset, and make minor adjustments according to your desired doneness.) and choose a shake reminder. Air fry for 6 minutes or until golden brown. Repeat steps 5 and 6 to air fry remaining French toast sticks. Serve with maple syrup.

## Cranberry Muffins

**Prep time: 10 minutes | Cook time: 30 minutes | Makes 8 muffins**

1½ cups bran cereal flakes
1 cup plus 2 tablespoons whole-wheat pastry flour
3 tablespoons packed brown sugar
1 teaspoon low-sodium baking

powder
1 cup 2 percent milk
3 tablespoons safflower oil or peanut oil
1 egg
½ cup dried cranberries

In a medium bowl, mix the cereal, pastry flour, brown sugar, and baking powder. In a small bowl, whisk the milk, oil, and egg until combined. Stir the egg mixture into the dry ingredients until just combined. Stir in the cranberries. Double up 16 foil muffin cups to make 8 cups. Put 4 cups into the air fryer and fill each three-fourths full with batter when your air fryer displays "READY" (select the cooking preset, and make minor adjustments according to your desired doneness.) and choose a shake reminder. Bake for about 15 minutes, or until the muffin tops spring back when lightly touched with your finger. Repeat with the remaining muffin cups and batter. Let cool on a wire rack for 10 minutes before serving.

## Eggs in a Basket Baked

**Prep time: 5 minutes | Cook time: 6 minutes | Serves 1**

1 thick slice country, sourdough, or Italian bread
2 tablespoons (28 g) unsalted

butter, melted
1 egg
Kosher salt and pepper, to taste

Preheat the air fryer to 300ºF (149ºC). Brush the bottom of the air fryer cake pan insert and both sides of the bread with melted butter. Using a small round cookie or biscuit cutter, cut a hole out of the middle of the bread and set it aside. Place the slice of bread in the air fryer cake pan insert. Crack the egg into the hole in the bread, taking care not to break the yolk. Season with salt and pepper. Place the cut-out bread hole next to the slice of bread. Place the cake pan insert into the air fryer when your air fryer displays "READY" (select the cooking preset, and make minor adjustments according to your desired doneness.) and choose a shake reminder. Bake at 300ºF (149ºC) for 6 to 8 minutes until the egg white is set but the yolk is still runny. Using a silicone spatula, remove the bread slice to a plate. Serve with the cut-out bread circle on the side or place it on top of the egg.

## Cream Cheese Glazed Cinnamon Rolls

**Prep time: 10 minutes | Cook time: 9 minutes | Serves 8**

1 pound (454 g) frozen bread dough, thawed
¼ cup butter, melted
**Cream Cheese Glaze:**
4 ounces (113 g) cream cheese, softened
2 tablespoons butter, softened

¾ cup brown sugar
1½ tablespoons ground cinnamon

1¼ cups powdered sugar
½ teaspoon vanilla extract

Let the bread dough come to room temperature on the counter. On a lightly floured surface, roll the dough into a 13-inch by 11-inch rectangle. Position the rectangle so the 13-inch side is facing you. Brush the melted butter all over the dough, leaving a 1-inch border uncovered along the edge farthest away from you. Combine the brown sugar and cinnamon in a small bowl. Sprinkle the mixture evenly over the buttered dough, keeping the 1-inch border uncovered. Roll the dough into a log, starting with the edge closest to you. Roll the dough tightly, rolling evenly, and push out any air pockets. When you get to the uncovered edge of the dough, press the dough onto the roll to seal it together. Cut the log into 8 pieces, slicing slowly with a sawing motion so you don't flatten the dough. Turn the slices on their sides and cover with a clean kitchen towel. Let the rolls sit in the warmest part of the kitchen for 1½ to 2 hours to rise. To make the glaze, place the cream cheese and butter in a microwave-safe bowl. Soften the mixture in the microwave for 30 seconds at a time until it is easy to stir. Gradually add the powdered sugar and stir to combine. Add the vanilla extract and whisk until smooth. Set aside. When the rolls have risen, preheat the air fryer to 350ºF (177ºC). Transfer 4 of the rolls to the air fryer basket when your air fryer displays "READY" (select the cooking preset, and make minor adjustments according to your desired doneness.) and choose a shake reminder. Air fry for 5 minutes. Turn the rolls over and air fry for another 4 minutes. Repeat with the remaining 4 rolls. Let the rolls cool for two minutes before glazing. Spread large dollops of cream cheese glaze on top of the warm cinnamon rolls, allowing some glaze to drip down the side of the rolls. Serve warm.

## Bacon and Egg English Muffins

**Prep time: 5 minutes | Cook time: 8 minutes | Serves 4**

4 eggs
Salt and pepper, to taste
Olive oil
4 English muffins, split

1 cup shredded Colby Jack cheese
4 slices ham or Canadian bacon

Preheat air fryer to 390ºF (199ºC). Beat together eggs and add salt and pepper to taste. Spray air fryer baking pan lightly with oil and add eggs when your air fryer displays "READY" (select the cooking preset, and make minor adjustments according to your desired doneness.) and choose a shake reminder. Cook for 2 minutes, stir, and continue cooking for 3 or 4 minutes, stirring every minute, until eggs are scrambled to your preference. Remove pan from air fryer. Place bottom halves of English muffins in air fryer basket. Take half of the shredded cheese and divide it among the muffins. Top each with a slice of ham and one-quarter of the eggs. Sprinkle remaining cheese on top of the eggs. Use a fork to press the cheese into the egg a little so it doesn't slip off before it melts. Cook at 360ºF (182ºC) for 1 minute. Add English muffin tops and cook for 2 to 4 minutes to heat through and toast the muffins.

## Creamy Cinnamon-Glazed Pecan Roll

**Prep time: 15 minutes | Cook time: 25 minutes | Serves 2**

8 ounces (227 g) pizza dough
All-purpose flour, for dusting
2 tablespoons unsalted butter, melted
¼ cup packed dark brown sugar
¼ cup chopped pecans
¼ teaspoon kosher salt

1 tablespoon maple syrup, or dark agave syrup
½ cup powdered sugar
1 ounce (28 g) cream cheese, at room temperature
1 tablespoon milk
⅛ teaspoon ground cinnamon

Preheat the air fryer to 325ºF (163ºC). Using a rolling pin, roll the pizza dough out on a lightly floured work surface into a rough 12 x 8-inch rectangle. Brush the dough all over with the melted butter, then sprinkle evenly with the brown sugar, pecans, and salt, then drizzle with the syrup. Using a pizza cutter or knife, cut the rectangle lengthwise into 8 equal strips. Roll up one strip like a snail shell, then continue rolling each spiral up in the next strip until you have one giant spiral. Cut a piece of parchment paper or foil to the size of the bottom of your air fryer basket and line the bottom with it. Carefully lay the spiral in the air fryer and cover with a round of foil cut to fit the size of the spiral when your air fryer displays "READY" (select the cooking preset, and make minor adjustments according to your desired doneness.) and choose a shake reminder. Cook at 325ºF (163ºC) for 15 minutes. Remove the foil round from the top and cook the roll until golden brown and cooked through in the middle, about 10 minutes more. Meanwhile, in a bowl, whisk together the powdered sugar, cream cheese, milk, and cinnamon until smooth. Once the roll is cooked, let it cool in the basket for 10 minutes, then carefully lift it out of the air fryer using the parchment paper bottom as an aid. Transfer the roll to a plate and pour the icing over the roll to cover it completely. Let the roll and icing cool together for at least 10 more minutes to set before cutting into wedges to serve.

## Coconut Pancakes

**Prep time: 5 minutes | Cook time: 5 minutes | Serves 1**

2 ounces (57 g) cream cheese
2 eggs
½ teaspoon cinnamon

1 tablespoon coconut flour
½ to 1 packet of sugar

Mix together all the ingredients until smooth. Heat up a non-stick pan or skillet with butter or coconut oil on medium-high. Make them as you would normal pancakes. Cook it on one side and then flip to cook the other side! Top with some butter and/or sugar.

## Tow Berries Breakfast Puffs

**Prep time: 10 minutes | Cook time: 15 minutes | Serves 4**

1 puff pastry sheet
1 tablespoon strawberries, mashed
1 tablespoon raspberries,

mashed
¼ teaspoon vanilla extract
1 cup cream cheese
1 tablespoon honey

Preheat air fryer to 375ºF (191ºC). Roll the puff pastry out on a lightly floured surface into a 1-inch thick rectangle. Cut into 4 squares. Spread the cream cheese evenly on them. In a bowl, combine the berries, honey, and vanilla. Spoon the mixture onto the pastry squares. Fold in the sides over the filling. Pinch the ends to form a puff. Place the puffs on a lined with waxed paper baking dish. When your air fryer displays "READY" (select the cooking preset, and make minor adjustments according to your desired doneness.) and choose a shake reminder. Bake in the air fryer for 15 minutes until the pastry is puffed and golden all over. Let it cool for 10 mins before serving.

## Mozzarella Sausage Pizza

**Prep time: 10 minutes | Cook time: 6 minutes | Serves 4**

2 tablespoons ketchup
1 pita bread
⅓ cup sausage
½ pound (227 g) Mozzarella

cheese
1 teaspoon garlic powder
1 tablespoon olive oil

Preheat the air fryer to 340ºF (171ºC). Spread the ketchup over the pita bread. Top with the sausage and cheese. Sprinkle with the garlic powder and olive oil. Put the pizza in the air fryer basket when your air fryer displays "READY" (select the cooking preset, and make minor adjustments according to your desired doneness.) and choose a shake reminder. Bake for 6 minutes. Serve warm.

## Egg and Bacon Muffins with Cheddar

**Prep time: 5 minutes | Cook time: 15 minutes | Serves 1**

2 eggs
Salt and ground black pepper, to taste
1 tablespoon green pesto

3 ounces (85 g) shredded Cheddar cheese
5 ounces (142 g) cooked bacon
1 scallion, chopped

Preheat the air fryer to 350ºF (177ºC). Line a cupcake tin with parchment paper. Beat the eggs with pepper, salt, and pesto in a bowl. Mix in the cheese. Pour the eggs into the cupcake tin and top with the bacon and scallion when your air fryer displays "READY" (select the cooking preset, and make minor adjustments according to your desired doneness.) and choose a shake reminder. Bake in the preheated air fryer for 15 minutes, or until the egg is set. Serve immediately.

## Egg Porridge

**Prep time: 5 minutes | Cook time: 10 minutes | Serves 1**

2 organic free-range eggs
⅓ cup organic heavy cream without food additives
2 packages of your preferred

sweetener
2 tablespoons grass-fed butter
Ground organic cinnamon, to taste

In a bowl add the eggs, cream and sweetener, and mix together. Melt the butter in a saucepan over a medium heat. Lower the heat once the butter is melted. Combine together with the egg and cream mixture. While Cooking, mix until it thickens and curdles. When you see the first signs of curdling, remove the saucepan immediately from the heat. Pour the porridge into a bowl. Sprinkle cinnamon on top and serve immediately.

## Parmesan Eggs Florentine

**Prep time: 5 minutes | Cook time: 15 minutes | Serves 2**

1 cup washed, fresh spinach leaves
2 tablespoons freshly grated Parmesan cheese

Sea salt and pepper, to taste
1 tablespoon white vinegar
2 eggs

Cook the spinach the microwave or steam until wilted. Sprinkle with Parmesan cheese and seasoning. Slice into bite-size pieces and place on a plate. Simmer a pan of water and add the vinegar. Stir quickly with a spoon. Break an egg into the center. Turn off the heat and cover until set. Repeat with the second egg. Place the eggs on top of the spinach and serve.

## Eggs in Pepper Rings with Salsa

**Prep time: 5 minutes | Cook time: 10 to 16 minutes | Serves 4**

1 large red, yellow, or orange bell pepper, cut into four ¾-inch rings
4 eggs
Salt and freshly ground black pepper, to taste
2 teaspoons salsa
Cooking spray

Preheat the air fryer to 350ºF (177ºC). Coat a baking pan lightly with cooking spray. Put 2 bell pepper rings in the prepared baking pan. Crack one egg into each bell pepper ring and sprinkle with salt and pepper. Top each egg with ½ teaspoon of salsa. Put the baking pan in the air fryer basket when your air fryer displays "READY" (select the cooking preset, and make minor adjustments according to your desired doneness.) and choose a shake reminder. Air fry for 5 to 8 minutes, or until the eggs are cooked to your desired doneness. Remove from the pan to a plate and repeat with the remaining bell pepper rings, eggs, and salsa. Serve warm.

## Potatoes with Onion and Bell Pepper

**Prep time: 10 minutes | Cook time: 23 minutes | Serves 4**

3 large russet potatoes
1 tablespoon canola oil
1 tablespoon extra-virgin olive oil
1 teaspoon paprika
Salt, to taste
Pepper, to taste
1 cup chopped onion
1 cup chopped red bell pepper
1 cup chopped green bell pepper

Cut the potatoes into ½-inch cubes. Place the potatoes in a large bowl of cold water and allow them to soak for at least 30 minutes, preferably an hour. Drain the potatoes and dry thoroughly with paper towels. Return them to the empty bowl. Add the canola and olive oils, paprika, and salt and pepper to taste. Toss to fully coat the potatoes. Transfer the potatoes to the air fryer. Cook for 20 minutes, shaking the air fryer basket every 5 minutes (a total of 4 times). Add the onion and red and green bell peppers to the air fryer basket. Cook for an additional 3 to 4 minutes, or until the potatoes are cooked through and the peppers are soft. Cool before serving.

## Kale, Olives, and Pecorino Baked Eggs

**Prep time: 5 minutes | Cook time: 10 to 12 minutes | Serves 2**

1 cup roughly chopped kale leaves, stems and center ribs removed
¼ cup grated pecorino cheese
¼ cup olive oil
1 garlic clove, peeled
3 tablespoons whole almonds
Kosher salt and freshly ground black pepper, to taste
4 large eggs
2 tablespoons heavy cream
3 tablespoons chopped pitted mixed olives

Place the kale, pecorino, olive oil, garlic, almonds, salt, and pepper in a small blender and blitz until well incorporated. Preheat the air fryer to 300ºF (149ºC). One at a time, crack the eggs in a baking pan. Drizzle the kale pesto on top of the egg whites. Top the yolks with the cream and swirl together the yolks and the pesto. Transfer the pan to the air fryer basket when your air fryer displays "READY" (select the cooking preset, and make minor adjustments according to your desired doneness.) and choose a shake reminder. Bake for 10 to 12 minutes, or until the top begins to brown and the eggs are set. Allow the eggs to cool for 5 minutes. Scatter the olives on top and serve warm.

## Cheddar Eggs with Bacon

**Prep time: 10 minutes | Cook time: 27 minutes | Serves 1**

1 teaspoon olive oil
2 tablespoons finely chopped onion
1 teaspoon chopped fresh oregano
pinch crushed red pepper flakes
1 (14-ounce / 397-g) can
crushed or diced tomatoes
Salt and freshly ground black pepper, to taste
2 slices of bacon, chopped
2 large eggs
¼ cup grated Cheddar cheese
Fresh parsley, chopped

Start by making the tomato sauce. Pre-heat a medium saucepan over medium heat on the stovetop. Add the olive oil and sauté the onion, oregano and pepper flakes for 5 minutes. Add the tomatoes and bring to a simmer. Season with salt and freshly ground black pepper and simmer for 10 minutes. Meanwhile, pre-heat the air fryer to 400ºF (204ºC) and pour a little water into the bottom of the air fryer drawer. (This will help prevent the grease that drips into the bottom drawer from burning and smoking.) Place the bacon in the air fryer basket when your air fryer displays "READY" (select the cooking preset, and make minor adjustments according to your desired doneness.) and choose a shake reminder. Air-Fry at 400ºF (204ºC) for 5 minutes, shaking the basket every once in a while. When the bacon is almost crispy, remove it to a paper-towel lined plate and rinse out the air fryer drawer, draining away the bacon grease. Transfer the tomato sauce to a shallow 7-inch pie dish. Crack the eggs on top of the sauce and scatter the cooked bacon back on top. Season with salt and freshly ground black pepper and transfer the pie dish into the air fryer basket. You can use an aluminum foil sling to help with this by taking a long piece of aluminum foil, folding it in half lengthwise twice until it is roughly 26-inches by 3-inches. Place this under the pie dish and hold the ends of the foil to move the pie dish in and out of the air fryer basket. Tuck the ends of the foil beside the pie dish while it cooks in the air fryer. Air-fry at 400ºF (204ºC) for 5 minutes, or until the eggs are almost cooked to your liking. Sprinkle cheese on top and air-fry for an additional 2 minutes. When the cheese has melted, remove the pie dish from the air fryer, sprinkle with a little chopped parsley and let the eggs cool for a few minutes – just enough time to toast some buttered bread in your air fryer!

## Cherry and Raisin Beignets

**Prep time: 10 minutes | Cook time: 8 minutes | Makes 16 beignets**

1 teaspoon active quick-rising dry yeast
⅓ cup buttermilk
3 tablespoons packed brown sugar
1 egg
1½ cups whole-wheat pastry flour
3 tablespoons chopped dried cherries
3 tablespoons chopped golden raisins
2 tablespoons unsalted butter, melted
Powdered sugar, for dusting (optional)

In a medium bowl, mix the yeast with 3 tablespoons of water. Let it stand for 5 minutes, or until it bubbles. Stir in the buttermilk, brown sugar, and egg until well mixed. Stir in the pastry flour until combined. With your hands, work the cherries and raisins into the dough. Let the mixture stand for 15 minutes. Pat the dough into an 8-by-8-inch square and cut into 16 pieces. Gently shape each piece into a ball. Drizzle the balls with the melted butter. Place them in a single layer in the air fryer basket so they don't touch. You may have to cook these in batches. Air-fry for 5 to 8 minutes, or until puffy and golden brown. Dust with powdered sugar before serving, if desired.

## English Pumpkin Egg Baked

**Prep time: 10 minutes | Cook time: 10 minutes | Serves 2**

2 eggs
½ cup milk
2 cups flour
2 tablespoons cider vinegar
2 teaspoons baking powder

1 tablespoon sugar
1 cup pumpkin purée
1 teaspoon cinnamon powder
1 teaspoon baking soda
1 tablespoon olive oil

Preheat the air fryer to 300ºF (149ºC). Crack the eggs into a bowl and beat with a whisk. Combine with the milk, flour, cider vinegar, baking powder, sugar, pumpkin purée, cinnamon powder, and baking soda, mixing well. Grease a baking tray with oil. Add the mixture and transfer into the air fryer when your air fryer displays "READY" (select the cooking preset, and make minor adjustments according to your desired doneness.) and choose a shake reminder. Bake for 10 minutes. Serve warm.

## Avocado Tempura

**Prep time: 5 minutes | Cook time: 10 minutes | Serves 4**

½ cup bread crumbs
½ teaspoons salt
1 Haas avocado, pitted, peeled

and sliced
Liquid from 1 can white beans

Preheat the air fryer to 350ºF (177ºC). Mix the bread crumbs and salt in a shallow bowl until well-incorporated. Dip the avocado slices in the bean liquid, then into the bread crumbs. Put the avocados in the air fryer, taking care not to overlap any slices when your air fryer displays "READY" (select the cooking preset, and make minor adjustments according to your desired doneness.) and choose a shake reminder. Air fry for 10 minutes, giving the basket a good shake at the halfway point. Serve immediately.

## Ham, Grit, and Cheddar Cheese Fritters

**Prep time: 15 minutes | Cook time: 20 minutes | Serves 6 to 8**

4 cups water
1 cup quick-cooking grits
¼ teaspoon salt
2 tablespoons butter
2 cups grated Cheddar cheese, divided
1 cup finely diced ham

1 tablespoon chopped chives
Salt and freshly ground black pepper, to taste
1 egg, beaten
2 cups panko bread crumbs
Cooking spray

Bring the water to a boil in a saucepan. Whisk in the grits and ¼ teaspoon of salt, and cook for 7 minutes until the grits are soft. Remove the pan from the heat and stir in the butter and 1 cup of the grated Cheddar cheese. Transfer the grits to a bowl and let them cool for 10 to 15 minutes. Stir the ham, chives and the rest of the cheese into the grits and season with salt and pepper to taste. Add the beaten egg and refrigerate the mixture for 30 minutes. Put the panko bread crumbs in a shallow dish. Measure out ¼-cup portions of the grits mixture and shape them into patties. Coat all sides of the patties with the panko bread crumbs, patting them with the hands so the crumbs adhere to the patties. You should have about 16 patties. Spritz both sides of the patties with cooking spray. Preheat the air fryer to 400ºF (204ºC). When your air fryer displays "READY" (select the cooking preset, and make minor adjustments according to your desired doneness.) and choose a shake reminder.In batches of 5 or 6, air fry the fritters for 8 minutes. Using a flat spatula, flip the fritters over and air fry for another 4 minutes. Serve hot.

## Quick Coffee Donuts

**Prep time: 5 minutes | Cook time: 6 minutes | Serves 6**

¼ cup sugar
½ teaspoon salt
1 cup flour
1 teaspoon baking powder

¼ cup coffee
1 tablespoon aquafaba
1 tablespoon sunflower oil

In a large bowl, combine the sugar, salt, flour, and baking powder. Add the coffee, aquafaba, and sunflower oil and mix until a dough is formed. Leave the dough to rest in and the refrigerator. Preheat the air fryer to 400ºF (204ºC). Remove the dough from the fridge and divide up, kneading each section into a doughnut. Put the doughnuts inside the air fryer when your air fryer displays "READY" (select the cooking preset, and make minor adjustments according to your desired doneness.) and choose a shake reminder. Air fry for 6 minutes. Serve immediately.

## Butter French Toast

**Prep time: 10 minutes | Cook time: 6 minutes | Serves 2**

4 slices bread of your choosing
2 tablespoons soft butter
2 eggs, lightly beaten
Pinch of salt
Pinch of cinnamon

Pinch of ground nutmeg
Pinch of ground cloves
Nonstick cooking spray
Sugar, for serving

In a shallow bowl, mix together the salt, spices and eggs. Butter each side of the slices of bread and slice into strips. You may also use cookie cutters for this step. Set your Air Fryer to 350ºF (177ºC) and allow to warm up briefly. Dredge each strip of bread in the egg and transfer to the fryer. Cook for 2 minutes, ensuring the toast turns golden brown. At this point, spritz the tops of the bread strips with cooking spray, flip, and cook for another 4 minutes on the other side. Top with a light dusting of sugar before serving.

## PB&J

**Prep time: 10 minutes | Cook time: 7 minutes | Serves 4**

½ cup cornflakes, crushed
¼ cup shredded coconut
8 slices oat nut bread or any whole-grain, oversize bread
6 tablespoons peanut butter
2 medium bananas, cut into

½-inch-thick slices
6 tablespoons pineapple preserves
1 egg, beaten
Oil for misting or cooking spray

Preheat air fryer to 360ºF (182ºC). In a shallow dish, mix together the cornflake crumbs and coconut. For each sandwich, spread one bread slice with 1½ tablespoons of peanut butter. Top with banana slices. Spread another bread slice with 1½ tablespoons of preserves. Combine to make a sandwich. Using a pastry brush, brush top of sandwich lightly with beaten egg. Sprinkle with about 1½ tablespoons of crumb coating, pressing it in to make it stick. Spray with oil. Turn sandwich over and repeat to coat and spray the other side. Cooking 2 at a time, place sandwiches in air fryer basket when your air fryer displays "READY" (select the cooking preset, and make minor adjustments according to your desired doneness.) and choose a shake reminder. Cook for 6 to 7 minutes or until coating is golden brown and crispy. If sandwich doesn't brown enough, spray with a little more oil and cook at 390ºF (199ºC) for another minute. Cut cooked sandwiches in half and serve warm.

## Easy French Toast Sticks

Prep time: 10 minutes | Cook time: 13 minutes | Makes 12 sticks

4 slices Texas toast (or any thick bread, such as challah)
1 tablespoon butter
1 egg
1 teaspoon stevia
1 teaspoon ground cinnamon
¼ cup milk
1 teaspoon vanilla extract
Cooking oil

Cut each slice of bread into 3 pieces (for 12 sticks total). Place the butter in a small, microwave-safe bowl. Microwave for 15 seconds, or until the butter has melted. Remove the bowl from the microwave. Add the egg, stevia, cinnamon, milk, and vanilla extract. Whisk until fully combined. Spray the air fryer basket with cooking oil. Dredge each of the bread sticks in the egg mixture. Place the French toast sticks in the air fryer. It is okay to stack them. Spray the French toast sticks with cooking oil. Cook for 8 minutes. Open the air fryer and flip each of the French toast sticks. Cook for an additional 4 minutes, or until the French toast sticks are crisp. Cool before serving.

## Another Version French Toast Sticks

Prep time: 10 minutes | Cook time: 15 minutes | Serves 4

2 eggs
½ cup milk
⅛ teaspoon salt
½ teaspoon pure vanilla extract
¾ cup crushed cornflakes
6 slices sandwich bread, each slice cut into 4 strips
Oil for misting or cooking spray
Maple syrup or honey, for serving

Preheat the air fryer to 390ºF (199ºC). In a small bowl, beat together eggs, milk, salt, and vanilla. Place crushed cornflakes on a plate or in a shallow dish. Dip bread strips in egg mixture, shake off excess, and roll in cornflake crumbs. Spray both sides of bread strips with oil. Place bread strips in air fryer basket in single layer when your air fryer displays "READY" (select the cooking preset, and make minor adjustments according to your desired doneness.) and choose a shake reminder. Cook at 390ºF (199ºC) for 5 to 7 minutes or until they're dark golden brown. Repeat steps 5 and 6 to cook remaining French toast sticks. Serve with maple syrup or honey for dipping.

## Fried Cheddar Grits

Prep time: 10 minutes | Cook time: 10 to 12 minutes | Serves 4

⅔ cup instant grits
1 teaspoon salt
1 teaspoon freshly ground black pepper
¾ cup whole or 2% milk
3 ounces (85 g) cream cheese,
at room temperature
1 large egg, beaten
1 tablespoon butter, melted
1 cup shredded mild Cheddar cheese
Cooking spray

Mix the grits, salt, and black pepper in a large bowl. Add the milk, cream cheese, beaten egg, and melted butter and whisk to combine. Fold in the Cheddar cheese and stir well. Preheat the air fryer to 400ºF (204ºC). Spray a baking pan with cooking spray. Spread the grits mixture into the baking pan and place in the air fryer basket when your air fryer displays "READY" (select the cooking preset, and make minor adjustments according to your desired doneness.) and choose a shake reminder. Air fry for 1o to 12 minutes, or until the grits are cooked and a knife inserted in the center comes out clean. Stir the mixture once halfway through the cooking time. Rest for 5 minutes and serve warm.

## Strawberry Toast

Prep time: 5 minutes | Cook time: 8 minutes | Makes 4 toasts

4 slices bread, ½-inch thick
1 cup sliced strawberries
1 teaspoon sugar
Cooking spray

Preheat the air fryer to 375ºF (191ºC). On a clean work surface, lay the bread slices and spritz one side of each slice of bread with cooking spray. Place the bread slices in the air fryer basket, sprayed side down when your air fryer displays "READY" (select the cooking preset, and make minor adjustments according to your desired doneness.) and choose a shake reminder. Top with the strawberries and a sprinkle of sugar. Air fry for 8 minutes until the toast is well browned on each side. Remove from the air fryer basket to a plate and serve.

## Gold Breaded Avocado

Prep time: 5 minutes | Cook time: 6 minutes | Serves 4

2 large avocados, sliced
¼ teaspoon paprika
Salt and ground black pepper, to taste
½ cup flour
2 eggs, beaten
1 cup bread crumbs

Preheat the air fryer to 400ºF (204ºC). Sprinkle paprika, salt and pepper on the slices of avocado. Lightly coat the avocados with flour. Dredge them in the eggs, before covering with bread crumbs. Transfer to the air fryer when your air fryer displays "READY" (select the cooking preset, and make minor adjustments according to your desired doneness.) and choose a shake reminder. Air fry for 6 minutes. Serve warm.

## Smoked Ham and Cheese Sandwiches

Prep time: 5 minutes | Cook time: 8 minutes | Serves 2

1 teaspoon butter
4 slices bread
4 slices smoked country ham
4 slices Cheddar cheese
4 thick slices tomato

Spread ½ teaspoon of butter onto one side of 2 slices of bread. Each sandwich will have 1 slice of bread with butter and 1 slice without. Assemble each sandwich by layering 2 slices of ham, 2 slices of cheese, and 2 slices of tomato on the unbuttered pieces of bread. Top with the other bread slices, buttered side up. Place the sandwiches in the air fryer buttered-side down. Cook for 4 minutes. Open the air fryer. Flip the grilled cheese sandwiches. Cook for an additional 4 minutes. Cool before serving. Cut each sandwich in half and enjoy.

## Hard-Cooked Eggs

Prep time: 5 minutes | Cook time: 15 minutes | Serves 6

6 large eggs

Preheat the air fryer to 250ºF (121ºC). Fit a rack into the air-fryer basket when your air fryer displays "READY" (select the cooking preset, and make minor adjustments according to your desired doneness.) and choose a shake reminder. Arrange the eggs on the rack. Set the air fryer to 250ºF (121ºC) for 15 minutes for large eggs (20 minutes for extra-large or jumbo eggs). Meanwhile, fill a large bowl with ice and water. At the end of the cooking time, very carefully remove the hot eggs from the rack and place them in the ice bath for 5 minutes. When the eggs are cool to the touch, drain them and store in the refrigerator for up to a week, or peel and eat them right away!

## Ham and Cheddar Cheese Toast

**Prep time: 5 minutes | Cook time: 6 minutes | Serves: 1**

1 slice bread
1 teaspoon butter, at room temperature
1 egg
Salt and freshly ground black

pepper, to taste
2 teaspoons diced ham
1 tablespoon grated Cheddar cheese

Preheat the air fryer to 325ºF (163ºC). On a clean work surface, use a 2½-inch biscuit cutter to make a hole in the center of the bread slice with about ½-inch of bread remaining. Spread the butter on both sides of the bread slice. Crack the egg into the hole and season with salt and pepper to taste. Transfer the bread to the air fryer basket when your air fryer displays "READY" (select the cooking preset, and make minor adjustments according to your desired doneness.) and choose a shake reminder. Air fry for 5 minutes. Scatter the cheese and diced ham on top and continue to cook for an additional 1 minute until the egg is set and the cheese has melted. Remove the toast from the basket to a plate and let cool for 5 minutes before serving.

## Ham and Cheddar Cheese Muffins

**Prep time: 10 minutes | Cook time: 6 minutes | Makes 8 muffins**

¾ cup yellow cornmeal
¼ cup flour
1½ teaspoons baking powder
¼ teaspoon salt
1 egg, beaten

2 tablespoons canola oil
½ cup milk
½ cup shredded sharp Cheddar cheese
½ cup diced ham

Preheat the air fryer to 390ºF (199ºC). In a medium bowl, stir together the cornmeal, flour, baking powder, and salt. Add the egg, oil, and milk to dry ingredients and mix well. Stir in shredded cheese and diced ham. Divide batter among 8 parchment paper-lined muffin cups. Put 4 filled muffin cups in air fryer basket when your air fryer displays "READY" (select the cooking preset, and make minor adjustments according to your desired doneness.) and choose a shake reminder. Bake for 5 minutes. Reduce temperature to 330ºF (166ºC) and bake for 1 minute or until a toothpick inserted in center of the muffin comes out clean. Repeat steps 6 and 7 to bake remaining muffins. Serve warm.

## Vanilla Walnut Pancake

**Prep time: 10 minutes | Cook time: 20 minutes | Serves 4**

3 tablespoons melted butter, divided
1 cup flour
2 tablespoons sugar
1½ teaspoons baking powder
¼ teaspoon salt

1 egg, beaten
¾ cup milk
1 teaspoon pure vanilla extract
½ cup roughly chopped walnuts
Maple syrup or fresh sliced fruit, for serving

Preheat the air fryer to 330ºF (166ºC). Grease a baking pan with 1 tablespoon of melted butter. Mix together the flour, sugar, baking powder, and salt in a medium bowl. Add the beaten egg, milk, the remaining 2 tablespoons of melted butter, and vanilla and stir until the batter is sticky but slightly lumpy. Slowly pour the batter into the greased baking pan and scatter with the walnuts. Place the pan in the air fryer basket when your air fryer displays "READY" (select the cooking preset, and make minor adjustments according to your desired doneness.) and choose a shake reminder. Bake for 20 minutes until golden brown and cooked through. Let the pancake rest for 5 minutes and serve topped with the maple syrup or fresh fruit, if desired.

## Buttermilk Pancake Muffins

**Prep time: 15 minutes | Cook time: 28 minutes | Serves 4**

1 cup flour
2 tablespoons sugar (optional)
½ teaspoon baking soda
1 teaspoon baking powder
¼ teaspoon salt
1 egg, beaten
**For the Suggested Fillings:**

1 cup buttermilk
2 tablespoons melted butter
1 teaspoon pure vanilla extract
24 foil muffin cups
Cooking spray

1 teaspoon of jelly or fruit preserves
1 tablespoon or less fresh blueberries; chopped fresh strawberries; chopped frozen

cherries; dark chocolate chips; chopped walnuts, pecans, or other nuts; cooked, crumbled bacon or sausage

Preheat the air fryer to 330ºF (166ºC). In a large bowl, stir together flour, optional sugar, baking soda, baking powder, and salt. In a small bowl, combine egg, buttermilk, butter, and vanilla. Mix well. Pour egg mixture into dry ingredients and stir to mix well but don't overbeat. Double up the muffin cups and remove the paper liners from the top cups. Spray the foil cups lightly with cooking spray. Place 6 sets of muffin cups in air fryer basket when your air fryer displays "READY" (select the cooking preset, and make minor adjustments according to your desired doneness.) and choose a shake reminder. Pour just enough batter into each cup to cover the bottom. Sprinkle with desired filling. Pour in more batter to cover the filling and fill the cups about ¾ full. Cook at 330ºF (166ºC) for 7 to 8 minutes. Repeat steps 5 and 6 for the remaining 6 pancake muffins.

## Shakshuka with Tomato Sauce

**Prep time: 15 minutes | Cook time: 30 minutes | Serves 2**

**For the Tomato Sauce:**
3 tablespoons extra-virgin olive oil
1 small yellow onion, diced
1 jalapeño pepper, seeded and minced
1 red bell pepper, diced
2 cloves garlic, minced
**For the Shakshuka:**
4 eggs
1 tablespoon heavy cream

1 teaspoon cumin
1 teaspoon sweet paprika
Pinch cayenne pepper
1 tablespoon tomato paste
1 can (28-ounce / 794-g) whole plum tomatoes with juice
2 teaspoons granulated sugar

1 tablespoon chopped cilantro
Kosher salt and pepper, to taste

Preheat the air fryer to 300ºF (149ºC). Heat the olive oil in a large, deep skillet over medium heat. Add the onion and peppers, season with salt, and sauté until softened, about 10 minutes. Add the garlic and spices and sauté a few additional minutes until fragrant. Add the tomato paste and stir to combine. Add the plum tomatoes along with their juice—breaking up the tomatoes with a spoon—and the sugar. Turn the heat to high and bring the mixture to a boil. Turn the heat down and simmer until the tomatoes are thickened, about 10 minutes. Turn off the heat. (May be done in advance. Refrigerate the sauce if not using right away.) Crack the eggs into a 7-inch round cake pan insert for the air fryer. Remove 1 cup of the tomato sauce from the skillet and spoon it over the egg whites only, leaving the yolks exposed. Drizzle the cream over the yolks. Place the cake pan in the air fryer when your air fryer displays "READY" (select the cooking preset, and make minor adjustments according to your desired doneness.) and choose a shake reminder. Cook at 300ºF (149ºC) for 10 to 12 minutes, until the egg whites are set and the yolks still runny. Remove the pan from the air fryer and garnish with chopped cilantro. Season with salt and pepper. Serve immediately with crusty bread to mop up the sauce.

## Maple Smoked Bacon Knots

**Prep time: 5 minutes | Cook time: 7 to 8 minutes | Serves 6**

1 pound (454 g) maple smoked center-cut bacon
¼ cup maple syrup

¼ cup brown sugar
Coarsely cracked black peppercorns, to taste

Preheat the air fryer to 390ºF (199ºC). On a clean work surface, tie each bacon strip in a loose knot. Stir together the maple syrup and brown sugar in a bowl. Generously brush this mixture over the bacon knots. Working in batches, arrange the bacon knots in the air fryer basket when your air fryer displays "READY" (select the cooking preset, and make minor adjustments according to your desired doneness.) and choose a shake reminder. Sprinkle with the coarsely cracked black peppercorns. Air fry for 5 minutes. Flip the bacon knots and continue cooking for 2 to 3 minutes more, or until the bacon is crisp. Remove from the basket to a paper towel-lined plate. Repeat with the remaining bacon knots. Let the bacon knots cool for a few minutes and serve warm.

## Mixed Berries Dutch Baby Pancake

**Prep time: 10 minutes | Cook time: 12 to 16 minutes | Serves 4**

1 tablespoon unsalted butter, at room temperature
1 egg
2 egg whites
½ cup 2% milk

½ cup whole-wheat pastry flour
1 teaspoon pure vanilla extract
1 cup sliced fresh strawberries
½ cup fresh raspberries
½ cup fresh blueberries

Preheat the air fryer to 330ºF (166ºC). Grease a baking pan with the butter. Using a hand mixer, beat together the egg, egg whites, milk, pastry flour, and vanilla in a medium mixing bowl until well incorporated. Pour the batter into the pan when your air fryer displays "READY" (select the cooking preset, and make minor adjustments according to your desired doneness.) and choose a shake reminder. Bake in the preheated air fryer for 12 to 16 minutes, or until the pancake puffs up in the center and the edges are golden brown. Allow the pancake to cool for 5 minutes and serve topped with the berries.

## Pork Sausage and Cheddar Quiche Cups

**Prep time: 5 minutes | Cook time: 22 minutes | Makes 10 quiche cups**

¼ pound all-natural ground pork sausage
3 eggs
¾ cup milk

20 foil muffin cups
Cooking spray
4 ounces (113 g) sharp Cheddar cheese, grated

Preheat the air fryer to 390ºF (199ºC). Divide sausage into 3 portions and shape each into a thin patty. Place patties in air fryer basket when your air fryer displays "READY" (select the cooking preset, and make minor adjustments according to your desired doneness.) and choose a shake reminder. Cook at 390ºF (199ºC) for 6 minutes. While sausage is cooking, prepare the egg mixture. A large measuring cup or bowl with a pouring lip works best. Combine the eggs and milk and whisk until well blended. Set aside. When sausage has cooked fully, remove patties from basket, drain well, and use a fork to crumble the meat into small pieces. Double the foil cups into 10 sets. Remove paper liners from the top muffin cups and spray the foil cups lightly with cooking spray. Divide crumbled sausage among the 10 muffin cup sets. Top each with grated cheese, divided evenly among the cups. Place 5 cups in air fryer basket. Pour egg mixture into each cup, filling until each cup is at least ⅔ full. Cook for 8 minutes and test for doneness. A knife inserted into the center shouldn't have any raw egg on it when removed. If needed, cook 1 to 2 more minutes, until egg completely sets. Repeat steps 8 through 11 for the remaining quiches.

## Lush Cheddar Biscuits

**Prep time: 10 minutes | Cook time: 22 minutes | Makes 8 biscuits**

2⅓ cups self-rising flour
2 tablespoons sugar
½ cup butter (1 stick), frozen for 15 minutes
½ cup grated Cheddar cheese,

plus more to melt on top
1⅓ cups buttermilk
1 cup all-purpose flour, for shaping
1 tablespoon butter, melted

Line a buttered 7-inch metal cake pan with parchment paper or a silicone liner. Combine the flour and sugar in a large mixing bowl. Grate the butter into the flour. Add the grated cheese and stir to coat the cheese and butter with flour. Then add the buttermilk and stir just until you can no longer see streaks of flour. The dough should be quite wet. Spread the all-purpose (not self-rising) flour out on a small cookie sheet. With a spoon, scoop 8 evenly sized balls of dough into the flour, making sure they don't touch each other. With floured hands, coat each dough ball with flour and toss them gently from hand to hand to shake off any excess flour. Put each floured dough ball into the prepared pan, right up next to the other. This will help the biscuits rise, rather than spreading out. Preheat the air fryer to 380ºF (193ºC). Transfer the cake pan to the basket of the air fryer. Let the ends of the aluminum foil sling hang across the cake pan before returning the basket to the air fryer when your air fryer displays "READY" (select the cooking preset, and make minor adjustments according to your desired doneness.) and choose a shake reminder. Air fry for 20 minutes. Check the biscuits twice to make sure they are not getting too brown on top. If they are, re-arrange the aluminum foil strips to cover any brown parts. After 20 minutes, check the biscuits by inserting a toothpick into the center of the biscuits. It should come out clean. If it needs a little more time, continue to air fry for two extra minutes. Brush the tops of the biscuits with some melted butter and sprinkle a little more grated cheese on top if desired. Pop the basket back into the air fryer for another 2 minutes. Remove the cake pan from the air fryer. Let the biscuits cool for just a minute or two and then turn them out onto a plate and pull apart. Serve immediately.

## Red Meat Rolls

**Prep time: 10 minutes | Cook time: 15 minutes | Serves 6**

7 cups minced meat
1 small onion, diced
1 packet spring roll sheets
2 ounces (57 g) Asian noodles
3 cloves garlic, crushed

1 cup mixed vegetables
1 tablespoon sesame oil
2 tablespoons water
1 teaspoon soy sauce

Cook the noodles in hot water until they turn soft. Drain and cut to your desired length. Grease the wok with sesame oil. Put it over a medium-high heat and fry the minced meat, mixed vegetables, garlic, and onion, stirring regularly to ensure the minced meat cooks through. The cooking time will vary depending on the pan you are using – allow 3 to 5 minutes if using a wok, and 7 to 10 if using a standard frying pan. Drizzle in the soy sauce and add to the noodles, tossing well to allow the juices to spread and absorb evenly. Spoon the stir-fry diagonally across a spring roll sheet and fold back the top point over the filling. Fold over the sides. Before folding back the bottom point, brush it with cold water, which will act as an adhesive. Repeat until all the filling and sheets are used. Pre-heat your Air Fryer at 360ºF (182ºC). If desired, drizzle a small amount of oil over the top of the spring rolls to enhance the taste and ensure crispiness. When your air fryer displays "READY" (select the cooking preset, and make minor adjustments according to your desired doneness.), choose a shake reminder. Cook the spring rolls in the fryer for 8 minutes, in multiple batches if necessary. Serve and enjoy.

# Chapter 3 Beef and Lamb

## Roasted Sirloin Steak with Mayo

**Prep time: 10 minutes | Cook time: 14 minutes | Serves 3**

1 pound (454 g) sirloin steak, cubed
½ cup mayonnaise
1 tablespoon red wine vinegar
½ teaspoon dried basil
1 teaspoon garlic, minced
½ teaspoon cayenne pepper
Kosher salt and ground black pepper, to season

Pat dry the sirloin steak with paper towels. In a small mixing dish, thoroughly combine the remaining ingredients until everything is well incorporated. Toss the cubed steak with the mayonnaise mixture and transfer to the Air Fryer cooking basket. When your air fryer displays "READY" (select the cooking preset, and make minor adjustments according to your desired doneness.) and choose a shake reminder. Cook in the preheated Air Fryer at 400ºF (204ºC) for 7 minutes. Shake the basket and continue to cook for a further 7 minutes. Enjoy!

## Beef Back Ribs

**Prep time: 5 minutes | Cook time: 29 minutes | Serves 4**

2 pounds (907 g) beef back ribs
1 tablespoon sunflower oil
½ teaspoon mixed peppercorns, cracked
1 teaspoon red pepper flakes
1 teaspoon dry mustard
Coarse sea salt, to taste

Trim the excess fat from the beef ribs. Mix the sunflower oil, cracked peppercorns, red pepper, dry mustard, and salt. Rub over the ribs. When your air fryer displays "READY" (select the cooking preset, and make minor adjustments according to your desired doneness.) and choose a shake reminder. Cook in the preheated Air Fryer at 395ºF (202ºC) for 11 minutes. Turn the heat to 330ºF (166ºC) and continue to cook for 18 minutes more. Serve warm.

## Beef Flank Steak Satay

**Prep time: 15 minutes | Cook time: 8 minutes | Serves 4**

1 pound (454 g) beef flank steak, thinly sliced into long strips
2 tablespoons vegetable oil
1 tablespoon fish sauce
1 tablespoon soy sauce
1 tablespoon minced fresh ginger
1 tablespoon minced garlic
1 tablespoon sugar
1 teaspoon sriracha or other hot sauce
1 teaspoon ground coriander
½ cup chopped fresh cilantro
¼ cup chopped roasted peanuts
Peanut sauce, for serving

Preheat the air fryer to 400ºF (204ºC). Place the beef strips in a large bowl or resealable plastic bag. Add the vegetable oil, fish sauce, soy sauce, ginger, garlic, sriracha, coriander, and ¼ cup of the cilantro to the bag. Seal and massage the bag to thoroughly coat and combine. Marinate at room temperature for 30 minutes, or cover and refrigerate for up to 24 hours. Using tongs, remove the beef strips from the bag and lay them flat in the air-fryer basket, minimizing overlap as much as possible; discard the marinade. When your air fryer displays "READY" (select the cooking preset, and make minor adjustments according to your desired doneness.) and choose a shake reminder. Set the air fryer to 400ºF (204ºC) for 8 minutes, turning the beef strips halfway through the cooking time. Transfer the meat to a serving platter. Sprinkle with the remaining ¼ cup cilantro and the peanuts. Serve with peanut sauce.

## Greek Roast Beef with Zucchini

**Prep time: 10 minutes | Cook time: 52 minutes | Serves 3**

1 clove garlic, halved
1½ pounds (680 g) beef eye round roast
1 zucchini, sliced lengthwise
2 teaspoons olive oil
1 teaspoon Greek spice mix
Sea salt, to season
½ cup Greek-style yogurt

Rub the beef eye round roast with garlic halves. Brush the beef eye round roast and zucchini with olive oil. Sprinkle with spices and place the beef in the cooking basket. When your air fryer displays "READY" (select the cooking preset, and make minor adjustments according to your desired doneness.) and choose a shake reminder. Roast in your Air Fryer at 400ºF (204ºC) for 40 minutes. Turn the beef over. Add the zucchini to the cooking basket and continue to cook for 12 minutes more or until cooked through. Serve warm, garnished with Greek-style yogurt. Enjoy!

## Fried Beef Sausages in Batter

**Prep time: 5 minutes | Cook time: 40 minutes | Serves 4**

6 beef sausages
1 tablespoon butter, melted
1 cup plain flour
A pinch of salt
2 eggs
1 cup semi-skimmed milk

When your air fryer displays "READY" (select the cooking preset, and make minor adjustments according to your desired doneness.) and choose a shake reminder. Cook the sausages in the preheated Air Fryer at 380ºF (193ºC) for 15 minutes, shaking halfway through the cooking time. Meanwhile, make up the batter mix. Tip the flour into a bowl with salt; make a well in the middle and crack the eggs into it. Mix with an electric whisk; now, slowly and gradually pour in the milk, whisking all the time. Place the sausages in a lightly greased baking pan. Pour the prepared batter over the sausages. Cook in the preheated Air Fryer at 370ºF (188ºC) approximately 25 minutes, until golden and risen. Serve with gravy if desired. Enjoy!

## Fast Carne Asada

**Prep time: 15 minutes | Cook time: 16 minutes | Serves 4**

Juice of 2 limes
1 orange, peeled and seeded
1 cup fresh cilantro leaves
1 jalapeño, diced
2 tablespoons vegetable oil
2 tablespoons apple cider vinegar
2 teaspoons ancho chile
powder
2 teaspoons sugar
1 teaspoon kosher salt
1 teaspoon cumin seeds
1 teaspoon coriander seeds
1½ pounds (680 g) skirt steak, cut into 3 pieces

In a blender, combine the lime juice, orange, cilantro, jalapeño, vegetable oil, vinegar, chile powder, sugar, salt, cumin, and coriander. Blend until smooth. Place the steak in a resealable plastic bag. Pour the marinade over the steak and seal the bag. Let stand at room temperature for 30 minutes or cover and refrigerate for up to 24 hours. Preheat the air fryer to 400ºF (204ºC). Place the steak pieces in the air-fryer basket when your air fryer displays "READY" (select the cooking preset, and make minor adjustments according to your desired doneness.) and choose a shake reminder.. Discard marinade. Set the air fryer to 400ºF (204ºC) for 8 minutes. Use a meat thermometer to ensure the steak has reached an internal temperature of 145ºF (63ºC). (It is critical to not overcook skirt steak to avoid toughening the meat.) Transfer the steak to a cutting board and let rest for 10 minutes. Slice across the grain and serve.

## Argentinian Cheesy Beef Empanadas
**Prep time: 10 minutes | Cook time: 8 minutes | Serves 2**

½ pound (227 g) ground chuck
½ yellow onion
1 teaspoon fresh garlic, minced
2 tablespoons piri piri sauce
1 tablespoon mustard
6 cubes Cotija cheese
6 Goya discos pastry dough

Heat a nonstick skillet over medium-high heat. Once hot, cook the ground beef, onion and garlic until tender, about 6 minutes. Crumble with a fork and stir in the piri piri sauce; stir to combine. Divide the sauce between empanadas. Top with mustard and cheese. Fold each of them in half and seal the edges. When your air fryer displays "READY" (select the cooking preset, and make minor adjustments according to your desired doneness.) and choose a shake reminder. Bake in the preheated Air Fryer at 340ºF (171ºC) for about 8 minutes, flipping them halfway through the cooking time. Serve with salsa sauce if desired. Enjoy!

## Beef Riblets with BBQ Glaze
**Prep time: 10 minutes | Cook time: 12 minutes | Serves 3**

1 pound (454 g) beef riblets
Sea salt and red pepper, to taste
¼ cup tomato paste
¼ cup Worcestershire sauce
2 tablespoons hot sauce
1 tablespoon oyster sauce
2 tablespoons rice vinegar
1 tablespoon stone-ground mustard

Combine all ingredients in a glass dish, cover and marinate at least 2 hours in your refrigerator. Discard the marinade and place riblets in the Air Fryer cooking basket. When your air fryer displays "READY" (select the cooking preset, and make minor adjustments according to your desired doneness.) and choose a shake reminder. Cook in the preheated Air Fryer at 360ºF (182ºC) for 12 minutes, shaking the basket halfway through to ensure even cooking. Heat the reserved marinade in a small skillet over a moderate flame; spoon the glaze over the riblets and serve immediately.

## Tangy Beef and Fruit Stir-Fry
**Prep time: 10 minutes | Cook time: 8 minutes | Serves 4**

12 ounces (340 g) sirloin tip steak, thinly sliced
1 tablespoon freshly squeezed lime juice
1 cup canned mandarin orange segments, drained, juice reserved
1 cup canned pineapple
chunks, drained, juice reserved
1 teaspoon low-sodium soy sauce
1 tablespoon cornstarch
1 teaspoon olive oil
2 scallions, white and green parts, sliced
Brown rice, cooked (optional)

In a medium bowl, mix the steak with the lime juice. Set aside. In a small bowl, thoroughly mix 3 tablespoons of reserved mandarin orange juice, 3 tablespoons of reserved pineapple juice, the soy sauce, and cornstarch. Drain the beef and transfer it to a medium metal bowl, reserving the juice. Stir the reserved juice into the mandarin-pineapple juice mixture. Set aside. Add the olive oil and scallions to the steak. Place the metal bowl in the air fryer and cook for 3 to 4 minutes, or until the steak is almost cooked, shaking the basket once during cooking. Stir in the mandarin oranges, pineapple, and juice mixture. Cook for 3 to 7 minutes more, or until the sauce is bubbling and the beef is tender and reaches at least 145ºF (63ºC) on a meat thermometer. Stir and serve over hot cooked brown rice, if desired.

## Stuffed Zucchini with Beef Sausage
**Prep time: 10 minutes | Cook time: 25 minutes | Serves 2**

½ pound (227 g) beef sausage, crumbled
½ cup tortilla chips, crushed
½ teaspoon garlic, pressed
¼ cup tomato paste
2 small-sized zucchini, halved lengthwise and seeds removed
½ cup sharp Cheddar cheese, grated

In a mixing bowl, thoroughly combine the beef sausage, tortilla chips, garlic and tomato paste. Divide the sausage mixture between the zucchini halves. When your air fryer displays "READY" (select the cooking preset, and make minor adjustments according to your desired doneness.) and choose a shake reminder. Bake in the preheated Air Fryer at 400ºF (204ºC) for 20 minutes. Top with grated Cheddar cheese and cook an additional 5 minutes. Enjoy!

## Reuben Beef Rolls
**Prep time: 15 minutes | Cook time: 10 minutes per batch | Makes 10 rolls**

½ pound (227 g) cooked corned beef, chopped
½ cup drained and chopped sauerkraut
1 (8-ounce / 227-g) package
**Thousand Island Sauce:**
¼ cup chopped dill pickles
¼ cup tomato sauce
¾ cup mayonnaise
Fresh thyme leaves, for garnish
cream cheese, softened
½ cup shredded Swiss cheese
20 slices prosciutto
Cooking spray

2 tablespoons sugar
⅛ teaspoon fine sea salt
Ground black pepper, to taste

Preheat the air fryer to 400ºF (204ºC) and spritz with cooking spray. Combine the beef, sauerkraut, cream cheese, and Swiss cheese in a large bowl. Stir to mix well. Unroll a slice of prosciutto on a clean work surface, then top with another slice of prosciutto crosswise. Scoop up 4 tablespoons of the beef mixture in the center. Fold the top slice sides over the filling as the ends of the roll, then roll up the long sides of the bottom prosciutto and make it into a roll shape. Overlap the sides by about 1 inch. Repeat with remaining filling and prosciutto. Arrange the rolls in the preheated air fryer, seam side down, and spritz with cooking spray. When your air fryer displays "READY" (select the cooking preset, and make minor adjustments according to your desired doneness.) and choose a shake reminder. Cook at the corresponding preset mode or Air Fry for 10 minutes or until golden and crispy. Flip the rolls halfway through. Work in batches to avoid overcrowding. Meanwhile, combine the ingredients for the sauce in a small bowl. Stir to mix well. Serve the rolls with the dipping sauce.

## Super Cheesy Beef Meatballs
**Prep time: 10 minutes | Cook time: 10 minutes | Serves 4**

1 pound (454 g) ground beef
¼ cup Grana Padano, grated
2 tablespoons scallion, chopped
2 garlic cloves, minced
2 stale crustless bread slices
1 tablespoon Italian seasoning
mix
1 egg, beaten
¼ cup Mozzarella cheese, shredded
Kosher salt and ground black pepper, to taste

In a mixing bowl, combine all ingredients. Then, shape the mixture into 8 meatballs. When your air fryer displays "READY" (select the cooking preset, and make minor adjustments according to your desired doneness.) and choose a shake reminder. Cook the meatballs at 370ºF (188ºC) for 10 minutes, shaking the basket halfway through the cooking time. Serve the meatballs in a sandwich if desired. Enjoy!

## Marinated Flank Steak

**Prep time: 10 minutes | Cook time: 12 minutes | Serves 4**

1½ pounds (680 g) flank steak
½ cup red wine
½ cup apple cider vinegar
2 tablespoons soy sauce
Salt, to taste
½ teaspoon ground black
pepper
½ teaspoon red pepper flakes,
crushed
½ teaspoon dried basil
1 teaspoon thyme

Add all ingredients to a large ceramic bowl. Cover and let it marinate for 3 hours in your refrigerator. Transfer the flank steak to the Air Fryer basket that is previously greased with nonstick cooking oil. When your air fryer displays "READY" (select the cooking preset, and make minor adjustments according to your desired doneness.) and choose a shake reminder. Cook in the preheated Air Fryer at 400ºF (204ºC) for 12 minutes, flipping over halfway through the cooking time. Enjoy!

## Dijon Flank Steak

**Prep time: 5 minutes | Cook time: 12 minutes | Serves 3**

1 pound (454 g) flank steak
½ teaspoon olive oil
Sea salt and red pepper flakes,
to taste
3 tablespoons butter
1 teaspoon Dijon mustard
1 teaspoon honey

Brush the flank steak with olive oil and season with salt and pepper. When your air fryer displays "READY" (select the cooking preset, and make minor adjustments according to your desired doneness.) and choose a shake reminder. Cook at 400ºF (204ºC) for 6 minutes. Then, turn the steak halfway through the cooking time and continue to cook for a further 6 minutes. In the meantime, prepare the Dijon honey butter by whisking the remaining ingredients. Serve the warm flank steak dolloped with the Dijon honey butter. Enjoy!

## Greek Lamb Pita with Yogurt Dressing

**Prep time: 15 minutes | Cook time: 6 minutes | Serves 4**

**Dressing:**
1 cup plain yogurt
1 tablespoon lemon juice
1 teaspoon dried dill weed,
crushed
1 teaspoon ground oregano
½ teaspoon salt
**Meatballs:**
½ pound (227 g) ground lamb
1 tablespoon diced onion
1 teaspoon dried parsley
1 teaspoon dried dill weed,
crushed
¼ teaspoon oregano
¼ teaspoon coriander
¼ teaspoon ground cumin
¼ teaspoon salt
4 pita halves
**Suggested Toppings:**
1 red onion, slivered
1 medium cucumber, deseeded,
thinly sliced
Crumbled feta cheese
Sliced black olives
Chopped fresh peppers

Preheat the air fryer to 390ºF (199ºC). Stir the dressing ingredients together in a small bowl and refrigerate while preparing lamb. Combine all meatball ingredients in a large bowl and stir to distribute seasonings. Shape meat mixture into 12 small meatballs, rounded or slightly flattened if you prefer. Transfer the meatballs in the preheated air fryer when your air fryer displays "READY" (select the cooking preset, and make minor adjustments according to your desired doneness.) and choose a shake reminder. Cook at the corresponding preset mode or Air Fry for 6 minutes, until well done. Remove and drain on paper towels. To serve, pile meatballs and the choice of toppings in pita pockets and drizzle with dressing.

## Filet Mignon with Button Mushrooms

**Prep time: 5 minutes | Cook time: 18 minutes | Serves 2**

1 pound (454 g) filet mignon
2 garlic cloves, halved
Salt and black pepper, to
season
1 bell pepper, sliced
6 ounces (170 g) button
mushrooms, cleaned and
halved
1 teaspoon olive oil

Rub your filet mignon with garlic halves. Season it with the Salt and black pepper, to taste. Place the filet mignon in a lightly greased cooking basket. When your air fryer displays "READY" (select the cooking preset, and make minor adjustments according to your desired doneness.) and choose a shake reminder. Top with peppers and air fry them at 400ºF (204ºC) for 10 minutes. Turn them over. Now, add in the mushrooms. Drizzle olive oil over the mushrooms and continue to cook for 8 minutes more. Serve warm. Enjoy!

## Warm Marinated London Broil

**Prep time: 10 minutes | Cook time: 20 minutes | Serves 2**

2 tablespoons soy sauce
2 garlic cloves, minced
1 teaspoon mustard
1 tablespoon olive oil
2 tablespoons wine vinegar
1 tablespoon honey
1 pound (454 g) London broil
½ teaspoon paprika
Salt and black pepper, to taste

In a ceramic dish, mix the soy sauce, garlic, mustard, oil, wine vinegar and honey. Add in the London broil and let it marinate for 2 hours in your refrigerator. Season the London broil with paprika, salt and pepper. When your air fryer displays "READY" (select the cooking preset, and make minor adjustments according to your desired doneness.) and choose a shake reminder. Cook in the preheated Air Fryer at 400ºF (204ºC) for 10 minutes; turn over and continue to cook for a further 10 minutes. Slice the London broil against the grain and eat warm. Enjoy!

## Salisbury Steak with Mushroom Gravy

**Prep time: 20 minutes | Cook time: 33 minutes | Serves 2**

**For the Mushroom Gravy:**
¾ cup sliced button mushrooms
¼ cup thinly sliced onions
¼ cup unsalted butter, melted
½ teaspoon fine sea salt
¼ cup beef broth
**For the Steaks:**
½ pound (227 g) ground beef
(85% lean)
1 tablespoon dry mustard
2 tablespoons tomato paste
¼ teaspoon garlic powder
½ teaspoon onion powder
½ teaspoon fine sea salt
¼ teaspoon ground black
pepper
Chopped fresh thyme leaves,
for garnish

Preheat the air fryer to 390ºF (199ºC). Toss the mushrooms and onions with butter in a baking pan to coat well, then sprinkle with salt. Place the baking pan in the preheated air fryer when your air fryer displays "READY" (select the cooking preset, and make minor adjustments according to your desired doneness.) and choose a shake reminder. Cook at the corresponding preset mode or Air Fry for 8 minutes or until the mushrooms are tender. Stir the mixture halfway through. Pour the broth in the baking pan and cook for 10 more minutes to make the gravy. Meanwhile, combine all the ingredients for the steaks, except for the thyme leaves, in a large bowl. Stir to mix well. Shape the mixture into two oval steaks. Arrange the steaks over the gravy and cook at the corresponding preset mode or Air Fry for 15 minutes or until the patties are browned. Flip the steaks halfway through. Transfer the steaks onto a plate and pour the gravy over. Sprinkle with fresh thyme and serve immediately.

## Barbecued Beef Ribs

**Prep time: 10 minutes | Cook time: 20 minutes | Serves 3**

1 pound (454 g) beef ribs
¼ cup ketchup
¼ cup tequila
1 tablespoon brown mustard

1 tablespoon brown sugar
2 tablespoons soy sauce
½ red onion, sliced
2 garlic cloves, pressed

Cut the ribs into serving size portions and transfer them to a ceramic dish. Add in the remaining ingredients, cover and allow it to marinate in your refrigerator overnight. Discard the marinade. When your air fryer displays "READY" (select the cooking preset, and make minor adjustments according to your desired doneness.) and choose a shake reminder. Grill in the preheated Air Fryer at 400ºF (204ºC) for 10 minutes. Turn them over and continue to cook for 10 minutes more. Meanwhile, make the sauce by warming the marinade ingredients in a nonstick pan. Spoon over the warm ribs and serve immediately.

## Japanese Gyudon

**Prep time: 10 minutes | Cook time: 14 minutes | Serves 4**

1 shallot, chopped
½ cup dashi
1 tablespoon mirin
1 teaspoon agave syrup

2 tablespoons Shoyu sauce
½ teaspoon wasabi
1 pound (454 g) rib eye, sliced

Add all ingredients to a lightly greased baking pan. Gently stir to combine. When your air fryer displays "READY" (select the cooking preset, and make minor adjustments according to your desired doneness.) and choose a shake reminder. Cook in the preheated Air Fryer at 400ºF (204ºC) for 7 minutes. Stir again and cook for a further 7 minutes. Serve with Japanese ramen noodles if desired. Enjoy!

## London Broil with Herb-Lemon Butter

**Prep time: 10 minutes | Cook time: 26 minutes | Serves 3**

1 pound (454 g) London broil
**For the Herb Butter:**
2 tablespoons butter, at room temperature
1 teaspoon basil, chopped
1 tablespoon cilantro, chopped

1 tablespoon chives, chopped
1 tablespoon lemon juice
Coarse sea salt and crushed black peppercorns, to taste

Pat the London broil dry with paper towels. Mix all ingredients for the herb butter. When your air fryer displays "READY" (select the cooking preset, and make minor adjustments according to your desired doneness.) and choose a shake reminder. Cook in the preheated Air Fryer at 400ºF (204ºC) for 14 minutes; turn over, brush with the herb butter and continue to cook for a further 12 minutes. Slice the London broil against the grain and serve warm.

## Ribeye Steak with Blue Cheese

**Prep time: 10 minutes | Cook time: 15 minutes | Serves 4**

1 pound (454 g) ribeye steak, bone-in
Sea salt and ground black pepper, to taste

2 tablespoons olive oil
½ teaspoon onion powder
1 teaspoon garlic powder
1 cup blue cheese, crumbled

Toss the ribeye steak with the salt, black pepper, olive oil, onion powder, and garlic powder; place the ribeye steak in the Air Fryer cooking basket. Cook the ribeye steak at 400ºF (204ºC) for 15 minutes, turning it over halfway through the cooking time. Top the ribeye steak with the cheese and serve warm. Bon appétit!

## American-Style Spiced Roast Beef

**Prep time: 10 minutes | Cook time: 15 minutes | Serves 3**

1 pound (454 g) beef eye of round roast
1 teaspoon sesame oil
1 teaspoon red pepper flakes
¼ teaspoon dried bay laurel

½ teaspoon cumin powder
Sea salt and black pepper, to taste
1 sprig thyme, crushed

Simply toss the beef with the remaining ingredients; toss until well coated on all sides. When your air fryer displays "READY" (select the cooking preset, and make minor adjustments according to your desired doneness.) and choose a shake reminder. Cook in the preheated Air Fryer at 390ºF (199ºC) for 15 to 20 minutes, flipping the meat halfway through to cook on the other side. Remove from the cooking basket, cover loosely with foil and let rest for 15 minutes before carving and serving. Enjoy!

## Smoked Beef Jerky

**Prep time: 10 minutes | Cook time: 4 minutes | Serves 4**

6 ounces (170 g) top round steak, cut into ⅛-inch thick strips
½ teaspoon fresh garlic, crushed
1 teaspoon onion powder

2 tablespoons Worcestershire sauce
½ tablespoon honey
1 teaspoon liquid smoke
1 teaspoon hot sauce

Transfer the strips of steak to a large Ziplock bag; add in the other ingredients, seal the bag and shake to combine well. Refrigerate for at least 30 minutes. When your air fryer displays "READY" (select the cooking preset, and make minor adjustments according to your desired doneness.) and choose a shake reminder. Cook in the preheated Air Fryer at 160ºF (71ºC) for about 4 minutes, until it is dry and firm. Refrigerate in an airtight container for up to 1 month. Enjoy!

## BBQ Beef Brisket

**Prep time: 5 minutes | Cook time: 1¼ hours | Serves 4**

1½ pounds (680 g) beef brisket
¼ cup barbecue sauce

2 tablespoons soy sauce

Preheat the air fryer to 390ºF (199ºC). Toss the beef with the remaining ingredients; place the beef in the Air Fryer cooking basket when your air fryer displays "READY" (select the cooking preset, and make minor adjustments according to your desired doneness.) and choose a shake reminder. Cook the beef at 390ºF (199ºC) for 15 minutes, turn the beef over and turn the temperature to 360ºF (182ºC). Continue to cook the beef for 55 minutes more. Bon appétit!

## Montreal Seasoned Ribeye Steak

**Prep time: 5 minutes | Cook time: 15 minutes | Serves 4**

1½ pounds (680 g) ribeye steak, bone-in
2 tablespoons butter

1 Montreal seasoning mix
Sea salt and ground black pepper, to taste

Preheat the air fryer to 400ºF (204ºC). Toss the ribeye steak with the remaining ingredients; place the ribeye steak in a lightly oiled Air Fryer cooking basket when your air fryer displays "READY" (select the cooking preset, and make minor adjustments according to your desired doneness.) and choose a shake reminder. Cook the ribeye steak at 400ºF (204ºC) for 15 minutes, turning it over halfway through the cooking time. Bon appétit!

## Beef Steak with Brussels Sprouts

**Prep time: 20 minutes | Cook time: 15 minutes | Serves 4**

1 pound (454 g) beef chuck shoulder steak
2 tablespoons vegetable oil
1 tablespoon red wine vinegar
1 teaspoon fine sea salt
½ teaspoon ground black pepper
1 teaspoon smoked paprika

1 teaspoon onion powder
½ teaspoon garlic powder
½ pound (227 g) Brussels sprouts, cleaned and halved
½ teaspoon fennel seeds
1 teaspoon dried basil
1 teaspoon dried sage

Massage the beef with the vegetable oil, wine vinegar, salt, black pepper, paprika, onion powder, and garlic powder, coating it well. Allow to marinate for a minimum of 3 hours. Preheat the air fryer to 390ºF (199ºC). Remove the beef from the marinade and put in the preheated air fryer when your air fryer displays "READY" (select the cooking preset, and make minor adjustments according to your desired doneness.) and choose a shake reminder. Cook at the corresponding preset mode or Air Fry for 10 minutes. Flip the beef halfway through. Put the prepared Brussels sprouts in the air fryer along with the fennel seeds, basil, and sage. Lower the heat to 380ºF (193ºC) and air fry everything for another 5 minutes. Give them a good stir. Cook for an additional 10 minutes. Serve immediately.

## Cheddar Beef Burger Egg Rolls

**Prep time: 15 minutes | Cook time: 8 minutes | Makes 6 egg rolls**

8 ounces (227 g) raw lean ground beef
½ cup chopped onion
½ cup chopped bell pepper
¼ teaspoon onion powder
¼ teaspoon garlic powder

3 tablespoons cream cheese
1 tablespoon yellow mustard
3 tablespoons shredded Cheddar cheese
6 chopped dill pickle chips
6 egg roll wrappers

Preheat the air fryer to 392ºF (200ºC). In a skillet, add the beef, onion, bell pepper, onion powder, and garlic powder. Stir and crumble beef until fully cooked, and vegetables are soft. Take skillet off the heat and add cream cheese, mustard, and Cheddar cheese, stirring until melted. Pour beef mixture into a bowl and fold in pickles. Lay out egg wrappers and divide the beef mixture into each one. Moisten egg roll wrapper edges with water. Fold sides to the middle and seal with water. Repeat with all other egg rolls. Put rolls into air fryer, one batch at a time. When your air fryer displays "READY" (select the cooking preset, and make minor adjustments according to your desired doneness.) and choose a shake reminder. Cook at the corresponding preset mode or Air Fry for 8 minutes. Serve immediately.

## Herb Lamb Chops with Asparagus

**Prep time: 5 minutes | Cook time: 15 minutes | Serves 4**

1 pound (454 g) lamb chops
2 tablespoons olive oil
2 teaspoons fresh thyme, chopped

1 garlic clove, minced
Salt and black pepper, to taste
1 pound (454 g) asparagus spears, trimmed

Preheat air fryer to 400ºF (205ºC). Drizzle the asparagus with some olive oil and sprinkle with salt. Season the lamb with salt and pepper. Brush with the remaining olive oil and place in the air fryer basket. When your air fryer displays "READY" (select the cooking preset, and make minor adjustments according to your desired doneness.) and choose a shake reminder. AirFry for 10 minutes, turn and add the asparagus. Cook for another 5 minutes. Serve topped with thyme.

## Italian Steak Piadina Sandwich

**Prep time: 5 minutes | Cook time: 15 minutes | Serves 2**

½ pound (227 g) ribeye steak
1 teaspoon sesame oil
Sea salt and red pepper, to taste

2 medium-sized piadinas
2 ounces (57 g) Fontina cheese, grated
4 tablespoons Giardiniera

Brush the ribeye steak with sesame oil and season with salt and red pepper. When your air fryer displays "READY" (select the cooking preset, and make minor adjustments according to your desired doneness.) and choose a shake reminder. Cook at 400ºF (204ºC) for 6 minutes. Then, turn the steak halfway through the cooking time and continue to cook for a further 6 minutes. Slice the ribeye steak into bite-sized strips. Top the piadinas with steak strips and cheese. Heat the sandwich in your Air Fryer at 380ºF (193ºC) for about 3 minutes until the cheese melts. Top with Giardiniera and serve. Enjoy!

## Steak with Broccoli and Mushroom

**Prep time: 10 minutes | Cook time: 15 minutes | Serves 4**

2 tablespoons cornstarch
½ cup low-sodium beef broth
1 teaspoon low-sodium soy sauce
12 ounces (340 g) sirloin strip steak, cut into 1-inch cubes

2½ cups broccoli florets
1 onion, chopped
1 cup sliced cremini mushrooms
1 tablespoon grated fresh ginger
Brown rice, cooked (optional)

In a medium bowl, stir together the cornstarch, beef broth, and soy sauce. Add the beef and toss to coat. Let stand for 5 minutes at room temperature. With a slotted spoon, transfer the beef from the broth mixture into a medium metal bowl. Reserve the broth. Add the broccoli, onion, mushrooms, and ginger to the beef. Place the bowl into the air fryer and cook for 12 to 15 minutes, or until the beef reaches at least 145ºF (63ºC) on a meat thermometer and the vegetables are tender. Add the reserved broth and cook for 2 to 3 minutes more, or until the sauce boils. Serve immediately over hot cooked brown rice, if desired.

## Beef Egg Rolls Wrappers

**Prep time: 15 minutes | Cook time: 12 minutes | Makes 8 egg rolls**

½ chopped onion
2 garlic cloves, chopped
½ packet taco seasoning
Salt and ground black pepper, to taste
1 pound (454 g) lean ground beef

½ can cilantro lime rotel
16 egg roll wrappers
1 cup shredded Mexican cheese
1 tablespoon olive oil
1 teaspoon cilantro

Preheat the air fryer to 400ºF (205ºC). Add onions and garlic to a skillet, cooking until fragrant. Then add taco seasoning, pepper, salt, and beef, cooking until beef is broke up into tiny pieces and cooked thoroughly. Add rotel and stir well. Lay out egg wrappers and brush with a touch of water to soften a bit. Load wrappers with beef filling and add cheese to each. Fold diagonally to close and use water to secure edges. Brush filled egg wrappers with olive oil and add to the air fryer when your air fryer displays "READY" (select the cooking preset, and make minor adjustments according to your desired doneness.) and choose a shake reminder. Cook at the corresponding preset mode or Air Fry for 8 minutes, flip, and cook for another 4 minutes. Serve sprinkled with cilantro.

## Cheesy Lasagna

**Prep time: 15 minutes | Cook time: 20 minutes | Serves 4**

**For the Meat Layer:**

Extra-virgin olive oil
1 pound (454 g) 85% lean ground beef
1 cup prepared marinara sauce
¼ cup diced celery
¼ cup diced red onion
½ teaspoon minced garlic
Kosher salt and black pepper, to taste

**For the Cheese Layer:**

8 ounces (227 g) ricotta cheese
1 cup shredded Mozzarella cheese
½ cup grated Parmesan cheese
2 large eggs
1 teaspoon dried Italian seasoning, crushed
½ teaspoon each minced garlic, garlic powder, and black pepper

Grease a 7½-inch barrel cake pan with 1 teaspoon olive oil. In a large bowl, combine the ground beef, marinara, celery, onion, garlic, salt, and pepper. Place the seasoned meat in the pan. Preheat the air fryer to 375ºF (190ºC). Place the pan in the air-fryer basket when your air fryer displays "READY" (select the cooking preset, and make minor adjustments according to your desired doneness.) and choose a shake reminder. Set the air fryer to 375ºF (190ºC) for 10 minutes. Meanwhile, in a medium bowl, combine the ricotta, half the Mozzarella, the Parmesan, lightly beaten eggs, Italian seasoning, minced garlic, garlic powder, and pepper. Stir until well blended. At the end of the cooking time, spread the cheese mixture over the meat mixture. Sprinkle with the remaining ½ cup Mozzarella. Set the air fryer to 375ºF (190ºC) for 10 minutes, or until the cheese is browned and bubbling. At the end of the cooking time, use a meat thermometer to ensure the meat has reached an internal temperature of 160ºF (71ºC). Drain the fat and liquid from the pan. Let stand for 5 minutes before serving.

## Thyme-Dijon Top Chuck

**Prep time: 10 minutes | Cook time: 50 minutes | Serves 3**

1½ pounds (680 g) top chuck
2 teaspoons olive oil
1 tablespoon Dijon mustard
Sea salt and ground black
pepper, to taste
1 teaspoon dried marjoram
1 teaspoon dried thyme
½ teaspoon fennel seeds

Start by preheating your Air Fryer to 380ºF (193ºC). Add all ingredients in a Ziploc bag; shake to mix well. Next, spritz the bottom of the Air Fryer basket with cooking spray. When your air fryer displays "READY" (select the cooking preset, and make minor adjustments according to your desired doneness.) and choose a shake reminder. Place the beef in the cooking basket and cook for 50 minutes, turning every 10 to 15 minutes. Let it rest for 5 to 7 minutes before slicing and serving. Enjoy!

## Christmas Beef Brisket

**Prep time: 10 minutes | Cook time: 1¼ hours | Serves 4**

1½ pounds (680 g) beef brisket
2 tablespoons olive oil
1 tablespoon smoked paprika
1 tablespoon English mustard
powder
1 teaspoon ground
1 teaspoon chili pepper flakes
2 garlic cloves, pressed

Preheat the air fryer to 390ºF (199ºC). Toss the beef with the remaining ingredients; place the beef in the Air Fryer cooking basket when your air fryer displays "READY" (select the cooking preset, and make minor adjustments according to your desired doneness.) and choose a shake reminder. Cook the beef at 390ºF (199ºC) for 15 minutes, turn the beef over and reduce the temperature to 360ºF (182ºC). Continue to cook the beef for 55 minutes more. Bon appétit!

## Mustard Buttered New York Strip

**Prep time: 10 minutes | Cook time: 14 minutes | Serves 4**

1 tablespoon peanut oil
2 pounds (907 g) New York Strip
1 teaspoon cayenne pepper
Sea salt and freshly cracked
black pepper, to taste
½ stick butter, softened
1 teaspoon whole-grain mustard
½ teaspoon honey

Rub the peanut oil all over the steak; season with cayenne pepper, salt, and black pepper. When your air fryer displays "READY" (select the cooking preset, and make minor adjustments according to your desired doneness.) and choose a shake reminder. Cook in the preheated Air Fryer at 400ºF (204ºC) for 7 minutes; turn over and cook an additional 7 minutes. Meanwhile, prepare the mustard butter by whisking the butter, whole-grain mustard, and honey. Serve the roasted New York Strip dolloped with the mustard butter. Enjoy!

## Minty Filet Mignon

**Prep time: 10 minutes | Cook time: 18 minutes | Serves 4**

2 tablespoons olive oil
2 tablespoons Worcestershire sauce
1 lemon, juiced
¼ cup fresh mint leaves,
chopped
4 cloves garlic, minced
Sea salt and ground black pepper, to taste
2 pounds (907 g) filet mignon

In a ceramic bowl, place the olive oil, Worcestershire sauce, lemon juice, mint leaves, garlic, salt, black pepper, and cayenne pepper. Add the fillet mignon and let it marinate for 2 hours in the refrigerator. When your air fryer displays "READY" (select the cooking preset, and make minor adjustments according to your desired doneness.) and choose a shake reminder. Roast in the preheated Air Fryer at 400ºF (204ºC) for 18 minutes, basting with the reserved marinade and flipping a couple of times. Serve warm. Enjoy!

## Stuffed Beef Tenderloin with Cheese

**Prep time: 10 minutes | Cook time: 10 minutes | Serves 4**

1½ pounds (680 g) beef tenderloin, pounded to ¼ inch thick
3 teaspoons sea salt
1 teaspoon ground black pepper
2 ounces (57 g) creamy goat cheese
½ cup crumbled feta cheese
¼ cup finely chopped onions
2 cloves garlic, minced
Cooking spray

Preheat the air fryer to 400ºF (204ºC). Spritz the air fryer basket with cooking spray. Unfold the beef tenderloin on a clean work surface. Rub the salt and pepper all over the beef tenderloin to season. Make the filling for the stuffed beef tenderloins: Combine the goat cheese, feta, onions, and garlic in a medium bowl. Stir until well blended. Spoon the mixture in the center of the tenderloin. Roll the tenderloin up tightly like rolling a burrito and use some kitchen twine to tie the tenderloin. Arrange the tenderloin in the air fryer basket when your air fryer displays "READY" (select the cooking preset, and make minor adjustments according to your desired doneness.) and choose a shake reminder. Cook at the corresponding preset mode or Air Fry for 10 minutes, flipping the tenderloin halfway through to ensure even cooking, or until an instant-read thermometer inserted in the center of the tenderloin registers 135ºF (57ºC) for medium-rare. Transfer to a platter and serve immediately.

## Easy BBQ Cheeseburgers

**Prep time: 5 minutes | Cook time: 15 minutes | Serves 3**

¾ pound (340.2 g) ground chuck
1 teaspoon garlic, minced
2 tablespoons BBQ sauce

Sea salt and ground black pepper, to taste
3 slices cheese
3 hamburger buns

Preheat the air fryer to 380ºF (193ºC). Mix the ground chuck, garlic, BBQ sauce, salt, and black pepper until everything is well combined. Form the mixture into four patties. When your air fryer displays "READY" (select the cooking preset, and make minor adjustments according to your desired doneness.) and choose a shake reminder. Cook the burgers at 380ºF (193ºC) for about 15 minutes or until cooked through; make sure to turn them over halfway through the cooking time. Top each burger with cheese. Serve your burgers on the prepared buns and enjoy!

## Beef, Tomato, and Rice Stuffed Peppers

**Prep time: 10 minutes | Cook time: 15 minutes | Serves 4**

4 medium bell peppers, any colors, rinsed, tops removed
1 medium onion, chopped
½ cup grated carrot
2 teaspoons olive oil
2 medium beefsteak tomatoes,

chopped
1 cup cooked brown rice
1 cup chopped cooked low-sodium roast beef
1 teaspoon dried marjoram

Remove the stems from the bell pepper tops and chop the tops. In a 6-by-2-inch pan, combine the chopped bell pepper tops, onion, carrot, and olive oil. Cook for 2 to 4 minutes, or until the vegetables are crisp-tender. Transfer the vegetables to a medium bowl. Add the tomatoes, brown rice, roast beef, and marjoram. Stir to mix. Stuff the vegetable mixture into the bell peppers. Place the bell peppers in the air fryer basket. Bake for 11 to 16 minutes, or until the peppers are tender and the filling is hot. Serve immediately.

## Beef and Vegetable Cubes

**Prep time: 15 minutes | Cook time: 17 minutes | Serves 4**

2 tablespoons olive oil
1 tablespoon apple cider vinegar
1 teaspoon fine sea salt
½ teaspoons ground black pepper
1 teaspoon shallot powder
¾ teaspoon smoked cayenne pepper
½ teaspoons garlic powder

¼ teaspoon ground cumin
1 pound (454 g) top round steak, cut into cubes
4 ounces (113 g) broccoli, cut into florets
4 ounces (113 g) mushrooms, sliced
1 teaspoon dried basil
1 teaspoon celery seeds

Massage the olive oil, vinegar, salt, black pepper, shallot powder, cayenne pepper, garlic powder, and cumin into the cubed steak, ensuring to coat each piece evenly. Allow to marinate for a minimum of 3 hours. Preheat the air fryer to 365ºF (185ºC). Put the beef cubes in the air fryer basket and cook at the corresponding preset mode or Air Fry for 12 minutes. When the steak is cooked through, place it in a bowl. Wipe the grease from the basket and pour in the vegetables. Season them with basil and celery seeds. Increase the temperature of the air fryer to 400ºF (204ºC) and cook at the corresponding preset mode or Air Fry for 5 to 6 minutes. When the vegetables are hot, serve them with the steak.

## Oregano Beef Burgers

**Prep time: 10 minutes | Cook time: 10 minutes | Serves 4**

1 pound (454 g) lean ground beef
1 teaspoon dried parsley
½ teaspoon dried oregano
½ teaspoon pepper
½ teaspoon salt

½ teaspoon onion powder
½ teaspoon garlic powder
Few drops of liquid smoke
1 teaspoon Worcestershire sauce

Ensure your air fryer is preheated to 350ºF (177ºC). Mix all seasonings together till combined. Place beef in a bowl and add seasonings. Mix well, but do not overmix. Make 4 patties from the mixture and using your thumb, making an indent in the center of each patty. Add patties to air fryer basket when your air fryer displays "READY" (select the cooking preset, and make minor adjustments according to your desired doneness.) and choose a shake reminder. Cook 10 minutes. No need to turn!

## Glazed Beef Cheese Cups

**Prep time: 10 minutes | Cook time: 25 minutes | Serves 4**

**For the Meatloaves:**
1 pound (454 g) ground beef
¼ cup seasoned breadcrumbs
¼ cup Parmesan cheese, grated
1 small onion, minced
**For the Glaze:**
4 tablespoons tomato sauce
1 tablespoon brown sugar

2 garlic cloves, pressed
1 egg, beaten
Sea salt and ground black pepper, to taste

1 tablespoon Dijon mustard

Preheat the air fryer to 380ºF (193ºC). Thoroughly combine all ingredients for the meatloaves until everything is well combined. Scrape the beef mixture into lightly oiled silicone cups and transfer them to the Air Fryer cooking basket when your air fryer displays "READY" (select the cooking preset, and make minor adjustments according to your desired doneness.) and choose a shake reminder. Cook the beef cups at 380ºF (193ºC) for 20 minutes. In the meantime, mix the remaining ingredients for the glaze. Then, spread the glaze on top of each muffin; continue to cook for another 5 minutes. Bon appétit!

## Bacon-Wrapped Beef and Mushrooms

**Prep time: 10 minutes | Cook time: 13 minutes per batch | Serves 8**

1 ounce (28 g) dried porcini mushrooms
½ teaspoon granulated white sugar
½ teaspoon salt
½ teaspoon ground white

pepper
8 (4-ounce / 113-g) filets mignons or beef tenderloin steaks
8 thin-cut bacon strips

Preheat the air fryer to 400ºF (204ºC). Put the mushrooms, sugar, salt, and white pepper in a spice grinder and grind to combine. On a clean work surface, rub the filets mignons with the mushroom mixture, then wrap each filet with a bacon strip. Secure with toothpicks if necessary. Arrange the bacon-wrapped filets mignons in the preheated air fryer basket, seam side down when your air fryer displays "READY" (select the cooking preset, and make minor adjustments according to your desired doneness.) and choose a shake reminder. Work in batches to avoid overcrowding. Cook at the corresponding preset mode or Air Fry for 13 minutes or until medium rare. Flip the filets halfway through. Serve immediately.

## Cheeseburgers with Ciabatta Rolls

**Prep time: 10 minutes | Cook time: 15 minutes | Serves 4**

¾ pound (340 g) ground beef
chuck
1 envelope onion soup mix
Kosher salt and freshly ground

black pepper, to taste
1 teaspoon paprika
4 slices Monterey Jack cheese
4 ciabatta rolls

In a bowl, stir together the ground chuck, onion soup mix, salt, black pepper, and paprika to combine well. Preheat the air fryer to 385ºF (196ºC). Take four equal portions of the mixture and mold each one into a patty. Transfer to the air fryer when your air fryer displays "READY" (select the cooking preset, and make minor adjustments according to your desired doneness.) and choose a shake reminder. Cook at the corresponding preset mode or Air Fry for 10 minutes. Put the slices of cheese on the top of the burgers. Cook for another minute before serving on ciabatta rolls.

## Hearty Beef Jerky

**Prep time: 10 minutes | Cook time: 1 hour | Serves 4**

1 cup beer
½ cup tamari sauce
1 teaspoon liquid smoke
2 garlic cloves, minced
Sea salt and ground black

pepper
1 teaspoon ancho chili powder
2 tablespoons honey
¾ pound (340 g) flank steak,
slice into strips

Place all ingredients in a ceramic dish; let it marinate for 3 hours in the refrigerator. Slice the beef into thin strips Marinate the beef in the refrigerator overnight. Now, discard the marinade and hang the meat in the cooking basket by using skewers. When your air fryer displays "READY" (select the cooking preset, and make minor adjustments according to your desired doneness.) and choose a shake reminder. Air Fry at 190ºF (88ºC) for 1 hour. Store it in an airtight container for up to 2 weeks. Enjoy!

## Mediterranean-Style Filet Mignon

**Prep time: 10 minutes | Cook time: 14 minutes | Serves 4**

1½ pounds (680 g) filet mignon
Sea salt and ground black
pepper, to taste
2 tablespoons olive oil

1 teaspoon dried rosemary
1 teaspoon dried thyme
1 teaspoon dried basil
2 cloves garlic, minced

Preheat the air fryer to 400ºF (204ºC). Toss the beef with the remaining ingredients; place the beef in the Air Fryer cooking basket when your air fryer displays "READY" (select the cooking preset, and make minor adjustments according to your desired doneness.) and choose a shake reminder. Cook the beef at 400ºF (204ºC) for 14 minutes, turning it over halfway through the cooking time. Enjoy!

## Easy Ribeye Steak

**Prep time: 5 minutes | Cook time: 13 minutes | Serves 4**

1 tablespoon olive oil
Pepper and salt, to taste

2 pounds (907 g) of ribeye
steak

Season meat on both sides with pepper and salt. Rub all sides of meat with olive oil. Preheat air fryer to 356ºF (180ºC) and spritz with olive oil. Add into the air fryer when your air fryer displays "READY" (select the cooking preset, and make minor adjustments according to your desired doneness.) and choose a shake reminder. Cook steak 7 minutes. Flip and cook an additional 6 minutes. Let meat sit 2 to 5 minutes to rest. Slice and serve with salad.

## African Mint Lamb Kofta

**Prep time: 10 minutes | Cook time: 10 minutes | Serves 4**

1 pound (454 g) ground lamb
1 teaspoon cumin
2 tablespoons mint, chopped
1 teaspoon garlic powder
1 teaspoon onion powder

1 tablespoon ras el hanout
½ teaspoon dried coriander
4 bamboo skewers
Salt and black pepper, to taste

In a bowl, mix ground lamb, cumin, garlic and onion powders, mint, ras el hanout, coriander, salt, and pepper. Mold into sausage shapes and place onto skewers. Let sit for 15 minutes in the fridge. Preheat air fryer to 380ºF (193ºC). Grease the frying basket with cooking spray. Arrange the skewers on the basket when your air fryer displays "READY" (select the cooking preset, and make minor adjustments according to your desired doneness.) and choose a shake reminder. AirFry for 10 to 12 minutes, turning once halfway through. Serve with yogurt dip.

## Panko-Calf's Liver Strips

**Prep time: 15 minutes | Cook time: 23 to 25 minutes | Serves 4**

1 pound (454 g) sliced calf's
liver, cut into ½-inch wide strips
2 eggs
2 tablespoons milk
½ cup whole wheat flour

2 cups panko breadcrumbs
Salt and ground black pepper,
to taste
Cooking spray

Preheat the air fryer to 390ºF (199ºC) and spritz with cooking spray. Rub the calf's liver strips with salt and ground black pepper on a clean work surface. Whisk the eggs with milk in a large bowl. Pour the flour in a shallow dish. Pour the panko on a separate shallow dish. Dunk the liver strips in the flour, then in the egg mixture. Shake the excess off and roll the strips over the panko to coat well. Arrange half of the liver strips in a single layer in the preheated air fryer and spritz with cooking spray. When your air fryer displays "READY" (select the cooking preset, and make minor adjustments according to your desired doneness.) and choose a shake reminder. Cook at the corresponding preset mode or Air Fry for 5 minutes or until browned. Flip the strips halfway through. Repeat with the remaining strips. Serve immediately.

## Teriyaki Rump Steak with Broccoli

**Prep time: 5 minutes | Cook time: 13 minutes | Serves 4**

½ pound (227 g) rump steak
⅓ cup teriyaki marinade
1½ teaspoons sesame oil
½ head broccoli, cut into florets

2 red capsicums, sliced
Fine sea salt and ground black
pepper, to taste
Cooking spray

Toss the rump steak in a large bowl with teriyaki marinade. Wrap the bowl in plastic and refrigerate to marinate for at least an hour. Preheat the air fryer to 400ºF (204ºC) and spritz with cooking spray. Discard the marinade and transfer the steak in the preheated air fryer when your air fryer displays "READY" (select the cooking preset, and make minor adjustments according to your desired doneness.) and choose a shake reminder. Spritz with cooking spray. Cook at the corresponding preset mode or Air Fry for 13 minutes or until well browned. Flip the steak halfway through. Meanwhile, heat the sesame oil in a nonstick skillet over medium heat. Add the broccoli and capsicum. Sprinkle with salt and ground black pepper. Sauté for 5 minutes or until the broccoli is tender. Transfer the air fried rump steak on a plate and top with the sautéed broccoli and capsicum. Serve hot.

## Beef Rib-Eye Steaks

**Prep time: 5 minutes | Cook time: 20 minutes | Serves 2**

2 beef rib-eye steaks
1 tablespoon balsamic vinegar
½ tablespoon Italian seasoning
2 tablespoons olive oil
Salt and black pepper, to taste

Preheat air fryer to 360ºF (182ºC). In a bowl, combine all ingredients, cover it, and place in the fridge for 30 minutes. Transfer the beef to the frying basket when your air fryer displays "READY" (select the cooking preset, and make minor adjustments according to your desired doneness.) and choose a shake reminder. Bake for 20 minutes, flipping once halfway through.

## Lamb Steaks with Red Potatoes

**Prep time: 5 minutes | Cook time: 14 minutes | Serves 2**

2 lamb steaks
2 tablespoons olive oil
2 garlic cloves, crushed
Salt and black pepper, to taste
2 tablespoons fresh thyme, chopped
2 red potatoes, sliced

Rub the steaks with 1 tablespoon olive oil, garlic, salt, and pepper. Place them in the greased air fryer basket. Season the potatoes with olive oil, salt, pepper, and thyme. Arrange the potatoes next to the steaks when your air fryer displays "READY" (select the cooking preset, and make minor adjustments according to your desired doneness.) and choose a shake reminder. Cook at 360ºF (182ºC) for 14 to 16 minutes, turning once halfway through cooking. Serve immediately.

## Thyme Beef Loin

**Prep time: 5 minutes | Cook time: 15 minutes | Serves 4**

1 tablespoon butter, melted
¼ dried thyme
1 teaspoon garlic salt
¼ teaspoon dried parsley
1 pound (454 g) beef loin

Preheat the air fryer to 400ºF (204ºC). In a bowl, combine the melted butter, thyme, garlic salt, and parsley. Cut the beef loin into slices and generously apply the seasoned butter using a brush. Transfer to the air fryer basket when your air fryer displays "READY" (select the cooking preset, and make minor adjustments according to your desired doneness.) and choose a shake reminder. Cook the beef at the corresponding preset mode or Air Fry for 15 minutes. Take care when removing it and serve hot.

## Oregano Beef with Zucchini

**Prep time: 5 minutes | Cook time: 12 minutes | Serves 4**

1½ pounds (680 g) ground beef
1 pound (454 g) chopped zucchini
2 tablespoons extra-virgin olive oil
1 teaspoon dried oregano
1 teaspoon dried basil
1 teaspoon dried rosemary
2 tablespoons fresh chives, chopped

Preheat the air fryer to 400ºF (204ºC). In a large bowl, combine all the ingredients, except for the chives, until well blended. Place the beef and zucchini mixture in the baking pan when your air fryer displays "READY" (select the cooking preset, and make minor adjustments according to your desired doneness.) and choose a shake reminder. Cook at the corresponding preset mode or Air Fry for 12 minutes, or until the beef is browned and the zucchini is tender. Divide the beef and zucchini mixture among four serving dishes. Top with fresh chives and serve hot.

## Lamb Satay

**Prep time: 5 minutes | Cook time: 8 minutes | Serves 2**

¼ teaspoon cumin
1 teaspoon ginger
½ teaspoons nutmeg
Salt and ground black pepper,
to taste
2 boneless lamb steaks
Cooking spray

Combine the cumin, ginger, nutmeg, salt and pepper in a bowl. Cube the lamb steaks and massage the spice mixture into each one. Leave to marinate for 10 minutes, then transfer onto metal skewers. Preheat the air fryer to 400ºF (204ºC). When your air fryer displays "READY" (select the cooking preset, and make minor adjustments according to your desired doneness.), choose a shake reminder. Spritz the skewers with the cooking spray, then cook at the corresponding preset mode or Air Fry for 8 minutes. Take care when removing them from the air fryer and serve.

## Balsamic-Mustard London Broil

**Prep time: 15 minutes | Cook time: 25 minutes | Serves 8**

2 pounds (907 g) London broil
3 large garlic cloves, minced
3 tablespoons balsamic vinegar
3 tablespoons whole-grain mustard
2 tablespoons olive oil
Sea salt and ground black pepper, to taste
½ teaspoons dried hot red pepper flakes

Wash and dry the London broil. Score its sides with a knife. Mix the remaining ingredients. Rub this mixture into the broil, coating it well. Allow to marinate for a minimum of 3 hours. Preheat the air fryer to 400ºF (204ºC). When your air fryer displays "READY" (select the cooking preset, and make minor adjustments according to your desired doneness.) and choose a shake reminder. Air fry the meat for 15 minutes. Turn it over and cook at the corresponding preset mode or Air Fry for an additional 10 minutes before serving.

## Paprika Flank Steak

**Prep time: 5 minutes | Cook time: 12 minutes | Serves 5**

2 pounds (907 g) flank steak
2 tablespoons olive oil
1 teaspoon paprika
Sea salt and ground black pepper, to taste

Preheat the air fryer to 400ºF (204ºC). Toss the steak with the remaining ingredients; place the steak in the Air Fryer cooking basket when your air fryer displays "READY" (select the cooking preset, and make minor adjustments according to your desired doneness.) and choose a shake reminder. Cook the steak at 400ºF (204ºC) for 12 minutes, turning over halfway through the cooking time. Bon appétit!

## Chinese Five-Spice Beef Tenderloin

**Prep time: 10 minutes | Cook time: 20 minutes | Serves 4**

1½ pounds (680 g) beef tenderloin, sliced
2 tablespoons sesame oil
1 teaspoon Five-spice powder
2 garlic cloves, minced
1 teaspoon fresh ginger, peeled and grated
2 tablespoons soy sauce

Preheat the air fryer to 400ºF (204ºC). Toss the beef tenderloin with the remaining ingredients; place the beef tenderloin in the Air Fryer cooking basket when your air fryer displays "READY" (select the cooking preset, and make minor adjustments according to your desired doneness.) and choose a shake reminder. Cook the beef tenderloin at 400ºF (204ºC) for 20 minutes, turning it over halfway through the cooking time. Enjoy!

## Chimichurri Flank Steak

**Prep time: 5 minutes | Cook time: 12 minutes | Serves 1**

1 flank steak
Salt and ground black pepper, to taste

2 avocados
2 tablespoons butter, melted
½ cup chimichurri sauce

Rub the flank steak with salt and pepper to taste and leave to sit for 20 minutes. Preheat the air fryer to 400ºF (204ºC). Halve the avocados and take out the pits. Spoon the flesh into a bowl and mash with a fork. Mix in the melted butter and chimichurri sauce, making sure everything is well combined. Put the steak in the air fryer basket when your air fryer displays "READY (select the cooking preset, and make minor adjustments according to your desired doneness.) and choose a shake reminder. Cook at the corresponding preset mode or Air Fry for 6 minutes. Flip over and allow to cook for another 6 minutes. Serve the steak with the avocado butter.

## Roast Beef with Tomato

**Prep time: 5 minutes | Cook time: 55 minutes | Serves 4**

1½ pounds (680 g) chuck eye roast
Sea salt and ground black pepper, to taste
1 teaspoon red pepper flakes,

crushed
2 tablespoons olive oil, melted
1 jalapeno pepper, chopped
1 large-sized tomato, sliced

Preheat the air fryer to 390ºF (199ºC). Toss the roast beef with the salt, black pepper, salt, red pepper flakes, and olive oil; place the roast beef in a lightly oiled Air Fryer cooking basket when your air fryer displays "READY" (select the cooking preset, and make minor adjustments according to your desired doneness.) and choose a shake reminder. Cook the roast beef at 390ºF (199ºC) for 45 minutes, turning it over halfway through the cooking time. Top the roast beef with the tomato and jalapeno pepper. Continue to cook for 10 minutes more. Enjoy!

## Beef Brisket

**Prep time: 10 minutes | Cook time: 1¼ hours | Serves 4**

1½ pounds (680 g) beef brisket
2 tablespoons olive oil
1 teaspoon onion powder
1 teaspoon garlic powder

Sea salt and ground black pepper, to taste
1 teaspoon dried parsley flakes
1 teaspoon dried thyme

Preheat the air fryer to 390ºF (199ºC). Toss the beef with the remaining ingredients; place the beef in the Air Fryer cooking basket when your air fryer displays "READY (select the cooking preset, and make minor adjustments according to your desired doneness.) and choose a shake reminder. Cook the beef at 390ºF (199ºC) for 15 minutes, turn the beef over and turn the temperature to 360ºF (182ºC). Continue to cook the beef for 55 minutes more. Bon appétit!

## Taco Bell Crunch Wraps

**Prep time: 10 minutes | Cook time: 2 minutes | Serves 6**

6 wheat tostadas
2 cups sour cream
2 cups Mexican blend cheese
2 cups shredded lettuce
12 ounces (340 g) low-sodium nacho cheese
3 Roma tomatoes

6 (12-inch) wheat tortillas
1⅓ cups water
2 packets low-sodium taco seasoning
2 pounds (907 g) of lean ground beef

Ensure your air fryer is preheated to 400ºF (204ºC). Make beef according to taco seasoning packets. Place ⅔ cup prepared beef, 4 tablespoons cheese, 1 tostada, ⅓ cup sour cream, ⅓ cup lettuce, ⅙ of tomatoes and ⅓ cup cheese on each tortilla. Fold up tortillas edges and repeat with remaining ingredients. Lay the folded sides of tortillas down into the air fryer and spray with olive oil. When your air fryer displays "READY" (select the cooking preset, and make minor adjustments according to your desired doneness.) and choose a shake reminder. Cook 2 minutes till browned.

## Delicious Coulotte Roast

**Prep time: 5 minutes | Cook time: 55 minutes | Serves 5**

2 pounds (907 g) Coulotte roast
2 tablespoons olive oil
1 tablespoon fresh parsley, finely chopped
1 tablespoon fresh cilantro,

finely chopped
2 garlic cloves, minced
Kosher salt and ground black pepper, to taste

Preheat the air fryer to 390ºF (199ºC). Toss the roast beef with the remaining ingredients; place the roast beef in the Air Fryer cooking basket when your air fryer displays "READY" (select the cooking preset, and make minor adjustments according to your desired doneness.) and choose a shake reminder. Cook the roast beef at 390ºF (199ºC) for 55 minutes, turning over halfway through the cooking time. Enjoy!

## Beef Steak Fingers

**Prep time: 5 minutes | Cook time: 8 minutes | Serves 4**

4 small beef cube steaks
Salt and ground black pepper, to taste

½ cup flour
Cooking spray

Preheat the air fryer to 390ºF (199ºC). Cut cube steaks into 1-inch-wide strips. Sprinkle lightly with salt and pepper to taste. Roll in flour to coat all sides. Spritz air fryer basket with cooking spray. Put steak strips in air fryer basket in a single layer when your air fryer displays "READY" (select the cooking preset, and make minor adjustments according to your desired doneness.) and choose a shake reminder. Spritz top of steak strips with cooking spray. Cook at the corresponding preset mode or Air Fry for 4 minutes, turn strips over, and spritz with cooking spray. Air fry 4 more minutes and test with fork for doneness. Steak fingers should be crispy outside with no red juices inside. Repeat steps 5 through 7 to air fry remaining strips. Serve immediately.

## London Broil with Garlic Butter

**Prep time: 10 minutes | Cook time: 28 minutes | Serves 4**

1½ pounds (680 g) London broil
Kosher salt and ground black pepper, to taste
¼ teaspoon ground bay leaf
3 tablespoons butter, cold

1 tablespoon Dijon mustard
1 teaspoon garlic, pressed
1 tablespoon fresh parsley, chopped

Preheat the air fryer to 400ºF (204ºC). Toss the beef with the salt and black pepper; place the beef in a lightly oiled Air Fryer cooking basket when your air fryer displays "READY" (select the cooking preset, and make minor adjustments according to your desired doneness.) and choose a shake reminder. Cook the beef at 400ºF (204ºC) for 28 minutes, turning over halfway through the cooking time. In the meantime, mix the butter with the remaining ingredients and place it in the refrigerator until well-chilled. Serve warm beef with the chilled garlic butter on the side. Bon appétit!

## Classic Beef Empanadas
**Prep time: 5 minutes | Cook time: 32 minutes | Serves 8**

1 teaspoon water
1 egg white
1 cup picadillo

8 Goya empanada discs (thawed)

Ensure your air fryer is preheated to 320ºF (160ºC). Spray basket with olive oil. Place 2 tablespoons of picadillo into the center of each disc. Fold disc in half and use a fork to seal edges. Repeat with all ingredients. Whisk egg white with water and brush tops of empanadas with egg wash. Add 2 to 3 empanadas to air fryer when your air fryer displays "READY" (select the cooking preset, and make minor adjustments according to your desired doneness.) and choose a shake reminder. Cook for 8 minutes until golden. Repeat till you cook all filled empanadas.

## Beef Risotto with Parmesan
**Prep time: 10 minutes | Cook time: 20 minutes | Serves 4**

2 teaspoons olive oil
1 onion, finely chopped
3 garlic cloves, minced
½ cup chopped red bell pepper
¾ cup short-grain rice

1¼ cups low-sodium beef broth
½ cup chopped cooked roast beef
3 tablespoons grated Parmesan cheese

In a 6-by-2-inch pan, combine the olive oil, onion, garlic, and red bell pepper. Place the pan in the air fryer for 2 minutes, or until the vegetables are crisp-tender. Remove from the air fryer. Add the rice, beef broth, and roast beef. Return the pan to the air fryer and bake for 18 to 22 minutes, stirring once during cooking, until the rice is tender and the beef reaches at least 145ºF (63ºC) on a meat thermometer. Remove the pan from the air fryer. Stir in the Parmesan cheese and serve immediately.

## Beef Shoulder
**Prep time: 10 minutes | Cook time: 55 minutes | Serves 4**

1½ pounds (680 g) beef shoulder
Sea salt and ground black pepper, to taste
1 teaspoon cayenne pepper

½ teaspoon ground cumin
2 tablespoons olive oil
2 cloves garlic, minced
1 teaspoon Dijon mustard
1 onion, cut into slices

Preheat the air fryer to 390ºF (199ºC). Toss the beef with the spices, garlic, mustard, and olive oil; place the beef in a lightly oiled Air Fryer cooking basket when your air fryer displays "READY" (select the cooking preset, and make minor adjustments according to your desired doneness.) and choose a shake reminder. Cook the beef at 390ºF (199ºC) for 45 minutes, turning it over halfway through the cooking time. Add in the onion and continue to cook an additional 10 minutes. Bon appétit!

## Beef with Fajita Veggies
**Prep time: 10 minutes | Cook time: 18 minutes | Serves 4 to 6**

**For the Beef:**
⅛ cup carne asada seasoning
2 pounds (907 g) beef flap meat

Diet 7-Up

**For the Fajita Veggies:**
1 teaspoon chili powder
1 to 2 teaspoons pepper
1 to 2 teaspoons salt

2 bell peppers, your choice of color
1 onion

Slice flap meat into manageable pieces and place into a bowl. Season meat with carne seasoning and pour diet soda over meat. Cover and chill overnight. Ensure your air fryer is preheated to 380ºF (193ºC). Place a parchment liner into air fryer basket and spray with olive oil when your air fryer displays "READY" (select the cooking preset, and make minor adjustments according to your desired doneness.) and choose a shake reminder. Place beef in layers into the basket. Cook 8 to 10 minutes, making sure to flip halfway through. Remove and set to the side. Slice up veggies and spray air fryer basket. Add veggies to the fryer and spray with olive oil. Cook 10 minutes at 400ºF (204ºC), shaking 1 to 2 times during cooking process. Serve meat and veggies on wheat tortillas and top with favorite keto fillings!

## Brandy Rump Roast with Cold Butter
**Prep time: 5 minutes | Cook time: 50 minutes | Serves 4**

1½ pounds (680 g) rump roast
Ground black pepper and kosher salt, to taste
1 teaspoon paprika

2 tablespoons olive oil
¼ cup brandy
2 tablespoons cold butter

Preheat the air fryer to 390ºF (199ºC). Toss the rump roast with the black pepper, salt, paprika, olive oil, and brandy; place the rump roast in a lightly oiled Air Fryer cooking basket when your air fryer displays "READY" (select the cooking preset, and make minor adjustments according to your desired doneness.) and choose a shake reminder. Cook the rump roast at 390ºF (199ºC) for 50 minutes, turning it over halfway through the cooking time. Serve with the cold butter and enjoy!

## Filet Mignon
**Prep time: 5 minutes | Cook time: 14 minutes | Serves 4**

1½ pounds (680 g) filet mignon
2 tablespoons soy sauce
2 tablespoons butter, melted
1 teaspoon mustard powder

1 teaspoon garlic powder
Sea salt and ground black pepper, to taste

Preheat the air fryer to 400ºF (204ºC). Toss the filet mignon with the remaining ingredients; place the filet mignon in the Air Fryer cooking basket when your air fryer displays "READY" (select the cooking preset, and make minor adjustments according to your desired doneness.) and choose a shake reminder. Cook the filet mignon at 400ºF (204ºC) for 14 minutes, turning it over halfway through the cooking time. Enjoy!

## Air-Fried Beef Ribs
**Prep time: 20 minutes | Cook time: 8 minutes | Serves 4**

1 pound (454 g) meaty beef ribs, rinsed and drained
3 tablespoons apple cider vinegar
1 cup coriander, finely chopped
1 tablespoon fresh basil leaves, chopped

2 garlic cloves, finely chopped
1 chipotle powder
1 teaspoon fennel seeds
1 teaspoon hot paprika
Kosher salt and black pepper, to taste
½ cup vegetable oil

Coat the ribs with the remaining ingredients and refrigerate for at least 3 hours. Preheat the air fryer to 360ºF (182ºC). Separate the ribs from the marinade and put them in the air fryer basket when your air fryer displays "READY" (select the cooking preset, and make minor adjustments according to your desired doneness.) and choose a shake reminder. Cook at the corresponding preset mode or Air Fry for 8 minutes. Pour the remaining marinade over the ribs before serving.

## Cheddar Beef Stuffed Peppers

**Prep time: 10 minutes | Cook time: 18 minutes | Serves 4**

4 ounces (113 g) shredded Cheddar cheese
½ teaspoon pepper
½ teaspoon salt
1 teaspoon Worcestershire sauce
½ cup tomato sauce

8 ounces (227 g) lean ground beef
1 teaspoon olive oil
1 minced garlic clove
½ chopped onion
2 green peppers

Ensure your air fryer is preheated to 390ºF (199ºC). Spray with olive oil. Cut stems off bell peppers and remove seeds. Cook in boiling salted water for 3 minutes. Sauté garlic and onion together in a skillet until golden in color. Take skillet off the heat. Mix pepper, salt, Worcestershire sauce, ¼ cup of tomato sauce, half of cheese and beef together. Divide meat mixture into pepper halves. Top filled peppers with remaining cheese and tomato sauce. Place filled peppers in air fryer when your air fryer displays "READY" (select the cooking preset, and make minor adjustments according to your desired doneness.) and choose a shake reminder. Bake 15 to 20 minutes.

## Beef and Baby Spinach Rolls

**Prep time: 10 minutes | Cook time: 14 minutes | Serves 2**

3 teaspoons pesto
2 pounds (907 g) beef flank steak
6 slices provolone cheese
3 ounces (85 g) roasted red bell

peppers
¾ cup baby spinach
1 teaspoon sea salt
1 teaspoon black pepper

Preheat the air fryer to 400ºF (204ºC). Spoon equal amounts of the pesto onto each flank steak and spread it across evenly. Put the cheese, roasted red peppers and spinach on top of the meat, about three-quarters of the way down. Roll the steak up, holding it in place with toothpicks. Sprinkle with the sea salt and pepper. Put inside the air fryer when your air fryer displays "READY" (select the cooking preset, and make minor adjustments according to your desired doneness.) and choose a shake reminder. Cook at the corresponding preset mode or Air Fry for 14 minutes, turning halfway through the cooking time. Allow the beef to rest for 10 minutes before slicing up and serving.

## Rosemary Lamb Rack

**Prep time: 5 minutes | Cook time: 10 minutes | Serves 4**

¼ cup freshly squeezed lemon juice
1 teaspoon oregano
2 teaspoons minced fresh rosemary
1 teaspoon minced fresh thyme

2 tablespoons minced garlic
Salt and freshly ground black pepper, to taste
2 to 4 tablespoons olive oil
1 lamb rib rack (7 to 8 ribs)

Preheat the air fryer to 360ºF (182ºC). In a small mixing bowl, combine the lemon juice, oregano, rosemary, thyme, garlic, salt, pepper, and olive oil and mix well. Rub the mixture over the lamb, covering all the meat. Put the rack of lamb in the air fryer when your air fryer displays "READY" (select the cooking preset, and make minor adjustments according to your desired doneness.) and choose a shake reminder. Cook at the corresponding preset mode or Air Fry for 10 minutes. Flip the rack halfway through. After 10 minutes, measure the internal temperature of the rack of lamb reaches at least 145ºF (63ºC). Serve immediately.

## Nice Steak with Gravy

**Prep time: 15 minutes | Cook time: 10 minutes | Serves 4**

½ cup flour
2 teaspoons salt, divided
Freshly ground black pepper, to taste
¼ teaspoon garlic powder
**For the Gravy:**
2 tablespoons butter or bacon drippings
¼ onion, minced
1 clove garlic, smashed
¼ teaspoon dried thyme
3 tablespoons flour

1 cup buttermilk
1 cup fine bread crumbs
4 (6-ounce / 170-g) tenderized top round steaks, ½-inch thick
Vegetable or canola oil

1 cup milk
Salt and freshly ground black pepper, to taste
Dashes of Worcestershire sauce

Set up a dredging station. Combine the flour, 1 teaspoon of salt, black pepper and garlic powder in a shallow bowl. Pour the buttermilk into a second shallow bowl. Finally, put the bread crumbs and 1 teaspoon of salt in a third shallow bowl. Dip the tenderized steaks into the flour, then the buttermilk, and then the bread crumb mixture, pressing the crumbs onto the steak. Put them on a baking sheet and spray both sides generously with vegetable or canola oil. Preheat the air fryer to 400ºF (204ºC). Transfer the steaks to the air fryer basket when your air fryer displays "READY" (select the cooking preset, and make minor adjustments according to your desired doneness.) and choose a shake reminder. Cook at the corresponding preset mode or Air Fry for 10 minutes, flipping the steaks over halfway through the cooking time. Hold the first batch of steaks warm in a 170ºF (77ºC) oven while you air fry the second batch. While the steaks are cooking, make the gravy. Melt the butter in a small saucepan over medium heat on the stovetop. Add the onion, garlic and thyme and cook for five minutes, until the onion is soft and just starting to brown. Stir in the flour and cook for another five minutes, stirring regularly, until the mixture starts to brown. Whisk in the milk and bring the mixture to a boil to thicken. Season to taste with salt, lots of freshly ground black pepper, and a few dashes of Worcestershire sauce. Pour the gravy over the chicken fried steaks and serve.

## Mexican-Flavor Carne Asada Tacos

**Prep time: 5 minutes | Cook time: 14 minutes | Serves 4**

⅓ cup olive oil
1½ pounds (680 g) flank steak
Salt and freshly ground black pepper, to taste
⅓ cup freshly squeezed lime

juice
½ cup chopped fresh cilantro
4 teaspoons minced garlic
1 teaspoon ground cumin
1 teaspoon chili powder

Brush the air fryer basket with olive oil. Put the flank steak in a large mixing bowl. Season with salt and pepper. Add the lime juice, cilantro, garlic, cumin, and chili powder and toss to coat the steak. For the best flavor, let the steak marinate in the refrigerator for about 1 hour. Preheat the air fryer to 400ºF (204ºC). Put the steak in the air fryer basket when your air fryer displays "READY" (select the cooking preset, and make minor adjustments according to your desired doneness.) and choose a shake reminder. Cook at the corresponding preset mode or Air Fry for 7 minutes. Flip the steak. Cook for 7 minutes more or until an internal temperature reaches at least 145ºF (63ºC). Let the steak rest for about 5 minutes, then cut into strips to serve.

## New York Strip

**Prep time: 5 minutes | Cook time: 14 minutes | Serves 4**

2 pounds (907 g) New York Strip
1 teaspoon cayenne pepper
1 tablespoon honey
1 tablespoon Dijon mustard
½ stick butter, softened
Sea salt and freshly ground black pepper, to taste
Cooking spray

Preheat the air fryer to 400ºF (204ºC) and spritz with cooking spray. Sprinkle the New York Strip with cayenne pepper, salt, and black pepper on a clean work surface. Arrange the New York Strip in the preheated air fryer and spritz with cooking spray when your air fryer displays "READY" (select the cooking preset, and make minor adjustments according to your desired doneness.) and choose a shake reminder. Cook at the corresponding preset mode or Air Fry for 14 minutes or until browned and reach your desired doneness. Flip the New York Strip halfway through. Meanwhile, combine the honey, mustard, and butter in a small bowl. Stir to mix well. Transfer the air fried New York Strip onto a plate and baste with the honey-mustard butter before serving.

## Mongolian Beef Tenderloin

**Prep time: 15 minutes | Cook time: 12 minutes | Serves 6 to 10**

Olive oil
½ cup almond flour
2 pounds (907 g) beef
**For the Sauce:**
½ cup chopped green onion
1 teaspoon red chili flakes
1 teaspoon almond flour
½ cup brown sugar
1 teaspoon hoisin sauce
½ cup water
tenderloin or beef chuck, sliced into strips

½ cup rice vinegar
½ cup low-sodium soy sauce
1 tablespoon chopped garlic
1 tablespoon finely chopped ginger
2 tablespoons olive oil

Preheat the air fryer to 300ºF (149ºC). Toss strips of beef in almond flour, ensuring they are coated well. Add to air fryer when your air fryer displays "READY" (select the cooking preset, and make minor adjustments according to your desired doneness.) and choose a shake reminder. Cook for 10 minutes at 300ºF (149ºC). Meanwhile, add all sauce ingredients to the pan and bring to a boil. Mix well. Add beef strips to the sauce and cook 2 minutes. Serve over cauliflower rice!

## Salsa Beef Meatballs

**Prep time: 10 minutes | Cook time: 10 minutes | Serves 4**

1 pound (454 g) ground beef (85% lean)
½ cup salsa
¼ cup diced green or red bell peppers
1 large egg, beaten
¼ cup chopped onions
½ teaspoon chili powder
1 clove garlic, minced
½ teaspoon ground cumin
1 teaspoon fine sea salt
Lime wedges, for serving
Cooking spray

Preheat the air fryer to 350ºF (177ºC) and spritz with cooking spray. Combine all the ingredients in a large bowl. Stir to mix well. Divide and shape the mixture into 1-inch balls. Arrange the balls in the preheated air fryer and spritz with cooking spray when your air fryer displays "READY" (select the cooking preset, and make minor adjustments according to your desired doneness.) and choose a shake reminder. Cook at the corresponding preset mode or Air Fry for 10 minutes or until the balls are well browned. Flip the balls with tongs halfway through. Transfer the balls on a plate and squeeze the lime wedges over before serving.

## Chateaubriand with French Wine

**Prep time: 5 minutes | Cook time: 14 minutes | Serves 4**

1 pound (454 g) beef filet mignon
Sea salt and ground black pepper, to taste
1 teaspoon cayenne pepper
3 tablespoons olive oil
1 tablespoon Dijon mustard
4 tablespoons dry French wine

Preheat the air fryer to 400ºF (204ºC). Toss the filet mignon with the rest of the ingredients; place the filet mignon in the Air Fryer cooking basket when your air fryer displays "READY" (select the cooking preset, and make minor adjustments according to your desired doneness.) and choose a shake reminder. Cook the filet mignon at 400ºF (204ºC) for 14 minutes, turning it over halfway through the cooking time. Enjoy!

## Chuck Roast with Red Wine

**Prep time: 10 minutes | Cook time: 55 minutes | Serves 5**

½ cup red wine
1 tablespoon Dijon mustard
1 tablespoon fresh garlic, minced
1 teaspoon red pepper flakes,
crushed
Sea salt and ground black pepper, to taste
2 pounds (907 g) chuck roast
1 tablespoon corn flour

Preheat the air fryer to 390ºF (199ºC). Place the wine, mustard, garlic, red pepper, salt, black pepper, and chuck roast in a ceramic bowl. Cover the bowl and let the meat marinate for 3 hours in your refrigerator. Toss the roast beef with the corn flour; place the roast beef in the Air Fryer cooking basket when your air fryer displays "READY" (select the cooking preset, and make minor adjustments according to your desired doneness.) and choose a shake reminder. Cook the roast beef at 390ºF (199ºC) for 55 minutes, turning them over halfway through the cooking time. Enjoy!

## Garlicky-Cheesy Beef Meatballs

**Prep time: 5 minutes | Cook time: 18 minutes | Serves 6**

1 pound (454 g) ground beef
½ cup grated Parmesan cheese
1 tablespoon minced garlic
½ cup Mozzarella cheese
1 teaspoon freshly ground pepper

Preheat the air fryer to 400ºF (204ºC). In a bowl, mix all the ingredients together. Roll the meat mixture into 5 generous meatballs. Put the meatballs into the air fryer when your air fryer displays "READY" (select the cooking preset, and make minor adjustments according to your desired doneness.) and choose a shake reminder. Cook at the corresponding preset mode or Air Fry at 165ºF (74ºC) for about 18 minutes. Serve immediately.

## Breaded Beef Schnitzel

**Prep time: 5 minutes | Cook time: 12 minutes | Serves 1**

½ cup friendly bread crumbs
2 tablespoons olive oil
Pepper and salt, to taste
1 egg, beaten
1 thin beef schnitzel

Preheat the air fryer to 350ºF (177ºC). In a shallow dish, combine the bread crumbs, oil, pepper, and salt. In a second shallow dish, place the beaten egg. Dredge the schnitzel in the egg before rolling it in the bread crumbs. Put the coated schnitzel in the air fryer basket when your air fryer displays "READY" (select the cooking preset, and make minor adjustments according to your desired doneness.) and choose a shake reminder. Cook at the corresponding preset mode or Air Fry for 12 minutes. Flip the schnitzel halfway through. Serve immediately.

## Golden Herb Filet Mignon

**Prep time: 15 minutes | Cook time: 12 minutes | Serves 4**

½ pound (227 g) filet mignon
Sea salt and ground black
pepper, to taste
½ teaspoon cayenne pepper
1 teaspoon dried basil

1 teaspoon dried rosemary
1 teaspoon dried thyme
1 tablespoon sesame oil
1 small egg, whisked
½ cup bread crumbs

Preheat the air fryer to 360ºF (182ºC). Cover the filet mignon with the salt, black pepper, cayenne pepper, basil, rosemary, and thyme. Coat with sesame oil. Put the egg in a shallow plate. Pour the bread crumbs in another plate. Dip the filet mignon into the egg. Roll it into the crumbs. Transfer the steak to the air fryer when your air fryer displays "READY" (select the cooking preset, and make minor adjustments according to your desired doneness.) and choose a shake reminder. Cook at the corresponding preset mode or Air Fry for 12 minutes or until it turns golden. Serve immediately.

## Peruvian Beef Sirloin with Fries

**Prep time: 10 minutes | Cook time: 32 minutes | Serves 4**

2 russet potatoes
1 pound (454 g) beef sirloin
2 cloves garlic, minced
2 tablespoons soy sauce, plus
more for serving
Juice of 1 lime
2 teaspoons aji amarillo

(Peruvian yellow chile powder
or paste)
½ red onion, sliced
2 tomatoes, cut into wedges
1 tablespoon vegetable oil plus
more for spraying
Kosher salt and pepper, to taste

Peel the potatoes and cut them into ¼-inch slices. Cut each slice into 4 or 5 thick fries. (Halve any especially long pieces. You're looking for fries the size of your finger.) Place the cut potatoes into a bowl of cold water and let them soak for at least 30 minutes to get rid of excess starch. While the potatoes are soaking, marinate the beef. Cut the beef sirloin into strips approximately ½ to 1 inch wide and 4 to 5 inches long. Whisk together the garlic, soy sauce, lime juice, and aji amarillo in a medium bowl. Add the beef and toss to combine. Marinate at room temperature for 15 minutes. While the beef is marinating, cook the onion and tomatoes. Preheat the air fryer to 375ºF (190ºC). Spray the basket of the air fryer with oil. Arrange the vegetables in a single layer in the basket and spray with oil when your air fryer displays "READY" (select the cooking preset, and make minor adjustments according to your desired doneness.) and choose a shake reminder. Season with salt and pepper. Cook until the vegetables begin to char and soften, 9 to 10 minutes. Remove the vegetables to a large bowl. Remove the beef from the marinade and, working in batches as necessary, arrange the beef in a single layer in the basket of the air fryer. Cook at 375ºF (190ºC) until the meat is browned on the outside but pink inside, about 3 to 4 minutes. Place the beef in the bowl with the vegetables. Drain the potatoes and dry them well. Toss the potatoes with the tablespoon of oil and salt. Arrange the potatoes in a single layer in the basket of the air fryer. (Depending on the size of your machine, you may have to work in 2 batches. Do not overcrowd the basket.) Cook for 10 minutes. Open the air fryer and shake the basket to redistribute the potatoes. Cook for an additional 10 to 12 minutes until all the potatoes are browned and crisp. Repeat with the remaining potatoes if necessary. Quickly reheat the meat and vegetables in a large skillet over medium heat. If desired, add the fries to the skillet and stir to combine. (You can also serve the fries on the side if you prefer. Both ways are common in Peru.) Taste and adjust the seasoning, adding more soy sauce, salt, and pepper if necessary. Serve immediately with rice.

## Beef Burger

**Prep time: 5 minutes | Cook time: 15 minutes | Serves 4**

1 pound (454 g) ground beef
½ teaspoon garlic powder
½ teaspoon onion powder
1 teaspoon paprika

Sea salt and ground black
pepper, to taste
8 dinner rolls

Preheat the air fryer to 380ºF (193ºC). Mix all ingredients, except for the dinner rolls. Shape the mixture into four patties. When your air fryer displays "READY" (select the cooking preset, and make minor adjustments according to your desired doneness.) and choose a shake reminder. Cook the burgers at 380ºF (193ºC) for about 15 minutes or until cooked through; make sure to turn them over halfway through the cooking time. Serve your burgers on the prepared dinner rolls and enjoy!

## Mexican Meatloaf

**Prep time: 10 minutes | Cook time: 25 minutes | Serves 4**

1½ pounds (680 g) ground
chuck
½ onion, chopped
1 teaspoon habanero pepper,
minced
¼ cup tortilla chips, crushed

1 teaspoon garlic, minced
Sea salt and ground black
pepper, to taste
2 tablespoons olive oil
1 egg, whisked

Preheat the air fryer to 390ºF (199ºC). Thoroughly combine all ingredients until everything is well combined. Scrape the beef mixture into a lightly oiled baking pan and transfer it to the Air Fryer cooking basket when your air fryer displays "READY" (select the cooking preset, and make minor adjustments according to your desired doneness.) and choose a shake reminder.. Cook your meatloaf at 390ºF (199ºC) for 25 minutes. Bon appétit!

## Paprika New York Strip Steak

**Prep time: 5 minutes | Cook time: 15 minutes | Serves 4**

1½ pounds (680 g) New York
strip steak
2 tablespoons butter, melted
Sea salt and ground black

pepper, to taste
1 teaspoon paprika
1 teaspoon dried thyme
1 teaspoon dried rosemary

Preheat the air fryer to 400ºF (204ºC). Toss the beef with the remaining ingredients; place the beef in the Air Fryer cooking basket when your air fryer displays "READY" (select the cooking preset, and make minor adjustments according to your desired doneness.) and choose a shake reminder. Cook the beef at 400ºF (204ºC) for 15 minutes, turning it over halfway through the cooking time. Enjoy!

## Filet Mignon with Italian Herb

**Prep time: 5 minutes | Cook time: 14 minutes | Serves 4**

1½ pounds (680 g) filet mignon
2 tablespoons olive oil
2 cloves garlic, pressed
1 tablespoon Italian herb mix

1 teaspoon cayenne pepper
Kosher salt and freshly ground
black pepper, to taste

Preheat the air fryer to 400ºF (204ºC). Toss the beef with the remaining ingredients; place the beef in the Air Fryer cooking basket when your air fryer displays "READY" (select the cooking preset, and make minor adjustments according to your desired doneness.) and choose a shake reminder. Cook the beef at 400ºF (204ºC) for 14 minutes, turning it over halfway through the cooking time. Enjoy!

## Greek Spiced Pulled Beef

**Prep time: 10 minutes | Cook time: 1¼ hours | Serves 4**

1½ pounds (680 g) beef brisket
2 tablespoons olive oil
Sea salt and freshly ground
black pepper, to season
1 teaspoon dried oregano

1 teaspoon mustard powder
½ teaspoon ground cumin
2 cloves garlic, minced
2 tablespoons chives, chopped
2 tablespoons cilantro, chopped

Preheat the air fryer to 390°F (199°C). Toss the beef brisket with the rest of the ingredients; now, place the beef brisket in the Air Fryer cooking basket when your air fryer displays "READY" (select the cooking preset, and make minor adjustments according to your desired doneness.) and choose a shake reminder. Cook the beef brisket at 390°F (199°C) for 15 minutes, turn the beef over and reduce the temperature to 360°F (182°C). Continue to cook the beef brisket for approximately 55 minutes or until cooked through. Shred the beef with two forks and serve with toppings of choice. Bon appétit!

## Rump Roast with Italian Herb

**Prep time: 10 minutes | Cook time: 55 minutes | Serves 4**

1½ pounds (680 g) rump roast
2 tablespoons olive oil
Sea salt and ground black
pepper, to taste
1 teaspoon Italian seasoning

mix
1 onion, sliced
2 cloves garlic, peeled
¼ cup red wine

Preheat the air fryer to 390°F (199°C). Toss the rump roast with the rest of the ingredients; place the rump roast in a lightly oiled Air Fryer cooking basket when your air fryer displays "READY" (select the cooking preset, and make minor adjustments according to your desired doneness.) and choose a shake reminder. Cook the rump roast at 390°F (199°C) for 55 minutes, turning it over halfway through the cooking time. Bon appétit!

## Juicy Tomahawk Steaks

**Prep time: 10 minutes | Cook time: 14 minutes | Serves 4**

1½ pounds (680 g) Tomahawk
steaks
2 bell peppers, sliced
2 tablespoons butter, melted
2 teaspoons Montreal steak

seasoning
2 tablespoons fish sauce
Sea salt and ground black
pepper, to taste

Preheat the air fryer to 400°F (204°C). Toss all ingredients in the Air Fryer cooking basket when your air fryer displays "READY" (select the cooking preset, and make minor adjustments according to your desired doneness.) and choose a shake reminder. Cook the steak and peppers at 400°F (204°C) for about 14 minutes, turning it over halfway through the cooking time. Bon appétit!

## Light Herbed Beef Meatballs

**Prep time: 10 minutes | Cook time: 15 minutes | Makes 24 meatballs**

1 medium onion, minced
2 garlic cloves, minced
1 teaspoon olive oil
1 slice low-sodium whole-wheat
bread, crumbled

3 tablespoons 1 percent milk
1 teaspoon dried marjoram
1 teaspoon dried basil
1 pound (454 g) 96 percent
lean ground beef

In a 6-by-2-inch pan, combine the onion, garlic, and olive oil. Air-fry for 2 to 4 minutes, or until the vegetables are crisp-tender. Transfer the vegetables to a medium bowl, and add the bread crumbs, milk, marjoram, and basil. Mix well. Add the ground beef. With your hands, work the mixture gently but thoroughly until combined. Form the meat mixture into about 24 (1-inch) meatballs. Bake the meatballs, in batches, in the air fryer basket for 12 to 17 minutes, or until they reach 160°F (71°C) on a meat thermometer. Serve immediately.

## Marinated London Broil

**Prep time: 10 minutes | Cook time: 28 minutes | Serves 4**

1 pound (454 g) London broil
Kosher salt and ground black
pepper, to taste
2 tablespoons olive oil
1 small lemon, freshly squeezed

3 cloves garlic, minced
1 tablespoon fresh parsley,
chopped
1 tablespoon fresh coriander,
chopped

Preheat the air fryer to 400°F (204°C). Toss the beef with the remaining ingredients and let it marinate for an hour. Place the beef in a lightly oiled Air Fryer cooking basket and discard the marinade when your air fryer displays "READY" (select the cooking preset, and make minor adjustments according to your desired doneness.) and choose a shake reminder. Cook the beef at 400°F (204°C) for 28 minutes, turning it over halfway through the cooking time. Bon appétit!

## Mexican Carnitas

**Prep time: 5 minutes | Cook time: 1¼ hours | Serves 4**

1½ pounds (680 g) beef brisket
2 tablespoons olive oil
Sea salt and ground black

pepper, to taste
1 teaspoon chili powder
4 medium-sized flour tortillas

Preheat the air fryer to 390°F (199°C). Toss the beef brisket with the olive oil, salt, black pepper, and chili powder; now, place the beef brisket in the Air Fryer cooking basket when your air fryer displays "READY" (select the cooking preset, and make minor adjustments according to your desired doneness.) and choose a shake reminder. Cook the beef brisket at 390°F (199°C) for 15 minutes, turn the beef over and reduce the temperature to 360°F (182°C). Continue to cook the beef brisket for approximately 55 minutes or until cooked through. Shred the beef with two forks and serve with tortillas and toppings of choice. Bon appétit!

## Chunk and Mushroom Patties

**Prep time: 10 minutes | Cook time: 15 minutes | Serves 4**

1 pound (454 g) ground chuck
2 garlic cloves, minced
1 small onion, chopped
1 cup mushrooms, chopped

1 teaspoon cayenne pepper
Sea salt and ground black
pepper, to taste
4 brioche rolls

Preheat the air fryer to 380°F (193°C). Mix the ground chuck, garlic, onion, mushrooms, cayenne pepper, salt, and black pepper until everything is well combined. Form the mixture into four patties. Add to air fryer when your air fryer displays "READY" (select the cooking preset, and make minor adjustments according to your desired doneness.) and choose a shake reminder. Cook the patties at 380°F (193°C) for about 15 minutes or until cooked through; make sure to turn them over halfway through the cooking time. Serve your patties on the prepared brioche rolls and enjoy!

## Minty Lamb Ribs

**Prep time: 5 minutes | Cook time: 18 minutes | Serves 4**

2 tablespoons mustard
1 pound (454 g) lamb ribs
1 teaspoon rosemary, chopped
Salt and ground black pepper,

to taste
¼ cup mint leaves, chopped
1 cup Greek yogurt

Preheat the air fryer to 350ºF (177ºC). Use a brush to apply the mustard to the lamb ribs, and season with rosemary, salt, and pepper. Add to air fryer when your air fryer displays "READY" (select the cooking preset, and make minor adjustments according to your desired doneness.) and choose a shake reminder. Cook the ribs in the air fryer at the corresponding preset mode or Air Fry for 18 minutes. Meanwhile, combine the mint leaves and yogurt in a bowl. Remove the lamb ribs from the air fryer when cooked and serve with the mint yogurt.

## Dijon Skirt Steak Sliders

**Prep time: 10 minutes | Cook time: 15 minutes | Serves 4**

1½ pounds (680 g) skirt steak
1 teaspoon steak dry rub
½ teaspoon cayenne pepper
Sea salt and ground black

pepper, to taste
2 tablespoons olive oil
2 tablespoons Dijon mustard
8 Hawaiian buns

Preheat the air fryer to 400ºF (204ºC). Toss the beef with the spices and olive oil; place the beef in the Air Fryer cooking basket when your air fryer displays "READY" (select the cooking preset, and make minor adjustments according to your desired doneness.) and choose a shake reminder. Cook the beef at 400ºF (204ºC) for 15 minutes, turning it over halfway through the cooking time. Cut the beef into slices and serve them with mustard and Hawaiian buns. Bon appétit!

## Old-Fashioned Herb Meatloaf

**Prep time: 10 minutes | Cook time: 25 minutes | Serves 4**

1½ pounds (680 g) ground
chuck
1 egg, beaten
2 tablespoons olive oil
4 tablespoons crackers,
crushed
½ cup shallots, minced

2 garlic cloves, minced
1 tablespoon fresh rosemary,
chopped
1 tablespoon fresh thyme,
chopped
Sea salt and ground black
pepper, to taste

Preheat the air fryer to 390ºF (199ºC). Thoroughly combine all ingredients until everything is well combined. Scrape the beef mixture into a lightly oiled baking pan and transfer it to the Air Fryer cooking basket when your air fryer displays "READY" (select the cooking preset, and make minor adjustments according to your desired doneness.) and choose a shake reminder. Cook your meatloaf at 390ºF (199ºC) for 25 minutes. Bon appétit!

## Oregano Roast Beef Slices

**Prep time: 10 minutes | Cook time: 50 minutes | Serves 4**

1½ pounds (680 g) bottom
round roast
2 tablespoons olive oil
2 garlic cloves, minced
1 teaspoon rosemary

1 teaspoon parsley
1 teaspoon oregano
Sea salt and freshly ground
black pepper, to taste

Preheat the air fryer to 390ºF (199ºC). Toss the beef with the spices, garlic, and olive oil; place the beef in the Air Fryer cooking basket when your air fryer displays "READY" (select the cooking preset, and make minor adjustments according to your desired doneness.) and choose a shake reminder. Cook the roast beef at 390ºF (199ºC) for 50 minutes, turning it over halfway through the cooking time. Cut the beef into slices and serve them with dinner rolls. Bon appétit!

## Pulled Beef with Ketchup and Mustard

**Prep time: 10 minutes | Cook time: 1¼ hours | Serves 4**

1½ pounds (680 g) beef brisket
2 tablespoons olive oil
3 garlic cloves, pressed
Sea salt and ground black
pepper, to taste

1 teaspoon red pepper flakes,
crushed
2 tablespoons tomato ketchup
2 tablespoons Dijon mustard

Preheat the air fryer to 390ºF (199ºC). Toss the beef brisket with the olive oil, garlic, salt, black pepper, and red pepper; now, place the beef brisket in the Air Fryer cooking basket when your air fryer displays "READY" (select the cooking preset, and make minor adjustments according to your desired doneness.) and choose a shake reminder. Cook the beef brisket at 390ºF (199ºC) for 15 minutes, turn the beef over and reduce the temperature to 360ºF (182ºC). Continue to cook the beef brisket for approximately 55 minutes or until cooked through. Shred the beef with two forks; add in the ketchup and mustard and stir to combine well. Bon appétit!

## Parmesan Chuck and Pork Sausage Meatloaf

**Prep time: 10 minutes | Cook time: 25 minutes | Serves 4**

¾ pound (340 g) ground chuck
4 ounces (113 g) ground pork
sausage
2 eggs, beaten
1 cup Parmesan cheese, grated
1 cup chopped shallot
3 tablespoons plain milk
1 tablespoon oyster sauce

1 tablespoon fresh parsley
1 teaspoon garlic paste
1 teaspoon chopped porcini
mushrooms
½ teaspoon cumin powder
Seasoned salt and crushed red
pepper flakes, to taste

Preheat the air fryer to 360ºF (182ºC). In a large bowl, combine all the ingredients until well blended. Place the meat mixture in the baking pan when your air fryer displays "READY" (select the cooking preset, and make minor adjustments according to your desired doneness.) and choose a shake reminder. Use a spatula to press the mixture to fill the pan. Cook at the corresponding preset mode or Air Fry for 25 minutes, or until well browned. Let the meatloaf rest for 5 minutes. Transfer to a serving dish and slice. Serve warm.

# Chapter 4 Pork

## Pork Loin with Roasted Peppers
**Prep time: 10 minutes | Cook time: 55 minutes | Serves 3**

3 red bell peppers
1½ pounds (680 g) pork loin
1 garlic clove, halved
1 teaspoon lard, melted
½ teaspoon cayenne pepper
¼ teaspoon cumin powder
¼ teaspoon ground bay laurel
Kosher
Salt and ground black pepper, to taste

Preheat your air fryer to 395ºF (202ºC). When your air fryer displays "READY" (select the cooking preset, and make minor adjustments according to your desired doneness.) and choose a shake reminder. Roast the peppers in the preheated Air Fryer at 395ºF (202ºC) for 10 minutes, flipping them halfway through the cooking time. Let them steam for 10 minutes; then, peel the skin and discard the stems and seeds. Slice the peppers into halves and add salt to taste. Rub the pork with garlic; brush with melted lard and season with spices until well coated on all sides. Place in the cooking basket and cook at 360ºF (182ºC) for 25 minutes. Turn the meat over and cook an additional 20 minutes. Serve with roasted peppers. Enjoy!

## Korean-Style Pork Bulgogi Bowl
**Prep time: 10 minutes | Cook time: 20 minutes | Serves 2**

2 pork loin chops
1 teaspoon stone-ground mustard
1 teaspoon cayenne pepper
Kosher salt and ground black pepper, to taste
2 stalks green onion
½ teaspoon fresh ginger, grated
1 garlic clove, pressed
1 tablespoon rice wine
2 tablespoons gochujang chili paste
1 teaspoon sesame oil
1 tablespoon sesame seeds, lightly toasted

Toss the pork loin chops with the mustard, cayenne pepper, salt and black pepper. When your air fryer displays "READY" (select the cooking preset, and make minor adjustments according to your desired doneness.) and choose a shake reminder. Cook in the preheated Air Fryer at 400ºF (204ºC) for 10 minutes. Check the pork chops halfway through the cooking time. Add the green onions to the cooking basket and continue to cook for a further 5 minutes. In the meantime, whisk the fresh ginger, garlic, wine, gochujang chili paste and sesame oil. Simmer the sauce for about 5 minutes until thoroughly warmed. Slice the pork loin chops into bite-sized strips and top with green onions and sauce. Garnish with sesame seeds. Enjoy!

## Festive Romano Pork with Apples
**Prep time: 10 minutes | Cook time: 15 minutes | Serves 3**

¼ cup chickpea flour
2 tablespoons Romano cheese, grated
1 teaspoon onion powder
1 teaspoon garlic powder
½ teaspoon ground cumin
1 teaspoon cayenne pepper
2 pork fillets (1 pound (454 g)
1 Granny Smiths apple, peeled and sliced
1 tablespoon lemon juice
1 ounce (28 g) butter, cold

Combine the flour, cheese, onions powder, garlic powder, cumin, and cayenne pepper in a ziploc bag; shake to mix well. Place the pork fillets in the bag. Shake to coat on all sides. Next, spritz the bottom of the Air Fryer basket with cooking spray. When your air fryer displays "READY" (select the cooking preset, and make minor adjustments according to your desired doneness.) and choose a shake reminder. Cook in the preheated Air Fryer at 370ºF (188ºC) for 10 minutes. Add the apples and drizzle with lemon juice; place the cold butter on top and cook an additional 5 minutes. Serve immediately.

## Dark Brown Suagr Pork Belly
**Prep time: 10 minutes | Cook time: 17 minutes | Serves 6**

1½ pounds (680 g) pork belly, cut into pieces
¼ cup tomato sauce
1 tablespoon tamari sauce
2 tablespoons dark brown
sugar
1 teaspoon garlic, minced
Sea salt and ground black pepper, to season

Toss all ingredients in your Air Fryer cooking basket. When your air fryer displays "READY" (select the cooking preset, and make minor adjustments according to your desired doneness.) and choose a shake reminder. Cook the pork belly at 400ºF (204ºC) for about 17 minutes, shaking the basket halfway through the cooking time. Bon appétit!

## Lechon Kawali
**Prep time: 10 minutes | Cook time: 30 minutes | Serves 4**

1 pound (454 g) pork belly, cut into three thick chunks
6 garlic cloves
2 bay leaves
2 tablespoons soy sauce
1 teaspoon kosher salt
1 teaspoon ground black pepper
3 cups water
Cooking spray

Put all the ingredients in a pressure cooker, then put the lid on and cook on high for 15 minutes. Natural release the pressure and release any remaining pressure, transfer the tender pork belly on a clean work surface. Allow to cool under room temperature until you can handle. Preheat the air fryer to 400ºF (204ºC). Generously spritz the air fryer basket with cooking spray. Cut each chunk into two slices, then put the pork slices in the preheated air fryer. When your air fryer displays "READY" (select the cooking preset, and make minor adjustments according to your desired doneness.) and choose a shake reminder. Cook at the corresponding preset mode or Air Fry for 15 minutes or until the pork fat is crispy. Spritz the pork with more cooking spray, if necessary. Serve immediately.

## Panko-Pork Chops
**Prep time: 10 minutes | Cook time: 24 minutes | Serves 8**

⅛ teaspoon pepper
¼ teaspoon chili powder
½ teaspoon onion powder
½ teaspoon garlic powder
1¼ teaspoons sweet paprika
2 tablespoons grated Parmesan cheese
⅓ cup crushed cornflake crumbs
½ cup panko breadcrumbs
1 beaten egg
6 center-cut boneless pork chops

Ensure that your air fryer is preheated to 400ºF (204ºC). Spray the basket with olive oil. With ½ teaspoon salt and pepper, season both sides of pork chops. Combine ¾ teaspoon salt with pepper, chili powder, onion powder, garlic powder, paprika, cornflake crumbs, panko breadcrumbs and Parmesan cheese. Beat egg in another bowl. Dip pork chops into the egg and then crumb mixture. Add pork chops to air fryer and spritz with olive oil. When your air fryer displays "READY" (select the cooking preset, and make minor adjustments according to your desired doneness.) and choose a shake reminder. Cook 12 minutes, making sure to flip over halfway through cooking process. Only add 3 chops in at a time and repeat the process with remaining pork chops.

## Japanese Tonkatsu

**Prep time: 5 minutes | Cook time: 10 minutes per batch | Serves 4**

⅔ cup all-purpose flour
2 large egg whites
1 cup panko breadcrumbs
4 (4-ounce / 113-g) center-cut

boneless pork loin chops (about ½ inch thick)
Cooking spray

Preheat the air fryer to 375ºF (191ºC). Spritz the air fryer basket with cooking spray. Pour the flour in a bowl. Whisk the egg whites in a separate bowl. Spread the breadcrumbs on a large plate. Dredge the pork loin chops in the flour first, press to coat well, then shake the excess off and dunk the chops in the eggs whites, and then roll the chops over the breadcrumbs. Shake the excess off. Arrange the pork chops in batches in a single layer in the preheated air fryer and spritz with cooking spray. When your air fryer displays "READY" (select the cooking preset, and make minor adjustments according to your desired doneness.) and choose a shake reminder. Cook at the corresponding preset mode or Air Fry for 10 minutes or until the pork chops are lightly browned and crunchy. Flip the chops halfway through. Repeat with remaining chops. Serve immediately.

## Herb-Crusted Pork Loin Roast

**Prep time: 10 minutes | Cook time: 55 minutes | Serves 2**

½ pound (227 g) pork loin
Salt and black pepper, to taste
½ teaspoon onion powder
½ teaspoon parsley flakes
½ teaspoon oregano

½ teaspoon thyme
½ teaspoon grated lemon peel
1 teaspoon garlic, minced
1 teaspoon butter, softened

Pat the pork loin dry with kitchen towels. Season it with salt and black pepper. In a bowl, mix the remaining ingredients until well combined. Coat the pork with the herb rub, pressing to adhere well. When your air fryer displays "READY" (select the cooking preset, and make minor adjustments according to your desired doneness.) and choose a shake reminder. Cook in the preheated Air Fryer at 360ºF (182ºC) for 30 minutes; turn it over and cook on the other side for 25 minutes more. Enjoy!

## Keto Crispy Pork Chops

**Prep time: 10 minutes | Cook time: 12 minutes | Serves 3**

3 center-cut pork chops, boneless
½ teaspoon paprika
Sea salt and ground black pepper, to taste
¼ cup Romano cheese, grated
¼ cup crushed pork rinds

½ teaspoon garlic powder
½ teaspoon mustard seeds
½ teaspoon dried marjoram
1 egg, beaten
1 tablespoon buttermilk
1 teaspoon peanut oil

Pat the pork chops dry with kitchen towels. Season them with paprika, salt and black pepper. Add the Romano cheese, crushed pork rinds, garlic powder, mustard seeds and marjoram to a rimmed plate. Beat the egg and buttermilk in another plate. Now, dip the pork chops in the egg, then in the cheese/pork rind mixture. Drizzle the pork with peanut oil. When your air fryer displays "READY" (select the cooking preset, and make minor adjustments according to your desired doneness.) and choose a shake reminder. Cook in the preheated Air Fryer at 400ºF (204ºC) for 12 minutes, flipping pork chops halfway through the cooking time. Serve with keto-friendly sides such as cauliflower rice Enjoy!

## Pork Butt and Mushroom Kabobs

**Prep time: 10 minutes | Cook time: 12 minutes | Serves 2**

1 pound (454 g) pork butt, cut into bite-sized cubes
8 button mushrooms
1 red bell pepper, sliced

1 green bell pepper, sliced
2 tablespoons soy sauce
2 tablespoons lime juice
Salt and black pepper, to taste

Toss all ingredients in a bowl until well coated. Thread the pork cubes, mushrooms and peppers onto skewers. When your air fryer displays "READY" (select the cooking preset, and make minor adjustments according to your desired doneness.) and choose a shake reminder. Cook in the preheated Air Fryer at 395ºF (202ºC) for 12 minutes, flipping halfway through the cooking time. Enjoy!

## Tenderloin with Brussels Sprouts

**Prep time: 10 minutes | Cook time: 15 minutes | Serves 3**

1 pound (454 g) Brussels sprouts, halved
1½ pounds (680 g) tenderloin
1 teaspoon peanut oil
1 teaspoon garlic powder

1 tablespoon coriander, minced
1 teaspoon smoked paprika
Sea salt and ground black pepper, to taste

Toss the Brussels sprouts and pork with oil and spices until well coated. Place in the Air Fryer cooking basket. When your air fryer displays "READY" (select the cooking preset, and make minor adjustments according to your desired doneness.) and choose a shake reminder. Cook in the preheated Air Fryer at 370ºF (188ºC) for 15 minutes. Taste and adjust seasonings. Eat warm. Enjoy!

## Classic Fried Bacon Slices

**Prep time: 5 minutes | Cook time: 8 minutes | Serves 4**

½ pound (227 g) bacon slices
½ cup tomato ketchup
¼ teaspoon cayenne pepper

¼ teaspoon dried marjoram
1 teaspoon Sriracha sauce

Place the bacon slices in the cooking basket. When your air fryer displays "READY" (select the cooking preset, and make minor adjustments according to your desired doneness.) and choose a shake reminder. Cook the bacon slices at 400ºF (204ºC) for about 8 minutes. Meanwhile, make the sauce by mixing the remaining ingredients. Serve the warm bacon with the sauce on the side. Enjoy!

## Pork and Parmesan Cheese Meatballs

**Prep time: 10 minutes | Cook time: 7 minutes | Serves 3**

1 pound (454 g) ground pork
2 tablespoons tamari sauce
1 teaspoon garlic, minced
2 tablespoons spring onions, finely chopped
1 tablespoon brown sugar

1 tablespoon olive oil
½ cup breadcrumbs
2 tablespoons parmesan cheese, preferably freshly grated

Combine the ground pork, tamari sauce, garlic, onions, and sugar in a mixing dish. Mix until everything is well incorporated. Form the mixture into small meatballs. In a shallow bowl, mix the olive oil, breadcrumbs, and parmesan. Roll the meatballs over the Parmesan mixture. When your air fryer displays "READY" (select the cooking preset, and make minor adjustments according to your desired doneness.) and choose a shake reminder. Cook at 380ºF (193ºC) for 3 minutes; shake the basket and cook an additional 4 minutes or until meatballs are browned on all sides. enjoy!

## Five-Spice Country-Style Pork Ribs

**Prep time: 10 minutes | Cook time: 34 minutes | Serves 3**

2½ pounds country-style pork ribs
1 teaspoon mustard powder
1 teaspoon cumin powder
1 teaspoon shallot powder

1 tablespoon Five-spice powder
Coarse sea salt and ground black pepper, to taste
1 teaspoon sesame oil
2 tablespoons soy sauce

Toss the country-style pork ribs with spices and sesame oil and transfer them to the Air Fryer cooking basket. When your air fryer displays "READY" (select the cooking preset, and make minor adjustments according to your desired doneness.) and choose a shake reminder. Cook at 360ºF (182ºC) for 20 minutes; flip them over and continue to cook an additional 14 to 15 minutes. Drizzle with soy sauce just before serving. Enjoy!

## Pork Cutlets with Cheese and Pearl Onions

**Prep time: 10 minutes | Cook time: 15 minutes | Serves 2**

2 pork cutlets
1 teaspoon onion powder
½ teaspoon cayenne pepper
Sea salt and black pepper, to taste

¼ cup flour
¼ cup Pecorino Romano cheese, grated
1 cup pearl onions

Toss the pork cutlets with the onion powder, cayenne pepper, salt, black pepper, flour and cheese. Transfer the pork cutlets to the lightly oiled cooking basket. Scatter pearl onions around the pork. When your air fryer displays "READY" (select the cooking preset, and make minor adjustments according to your desired doneness.) and choose a shake reminder. Cook in the preheated Air Fryer at 360ºF (182ºC) for 15 minutes, turning over halfway through the cooking time. Enjoy!

## BBQ Pork Butt

**Prep time: 5 minutes | Cook time: 55 minutes | Serves 5**

2 pounds (907 g) pork butt
1 tablespoon olive oil
Kosher salt and ground black

pepper, to taste
1 teaspoon ground cumin
½ cup BBQ sauce

Toss all ingredients in a lightly greased Air Fryer cooking basket. When your air fryer displays "READY" (select the cooking preset, and make minor adjustments according to your desired doneness.) and choose a shake reminder. Cook the pork butt at 360ºF (182ºC) for 55 minutes, turning it over halfway through the cooking time. Serve warm and enjoy!

## Barbecue Pork Steaks

**Prep time: 5 minutes | Cook time: 15 minutes | Serves 4**

4 pork steaks
1 tablespoon Cajun seasoning
2 tablespoons BBQ sauce
1 tablespoon vinegar

1 teaspoon soy sauce
½ cup brown sugar
½ cup ketchup

Preheat the air fryer to 290ºF (143ºC). Sprinkle pork steaks with Cajun seasoning. Combine remaining ingredients and brush onto steaks. Add coated steaks to air fryer. When your air fryer displays "READY" (select the cooking preset, and make minor adjustments according to your desired doneness.) and choose a shake reminder. Cook at the corresponding preset mode or Air Fry for 15 minutes until just browned. Serve immediately.

## Beer Pork Loin

**Prep time: 5 minutes | Cook time: 55 minutes | Serves 5**

4 tablespoons beer
1 tablespoon garlic, crushed
1 teaspoon paprika

Sea salt and ground black pepper, to taste
2 pounds (907 g) pork loin

Toss all ingredients in a lightly greased Air Fryer cooking basket. When your air fryer displays "READY" (select the cooking preset, and make minor adjustments according to your desired doneness.) and choose a shake reminder. Cook the pork at 360ºF (182ºC) for 55 minutes, turning it over halfway through the cooking time. Serve warm and enjoy!

## Boneless Pork Shoulder with Molasses Sauce

**Prep time: 10 minutes | Cook time: 14 minutes | Serves 3**

2 tablespoons molasses
2 tablespoons soy sauce
2 tablespoons Shaoxing wine
2 garlic cloves, minced
1 teaspoon fresh ginger, minced

1 tablespoon cilantro stems and leaves, finely chopped
1 pound (454 g) boneless pork shoulder
2 tablespoons sesame oil

In a large-sized ceramic dish, thoroughly combine the molasses, soy sauce, wine, garlic, ginger, and cilantro; add the pork shoulder and allow it to marinate for 2 hours in the refrigerator. Then, grease the cooking basket with sesame oil. Place the pork shoulder in the cooking basket; reserve the marinade. When your air fryer displays "READY" (select the cooking preset, and make minor adjustments according to your desired doneness.) and choose a shake reminder. Cook in the preheated Air Fryer at 395ºF (202ºC) for 14 to 17 minutes, flipping and basting with the marinade halfway through. Let it rest for 5 to 6 minutes before slicing and serving. While the pork is roasting, cook the marinade in a preheated skillet over medium heat; cook until it has thickened. Brush the pork shoulder with the sauce and enjoy!

## Sesame Pork with Aloha Salsa

**Prep time: 15 minutes | Cook time: 7 minutes | Serves 4**

2 eggs
2 tablespoons milk
¼ cup flour
¼ cup panko breadcrumbs
4 teaspoons sesame seeds
**For the Aloha Salsa:**
1 cup fresh pineapple, chopped in small pieces
¼ cup red onion, finely chopped
¼ cup green or red bell pepper, chopped
½ teaspoon ground cinnamon

1 pound (454 g) boneless, thin pork cutlets (⅜- to ½-inch thick)
Lemon pepper and salt
¼ cup cornstarch
Oil for misting or cooking spray

1 teaspoon low-sodium soy sauce
⅛ teaspoon crushed red pepper
⅛ teaspoon ground black pepper

In a medium bowl, stir together all ingredients for salsa. Cover and refrigerate while cooking pork. Preheat air fryer to 390ºF (199ºC). Beat together eggs and milk in shallow dish. In another shallow dish, mix together the flour, panko, and sesame seeds. Sprinkle pork cutlets with lemon pepper and salt to taste. Most lemon pepper seasoning contains salt, so go easy adding extra. Dip pork cutlets in cornstarch, egg mixture, and then panko coating. Spray both sides with oil or cooking spray. When your air fryer displays "READY" (select the cooking preset, and make minor adjustments according to your desired doneness.) and choose a shake reminder. Cook cutlets for 3 minutes. Turn cutlets over, spraying both sides, and continue cooking for 4 to 6 minutes or until well done. Serve fried cutlets with salsa on the side.

## Pork Bulgogi

**Prep time: 15 minutes | Cook time: 15 minutes | Serves 4**

1 onion, thinly sliced
2 tablespoons gochujang (Korean red chile paste)
1 tablespoon minced fresh ginger
1 tablespoon minced garlic
1 tablespoon soy sauce
1 tablespoon Shaoxing wine (rice cooking wine)
1 tablespoon toasted sesame

oil
1 teaspoon sugar
¼ to 1 teaspoon cayenne pepper or gochugaru (Korean ground red pepper)
1 pound (454 g) boneless pork shoulder, cut into ½-inch-thick slices
1 tablespoon sesame seeds
¼ cup sliced scallions

In a large bowl, combine the onion, gochujang, ginger, garlic, soy sauce, wine, sesame oil, sugar, and cayenne. Add the pork and toss to coat. Marinate at room temperature for 30 minutes, or cover and refrigerate for up to 24 hours. Arrange the pork and onion slices in the air-fryer basket; discard the marinade. When your air fryer displays "READY" (select the cooking preset, and make minor adjustments according to your desired doneness.) and choose a shake reminder. Set the air fryer to 400ºF (204ºC) for 15 minutes, turning the pork halfway through the cooking time. Arrange the pork on a serving platter. Sprinkle with the sesame seeds and scallions and serve.

## Dried Herb Center Cut Pork Roast

**Prep time: 10 minutes | Cook time: 55 minutes | Serves 4**

1½ pounds (680 g) center-cut pork roast
1 tablespoon olive oil
Sea salt and freshly ground black pepper, to taste

1 teaspoon garlic powder
1 teaspoon hot paprika
½ teaspoon dried parsley flakes
½ teaspoon dried rosemary

Toss all ingredients in a lightly greased Air Fryer cooking basket. When your air fryer displays "READY" (select the cooking preset, and make minor adjustments according to your desired doneness.) and choose a shake reminder. Cook the pork at 360ºF (182ºC) for 55 minutes, turning it over halfway through the cooking time. Serve warm and enjoy!

## Pork Stuffed Bell Peppers with Cheese

**Prep time: 10 minutes | Cook time: 19 minutes | Serves 3**

3 bell peppers, stems and seeds removed
1 tablespoon olive oil
3 scallions, chopped
1 teaspoon fresh garlic, minced
12 ounces (340 g) lean pork, ground

½ teaspoon sea salt
½ teaspoon black pepper
1 tablespoon fish sauce
2 ripe tomatoes, pureed
3 ounces (85 g) Monterey Jack cheese, grated

Cook the peppers in boiling salted water for 4 minutes In a nonstick skillet, heat the olive oil over medium heat. Then, sauté the scallions and garlic until tender and fragrant. Stir in the ground pork and continue sautéing until the pork has browned; drain off the excess fat. Add the salt, black pepper, fish sauce, and 1 pureed tomato; give it a good stir. Divide the filling among the bell peppers. Arrange the peppers in a baking dish lightly greased with cooking oil. Place the remaining tomato puree around the peppers. When your air fryer displays "READY" (select the cooking preset, and make minor adjustments according to your desired doneness.) and choose a shake reminder. Bake in the preheated Air Fryer at 380ºF (193ºC) for 13 minutes. Top with grated cheese and bake another 6 minutes. Serve warm and enjoy!

## Boston Butt with Salsa Verde

**Prep time: 10 minutes | Cook time: 28 minutes | Serves 4**

1 pound (454 g) Boston butt, thinly sliced across the grain into 2-inch-long strips
½ teaspoon red pepper flakes, crushed
Sea salt and ground black pepper, to taste
½ pound (227 g) tomatillos,

chopped
1 small-sized onion, chopped
2 chili peppers, chopped
2 cloves garlic
2 tablespoons fresh cilantro, chopped
1 tablespoon olive oil
1 teaspoon sea salt

Rub the Boston butt with red pepper, salt, and black pepper. Spritz the bottom of the cooking basket with a nonstick cooking spray. When your air fryer displays "READY" (select the cooking preset, and make minor adjustments according to your desired doneness.) and choose a shake reminder. Roast the Boston butt in the preheated Air Fryer at 390ºF (199ºC) for 10 minutes. Shake the basket and cook another 10 minutes. While the pork is roasting, make the salsa. Blend the remaining ingredients until smooth and uniform. Transfer the mixture to a saucepan and add 1 cup of water. Bring to a boil; reduce the heat and simmer for 8 to 12 minutes. Serve the roasted pork with the salsa verde on the side. Enjoy!

## Creole Pork with Plum Sauce

**Prep time: 10 minutes | Cook time: 13 minutes | Serves 4**

4 pork cutlets
2 teaspoosn sesame oil
½ teaspoon ground black pepper
Salt, to taste

1 tablespoon Creole seasoning
2 tablespoons aged balsamic vinegar
2 tablespoons soy sauce
6 ripe plums, pitted and diced

Preheat your Air Fryer to 390ºF (199ºC). Toss the pork cutlets with the sesame oil, black pepper, salt, Creole seasoning, vinegar, and soy sauce. Transfer them to a lightly greased baking pan; lower the pan onto the cooking basket. When your air fryer displays "READY" (select the cooking preset, and make minor adjustments according to your desired doneness.) and choose a shake reminder. Cook for 13 minutes in the preheated Air Fryer, flipping them halfway through the cooking time. Serve warm.

## Spanish Pork Loin with Padrón Peppers

**Prep time: 10 minutes | Cook time: 26 minutes | Serves 4**

1 tablespoon olive oil
8 ounces (227 g) Padrón peppers
2 pounds (907 g) pork loin, sliced
1 teaspoon Celtic salt

1 teaspoon paprika
1 heaped tablespoon capers, drained
8 green olives, pitted and halved

Drizzle olive oil all over the Padrón peppers; when your air fryer displays "READY" (select the cooking preset, and make minor adjustments according to your desired doneness.) and choose a shake reminder. Cook them in the preheated Air Fryer at 400ºF (204ºC) for 10 minutes, turning occasionally, until well blistered all over and tender-crisp. Then, turn the temperature to 360ºF (182ºC). Season the pork loin with salt and paprika. Add the capers and cook for 16 minutes, turning them over halfway through the cooking time. Serve with olives and the reserved Padrón peppers.

## Pork Loin Chops

**Prep time: 5 minutes | Cook time: 12 minutes | Serves 2**

1 egg
¼ cup cornmeal
¼ cup crackers, crushed
½ teaspoon garlic powder
½ teaspoon cayenne pepper
Salt and black pepper, to taste
2 (6-ounce / 170-g) boneless pork loin chops, about 1-inch thick

In a shallow mixing bowl, whisk the egg until pale and frothy. In another bowl, mix the cornmeal, crushed crackers, garlic powder, cayenne pepper, salt and black pepper. Dip each pork loin chop in the beaten egg. Then, roll them over the cornmeal mixture. Spritz the bottom of the cooking basket with cooking oil. Add the breaded pork cutlets when your air fryer displays "READY" (select the cooking preset, and make minor adjustments according to your desired doneness.) and choose a shake reminder. Cook at 395ºF (202ºC) for 6 minutes. Flip and cook for 6 minutes on the other side. Serve warm.

## Pork Sausage with Baby Potato

**Prep time: 5 minutes | Cook time: 15 minutes | Serves 3**

1 pound (454 g) pork sausage, uncooked
1 pound (454 g) baby potatoes
¼ teaspoon paprika
½ teaspoon dried rosemary leaves, crushed
Himalayan salt and black pepper, to taste

Put the sausage into the Air Fryer cooking basket. Cook in the preheated Air Fryer at 380ºF (193ºC) for 15 minutes; reserve. Season the baby potatoes with paprika, rosemary, salt and black pepper. Add the baby potatoes to the cooking basket. When your air fryer displays "READY" (select the cooking preset, and make minor adjustments according to your desired doneness.) and choose a shake reminder. Cook the potatoes at 400ºF (204ºC) for 15 minutes, shaking the basket once or twice. Serve warm sausages with baby potatoes and enjoy!

## Bacon-Wrapped Pork with Apple Gravy

**Prep time: 10 minutes | Cook time: 25 minutes | Serves 4**

**Pork:**
1 tablespoons Dijon mustard
1 pork tenderloin
3 strips bacon
**Apple Gravy:**
3 tablespoons ghee, divided
1 small shallot, chopped
2 apples
1 tablespoon almond flour
1 cup vegetable broth
½ teaspoon Dijon mustard

Preheat the air fryer to 360ºF (182ºC). Spread Dijon mustard all over tenderloin and wrap with strips of bacon. Put into air fryer when your air fryer displays "READY" (select the cooking preset, and make minor adjustments according to your desired doneness.) and choose a shake reminder. Cook at the corresponding preset mode or Air Fry for 12 minutes. Use a meat thermometer to check for doneness. To make sauce, heat 1 tablespoons of ghee in a pan and add shallots. Cook for 1 minute. Then add apples, cooking for 4 minutes until softened. Add flour and 2 tablespoons of ghee to make a roux. Add broth and mustard, stirring well to combine. When sauce starts to bubble, add 1 cup of sautéed apples, cooking until sauce thickens. Once pork tenderloin is cooked, allow to sit 8 minutes to rest before slicing. Serve topped with apple gravy.

## Ritzy Stuffed Pork Chops

**Prep time: 20 minutes | Cook time: 24 minutes | Serves 3**

4 slices bacon, chopped
1 tablespoon butter
½ cup finely diced onion
⅓ cup chicken stock
1½ cups seasoned stuffing cubes
1 egg, beaten
½ teaspoon dried thyme
½ teaspoon salt
⅛ teaspoon freshly ground black pepper
1 pear, finely diced
⅓ cup crumbled blue cheese
3 boneless center-cut pork chops (2-inch thick)
Olive oil, for greasing
Salt and freshly ground black pepper, to taste

Preheat the air fryer to 400ºF (204ºC). Put the bacon into the air fryer basket and cook at the corresponding preset mode or Air Fry for 6 minutes, stirring halfway through the cooking time. Remove the bacon and set it aside on a paper towel. Pour out the grease from the bottom of the air fryer. To make the stuffing, melt the butter in a medium saucepan over medium heat on the stovetop. Add the onion and sauté for a few minutes until it starts to soften. Add the chicken stock and simmer for 1 minute. Remove the pan from the heat and add the stuffing cubes. Stir until the stock has been absorbed. Add the egg, dried thyme, salt and freshly ground black pepper, and stir until combined. Fold in the diced pear and crumbled blue cheese. Put the pork chops on a cutting board. Using the palm of the hand to hold the chop flat and steady, slice into the side of the pork chop to make a pocket in the center of the chop. Leave about an inch of chop uncut and make sure you don't cut all the way through the pork chop. Brush both sides of the pork chops with olive oil and season with salt and freshly ground black pepper. Stuff each pork chop with a third of the stuffing, packing the stuffing tightly inside the pocket. Adjust the temperature to 360ºF (182ºC). Spray or brush the sides of the air fryer basket with oil. Put the pork chops in the air fryer basket with the open, stuffed edge of the pork chop facing the outside edges of the basket. Cook the pork chops at the corresponding preset mode or Air Fry for 18 minutes, turning the pork chops over halfway through the cooking time. When the chops are done, let them rest for 5 minutes and then transfer to a serving platter.

## Pork Chops with Vegetable

**Prep time: 10 minutes | Cook time: 15 to 18 minutes | Serves 4**

2 carrots, cut into sticks
1 cup mushrooms, sliced
2 garlic cloves, minced
2 tablespoons olive oil
1 pound (454 g) boneless pork chops
1 teaspoon dried oregano
1 teaspoon dried thyme
1 teaspoon cayenne pepper
Salt and ground black pepper, to taste
Cooking spray

Preheat air fryer to 360ºF (182ºC). Spritz the air fryer basket with cooking spray. In a mixing bowl, toss together the carrots, mushrooms, garlic, olive oil and salt until well combined. Add the pork chops to a different bowl and season with oregano, thyme, cayenne pepper, salt and black pepper. Lower the vegetable mixture in the prepared air fryer basket. Place the seasoned pork chops on top. When your air fryer displays "READY" (select the cooking preset, and make minor adjustments according to your desired doneness.) and choose a shake reminder. Cook at the corresponding preset mode or Air Fry for 15 to 18 minutes, or until the pork is well browned and the vegetables are tender, flipping the pork and shaking the basket once halfway through. Transfer the pork chops to the serving dishes and let cool for 5 minutes. Serve warm with vegetable on the side.

## Char Siu

**Prep time: 10 minutes | Cook time: 35 minutes | Serves 3**

1 pound (454 g) pork shoulder, cut into long strips
½ teaspoon Chinese five-spice powder
¼ teaspoon Szechuan pepper
1 tablespoon hoisin sauce
2 tablespoons hot water
1 teaspoon sesame oil
1 tablespoon Shaoxing wine
1 tablespoon molasses

Place all ingredients in a ceramic dish and let it marinate for 2 hours in the refrigerator. When your air fryer displays "READY" (select the cooking preset, and make minor adjustments according to your desired doneness.) and choose a shake reminder. Cook in the preheated Air Fryer at 390ºF (199ºC) for 20 minutes, shaking the basket halfway through the cooking time. Heat the reserved marinade in a wok for about 15 minutes or until the sauce has thickened. Spoon the sauce over the warm pork shoulder and serve with rice if desired. Enjoy!

## Pork Chops with Applesauce

**Prep time: 10 minutes | Cook time: 23 minutes | Serves 4**

4 pork chops, bone-in
Sea salt and ground black pepper, to taste
½ teaspoon onion powder
½ teaspoon paprika
½ teaspoon celery seeds
2 cooking apples, peeled and sliced
1 tablespoon honey
1 tablespoon peanut oil

Place the pork in a lightly greased baking pan. Season with salt and pepper, and transfer the pan to the cooking basket. When your air fryer displays "READY" (select the cooking preset, and make minor adjustments according to your desired doneness.) and choose a shake reminder. Cook in the preheated Air Fryer at 370ºF (188ºC) for 10 minutes. Meanwhile, in a saucepan, simmer the remaining ingredients over medium heat for about 8 minutes or until the apples are softened. Pour the applesauce over the prepared pork chops. Add to the Air Fryer and bake for 5 minutes more. Enjoy!

## Porterhouse Steaks

**Prep time: 10 minutes | Cook time: 12 minutes | Serves 2**

1 pound (454 g) porterhouse steak, cut meat from bone in 2 pieces
½ teaspoon ground black pepper
1 teaspoon cayenne pepper
½ teaspoon salt
1 teaspoon garlic powder
½ teaspoon dried thyme
½ teaspoon dried marjoram
1 teaspoon Dijon mustard
1 tablespoon butter, melted

Sprinkle the porterhouse steak with all the seasonings. Spread the mustard and butter evenly over the meat. When your air fryer displays "READY" (select the cooking preset, and make minor adjustments according to your desired doneness.) and choose a shake reminder. Cook in the preheated Air Fryer at 390ºF (199ºC) for 12 to 14 minutes. Taste for doneness with a meat thermometer and serve immediately.

## Dijon Honey Roasted Pork Cutlets

**Prep time: 5 minutes | Cook time: 12 minutes | Serves 2**

1 pound (454 g) pork cutlets
1 teaspoon cayenne pepper
Kosher salt and ground black pepper, to season
½ teaspoon garlic powder
1 tablespoon honey
1 teaspoon Dijon mustard

Spritz the sides and bottom of the cooking basket with a nonstick cooking spray. Place the pork cutlets in the cooking basket; sprinkle with cayenne pepper, salt, black pepper and garlic powder. In a mixing dish, thoroughly combine the honey and Dijon mustard. When your air fryer displays "READY" (select the cooking preset, and make minor adjustments according to your desired doneness.) and choose a shake reminder. Cook the pork cutlets at 390ºF (199ºC) for 6 minutes. Flip halfway through, rub with the honey mixture and continue to cook for 6 minutes more. Serve immediately.

## Balsamic Pork Loin Chops with Asparagus

**Prep time: 10 minutes | Cook time: 12 minutes | Serves 2**

2 pork loin chops
1 pound (454 g) asparagus spears, cleaned and trimmed
1 teaspoon sesame oil
2 tablespoons balsamic vinegar
1 teaspoon yellow mustard
½ teaspoon garlic, minced
½ teaspoon smoked pepper
¼ teaspoon dried dill
Salt and black pepper, to taste

Toss the pork loin chops and asparagus with the other ingredients until well coated on all sides. Place the pork in the Air Fryer cooking basket when your air fryer displays "READY" (select the cooking preset, and make minor adjustments according to your desired doneness.) and choose a shake reminder. Cook at 400ºF (204ºC) for 7 minutes; turn them over, top with the asparagus and continue to cook for a further 5 minutes. Serve warm with mayo, sriracha sauce, or sour cream if desired. Enjoy!

## Tender Pork Spare Ribs

**Prep time: 10 minutes | Cook time: 31 minutes | Serves 4**

1 rack pork spareribs, fat trimmed and cut in half
2 tablespoons fajita seasoning
2 tablespoons smoked paprika
Sea salt and pepper, to taste
1 tablespoon prepared brown
mustard
3 tablespoons Worcestershire sauce
½ cup beer
1 tablespoon peanut oil

Toss the spareribs with the fajita seasoning, paprika, salt, pepper, mustard, and Worcestershire sauce. Pour in the beer and let it marinate for 1 hour in your refrigerator. Rub the sides and bottom of the cooking basket with peanut oil. When your air fryer displays "READY" (select the cooking preset, and make minor adjustments according to your desired doneness.) and choose a shake reminder. Cook the spareribs in the preheated Air Fryer at 365ºF (185ºC) for 17 minutes. Turn the ribs over and cook an additional 14 to 15 minutes. Serve warm. Enjoy!

## Rosemary Pork Loin Roast

**Prep time: 5 minutes | Cook time: 55 minutes | Serves 4**

1½ pounds (680 g) pork loin roast
2 tablespoons butter, melted
Sea salt and ground black
pepper, to taste
1 teaspoon cayenne pepper
1 teaspoon garlic, pressed
1 teaspoon dried rosemary

Toss all ingredients in a lightly greased Air Fryer cooking basket. When your air fryer displays "READY" (select the cooking preset, and make minor adjustments according to your desired doneness.) and choose a shake reminder. Cook the pork at 360ºF (182ºC) for 55 minutes, turning it over halfway through the cooking time. Serve warm and enjoy!

## Cracker Pork Chops
**Prep time: 10 minutes | Cook time: 14 minutes | Serves 3**

¼ cup all-purpose flour
1 teaspoon turmeric powder
1 egg
1 teaspoon mustard
Kosher salt, to taste
¼ teaspoon freshly ground

black pepper
2 cups crackers, crushed
½ teaspoon porcini powder
1 teaspoon shallot powder
3 center-cut loin pork chops

Place the flour and turmeric in a shallow bowl. In another bowl, whisk the eggs, mustard, salt, and black pepper. In the third bowl, mix the crushed crackers with the porcini powder and shallot powder. Preheat your Air Fryer to 390ºF (199ºC). Dredge the pork chops in the flour mixture, then in the egg, followed by the cracker mixture. When your air fryer displays "READY" (select the cooking preset, and make minor adjustments according to your desired doneness.) and choose a shake reminder. Cook the pork chops for 7 minutes per side, spraying with cooking oil. Enjoy!

## Honey Bratwurst with Brussels Sprouts
**Prep time: 10 minutes | Cook time: 15 minutes | Serves 4**

1 pound (454 g) bratwurst
1 pound (454 g) Brussels sprouts
1 large onion, cut into wedges

1 teaspoon garlic, minced
1 tablespoon mustard
2 tablespoons honey

Toss all ingredients in a lightly greased Air Fryer cooking basket. When your air fryer displays "READY" (select the cooking preset, and make minor adjustments according to your desired doneness.) and choose a shake reminder. Air fry the sausage at 380ºF (193ºC) for approximately 15 minutes, tossing the basket halfway through the cooking time. Bon appétit!

## Breaded Pecorino Sirloin Chops
**Prep time: 10 minutes | Cook time: 15 minutes | Serves 3**

1 pound (454 g) sirloin chops
1 egg
2 tablespoons butter, at room temperature
Sea salt and ground black pepper, to taste

3 tablespoons Pecorino cheese, grated
½ cup breadcrumbs
1 teaspoon paprika
1 teaspoon garlic powder

Pat the pork sirloin chops dry with kitchen towels. In a shallow bowl, whisk the egg until pale and frothy. In another shallow bowl, thoroughly combine the remaining ingredients. Dip the pork chops into the egg, then the cheese/crumb mixture. Place the pork sirloin chops in a lightly oiled Air Fryer cooking basket. When your air fryer displays "READY" (select the cooking preset, and make minor adjustments according to your desired doneness.) and choose a shake reminder. Cook the pork sirloin chops at 400ºF (204ºC) for 15 minutes, turning them over halfway through the cooking time. Bon appétit!

## Brown Sugar Pulled Pork Rolls
**Prep time: 10 minutes | Cook time: 55 minutes | Serves 4**

1 pound (454 g) pork shoulder
1 tablespoon olive oil
2 cloves garlic, minced
1 teaspoon cayenne pepper
1 tablespoon fresh sage, chopped
1 tablespoon fresh thyme,

chopped
1 tablespoon brown sugar
2 tablespoons fish sauce
Kosher salt and freshly ground pepper, to taste
8 dinner rolls

Toss all ingredients, except for the dinner rolls, in a lightly greased Air Fryer cooking basket. When your air fryer displays "READY" (select the cooking preset, and make minor adjustments according to your desired doneness.) and choose a shake reminder. Cook the pork at 360ºF (182ºC) for 55 minutes, turning it over halfway through the cooking time. Serve on dinner rolls and enjoy!

## Country-Style Ribs with Red Wine
**Prep time: 10 minutes | Cook time: 35 minutes | Serves 5**

2 pounds (907 g) Country-style ribs
Coarse sea salt and ground black pepper, to taste
1 teaspoon smoked paprika

1 teaspoon mustard powder
1 tablespoon butter, melted
1 teaspoon chili sauce
4 tablespoons dry red wine

Toss all ingredients in a lightly greased Air Fryer cooking basket. When your air fryer displays "READY" (select the cooking preset, and make minor adjustments according to your desired doneness.) and choose a shake reminder. Cook the pork ribs at 350ºF (177ºC) for 35 minutes, turning them over halfway through the cooking time. Bon appétit!

## Caribbean Pork Patties with Brioche
**Prep time: 10 minutes | Cook time: 15 minutes | Serves 4**

1 pound (454 g) ground pork
Kosher salt and ground black pepper, to taste
1 tablespoon fresh parsley, chopped
1 tablespoon fresh coriander, chopped

1 teaspoon habanero pepper, sliced
1 tablespoon teriyaki sauce
1 small onion, chopped
1 clove garlic, minced
4 brioche hamburger buns, lightly toasted

In a mixing bowl, thoroughly combine the pork, spices, habanero pepper, teriyaki sauce, onion, and garlic. Then, roll the mixture into four patties. When your air fryer displays "READY" (select the cooking preset, and make minor adjustments according to your desired doneness.) and choose a shake reminder. Cook the pork patties at 380ºF (193ºC) for about 15 minutes or until cooked through; make sure to turn them over halfway through the cooking time. Serve the patties with the brioche hamburger buns. Enjoy!

## Cheddar Bacon Burst with Spinach
**Prep time: 5 minutes | Cook time: 60 minutes | Serves 8**

30 slices bacon
1 tablespoon Chipotle seasoning

2 teaspoons Italian seasoning
2½ cups Cheddar cheese
4 cups raw spinach

Preheat the air fryer to 375ºF (191ºC). Weave the bacon into 15 vertical pieces and 12 horizontal pieces. Cut the extra 3 in half to fill in the rest, horizontally. Season the bacon with Chipotle seasoning and Italian seasoning. Add the cheese to the bacon. Add the spinach and press down to compress. Tightly roll up the woven bacon. Line a baking sheet with kitchen foil and add plenty of salt to it. Put the bacon on top of a cooling rack and put that on top of the baking sheet. When your air fryer displays "READY" (select the cooking preset, and make minor adjustments according to your desired doneness.) and choose a shake reminder. Cook at the corresponding preset mode or Air Fry for 60 minutes. Let cool for 15 minutes before slicing and serving.

## Colby Pork Sausage with Cauliflower Mash

**Prep time: 5 minutes | Cook time: 27 minutes | Serves 6**

1 pound (454 g) cauliflower, chopped
6 pork sausages, chopped
½ onion, sliced
3 eggs, beaten
⅓ cup Colby cheese
1 teaspoon cumin powder
½ teaspoon tarragon
½ teaspoon sea salt
½ teaspoon ground black pepper
Cooking spray

Preheat the air fryer to 365ºF (185ºC). Spritz a baking pan with cooking spray. In a saucepan over medium heat, boil the cauliflower until tender. Place the boiled cauliflower in a food processor and pulse until puréed. Transfer to a large bowl and combine with remaining ingredients until well blended. Pour the cauliflower and sausage mixture into the baking pan. When your air fryer displays "READY" (select the cooking preset, and make minor adjustments according to your desired doneness.) and choose a shake reminder. Cook in the preheated air fryer at the corresponding preset mode or Air Fry for 27 minutes, or until lightly browned. Divide the mixture among six serving dishes and serve warm.

## Red Chili Pork Meatballs

**Prep time: 5 minutes | Cook time: 15 minutes | Serves 4**

1 pound (454 g) ground pork
2 cloves garlic, finely minced
1 cup scallions, finely chopped
1½ tablespoons Worcestershire sauce
½ teaspoon freshly grated
ginger root
1 teaspoon turmeric powder
1 tablespoon oyster sauce
1 small sliced red chili, for garnish
Cooking spray

Preheat the air fryer to 350ºF (177ºC). Spritz the air fryer basket with cooking spray. Combine all the ingredients, except for the red chili in a large bowl. Toss to mix well. Shape the mixture into equally sized balls, then arrange them in the preheated air fryer and spritz with cooking spray. When your air fryer displays "READY" (select the cooking preset, and make minor adjustments according to your desired doneness.) and choose a shake reminder. Cook at the corresponding preset mode or Air Fry for 15 minutes or until the balls are lightly browned. Flip the balls halfway through. Serve the pork meatballs with red chili on top.

## Famous Chinese Char Siew

**Prep time: 10 minutes | Cook time: 20 minutes | Serves 4 to 6**

1 strip of pork shoulder butt with a good amount of fat marbling
Olive oil, for brushing the pan
**Marinade:**
1 teaspoon sesame oil
4 tablespoons raw honey
1 teaspoon low-sodium dark soy sauce
1 teaspoon light soy sauce
1 tablespoon rose wine
2 tablespoons Hoisin sauce

Combine all the marinade ingredients together in a Ziploc bag. Put pork in bag, making sure all sections of pork strip are engulfed in the marinade. Chill for 3 to 24 hours. Take out the strip 30 minutes before planning to roast and preheat the air fryer to 350ºF (177ºC). Put foil on small pan and brush with olive oil. Put marinated pork strip onto prepared pan. When your air fryer displays "READY" (select the cooking preset, and make minor adjustments according to your desired doneness.) and choose a shake reminder. Cook in the preheated air fryer at the corresponding preset mode or Air Fry for 20 minutes. Glaze with marinade every 5 to 10 minutes. Remove strip and leave to cool a few minutes before slicing. Serve immediately.

## Authentic Chinese Pork Loin Porterhouse

**Prep time: 10 minutes | Cook time: 15 minutes | Serves 4**

1½ pounds (680 g) pork loin porterhouse, cut into four slices
1½ tablespoons sesame oil
½ teaspoon Five-spice powder
2 garlic cloves, crushed
1 tablespoon soy sauce
1 tablespoon hoisin sauce
2 tablespoons Shaoxing wine

Place all ingredients in a lightly greased Air Fryer cooking basket. When your air fryer displays "READY" (select the cooking preset, and make minor adjustments according to your desired doneness.) and choose a shake reminder. Cook the pork loin chops at 400ºF (204ºC) for 15 minutes, turning them over halfway through the cooking time. Bon appétit!

## Slab Baby Back Ribs

**Prep time: 10 minutes | Cook time: 30 minutes | Serves 4**

1 tablespoon toasted sesame oil
1 tablespoon fermented black bean paste
1 tablespoon Shaoxing wine (rice cooking wine)
1 tablespoon dark soy sauce
1 tablespoon agave nectar or honey
1 teaspoon minced garlic
1 teaspoon minced fresh ginger
1 (1½-pound / 680-g) slab baby back ribs, cut into individual ribs

In a large bowl, stir together the sesame oil, black bean paste, wine, soy sauce, agave, garlic, and ginger. Add the ribs and toss well to coat. Marinate at room temperature for 30 minutes, or cover and refrigerate for up to 24 hours. Place the ribs in the air-fryer basket; discard the marinade. When your air fryer displays "READY" (select the cooking preset, and make minor adjustments according to your desired doneness.) and choose a shake reminder. Set the air fryer to 350ºF (177ºC) for 30 minutes.

## Sunday Pork Belly

**Prep time: 5 minutes | Cook time: 20 minutes | Serves 5**

1 pound (454 g) pork belly
1 tablespoon tomato sauce
2 tablespoons rice vinegar
1 teaspoon dried thyme
1 teaspoon dried rosemary

Toss all ingredients in a lightly greased Air Fryer cooking basket. When your air fryer displays "READY" (select the cooking preset, and make minor adjustments according to your desired doneness.) and choose a shake reminder. Cook the pork belly at 320ºF (160ºC) for 20 minutes. Now, turn it over and continue cooking for a further 25 minutes. Serve warm and enjoy!

## Pork Rib Roast

**Prep time: 10 minutes | Cook time: 55 minutes | Serves 4**

1½ pounds (680 g) pork center cut rib roast
2 teaspoons butter, melted
1 teaspoon red chili powder
1 teaspoon paprika
1 teaspoon garlic powder
½ teaspoon onion powder
Sea salt and ground black pepper, to taste
2 tablespoons tamari sauce

Toss all ingredients in a lightly greased Air Fryer cooking basket. When your air fryer displays "READY" (select the cooking preset, and make minor adjustments according to your desired doneness.) and choose a shake reminder. Cook the pork at 360ºF (182ºC) for 55 minutes, turning it over halfway through the cooking time. Serve warm and enjoy!

## Pork Schnitzels with Sour Cream-Dill Sauce

**Prep time: 5 minutes | Cook time: 24 minutes | Serves 4 to 6**

½ cup flour
1½ teaspoons salt
Freshly ground black pepper, to taste
2 eggs
½ cup milk
1½ cups toasted breadcrumbs
1 teaspoon paprika
6 boneless, center cut pork chops (about 1½ pounds / 680 g), fat trimmed, pound to ½-inch thick

2 tablespoons olive oil
3 tablespoons melted butter
Lemon wedges, for serving
Sour Cream and Dill Sauce:
1 cup chicken stock
1½ tablespoons cornstarch
⅓ cup sour cream
1½ tablespoons chopped fresh dill
Salt and ground black pepper, to taste

Preheat the air fryer to 400ºF (204ºC). Combine the flour with salt and black pepper in a large bowl. Stir to mix well. Whisk the egg with milk in a second bowl. Stir the breadcrumbs and paprika in a third bowl. Dredge the pork chops in the flour bowl, then in the egg milk, and then into the breadcrumbs bowl. Press to coat well. Shake the excess off. Arrange one pork chop in the preheated air fryer each time, then brush with olive oil and butter on all sides. When your air fryer displays "READY" (select the cooking preset, and make minor adjustments according to your desired doneness.) and choose a shake reminder. Cook each pork chop at the corresponding preset mode or Air Fry for 4 minutes or until golden brown and crispy. Flip the chop halfway through the cooking time. Transfer the cooked pork chop (schnitzel) to a baking pan in the oven and keep warm over low heat while air frying the remaining pork chops. Meanwhile, combine the chicken stock and cornstarch in a small saucepan and bring to a boil over medium-high heat. Simmer for 2 more minutes. Turn off the heat, then mix in the sour cream, fresh dill, salt, and black pepper. Remove the schnitzels from the air fryer to a plate and baste with sour cream and dill sauce. Squeeze the lemon wedges over and slice to serve.

## Coconut Buttery Pork Chops

**Prep time: 5 minutes | Cook time: 15 minutes | Serves 4**

2 teaspoons parsley
2 teaspoons grated garlic cloves

1 tablespoon coconut oil
1 tablespoon coconut butter
4 pork chops

Ensure your air fryer is preheated to 350ºF (177ºC). Mix butter, coconut oil, and all seasoning together. Then rub seasoning mixture over all sides of pork chops. Place in foil, seal, and chill for 1 hour. Remove pork chops from foil and place into air fryer. When your air fryer displays "READY" (select the cooking preset, and make minor adjustments according to your desired doneness.) and choose a shake reminder. Cook 7 minutes on one side and 8 minutes on the other. Drizzle with olive oil and serve alongside a green salad.

## Chinese-Flavor Back Ribs

**Prep time: 10 minutes | Cook time: 35 minutes | Serves 4**

1 tablespoon sesame oil
1½ pounds (680 g) back ribs
½ cup tomato sauce

1 tablespoon soy sauce
2 tablespoons agave syrup
2 tablespoons rice wine

Toss all ingredients in a lightly greased Air Fryer cooking basket. When your air fryer displays "READY" (select the cooking preset, and make minor adjustments according to your desired doneness.) and choose a shake reminder. Cook the pork ribs at 350ºF (177ºC) for 35 minutes, turning them over halfway through the cooking time. Bon appétit!

## Cuban Pork Butt Sandwich

**Prep time: 10 minutes | Cook time: 55 minutes | Serves 4**

1½ pounds (680 g) pork butt
1 teaspoon stone-ground mustard
½ teaspoon ground cumin
2 cloves garlic, crushed
Kosher salt and freshly ground black pepper, to season

½ teaspoon ground allspice
2 tablespoons fresh pineapple juice
2 ounces Swiss cheese, sliced
16 ounces (454 g) Cuban bread loaf, sliced

Toss all ingredients, except for the cheese and bread, in a lightly greased Air Fryer cooking basket. When your air fryer displays "READY" (select the cooking preset, and make minor adjustments according to your desired doneness.) and choose a shake reminder. Air fry the pork butt at 360ºF (182ºC) for 55 minutes, turning it over halfway through the cooking time. Using two forks, shred the pork; assemble your sandwiches with cheese and bread. Serve warm and enjoy!

## Mustard Pork Loin Roast

**Prep time: 5 minutes | Cook time: 15 minutes | Serves 4**

1½ pounds (680 g) top loin roasts, sliced into four pieces
2 tablespoons olive oil
1 teaspoon hot paprika

Sea salt and ground black pepper
1 tablespoon Dijon mustard
1 teaspoon garlic, pressed

Place all ingredients in a lightly greased Air Fryer cooking basket. When your air fryer displays "READY" (select the cooking preset, and make minor adjustments according to your desired doneness.) and choose a shake reminder. Cook the pork at 400ºF (204ºC) for 15 minutes, turning it over halfway through the cooking time. Bon appétit!

## Fried Pork Loin

**Prep time: 10 minutes | Cook time: 55 minutes | Serves 4**

1½ pounds (680 g) pork top loin
1 tablespoon olive oil
1 tablespoon Dijon mustard
2 cloves garlic, crushed
1 tablespoon parsley

1 tablespoon coriander
½ teaspoon red pepper flakes, crushed
Kosher salt and ground black pepper, to taste

Toss all ingredients in a lightly greased Air Fryer cooking basket. When your air fryer displays "READY" (select the cooking preset, and make minor adjustments according to your desired doneness.) and choose a shake reminder. Cook the pork at 360ºF (182ºC) for 55 minutes, turning it over halfway through the cooking time. Serve warm and enjoy!

## St. Louis-Style Ribs

**Prep time: 5 minutes | Cook time: 35 minutes | Serves 4**

1½ pounds (680 g) St. Louis-style ribs
1 teaspoon hot sauce
1 tablespoon canola oil

Kosher salt and ground black pepper, to taste
2 garlic cloves, minced

Toss all ingredients in a lightly greased Air Fryer cooking basket. When your air fryer displays "READY" (select the cooking preset, and make minor adjustments according to your desired doneness.) and choose a shake reminder. Cook the pork ribs at 350ºF (177ºC) for 35 minutes, turning them over halfway through the cooking time. Bon appétit!

## Espresso Pork Tenderloin

**Prep time: 10 minutes | Cook time: 10 minutes | Serves 4**

1 tablespoon packed brown sugar
2 teaspoons espresso powder
1 teaspoon ground paprika
½ teaspoon dried marjoram
1 tablespoon honey

1 tablespoon freshly squeezed lemon juice
2 teaspoons olive oil
1 (1-pound / 227-g) pork tenderloin

In a small bowl, mix the brown sugar, espresso powder, paprika, and marjoram. Stir in the honey, lemon juice, and olive oil until well mixed. Spread the honey mixture over the pork and let stand for 10 minutes at room temperature. When your air fryer displays "READY" (select the cooking preset, and make minor adjustments according to your desired doneness.) and choose a shake reminder. Roast the tenderloin in the air fryer basket for 9 to 11 minutes, or until the pork registers at least 145ºF (63ºC) on a meat thermometer. Slice the meat to serve.

## Pork Tenderloin and Creamer Potatoes

**Prep time: 10 minutes | Cook time: 25 minutes | Serves 4**

2 cups creamer potatoes, rinsed and dried
2 teaspoons olive oil
1 (1-pound / 227-g) pork tenderloin, cut into 1-inch cubes
1 onion, chopped

1 red bell pepper, chopped
2 garlic cloves, minced
½ teaspoon dried oregano
2 tablespoons low-sodium chicken broth

In a medium bowl, toss the potatoes and olive oil to coat. Transfer the potatoes to the air fryer basket. When your air fryer displays "READY" (select the cooking preset, and make minor adjustments according to your desired doneness.) and choose a shake reminder. Roast for 15 minutes. In a medium metal bowl, mix the potatoes, pork, onion, red bell pepper, garlic, and oregano. Drizzle with the chicken broth. Put the bowl in the air fryer basket. Roast for about 10 minutes more, shaking the basket once during cooking, until the pork reaches at least 145ºF (63ºC) on a meat thermometer and the potatoes are tender. Serve immediately.

## Panko-Crusted Pork Schnitzel

**Prep time: 15 minutes | Cook time: 15 minutes | Serves 4**

4 thin boneless pork loin chops
2 tablespoons lemon juice
½ cup flour
¼ teaspoon marjoram
1 teaspoon salt

1 cup panko breadcrumbs
2 eggs
Lemon wedges, for serving
Cooking spray

Preheat the air fryer to 390ºF (199ºC) and spritz with cooking spray. On a clean work surface, drizzle the pork chops with lemon juice on both sides. Combine the flour with marjoram and salt on a shallow plate. Pour the breadcrumbs on a separate shallow dish. Beat the eggs in a large bowl. Dredge the pork chops in the flour, then dunk in the beaten eggs to coat well. Shake the excess off and roll over the breadcrumbs. Arrange the chops in the preheated air fryer and spritz with cooking spray. When your air fryer displays "READY" (select the cooking preset, and make minor adjustments according to your desired doneness.) and choose a shake reminder. Cook at the corresponding preset mode or Air Fry for 15 minutes or until the chops are golden and crispy. Flip the chops halfway through. Squeeze the lemon wedges over the fried chops and serve immediately.

## Garlic Baby Back Ribs

**Prep time: 5 minutes | Cook time: 30 minutes | Serves 2**

2 teaspoons red pepper flakes
¾ ground ginger
3 cloves minced garlic

Salt and ground black pepper, to taste
2 baby back ribs

Preheat the air fryer to 350ºF (177ºC). Combine the red pepper flakes, ginger, garlic, salt and pepper in a bowl, making sure to mix well. Massage the mixture into the baby back ribs. When your air fryer displays "READY" (select the cooking preset, and make minor adjustments according to your desired doneness.) and choose a shake reminder. Cook the ribs in the air fryer at the corresponding preset mode or Air Fry for 30 minutes. Take care when taking the rubs out of the air fryer. Put them on a serving dish and serve.

## Greek-Style Souvlaki

**Prep time: 10 minutes | Cook time: 15 minutes | Serves 4**

1 tablespoon olive oil
½ teaspoon sweet paprika
1 pound (454 g) pork tenderloin, cubed

1 small lemon, freshly juiced
1 eggplant, diced
2 bell peppers, diced
½ pound (227 g) fennel, diced

Toss all ingredients in a mixing bowl until well coated on all sides. Thread the ingredients onto skewers and place them in the Air Fryer cooking basket. When your air fryer displays "READY" (select the cooking preset, and make minor adjustments according to your desired doneness.) and choose a shake reminder. Then, cook the skewers at 400ºF (204ºC) for approximately 15 minutes, turning them over halfway through the cooking time. Bon appétit!

## Pork Center Cut with Italian Herb

**Prep time: 5 minutes | Cook time: 55 minutes | Serves 5**

2 pounds (907 g) pork center cut
2 tablespoons olive oil
1 tablespoon Italian herb mix

1 teaspoon red pepper flakes, crushed
Sea salt and freshly ground black pepper, to taste

Toss all ingredients in a lightly greased Air Fryer cooking basket. When your air fryer displays "READY" (select the cooking preset, and make minor adjustments according to your desired doneness.) and choose a shake reminder. Cook the pork at 360ºF (182ºC) for 55 minutes, turning it over halfway through the cooking time. Serve warm and enjoy!

## Greek Spice Pork Shoulder

**Prep time: 10 minutes | Cook time: 55 minutes | Serves 4**

1 pound (454 g) pork shoulder
1 teaspoon smoked paprika
½ teaspoon onion powder
1 teaspoon garlic powder
½ teaspoon ground cumin

½ teaspoon ground bay leaf
Sea salt and ground black pepper, to taste
4 pitta bread, warmed

Toss the pork on all sides, top and bottom, with the spices. Place the pork in a lightly greased Air Fryer cooking basket. When your air fryer displays "READY" (select the cooking preset, and make minor adjustments according to your desired doneness.) and choose a shake reminder. Cook the pork at 360ºF (182ºC) for 55 minutes, turning it over halfway through the cooking time. Shred the pork with two forks and serve on warmed pitta bread and some extra toppings of choice. Enjoy!

### Ham and Provolone Cheese Roll-Ups
**Prep time: 10 minutes | Cook time: 15 minutes | Serves 12**

2 teaspoons raw honey
2 teaspoons dried parsley
1 tablespoon poppy seeds
½ cup melted coconut oil
¼ cup spicy brown mustard

9 slices of provolone cheese
10 ounces (283 g) of thinly sliced Black Forest Ham
1 tube of crescent rolls

Roll out dough into a rectangle. Spread 2 to 3 tablespoons of spicy mustard onto dough, then layer provolone cheese and ham slices. Roll the filled dough up as tight as you can and slice into 12 to 15 pieces. Melt coconut oil and mix with a pinch of salt and pepper, parsley, honey, and remaining mustard. Brush mustard mixture over roll-ups and sprinkle with poppy seeds. Grease air fryer basket liberally with olive oil and add rollups. When your air fryer displays "READY" (select the cooking preset, and make minor adjustments according to your desired doneness.) and choose a shake reminder. Cook 15 minutes at 350ºF (177ºC). Serve!

### Parmesan Pork Burgers
**Prep time: 10 minutes | Cook time: 15 minutes | Serves 4**

1 pound (454 g) ground pork
Sea salt and ground black pepper, to taste
1 tablespoon Italian herb mix
1 small onion, chopped
1 teaspoon garlic, minced
¼ cup Parmesan cheese,

grated
¼ cup seasoned breadcrumbs
1 egg
4 hamburger buns
4 teaspoons Dijon mustard
4 tablespoons mayonnaise

In a mixing bowl, thoroughly combine the pork, spices, onion, garlic, Parmesan, breadcrumbs, and egg. Form the mixture into four patties. When your air fryer displays "READY" (select the cooking preset, and make minor adjustments according to your desired doneness.) and choose a shake reminder. Cook the burgers at 380ºF (193ºC) for about 15 minutes or until cooked through; make sure to turn them over halfway through the cooking time. Serve your burgers with hamburger buns, mustard, and mayonnaise. Enjoy!

### Lush Pork Sausage with Ratatouille
**Prep time: 10 minutes | Cook time: 25 minutes | Serves 4**

4 pork sausages
**Ratatouille:**
2 zucchinis, sliced
1 eggplant, sliced
15 ounces (425 g) tomatoes, sliced
1 red bell pepper, sliced
1 medium red onion, sliced
1 cup canned butter beans,

drained
1 tablespoon balsamic vinegar
2 garlic cloves, minced
1 red chili, chopped
2 tablespoons fresh thyme, chopped
2 tablespoons olive oil

Preheat the air fryer to 390ºF (199ºC). Place the sausages in the preheated air fryer when your air fryer displays "READY" (select the cooking preset, and make minor adjustments according to your desired doneness.) and choose a shake reminder. Cook at the corresponding preset mode or Air Fry for 10 minutes or until the sausage is lightly browned. Flip the sausages halfway through. Meanwhile, make the ratatouille: arrange the vegetable slices on the prepared baking pan alternatively, then add the remaining ingredients on top. Transfer the air fried sausage to a plate, then arrange the baking pan in the air fryer and cook at the corresponding preset mode or Air Fry for 15 minutes or until the vegetables are tender. Serve the ratatouille with the sausage on top.

### Pork Ribs with Zucchini
**Prep time: 10 minutes | Cook time: 37 minutes | Serves 4**

1½ pounds (680 g) pork loin ribs
2 cloves garlic, minced
1 tablespoon olive oil
4 tablespoons whiskey

1 teaspoon onion powder
Sea salt and ground black pepper, to taste
½ pound (227 g) zucchini, sliced

Toss the pork ribs with the garlic, olive oil, whiskey and spices; place the ingredients in a lightly greased Air Fryer cooking basket. When your air fryer displays "READY" (select the cooking preset, and make minor adjustments according to your desired doneness.) and choose a shake reminder. Cook the pork ribs at 350ºF (177ºC) for 25 minutes, turning them over halfway through the cooking time. Top the pork ribs with the sliced zucchini and continue cooking an additional 12 minutes. Serve immediately. Bon appétit!

### Mexican Street Pork Tacos
**Prep time: 10 minutes | Cook time: 55 minutes | Serves 4**

2 ancho chiles, seeded and minced
2 garlic cloves, chopped
1 tablespoon olive oil
Kosher salt and freshly ground

black pepper, to season
1 teaspoon dried Mexican oregano
1½ pounds (680 g) pork butt
4 corn tortillas, warmed

Toss all ingredients, except for the tortillas, in a lightly greased Air Fryer cooking basket. When your air fryer displays "READY" (select the cooking preset, and make minor adjustments according to your desired doneness.) and choose a shake reminder. Air fry the pork butt at 360ºF (182ºC) for 55 minutes, turning it over halfway through the cooking time. Using two forks, shred the pork and serve in tortillas with toppings of choice. Serve immediately!

### Holiday Pork Butt
**Prep time: 10 minutes | Cook time: 55 minutes | Serves 4**

1½ pounds (680 g) pork butt
1 teaspoon olive oil
1 teaspoon dried rosemary
1 teaspoon dried thyme
1 teaspoon dried oregano

1 teaspoon dried basil
1 teaspoon cayenne pepper
Sea salt and ground black pepper, to taste

Toss all ingredients in a lightly greased Air Fryer cooking basket. When your air fryer displays "READY" (select the cooking preset, and make minor adjustments according to your desired doneness.) and choose a shake reminder. Cook the pork at 360ºF (182ºC) for 55 minutes, turning it over halfway through the cooking time. Serve warm and enjoy!

### Paprika Pork Loin Chops
**Prep time: 5 minutes | Cook time: 15 minutes | Serves 4**

1 pound (454 g) pork loin chops
1 tablespoon olive oil
Sea salt and ground black

pepper, to taste
1 tablespoon smoked paprika

Place all ingredients in a lightly greased Air Fryer cooking basket. When your air fryer displays "READY" (select the cooking preset, and make minor adjustments according to your desired doneness.) and choose a shake reminder. Cook the pork loin chops at 400ºF (204ºC) for 15 minutes, turning them over halfway through the cooking time. Bon appétit!

## Pork Tenderloin with Walnut

**Prep time: 10 minutes | Cook time: 14 minutes | Serves 4**

3 tablespoons low-sodium grainy mustard
2 teaspoons olive oil
¼ teaspoon dry mustard powder
1 (1-pound / 227-g) pork tenderloin, silverskin and

excess fat trimmed and discarded
2 slices low-sodium whole-wheat bread, crumbled
¼ cup ground walnuts
2 tablespoons cornstarch

In a small bowl, stir together the mustard, olive oil, and mustard powder. Spread this mixture over the pork. On a plate, mix the bread crumbs, walnuts, and cornstarch. Dip the mustard-coated pork into the crumb mixture to coat. When your air fryer displays "READY" (select the cooking preset, and make minor adjustments according to your desired doneness.) and choose a shake reminder. Air-fry the pork for 12 to 16 minutes, or until it registers at least 145ºF (63ºC) on a meat thermometer. Slice to serve.

## Parmesan-Crusted Boneless Pork Chops

**Prep time: 10 minutes | Cook time: 12 minutes | Serves 4 to 6**

¼ teaspoon pepper
½ teaspoons salt
4 to 6 thick boneless pork chops
1 cup pork rind crumbs
¼ teaspoon chili powder

½ teaspoons onion powder
1 teaspoon smoked paprika
2 beaten eggs
3 tablespoons grated Parmesan cheese
Cooking spray

Preheat the air fryer to 400ºF (205ºC). Rub the pepper and salt on both sides of pork chops. In a food processor, pulse pork rinds into crumbs. Mix crumbs with chili powder, onion powder, and paprika in a bowl. Beat eggs in another bowl. Dip pork chops into eggs then into pork rind crumb mixture. Spritz the air fryer basket with cooking spray and add pork chops to the basket. When your air fryer displays "READY" (select the cooking preset, and make minor adjustments according to your desired doneness.) and choose a shake reminder. Cook at the corresponding preset mode or Air Fry for 12 minutes. Serve garnished with the Parmesan cheese.

## Rosemary Pork Rack

**Prep time: 5 minutes | Cook time: 35 minutes | Serves 2**

1 clove garlic, minced
2 tablespoons olive oil
1 pound (454 g) rack of pork
1 cup chopped macadamia nuts
1 tablespoon breadcrumbs

1 tablespoon rosemary, chopped
1 egg
Salt and ground black pepper, to taste

Preheat the air fryer to 350ºF (177ºC). Combine the garlic and olive oil in a small bowl. Stir to mix well. On a clean work surface, rub the pork rack with the garlic oil and sprinkle with salt and black pepper on both sides. Combine the macadamia nuts, breadcrumbs, and rosemary in a shallow dish. Whisk the egg in a large bowl. Dredge the pork in the egg, then roll the pork over the macadamia nut mixture to coat well. Shake the excess off. Arrange the pork in the preheated air fryer when your air fryer displays "READY" (select the cooking preset, and make minor adjustments according to your desired doneness.) and choose a shake reminder. Cook at the corresponding preset mode or Air Fry for 30 minutes on both sides. Increase to 390ºF (199ºC) and fry for 5 more minutes or until the pork is well browned. Serve immediately.

## Picnic Ham with Tamari Sauce

**Prep time: 5 minutes | Cook time: 45 minutes | Serves 4**

1½ pounds (680 g) picnic ham
2 tablespoons olive oil
2 garlic cloves, minced

2 tablespoons rice vinegar
1 tablespoon tamari sauce

Start by preheating your Air Fryer to 400ºF (204ºC) for about 13 minutes. Toss the ham with the remaining ingredients; wrap the ham in a piece of aluminum foil and lower it into the Air Fryer cooking basket. When your air fryer displays "READY" (select the cooking preset, and make minor adjustments according to your desired doneness.) and choose a shake reminder. Reduce the temperature to 375ºF (191ºC) and cook the ham for about 30 minutes. Remove the foil, turn the temperature to 400ºF (204ºC), and continue to cook an additional 15 minutes or until cooked through. Bon appétit!

## Pork and Vegetable Skewers

**Prep time: 10 minutes | Cook time: 15 minutes | Serves 4**

1 pound (454 g) pork tenderloin, cubed
1 pound (454 g) bell peppers, diced
1 pound (454 g) eggplant, diced

1 tablespoon olive oil
1 tablespoon parsley, chopped
1 tablespoon cilantro, chopped
Sea salt and ground black pepper, to taste

Toss all ingredients in a mixing bowl until well coated on all sides. Thread the ingredients onto skewers and place them in the Air Fryer cooking basket. When your air fryer displays "READY" (select the cooking preset, and make minor adjustments according to your desired doneness.) and choose a shake reminder. Then, cook the skewers at 400ºF (204ºC) for approximately 15 minutes, turning them over halfway through the cooking time. Bon appétit!

## Rosemary Pork Butt

**Prep time: 5 minutes | Cook time: 55 minutes | Serves 4**

1½ pounds (680 g) pork butt
1 teaspoon butter, melted
2 garlic cloves, pressed
2 tablespoons fresh rosemary,

chopped
Coarse sea salt and freshly ground black pepper, to taste

Toss all ingredients in a lightly greased Air Fryer cooking basket. When your air fryer displays "READY" (select the cooking preset, and make minor adjustments according to your desired doneness.) and choose a shake reminder. Cook the pork at 360ºF (182ºC) for 55 minutes, turning it over halfway through the cooking time. Serve warm and enjoy!

## Smoked Pork Sausage with Onions Rings

**Prep time: 5 minutes | Cook time: 15 minutes | Serves 4**

1 pound (454 g) pork sausage, smoked
4 ounces (113 g) onion rings

Place the sausage in a lightly greased Air fryer cooking basket. When your air fryer displays "READY" (select the cooking preset, and make minor adjustments according to your desired doneness.) and choose a shake reminder. Air fry the sausage at 370ºF (188ºC) for approximately 7 minutes, tossing the basket halfway through the cooking time. Add in the onion rings and continue to cook for 8 minutes more. Bon appétit!

## Rib Chops with Bell Peppers

**Prep time: 10 minutes | Cook time: 15 minutes | Serves 4**

1½ pounds (680 g) center-cut rib chops
2 bell peppers, seeded and sliced
2 tablespoons olive oil
½ teaspoon mustard powder

Kosher salt and freshly ground black pepper, to taste
1 teaspoon fresh rosemary, chopped
1 teaspoon fresh basil, chopped

Toss all ingredients in a lightly greased Air Fryer cooking basket. When your air fryer displays "READY" (select the cooking preset, and make minor adjustments according to your desired doneness.) and choose a shake reminder. Cook the pork chops and bell peppers at 400ºF (204ºC) for 15 minutes, turning them over halfway through the cooking time. Bon appétit!

## Orange Glazed Pork Chops

**Prep time: 5 minutes | Cook time: 15 minutes | Serves 3**

1 pound (454 g) rib pork chops
1½ tablespoons butter, melted
2 tablespoons orange juice, freshly squeezed

1 teaspoon rosemary, chopped
Sea salt and cayenne pepper, to taste

Toss all ingredients in a lightly greased Air Fryer cooking basket. When your air fryer displays "READY" (select the cooking preset, and make minor adjustments according to your desired doneness.) and choose a shake reminder. Cook the pork chops at 400ºF (204ºC) for 15 minutes, turning them over halfway through the cooking time. Bon appétit!

## Pork with Worcestershire Sauce

**Prep time: 5 minutes | Cook time: 16 minutes | Serves 2**

2 (10-ounce / 283-g) bone-in, center-cut pork chops, 1-inch thick
2 teaspoons Worcestershire

sauce
Salt and pepper, to taste
Cooking spray

Rub the Worcestershire sauce into both sides of pork chops. Season with salt and pepper to taste. Spray air fryer basket with cooking spray and place the chops in basket side by side. When your air fryer displays "READY" (select the cooking preset, and make minor adjustments according to your desired doneness.) and choose a shake reminder. Cook at 360ºF (182ºC) for 16 to 20 minutes or until well done. Let rest for 5 minutes before serving.

## Pork Dinner Rolls

**Prep time: 10 minutes | Cook time: 15 minutes | Serves 4**

1 pound (454 g) ground pork
Sea salt and freshly ground black pepper, to taste
1 teaspoon red pepper flakes, crushed

½ cup scallions, chopped
2 garlic cloves, minced
1 tablespoon olive oil
1 tablespoon soy sauce
8 dinner rolls, split

In a mixing bowl, thoroughly combine the pork, spices, scallions, garlic, olive oil, and soy sauce. Form the mixture into four patties. When your air fryer displays "READY" (select the cooking preset, and make minor adjustments according to your desired doneness.) and choose a shake reminder. Cook the patties at 380ºF (193ºC) for about 15 minutes or until cooked through; make sure to turn them over halfway through the cooking time. Serve the patties in dinner rolls and enjoy!

## Pork Chops with Onions

**Prep time: 5 minutes | Cook time: 15 minutes | Serves 4**

1½ pounds (680 g) pork loin chops, boneless
2 tablespoons olive oil
½ teaspoon cayenne pepper

1 teaspoon garlic powder
Sea salt and ground black pepper, to taste
1 onion, cut into wedges

Place all ingredients in a lightly greased Air Fryer cooking basket. When your air fryer displays "READY" (select the cooking preset, and make minor adjustments according to your desired doneness.) and choose a shake reminder. Cook the pork loin chops at 400ºF (204ºC) for 15 minutes, turning them over halfway through the cooking time. Bon appétit!

## Mushroom-Pork Loin Filets with Blue Cheese

**Prep time: 5 minutes | Cook time: 15 minutes | Serves 4**

1½ pounds (680 g) pork loin filets
Sea salt and ground black pepper, to taste

2 tablespoons olive oil
1 pound (454 g) mushrooms, sliced
2 ounces (57 g) blue cheese

Place the pork, salt, black pepper, and olive oil in a lightly greased Air Fryer cooking basket. When your air fryer displays "READY" (select the cooking preset, and make minor adjustments according to your desired doneness.) and choose a shake reminder. Cook the pork loin filets at 400ºF (204ºC) for 10 minutes, turning them over halfway through the cooking time. Top the pork loin filets with the mushrooms. Continue to cook for about 5 minutes longer. Top the warm pork with blue cheese. Bon appétit!

## Sausage with Brussels Sprouts

**Prep time: 10 minutes | Cook time: 15 minutes | Serves 4**

1 pound (454 g) sausage links, uncooked
1 pound (454 g) Brussels sprouts, halved

1 teaspoon dried thyme
1 teaspoon dried rosemary
1 teaspoon dried parsley flakes
1 teaspoon garlic powder

Place the sausage and Brussels sprouts in a lightly greased Air Fryer cooking basket. When your air fryer displays "READY" (select the cooking preset, and make minor adjustments according to your desired doneness.) and choose a shake reminder. Air fry the sausage and Brussels sprouts at 380ºF (193ºC) for approximately 15 minutes tossing the basket halfway through the cooking time. Bon appétit!

## Air-Fried Baby Back Ribs

**Prep time: 10 minutes | Cook time: 35 minutes | Serves 4**

1½ pounds (680 g) baby back ribs
2 tablespoons olive oil
1 teaspoon smoked paprika
1 teaspoon garlic powder
1 teaspoon onion powder

½ teaspoon ground cumin
1 teaspoon mustard powder
1 teaspoon dried thyme
Coarse sea salt and freshly cracked black pepper, to season

Toss all ingredients in a lightly greased Air Fryer cooking basket. When your air fryer displays "READY" (select the cooking preset, and make minor adjustments according to your desired doneness.) and choose a shake reminder. Cook the pork ribs at 350ºF (177ºC) for 35 minutes, turning them over halfway through the cooking time. Bon appétit!

## Hot Pork Spareribs

**Prep time: 10 minutes | Cook time: 35 minutes | Serves 4**

2 pounds (907 g) pork spareribs
1 teaspoon coarse sea salt
⅓ teaspoon freshly ground
black pepper
1 tablespoon brown sugar
1 teaspoon cayenne pepper
1 teaspoon garlic powder
1 teaspoon mustard powder

Toss all ingredients in a lightly greased Air Fryer cooking basket. When your air fryer displays "READY" (select the cooking preset, and make minor adjustments according to your desired doneness.) and choose a shake reminder. Cook the pork ribs at 350ºF (177ºC) for 35 minutes, turning them over halfway through the cooking time. Bon appétit!

## Lime Pork Taquitos

**Prep time: 5 minutes | Cook time: 10 minutes | Serves 8**

1 juiced lime
10 whole wheat tortillas
2½ cups shredded Mozzarella
cheese
30 ounces (850.5 g) of cooked
and shredded pork tenderloin

Ensure your air fryer is preheated to 380ºF (193ºC). Drizzle pork with lime juice and gently mix. Heat up tortillas in the microwave with a dampened paper towel to soften. Add about 3 ounces of pork and ¼ cup of shredded cheese to each tortilla. Tightly roll them up. Spray the air fryer basket with a bit of olive oil. When your air fryer displays "READY" (select the cooking preset, and make minor adjustments according to your desired doneness.) and choose a shake reminder. Air fry taquitos 7-10 minutes till tortillas turn a slight golden color, making sure to flip halfway through cooking process.

## Mustard Pork Sausage with Fennel

**Prep time: 5 minutes | Cook time: 15 minutes | Serves 4**

1 pound (454 g) pork sausage
1 pound (454 g) fennel,
quartered
1 teaspoon garlic powder
½ teaspoon onion powder
2 teaspoons mustard

Place all ingredients in a lightly greased Air Fryer cooking basket. When your air fryer displays "READY" (select the cooking preset, and make minor adjustments according to your desired doneness.) and choose a shake reminder. Air fry the sausage and fennel at 370ºF (188ºC) for approximately 15 minutes, tossing the basket halfway through the cooking time. Bon appétit!

## Pork, Plums, and Apricots Kebabs

**Prep time: 10 minutes | Cook time: 10 minutes | Serves 4**

⅓ cup apricot jam
2 tablespoons freshly squeezed
lemon juice
2 teaspoons olive oil
½ teaspoon dried tarragon
1 (1-pound / 227-g) pork
tenderloin, cut into 1-inch cubes
4 plums, pitted and quartered
4 small apricots, pitted and
halved

In a large bowl, mix the jam, lemon juice, olive oil, and tarragon. Add the pork and stir to coat. Let stand for 10 minutes at room temperature. Alternating the items, thread the pork, plums, and apricots onto 4 metal skewers that fit into the air fryer. Brush with any remaining jam mixture. Discard any remaining marinade. When your air fryer displays "READY" (select the cooking preset, and make minor adjustments according to your desired doneness.) and choose a shake reminder. Grill the kebabs in the air fryer for 9 to 12 minutes, or until the pork reaches 145ºF (63ºC) on a meat thermometer and the fruit is tender. Serve immediately.

## Pork Tenderloin with Greens Salad

**Prep time: 10 minutes | Cook time: 5 minutes | Serves 4**

2 pounds (907 g) pork
tenderloin, cut into 1-inch slices
1 teaspoon olive oil
1 teaspoon dried marjoram
⅛ teaspoon freshly ground
black pepper
6 cups mixed salad greens
1 red bell pepper, sliced
1 (8-ounce / 227-g) package
button mushrooms, sliced
⅓ cup low-sodium low-fat
vinaigrette dressing

In a medium bowl, mix the pork slices and olive oil. Toss to coat. Sprinkle with the marjoram and pepper and rub these into the pork. When your air fryer displays "READY" (select the cooking preset, and make minor adjustments according to your desired doneness.) and choose a shake reminder. Grill the pork in the air fryer, in batches, for about 4 to 6 minutes, or until the pork reaches at least 145ºF (63ºC) on a meat thermometer. Meanwhile, in a serving bowl, mix the salad greens, red bell pepper, and mushrooms. Toss gently. When the pork is cooked, add the slices to the salad. Drizzle with the vinaigrette and toss gently. Serve immediately.

## Pork Shoulder Chops

**Prep time: 5 minutes | Cook time: 15 minutes | Serves 4**

1½ pounds (680 g) pork
shoulder chops
2 tablespoons olive oil
Kosher salt and ground black
pepper, to taste
2 sprigs rosemary, leaves
picked and chopped
1 teaspoon garlic, pressed

Toss all ingredients in a lightly greased Air Fryer cooking basket. When your air fryer displays "READY" (select the cooking preset, and make minor adjustments according to your desired doneness.) and choose a shake reminder. Cook the pork shoulder chops at 400ºF (204ºC) for 15 minutes, turning them over halfway through the cooking time. Bon appétit!

## Pork Tenderloin and Veggies Kabobs

**Prep time: 25 minutes | Cook time: 15 minutes | Serves 4**

1 pound (454 g) pork tenderloin,
cubed
1 teaspoon smoked paprika
Salt and ground black pepper,
to taste
1 green bell pepper, cut into
chunks
1 zucchini, cut into chunks
1 red onion, sliced
1 tablespoon oregano
Cooking spray

**Special Equipment:**
Small bamboo skewers, soaked in water for 20 minutes to keep them from burning while cooking

Preheat the air fryer to 350ºF (177ºC). Spritz the air fryer basket with cooking spray. Add the pork to a bowl and season with the smoked paprika, salt and black pepper. Thread the seasoned pork cubes and vegetables alternately onto the soaked skewers. Arrange the skewers in the prepared air fryer basket and spray with cooking spray. When your air fryer displays "READY" (select the cooking preset, and make minor adjustments according to your desired doneness.) and choose a shake reminder. Cook at the corresponding preset mode or Air Fry for 15 minutes, or until the pork is well browned and the vegetables are tender, flipping once halfway through. Transfer the skewers to the serving dishes and sprinkle with oregano. Serve hot.

## Sweet-Sour Pork Cubes

**Prep time: 20 minutes | Cook time: 14 minutes | Serves 2 to 4**

⅓ cup all-purpose flour
⅓ cup cornstarch
2 teaspoons Chinese five-spice powder
1 teaspoon salt
Freshly ground black pepper,to taste
1 egg
2 tablespoons milk
¾ pound (340 g) boneless pork, cut into 1-inch cubes
Vegetable or canola oil

1½ cups large chunks of red and green peppers
½ cup ketchup
2 tablespoons rice wine vinegar or apple cider vinegar
2 tablespoons brown sugar
¼ cup orange juice
1 tablespoon soy sauce
1 clove garlic, minced
1 cup cubed pineapple
Chopped scallions, for garnish

Set up a dredging station with two bowls. Combine the flour, cornstarch, Chinese five-spice powder, salt and pepper in one large bowl. Whisk the egg and milk together in a second bowl. Dredge the pork cubes in the flour mixture first, then dip them into the egg and then back into the flour to coat on all sides. Spray the coated pork cubes with vegetable or canola oil. Preheat the air fryer to 400ºF (204ºC). Toss the pepper chunks with a little oil. When your air fryer displays "READY" (select the cooking preset, and make minor adjustments according to your desired doneness.) and choose a shake reminder. Cook at the corresponding preset mode or Air Fry for 5 minutes, shaking the basket halfway through the cooking time. While the peppers are cooking, start making the sauce. Combine the ketchup, rice wine vinegar, brown sugar, orange juice, soy sauce, and garlic in a medium saucepan and bring the mixture to a boil on the stovetop. Reduce the heat and simmer for 5 minutes. When the peppers have finished air frying, add them to the saucepan along with the pineapple chunks. Simmer the peppers and pineapple in the sauce for an additional 2 minutes. Set aside and keep warm. Add the dredged pork cubes to the air fryer basket and air fry at 400ºF (204ºC) for 6 minutes, shaking the basket to turn the cubes over for the last minute of the cooking process. When ready to serve, toss the cooked pork with the pineapple, peppers and sauce. Serve garnished with chopped scallions.

## Balsamic Pork Loin

**Prep time: 10 minutes | Cook time: 25 minutes | Serves 6 to 8**

Balsamic vinegar
1 teaspoon parsley
½ teaspoon red pepper flakes
½ teaspoon garlic powder

1 teaspoon pepper
1 teaspoon sat
2 pounds (907 g) pork loin

Sprinkle pork loin with seasonings and brush with vinegar. Place pork in your air fryer. When your air fryer displays "READY" (select the cooking preset, and make minor adjustments according to your desired doneness.) and choose a shake reminder. Cook 25 minutes at 340ºF (171ºC). Remove from air fryer and let rest 10 minutes before slicing.

## Pork Leg Roast with Candy Onions

**Prep time: 10 minutes | Cook time: 52 minutes | Serves 4**

2 teaspoons sesame oil
1 teaspoon dried sage, crushed
1 teaspoon cayenne pepper
1 rosemary sprig, chopped
1 thyme sprig, chopped
Sea salt and ground black pepper, to taste

2 pounds (907 g) pork leg roast, scored
½ pound (227 g) candy onions, sliced
4 cloves garlic, finely chopped
2 chili peppers, minced

Preheat the air fryer to 400ºF (204ºC). In a mixing bowl, combine the sesame oil, sage, cayenne pepper, rosemary, thyme, salt and black pepper until well mixed. In another bowl, place the pork leg and brush with the seasoning mixture. Place the seasoned pork leg in a baking pan when your air fryer displays "READY" (select the cooking preset, and make minor adjustments according to your desired doneness.) and choose a shake reminder. Cook at the corresponding preset mode or Air Fry for 40 minutes, or until lightly browned, flipping halfway through. Add the candy onions, garlic and chili peppers to the pan and cook for another 12 minutes. Transfer the pork leg to a plate. Let cool for 5 minutes and slice. Spread the juices left in the pan over the pork and serve warm with the candy onions.

## Bourbon Country-Style Ribs

**Prep time: 5 minutes | Cook time: 35 minutes | Serves 5**

2 pounds (907 g) Country-style ribs
¼ cup Sriracha sauce
2 tablespoons bourbon

1 tablespoon honey
1 teaspoon stone-ground mustard

Toss all ingredients in a lightly greased Air Fryer cooking basket. When your air fryer displays "READY" (select the cooking preset, and make minor adjustments according to your desired doneness.) and choose a shake reminder. Cook the pork ribs at 350ºF (177ºC) for 35 minutes, turning them over halfway through the cooking time. Bon appétit!

## Spareribs with Sriracha Sauce

**Prep time: 5 minutes | Cook time: 35 minutes | Serves 5**

2 pounds (907 g) spareribs
¼ cup Sriracha sauce
1 teaspoon paprika

Sea salt and ground black pepper, to taste

Toss all ingredients in a lightly greased Air Fryer cooking basket. When your air fryer displays "READY" (select the cooking preset, and make minor adjustments according to your desired doneness.) and choose a shake reminder. Cook the pork ribs at 350ºF (177ºC) for 35 minutes, turning them over halfway through the cooking time. Bon appétit!

## Lime Pork Loin Roast

**Prep time: 10 minutes | Cook time: 45 minutes | Serves 8**

1 tablespoon lime juice
1 tablespoon orange marmalade
1 teaspoon coarse brown mustard
1 teaspoon curry powder

1 teaspoon dried lemongrass
2 pound (907 g) boneless pork loin roast
Salt and ground black pepper, to taste
Cooking spray

Preheat the air fryer to 360ºF (182ºC). Mix the lime juice, marmalade, mustard, curry powder, and lemongrass. Rub mixture all over the surface of the pork loin. Season with salt and pepper. Spray air fryer basket with cooking spray and place pork roast diagonally in the basket. When your air fryer displays "READY" (select the cooking preset, and make minor adjustments according to your desired doneness.) and choose a shake reminder. Cook at the corresponding preset mode or Air Fry for approximately 45 minutes, until the internal temperature reaches at least 145ºF (63ºC). Wrap roast in foil and let rest for 10 minutes before slicing. Serve immediately.

## Pork with Sweet and Sour Sauce

**Prep time: 15 minutes | Cook time: 10 minutes | Serves 4 to 6**

3 tablespoons olive oil
$\frac{1}{16}$ teaspoon Chinese Five
Spice
¼ teaspoon pepper
½ teaspoon sea salt
**For the Sweet and Sour Sauce:**
¼ teaspoon sea salt
½ teaspoon garlic powder
1 tablespoon low-sodium soy
sauce

1 teaspoon pure sesame oil
2 eggs
1 cup almond flour
2 pounds (907 g) pork, sliced
into chunks

½ cup rice vinegar
5 tablespoons tomato paste
⅛ teaspoon water
½ cup sweetener of choice

To make the dipping sauce, whisk all sauce ingredients together over medium heat, stirring 5 minutes. Simmer uncovered 5 minutes till thickened. Meanwhile, combine almond flour, five spice, pepper, and salt. In another bowl, mix eggs with sesame oil. Dredge pork in flour mixture and then in egg mixture. Shake any excess off before adding to air fryer basket. When your air fryer displays "READY" (select the cooking preset, and make minor adjustments according to your desired doneness.) and choose a shake reminder. Cook 8 to 12 minutes at 340ºF (171ºC). Serve with sweet and sour dipping sauce!

## Tortilla Chips-Crusted Pork

**Prep time: 5 minutes | Cook time: 15 minutes | Serves 4**

1½ pounds (680 g) pork cutlets
Salt and ground black pepper,
to taste

1 cup tortilla chips, crushed
½ teaspoon cayenne pepper
2 tablespoons olive oil

Toss the pork cutlets with the remaining ingredients; place them in a lightly oiled Air Fryer cooking basket. When your air fryer displays "READY" (select the cooking preset, and make minor adjustments according to your desired doneness.) and choose a shake reminder. Cook the pork cutlets at 400ºF (204ºC) for 15 minutes, turning them over halfway through the cooking time. Bon appétit!

## Vietnamese Pork Shoulder with Peanuts

**Prep time: 10 minutes | Cook time: 20 minutes | Serves 6**

¼ cup minced yellow onion
2 tablespoons sugar
2 tablespoons vegetable oil
1 tablespoon minced garlic
1 tablespoon fish sauce
1 tablespoon minced fresh
lemongrass
2 teaspoons dark soy sauce

½ teaspoon black pepper
1½ pounds (680 g) boneless
pork shoulder, cut into ½-inch-
thick slices
¼ cup chopped salted roasted
peanuts
2 tablespoons chopped fresh
cilantro or parsley

In a large bowl, combine the onion, sugar, vegetable oil, garlic, fish sauce, lemongrass, soy sauce, and pepper. Add the pork and toss to coat. Marinate at room temperature for 30 minutes, or cover and refrigerate for up to 24 hours. Arrange the pork slices in the air-fryer basket; discard the marinade. When your air fryer displays "READY" (select the cooking preset, and make minor adjustments according to your desired doneness.) and choose a shake reminder. Set the air fryer to 400ºF (204ºC) for 20 minutes, turning the pork halfway through the cooking time. Transfer the pork to a serving platter. Sprinkle with the peanuts and cilantro and serve.

## Holiday Pork Sausages

**Prep time: 15 minutes | Cook time: 15 minutes | Serves 4**

**For the Sausages:**
1 heaping tablespoon jasmine
rice
2 tablespoons fish sauce
2 garlic cloves, minced
1 tablespoon sugar
**For Serving:**
Hot cooked rice or rice noodles
Shredded lettuce
Fresh mint and basil leaves

½ teaspoon black pepper
½ teaspoon kosher salt
½ teaspoon baking powder
1 pound (454 g) finely ground
pork

Sliced cucumber
Sliced scallions
Dipping Sauce

Place the rice in a small heavy-bottomed skillet. Toast over medium heat, stirring continuously, until it turns a deep golden yellow color, 5 to 8 minutes. Pour the rice onto a plate to cool completely. Grind in a spice or coffee grinder to a fine powder. In a large bowl, stir together the rice powder, fish sauce, garlic, sugar, pepper, salt, and baking powder until thoroughly combined. Add the pork and mix gently until the seasonings are incorporated. Divide the meat mixture into eight equal pieces. Roll each into a 3-inch-long log. Cover lightly with plastic wrap. Refrigerate for at least 30 minutes or up to 24 hours. Arrange the sausages in the air-fryer basket. When your air fryer displays "READY" (select the cooking preset, and make minor adjustments according to your desired doneness.) and choose a shake reminder. Set the air fryer to 375ºF (190ºC) for 15 minutes. Use a meat thermometer to ensure the sausages have reached an internal temperature of 160ºF (71ºC). Arrange the sausages, lettuce, mint, basil, cucumbers, and scallions over the rice. Serve with the dipping sauce.
Thinly slice 3 fresh Thai bird chiles (or 1 serrano chile) on an angle. Set aside one-third of the chiles. In a mortar, combine the chiles; 1 garlic clove, sliced; and 3 tablespoons sugar. Pound to a paste. Transfer to a small bowl. Add ⅔ cup warm water, 5 tablespoons fish sauce, 2 tablespoons finely shredded carrot, 1½ tablespoons fresh lime juice, and the reserved chile slices. Let stand for 10 minutes before serving.

## Wiener Pork Schnitzel

**Prep time: 10 minutes | Cook time: 14 minutes | Serves 4**

4 thin boneless pork loin chops
2 tablespoons lemon juice
½ cup flour
1 teaspoon salt

¼ teaspoon marjoram
1 cup plain breadcrumbs
2 eggs, beaten
Oil for misting or cooking spray

Rub the lemon juice into all sides of pork chops. Mix together the flour, salt, and marjoram. Place flour mixture on a sheet of wax paper. Place breadcrumbs on another sheet of wax paper. Roll pork chops in flour, dip in beaten eggs, then roll in breadcrumbs. Mist all sides with oil or cooking spray. Spray air fryer basket with nonstick cooking spray and place pork chops in basket. When your air fryer displays "READY" (select the cooking preset, and make minor adjustments according to your desired doneness.) and choose a shake reminder. Cook at 390ºF (199ºC) for 7 minutes. Turn, mist again, and cook for another 7 or 8 minutes, until well done. Serve with lemon wedges.

# Chapter 5 Poultry

## Parmesan Chicken Wings

**Prep time: 10 minutes | Cook time: 15 minutes | Serves 4**

8 chicken wings
1 teaspoon Dijon mustard
Salt to taste
2 tablespoons olive oil
2 cloves garlic, crushed

4 tablespoons Parmesan cheese, grated
2 teaspoons fresh parsley, chopped

Preheat air fryer to 380ºF (193ºC). Grease the frying basket. Season the wings with salt and black pepper. Brush them with mustard. On a plate, pour 2 tablespoons of the Parmesan cheese. Coat the wings with Parmesan cheese, drizzle with olive oil, and place in the air fryer basket. When your air fryer displays "READY" (select the cooking preset, and make minor adjustments according to your desired doneness.) and choose a shake reminder. AirFry for 15 minutes, turning once. Top with the remaining Parmesan cheese and parsley to serve.

## Coconut Chicken Breasts

**Prep time: 5 minutes | Cook time: 16 minutes | Serves 4**

2 cups coconut flakes
4 chicken breasts, cut into strips

½ cup cornstarch
Salt and black pepper, to taste
2 eggs, beaten

Preheat air fryer to 350ºF (180ºC). Mix salt, pepper, and cornstarch in a bowl. Line a frying basket with parchment paper. Dip the chicken first in the cornstarch, then into the eggs, and finally, coat with coconut flakes. Arrange in the air fryer when your air fryer displays "READY" (select the cooking preset, and make minor adjustments according to your desired doneness.) and choose a shake reminder. Bake for 16 minutes, flipping once until crispy. Serve with berry sauce.

## Chicken Breasts with Sweet Chili Adobo

**Prep time: 5 minutes | Cook time: 12 minutes | Serves 4**

2 chicken breasts, halved
Salt and black pepper, to taste

¼ cup sweet chili sauce
1 teaspoon turmeric

Preheat air fryer to 390ºF (199ºC). In a bowl, add salt, black pepper, sweet chili sauce, and turmeric; mix well. Lightly brush the chicken with the mixture and place it in the frying basket. When your air fryer displays "READY" (select the cooking preset, and make minor adjustments according to your desired doneness.) and choose a shake reminder. AirFry for 12 to 14 minutes, turning once halfway through. Serve with a side of steamed greens.

## Fried Chicken Legs

**Prep time: 5 minutes | Cook time: 14 minutes | Serves 4**

4 chicken legs
2 lemons, halved
1 tablespoon garlic powder

½ teaspoon dried oregano
⅓ cup olive oil
Salt and black pepper, to taste

Preheat the air fryer to 350ºF (180ºC). Brush the chicken legs with olive oil. Sprinkle with lemon juice and arrange in the frying basket when your air fryer displays "READY" (select the cooking preset, and make minor adjustments according to your desired doneness.) and choose a shake reminder. In a bowl, mix oregano, garlic powder, salt, and pepper. Scatter the seasoning mixture over the chicken and Bake the legs in the air fryer for 14 to 16 minutes, shaking once.

## Mozzarella Chicken Enchiladas

**Prep time: 10 minutes | Cook time: 24 minutes | Serves 4**

1 pound (454 g) chicken breasts, chopped
1 cup Mozzarella cheese, grated

½ cup salsa
1 can green chilies, chopped
8 flour tortillas
1 cup enchilada sauce

Preheat the air fryer to 400ºF (205ºC). In a bowl, mix salsa and enchilada sauce. Toss in the chopped chicken to coat. Place the chicken in a baking dish when your air fryer displays "READY" (select the cooking preset, and make minor adjustments according to your desired doneness.) and choose a shake reminder. Bake in the air fryer for 14 to 18 minutes, shaking once. Remove and divide between the tortillas. Top with cheese and roll the tortillas. Place in the air fryer basket and Bake for 10 minutes. Serve with guacamole.

## Sweet Wasabi Chicken Breasts

**Prep time: 5 minutes | Cook time: 16 minutes | Serves 2**

2 tablespoons wasabi
1 tablespoon agave syrup
2 teaspoons black sesame seeds

Salt and black pepper, to taste
2 chicken breasts, cut into large chunks

In a bowl, mix wasabi, agave syrup, sesame seed, salt, and pepper. Rub the mixture onto the breasts. Arrange the breasts on a greased frying basket when your air fryer displays "READY" (select the cooking preset, and make minor adjustments according to your desired doneness.) and choose a shake reminder. Cook for 16 minutes, turning once halfway through.

## Tropical Coconut Chicken

**Prep time: 5 minutes | Cook time: 12 minutes | Serves 4**

1 tablespoon curry powder
4 tablespoons mango chutney
Salt and black pepper, to taste

¾ cup coconut, shredded
1 pound (454 g) chicken thighs

Preheat air fryer to 400ºF (205ºC). In a bowl, mix curry powder, mango chutney, salt, and black pepper. Brush the thighs with the glaze and roll the chicken thighs in shredded coconut. Grease a baking dish with cooking spray and arrange the thing in. When your air fryer displays "READY" (select the cooking preset, and make minor adjustments according to your desired doneness.) and choose a shake reminder. Bake them in the air fryer for 12 to 14 minutes, turning once, until golden brown.

## Honey Mustard Chicken Thighs

**Prep time: 5 minutes | Cook time: 16 minutes | Serves 4**

4 chicken thighs, skin-on
1 tablespoon honey

1 teaspoon Dijon mustard
Salt and garlic powder to taste

In a bowl, mix honey, mustard, garlic powder, and salt. Brush the thighs with the mixture and place them into the air fryer basket when your air fryer displays "READY" (select the cooking preset, and make minor adjustments according to your desired doneness.) and choose a shake reminder. AirFry them for 16 minutes at 400ºF (205ºC), turning once halfway through. Serve hot.

## Sweet Chili Chicken Wings
**Prep time: 5 minutes | Cook time: 14 minutes | Serves 4**

1 pound (454 g) chicken wings
1 teaspoon ginger root powder

1 tablespoon tamarind powder
¼ cup sweet chili sauce

Preheat air fryer to 390ºF (199ºC). Rub the chicken wings with tamarind and ginger root powders. Spray with cooking spray and place in the air fryer basket. When your air fryer displays "READY" (select the cooking preset, and make minor adjustments according to your desired doneness.) and choose a shake reminder. Cook for 6 minutes. Slide-out the basket and cover with sweet chili sauce; cook for 8 more minutes. Serve warm.

## Yellow Mustard Chicken Breasts
**Prep time: 5 minutes | Cook time: 15 minutes | Serves 4**

4 chicken breasts, sliced
1 tablespoon Worcestershire sauce
¼ cup onions, chopped

1 tablespoon brown sugar
¼ cup yellow mustard
½ cup ketchup

Preheat air fryer to 360ºF (182ºC). In a bowl, mix sugar, 1 cup of water, ketchup, onions, mustard, Worcestershire sauce, and salt. Place the chicken into the mixture and let marinate for 10 minutes. Transfer the chicken to the frying basket when your air fryer displays "READY" (select the cooking preset, and make minor adjustments according to your desired doneness.) and choose a shake reminder. AirFry for 15 minutes, flipping once. Serve with the sauce.

## Breaded Chicken Tenderloins
**Prep time: 5 minutes | Cook time: 14 minutes | Serves 4**

8 chicken tenderloins
2 tablespoons butter, melted

1 cup seasoned breadcrumbs

Preheat air fryer to 380ºF (193ºC). Dip the chicken in the eggs, then coat with the seasoned crumbs. Coat the air fryer basket with some butter and place in the chicken when your air fryer displays "READY" (select the cooking preset, and make minor adjustments according to your desired doneness.) and choose a shake reminder. Brush with the remaining butter and cook for 14 to 16 minutes, shaking once halfway through. Serve with your favorite dip.

## Gluten-Free Cheddar Chicken
**Prep time: 10 minutes | Cook time: 18 minutes | Serves 4**

2 garlic cloves, minced
1 pound (454 g) chicken breasts, sliced
½ teaspoon dried thyme
1 cup potato flakes

Salt and black pepper, to taste
½ cup Cheddar cheese, grated
½ cup mayonnaise
1 lemon, zested

Preheat air fryer to 350ºF (180ºC). In a bowl, mix garlic, potato flakes, Cheddar cheese, thyme, lemon zest, salt, and pepper. Brush the chicken with mayonnaise, then roll in the potato mixture. Place in the greased air fryer basket when your air fryer displays "READY" (select the cooking preset, and make minor adjustments according to your desired doneness.) and choose a shake reminder. AirFry for 18 to 20 minutes, shaking once halfway through. Serve warm.

## Chicken Breast Bowl with Black Beans
**Prep time: 10 minutes | Cook time: 18 minutes | Serves 4**

4 chicken breasts, cubed
1 can sweet corn
1 can black beans, rinsed and drained

1 cup red and green peppers, stripes, cooked
1 tablespoon vegetable oil
1 teaspoon chili powder

Preheat the air fryer to 380ºF (193ºC). Coat the chicken with salt, black pepper, and a bit of oil. When your air fryer displays "READY" (select the cooking preset, and make minor adjustments according to your desired doneness.) and choose a shake reminder. AirFry for 15 minutes at 380ºF (193ºC). In a deep skillet, pour 1 tablespoon of oil and stir in chili powder, corn, peppers, and beans. Add a little bit of hot water and keep stirring for 3 minutes. Transfer the veggies to a serving platter and top with the fried chicken.

## Parmesan Crusted Chicken Thighs
**Prep time: 5 minutes | Cook time: 10 minutes | Serves 4**

½ cup Italian breadcrumbs
2 tablespoons Parmesan cheese, grated
1 tablespoon butter, melted

4 chicken thighs
½ cup marinara sauce
½ cup Monterrey jack cheese, shredded

Preheat air fryer to 380ºF (193ºC). In a bowl, mix the crumbs with Parmesan cheese. Brush the thighs with butter. Dip each thigh into the crumb mixture. Arrange them on the greased air fryer basket. When your air fryer displays "READY" (select the cooking preset, and make minor adjustments according to your desired doneness.) and choose a shake reminder. AirFry for 6 to 7 minutes at 380ºF (193ºC), flip, top with marinara sauce and shredded Monterrey Jack cheese, and continue to cook for another 4 to 5 minutes. Serve immediately

## Israeli Chicken Schnitzel
**Prep time: 5 minutes | Cook time: 10 minutes | Serves 4**

2 large boneless, skinless chicken breasts, each weighing about 1 pound (454 g)
1 cup all-purpose flour
2 teaspoons garlic powder
2 teaspoons kosher salt
1 teaspoon black pepper

1 teaspoon paprika
2 eggs beaten with 2 tablespoons water
2 cups panko bread crumbs
Vegetable oil spray
Lemon juice, for serving

Preheat the air fryer to 375ºF (191ºC). Place 1 chicken breast between 2 pieces of plastic wrap. Use a mallet or a rolling pin to pound the chicken until it is ¼ inch thick. Set aside. Repeat with the second breast. Whisk together the flour, garlic powder, salt, pepper, and paprika on a large plate. Place the panko in a separate shallow bowl or pie plate. Dredge 1 chicken breast in the flour, shaking off any excess, then dip it in the egg mixture. Dredge the chicken breast in the panko, making sure to coat it completely. Shake off any excess panko. Place the battered chicken breast on a plate. Repeat with the second chicken breast. Spray the air fryer basket with oil spray. Place 1 of the battered chicken breasts in the basket and spray the top with oil spray. When your air fryer displays "READY" (select the cooking preset, and make minor adjustments according to your desired doneness.) and choose a shake reminder. Cook at the corresponding preset mode or Air Fry until the top is browned, about 5 minutes. Flip the chicken and spray the second side with oil spray. Cook until the second side is browned and crispy and the internal temperature reaches 165ºF (74ºC). Remove the first chicken breast from the air fryer and repeat with the second chicken breast. Serve hot with lemon juice.

## Chicken Breasts and Fingerling Potatoes
**Prep time: 15 minutes | Cook time: 25 minutes | Serves 2**

2 teaspoons minced fresh oregano, divided
2 teaspoons minced fresh thyme, divided
2 teaspoons extra-virgin olive oil, plus extra as needed
1 pound (454 g) fingerling potatoes, unpeeled
2 (12-ounce / 340-g) bone-in split chicken breasts, trimmed
1 garlic clove, minced
¼ cup oil-packed sun-dried tomatoes, patted dry and chopped
1½ tablespoons red wine vinegar
1 tablespoon capers, rinsed and minced
1 small shallot, minced
Salt and ground black pepper, to taste

Preheat the air fryer to 350ºF (177ºC). Combine 1 teaspoon of oregano, 1 teaspoon of thyme, ¼ teaspoon of salt, ¼ teaspoon of ground black pepper, 1 teaspoons of olive oil in a large bowl. Add the potatoes and toss to coat well. Combine the chicken with remaining thyme, oregano, and olive oil. Sprinkle with garlic, salt, and pepper. Toss to coat well. Place the potatoes in the preheated air fryer, then arrange the chicken on top of the potatoes. When your air fryer displays "READY" (select the cooking preset, and make minor adjustments according to your desired doneness.) and choose a shake reminder. Cook at the corresponding preset mode or Air Fry for 25 minutes or until the internal temperature of the chicken reaches at least 165ºF (74ºC) and the potatoes are wilted. Flip the chicken and potatoes halfway through. Meanwhile, combine the sun-dried tomatoes, vinegar, capers, and shallot in a separate large bowl. Sprinkle with salt and ground black pepper. Toss to mix well. Remove the chicken and potatoes from the air fryer and allow to cool for 10 minutes. Serve with the sun-dried tomato mix.

## Gluten-Free Barbecue Chicken
**Prep time: 5 minutes | Cook time: 15 minutes | Serves 4**

6 boneless, skinless chicken thighs
¼ cup gluten-free barbecue sauce
2 cloves garlic, minced
2 tablespoons lemon juice

In a medium bowl, combine the chicken, barbecue sauce, cloves, and lemon juice, and mix well. Let marinate for 10 minutes. Remove the chicken thighs from the bowl and shake off excess sauce. Put the chicken pieces in the air fryer, leaving a bit of space between each one. When your air fryer displays "READY" (select the cooking preset, and make minor adjustments according to your desired doneness.) and choose a shake reminder. Grill for 15 to 18 minutes or until the chicken is 165ºF (74ºC) on an instant-read meat thermometer.

## Creamy Asiago Chicken Breasts
**Prep time: 5 minutes | Cook time: 15 minutes | Serves 4**

4 chicken breasts, cubed
½ teaspoon garlic powder
1 cup mayonnaise
½ cup Asiago cheese, grated
Salt and black pepper, to taste
2 tablespoons fresh basil, chopped

Preheat air fryer to 380ºF (193ºC). In a bowl, mix Asiago cheese, mayonnaise, garlic powder, and salt. Add in the chicken and toss to coat. Place the coated chicken in the greased frying basket when your air fryer displays "READY" (select the cooking preset, and make minor adjustments according to your desired doneness.) and choose a shake reminder. Bake for 15 minutes, shaking once. Serve sprinkled with freshly chopped basil.

## Chipotle Buttered Turkey Breast
**Prep time: 5 minutes | Cook time: 10 minutes | Serves 4**

1 pound (454 g) turkey breast, sliced
2 cups panko breadcrumbs
½ teaspoon chipotle chili
pepper
Salt and black pepper, to taste
1 stick butter, melted

In a bowl, combine panko and chipotle chili pepper. Sprinkle turkey with salt and black pepper, and brush with some butter. Coat the turkey with the panko mixture. Transfer to the frying basket dish and top with butter. When your air fryer displays "READY" (select the cooking preset, and make minor adjustments according to your desired doneness.) and choose a shake reminder. AirFry for 10 minutes at 390ºF (199ºC). Shake, drizzle the remaining butter, and Bake for 5 more minutes, until nice and crispy. Serve with enchilada sauce.

## Thai Tom Yum Chicken Wings
**Prep time: 5 minutes | Cook time: 12 minutes | Serves 2**

8 chicken wings
1 tablespoon water
½ cup flour
2 tablespoons cornstarch
2 tablespoons tom yum paste
½ tablespoon baking powder

Combine the tom yum paste and water in a small bowl. Place the wings in a large bowl, add the tom yum mixture, and mix to coat well. Cover the bowl and refrigerate for 2 hours. Preheat air fryer to 370ºF (188ºC). Mix baking powder, cornstarch, and flour. Dip the wings in the starch mixture. Place on the greased frying basket when your air fryer displays "READY" (select the cooking preset, and make minor adjustments according to your desired doneness.) and choose a shake reminder. AirFry for 7 to 8 minutes. Flip and cook for 5 to 6 minutes. Serve.

## BBQ Whole Small Chicken
**Prep time: 5 minutes | Cook time: 23 minutes | Serves 3**

1 whole small chicken, cut into pieces
Salt to taste
½ teaspoon smoked paprika
½ teaspoon garlic powder
1 cup BBQ sauce

Mix salt, paprika, and garlic powder and coat the chicken pieces. Place in the air fryer basket when your air fryer displays "READY" (select the cooking preset, and make minor adjustments according to your desired doneness.) and choose a shake reminder. Bake for 18 minutes at 400ºF (205ºC). Remove to a plate and brush with barbecue sauce. Wipe the fryer clean from the chicken fat. Return the chicken to the fryer, skin-side up, and Bake for 5 more minutes at 340ºF (171ºC).

## Ginger Chili Chicken Wings
**Prep time: 5 minutes | Cook time: 14 minutes | Serves 2**

8 chicken wings
1 cup cornflour
½ cup white wine
1 teaspoon chili paste
1-inch fresh ginger, grated
1 tablespoon olive oil

Preheat air fryer to 360ºF (182ºC). In a bowl, mix ginger, chili paste, and wine. Add in the chicken wings and marinate for 30 minutes. Remove the chicken, drain, and coat with cornflour. Brush with olive oil and place in the frying basket. When your air fryer displays "READY" (select the cooking preset, and make minor adjustments according to your desired doneness.) and choose a shake reminder. AirFry for 14 to 16 minutes, shaking once until crispy on the outside. Serve

## Jerusalem Matzah and Chicken Schnitzels

**Prep time: 5 minutes | Cook time: 14 minutes | Serves 4**

4 chicken breasts
1 cup panko breadcrumbs
2 tablespoons Parmesan cheese, grated

6 sage leaves, chopped
½ cup fine matzah meal
2 beaten eggs

Pound the chicken to ¼-inch thickness using a rolling pin. In a bowl, add Parmesan cheese, sage, and breadcrumbs. Toss chicken with matzah meal, dip in eggs, then coat well with bread crumbs. Preheat air fryer to 390ºF (199ºC). When your air fryer displays "READY" (select the cooking preset, and make minor adjustments according to your desired doneness.) and choose a shake reminder. Spray both sides of chicken breasts with cooking spray and AirFry in the frying basket for 14 to 16 minutes, turning once halfway through until golden. Serve warm.

## Crumbed Sage Chicken Scallopini

**Prep time: 5 minutes | Cook time: 14 minutes | Serves 4**

4 chicken breasts
3 ounces (85 g) breadcrumbs
2 tablespoons Parmesan cheese, grated
2 ounces (57 g) flour 2 eggs,

beaten
1 tablespoon fresh sage, chopped
1 lemon, cut into wedges

Preheat air fryer to 370ºF (188ºC). Place some plastic wrap underneath and on top of the breasts. Using a rolling pin, beat the meat until it becomes skinny. In a bowl, combine Parmesan cheese, sage, and breadcrumbs. Dip the chicken in the egg first, and then in the flour. When your air fryer displays "READY" (select the cooking preset, and make minor adjustments according to your desired doneness.) and choose a shake reminder. Spray with cooking spray and AirFry for 14 to 16 minutes, flipping once halfway through. Serve with lemon wedges.

## Super Cheesy Chicken Breast

**Prep time: 10 minutes | Cook time: 12 minutes | Serves 4**

1 egg
1 tablespoon mayonnaise
1 cup panko bread crumbs
½ cup freshly grated Parmesan cheese
1 teaspoon Italian seasoning
1 pound (454 g) boneless, skinless hand-filleted chicken

breasts or regular breasts sliced in half crosswise to create 4 thin breasts
Vegetable oil for spraying
¼ cup Marinara Sauce
6 tablespoons grated Mozzarella cheese

Mix the egg and mayonnaise in a shallow bowl until smooth. In another bowl, combine the panko, Parmesan cheese, and Italian seasoning. Dip each piece of chicken in the mayonnaise mixture, shaking off any excess, then dredge in the panko mixture until both sides are coated. Place the breaded chicken on a plate or rack. Preheat the air fryer to 350ºF (177ºC) for 3 minutes. Spray the basket of the air fryer with oil and place 2 pieces of chicken in the basket. Spray the chicken cutlets with oil. When your air fryer displays "READY" (select the cooking preset, and make minor adjustments according to your desired doneness.) and choose a shake reminder. Cook the cutlets for 6 minutes, then turn them over. Top each piece of chicken with 1 tablespoon of marinara sauce and 1½ tablespoons of grated Mozzarella cheese. Cook the chicken until the cheese is melted, about 3 additional minutes. Remove the cooked chicken to a serving dish and keep warm. Cook the remaining pieces of chicken in the same manner. Serve warm with pasta on the side.

## Bacon-Wrapped Cream Cheese Chicken

**Prep time: 10 minutes | Cook time: 20 minutes | Serves 4**

4 (5-ounce / 142-g) boneless, skinless chicken breasts, pounded to ¼ inch thick
1 cup cream cheese
2 tablespoons chopped fresh

chives
8 slices thin-cut bacon
Sprig of fresh cilantro, for garnish
Cooking spray

Preheat the air fryer to 400ºF (204ºC). Spritz the air fryer basket with cooking spray. On a clean work surface, slice the chicken horizontally to make a 1-inch incision on top of each chicken breast with a knife, then cut into the chicken to make a pocket. Leave a ½-inch border along the sides and bottom. Combine the cream cheese and chives in a bowl. Stir to mix well, then gently pour the mixture into the chicken pockets. Wrap each stuffed chicken breast with 2 bacon slices, then secure the ends with toothpicks. Arrange them in the preheated air fryer basket when your air fryer displays "READY" (select the cooking preset, and make minor adjustments according to your desired doneness.) and choose a shake reminder. Cook at the corresponding preset mode or Air Fry for 20 minutes or until the bacon is lightly browned and crispy. Flip the bacon-wrapped chicken halfway through the cooking time. Transfer them on a large plate and serve with cilantro on top.

## Buffalo Chicken Wings

**Prep time: 5 minutes | Cook time: 30 minutes | Serves 6 to 8**

1 teaspoon salt
1 to 2 tablespoons brown sugar
1 tablespoon Worcestershire sauce

½ cup vegan butter
½ cup cayenne pepper sauce
4 pounds (1.8 kg) chicken wings

Whisk salt, brown sugar, Worcestershire sauce, butter, and hot sauce together and set to the side. Dry wings and add to air fryer basket. When your air fryer displays "READY" (select the cooking preset, and make minor adjustments according to your desired doneness.) and choose a shake reminder. Cook 25 minutes at 380ºF (193ºC), tossing halfway through. When timer sounds, shake wings and bump up the temperature to 400ºF (204ºC) and cook another 5 minutes. Take out wings and place into a big bowl. Add sauce and toss well. Serve alongside celery sticks!

## Chicken Tenderloins with Peanuts

**Prep time: 10 minutes | Cook time: 25 minutes | Serves 4**

½ cup grated Parmesan cheese
½ teaspoon garlic powder
1 teaspoon red pepper flakes
Sea salt and ground black pepper, to taste
2 tablespoons peanut oil

1½ pounds (680 g) chicken tenderloins
2 tablespoons peanuts, roasted and roughly chopped
Cooking spray

Preheat the air fryer to 360ºF (182ºC). Spritz the air fryer basket with cooking spray. Combine the Parmesan cheese, garlic powder, red pepper flakes, salt, black pepper, and peanut oil in a large bow. Stir to mix well. Dip the chicken tenderloins in the cheese mixture, then press to coat well. Shake the excess off. Transfer the chicken tenderloins in the air fryer basket. When your air fryer displays "READY" (select the cooking preset, and make minor adjustments according to your desired doneness.) and choose a shake reminder. Cook at the corresponding preset mode or Air Fry for 12 minutes or until well browned. Flip the tenderloin halfway through. You may need to work in batches to avoid overcrowding. Transfer the chicken tenderloins on a large plate and top with roasted peanuts before serving.

## Creamy Onion Chicken Breasts

**Prep time: 5 minutes | Cook time: 15 minutes | Serves 4**

4 chicken breasts, cubed
1½ cups onion soup mix

1 cup mushroom soup
½ cup heavy cream

Preheat air fryer to 400ºF (205ºC). Warm mushroom soup, onion mix, and heavy cream in a frying pan over low heat for 1 minute. Pour the mixture over the chicken and let sit for 25 minutes. Transfer the chicken to the air fryer when your air fryer displays "READY" (select the cooking preset, and make minor adjustments according to your desired doneness.) and choose a shake reminder. Bake for 15 minutes, shaking once. Serve topped with the remaining sauce.

## Shredded Chicken and Jalapeño Quesadilla

**Prep time: 5 minutes | Cook time: 12 minutes | Serves 4**

8 tortillas
2 cups Monterey Jack cheese, shredded
½ cup cooked chicken,

shredded
1 cup canned fire-roasted jalapeño peppers, chopped
1 beaten egg, to seal tortillas

Preheat air fryer to 390ºF (199ºC). Divide chicken, cheese, and jalapeño peppers between 4 tortillas. Seal the tortillas with beaten egg. Grease with cooking spray. In batches, place in the air fryer basket when your air fryer displays "READY" (select the cooking preset, and make minor adjustments according to your desired doneness.) and choose a shake reminder. Bake for 12 minutes, turning once halfway through. Serve with green salsa.

## Sticky Chicken Drumsticks

**Prep time: 5 minutes | Cook time: 15 minutes | Serves 2**

2 chicken drumsticks, skin removed
2 tablespoons canola oil

1 tablespoon Agave nectar
1 garlic clove, minced

Add all ingredients to a resealable bag and massage until well-coated. Allow the chicken to marinate for 30 minutes. Preheat the air fryer to 380ºF (193ºC). Add the chicken to the frying basket when your air fryer displays "READY" (select the cooking preset, and make minor adjustments according to your desired doneness.) and choose a shake reminder. Bake for 15 minutes, shaking once. Serve warm

## BBQ Chicken Drumsticks

**Prep time: 5 minutes | Cook time: 40 minutes | Serves 5**

1 tablespoon olive oil
10 chicken drumsticks
Chicken seasoning or rub, to taste

Salt and ground black pepper, to taste
1 cup barbecue sauce
¼ cup honey

Preheat the air fryer to 390ºF (199ºC). Grease the air fryer basket with olive oil. Rub the chicken drumsticks with chicken seasoning or rub, salt and ground black pepper on a clean work surface. Arrange the chicken drumsticks in a single layer in the air fryer when your air fryer displays "READY" (select the cooking preset, and make minor adjustments according to your desired doneness.) and choose a shake reminder. Cook at the corresponding preset mode or Air Fry for 18 minutes or until lightly browned. Flip the drumsticks halfway through. You may need to work in batches to avoid overcrowding. Meanwhile, combine the barbecue sauce and honey in a small bowl. Stir to mix well. Remove the drumsticks from the air fryer and baste with the sauce mixture to serve.

## Cranberry Glazed Turkey Fingers

**Prep time: 5 minutes | Cook time: 15 minutes | Serves 4**

1 pound (454 g) turkey breast, cut into strips
1 tablespoon chicken seasoning

Salt and black pepper, to taste
½ cup cranberry sauce

Preheat air fryer to 390ºF (199ºC). Season the turkey with chicken seasoning, salt, and pepper. When your air fryer displays "READY" (select the cooking preset, and make minor adjustments according to your desired doneness.) and choose a shake reminder. Spray with cooking spray and AirFry in the frying basket for 10 to 12 minutes, flipping once halfway through. Put a saucepan over low heat, and add the cranberry sauce and ¼ cup of water. Simmer for 5 minutes, stirring continuously. Serve the turkey drizzled with cranberry sauce. Yummy!

## Cajun Chicken Drumsticks

**Prep time: 5 minutes | Cook time: 40 minutes | Serves 5**

1 tablespoon olive oil
10 chicken drumsticks
1½ tablespoons Cajun

seasoning
Salt and ground black pepper, to taste

Preheat the air fryer to 390ºF (199ºC). Grease the air fryer basket with olive oil. On a clean work surface, rub the chicken drumsticks with Cajun seasoning, salt, and ground black pepper. Arrange the seasoned chicken drumsticks in a single layer in the air fryer. When your air fryer displays "READY" (select the cooking preset, and make minor adjustments according to your desired doneness.) and choose a shake reminder. You need to work in batches to avoid overcrowding. Cook at the corresponding preset mode or Air Fry for 18 minutes or until lightly browned. Flip the drumsticks halfway through. Remove the chicken drumsticks from the air fryer. Serve immediately.

## BBQ Tostadas with Coleslaw

**Prep time: 15 minutes | Cook time: 40 minutes | Makes 4 tostadas**

**Coleslaw:**
¼ cup sour cream
¼ small green cabbage, finely chopped
½ tablespoon white vinegar
**Tostadas:**
2 cups pulled rotisserie chicken
½ cup barbecue sauce
4 corn tortillas

½ teaspoon garlic powder
½ teaspoon salt
¼ teaspoon ground black pepper

½ cup shredded Mozzarella cheese
Cooking spray

Combine the ingredients for the coleslaw in a large bowl. Toss to mix well. Refrigerate until ready to serve. Preheat the air fryer to 370ºF (188ºC). Spritz the air fryer basket with cooking spray. Toss the chicken with barbecue sauce in a separate large bowl to combine well. Set aside. Place one tortilla in the preheated air fryer and spritz with cooking spray. Work in batches to avoid overcrowding. When your air fryer displays "READY" (select the cooking preset, and make minor adjustments according to your desired doneness.) and choose a shake reminder. Air fry the tortilla for 5 minutes or until lightly browned, then spread a quarter of the barbecue chicken and cheese over. Cook at the corresponding preset mode or Air Fry for another 5 minutes or until the cheese melts. Repeat with remaining tortillas, chicken, and cheese. Serve the tostadas with coleslaw on top.

## Turkey and Black Bean Burgers
**Prep time: 15 minutes | Cook time: 21 minutes | Serves 2**

| | |
|---|---|
| 1 cup canned black beans, drained and rinsed | breadcrumbs |
| ¾ pound (340.2 g) lean ground turkey | ½ teaspoon chili powder |
| | ¼ teaspoon cayenne pepper |
| 2 tablespoons minced red onion | Salt, to taste |
| 1 Jalapeño pepper, seeded and minced | Olive or vegetable oil |
| | 2 slices pepper jack cheese |
| 2 tablespoons plain | Toasted burger rolls, sliced tomatoes, lettuce leaves |

**For the Cumin-Avocado Spread:**

| | |
|---|---|
| 1 ripe avocado | 1 tablespoon chopped fresh cilantro |
| Juice of 1 lime | |
| 1 teaspoon ground cumin | Freshly ground black pepper, to taste |
| ½ teaspoon salt | |

Place the black beans in a large bowl and smash them slightly with the back of a fork. Add the ground turkey, red onion, Jalapeño pepper, breadcrumbs, chili powder and cayenne pepper. Season with salt. Mix with your hands to combine all the ingredients and then shape them into 2 patties. Brush both sides of the burger patties with a little olive or vegetable oil. Pre-heat the air fryer to 380ºF (193ºC). Transfer the burgers to the air fryer basket and air-fry for 20 minutes, flipping them over halfway through the cooking process. Top the burgers with the pepper jack cheese (securing the slices to the burgers with a toothpick) for the last 2 minutes of the cooking process. While the burgers are cooking, make the cumin avocado spread. Place the avocado, lime juice, cumin and salt in food processor and process until smooth. (For a chunkier spread, you can mash this by hand in a bowl.) Stir in the cilantro and season with freshly ground black pepper. Chill the spread until you are ready to serve. When the burgers have finished cooking, remove them from the air fryer and let them rest on a plate, covered gently with aluminum foil. Brush a little olive oil on the insides of the burger rolls. Place the rolls, cut side up, into the air fryer basket when your air fryer displays "READY" (select the cooking preset, and make minor adjustments according to your desired doneness.) and choose a shake reminder. Air-fry at 400ºF (204ºC) for 1 minute to toast and warm them. Spread the cumin-avocado spread on the rolls and build your burgers with lettuce and sliced tomatoes and any other ingredient you like. Serve warm with a side of sweet potato fries.

## Parmesan Chicken Wings
**Prep time: 15 minutes | Cook time: 16 to 18 minutes | Serves 4**

| | |
|---|---|
| 1¼ cups grated Parmesan cheese | ¾ cup all-purpose flour |
| | 1 large egg, beaten |
| 1 tablespoon garlic powder | 12 chicken wings (about 1 pound / 454 g) |
| 1 teaspoon salt | |
| ½ teaspoon freshly ground black pepper | Cooking spray |

Preheat the air fryer to 390ºF (199ºC). Line the air fryer basket with parchment paper. In a shallow bowl, whisk the Parmesan cheese, garlic powder, salt, and pepper until blended. Place the flour in a second shallow bowl and the beaten egg in a third shallow bowl. One at a time, dip the chicken wings into the flour, the beaten egg, and the Parmesan cheese mixture, coating thoroughly. Place the chicken wings on the parchment and spritz with cooking spray. When your air fryer displays "READY" (select the cooking preset, and make minor adjustments according to your desired doneness.) and choose a shake reminder. Cook at the corresponding preset mode or Air Fry for 8 minutes. Flip the chicken, spritz it with cooking spray, and cook for 8 to 10 minutes more until the internal temperature reaches 165ºF (74ºC) and the insides are no longer pink. Let sit for 5 minutes before serving.

## Breaded Chicken Breast
**Prep time: 10 minutes | Cook time: 12 minutes | Serves 4**

| | |
|---|---|
| 1 pound (454 g) chicken breasts, boneless and skinless | 1 teaspoon cayenne pepper |
| | 1 teaspoon garlic powder |
| 1 tablespoon butter, room temperature | Kosher salt and ground black pepper, to taste |
| 1 egg, whisked | ½ cup breadcrumbs |

Pat the chicken dry with paper towels. In a bowl, thoroughly combine the butter, egg, cayenne pepper, garlic powder, kosher salt, black pepper. Dip the chicken breasts into the egg mixture. Then, roll the chicken breasts over the breadcrumbs. When your air fryer displays "READY" (select the cooking preset, and make minor adjustments according to your desired doneness.) and choose a shake reminder. Cook the chicken at 380ºF (193ºC) for 12 minutes, turning them over halfway through the cooking time. Bon appétit!

## Chicken Egg Rolls with Blue Cheese
**Prep time: 15 minutes | Cook time: 18 minutes | Makes 8 egg rolls**

| | |
|---|---|
| 1 teaspoon water | ⅓ cup chopped green onion |
| 1 tablespoon cornstarch | ⅓ cup diced celery |
| 1 egg | ⅓ cup buffalo wing sauce |
| 2½ cups cooked chicken, diced or shredded | 8 egg roll wraps |
| | Oil for misting or cooking spray |

**For the Blue Cheese Dip:**

| | |
|---|---|
| 3 ounces (85 g) cream cheese, softened | sauce |
| | ¼ teaspoon garlic powder |
| ⅓ cup blue cheese, crumbled | ¼ cup buttermilk (or sour cream) |
| 1 teaspoon Worcestershire | |

Mix water and cornstarch in a small bowl until dissolved. Add egg, beat well, and set aside. In a medium size bowl, mix together chicken, green onion, celery, and buffalo wing sauce. Divide chicken mixture evenly among 8 egg roll wraps, spooning ½ inch from one edge. Moisten all edges of each wrap with beaten egg wash. Fold the short ends over filling, then roll up tightly and press to seal edges. Brush outside of wraps with egg wash, then spritz with oil or cooking spray. Place 4 egg rolls in air fryer basket. When your air fryer displays "READY" (select the cooking preset, and make minor adjustments according to your desired doneness.) and choose a shake reminder. Cook at 390ºF (199ºC) for 9 minutes or until outside is brown and crispy. While the rolls are cooking, prepare the Blue Cheese Dip. With a fork, mash together cream cheese and blue cheese. Stir in remaining ingredients. Dip should be just thick enough to slightly cling to egg rolls. If too thick, stir in buttermilk or milk 1 tablespoon at a time until you reach the desired consistency. Cook remaining 4 egg rolls as in steps 7 and 8. Serve while hot with blue cheese dip, more buffalo wing sauce, or both.

## Asian Spiced Chicken Drumsticks
**Prep time: 5 minutes | Cook time: 22 minutes | Serves 3**

| | |
|---|---|
| 3 chicken drumsticks | pepper, to taste |
| 2 tablespoons sesame oil | 1 tablespoon soy sauce |
| Kosher salt and ground black | 1 teaspoon Five-spice powder |

Pat the chicken drumsticks dry with paper towels. Toss the chicken drumsticks with the remaining ingredients. When your air fryer displays "READY" (select the cooking preset, and make minor adjustments according to your desired doneness.) and choose a shake reminder. Cook the chicken drumsticks at 370ºF (188ºC) for 22 minutes, turning them over halfway through the cooking time. Bon appétit!

## Easy Chicken Breast

**Prep time: 5 minutes | Cook time: 14 minutes | Serves 2**

2 (8-ounce / 227-g) boneless, skinless chicken breasts
1 sleeve Ritz crackers
4 tablespoons cold unsalted butter, cut into 1-tablespoon slices

Spray the air fryer basket with olive oil, or spray an air fryer–size baking sheet with olive oil or cooking spray. Dip the chicken breasts in water. Put the crackers in a resealable plastic bag. Using a mallet or your hands, crush the crackers. Place the chicken breasts inside the bag one at a time and coat them with the cracker crumbs. Place the chicken in the greased air fryer basket, or on the greased baking sheet set into the air fryer basket. Put 1 to 2 dabs of butter onto each piece of chicken. When your air fryer displays "READY" (select the cooking preset, and make minor adjustments according to your desired doneness.) and choose a shake reminder. Set the temperature to 370ºF (188ºC). Set the timer and bake for 7 minutes. Using tongs, flip the chicken. Spray the chicken generously with olive oil to avoid uncooked breading. Reset the timer and bake for 7 minutes more. Check that the chicken has reached an internal temperature of 165ºF (74ºC). Add cooking time if needed. Using tongs, remove the chicken from the air fryer and serve.

## Asian Duck Breast

**Prep time: 5 minutes | Cook time: 30 minutes | Serves 3**

1 pound (454 g) duck breast
1 tablespoon Hoisin sauce
1 tablespoon Five-spice powder
Sea salt and black pepper, to taste
¼ teaspoon ground cinnamon

Pat the duck breasts dry with paper towels. Toss the duck breast with the remaining ingredients. When your air fryer displays "READY" (select the cooking preset, and make minor adjustments according to your desired doneness.) and choose a shake reminder. Cook the duck breast at 330ºF (166ºC) for 15 minutes, turning them over halfway through the cooking time. Turn the heat to 350ºF (177ºC); continue to cook for about 15 minutes or until cooked through. Let it rest for 10 minutes before carving and serving. Bon appétit!

## Parmesan Potato-Crusted Chicken

**Prep time: 15 minutes | Cook time: 22 to 25 minutes | Serves 4**

¼ cup buttermilk
1 large egg, beaten
1 cup instant potato flakes
¼ cup grated Parmesan cheese
1 teaspoon salt
½ teaspoon freshly ground
black pepper
2 whole boneless, skinless chicken breasts (about 1 pound / 454 g each), halved
Cooking spray

Preheat the air fryer to 325ºF (163ºC). Line the air fryer basket with parchment paper. In a shallow bowl, whisk the buttermilk and egg until blended. In another shallow bowl, stir together the potato flakes, cheese, salt, and pepper. One at a time, dip the chicken pieces in the buttermilk mixture and the potato flake mixture, coating thoroughly. Place the coated chicken on the parchment and spritz with cooking spray. When your air fryer displays "READY" (select the cooking preset, and make minor adjustments according to your desired doneness.) and choose a shake reminder. Cook at the corresponding preset mode or Air Fry for 15 minutes. Flip the chicken, spritz it with cooking spray, and cook for 7 to 10 minutes more until the outside is crispy and the inside is no longer pink. Serve immediately.

## Buttermilk Fried Chicken

**Prep time: 10 minutes | Cook time: 47 minutes | Serves 4**

1 (4-pound / 1.8-kg) chicken, cut into 8 pieces
2 cups buttermilk
Hot sauce (optional)
1½ cups flour
2 teaspoons paprika
1 teaspoon salt
Freshly ground black pepper, to taste
2 eggs, lightly beaten
Vegetable oil, in a spray bottle

Cut the chicken into 8 pieces and submerge them in the buttermilk and hot sauce, if using. A zipper-sealable plastic bag works well for this. Let the chicken soak in the buttermilk for at least one hour or even overnight in the refrigerator. Set up a dredging station. Mix the flour, paprika, salt and black pepper in a clean zipper-sealable plastic bag. Whisk the eggs and place them in a shallow dish. Remove four pieces of chicken from the buttermilk and transfer them to the bag with the flour. Shake them around to coat on all sides. Remove the chicken from the flour, shaking off any excess flour, and dip them into the beaten egg. Return the chicken to the bag of seasoned flour and shake again. Set the coated chicken aside and repeat with the remaining four pieces of chicken. Pre-heat the air fryer to 370ºF (188ºC). Spray the chicken on all sides with the vegetable oil and then transfer one batch to the air fryer basket. When your air fryer displays "READY" (select the cooking preset, and make minor adjustments according to your desired doneness.) and choose a shake reminder. Air-fry the chicken at 370ºF (188ºC) for 20 minutes, flipping the pieces over halfway through the cooking process, taking care not to knock off the breading. Transfer the chicken to a plate, but do not cover. Repeat with the second batch of chicken. Lower the temperature on the air fryer to 340ºF (171ºC). Flip the chicken back over and place the first batch of chicken on top of the second batch already in the basket. Air-fry for another 7 minutes and serve warm.

## Chicken and Ham Meatballs

**Prep time: 10 minutes | Cook time: 15 minutes | Serves 4**

**Meatballs:**
½ pound (227 g) ham, diced
½ pound (227 g) ground chicken
½ cup grated Swiss cheese
1 large egg, beaten
3 cloves garlic, minced
¼ cup chopped onions
1½ teaspoons sea salt
1 teaspoon ground black pepper
Cooking spray

**Dijon Sauce:**
3 tablespoons Dijon mustard
2 tablespoons lemon juice
¼ cup chicken broth, warmed
¾ teaspoon sea salt
¼ teaspoon ground black pepper
Chopped fresh thyme leaves, for garnish

Preheat the air fryer to 390ºF (199ºC). Spritz the air fryer basket with cooking spray. Combine the ingredients for the meatballs in a large bowl. Stir to mix well, then shape the mixture in twelve 1½-inch meatballs. Arrange the meatballs in a single layer in the air fryer basket. When your air fryer displays "READY" (select the cooking preset, and make minor adjustments according to your desired doneness.) and choose a shake reminder. Cook at the corresponding preset mode or Air Fry for 15 minutes or until lightly browned. Flip the balls halfway through. You may need to work in batches to avoid overcrowding. Meanwhile, combine the ingredients, except for the thyme leaves, for the sauce in a small bowl. Stir to mix well. Transfer the cooked meatballs on a large plate, then baste the sauce over. Garnish with thyme leaves and serve.

## Panko-Chicken Drumsticks

**Prep time: 10 minutes | Cook time: 20 minutes | Serves 2**

1 egg
½ cup buttermilk
¾ cup self-rising flour
¾ cup seasoned panko
breadcrumbs

1 teaspoon salt
¼ teaspoon ground black
pepper (to mix into coating)
4 chicken drumsticks, skin on
Oil for misting or cooking spray

Beat together egg and buttermilk in shallow dish. In a second shallow dish, combine the flour, panko crumbs, salt, and pepper. Sprinkle chicken legs with additional salt and pepper to taste. Dip legs in buttermilk mixture, then roll in panko mixture, pressing in crumbs to make coating stick. Mist with oil or cooking spray. Spray air fryer basket with cooking spray. When your air fryer displays "READY" (select the cooking preset, and make minor adjustments according to your desired doneness.) and choose a shake reminder. Cook drumsticks at 360ºF (182ºC) for 10 minutes. Turn pieces over and cook an additional 10 minutes. Turn pieces to check for browning. If you have any white spots that haven't begun to brown, spritz them with oil or cooking spray. Continue cooking for 5 more minutes or until crust is golden brown and juices run clear. Larger, meatier drumsticks will take longer to cook than small ones.

## Salsa Turkey Burgers

**Prep time: 10 minutes | Cook time: 14 to 16 minutes | Serves 4**

⅓ cup finely crushed corn
tortilla chips
1 egg, beaten
¼ cup salsa
⅓ cup shredded pepper Jack
cheese

Pinch salt
Freshly ground black pepper, to
taste
1 pound (454 g) ground turkey
1 tablespoon olive oil
1 teaspoon paprika

Preheat the air fryer to 330ºF (166ºC). In a medium bowl, combine the tortilla chips, egg, salsa, cheese, salt, and pepper, and mix well. Add the turkey and mix gently but thoroughly with clean hands. Form the meat mixture into patties about ½ inch thick. Make an indentation in the center of each patty with your thumb so the burgers don't puff up while cooking. Brush the patties on both sides with the olive oil and sprinkle with paprika. Put in the air fryer basket when your air fryer displays "READY" (select the cooking preset, and make minor adjustments according to your desired doneness.) and choose a shake reminder. Cook at the corresponding preset mode or Air Fry for 14 to 16 minutes or until the meat registers at least 165ºF (74ºC). Let sit for 5 minutes before serving.

## Chinese Chili Chicken Patties

**Prep time: 5 minutes | Cook time: 17 minutes | Serves 4**

1 pound (454 g) chicken,
ground
1 tablespoon olive oil
1 small onion, chopped

1 teaspoon garlic, minced
1 tablespoon chili sauce
Kosher salt and ground black
pepper, to taste

Mix all ingredients until everything is well combined. Form the mixture into four patties. When your air fryer displays "READY" (select the cooking preset, and make minor adjustments according to your desired doneness.) and choose a shake reminder. Cook the patties at 380ºF (193ºC) for about 17 minutes or until cooked through; make sure to turn them over halfway through the cooking time. Bon appétit!

## Turkey and Cranberry Quesadillas

**Prep time: 7 minutes | Cook time: 4 to 8 minutes | Serves 4**

6 low-sodium whole-wheat
tortillas
⅓ cup shredded low-sodium
low-fat Swiss cheese
¾ cup shredded cooked low-
sodium turkey breast

2 tablespoons cranberry sauce
2 tablespoons dried cranberries
½ teaspoon dried basil
Olive oil spray, for spraying the
tortillas

Preheat the air fryer to 400ºF (204ºC). Put 3 tortillas on a work surface. Evenly divide the Swiss cheese, turkey, cranberry sauce, and dried cranberries among the tortillas. Sprinkle with the basil and top with the remaining tortillas. Spray the outsides of the tortillas with olive oil spray. When your air fryer displays "READY" (select the cooking preset, and make minor adjustments according to your desired doneness.) and choose a shake reminder. One at a time, cook the quesadillas at the corresponding preset mode or Air Fry for 4 to 8 minutes, or until crisp and the cheese is melted. Cut into quarters and serve.

## Turkey and HummusWraps

**Prep time: 10 minutes | Cook time: 3 to 4 minutes | Serves 4**

4 large whole wheat wraps
½ cup hummus
16 thin slices deli turkey

8 slices provolone cheese
1 cup fresh baby spinach, or
more to taste

Preheat the air fryer to 360ºF (182ºC). To assemble, place 2 tablespoons of hummus on each wrap and spread to within about a half inch from edges. Top with 4 slices of turkey and 2 slices of provolone. Finish with ¼ cup of baby spinach, or pile on as much as you like. Roll up each wrap. You don't need to fold or seal the ends. Place 2 wraps in air fryer basket, seam-side down. When your air fryer displays "READY" (select the cooking preset, and make minor adjustments according to your desired doneness.) and choose a shake reminder. Cook at the corresponding preset mode or Air Fry for 3 to 4 minutes to warm filling and melt cheese. Repeat step 4 to air fry the remaining wraps. Serve immediately.

## Chicken Breast with Parmesan Cheese

**Prep time: 10 minutes | Cook time: 20 minutes | Serves 4**

1 egg
2 tablespoons lemon juice
2 teaspoons minced garlic
½ teaspoon salt
½ teaspoon freshly ground
black pepper

4 boneless, skinless chicken
breasts, thin cut
Olive oil spray
½ cup whole-wheat bread
crumbs
¼ cup grated Parmesan cheese

In a medium bowl, whisk together the egg, lemon juice, garlic, salt, and pepper. Add the chicken breasts, cover, and refrigerate for up to 1 hour. In a shallow bowl, combine the bread crumbs and Parmesan cheese. Preheat the air fryer to 360ºF (182ºC). Spray the air fryer basket lightly with olive oil spray. Remove the chicken breasts from the egg mixture, then dredge them in the bread crumb mixture, and place in the air fryer basket in a single layer. Lightly spray the chicken breasts with olive oil spray. You may need to cook the chicken in batches. When your air fryer displays "READY" (select the cooking preset, and make minor adjustments according to your desired doneness.) and choose a shake reminder. Cook at the corresponding preset mode or Air Fry for 8 minutes. Flip the chicken over, lightly spray with olive oil spray, and cook until the chicken reaches an internal temperature of 165ºF (74ºC), for an additional 7 to 12 minutes. Serve warm.

## Chicken Breast and Carrot Salad

**Prep time: 5 minutes | Cook time: 12 minutes | Serves 3**

| | |
|---|---|
| 1 pound (454 g) chicken breast | ½ cup mayonnaise |
| 2 tablespoons scallions, chopped | 1 tablespoon mustard |
| 1 carrot, shredded | Sea salt and ground black pepper, to taste |

Pat the chicken dry with kitchen towels. Place the chicken in a lightly oiled cooking basket. When your air fryer displays "READY" (select the cooking preset, and make minor adjustments according to your desired doneness.) and choose a shake reminder. Cook the chicken at 380ºF (193ºC) for 12 minutes, turning them over halfway through the cooking time. Chop the chicken breasts and transfer it to a salad bowl; add in the remaining ingredients and toss to combine well. Bon appétit!

## Fried Chicken with Buttermilk Waffles

**Prep time: 20 minutes | Cook time: 32 minutes | Serves 4**

**For the Fried Chicken:**

| | |
|---|---|
| 4 (2-pound / 907-g) small boneless, skinless chicken breasts | 1 egg |
| | 2 tablespoons buttermilk |
| | Dash hot sauce |
| ½ cup all-purpose flour | 1½ cups panko bread crumbs |
| 1 teaspoon kosher salt | Vegetable oil for spraying |
| ½ teaspoon cayenne pepper | |

**For the Buttermilk Waffles:**

| | |
|---|---|
| 1¾ cups all-purpose flour | 1¾ cups buttermilk |
| 2 teaspoons baking powder | 2 eggs |
| 1 teaspoon granulated sugar | ½ cup unsalted butter, melted and cooled |
| 1 teaspoon baking soda | |
| 1 teaspoon kosher salt | Maple syrup or honey to serve |

To make the chicken, cut each chicken breast in half lengthwise to make 2 long chicken tenders. Whisk together the flour, salt, and cayenne pepper on a large plate. Beat the egg with the buttermilk and hot sauce in a large, shallow bowl. Place the panko in a separate shallow bowl or pie plate. Dredge the chicken tenders in the flour, shaking off any excess, then dip them in the egg mixture. Dredge the chicken tenders in the panko, making sure to coat them completely. Shake off any excess panko. Place the battered chicken tenders on a plate. Preheat the air fryer to 375ºF (190ºC). Spray the basket lightly with oil. Arrange half the chicken tenders in the basket of the air fryer and spray the tops with oil. When your air fryer displays "READY" (select the cooking preset, and make minor adjustments according to your desired doneness.) and choose a shake reminder. Cook at 375ºF (190ºC) until the top side of the tenders is browned and crispy, 8 to 10 minutes. Flip the tenders and spray the second side with oil. Cook until the second side is browned and crispy and the internal temperature reaches 165ºF (74ºC), another 8 to 10 minutes. Remove the first batch of tenders and keep it warm. Cook the second batch in the same manner. While the tenders are cooking, make the waffles. In a large bowl, whisk together the flour, baking powder, sugar, baking soda, and salt. In a separate bowl, whisk together the buttermilk, eggs, and melted butter, reserving a small amount of butter to brush on the waffle iron. Add the wet ingredients to the dry ingredients and stir with a fork until just combined. Allow the batter to rest for at least 5 minutes. Brush the waffle iron with reserved melted butter and preheat according to the manufacturer's instructions. Scoop ⅓ to ½ cup of batter into each grid of the waffle iron and cook according to your waffle iron's instructions. (You should be able to make 8 waffles.) To serve, place 2 chicken tenders on top of 1 or 2 waffles, depending on the person's appetite. Serve with maple syrup or honey and additional hot sauce.

## Chicken Leg Quarters

**Prep time: 8 minutes | Cook time: 27 minutes | Serves 2**

| | |
|---|---|
| 1 tablespoon packed brown sugar | ¼ teaspoon cayenne pepper |
| 1 teaspoon ground allspice | 2 (10-ounce / 284-g) chicken leg quarters, trimmed |
| 1 teaspoon pepper | 1 teaspoon vegetable oil |
| 1 teaspoon garlic powder | 1 scallion, green part only, sliced thin |
| ¾ teaspoon dry mustard | Lime wedges |
| ¾ teaspoon dried thyme | |
| ½ teaspoon salt | |

Preheat the air fryer to 400ºF (204ºC). Combine sugar, allspice, pepper, garlic powder, mustard, thyme, salt, and cayenne in a bowl. Pat chicken dry with paper towels. Using metal skewer, poke 10 to 15 holes in skin of each chicken leg. Rub with oil and sprinkle evenly with spice mixture. Arrange chicken skin-side up in the air fryer basket, spaced evenly apart. When your air fryer displays "READY" (select the cooking preset, and make minor adjustments according to your desired doneness.) and choose a shake reminder. Cook at the corresponding preset mode or Air Fry until chicken is well browned and crisp, 27 to 30 minutes, rotating chicken halfway through cooking (do not flip). Transfer chicken to plate, tent loosely with aluminum foil, and let rest for 5 minutes. Sprinkle with scallion. Serve with lime wedges.

## Crispy Chicken Livers

**Prep time: 10 minutes | Cook time: 20 minutes | Serves 4**

| | |
|---|---|
| 2 eggs | ½ teaspoon ground black pepper |
| 2 tablespoons water | |
| ¾ cup flour | 20 ounces (567 g) chicken livers |
| 2 cups panko breadcrumbs | |
| 1 teaspoon salt | Cooking spray |

Preheat the air fryer to 390ºF (199ºC). Spritz the air fryer basket with cooking spray. Whisk the eggs with water in a large bowl. Pour the flour in a separate bowl. Pour the panko on a shallow dish and sprinkle with salt and pepper. Dredge the chicken livers in the flour. Shake the excess off, then dunk the livers in the whisked eggs, and then roll the livers over the panko to coat well. Arrange the livers in the preheated air fryer and spritz with cooking spray. Work in batches to avoid overcrowding. When your air fryer displays "READY" (select the cooking preset, and make minor adjustments according to your desired doneness.) and choose a shake reminder. Cook at the corresponding preset mode or Air Fry for 10 minutes or until the livers are golden and crispy. Flip the livers halfway through. Repeat with remaining livers. Serve immediately.

## Air-Fried Chicken Skin

**Prep time: 5 minutes | Cook time: 6 minutes | Serves 4**

| | |
|---|---|
| 1 pound (454 g) chicken skin, cut into slices | 1 teaspoon dried dill |
| 1 teaspoon melted butter | Salt and ground black pepper, to taste |
| ½ teaspoon crushed chili flakes | |

Preheat the fryer to 360ºF (182ºC). Combine all the ingredients in a large bowl. Toss to coat the chicken skin well. Transfer the skin in the preheated air fryer. When your air fryer displays "READY" (select the cooking preset, and make minor adjustments according to your desired doneness.) and choose a shake reminder. Cook at the corresponding preset mode or Air Fry for 6 minutes or until the skin is crispy. Shake the basket halfway through. Serve immediately.

## Authentic Chicken Cordon Bleu

**Prep time: 10 minutes | Cook time: 16 minutes | Serves 4**

4 small boneless, skinless chicken breasts
Salt and pepper, to taste
4 slices deli ham
4 (3- to 4-inch square) slices

deli Swiss cheese
2 tablespoons olive oil
2 teaspoons marjoram
¼ teaspoon paprika

Split each chicken breast horizontally almost in two, leaving one edge intact. Lay breasts open flat and sprinkle with salt and pepper to taste. Place a ham slice on top of each chicken breast. Cut cheese slices in half and place one half atop each breast. Set aside remaining halves of cheese slices. Roll up chicken breasts to enclose cheese and ham and secure with toothpicks. Mix together the olive oil, marjoram, and paprika. Rub all over outsides of chicken breasts. Place chicken in air fryer basket when your air fryer displays "READY" (select the cooking preset, and make minor adjustments according to your desired doneness.) and choose a shake reminder. Cook at 360ºF (182ºC) for 15 to 20 minutes, until well done and juices run clear. Remove all toothpicks. To avoid burns, place chicken breasts on a plate to remove toothpicks, then immediately return them to the air fryer basket. Place a half cheese slice on top of each chicken breast and cook for a minute or so just to melt cheese.

## Drumettes with Buffalo Sauce

**Prep time: 10 minutes | Cook time: 20 minutes | Serves 6**

16 chicken drumettes (party wings)
Chicken seasoning or rub, to taste

1 teaspoon garlic powder
Ground black pepper, to taste
¼ cup buffalo wings sauce
Cooking spray

Preheat the air fryer to 400ºF (204ºC). Spritz the air fryer basket with cooking spray. Rub the chicken wings with chicken seasoning, garlic powder, and ground black pepper on a clean work surface. Arrange the chicken wings in the preheated air fryer. Spritz with cooking spray. When your air fryer displays "READY" (select the cooking preset, and make minor adjustments according to your desired doneness.) and choose a shake reminder. Cook at the corresponding preset mode or Air Fry for 10 minutes or until lightly browned. Shake the basket halfway through. Transfer the chicken wings in a large bowl, then pour in the buffalo wings sauce and toss to coat well. Put the wings back to the air fryer and cook for an additional 7 minutes. Serve immediately.

## Chicken Breasts with Vegetable

**Prep time: 20 minutes | Cook time: 25 minutes | Serves 2**

1 cup canned cannellini beans, rinsed
1½ tablespoons red wine vinegar
1 garlic clove, minced
2 tablespoons extra-virgin olive oil, divided
Salt and ground black pepper, to taste
½ red onion, sliced thinly

8 ounces (227 g) asparagus, trimmed and cut into 1-inch lengths
2 (8-ounce / 227-g) boneless, skinless chicken breasts, trimmed
¼ teaspoon paprika
½ teaspoon ground coriander
2 ounces (57 g) baby arugula, rinsed and drained

Preheat the air fryer to 400ºF (204ºC). Warm the beans in microwave for 1 minutes and combine with red wine vinegar, garlic, 1 tablespoon of olive oil, ¼ teaspoon of salt, and ¼ teaspoon of ground black pepper in a bowl. Stir to mix well. Combine the onion with ⅛ teaspoon of salt, ⅛ teaspoon of

ground black pepper, and 2 teaspoons of olive oil in a separate bowl. Toss to coat well. Place the onion in the air fryer and cook at the corresponding preset mode or Air Fry for 2 minutes, then add the asparagus and cook for 8 more minutes or until the asparagus is tender. Shake the basket halfway through. Transfer the onion and asparagus to the bowl with beans. Set aside. Toss the chicken breasts with remaining ingredients, except for the baby arugula, in a large bowl. Put the chicken breasts in the air fryer when your air fryer displays "READY" (select the cooking preset, and make minor adjustments according to your desired doneness.) and choose a shake reminder. Cook at the corresponding preset mode or Air Fry for 14 minutes or until the internal temperature of the chicken reaches at least 165ºF (74ºC). Flip the breasts halfway through. Remove the chicken from the air fryer and serve on an aluminum foil with asparagus, beans, onion, and arugula. Sprinkle with salt and ground black pepper. Toss to serve.

## Chicken Drumsticks with Sweet Rub

**Prep time: 10 minutes | Cook time: 20 minutes | Serves 4**

¼ cup brown sugar
1 tablespoon salt
½ teaspoon freshly ground black pepper
1 teaspoon chili powder
1 teaspoon smoked paprika

1 teaspoon dry mustard
1 teaspoon garlic powder
1 teaspoon onion powder
4 to 6 chicken drumsticks
2 tablespoons olive oil

In a small mixing bowl, combine the brown sugar, salt, pepper, chili powder, paprika, mustard, garlic powder, and onion powder. Using a paper towel, wipe any moisture off the chicken. Put the chicken drumsticks into a large resealable plastic bag, then pour in the dry rub. Seal the bag. Shake the bag to coat the chicken. Place the drumsticks in the air fryer basket. Brush the drumsticks with olive oil. When your air fryer displays "READY" (select the cooking preset, and make minor adjustments according to your desired doneness.) and choose a shake reminder. Set the temperature to 390ºF (199ºC). Set the timer and bake for 10 minutes. Using tongs, flip the drumsticks, and brush them with olive oil. Reset the timer and bake for 10 minutes more. Check that the chicken has reached an internal temperature of 165ºF (74ºC). Add cooking time if needed. Once the chicken is fully cooked, transfer it to a platter and serve.

## Chicken Breast with Pineapple

**Prep time: 10 minutes | Cook time: 11 minutes | Serves 4**

2 boneless, skinless chicken breasts
2 tablespoons cornstarch
1 egg white, lightly beaten
1 tablespoon olive or peanut oil
1 onion, sliced

1 red bell pepper, chopped
1 (8-ounce / 227-g) can pineapple tidbits, drained, juice reserved
2 tablespoons reduced-sodium soy sauce

Cut the chicken breasts into cubes and put into a medium bowl. Add the cornstarch and egg white and mix together thoroughly. Set aside. In a 6-inch metal bowl, combine the oil and the onion. When your air fryer displays "READY" (select the cooking preset, and make minor adjustments according to your desired doneness.) and choose a shake reminder. Cook in the air fryer for 2 to 3 minutes or until the onion is crisp and tender. Drain the chicken and add to the bowl with the onions; stir well. Cook for 7 to 9 minutes or until the chicken is thoroughly cooked to 165ºF (74ºC). Stir the chicken mixture, then add the pepper, pineapple tidbits, 3 tablespoons of the reserved pineapple liquid, and the soy sauce, and stir again. Cook for 2 to 3 minutes or until the food is cooked and the sauce is slightly thickened.

## Chicken Fajita Rolls

**Prep time: 10 minutes | Cook time: 24 minutes | Serves 6 to 8**

½ teaspoon oregano
½ teaspoon cayenne pepper
1 teaspoon cumin
1 teaspoon garlic powder
2 teaspoons paprika
½ sliced red onion
½ yellow bell pepper, sliced into

strips
½ green bell pepper, sliced into strips
½ red bell pepper, sliced into strips
3 chicken breasts

Mix oregano, cayenne pepper, garlic powder, cumin and paprika along with a pinch or two of pepper and salt. Set to the side. Slice chicken breasts lengthwise into 2 slices. Between two pieces of parchment paper, add breast slices and pound till they are ¼-inch thick. With seasoning, liberally season both sides of chicken slices. Put 2 strips of each color of bell pepper and a few onion slices onto chicken pieces. Roll up tightly and secure with toothpicks.

Repeat with remaining ingredients and sprinkle and rub mixture that is left over the chicken rolls. Lightly grease your air fryer basket and place 3 rollups into the fryer. When your air fryer displays "READY" (select the cooking preset, and make minor adjustments according to your desired doneness.) and choose a shake reminder. Cook 12 minutes at 400ºF (204ºC). Repeat with remaining rollups. Serve with salad!

## Chicken and Veggie Hand Pies

**Prep time: 10 minutes | Cook time: 15 minutes | Makes 8 pies**

¾ cup chicken broth
¾ cup frozen mixed peas and carrots
1 cup cooked chicken, chopped
1 tablespoon cornstarch

1 tablespoon milk
Salt and pepper, to taste
1 can organic flaky biscuits
Oil for misting or cooking spray

In a medium saucepan, bring chicken broth to a boil. Stir in the frozen peas and carrots and cook for 5 minutes over medium heat. Stir in chicken. Mix the cornstarch into the milk until it dissolves. Stir it into the simmering chicken broth mixture and cook just until thickened. Remove from heat, add salt and pepper to taste, and let cool slightly. Lay biscuits out on wax paper. Peel each biscuit apart in the middle to make 2 rounds so you have 16 rounds total. Using your hands or a rolling pin, flatten each biscuit round slightly to make it larger and thinner. Divide chicken filling among 8 of the biscuit rounds. Place remaining biscuit rounds on top and press edges all around. Use the tines of a fork to crimp biscuit edges and make sure they are sealed well. Spray both sides lightly with oil or cooking spray. When your air fryer displays "READY" (select the cooking preset, and make minor adjustments according to your desired doneness.) and choose a shake reminder. Cook in a single layer, 4 at a time, at 330ºF (166ºC) for 10 minutes or until biscuit dough is cooked through and golden brown.

## Fiesta Chicken Plate

**Prep time: 15 minutes | Cook time: 15 minutes | Serves 4**

1 pound (454 g) boneless, skinless chicken breasts (2 large breasts)
2 tablespoons lime juice
1 teaspoon cumin
½ teaspoon salt
½ cup grated Pepper Jack cheese
1 (16-ounce / 454-g) can refried

beans
½ cup salsa
2 cups shredded lettuce
1 medium tomato, chopped
2 avocados, peeled and sliced
1 small onion, sliced into thin rings
Sour cream
Tortilla chips (optional)

Split each chicken breast in half lengthwise. Mix lime juice, cumin, and salt together and brush on all surfaces of chicken breasts. Place in air fryer basket when your air fryer displays "READY" (select the cooking preset, and make minor adjustments according to your desired doneness.) and choose a shake reminder. Cook at 390ºF (199ºC) for 12 to 15 minutes, until well done. Divide the cheese evenly over chicken breasts and cook for an additional minute to melt cheese. While chicken is cooking, heat refried beans on stovetop or in microwave. When ready to serve, divide beans among 4 plates. Place chicken breasts on top of beans and spoon salsa over. Arrange the lettuce, tomatoes, and avocados artfully on each plate and scatter with the onion rings. Pass sour cream at the table and serve with tortilla chips if desired.

## Cumin Chicken Tender

**Prep time: 5 minutes | Cook time: 8 minutes | Makes 2½ cups**

1 pound (454 g) chicken tenders, skinless and boneless
½ teaspoon ground cumin

½ teaspoon garlic powder
Cooking spray

Sprinkle raw chicken tenders with seasonings. Spray air fryer basket lightly with cooking spray to prevent sticking. Place chicken in air fryer basket in single layer. When your air fryer displays "READY" (select the cooking preset, and make minor adjustments according to your desired doneness.) and choose a shake reminder. Cook at 390ºF (199ºC) for 4 minutes, turn chicken strips over, and cook for an additional 4 minutes. Test for doneness. Thick tenders may require an additional minute or two.

## Roasted Chicken with Lemon Sage

**Prep time: 5 minutes | Cook time: 1 hour | Serves 4**

1 (4-pound / 1.8-kg) chicken
1 bunch sage, divided
1 lemon, zest and juice

Salt and freshly ground black pepper, to taste

Pre-heat the air fryer to 350ºF (177ºC) and pour a little water into the bottom of the air fryer drawer. (This will help prevent the grease that drips into the bottom drawer from burning and smoking.) Run your fingers between the skin and flesh of the chicken breasts and thighs. Push a couple of sage leaves up underneath the skin of the chicken on each breast and each thigh. Push some of the lemon zest up under the skin of the chicken next to the sage. Sprinkle some of the zest inside the chicken cavity, and reserve any leftover zest. Squeeze the lemon juice all over the chicken and in the cavity as well. Season the chicken, inside and out, with the salt and freshly ground black pepper. Set a few sage leaves aside for the final garnish. Crumple up the remaining sage leaves and push them into the cavity of the chicken, along with one of the squeezed lemon halves. Place the chicken breast side up into the air fryer basket when your air fryer displays "READY" (select the cooking preset, and make minor adjustments according to your desired doneness.) and choose a shake reminder. Air-fry for 20 minutes at 350ºF (177ºC). Flip the chicken over so that it is breast side down and continue to air-fry for another 20 minutes. Return the chicken to breast side up and finish air-frying for 20 more minutes. The internal temperature of the chicken should register 165ºF (74ºC) in the thickest part of the thigh when fully cooked. Remove the chicken from the air fryer and let it rest on a cutting board for at least 5 minutes. Cut the rested chicken into pieces, sprinkle with the reserved lemon zest and garnish with the reserved sage leaves.

## Pecan-Crusted Chicken Tenders

**Prep time: 5 minutes | Cook time: 12 minutes | Serves 4**

1 pound (454 g) chicken tenders
1 teaspoon kosher salt
1 teaspoon black pepper
½ teaspoon smoked paprika
¼ cup coarse mustard
2 tablespoons honey
1 cup finely crushed pecans

Preheat the air fryer to 350ºF (177ºC). Place the chicken in a large bowl. Sprinkle with the salt, pepper, and paprika. Toss until the chicken is coated with the spices. Add the mustard and honey and toss until the chicken is coated. Place the pecans on a plate. Working with one piece of chicken at a time, roll the chicken in the pecans until both sides are coated. Lightly brush off any loose pecans. Place the chicken in the air fryer basket. When your air fryer displays "READY" (select the cooking preset, and make minor adjustments according to your desired doneness.) and choose a shake reminder. Cook at the corresponding preset mode or Air Fry for 12 minutes, or until the chicken is cooked through and the pecans are golden brown. Serve warm.

## Balsamic Chicken Breast

**Prep time: 10 minutes | Cook time: 20 minutes | Serves 4**

¼ cup balsamic vinegar
¼ cup honey
2 tablespoons olive oil
1 tablespoon dried rosemary leaves
1 teaspoon salt
½ teaspoon freshly ground black pepper
2 whole boneless, skinless chicken breasts (about 1 pound / 454 g each), halved
Cooking spray

In a large resealable bag, combine the vinegar, honey, olive oil, rosemary, salt, and pepper. Add the chicken pieces, seal the bag, and refrigerate to marinate for at least 2 hours. Preheat the air fryer to 325ºF (163ºC). Line the air fryer basket with parchment paper. Remove the chicken from the marinade and place it on the parchment. Spritz with cooking spray. When your air fryer displays "READY" (select the cooking preset, and make minor adjustments according to your desired doneness.) and choose a shake reminder. Cook at the corresponding preset mode or Air Fry for 10 minutes. Flip the chicken, spritz it with cooking spray, and cook for 10 minutes more until the internal temperature reaches 165ºF (74ºC) and the chicken is no longer pink inside. Let sit for 5 minutes before serving.

## Glazed Cornish Hens

**Prep time: 5 minutes | Cook time: 25 minutes | Serves 2 to 3**

1 (1½- to 2-pound / 680- to 907-g) Cornish game hen
1 tablespoon honey
1 tablespoon lime juice
1 teaspoon poultry seasoning
Salt and pepper, to taste
Cooking spray

To split the hen into halves, cut through breast bone and down one side of the backbone. Mix the honey, lime juice, and poultry seasoning together and brush or rub onto all sides of the hen. Season to taste with salt and pepper. Spray air fryer basket with cooking spray and place hen halves in the basket, skin-side down. When your air fryer displays "READY" (select the cooking preset, and make minor adjustments according to your desired doneness.) and choose a shake reminder. Cook at 330ºF (166ºC) for 25 to 30 minutes. Hen will be done when juices run clear when pierced at leg joint with a fork. Let hen rest for 5 to 10 minutes.

## Turkey Breasts with Italian Herb

**Prep time: 5 minutes | Cook time: 1 hour | Serves 4**

1 tablespoon butter, room temperature
Kosher salt and ground black pepper, to taste
1 teaspoon cayenne pepper
1 teaspoon Italian herb mix
1 pound (454 g) turkey breast, bone-in

In a mixing bowl, thoroughly combine the butter, salt, black pepper, cayenne pepper, and herb mix. Rub the mixture all over the turkey breast. When your air fryer displays "READY" (select the cooking preset, and make minor adjustments according to your desired doneness.) and choose a shake reminder. Cook the turkey breast at 350ºF (177ºC) for 1 hour, turning them over every 20 minutes. Bon appétit!

## Bacon-Wrapped Chicken Rolls

**Prep time: 10 minutes | Cook time: 15 minutes | Serves 4**

¼ cup chopped fresh chives
2 tablespoons lemon juice
1 teaspoon dried sage
1 teaspoon fresh rosemary leaves
½ cup fresh parsley leaves
4 cloves garlic, peeled
1 teaspoon ground fennel
3 teaspoons sea salt
½ teaspoon red pepper flakes
4 (4-ounce / 113-g) boneless, skinless chicken breasts, pounded to ¼ inch thick
8 slices bacon
Sprigs of fresh rosemary, for garnish
Cooking spray

Preheat the air fryer to 340ºF (171ºC). Spritz the air fryer basket with cooking spray. Put the chives, lemon juice, sage, rosemary, parsley, garlic, fennel, salt, and red pepper flakes in a food processor, then pulse to purée until smooth. Unfold the chicken breasts on a clean work surface, then brush the top side of the chicken breasts with the sauce. Roll the chicken breasts up from the shorter side, then wrap each chicken rolls with 2 bacon slices to cover. Secure with toothpicks. Arrange the rolls in the preheated air fryer when your air fryer displays "READY" (select the cooking preset, and make minor adjustments according to your desired doneness.) and choose a shake reminder. Cook for 10 minutes. Flip the rolls halfway through. Increase the heat to 390ºF (199ºC) and cook at the corresponding preset mode or Air Fry for 5 more minutes or until the bacon is browned and crispy. Transfer the rolls to a large plate. Discard the toothpicks and spread with rosemary sprigs before serving.

## Marinaded Chicken Tenders

**Prep time: 10 minutes | Cook time: 12 minutes | Serves 4**

1 pound (454 g) chicken tenders
**For the Marinade:**
¼ cup olive oil
2 tablespoons water
2 tablespoons honey
2 tablespoons white vinegar
½ teaspoon salt
½ teaspoon crushed red pepper
1 teaspoon garlic powder
1 teaspoon onion powder
½ teaspoon paprika

Combine all marinade ingredients and mix well. Add chicken and stir to coat. Cover tightly and let marinate in refrigerator for 30 minutes. Remove tenders from marinade and place them in a single layer in the air fryer basket. When your air fryer displays "READY" (select the cooking preset, and make minor adjustments according to your desired doneness.) and choose a shake reminder. Cook at 390ºF (199ºC) for 3 minutes. Turn tenders over and cook for 3 to 5 minutes longer or until chicken is done and juices run clear. Repeat step 4 to cook remaining tenders.

## Chicken with Nashville Hot Sauce

**Prep time: 15 minutes | Cook time: 47 minutes | Serves 4**

1 (4-pound / 1.8-kg) chicken, cut into 6 pieces (2 breasts, 2 thighs and 2 drumsticks)
2 eggs
1 cup buttermilk
2 cups all-purpose flour
2 tablespoons paprika
1 teaspoon garlic powder
1 teaspoon onion powder
2 teaspoons salt
1 teaspoon freshly ground black pepper
Vegetable oil, in a spray bottle
**For the Nashville Hot Sauce:**
1 tablespoon cayenne pepper
1 teaspoon salt
¼ cup vegetable oil
4 slices white bread
Dill pickle slices

Cut the chicken breasts into 2 pieces so that you have a total of 8 pieces of chicken. Set up a two-stage dredging station. Whisk the eggs and buttermilk together in a bowl. Combine the flour, paprika, garlic powder, onion powder, salt and black pepper in a zipper-sealable plastic bag. Dip the chicken pieces into the egg-buttermilk mixture, then toss them in the seasoned flour, coating all sides. Repeat this procedure (egg mixture and then flour mixture) one more time. This can be a little messy, but make sure all sides of the chicken are completely covered. Spray the chicken with vegetable oil and set aside. Pre-heat the air fryer to 370ºF (188ºC). Spray or brush the bottom of the air-fryer basket with a little vegetable oil. When your air fryer displays "READY" (select the cooking preset, and make minor adjustments according to your desired doneness.) and choose a shake reminder. Air-fry the chicken in two batches at 370ºF (188ºC) for 20 minutes, flipping the pieces over halfway through the cooking process. Transfer the chicken to a plate, but do not cover. Repeat with the second batch of chicken. Lower the temperature on the air fryer to 340ºF (171ºC). Flip the chicken back over and place the first batch of chicken on top of the second batch already in the basket. Air-fry for another 7 minutes. While the chicken is air-frying, combine the cayenne pepper and salt in a bowl. Heat the vegetable oil in a small saucepan and when it is very hot, add it to the spice mix, whisking until smooth. It will sizzle briefly when you add it to the spices. Place the fried chicken on top of the white bread slices and brush the hot sauce all over chicken. Top with the pickle slices and serve warm. Enjoy the heat and the flavor!

## Chicken Drumsticks with Dijon Glaze

**Prep time: 15 minutes | Cook time: 30 minutes | Makes 6 drumsticks**

**For the Glaze:**
½ cup apricot preserves
½ teaspoon tamari
**For the Chicken:**
6 chicken drumsticks
½ teaspoon seasoning salt
1 teaspoon salt
¼ teaspoon chili powder
2 teaspoons Dijon mustard

½ teaspoon ground black pepper
Cooking spray

Combine the ingredients for the glaze in a saucepan, then heat over low heat for 10 minutes or until thickened. Turn off the heat and sit until ready to use. Preheat the air fryer to 370ºF (188ºC). Spritz the air fryer basket with cooking spray. Combine the seasoning salt, salt, and pepper in a small bowl. Stir to mix well. Place the chicken drumsticks in the preheated air fryer. Spritz with cooking spray and sprinkle with the salt mixture on both sides. When your air fryer displays "READY" (select the cooking preset, and make minor adjustments according to your desired doneness.) and choose a shake reminder. Cook at the corresponding preset mode or Air Fry for 20 minutes or until well browned. Flip the chicken halfway through. Baste the chicken with the glaze and air fryer for 2 more minutes or until the chicken tenderloin is glossy. Serve immediately.

## Pepperoni and Chicken Cheese Pizza

**Prep time: 15 minutes | Cook time: 15 minutes | Serves 6**

2 cups cooked chicken, cubed
1 cup pizza sauce
20 slices pepperoni
¼ cup grated Parmesan cheese
1 cup shredded Mozzarella cheese
Cooking spray

Preheat the air fryer to 375ºF (191ºC). Spritz a baking pan with cooking spray. Arrange the chicken cubes in the prepared baking pan, then top the cubes with pizza sauce and pepperoni. Stir to coat the cubes and pepperoni with sauce. Scatter the cheeses on top, then place the baking pan in the preheated air fryer. When your air fryer displays "READY" (select the cooking preset, and make minor adjustments according to your desired doneness.) and choose a shake reminder. Cook at the corresponding preset mode or Air Fry for 15 minutes or until frothy and the cheeses melt. Serve immediately.

## Montreal Chicken Seasoned Cornish Hen

**Prep time: 5 minutes | Cook time: 30 minutes | Serves 2**

2 tablespoons Montreal chicken seasoning
1 (1½- to 2-pound / 680- to 907-g) Cornish hen

Preheat the air fryer to 390ºF (199ºC). Rub the seasoning over the chicken, coating it thoroughly. Place the chicken in the air fryer basket. When your air fryer displays "READY" (select the cooking preset, and make minor adjustments according to your desired doneness.) and choose a shake reminder. Set the timer and roast for 15 minutes. Flip the chicken and cook for another 15 minutes. Check that the chicken has reached an internal temperature of 165ºF (74ºC). Add cooking time if needed.

## Spiced Chicken Thight

**Prep time: 10 minutes | Cook time: 15 minutes | Serves 4**

1 pound (454 g) boneless, skinless chicken thighs, cut crosswise into thirds
1 yellow onion, cut into 1½-inch-thick slices
1 tablespoon coconut oil, melted
2 teaspoons minced fresh ginger
2 teaspoons minced garlic
1 teaspoon smoked paprika
1 teaspoon ground fennel
1 teaspoon garam masala
1 teaspoon ground turmeric
1 teaspoon kosher salt
½ to 1 teaspoon cayenne pepper
Vegetable oil spray
2 teaspoons fresh lemon juice
¼ cup chopped fresh cilantro or parsley

Use a fork to pierce the chicken all over to allow the marinade to penetrate better. In a large bowl, combine the onion, coconut oil, ginger, garlic, paprika, fennel, garam masala, turmeric, salt, and cayenne. Add the chicken, toss to combine, and marinate at room temperature for 30 minutes, or cover and refrigerate for up to 24 hours. Preheat the air fryer to 350ºF (177ºC). Place the chicken and onion in the air fryer basket. (Discard remaining marinade.) Spray with some vegetable oil spray. When your air fryer displays "READY" (select the cooking preset, and make minor adjustments according to your desired doneness.) and choose a shake reminder. Cook at the corresponding preset mode or Air Fry for 15 minutes. Halfway through the cooking time, remove the basket, spray the chicken and onion with more vegetable oil spray, and toss gently to coat. At the end of the cooking time, use a meat thermometer to ensure the chicken has reached an internal temperature of 165ºF (74ºC). Transfer the chicken and onion to a serving platter. Sprinkle with the lemon juice and cilantro and serve.

## Chicken Rochambeau
**Prep time: 25 minutes | Cook time: 30 minutes | Serves 4**

1 tablespoon butter
¼ cup all-purpose flour
4 chicken tenders, cut in half crosswise
4 slices ham, ¼-inch thick, large enough to cover an English
**Mushroom Sauce:**
2 tablespoons butter
½ cup chopped mushrooms
½ cup chopped green onions
2 tablespoons flour

muffin
2 English muffins, split in halves
Salt and ground black pepper, to taste
Cooking spray

1 cup chicken broth
1½ teaspoons Worcestershire sauce
¼ teaspoon garlic powder

Preheat the air fryer to 390ºF (199ºC). Put the butter in a baking pan and heat in the preheated air fryer for 2 minutes until melted. Combine the flour, salt, and ground black pepper in a shallow dish. Roll the chicken tenders over to coat well. Arrange the chicken in the baking pan and flip to coat with the melted butter. Broil in the air fryer for 10 minutes or until the juices just run clear. Flip the tenders halfway through. Meanwhile, make the mushroom sauce: melt 2 tablespoons of butter in a saucepan over medium-high heat. Add the mushrooms and onions to the saucepan and sauté for 3 minutes or until the onions are translucent. Gently mix in the flour, broth, Worcestershire sauce, and garlic powder until smooth. Reduce the heat to low and simmer for 5 minutes or until it has a thick consistency. Set the sauce aside until ready to serve. When the broiling of the chicken is complete, remove the baking pan from the air fryer and set the ham slices into the air fryer basket. When your air fryer displays "READY" (select the cooking preset, and make minor adjustments according to your desired doneness.) and choose a shake reminder. Cook at the corresponding preset mode or Air Fry for 5 minutes or until heated through, then remove from the air fryer and set in the English muffin halves and warm for 1 minute. Arrange each ham slice on top of each muffin half, then place each chicken tender over the ham slice. Cook for 2 more minutes to heat through. Serve with the sauce on top.

## Tempero Baiano Brazilian Chicken
**Prep time: 5 minutes | Cook time: 20 minutes | Serves 4**

1 teaspoon cumin seeds
1 teaspoon dried oregano
1 teaspoon dried parsley
1 teaspoon ground turmeric
½ teaspoon coriander seeds
1 teaspoon kosher salt

½ teaspoon black peppercorns
½ teaspoon cayenne pepper
¼ cup fresh lime juice
2 tablespoons olive oil
1½ pounds (680 g) chicken drumsticks

In a clean coffee grinder or spice mill, combine the cumin, oregano, parsley, turmeric, coriander seeds, salt, peppercorns, and cayenne. Process until finely ground. In a small bowl, combine the ground spices with the lime juice and oil. Place the chicken in a resealable plastic bag. Add the marinade, seal, and massage until the chicken is well coated. Marinate at room temperature for 30 minutes or in the refrigerator for up to 24 hours. Preheat the air fryer to 400ºF (204ºC). Place the drumsticks skin-side up in the air fryer basket when your air fryer displays "READY" (select the cooking preset, and make minor adjustments according to your desired doneness.) and choose a shake reminder. Cook at the corresponding preset mode or Air Fry for 20 to 25 minutes, turning the drumsticks halfway through the cooking time. Use a meat thermometer to ensure that the chicken has reached an internal temperature of 165ºF (74ºC). Serve immediately.

## Turkish Chicken Thighs Kebabs
**Prep time: 15 minutes | Cook time: 15 minutes | Serves 4**

¼ cup plain Greek yogurt
1 tablespoon minced garlic
1 tablespoon tomato paste
1 tablespoon fresh lemon juice
1 tablespoon vegetable oil
1 teaspoon kosher salt
1 teaspoon ground cumin
1 teaspoon sweet Hungarian

paprika
½ teaspoon ground cinnamon
½ teaspoon black pepper
½ teaspoon cayenne pepper
1 pound (454 g) boneless, skinless chicken thighs, quartered crosswise

In a large bowl, combine the yogurt, garlic, tomato paste, lemon juice, vegetable oil, salt, cumin, paprika, cinnamon, black pepper, and cayenne. Stir until the spices are blended into the yogurt. Add the chicken to the bowl and toss until well coated. Marinate at room temperature for 30 minutes, or cover and refrigerate for up to 24 hours. Preheat the air fryer to 375ºF (191ºC). Arrange the chicken in a single layer in the air fryer basket. When your air fryer displays "READY" (select the cooking preset, and make minor adjustments according to your desired doneness.) and choose a shake reminder. Cook at the corresponding preset mode or Air Fry for 10 minutes. Turn the chicken and cook for 5 minutes more. Use a meat thermometer to ensure the chicken has reached an internal temperature of 165ºF (74ºC). Serve warm.

## Lush Chicken with Coconut Rice
**Prep time: 15 minutes | Cook time: 1¼ hours | Serves 4**

1 (14-ounce / 397-g) can coconut milk
2 tablespoons green or red curry paste
Zest and juice of one lime
1 clove garlic, minced
1 tablespoon grated fresh ginger
**For the Rice:**
1 cup basmati or jasmine rice
1 cup water
1 cup coconut milk

1 teaspoon ground cumin
1 (3- to 4-pound / 1.4- to 1.8-kg) chicken, cut into 8 pieces
Vegetable or olive oil
Salt and freshly ground black pepper, to taste
Fresh cilantro leaves

½ teaspoon salt
Freshly ground black pepper, to taste

Make the marinade by combining the coconut milk, curry paste, lime zest and juice, garlic, ginger and cumin. Coat the chicken on all sides with the marinade and marinate the chicken for 1 hour to overnight in the refrigerator. Pre-heat the air fryer to 380ºF (193ºC). Brush the bottom of the air fryer basket with oil. Transfer the chicken thighs and drumsticks from the marinade to the air fryer basket, letting most of the marinade drip off. Season to taste with salt and freshly ground black pepper. When your air fryer displays "READY" (select the cooking preset, and make minor adjustments according to your desired doneness.) and choose a shake reminder. Air-fry the chicken drumsticks and thighs at 380ºF (193ºC) for 12 minutes. Flip the chicken over and continue to air-fry for another 12 minutes. Set aside and air-fry the chicken breast pieces at 380ºF (193ºC) for 15 minutes. Turn the chicken breast pieces over and air-fry for another 12 minutes. Return the chicken thighs and drumsticks to the air fryer and air-fry for an additional 5 minutes. While the chicken is cooking, make the coconut rice. Rinse the rice kernels with water and drain well. Place the rice in a medium saucepan with a tight fitting lid, along with the water, coconut milk, salt and freshly ground black pepper. Bring the mixture to a boil and then cover, reduce the heat and let it cook gently for 20 minutes without lifting the lid. When the time is up, lift the lid, fluff with a fork and set aside. Remove the chicken from the air fryer and serve warm with the coconut rice and fresh cilantro scattered around.

## Hawaiian Chicken Bites with Pineapple

**Prep time: 1 hour 15 minutes | Cook time: 15 minutes | Serves 4**

½ cup pineapple juice
2 tablespoons apple cider vinegar
½ tablespoon minced ginger
½ cup ketchup
2 garlic cloves, minced

½ cup brown sugar
2 tablespoons sherry
½ cup soy sauce
4 chicken breasts, cubed
Cooking spray

Combine the pineapple juice, cider vinegar, ginger, ketchup, garlic, and sugar in a saucepan. Stir to mix well. Heat over low heat for 5 minutes or until thickened. Fold in the sherry and soy sauce. Dunk the chicken cubes in the mixture. Press to submerge. Wrap the bowl in plastic and refrigerate to marinate for at least an hour. Preheat the air fryer to 360ºF (182ºC). Spritz the air fryer basket with cooking spray. Remove the chicken cubes from the marinade. Shake the excess off and put in the preheated air fryer. Spritz with cooking spray. When your air fryer displays "READY" (select the cooking preset, and make minor adjustments according to your desired doneness.) and choose a shake reminder. Cook at the corresponding preset mode or Air Fry for 15 minutes or until the chicken cubes are glazed and well browned. Shake the basket at least three times during the frying. Serve immediately.

## Light Breaded Chicken Breasts

**Prep time: 5 minutes | Cook time: 14 minutes | Serves 2**

2 large eggs
1 cup bread crumbs or panko bread crumbs
1 teaspoon Italian seasoning

4 to 5 tablespoons vegetable oil
2 (8-ounce / 227-g) boneless, skinless chicken breasts

Preheat the air fryer to 370ºF (188ºC). Spray the air fryer basket (or an air fryer–size baking sheet) with olive oil or cooking spray. In a small mixing bowl, beat the eggs until frothy. In a separate small mixing bowl, mix together the bread crumbs, Italian seasoning, and oil. Dip the chicken in the egg mixture, then in the bread crumb mixture. Place the chicken directly into the greased air fryer basket, or on the greased baking sheet set into the basket. Spray the chicken generously and thoroughly with olive oil to avoid powdery, uncooked breading. When your air fryer displays "READY" (select the cooking preset, and make minor adjustments according to your desired doneness.) and choose a shake reminder. Set the timer and fry for 7 minutes. Using tongs, flip the chicken and generously spray it with olive oil. Reset the timer and fry for 7 minutes more. Check that the chicken has reached an internal temperature of 165ºF (74ºC). Add cooking time if needed. Once the chicken is fully cooked, use tongs to remove it from the air fryer and serve.

## Coconut Chicken with Apricot-Ginger Sauce

**Prep time: 15 minutes | Cook time: 14 minutes | Serves 4**

1½ pounds (680 g) boneless, skinless chicken tenders, cut in large chunks (1¼ inches)
Salt and pepper, to taste
½ cup cornstarch
**For the Apricot-Ginger Sauce:**
½ cup apricot preserves
2 tablespoons white vinegar
¼ teaspoon ground ginger
¼ teaspoon low-sodium soy

2 eggs
1 tablespoon milk
3 cups shredded coconut
Oil for misting or cooking spray

sauce
2 teaspoons white or yellow onion, grated or finely minced

Mix all ingredients for the Apricot-Ginger Sauce well and let sit for flavors to blend while you cook the chicken. Season chicken chunks with salt and pepper to taste. Place cornstarch in a shallow dish. In another shallow dish, beat together eggs and milk. Place coconut in a third shallow dish. (If also using panko breadcrumbs, as suggested below, stir them to mix well.) Spray air fryer basket with oil or cooking spray. Dip each chicken chunk into cornstarch, shake off excess, and dip in egg mixture. Shake off excess egg mixture and roll lightly in coconut or coconut mixture. Spray with oil. Place coated chicken chunks in air fryer basket in a single layer, close together but without sides touching. When your air fryer displays "READY" (select the cooking preset, and make minor adjustments according to your desired doneness.) and choose a shake reminder. Cook at 360ºF (182ºC) for 4 minutes, stop, and turn chunks over. Cook an additional 3 to 4 minutes or until chicken is done inside and coating is crispy brown. Repeat steps 9 through 11 to cook remaining chicken chunks.

## Greek Chicken Breast Salad

**Prep time: 10 minutes | Cook time: 12 minutes | Serves 4**

1 pound (454 g) chicken breasts, boneless, skinless
1 red onion, thinly sliced
1 bell pepper, sliced
4 Kalamata olives, pitted and minced
1 small Greek cucumber, grated

and squeezed
4 tablespoons Greek yogurt
4 tablespoons mayonnaise
1 tablespoon fresh lemon juice
Coarse sea salt and red pepper flakes, to taste

Pat the chicken dry with paper towels. Place the chicken breasts in a lightly oiled Air Fryer basket. When your air fryer displays "READY" (select the cooking preset, and make minor adjustments according to your desired doneness.) and choose a shake reminder. Cook the chicken at 380ºF (193ºC) for 12 minutes, turning them over halfway through the cooking time. Chop the chicken breasts and transfer it to a salad bowl; add in the remaining ingredients and toss to combine well. Serve well-chilled and enjoy!

## Chicken Schnitzel

**Prep time: 15 minutes | Cook time: 5 minutes | Serves 4**

½ cup all-purpose flour
1 teaspoon marjoram
½ teaspoon thyme
1 teaspoon dried parsley flakes
½ teaspoon salt
1 egg

1 teaspoon lemon juice
1 teaspoon water
1 cup breadcrumbs
4 chicken tenders, pounded thin, cut in half lengthwise
Cooking spray

Preheat the air fryer to 390ºF (199ºC) and spritz with cooking spray. Combine the flour, marjoram, thyme, parsley, and salt in a shallow dish. Stir to mix well. Whisk the egg with lemon juice and water in a large bowl. Pour the breadcrumbs in a separate shallow dish. Roll the chicken halves in the flour mixture first, then in the egg mixture, and then roll over the breadcrumbs to coat well. Shake the excess off. Arrange the chicken halves in the preheated air fryer and spritz with cooking spray on both sides. When your air fryer displays "READY" (select the cooking preset, and make minor adjustments according to your desired doneness.) and choose a shake reminder. Cook at the corresponding preset mode or Air Fry for 5 minutes or until the chicken halves are golden brown and crispy. Flip the halves halfway through. Serve immediately.

## Chicken Wings with Gochujang Sauce

**Prep time: 15 minutes | Cook time: 25 minutes | Serves 4**

**For the Wings:**

2 pounds (907 g) chicken wings
1 teaspoon kosher salt

1 teaspoon black pepper or gochugaru (Korean red pepper)

**For the Sauce:**

2 tablespoons gochujang (Korean chile paste)
1 tablespoon mayonnaise
1 tablespoon toasted sesame oil
1 tablespoon minced fresh

ginger
1 tablespoon minced garlic
1 teaspoon sugar
1 teaspoon agave nectar or honey

**For Serving:**

1 teaspoon sesame seeds

¼ cup chopped scallions

Season the wings with the salt and pepper and place in the air-fryer basket. When your air fryer displays "READY" (select the cooking preset, and make minor adjustments according to your desired doneness.) and choose a shake reminder. Set the air fryer to 400ºF (204ºC) for 20 minutes, turning the wings halfway through the cooking time. In a small bowl, combine the gochujang, mayonnaise, sesame oil, ginger, garlic, sugar, and agave; set aside. As you near the 20-minute mark, use a meat thermometer to check the meat. When the wings reach 160ºF (71ºC), transfer them to a large bowl. Pour about half the sauce on the wings; toss to coat (serve the remaining sauce as a dip). Return the wings to the air-fryer basket and cook for 5 minutes, until the sauce has glazed. Transfer the wings to a serving platter. Sprinkle with the sesame seeds and scallions. Serve with the reserved sauce on the side for dipping.

## Lemon Chicken Breast

**Prep time: 10 minutes | Cook time: 16 to 19 minutes | Serves 4**

4 (5-ounce / 142-g) low-sodium boneless, skinless chicken breasts, cut into 4-by-½-inch strips
2 teaspoons olive oil
2 tablespoons cornstarch
3 garlic cloves, minced

½ cup low-sodium chicken broth
¼ cup freshly squeezed lemon juice
1 tablespoon honey
½ teaspoon dried thyme
Brown rice, cooked (optional)

Preheat the air fryer to 400ºF (204ºC). In a large bowl, mix the chicken and olive oil. Sprinkle with the cornstarch. Toss to coat. Add the garlic and transfer to a metal pan. Bake in the air fryer for 10 minutes, stirring once during cooking. Add the chicken broth, lemon juice, honey, and thyme to the chicken mixture. When your air fryer displays "READY" (select the cooking preset, and make minor adjustments according to your desired doneness.) and choose a shake reminder. Cook at the corresponding preset mode or Air Fry for 6 to 9 minutes more, or until the sauce is slightly thickened and the chicken reaches an internal temperature of 165ºF (74ºC) on a meat thermometer. Serve over hot cooked brown rice, if desired.

## Honey-Glazed Chicken Breasts

**Prep time: 5 minutes | Cook time: 20 minutes | Serves 4**

4 (4-ounce / 113-g) boneless, skinless chicken breasts
Chicken seasoning or rub, to taste
Salt and ground black pepper, to taste

¼ cup honey
2 tablespoons soy sauce
2 teaspoons grated fresh ginger
2 garlic cloves, minced
Cooking spray

Preheat the air fryer to 400ºF (204ºC). Spritz the air fryer basket with cooking spray. Rub the chicken breasts with chicken seasoning, salt, and black pepper on a clean work surface. Arrange the chicken breasts in a single layer in the air fryer and spritz with another layer of cooking spray. You may need to work in batches to avoid overcrowding. When your air fryer displays "READY" (select the cooking preset, and make minor adjustments according to your desired doneness.) and choose a shake reminder. Cook at the corresponding preset mode or Air Fry for 10 minutes or until the internal temperature of the chicken reaches at least 165ºF (74ºC). Flip the chicken breasts halfway through. Meanwhile, combine the honey, soy sauce, ginger, and garlic in a saucepan and heat over medium-high heat for 3 minutes or until thickened. Stir constantly. Remove the chicken from the air fryer and serve with the honey glaze.

## Chicken Souvlaki

**Prep time: 10 minutes | Cook time: 15 minutes | Serves 3 or 4**

**For the Chicken:**

Grated zest and juice of 1 lemon
2 tablespoons extra-virgin olive oil
1 tablespoon Greek souvlaki

seasoning
1 pound (454 g) boneless, skinless chicken breast, cut into 2-inch chunks
Vegetable oil spray

**For Serving:**

Warm pita bread or hot cooked rice
Sliced ripe tomatoes
Sliced cucumbers

Thinly sliced red onion
Kalamata olives
Tzatziki

In a small bowl, combine the lemon zest, lemon juice, olive oil, and souvlaki seasoning. Place the chicken in a gallon-size resealable plastic bag. Pour the marinade over chicken. Seal bag and massage to coat. Place the bag in a large bowl and marinate for 30 minutes, or cover and refrigerate up to 24 hours, turning the bag occasionally. Place the chicken a single layer in the air-fryer basket. When your air fryer displays "READY" (select the cooking preset, and make minor adjustments according to your desired doneness.) and choose a shake reminder. Set the air fryer to 350ºF (177ºC) for 10 minutes, turning the chicken and spraying with a little vegetable oil spray halfway through the cooking time. Increase the air-fryer temperature to 400ºF (204ºC) for 5 minutes to allow the chicken to crisp and brown a little. Transfer the chicken to a serving platter and serve with pita bread or rice, tomatoes, cucumbers, onion, olives and tzatziki.

## Mayo-Mustard Baked Chicken Tenders

**Prep time: 10 minutes | Cook time: 15 minutes | Serves 4**

6 tablespoons mayonnaise
2 tablespoons coarse-ground mustard
2 teaspoons honey (optional)
2 teaspoons curry powder

1 teaspoon kosher salt
1 teaspoon cayenne pepper
1 pound (454 g) chicken tenders

Preheat the air fryer to 350ºF (177ºC). In a large bowl, whisk together the mayonnaise, mustard, honey (if using), curry powder, salt, and cayenne. Transfer half of the mixture to a serving bowl to serve as a dipping sauce. Add the chicken tenders to the large bowl and toss until well coated. Place the tenders in the air fryer basket when your air fryer displays "READY" (select the cooking preset, and make minor adjustments according to your desired doneness.) and choose a shake reminder. Cook at the corresponding preset mode or Air Fry for 15 minutes. Use a meat thermometer to ensure the chicken has reached an internal temperature of 165ºF (74ºC). Serve the chicken with the dipping sauce.

## Turkey Meatballs

**Prep time: 15 minutes | Cook time: 15 minutes | Serves 6**

1 pound (454 g) lean ground turkey
½ cup whole-wheat panko bread crumbs
1 egg, beaten
1 tablespoon soy sauce
¼ cup plus 1 tablespoon hoisin

sauce, divided
2 teaspoons minced garlic
⅛ teaspoon salt
⅛ teaspoon freshly ground black pepper
1 teaspoon sriracha
Olive oil spray

Preheat the air fryer to 350°F (177°C). Spray the air fryer basket lightly with olive oil spray. In a large bowl, mix together the turkey, panko bread crumbs, egg, soy sauce, 1 tablespoon of hoisin sauce, garlic, salt, and black pepper. Using a tablespoon, form the mixture into 24 meatballs. In a small bowl, combine the remaining ¼ cup of hoisin sauce and sriracha to make a glaze and set aside. Place the meatballs in the air fryer basket in a single layer. When your air fryer displays "READY" (select the cooking preset, and make minor adjustments according to your desired doneness.) and choose a shake reminder. You may need to cook them in batches. Cook at the corresponding preset mode or Air Fry for 8 minutes. Brush the meatballs generously with the glaze and cook until cooked through, an additional 4 to 7 minutes. Serve warm.

## Hoisin Turkey Burgers

**Prep time: 10 minutes | Cook time: 20 minutes | Serves 4**

1 pound (454 g) lean ground turkey
¼ cup whole-wheat bread crumbs

¼ cup hoisin sauce
2 tablespoons soy sauce
4 whole-wheat buns
Olive oil spray

In a large bowl, mix together the turkey, bread crumbs, hoisin sauce, and soy sauce. Form the mixture into 4 equal patties. Cover with plastic wrap and refrigerate the patties for 30 minutes. Preheat the air fryer to 370°F (188°C). Spray the air fryer basket lightly with olive oil spray. Place the patties in the air fryer basket in a single layer. Spray the patties lightly with olive oil spray. When your air fryer displays "READY" (select the cooking preset, and make minor adjustments according to your desired doneness.) and choose a shake reminder. Cook at the corresponding preset mode or Air Fry for 10 minutes. Flip the patties over, lightly spray with olive oil spray, and cook for an additional 5 to 10 minutes, until golden brown. Place the patties on buns and top with your choice of low-calorie burger toppings like sliced tomatoes, onions, and cabbage slaw. Serve immediately.

## Chicken Thighs in Waffles

**Prep time: 1 hour 20 minutes | Cook time: 40 minutes | Serves 4**

**For the chicken:**
4 chicken thighs, skin on
1 cup low-fat buttermilk
½ cup all-purpose flour
½ teaspoon garlic powder
½ teaspoon mustard powder

1 teaspoon kosher salt
½ teaspoon freshly ground black pepper
¼ cup honey, for serving
Cooking spray

**For the waffles:**
½ cup all-purpose flour
½ cup whole wheat pastry flour
1 large egg, beaten
1 cup low-fat buttermilk

1 teaspoon baking powder
2 tablespoons canola oil
½ teaspoon kosher salt
1 tablespoon granulated sugar

Combine the chicken thighs with buttermilk in a large bowl. Wrap the bowl in plastic and refrigerate to marinate for at least an hour. Preheat the air fryer to 360°F (182°C). Spritz the air fryer basket with cooking spray. Combine the flour, mustard powder, garlic powder, salt, and black pepper in a shallow dish. Stir to mix well. Remove the thighs from the buttermilk and pat dry with paper towels. Sit the bowl of buttermilk aside. Dip the thighs in the flour mixture first, then into the buttermilk, and then into the flour mixture. Shake the excess off. Arrange 2 thighs in the preheated air fryer and spritz with cooking spray. When your air fryer displays "READY" (select the cooking preset, and make minor adjustments according to your desired doneness.) and choose a shake reminder. Cook at the corresponding preset mode or Air Fry for 20 minutes or until an instant-read thermometer inserted in the thickest part of the chicken thighs registers at least 165°F (74°C). flip the thighs halfway through. Repeat with remaining thighs. Meanwhile, make the waffles: combine the ingredients for the waffles in a large bowl. Stir to mix well, then arrange the mixture in a waffle iron and cook until a golden and fragrant waffle forms. Remove the waffles from the waffle iron and slice into 4 pieces. Remove the chicken thighs from the air fryer and allow to cool for 5 minutes. Arrange each chicken thigh on each waffle piece and drizzle with 1 tablespoon of honey. Serve warm.

## Tangy Chicken Thighs

**Prep time: 10 minutes | Cook time: 20 minutes | Serves 4**

4 to 6 chicken thighs
1 teaspoon salt
1 teaspoon freshly ground black pepper
2 tablespoons olive oil

2 tablespoons Italian seasoning
2 tablespoons freshly squeezed lemon juice
1 lemon, sliced

Place the chicken thighs in a medium mixing bowl and season them with the salt and pepper. Add the olive oil, Italian seasoning, and lemon juice and toss until the chicken thighs are thoroughly coated with oil. Add the sliced lemons. Place the chicken thighs into the air fryer basket in a single layer. When your air fryer displays "READY" (select the cooking preset, and make minor adjustments according to your desired doneness.) and choose a shake reminder. Set the temperature to 350°F (177°C). Set the timer and cook for 10 minutes. Using tongs, flip the chicken. Reset the timer and cook for 10 minutes more. Check that the chicken has reached an internal temperature of 165°F (74°C). Add cooking time if needed. Once the chicken is fully cooked, plate, serve, and enjoy!

## Super Garlicky Chicken Breast

**Prep time: 5 minutes | Cook time: 25 minutes | Serves 4**

4 (5-ounce / 142-g) low-sodium bone-in skinless chicken breasts
1 tablespoon olive oil
1 tablespoon freshly squeezed lemon juice

3 tablespoons cornstarch
1 teaspoon dried basil leaves
⅛ teaspoon freshly ground black pepper
20 garlic cloves, unpeeled

Preheat the air fryer to 370°F (188°C). Rub the chicken with the olive oil and lemon juice on both sides and sprinkle with the cornstarch, basil, and pepper. Place the seasoned chicken in the air fryer basket and top with the garlic cloves. When your air fryer displays "READY" (select the cooking preset, and make minor adjustments according to your desired doneness.) and choose a shake reminder. Cook at the corresponding preset mode or Air Fry for about 25 minutes, or until the garlic is soft and the chicken reaches an internal temperature of 165°F (74°C) on a meat thermometer. Serve immediately.

## Thai Curry Chicken Meatballs

**Prep time: 10 minutes | Cook time: 10 minutes | Serves 4**

| | |
|---|---|
| 1 pound (454 g) ground chicken | 2 garlic cloves, minced |
| ¼ cup chopped fresh cilantro | 2 teaspoons minced fresh |
| 1 teaspoon chopped fresh mint | ginger |
| 1 tablespoon fresh lime juice | ½ teaspoon kosher salt |
| 1 tablespoon Thai red, green, | ½ teaspoon black pepper |
| or yellow curry paste | ¼ teaspoon red pepper flakes |
| 1 tablespoon fish sauce | |

Preheat the air fryer to 400ºF (204ºC). In a large bowl, gently mix the ground chicken, cilantro, mint, lime juice, curry paste, fish sauce, garlic, ginger, salt, black pepper, and red pepper flakes until thoroughly combined. Form the mixture into 16 meatballs. Place the meatballs in a single layer in the air fryer basket. When your air fryer displays "READY" (select the cooking preset, and make minor adjustments according to your desired doneness.) and choose a shake reminder. Cook at the corresponding preset mode or Air Fry for 10 minutes, turning the meatballs halfway through the cooking time. Use a meat thermometer to ensure the meatballs have reached an internal temperature of 165ºF (74ºC). Serve immediately.

## Honey Chicken Tenders with Vegetable

**Prep time: 10 minutes | Cook time: 18 to 20 minutes | Serves 4**

| | |
|---|---|
| 1 pound (454 g) chicken tenders | ½ cup soft fresh bread crumbs |
| 1 tablespoon honey | ½ teaspoon dried thyme |
| Pinch salt | 1 tablespoon olive oil |
| Freshly ground black pepper, to taste | 2 carrots, sliced |
| | 12 small red potatoes |

Preheat the air fryer to 380ºF (193ºC). In a medium bowl, toss the chicken tenders with the honey, salt, and pepper. In a shallow bowl, combine the bread crumbs, thyme, and olive oil, and mix. Coat the tenders in the bread crumbs, pressing firmly onto the meat. Place the carrots and potatoes in the air fryer basket and top with the chicken tenders. When your air fryer displays "READY" (select the cooking preset, and make minor adjustments according to your desired doneness.) and choose a shake reminder. Cook at the corresponding preset mode or Air Fry for 18 to 20 minutes or until the chicken is cooked to 165ºF (74ºC) and the vegetables are tender, shaking the basket halfway during the cooking time. Serve warm.

## Honey Chicken Wings

**Prep time: 10 minutes | Cook time: 55 minutes | Serves 8**

| | |
|---|---|
| ⅛ cup water | ¼ cup raw honey |
| ½ teaspoon salt | ¾ cup almond flour |
| 4 tablespoons minced garlic | 16 chicken wings |
| ¼ cup vegan butter | |

Rinse off and dry chicken wings well. Spray air fryer basket with olive oil. Coat chicken wings with almond flour and add coated wings to air fryer. When your air fryer displays "READY" (select the cooking preset, and make minor adjustments according to your desired doneness.) and choose a shake reminder. Cook 25 minutes at 380ºF (193ºC), shaking every 5 minutes. When the timer goes off, cook 5 to 10 minutes at 400ºF (204ºC) till skin becomes crispy and dry. As chicken cooks, melt butter in a saucepan and add garlic. Sauté garlic 5 minutes. Add salt and honey, simmering 20 minutes. Make sure to stir every so often, so the sauce does not burn. Add a bit of water after 15 minutes to ensure sauce does not harden. Take out chicken wings from air fryer and coat in sauce. Enjoy!

## Grandmom' Merguez Meatballs

**Prep time: 10 minutes | Cook time: 10 minutes | Serves 4**

| | |
|---|---|
| 1 pound (454 g) ground chicken | 1 teaspoon ground cumin |
| 2 garlic cloves, finely minced | ½ teaspoon black pepper |
| 1 tablespoon sweet Hungarian paprika | ½ teaspoon ground fennel |
| 1 teaspoon kosher salt | ½ teaspoon ground coriander |
| 1 teaspoon sugar | ½ teaspoon cayenne pepper |
| | ¼ teaspoon ground allspice |

In a large bowl, gently mix the chicken, garlic, paprika, salt, sugar, cumin, black pepper, fennel, coriander, cayenne, and allspice until all the ingredients are incorporated. Let stand for 30 minutes at room temperature, or cover and refrigerate for up to 24 hours. Preheat the air fryer to 400ºF (204ºC). Form the mixture into 16 meatballs. Arrange them in a single layer in the air fryer basket. When your air fryer displays "READY" (select the cooking preset, and make minor adjustments according to your desired doneness.) and choose a shake reminder. Cook at the corresponding preset mode or Air Fry for 10 minutes, turning the meatballs halfway through the cooking time. Use a meat thermometer to ensure the meatballs have reached an internal temperature of 165ºF (74ºC). Serve warm.

## General Tso's Chicken Breast

**Prep time: 15 minutes | Cook time: 25 minutes | Serves 4**

| | |
|---|---|
| 2 pounds (907 g) boneless, skinless chicken breast, cut into bite-size cubes | 2 cloves garlic, minced |
| ½ cup soy sauce, divided | 1 tablespoon grated fresh ginger |
| ½ cup mirin or rice wine, divided | 12 dried red chiles |
| ½ cup plus ½ tablespoon cornstarch | ¼ cup rice vinegar |
| 2 tablespoons vegetable or canola oil plus additional oil for spraying | ¼ cup granulated sugar |
| | 2 teaspoons hoisin sauce (optional) |
| | 2 scallions, white and light green part only, sliced |
| | 1 teaspoon sesame seeds |

Toss the chicken with ¼ cup of the soy sauce and ¼ cup of the mirin in a glass bowl or baking dish. Cover and refrigerate for at least 15 and up to 30 minutes. Spread ½ cup of cornstarch on a plate. Take 2 pieces of chicken and dredge them in the cornstarch, then tap them against each other to remove any excess. Repeat until you have dredged one-third of the chicken in the cornstarch. Spray the basket of the air fryer with oil. Arrange the dredged chicken pieces in the basket in a single layer. Spray with oil. When your air fryer displays "READY" (select the cooking preset, and make minor adjustments according to your desired doneness.) and choose a shake reminder. Cook at 400ºF (204ºC) for 8 minutes, turning once, spraying with additional oil if there are dry patches of cornstarch. Set aside. While the first batch of chicken is cooking, dredge the second third of the chicken in the cornstarch. Spray the basket of the air fryer with oil and cook the second batch of chicken in the same manner. While the second batch is cooking, dredge the remaining chicken in the cornstarch. Cook the last third of the chicken in the same manner as the others. Set the cooked chicken aside. Whisk together the remaining ½ tablespoon of cornstarch with ½ tablespoon of water to create a slurry and set aside. Heat the 2 tablespoons of oil in a large, deep skillet over medium heat. Add the garlic, ginger, and dried red chiles and sauté for 1 minute until fragrant but not browned. Add the remaining soy sauce, mirin, rice vinegar, sugar, and hoisin sauce, if using, and bring to a boil, stirring to dissolve the sugar. Add the cornstarch slurry and cook until the mixture begins to thicken, 1 to 2 minutes. Add the chicken to the sauce in the pan and toss to coat. Cook until the chicken is heated through. Remove the chicken and sauce to a platter and garnish with scallions and sesame seeds. Serve immediately.

## Chicken Breast and Veggies Salad

**Prep time: 10 minutes | Cook time: 10 to 13 minutes | Serves 4**

3 (4-ounce / 113-g) low-sodium boneless, skinless chicken breasts, cut into 1-inch cubes
1 small red onion, sliced
1 red bell pepper, sliced
1 cup green beans, cut into 1-inch pieces
2 tablespoons low-fat ranch salad dressing
2 tablespoons freshly squeezed lemon juice
½ teaspoon dried basil
4 cups mixed lettuce

Preheat the air fryer to 400ºF (204ºC). In the air fryer basket when your air fryer displays "READY" (select the cooking preset, and make minor adjustments according to your desired doneness.) and choose a shake reminder. Cook the chicken, red onion, red bell pepper, and green beans at the corresponding preset mode or Air Fry for 10 to 13 minutes, or until the chicken reaches an internal temperature of 165ºF (74ºC) on a meat thermometer, tossing the food in the basket once during cooking. While the chicken cooks, in a serving bowl, mix the ranch dressing, lemon juice, and basil. Transfer the chicken and vegetables to a serving bowl and toss with the dressing to coat. Serve immediately on lettuce leaves.

## Chicken Breast with Spinach

**Prep time: 10 minutes | Cook time: 16 to 20 minutes | Serves 4**

3 (5-ounce / 142-g) low-sodium boneless, skinless chicken breasts, cut into 1-inch cubes
5 teaspoons olive oil
½ teaspoon dried thyme
1 medium red onion, sliced
1 red bell pepper, sliced
1 small zucchini, cut into strips
3 tablespoons freshly squeezed lemon juice
6 cups fresh baby spinach

Preheat the air fryer to 400ºF (204ºC). In a large bowl, mix the chicken with the olive oil and thyme. Toss to coat. Transfer to a medium metal bowl and cook at the corresponding preset mode or Air Fry for 8 minutes in the air fryer. Add the red onion, red bell pepper, and zucchini. When your air fryer displays "READY" (select the cooking preset, and make minor adjustments according to your desired doneness.) and choose a shake reminder. Cook at the corresponding preset mode or Air Fry for 8 to 12 minutes more, stirring once during cooking, or until the chicken reaches an internal temperature of 165ºF (74ºC) on a meat thermometer. Remove the bowl from the air fryer and stir in the lemon juice. Put the spinach in a serving bowl and top with the chicken mixture. Toss to combine and serve immediately.

## Chicken Fritters with Garlic Dip

**Prep time: 15 minutes | Cook time: 20 minutes | Make 16 to 18 fritters**

**For the Chicken Fritters:**
½ teaspoon salt
⅛ teaspoon pepper
1½ tablespoons fresh dill
1⅓ cups shredded Mozzarella cheese
⅓ cup coconut flour
⅓ cup vegan mayo
2 eggs
1½ pounds (680 g) chicken breasts

**For the Garlic Dip:**
⅛ teaspoon pepper
¼ teaspoon salt
½ tablespoon lemon juice
1 pressed garlic cloves
⅓ cup vegan mayo

Slice chicken breasts into ⅓" pieces and place in a bowl. Add all remaining fritter ingredients to the bowl and stir well. Cover and chill 2 hours or overnight. Ensure your air fryer is preheated to 350ºF (177ºC). Spray basket with a bit of olive oil. Add marinated chicken to air fryer when your air fryer displays "READY" (select the cooking preset, and make minor adjustments according to your desired doneness.) and choose a shake reminder. Cook for 20 minutes, making sure to turn halfway through cooking process. To make the dipping sauce, combine all the dip ingredients until smooth.

## French-Style Chicken Thighs

**Prep time: 10 minutes | Cook time: 27 minutes | Serves 4**

2 tablespoon extra-virgin olive oil
1 tablespoon Dijon mustard
1 tablespoon apple cider vinegar
3 cloves garlic, minced
2 teaspoons herbes de Provence
½ teaspoon kosher salt
1 teaspoon black pepper
1 pound (454 g) boneless, skinless chicken thighs, halved crosswise
2 tablespoons butter
8 cloves garlic, chopped
¼ cup heavy whipping cream

In a small bowl, combine the olive oil, mustard, vinegar, minced garlic, herbes de Provence, salt, and pepper. Use a wire whisk to emulsify the mixture. Pierce the chicken all over with a fork to allow the marinade to penetrate better. Place the chicken in a resealable plastic bag, pour the marinade over, and seal. Massage until the chicken is well coated. Marinate at room temperature for 30 minutes or in the refrigerator for up to 24 hours. When you are ready to cook, place the butter and chopped garlic ina 7 × 3-inch round heatproof pan and place it in the air fryer basket. When your air fryer displays "READY" (select the cooking preset, and make minor adjustments according to your desired doneness.) and choose a shake reminder. Set the air fryer to 400ºF (204ºC) for 5 minutes, or until the butter has melted and the garlic is sizzling. Add the chicken and the marinade to the seasoned butter. Set the air fryer to 350ºF (177ºC) for 15 minutes. Use a meat thermometer to ensure the chicken has reached an internal temperature of 165ºF (74ºC). Transfer the chicken to a plate and cover lightly with foil to keep warm. Add the cream to the pan, stirring to combine with the garlic, butter, and cooking juices. Place the pan in the air fryer basket. Set the air fryer to 350ºF (177ºC) for 7 minutes. Pour the thickened sauce over the chicken and serve.

# Chapter 6 Fish and Seafood

## Cod Fish Fillets
**Prep time: 5 minutes | Cook time: 9 minutes | Serves 4**

4 cod fillets
2 tablespoons olive oil
2 eggs, beaten
1 cup breadcrumbs
A pinch of salt
1 cup flour

Preheat air fryer to 390ºF (199ºC). Mix breadcrumbs, olive oil, and salt in a bowl. In another bowl, place the eggs. Put the flour into a third bowl. Toss the cod fillets in the flour, then in the eggs, and then in the breadcrumb mixture. Place them in the greased frying basket when your air fryer displays "READY" (select the cooking preset, and make minor adjustments according to your desired doneness.) and choose a shake reminder. AirFry for 9 minutes. At the 5-minute mark, quickly turn the fillets. Once done, remove to a plate and serve with cilantro-yogurt sauce.

## Tandoori Salmon Fillet
**Prep time: 10 minutes | Cook time: 12 minutes | Serves 2**

2 salmon fillets
1 teaspoon ginger powder
1 garlic clove, minced
½ green bell pepper, sliced
1 teaspoon sweet paprika, minced
1 teaspoon honey
1 teaspoon garam masala
1 tablespoon fresh cilantro, chopped
¼ cup yogurt Juice and zest from
1 lime

In a bowl, mix all the ingredients, except for salmon and yogurt. Season to taste and stir in the yogurt. Top the fillets with the mixture and let sit for 15 minutes. Preheat air fryer to 400ºF (205ºC). Place the fillets into the greased frying basket when your air fryer displays "READY" (select the cooking preset, and make minor adjustments according to your desired doneness.) and choose a shake reminder. Bake for 12 to 15 minutes until nice and crispy. Serve on a bed of rice.

## Salmon and Veggie Balls
**Prep time: 10 minutes | Cook time: 8 minutes | Serves 2**

1 cup tinned salmon
¼ celery stalk, chopped
1 spring onion, sliced
4 tablespoons wheat germ
2 tablespoons olive oil
1 large egg
1 tablespoon fresh dill, chopped
½ teaspoon garlic powder

Preheat air fryer to 390ºF (199ºC). In a large bowl, mix tinned salmon, egg, celery, onion, dill, and garlic. Shape the mixture into balls and roll them in wheat germ. Carefully flatten and place in them the greased air fryer basket. When your air fryer displays "READY" (select the cooking preset, and make minor adjustments according to your desired doneness.) and choose a shake reminder. AirFry for 8 to 10 minutes, flipping once halfway through until golden. Serve warm.

## Buttered Crab Legs with Parsley
**Prep time: 5 minutes | Cook time: 10 minutes | Serves 4**

3 pounds (1.4kg) crab legs
2 tablespoons butter, melted
1 tablespoon fresh parsley

Preheat air fryer to 380ºF (193ºC). Place the crab legs in the greased air fryer basket when your air fryer displays "READY" (select the cooking preset, and make minor adjustments according to your desired doneness.) and choose a shake reminder. AirFry for 10 minutes, shaking once. Pour the butter over crab legs, sprinkle with parsley, and serve.

## Lovely Catfish Fillet
**Prep time: 5 minutes | Cook time: 15 minutes | Serves 2**

2 catfish fillets
2 teaspoons blackening seasoning
Juice of 1 lime
2 tablespoons butter, melted
1 garlic clove, minced
2 tablespoons fresh cilantro, chopped

Preheat air fryer to 360ºF (182ºC). In a bowl, mix garlic, lime juice, cilantro, and butter. Divide the sauce into two parts, rub 1 part of the sauce onto fish fillets and sprinkle with the seasoning. Place the fillets in the greased frying basket when your air fryer displays "READY" (select the cooking preset, and make minor adjustments according to your desired doneness.) and choose a shake reminder. Bake for 15 minutes, flipping once. Serve with the remaining sauce.

## Rosemary Catfish Fillet
**Prep time: 5 minutes | Cook time: 12 minutes | Serves 4**

4 catfish fillets
¼ cup seasoned fish fry
1 tablespoon olive oil
1 tablespoon fresh rosemary, chopped

Preheat air fryer to 400ºF (205ºC). Add the seasoned fish fry and the fillets to a large Ziploc bag; massage well to coat. Place the fillets in the greased frying basket when your air fryer displays "READY" (select the cooking preset, and make minor adjustments according to your desired doneness.) and choose a shake reminder. AirFry for 10 to 12 minutes. Flip the fillets and cook for 2 to 3 more minutes until crispy. Top with freshly chopped rosemary and serve.

## Old Bay Tilapia Fillet
**Prep time: 5 minutes | Cook time: 10 minutes | Serves 4**

1 pound (454 g) tilapia fillets
1 teaspoon old bay seasoning
2 tablespoons canola oil
2 tablespoons lemon pepper
Salt, to taste
2 butter buds

Preheat air fryer to 400ºF (205ºC). Drizzle canola oil over tilapia. In a bowl, mix salt, lemon pepper, butter buds, and old bay seasoning; spread on the fish. Place the fillets in the fryer when your air fryer displays "READY" (select the cooking preset, and make minor adjustments according to your desired doneness.) and choose a shake reminder. AirFry for 10 to 12 minutes, turning once, until crispy. Serve with green salad.

## Cornmeal-Coated Tilapia Fillet
**Prep time: 5 minutes | Cook time: 16 minutes | Serves 5**

5 tablespoons all-purpose flour
Sea salt and white pepper, to taste
1 teaspoon garlic paste
2 tablespoons extra virgin olive oil
½ cup cornmeal
5 tilapia fillets, slice into halves

Combine the flour, salt, white pepper, garlic paste, olive oil, and cornmeal in a Ziploc bag. Add the fish fillets and shake to coat well. Spritz the Air Fryer basket with cooking spray. When your air fryer displays "READY" (select the cooking preset, and make minor adjustments according to your desired doneness.) and choose a shake reminder. Cook in the preheated Air Fryer at 400ºF (204ºC) for 10 minutes; turn them over and cook for 6 minutes more. Work in batches. Serve with lemon wedges if desired. Enjoy!

## Basil White Fish with Romano

**Prep time: 5 minutes | Cook time: 8 minutes | Serves 4**

2 tablespoons fresh basil, chopped
1 teaspoon garlic powder
2 tablespoons Romano cheese,
grated
Salt and black pepper, to taste
4 white fish fillets

Preheat air fryer to 350ºF (180ºC). Season fillets with garlic, salt, and black pepper. Place in the greased frying basket when your air fryer displays "READY" (select the cooking preset, and make minor adjustments according to your desired doneness.) and choose a shake reminder. AirFry them for 8 to 10 minutes, flipping once. Serve topped with Romano cheese and basil.

## Salmon Fillet with Creamy Parsley Sauce

**Prep time: 5 minutes | Cook time: 15 minutes | Serves 4**

4 Alaskan wild salmon fillets
2 teaspoons olive oil Salt to taste
½ cup heavy cream
½ cup milk
2 tablespoons fresh parsley, chopped

Preheat air fryer to 380ºF (193ºC). Drizzle the fillets with olive oil, and season with salt and black pepper. Place salmon in the frying basket when your air fryer displays "READY" (select the cooking preset, and make minor adjustments according to your desired doneness.) and choose a shake reminder. Bake for 15 minutes, turning once until tender and crispy. In a bowl, mix milk, parsley, salt, and whipped cream. Serve the salmon with the sauce.

## Catfish Fillet with Parsley

**Prep time: 5 minutes | Cook time: 11 minutes | Serves 2**

2 catfish fillets
½ cup breadcrumbs
¼ teaspoon cayenne pepper
¼ teaspoon fish seasoning
1 tablespoon fresh parsley, chopped
Salt to taste

Preheat air fryer to 400ºF (205ºC). Pour all the dry ingredients, except for the parsley, in a bowl. Add in the fish pieces and toss to coat. Lightly spray the fish with olive oil. Put the fillets in the fryer basket when your air fryer displays "READY" (select the cooking preset, and make minor adjustments according to your desired doneness.) and choose a shake reminder. AirFry for 6 to 7 minutes. Flip and cook further for 5 minutes. Garnish with freshly chopped parsley and serve.

## Hot Spiced Prawns

**Prep time: 5 minutes | Cook time: 8 minutes | Serves 4**

8 prawns, cleaned
Salt and black pepper, to taste
½ teaspoon ground cayenne pepper
½ teaspoon red chili flakes
½ teaspoon ground cumin
½ teaspoon garlic powder

In a bowl, season the prawns with salt and black pepper. Sprinkle with cayenne pepper, chili flakes, cumin, and garlic, and stir to coat. Spray the frying basket with oil and lay the prawns in an even layer. When your air fryer displays "READY" (select the cooking preset, and make minor adjustments according to your desired doneness.) and choose a shake reminder. AirFry for 8 minutes at 340ºF (171ºC), turning once halfway through. Serve with fresh sweet chili sauce.

## Buttery Lobster Tails

**Prep time: 5 minutes | Cook time: 10 minutes | Serves 4**

4 ounces (113 g) lobster tails, halved
1 garlic clove, minced
1 tablespoon butter
Salt and black pepper, to taste
½ tablespoon lemon Juice

Blend all ingredients, except for lobster, in a food processor. Clean the skin of the lobster and cover it with the mixture. Preheat air fryer to 380ºF (193ºC). Place the lobster in the frying basket when your air fryer displays "READY" (select the cooking preset, and make minor adjustments according to your desired doneness.) and choose a shake reminder. AirFry for 10 minutes, turning once halfway through. Serve with fresh herbs.

## Old Bay Shrimp

**Prep time: 5 minutes | Cook time: 8 minutes | Serves 2**

1 pound (454 g) jumbo shrimp, deveined
Salt to taste
¼ teaspoon old bay seasoning
⅓ tsp smoked paprika
¼ teaspoon cayenne pepper
1 tablespoon olive oil

Preheat air fryer to 390 degrees. In a bowl, add shrimp, paprika, olive oil, salt, old bay seasoning, and cayenne pepper; mix well. Place the shrimp in the fryer when your air fryer displays "READY" (select the cooking preset, and make minor adjustments according to your desired doneness.) and choose a shake reminder. AirFry for 8 to 10 minutes, shaking once.

## Breaded Scallops

**Prep time: 10 minutes | Cook time: 6 minutes | Serves 4**

1 pound (454 g) fresh scallops
3 tablespoons flour
Salt and black pepper, to taste
1 egg, lightly beaten
1 cup breadcrumbs
2 tablespoons olive oil
½ teaspoon fresh parsley, chopped

Coat the scallops with flour. Dip into the egg, then into the breadcrumbs. Brush with olive oil and place into the frying basket. When your air fryer displays "READY" (select the cooking preset, and make minor adjustments according to your desired doneness.) and choose a shake reminder. AirFry for 6 to 8 minutes at 360ºF (182ºC), shaking once. Serve topped with parsley. Enjoy!

## Rosemary Cashew-Crusted Shrimp

**Prep time: 10 minutes | Cook time: 6 minutes | Serves 4**

3 ounces (85 g) cashews, chopped
1 tablespoon fresh rosemary, chopped
1½ pounds (680 g) shrimp
1 garlic clove, minced
1 tablespoon breadcrumbs
1 egg, beaten
1 tablespoon olive oil
Salt and black pepper, to taste

Preheat air fryer to 320ºF (160ºC). Combine olive oil with garlic and brush onto the shrimp. Combine rosemary, cashews, and crumbs in a bowl. Dip shrimp in the egg and coat it in the cashew mixture. Place in the frying basket when your air fryer displays "READY" (select the cooking preset, and make minor adjustments according to your desired doneness.) and choose a shake reminder. Bake for 25 minutes. Increase the temperature to 390ºF (199ºC) and cook for 5 more minutes. Cover with a foil and let sit for a couple of minutes before serving.

## Mediterranean Salmon Fillet

**Prep time: 5 minutes | Cook time: 10 minutes | Serves 2**

2 salmon fillets
Salt and black pepper, to taste

1 lemon, cut into wedges
8 asparagus spears, trimmed

Rinse and pat dry the fillets with a paper towel. Coat the fish generously on both sides with cooking spray. Season fish and asparagus with salt and pepper. Arrange fish in the frying basket and lay the asparagus around the fish when your air fryer displays "READY" (select the cooking preset, and make minor adjustments according to your desired doneness.) and choose a shake reminder. AirFry for 10 to 12 minutes at 350ºF (180ºC), flipping once. Serve with lemon wedges.

## Cajun Mango Salmon Fillet

**Prep time: 10 minutes | Cook time: 12 minutes | Serves 4**

4 salmon fillets
½ teaspoon brown sugar
1 tablespoon Cajun seasoning
1 lemon, zested and juiced

1 tablespoon fresh parsley, chopped
2 tablespoons mango salsa

Preheat air fryer to 350ºF (180ºC). In a bowl, mix sugar, Cajun seasoning, lemon juice and zest, and coat the salmon with the mixture. Line with parchment paper the frying basket and place in the fish when your air fryer displays "READY" (select the cooking preset, and make minor adjustments according to your desired doneness.) and choose a shake reminder. Bake for 12 minutes, turning once halfway through. Top with parsley and mango salsa to serve.

## Creole Trout Fillet

**Prep time: 5 minutes | Cook time: 10 minutes | Serves 4**

4 skin-on trout fillets
2 teaspoons creole seasoning
2 tablespoons fresh dill,

chopped
1 lemon, sliced

Preheat air fryer to 350ºF (180ºC). Season the trout with creole seasoning on both sides and spray with cooking spray. Place in the frying basket when your air fryer displays "READY" (select the cooking preset, and make minor adjustments according to your desired doneness.) and choose a shake reminder. Bake for 10 to 12 minutes, flipping once. Serve sprinkled with dill and garnished with lemon slices. Enjoy!

## Spicy Curry King Prawns

**Prep time: 10 minutes | Cook time: 8 minutes | Serves 2**

12 king prawns, rinsed
1 tablespoon coconut oil
½ teaspoon piri piri powder
Salt and ground black pepper, to taste

1 teaspoon garlic paste
1 teaspoon onion powder
½ teaspoon cumin powder
1 teaspoon curry powder

In a mixing bowl, toss all ingredient until the prawns are well coated on all sides. When your air fryer displays "READY" (select the cooking preset, and make minor adjustments according to your desired doneness.) and choose a shake reminder. Cook in the preheated Air Fryer at 360ºF (182ºC) for 4 minutes. Shake the basket and cook for 4 minutes more. Serve over hot rice if desired. Enjoy!

## Lemony Shrimp

**Prep time: 10 minutes | Cook time: 7 to 8 minutes | Serves 4**

1 pound (454 g) shrimp, deveined
4 tablespoons olive oil
1½ tablespoons lemon juice
1½ tablespoons fresh parsley, roughly chopped

2 cloves garlic, finely minced
1 teaspoon crushed red pepper flakes, or more to taste
Garlic pepper, to taste
Sea salt flakes, to taste

Preheat the air fryer to 385ºF (196ºC). Toss all the ingredients in a large bowl until the shrimp are coated on all sides. Arrange the shrimp in the air fryer basket when your air fryer displays "READY" (select the cooking preset, and make minor adjustments according to your desired doneness.) and choose a shake reminder. Cook at the corresponding preset mode or Air Fry for 7 to 8 minutes, or until the shrimp are pink and cooked through. Serve warm.

## Peppery Shrimp

**Prep time: 5 minutes | Cook time: 6 minutes | Serves 4**

1½ pounds (680 g) raw shrimp, peeled and deveined
1 tablespoon olive oil
1 teaspoon garlic, minced

1 teaspoon cayenne pepper
½ teaspoon lemon pepper
Sea salt, to taste

Toss all ingredients in a lightly greased Air Fryer cooking basket. When your air fryer displays "READY" (select the cooking preset, and make minor adjustments according to your desired doneness.) and choose a shake reminder. Cook the shrimp at 400ºF (204ºC) for 6 minutes, tossing the basket halfway through the cooking time. Bon appétit!

## Shrimp and Veggie Spring Rolls

**Prep time: 10 minutes | Cook time: 17 to 22 minutes | Serves 4**

2 teaspoons minced garlic
2 cups finely sliced cabbage
1 cup matchstick cut carrots
2 (4-ounce / 113-g) cans tiny shrimp, drained

4 teaspoons soy sauce
Salt and freshly ground black pepper, to taste
16 square spring roll wrappers
Cooking spray

Preheat the air fryer to 370ºF (188ºC). Spray the air fryer basket lightly with cooking spray. Spray a medium sauté pan with cooking spray. Add the garlic to the sauté pan and cook over medium heat until fragrant, 30 to 45 seconds. Add the cabbage and carrots and sauté until the vegetables are slightly tender, about 5 minutes. Add the shrimp and soy sauce and season with salt and pepper, then stir to combine. Sauté until the moisture has evaporated, 2 more minutes. Set aside to cool. Place a spring roll wrapper on a work surface so it looks like a diamond. Place 1 tablespoon of the shrimp mixture on the lower end of the wrapper. Roll the wrapper away from you halfway, then fold in the right and left sides, like an envelope. Continue to roll to the very end, using a little water to seal the edge. Repeat with the remaining wrappers and filling. Place the spring rolls in the air fryer basket in a single layer, leaving room between each roll. Lightly spray with cooking spray. You may need to cook them in batches. When your air fryer displays "READY" (select the cooking preset, and make minor adjustments according to your desired doneness.) and choose a shake reminder. Cook at the corresponding preset mode or Air Fry for 5 minutes. Turn the rolls over, lightly spray with cooking spray, and cook until heated through and the rolls start to brown, 5 to 10 more minutes. Cool for 5 minutes before serving.

## Salmon Fillet with Herb and Garlic
**Prep time: 10 minutes | Cook time: 12 minutes | Serves 3**

1 pound (454 g) salmon fillets
Sea salt and ground black
pepper, to taste
1 tablespoon olive oil
1 sprig thyme
2 sprigs rosemary
2 cloves garlic, minced
1 lemon, sliced

Pat the salmon fillets dry and season them with salt and pepper; drizzle salmon fillets with olive oil and place in the Air Fryer cooking basket. When your air fryer displays "READY" (select the cooking preset, and make minor adjustments according to your desired doneness.) and choose a shake reminder. Cook the salmon fillets at 380ºF (193ºC) for 7 minutes; turn them over, top with thyme, rosemary and garlic and continue to cook for 5 minutes more. Serve topped with lemon slices and enjoy

## Seeds-Crusted Codfish Fillet
**Prep time: 5 minutes | Cook time: 12 minutes | Serves 2**

2 codfish fillets
1 teaspoon sesame oil
Sea salt and black pepper, to
taste
1 teaspoon sesame seeds
1 tablespoon chia seeds

Start by preheating your Air Fryer to 380ºF (193ºC). Add the sesame oil, salt, black pepper, sesame seeds and chia seeds to a rimmed plate. Coat the top of the codfish with the seed mixture, pressing it down to adhere. Lower the codfish fillets, seed side down, into the cooking basket. When your air fryer displays "READY" (select the cooking preset, and make minor adjustments according to your desired doneness.) and choose a shake reminder. Cook for 6 minutes. Turn the fish fillets over and cook for a further 6 minutes. Serve warm and enjoy!

## Blackened Shrimp Tacos
**Prep time: 10 minutes | Cook time: 10 to 15 minutes | Serves 4**

12 ounces (340 g) medium
shrimp, deveined, with tails off
1 teaspoon olive oil
1 to 2 teaspoons Blackened
seasoning
8 corn tortillas, warmed
1 (14-ounce / 397-g) bag
coleslaw mix
2 limes, cut in half
Cooking spray

Preheat the air fryer to 400ºF (204ºC). Spray the air fryer basket lightly with cooking spray. Dry the shrimp with a paper towel to remove excess water. In a medium bowl, toss the shrimp with olive oil and Blackened seasoning. Place the shrimp in the air fryer basket when your air fryer displays "READY" (select the cooking preset, and make minor adjustments according to your desired doneness.) and choose a shake reminder. Cook at the corresponding preset mode or Air Fry for 5 minutes. Shake the basket, lightly spray with cooking spray, and cook until the shrimp are cooked through and starting to brown, 5 to 10 more minutes. Fill each tortilla with the coleslaw mix and top with the blackened shrimp. Squeeze fresh lime juice over top and serve.

## Lobster Tails with Green Olives
**Prep time: 10 minutes | Cook time: 12 minutes | Serves 5**

2 pounds (907 g) fresh lobster
tails, cleaned and halved, in
shells
2 tablespoons butter, melted
1 teaspoon onion powder
1 teaspoon cayenne pepper
Salt and ground black pepper,
to taste
2 garlic cloves, minced
1 cup cornmeal
1 cup green olives

In a plastic closeable bag, thoroughly combine all ingredients; shake to combine well. Transfer the coated lobster tails to the greased cooking basket. When your air fryer displays "READY" (select the cooking preset, and make minor adjustments according to your desired doneness.) and choose a shake reminder. Cook in the preheated Air Fryer at 390ºF (199ºC) for 6 to 7 minutes, shaking the basket halfway through. Work in batches. Serve with green olives and enjoy!

## Rosemary-Infused Butter Sea Scallops
**Prep time: 5 minutes | Cook time: 14 minutes | Serves 4**

2 pounds (907 g) sea scallops
½ cup beer
4 tablespoons butter
2 sprigs rosemary, only leaves
Sea salt and freshly cracked
black pepper, to taste

In a ceramic dish, mix the sea scallops with beer; let it marinate for 1 hour. Meanwhile, preheat your Air Fryer to 400ºF (204ºC). Melt the butter and add the rosemary leaves. Stir for a few minutes. Discard the marinade and transfer the sea scallops to the Air Fryer basket. Season with salt and black pepper. When your air fryer displays "READY" (select the cooking preset, and make minor adjustments according to your desired doneness.) and choose a shake reminder. Cook the scallops in the preheated Air Fryer for 7 minutes, shaking the basket halfway through the cooking time. Work in batches.

## Piri Piri King Prawns
**Prep time: 10 minutes | Cook time: 8 minutes | Serves 2**

12 king prawns, rinsed
1 tablespoon coconut oil
Salt and ground black pepper,
to taste
1 teaspoon onion powder
1 teaspoon garlic paste
1 teaspoon curry powder
½ teaspoon piri piri powder
½ teaspoon cumin powder

Preheat the air fryer to 360ºF (182ºC). Combine all the ingredients in a large bowl and toss until the prawns are completely coated. Place the prawns in the air fryer basket when your air fryer displays "READY" (select the cooking preset, and make minor adjustments according to your desired doneness.) and choose a shake reminder. Cook at the corresponding preset mode or Air Fry for 8 minutes, shaking the basket halfway through, or until the prawns turn pink.
Serve hot.

## Romano Monkfish Fillet
**Prep time: 10 minutes | Cook time: 9 minutes | Serves 2**

2 monkfish fillets
1 teaspoon garlic paste
2 tablespoons butter, melted
½ teaspoon Aleppo chili powder
½ teaspoon dried rosemary
¼ teaspoon cracked black
pepper
½ teaspoon sea salt
4 tablespoons Romano cheese,
grated

Start by preheating the Air Fryer to 320ºF (160ºC). Spritz the Air Fryer basket with cooking oil. Spread the garlic paste all over the fish fillets. Brush the monkfish fillets with the melted butter on both sides. Sprinkle with the chili powder, rosemary, black pepper, and salt. When your air fryer displays "READY" (select the cooking preset, and make minor adjustments according to your desired doneness.) and choose a shake reminder. Cook for 7 minutes in the preheated Air Fryer. Top with the Romano cheese and continue to cook for 2 minutes more or until heated through. Serve and enjoy!

## Asian-Flavor Steamed Tuna Steak

**Prep time: 10 minutes | Cook time: 9 minutes | Serves 4**

4 small tuna steaks
2 tablespoons low-sodium soy sauce
2 teaspoons sesame oil
2 teaspoons rice wine vinegar
1 teaspoon grated fresh ginger
⅛ teaspoon pepper
1 stalk lemongrass, bent in half
3 tablespoons lemon juice

Place the tuna steaks on a plate. In a small bowl, combine the soy sauce, sesame oil, rice wine vinegar, and ginger, and mix well. Pour this mixture over the tuna and marinate for 10 minutes. Rub the soy sauce mixture gently into both sides of the tuna. Sprinkle with the pepper. Place the lemongrass on the air fryer basket and top with the steaks. Put the lemon juice and 1 tablespoon water in the pan below the basket. When your air fryer displays "READY" (select the cooking preset, and make minor adjustments according to your desired doneness.) and choose a shake reminder. Steam the fish for 8 to 10 minutes or until the tuna registers at least 145°F (63°C). Discard the lemongrass and serve the tuna.

## Mediterranean-Style Calamari

**Prep time: 10 minutes | Cook time: 5 minutes | Serves 4**

1 pound (454 g) calamari, sliced into rings
2 garlic cloves, minced
1 teaspoon red pepper flakes
2 tablespoons dry white wine
2 tablespoons olive oil
2 tablespoons fresh lemon juice
1 teaspoon basil, chopped
1 teaspoon dill, chopped
1 teaspoon parsley, chopped
Coarse sea salt and freshly cracked black pepper, to taste

Toss all ingredients in a lightly greased Air Fryer cooking basket. When your air fryer displays "READY" (select the cooking preset, and make minor adjustments according to your desired doneness.) and choose a shake reminder. Cook your calamari at 400°F (204°C) for 5 minutes, tossing the basket halfway through the cooking time. Bon appétit!

## Shrimp with Chili Mayo

**Prep time: 10 minutes | Cook time: 14 minutes | Serves 4**

**For the Sauce:**
½ cup mayonnaise
¼ cup sweet chili sauce
**For the Shrimp:**
1 pound (454 g) jumbo raw shrimp, peeled and deveined
2 tablespoons cornstarch or
2 to 4 tablespoons sriracha
1 teaspoon minced fresh ginger

rice flour
½ teaspoon kosher salt
Vegetable oil spray

In a large bowl, combine the mayonnaise, chili sauce, sriracha, and ginger. Stir until well combined. Remove half of the sauce to serve as a dipping sauce. Place the shrimp in a medium bowl. Sprinkle the cornstarch and salt over the shrimp and toss until well coated. Place the shrimp in the air fryer basket in a single layer. (If they won't fit in a single layer, set a rack or trivet on top of the bottom layer of shrimp and place the rest of the shrimp on the rack.) Spray generously with vegetable oil spray. When your air fryer displays "READY" (select the cooking preset, and make minor adjustments according to your desired doneness.) and choose a shake reminder. Set the air fryer to 350°F (177°C) for 10 minutes, turning and spraying with additional oil spray halfway through the cooking time. Remove the shrimp and toss in the bowl with half of the sauce. Place the shrimp back in the air fryer basket. Set the air fryer to 350°F (177°C) for an additional 4 to 5 minutes, or until the sauce has formed a glaze. Serve the hot shrimp with the reserved sauce for dipping.

## Bacon-Wrapped Sea Scallops

**Prep time: 10 minutes | Cook time: 12 minutes | Serves 4**

12 slices bacon
24 large sea scallops, tendons removed
1 teaspoon plus 2 tablespoons extra-virgin olive oil, divided
Salt and pepper, to taste
6 (6-inch) wooden skewers
1 tablespoon cider vinegar
1 teaspoon Dijon mustard
5 ounces (142 g) baby spinach
1 fennel bulb, stalks discarded, bulb halved, cored, and sliced thin
5 ounces (142 g) raspberries

Preheat the air fryer to 350°F (177°C). Line large plate with 4 layers of paper towels and arrange 6 slices bacon over towels in a single layer. Top with 4 more layers of paper towels and remaining 6 slices bacon. Cover with 2 layers of paper towels, place a second large plate on top, and press gently to flatten. Microwave until fat begins to render but bacon is still pliable, about 5 minutes. Pat scallops dry with paper towels and toss with 1 teaspoon oil, ⅛ teaspoon salt, and ⅛ teaspoon pepper in a bowl until evenly coated. Arrange 2 scallops side to side, flat side down, on the cutting board. Starting at narrow end, wrap 1 slice bacon tightly around sides of scallop bundle. (Bacon should overlap slightly; trim excess as needed.) Thread scallop bundle onto skewer through bacon. Repeat with remaining scallops and bacon, threading 2 bundles onto each skewer. Arrange 3 skewers in air fryer basket, parallel to each other and spaced evenly apart. Arrange remaining 3 skewers on top, perpendicular to the bottom layer. When your air fryer displays "READY" (select the cooking preset, and make minor adjustments according to your desired doneness.) and choose a shake reminder. Cook at the corresponding preset mode or Air Fry until bacon is crisp and scallops are firm and centers are opaque, 12 to 16 minutes, flipping and rotating skewers halfway through cooking. Meanwhile, whisk remaining 2 tablespoons oil, vinegar, mustard, ⅛ teaspoon salt, and ⅛ teaspoon pepper in large serving bowl until combined. Add spinach, fennel, and raspberries and gently toss to coat. Serve skewers with salad.

## Lime Shrimp Empanadas

**Prep time: 10 minutes | Cook time: 8 minutes | Serves 5**

½ pound (227g) raw shrimp, peeled, deveined and chopped
¼ cup chopped red onion
1 scallion, chopped
2 garlic cloves, minced
2 tablespoons minced red bell pepper
2 tablespoons chopped fresh cilantro
½ tablespoon fresh lime juice
¼ teaspoon sweet paprika
⅛ teaspoon kosher salt
⅛ teaspoon crushed red pepper flakes (optional)
1 large egg, beaten
10 frozen Goya Empanada Discos, thawed
Cooking spray

In a medium bowl, combine the shrimp, red onion, scallion, garlic, bell pepper, cilantro, lime juice, paprika, salt, and pepper flakes (if using). In a small bowl, beat the egg with 1 teaspoon water until smooth. Place an empanada disc on a work surface and put 2 tablespoons of the shrimp mixture in the center. Brush the outer edges of the disc with the egg wash. Fold the disc over and gently press the edges to seal. Use a fork and press around the edges to crimp and seal completely. Brush the tops of the empanadas with the egg wash. Preheat the air fryer to 380°F (193°C). Spray the bottom of the air fryer basket with cooking spray to prevent sticking. Working in batches, arrange a single layer of the empanadas in the air fryer basket when your air fryer displays "READY" (select the cooking preset, and make minor adjustments according to your desired doneness.) and choose a shake reminder. Cook at the corresponding preset mode or Air Fry for about 8 minutes, flipping halfway, until golden brown and crispy. Serve hot.

## Coconut-Shrimp Po' Boys

**Prep time: 10 minutes | Cook time: 12 minutes | Serves 4**

½ cup cornstarch
2 eggs
2 tablespoons milk
¾ cup shredded coconut
½ cup panko breadcrumbs
1 pound (454 g) shrimp, peeled and deveined
Old Bay seasoning, to taste
Oil for misting or cooking spray
2 large hoagie rolls
Honey mustard or light mayonnaise
1½ cups shredded lettuce
1 large tomato, thinly sliced

Place cornstarch in a shallow dish or plate. In another shallow dish, beat together eggs and milk. In a third dish mix the coconut and panko crumbs. Sprinkle shrimp with Old Bay seasoning. Dip shrimp in cornstarch to coat lightly, dip in egg mixture, shake off excess, and roll in coconut mixture to coat well. Spray both sides of coated shrimp with oil or cooking spray. When your air fryer displays "READY" (select the cooking preset, and make minor adjustments according to your desired doneness.) and choose a shake reminder. Cook half the shrimp in a single layer at 390°F (199°C) for 5 minutes. Repeat to cook remaining shrimp. Split each hoagie lengthwise, leaving one long edge intact. Place in air fryer basket and cook at 390°F (199°C) for 1 to 2 minutes or until heated through. Remove buns, break apart, and place on 4 plates, cut side up. Spread with honey mustard and/or mayonnaise. Top with shredded lettuce, tomato slices, and coconut shrimp.

## Sherry Calamari

**Prep time: 10 minutes | Cook time: 5 minutes | Serves 4**

1 pound (454 g) calamari, sliced into rings
2 tablespoons butter, melted
4 garlic cloves, smashed
2 tablespoons sherry wine
2 tablespoons fresh lemon juice
Coarse sea salt and ground black pepper, to taste
1 teaspoon paprika
1 teaspoon dried oregano

Toss all ingredients in a lightly greased Air Fryer cooking basket. When your air fryer displays "READY" (select the cooking preset, and make minor adjustments according to your desired doneness.) and choose a shake reminder. Cook your calamari at 400°F (204°C) for 5 minutes, tossing the basket halfway through the cooking time. Bon appétit!

## Cheddar Crawfish Casserole

**Prep time: 20 minutes | Cook time: 25 minutes | Serves 4**

1½ cups crawfish meat
½ cup chopped celery
½ cup chopped onion
½ cup chopped green bell pepper
2 large eggs, beaten
1 cup half-and-half
1 tablespoon butter, melted
1 tablespoon cornstarch
1 teaspoon Creole seasoning
¾ teaspoon salt
½ teaspoon freshly ground black pepper
1 cup shredded Cheddar cheese
Cooking spray

In a medium bowl, stir together the crawfish, celery, onion, and green pepper. In another medium bowl, whisk the eggs, half-and-half, butter, cornstarch, Creole seasoning, salt, and pepper until blended. Stir the egg mixture into the crawfish mixture. Add the cheese and stir to combine. Preheat the air fryer to 300°F (149°C). Spritz a baking pan with oil. Transfer the crawfish mixture to the prepared pan and place it in the air fryer basket. When your air fryer displays "READY" (select the cooking preset, and make minor adjustments according to your desired doneness.) and choose a shake reminder. Cook at the corresponding preset mode or Air Fry for 25 minutes, stirring every 10 minutes, until a knife inserted into the center comes out clean. Serve immediately.

## Baja Tilapia Fillet Tacos

**Prep time: 15 minutes | Cook time: 10 minutes | Serves 4**

**Fried Fish:**
1 pound (454 g) tilapia fillets (or other mild white fish)
½ cup all-purpose flour
1 teaspoon garlic powder
1 teaspoon kosher salt
**Tacos:**
8 corn tortillas
¼ head red or green cabbage, shredded
1 ripe avocado, halved and each half cut into 4 slices
¼ teaspoon cayenne pepper
½ cup mayonnaise
3 tablespoons milk
1¾ cups panko bread crumbs
Vegetable oil, for spraying

12 ounces (340 g) pico de gallo or other fresh salsa
Dollop of Mexican crema
1 lime, cut into wedges

To make the fish, cut the fish fillets into strips 3 to 4 inches long and 1 inch wide. Combine the flour, garlic powder, salt, and cayenne pepper on a plate and whisk to combine. In a shallow bowl, whisk the mayonnaise and milk together. Place the panko on a separate plate. Dredge the fish strips in the seasoned flour, shaking off any excess. Dip the strips in the mayonnaise mixture, coating them completely, then dredge in the panko, shaking off any excess. Place the fish strips on a plate or rack. Preheat the air fryer to 400°F (204°C). Working in batches, spray half the fish strips with oil and arrange them in the air fryer basket, taking care not to crowd them. When your air fryer displays "READY" (select the cooking preset, and make minor adjustments according to your desired doneness.) and choose a shake reminder. Cook at the corresponding preset mode or Air Fry for 4 minutes, then flip and cook for another 3 to 4 minutes until the outside is brown and crisp and the inside is opaque and flakes easily with a fork. Repeat with the remaining strips. Heat the tortillas in the microwave or on the stovetop. To assemble the tacos, place 2 fish strips inside each tortilla. Top with shredded cabbage, a slice of avocado, pico de gallo, and a dollop of crema. Serve with a lime wedge on the side.

## Butter and Parsley Calamari Rings

**Prep time: 5 minutes | Cook time: 5 minutes | Serves 4**

1 pound (454 g) calamari, sliced into rings
2 tablespoons butter
2 tablespoons parsley, chopped
2 garlic cloves, minced
1 teaspoon cayenne pepper
Sea salt and freshly ground black pepper, to taste

Toss all ingredients in a lightly greased Air Fryer cooking basket. When your air fryer displays "READY" (select the cooking preset, and make minor adjustments according to your desired doneness.) and choose a shake reminder. Cook your calamari at 400°F (204°C) for 5 minutes, tossing the basket halfway through the cooking time. Bon appétit!

## Italian Sea Bass

**Prep time: 5 minutes | Cook time: 10 minutes | Serves 4**

1 pound (454 g) sea bass
2 garlic cloves, minced
2 tablespoons olive oil
1 tablespoon Italian seasoning mix
Sea salt and ground black pepper, to taste
¼ cup dry white wine

Toss the fish with the remaining ingredients; place them in a lightly oiled Air Fryer cooking basket. When your air fryer displays "READY" (select the cooking preset, and make minor adjustments according to your desired doneness.) and choose a shake reminder. Cook the fish at 400°F (204°C) for about 10 minutes, turning them over halfway through the cooking time. Bon appétit!

## Balsamic Coconut Shrimp

**Prep time: 15 minutes | Cook time: 7 to 8 minutes | Serves 2**

1 pound (454 g) shrimp, deveined
1½ tablespoons olive oil
1½ tablespoons balsamic vinegar
1 tablespoon coconut aminos
½ tablespoon fresh parsley, roughly chopped

Sea salt flakes, to taste
1 teaspoon Dijon mustard
½ teaspoon smoked cayenne pepper
½ teaspoon garlic powder
Salt and ground black peppercorns, to taste
1 cup shredded goat cheese

Preheat the air fryer to 385ºF (196ºC). Except for the cheese, stir together all the ingredients in a large bowl until the shrimp are evenly coated. Arrange the shrimp in the air fryer basket when your air fryer displays "READY" (select the cooking preset, and make minor adjustments according to your desired doneness.) and choose a shake reminder. Cook at the corresponding preset mode or Air Fry for 7 to 8 minutes, shaking the basket halfway through, or until the shrimp are pink and cooked through. Serve the shrimp with the shredded goat cheese sprinkled on top.

## Bang Bang Shrimp

**Prep time: 10 minutes | Cook time: 8 minutes | Serves 4**

1 teaspoon paprika
Montreal chicken seasoning
¾ cup panko bread crumbs
½ cup almond flour
**For the Bang Bang Sauce:**
¼ cup sweet chili sauce
2 tablespoons sriracha sauce

1 egg white
1 pound (454 g) raw shrimp (peeled and deveined)

⅓ cup plain Greek yogurt

Ensure your air fryer is preheated to 400ºF (204ºC). Season all shrimp with seasonings. Add flour to one bowl, egg white in another, and breadcrumbs to a third. Dip seasoned shrimp in flour, then egg whites, and then breadcrumbs. Spray coated shrimp with olive oil and add to air fryer basket. When your air fryer displays "READY" (select the cooking preset, and make minor adjustments according to your desired doneness.) and choose a shake reminder. Cook 4 minutes, flip, and cook an additional 4 minutes. To make the sauce, mix together all sauce ingredients until smooth.

## Parmesan Halibut Fillet

**Prep time: 5 minutes | Cook time: 10 minutes | Serves 4**

2 medium-sized halibut fillets
Dash of tabasco sauce
1 teaspoon curry powder
½ teaspoon ground coriander
½ teaspoon hot paprika

Kosher salt and freshly cracked mixed peppercorns, to taste
2 eggs
1½ tablespoons olive oil
½ cup grated Parmesan cheese

Preheat the air fryer to 365ºF (185ºC). On a clean work surface, drizzle the halibut fillets with the tabasco sauce. Sprinkle with the curry powder, coriander, hot paprika, salt, and cracked mixed peppercorns. Set aside.
In a shallow bowl, beat the eggs until frothy. In another shallow bowl, combine the olive oil and Parmesan cheese. One at a time, dredge the halibut fillets in the beaten eggs, shaking off any excess, then roll them over the Parmesan cheese until evenly coated. Arrange the halibut fillets in the air fryer basket in a single layer when your air fryer displays "READY" (select the cooking preset, and make minor adjustments according to your desired doneness.) and choose a shake reminder. Cook at the corresponding preset mode or Air Fry for 10 minutes, or until the fish is golden brown and crisp. Cool for 5 minutes before serving.

## Blackened Tilapia

**Prep time: 15 minutes | Cook time: 8 minutes | Serves 4**

1 large egg, beaten
Blackened seasoning, as needed

2 tablespoons light brown sugar
4 (4-ounce / 113- g) tilapia fillets
Cooking spray

In a shallow bowl, place the beaten egg. In a second shallow bowl, stir together the Blackened seasoning and the brown sugar. One at a time, dip the fish fillets in the egg, then the brown sugar mixture, coating thoroughly. Preheat the air fryer to 300ºF (149ºC). Line the air fryer basket with parchment paper. Place the coated fish on the parchment and spritz with oil. When your air fryer displays "READY" (select the cooking preset, and make minor adjustments according to your desired doneness.) and choose a shake reminder. Cook at the corresponding preset mode or Air Fry for 4 minutes. Flip the fish, spritz it with oil, and cook for 4 to 6 minutes more until the fish is white inside and flakes easily with a fork. Serve immediately.

## Breaded Coconut Shrimp

**Prep time: 5 minutes | Cook time: 10 minutes | Serves 3**

1 cup almond flour
1 cup panko breadcrumbs
1 tablespoon coconut flour
1 cup unsweetened, dried

coconut
1 egg white
12 raw large shrimp

Put shrimp on paper towels to drain. Mix coconut and panko breadcrumbs together. Then mix in coconut flour and almond flour in a different bowl. Set to the side. Dip shrimp into flour mixture, then into egg white, and then into coconut mixture. Place into air fryer basket. Repeat with remaining shrimp. When your air fryer displays "READY" (select the cooking preset, and make minor adjustments according to your desired doneness.) and choose a shake reminder. Cook 10 minutes at 350ºF (177ºC). Turn halfway through cooking process.

## Tasty Shrimp and Cherry Tomato Kebabs

**Prep time: 15 minutes | Cook time: 5 minutes | Serves 4**

1½ pounds (680 g) jumbo shrimp, cleaned, shelled and deveined
1 pound (454 g) cherry tomatoes
2 tablespoons butter, melted
1 tablespoons Sriracha sauce

Sea salt and ground black pepper, to taste
1 teaspoon dried parsley flakes
½ teaspoon dried basil
½ teaspoon dried oregano
½ teaspoon mustard seeds
½ teaspoon marjoram

**Special Equipment:**
4 to 6 wooden skewers, soaked in water for 30 minutes

Preheat the air fryer to 400ºF (204ºC). Put all the ingredients in a large bowl and toss to coat well. Make the kebabs: Thread, alternating jumbo shrimp and cherry tomatoes, onto the wooden skewers that fit into the air fryer. Arrange the kebabs in the air fryer basket. You may need to cook in batches depending on the size of your air fryer basket. When your air fryer displays "READY" (select the cooking preset, and make minor adjustments according to your desired doneness.) and choose a shake reminder. Cook at the corresponding preset mode or Air Fry for 5 minutes, or until the shrimp are pink and the cherry tomatoes are softened. Repeat with the remaining kebabs. Let the shrimp and cherry tomato kebabs cool for 5 minutes and serve hot.

## Cod Fillet Cakes with Greens

Prep time: 15 minutes | Cook time: 12 minutes | Serves 4

| | |
|---|---|
| 1 pound (454 g) cod fillets, cut into chunks | ¼ teaspoon salt |
| ⅓ cup packed fresh basil leaves | ¼ teaspoon pepper |
| | 1 large egg, beaten |
| 3 cloves garlic, crushed | 1 cup panko bread crumbs |
| ½ teaspoon smoked paprika | Cooking spray |
| | Salad greens, for serving |

In a food processor, pulse cod, basil, garlic, smoked paprika, salt, and pepper until cod is finely chopped, stirring occasionally. Form into 8 patties, about 2 inches in diameter. Dip each first into the egg, then into the panko, patting to adhere. Spray with oil on one side. Preheat the air fryer to 400ºF (204ºC). Working in batches, place half the cakes in the basket, oil-side down; spray with oil. When your air fryer displays "READY" (select the cooking preset, and make minor adjustments according to your desired doneness.) and choose a shake reminder. Cook at the corresponding preset mode or Air Fry for 12 minutes, until golden brown and cooked through. Serve cod cakes with salad greens.

## Air-Fried Breaded Fish Sticks

Prep time: 10 minutes | Cook time: 6 to 8 minutes | Makes 8 fish sticks

| | |
|---|---|
| 8 ounces (227 g) fish fillets (pollock or cod), cut into ½×3-inch strips | Salt, to taste (optional) |
| | ½ cup plain bread crumbs |
| | Cooking spray |

Preheat the air fryer to 390ºF (199ºC). Season the fish strips with salt to taste, if desired. Place the bread crumbs on a plate. Roll the fish strips in the bread crumbs to coat. Spritz the fish strips with cooking spray. Arrange the fish strips in the air fryer basket in a single layer when your air fryer displays "READY" (select the cooking preset, and make minor adjustments according to your desired doneness.) and choose a shake reminder. Cook at the corresponding preset mode or Air Fry for 6 to 8 minutes or until golden brown. Cool for 5 minutes before serving.

## Dijon Catfish Fillets

Prep time: 20 minutes | Cook time: 7 minutes | Serves 4

| | |
|---|---|
| 4 tablespoons butter, melted | 4 (4-ounce / 113-g) catfish fillets |
| 2 teaspoons Worcestershire sauce, divided | Cooking spray |
| | ½ cup sour cream |
| 1 teaspoon lemon pepper | 1 tablespoon Dijon mustard |
| 1 cup panko bread crumbs | |

In a shallow bowl, stir together the melted butter, 1 teaspoon of Worcestershire sauce, and the lemon pepper. Place the bread crumbs in another shallow bowl. One at a time, dip both sides of the fillets in the butter mixture, then the bread crumbs, coating thoroughly. Preheat the air fryer to 300ºF (149ºC). Line the air fryer basket with parchment paper. Place the coated fish on the parchment and spritz with oil. When your air fryer displays "READY" (select the cooking preset, and make minor adjustments according to your desired doneness.) and choose a shake reminder. Cook at the corresponding preset mode or Air Fry for 4 minutes. Flip the fish, spritz it with oil, and cook for 3 to 6 minutes more, depending on the thickness of the fillets, until the fish flakes easily with a fork. In a small bowl, stir together the sour cream, Dijon, and remaining 1 teaspoon of Worcestershire sauce. This sauce can be made 1 day in advance and refrigerated before serving. Serve with the fried fish.

## Fried Buttermilk Tilapia Fillet

Prep time: 10 minutes | Cook time: 10 minutes | Serves 4

| | |
|---|---|
| ½ cup all-purpose flour | Sea salt and ground black pepper, to taste |
| 1 large egg | |
| 2 tablespoons buttermilk | ½ teaspoon cayenne pepper |
| ½ cup crackers, crushed | 1 pound (454 g) tilapia fillets, cut into strips |
| 1 teaspoon garlic powder | |

In a shallow bowl, place the flour. Whisk the egg and buttermilk in a second bowl, and mix the crushed crackers and spices in a third bowl. Dip the fish strips in the flour mixture, then in the whisked eggs; finally, roll the fish strips over the cracker mixture until they are well coated on all sides. Arrange the fish sticks in the Air Fryer basket. When your air fryer displays "READY" (select the cooking preset, and make minor adjustments according to your desired doneness.) and choose a shake reminder. Cook the fish sticks at 400ºF (204ºC) for about 10 minutes, shaking the basket halfway through the cooking time. Bon appétit!

## Cajun Seasoned Catfish Fillet

Prep time: 15 minutes | Cook time: 6 minutes | Serves 4

| | |
|---|---|
| ¾ cup all-purpose flour | ¼ cup Cajun seasoning |
| ¼ cup yellow cornmeal | 4 (4-ounce / 113-g) catfish fillets |
| 1 large egg, beaten | Cooking spray |

In a shallow bowl, whisk the flour and cornmeal until blended. Place the egg in a second shallow bowl and the Cajun seasoning in a third shallow bowl. One at a time, dip the catfish fillets in the breading, the egg, and the Cajun seasoning, coating thoroughly. Preheat the air fryer to 300ºF (149ºC). Line the air fryer basket with parchment paper. Place the coated fish on the parchment and spritz with oil. When your air fryer displays "READY" (select the cooking preset, and make minor adjustments according to your desired doneness.) and choose a shake reminder. Cook at the corresponding preset mode or Air Fry for 3 minutes. Flip the fish, spritz it with oil, and cook for 3 to 5 minutes more until the fish flakes easily with a fork and reaches an internal temperature of 145ºF (63ºC). Serve warm.

## Crunchy Catfish Strips

Prep time: 5 minutes | Cook time: 16 to 18 minutes | Serves 4

| | |
|---|---|
| 1 cup buttermilk | 1 cup cornmeal |
| 5 catfish fillets, cut into 1½-inch strips | 1 tablespoon Creole, Cajun, or Old Bay seasoning |
| Cooking spray | |

Pour the buttermilk into a shallow baking dish. Place the catfish in the dish and refrigerate for at least 1 hour to help remove any fishy taste. Preheat the air fryer to 400ºF (204ºC). Spray the air fryer basket lightly with cooking spray. In a shallow bowl, combine cornmeal and Creole seasoning. Shake any excess buttermilk off the catfish. Place each strip in the cornmeal mixture and coat completely. Press the cornmeal into the catfish gently to help it stick. Place the strips in the air fryer basket in a single layer. Lightly spray the catfish with cooking spray. You may need to cook the catfish in more than one batch. When your air fryer displays "READY" (select the cooking preset, and make minor adjustments according to your desired doneness.) and choose a shake reminder. Cook at the corresponding preset mode or Air Fry for 8 minutes. Turn the catfish strips over and lightly spray with cooking spray. Cook until golden brown and crispy, 8 to 10 more minutes. Serve warm.

## Cajun Shrimp with Remoulade

Prep time: 20 minutes | Cook time: 8 minutes | Serves 4

**For the Remoulade:**
½ cup mayonnaise
1 green onion, finely chopped
1 clove garlic, minced
1 tablespoon sweet pickle relish
2 tablespoons Creole mustard
2 teaspoons fresh lemon juice
½ teaspoon hot pepper sauce
½ teaspoon Worcestershire sauce
¼ teaspoon smoked paprika
¼ teaspoon kosher salt

**For the Shrimp:**
1½ cups buttermilk
1 large egg
3 teaspoons salt-free Cajun seasoning
1 pound (454 g) jumbo raw
shrimp, peeled and deveined
2 cups finely ground cornmeal
Kosher salt and black pepper
Vegetable oil spray

In a small bowl, stir together all the ingredients until well combined. Cover the sauce and chill until serving time. In a large bowl, whisk together the buttermilk, egg, and 1 teaspoon of the Cajun seasoning. Add the shrimp and toss gently to combine. Refrigerate for at least 15 minutes, or up to 1 hour. Meanwhile, in a shallow dish, whisk together the remaining 2 teaspoons Cajun seasoning, cornmeal, and salt and pepper to taste. Spray the air fryer basket with the vegetable oil spray. Dredge the shrimp in the cornmeal mixture until well coated. Shake off any excess and arrange the shrimp in the air fryer basket. Spray with oil spray. When your air fryer displays "READY" (select the cooking preset, and make minor adjustments according to your desired doneness.) and choose a shake reminder. Set the air fryer to 350ºF (177ºC) for 8 minutes, carefully turning and spraying the shrimp with the oil spray halfway through the cooking time. Serve the shrimp with the remoulade.

## Fish Croquettes with Lemon-Dill Aioli

Prep time: 15 minutes | Cook time: 10 minutes | Serves 4

**Croquettes:**
3 large eggs, divided
12 ounces (340 g) raw cod fillet, flaked apart with two forks
¼ cup 1% milk
½ cup boxed instant mashed potatoes
2 teaspoons olive oil
⅓ cup chopped fresh dill
1 shallot, minced
1 large garlic clove, minced
¾ cup plus 2 tablespoons bread crumbs, divided
1 teaspoon fresh lemon juice
1 teaspoon kosher salt
½ teaspoon dried thyme
¼ teaspoon freshly ground black pepper
Cooking spray

**Lemon-Dill Aioli:**
5 tablespoons mayonnaise
Juice of ½ lemon
1 tablespoon chopped fresh dill

For the croquettes: In a medium bowl, lightly beat 2 of the eggs. Add the fish, milk, instant mashed potatoes, olive oil, dill, shallot, garlic, 2 tablespoons of the bread crumbs, lemon juice, salt, thyme, and pepper. Mix to thoroughly combine. Place in the refrigerator for 30 minutes. For the lemon-dill aioli: In a small bowl, combine the mayonnaise, lemon juice, and dill. Set aside. Measure out about 3½ tablespoons of the fish mixture and gently roll in your hands to form a log about 3 inches long. Repeat to make a total of 12 logs. Beat the remaining egg in a small bowl. Place the remaining ¾ cup bread crumbs in a separate bowl. Dip the croquettes in the egg, then coat in the bread crumbs, gently pressing to adhere. Place on a work surface and spray both sides with cooking spray. Preheat the air fryer to 350ºF (177ºC). Working in batches, arrange a single layer of the croquettes in the air fryer basket. When your air fryer displays "READY" (select the cooking preset, and make minor adjustments according to your desired doneness.) and choose a shake reminder. Cook at the corresponding preset mode or Air Fry for about 10 minutes, flipping halfway, until golden. Serve with the aioli for dipping.

## Crab Cakes with Veggie Salad

Prep time: 10 minutes | Cook time: 13 minutes | Serves 2

8 ounces (227 g) lump crab meat, picked over for shells
2 tablespoons panko bread crumbs
1 scallion, minced
1 large egg
1 tablespoon mayonnaise
1½ teaspoons Dijon mustard
Pinch of cayenne pepper
2 shallots, sliced thin
1 tablespoon extra-virgin olive oil, divided
1 teaspoon lemon juice, plus lemon wedges for serving
⅛ teaspoon salt
Pinch of pepper
½ (3-ounce / 85-g) small head Bibb lettuce, torn into bite-size pieces
½ apple, cored and sliced thin

Preheat the air fryer to 400ºF (204ºC). Line large plate with triple layer of paper towels. Transfer crab meat to prepared plate and pat dry with additional paper towels. Combine panko, scallion, egg, mayonnaise, mustard, and cayenne in a bowl. Using a rubber spatula, gently fold in crab meat until combined; discard paper towels. Divide crab mixture into 4 tightly packed balls, then flatten each into 1-inch-thick cake (cakes will be delicate). Transfer cakes to plate and refrigerate until firm, about 10 minutes. Toss shallots with ½ teaspoon oil in separate bowl; transfer to air fryer basket. When your air fryer displays "READY" (select the cooking preset, and make minor adjustments according to your desired doneness.) and choose a shake reminder. Cook at the corresponding preset mode or Air Fry until shallots are browned, 5 to 7 minutes, tossing once halfway through cooking. Return shallots to now-empty bowl and set aside. Arrange crab cakes in air fryer basket, spaced evenly apart. Return basket to air fryer and cook until crab cakes are light golden brown on both sides, 8 to 10 minutes, flipping and rotating cakes halfway through cooking. Meanwhile, whisk remaining 2½ teaspoons oil, lemon juice, salt, and pepper together in large bowl. Add lettuce, apple, and shallots and toss to coat. Serve crab cakes with salad, passing lemon wedges separately.

## Tuna Steak and Fruit Kebabs

Prep time: 15 minutes | Cook time: 8 to 12 minutes | Serves 4

**Kebabs:**
1 pound (454 g) tuna steaks, cut into 1-inch cubes
½ cup canned pineapple
chunks, drained, juice reserved
½ cup large red grapes

**Marinade:**
1 tablespoon honey
1 teaspoon olive oil
2 teaspoons grated fresh ginger
Pinch cayenne pepper

**Special Equipment:**
4 metal skewers

Make the kebabs: Thread, alternating tuna cubes, pineapple chunks, and red grapes, onto the metal skewers that fit into the air fryer. Make the marinade: Whisk together the honey, olive oil, ginger, and cayenne pepper in a small bowl. Brush generously the marinade over the kebabs and allow to sit for 10 minutes. Preheat the air fryer to 370ºF (188ºC). Transfer the kebabs to the air fryer basket when your air fryer displays "READY" (select the cooking preset, and make minor adjustments according to your desired doneness.) and choose a shake reminder. Cook at the corresponding preset mode or Air Fry for 4 to 6 minutes. Flip the kebabs and brush with the remaining marinade. Air fry for another 4 to 6 minutes, or until the internal temperature registers 145ºF (63ºC) on a meat thermometer and the fruit is glazed. Discard any remaining marinade. Serve hot.

## Cajun Tilapia Fillet Tacos

**Prep time: 5 minutes | Cook time: 10 to 15 minutes | Serves 6**

| | |
|---|---|
| 2 teaspoons avocado oil | coleslaw mix |
| 1 tablespoon Cajun seasoning | 12 corn tortillas |
| 4 tilapia fillets | 2 limes, cut into wedges |
| 1 (14-ounce / 397-g) package | |

Preheat the air fryer to 380°F (193°C). Line the air fryer basket with parchment paper. In a medium, shallow bowl, mix the avocado oil and the Cajun seasoning to make a marinade. Add the tilapia fillets and coat evenly. Place the fillets in the basket in a single layer, leaving room between each fillet. You may need to cook in batches. When your air fryer displays "READY" (select the cooking preset, and make minor adjustments according to your desired doneness.) and choose a shake reminder. Cook at the corresponding preset mode or Air Fry until the fish is cooked and easily flakes with a fork, 10 to 15 minutes. Assemble the tacos by placing some of the coleslaw mix in each tortilla. Add ⅓ of a tilapia fillet to each tortilla. Squeeze some lime juice over the top of each taco and serve.

## Spicy Squid with Capers

**Prep time: 10 minutes | Cook time: 5 minutes | Serves 5**

| | |
|---|---|
| 1½ pounds (680 g) squid, cut into pieces | 1 tablespoon coriander, chopped |
| 1 chili pepper, chopped | 2 tablespoons parsley, chopped |
| 1 small lemon, squeezed | 1 teaspoon sweet paprika |
| 2 tablespoons olive oil | Sea salt and ground black pepper, to taste |
| 1 tablespoon capers, drained | |
| 2 garlic cloves, minced | |

Toss all ingredients in a lightly greased Air Fryer cooking basket. When your air fryer displays "READY" (select the cooking preset, and make minor adjustments according to your desired doneness.) and choose a shake reminder. Cook your squid at 400°F (204°C) for 5 minutes, tossing the basket halfway through the cooking time.
Bon appétit!

## Marinaded Shrimp

**Prep time: 10 minutes | Cook time: 16 minutes | Serves 4**

1 pound (454 g) shrimp, peeled, deveined, and butterflied (last tail section of shell intact)
**For the Marinade:**

| | |
|---|---|
| 1 (5-ounce / 142-g) can evaporated milk | 2 tablespoons white vinegar |
| 2 eggs, beaten | 1 tablespoon baking powder |

**For the Coating:**

| | |
|---|---|
| 1 cup crushed panko breadcrumbs | ½ teaspoon Old Bay seasoning |
| ½ teaspoon paprika | ¼ teaspoon garlic powder |
| | Oil for misting or cooking spray |

Stir together all marinade ingredients until well mixed. Add shrimp and stir to coat. Refrigerate for 1 hour. When ready to cook, preheat air fryer to 390°F (199°C). Combine coating ingredients in shallow dish. Remove shrimp from marinade, roll in crumb mixture, and spray with olive oil or cooking spray. Cooking in two batches, place shrimp in air fryer basket in single layer, close but not overlapping. When your air fryer displays "READY" (select the cooking preset, and make minor adjustments according to your desired doneness.) and choose a shake reminder. Cook at 390°F (199°C) for 6 to 8 minutes, until light golden brown and crispy. Repeat step 5 to cook remaining shrimp.

## Paprika Calamari

**Prep time: 10 minutes | Cook time: 5 minutes | Serves 4**

| | |
|---|---|
| ½ cup milk | black, to taste |
| 1 cup all-purpose flour | 1 teaspoon paprika |
| 2 tablespoons olive oil | 1 red chili, minced |
| 1 teaspoon turmeric powder | 1 pound (454 g) calamari, cut into rings |
| Sea salt flakes and ground | |

In a mixing bowl, thoroughly combine the milk, flour, olive oil, turmeric powder, salt, black pepper, paprika, and red chili. Mix to combine well. Now, dip your calamari into the flour mixture to coat. When your air fryer displays "READY" (select the cooking preset, and make minor adjustments according to your desired doneness.) and choose a shake reminder. Cook your calamari at 400°F (204°C) for 5 minutes, turning them over halfway through the cooking time. Bon appétit!

## Tangy Chimichurri Mackerel Fillet

**Prep time: 5 minutes | Cook time: 14 minutes | Serves 4**

| | |
|---|---|
| 1 tablespoon olive oil, or more to taste | pepper, taste |
| | 2 tablespoons parsley |
| 1½ pounds (680 g) mackerel fillets | 2 garlic cloves, minced |
| | 2 tablespoons fresh lime juice |
| Sea salt and ground black | |

Toss the fish fillets with the remaining ingredients and place them in a lightly oiled Air Fryer cooking basket. When your air fryer displays "READY" (select the cooking preset, and make minor adjustments according to your desired doneness.) and choose a shake reminder. Cook the fish fillets at 400°F (204°C) for about 14 minutes, turning them over halfway through the cooking time. Bon appétit!

## Trout Fingers

**Prep time: 15 minutes | Cook time: 6 minutes | Serves 2**

| | |
|---|---|
| ½ cup yellow cornmeal, medium or finely ground (not coarse) | ¾ pound (340 g) skinless trout fillets, cut into strips 1 inch wide and 3 inches long |
| ⅓ cup all-purpose flour | 3 large eggs, lightly beaten |
| 1½ teaspoons baking powder | Cooking spray |
| 1 teaspoon kosher salt, plus more as needed | ½ cup mayonnaise |
| ½ teaspoon freshly ground black pepper, plus more as needed | 2 tablespoons capers, rinsed and finely chopped |
| ⅛ teaspoon cayenne pepper | 1 tablespoon fresh tarragon |
| | 1 teaspoon fresh lemon juice, plus lemon wedges, for serving |

Preheat the air fryer to 400°F (204°C). In a large bowl, whisk together the cornmeal, flour, baking powder, salt, black pepper, and cayenne. Dip the trout strips in the egg, then toss them in the cornmeal mixture until fully coated. Transfer the trout to a rack set over a baking sheet and liberally spray all over with cooking spray. Transfer half the fish to the air fryer when your air fryer displays "READY" (select the cooking preset, and make minor adjustments according to your desired doneness.) and choose a shake reminder. Cook at the corresponding preset mode or Air Fry until the fish is cooked through and golden brown, about 6 minutes. Transfer the fish sticks to a plate and repeat with the remaining fish. Meanwhile, in a bowl, whisk together the mayonnaise, capers, tarragon, and lemon juice. Season the tartar sauce with salt and black pepper. Serve the trout fingers hot along with the tartar sauce and lemon wedges.

## Codfish and Avocado Tacos

Prep time: 10 minutes | Cook time: 14 minutes | Serves 4

1 pound (454 g) codfish fillets
1 tablespoon olive oil
1 avocado, pitted, peeled and mashed
4 tablespoons mayonnaise

1 teaspoon mustard
1 shallot, chopped
1 habanero pepper, chopped
8 small corn tortillas

Toss the fish fillets with the olive oil; place them in a lightly oiled Air Fryer cooking basket. When your air fryer displays "READY" (select the cooking preset, and make minor adjustments according to your desired doneness.) and choose a shake reminder. Cook the fish fillets at 400ºF (204ºC) for about 14 minutes, turning them over halfway through the cooking time. Assemble your tacos with the chopped fish and remaining ingredients and serve warm. Bon appétit!

## Pink Salmon Burgers

Prep time: 10 minutes | Cook time: 10 to 15 minutes | Serves 4

4 (5-ounce / 142-g) cans pink salmon in water, any skin and bones removed, drained
2 eggs, beaten
1 cup whole-wheat bread crumbs

4 tablespoons light mayonnaise
2 teaspoons Cajun seasoning
2 teaspoons dry mustard
4 whole-wheat buns
Cooking spray

In a medium bowl, mix the salmon, egg, bread crumbs, mayonnaise, Cajun seasoning, and dry mustard. Cover with plastic wrap and refrigerate for 30 minutes. Preheat the air fryer to 360ºF (182ºC). Spray the air fryer basket lightly with cooking spray. Shape the mixture into four ½-inch-thick patties about the same size as the buns. Place the salmon patties in the air fryer basket in a single layer and lightly spray the tops with cooking spray. You may need to cook them in batches. When your air fryer displays "READY" (select the cooking preset, and make minor adjustments according to your desired doneness.) and choose a shake reminder. Cook at the corresponding preset mode or Air Fry for 6 to 8 minutes. Turn the patties over and lightly spray with cooking spray. Cook until crispy on the outside, 4 to 7 more minutes. Serve on whole-wheat buns.

## Creole Shrimp with Remoulade Sauce

Prep time: 15 minutes | Cook time: 10 minutes | Serves 4

1 teaspoon creole seasoning
8 slices of tomato
Lettuce leaves
¼ cup buttermilk
**For the Remoulade Sauce:**
1 chopped green onion
1 teaspoon hot sauce
1 teaspoon Dijon mustard
½ teaspoon creole seasoning

½ cup Louisiana Fish Fry
1 pound (454 g) deveined shrimp

1 teaspoon Worcestershire sauce
Juice of ½ a lemon
½ cup vegan mayo

Combine all sauce ingredients until well incorporated. Chill while you cook shrimp. Mix seasonings together and liberally season shrimp. Add buttermilk to a bowl. Dip each shrimp into milk and place in a Ziploc bag. Chill half an hour to marinate. Add fish fry to a bowl. Take shrimp from marinating bag and dip into fish fry, then add to air fryer. Ensure your air fryer is preheated to 400ºC (204ºC). Spray shrimp with olive oil. When your air fryer displays "READY" (select the cooking preset, and make minor adjustments according to your desired doneness.) and choose a shake reminder. Cook 5 minutes, flip and then cook another 5 minutes. Assemble "Keto" Po Boy by adding sauce to lettuce leaves, along with shrimp and tomato.

## Spanish Paprika Swordfish Steak

Prep time: 10 minutes | Cook time: 10 minutes | Serves 4

1 pound (454 g) swordfish steaks
4 garlic cloves, peeled
4 tablespoons olive oil
2 tablespoons fresh lemon juice, more for later

1 tablespoon fresh cilantro, roughly chopped
1 teaspoon Spanish paprika
Sea salt and ground black pepper, to taste

Toss the swordfish steaks with the remaining ingredients and place them in a lightly oiled Air Fryer cooking basket. When your air fryer displays "READY" (select the cooking preset, and make minor adjustments according to your desired doneness.) and choose a shake reminder. Cook the swordfish steaks at 400ºF (204ºC) for about 10 minutes, turning them over halfway through the cooking time. Bon appétit!

## Peppery Tiger Shrimp

Prep time: 5 minutes | Cook time: 10 minutes | Serves 4

1 pound (454 g) tiger shrimp
2 tablespoons olive oil
½ tablespoon old bay seasoning

¼ tablespoon smoked paprika
¼ teaspoon cayenne pepper
A pinch of sea salt

Preheat air fryer to 380ºF (193ºC). Toss all the ingredients in a large bowl until the shrimp are evenly coated. Arrange the shrimp in the air fryer basket when your air fryer displays "READY" (select the cooking preset, and make minor adjustments according to your desired doneness.) and choose a shake reminder. Cook at the corresponding preset mode or Air Fry for 10 minutes, shaking the basket halfway through, or until the shrimp are pink and cooked through. Serve hot.

## Buttery Lobster Tail with Spring Onions

Prep time: 5 minutes | Cook time: 8 minutes | Serves 4

1 pound (454 g) lobster tails
4 tablespoons butter, room temperature
2 garlic cloves, minced

Coarse sea salt and freshly cracked black pepper, to taste
4 tablespoons springs onions
1 tablespoon fresh lime juice

Butterfly the lobster tails by cutting through the shell and place them in a lightly oiled Air Fryer basket. In a mixing bowl, thoroughly combine the remaining ingredients. Now, spread ½ of the butter mixture over the top of the lobster meat. When your air fryer displays "READY" (select the cooking preset, and make minor adjustments according to your desired doneness.) and choose a shake reminder. Air fry the lobster tails at 380ºF (193ºC) for 4 minutes. After that, spread another ½ of the butter mixture on top; continue to cook for a further 4 minutes. Bon appétit!

## Jumbo Shrimp with Cilantro

Prep time: 5 minutes | Cook time: 8 minutes | Serves 4

1 pound (454 g) jumbo shrimp
2 tablespoons butter, at room temperature
Coarse sea salt and lemon pepper, to taste

2 tablespoons fresh cilantro, chopped
2 tablespoons fresh chives, chopped
2 garlic cloves, crushed

Toss all ingredients in a lightly greased Air Fryer cooking basket. When your air fryer displays "READY" (select the cooking preset, and make minor adjustments according to your desired doneness.) and choose a shake reminder. Cook the shrimp at 400ºF (204ºC) for 8 minutes, tossing the basket halfway through the cooking time. Bon appétit!

## Cod Fingers

**Prep time: 10 minutes | Cook time: 10 minutes | Serves 4**

2 eggs
½ cup all-purpose flour
Sea salt and ground black pepper, to taste
½ teaspoon onion powder
¼ teaspoon garlic powder
¼ cup plain breadcrumbs
1½ tablespoons olive oil
1 pound (454 g) cod fish fillets, slice into pieces

In a mixing bowl, thoroughly combine the eggs, flour, and spices. In a separate bowl, thoroughly combine the breadcrumbs and olive oil. Mix to combine well. Now, dip the fish pieces into the flour mixture to coat; roll the fish pieces over the breadcrumb mixture until they are well coated on all sides. When your air fryer displays "READY" (select the cooking preset, and make minor adjustments according to your desired doneness.) and choose a shake reminder. Cook the fish fingers at 400ºF (204ºC) for 10 minutes, turning them over halfway through the cooking time. Bon appétit!

## Beer-Battered Cod Fillet

**Prep time: 5 minutes | Cook time: 15 minutes | Serves 4**

2 eggs
1 cup malty beer
1 cup all-purpose flour
½ cup cornstarch
1 teaspoon garlic powder
Salt and pepper, to taste
4 (4-ounce / 113-g) cod fillets
Cooking spray

Preheat the air fryer to 400ºF (204ºC). In a shallow bowl, beat together the eggs with the beer. In another shallow bowl, thoroughly combine the flour and cornstarch. Sprinkle with the garlic powder, salt, and pepper. Dredge each cod fillet in the flour mixture, then in the egg mixture. Dip each piece of fish in the flour mixture a second time. Spritz the air fryer basket with cooking spray. Arrange the cod fillets in the basket in a single layer. When your air fryer displays "READY" (select the cooking preset, and make minor adjustments according to your desired doneness.) and choose a shake reminder. Cook at the corresponding preset mode or Air Fry in batches for 15 minutes until the cod reaches an internal temperature of 145ºF (63ºC) on a meat thermometer and the outside is crispy. Flip the fillets halfway through the cooking time. Let the fish cool for 5 minutes and serve.

## Catfish Nuggets

**Prep time: 10 minutes | Cook time: 7 to 8 minutes | Serves 4**

2 medium catfish fillets, cut into chunks (approximately 1 × 2 inch)
Salt and pepper, to taste
2 eggs
2 tablespoons skim milk
½ cup cornstarch
1 cup panko bread crumbs
Cooking spray

Preheat the air fryer to 390ºF (199ºC). In a medium bowl, season the fish chunks with salt and pepper to taste. In a small bowl, beat together the eggs with milk until well combined. Place the cornstarch and bread crumbs into separate shallow dishes. Dredge the fish chunks one at a time in the cornstarch, coating well on both sides, then dip in the egg mixture, shaking off any excess, finally press well into the bread crumbs. Spritz the fish chunks with cooking spray. Arrange the fish chunks in the air fryer basket in a single layer. You may need to cook in batches depending on the size of your air fryer basket. When your air fryer displays "READY" (select the cooking preset, and make minor adjustments according to your desired doneness.) and choose a shake reminder. Cook the fish chunks at the corresponding preset mode or Air Fry for 7 to 8 minutes until they are no longer translucent in the center and golden brown. Shake the basket once during cooking. Remove the fish chunks from the basket to a plate. Repeat with the remaining fish chunks. Serve warm.

## Shrimp with Peanut Mix

**Prep time: 10 minutes | Cook time: 10 minutes | Serves 4**

**For the Peanut Mix:**
1 cup roasted and salted red-skinned Spanish peanuts
8 cloves garlic, smashed and peeled
**For the Shrimp:**
1 pound (454 g) jumbo raw shrimp, peeled and deveined
3 dried red arbol chiles, broken into pieces
1 tablespoon cumin seeds
2 teaspoons vegetable oil

2 tablespoons vegetable oil
Lime wedges, for serving

In a 6 × 3-inch round heatproof pan, combine all the ingredients and toss. Place the pan in the air fryer basket. When your air fryer displays "READY" (select the cooking preset, and make minor adjustments according to your desired doneness.) and choose a shake reminder. Set the air fryer to 400ºF (204ºC) for 5 minutes, or until all the spices are toasted. Remove the pan from the air fryer and let the mixture cool. When completely cool, transfer the mixture to a mortar and pestle or clean coffee or spice grinder; crush or pulse to a very coarse texture that won't fall through the grate of the air fryer basket. In a large bowl, combine the shrimp and oil. Toss until well combined. Add the peanut mix and toss again. Place the shrimp and peanut mix in the air fryer basket. Set the air fryer to 350ºF (177ºC) for 5 minutes. Transfer to a serving dish. Cover and allow the shrimp to finish cooking in the residual heat, about 5 minutes. Serve with lime wedges.

## Exotic Fried Prawns

**Prep time: 10 minutes | Cook time: 9 minutes | Serves 4**

1½ pounds (680 g) prawns, peeled and deveined
2 garlic cloves, minced
2 tablespoons fresh chives, chopped
½ cup whole-wheat flour
½ teaspoon sweet paprika
1 teaspoon hot paprika
Salt and freshly ground black pepper, to taste
2 tablespoons coconut oil
2 tablespoons lemon juice

Toss all ingredients in a lightly greased Air Fryer cooking basket. When your air fryer displays "READY" (select the cooking preset, and make minor adjustments according to your desired doneness.) and choose a shake reminder. Cook the prawns at 400ºF (204ºC) for 9 minutes, tossing the basket halfway through the cooking time. Bon appétit!

## Mustard Fish Fillet

**Prep time: 10 minutes | Cook time: 6 minutes | Serves 4**

1 pound (454 g) fish fillets
½ teaspoon hot sauce
1 tablespoon coarse brown mustard
**For the Crumb Coating:**
¾ cup panko breadcrumbs
¼ cup stone-ground cornmeal
1 teaspoon Worcestershire sauce
Salt, to taste

¼ teaspoon salt
Oil for misting or cooking spray

Cut fish fillets crosswise into slices 1-inch wide. Mix the hot sauce, mustard, and Worcestershire sauce together to make a paste and rub on all sides of the fish. Season to taste with salt. Mix crumb coating ingredients together and spread on a sheet of wax paper. Roll the fish fillets in the crumb mixture. Spray all sides with olive oil or cooking spray and place in air fryer basket in a single layer. When your air fryer displays "READY" (select the cooking preset, and make minor adjustments according to your desired doneness.) and choose a shake reminder. Cook at 390ºF (199ºC) for 6 to 9 minutes, until fish flakes easily.

## Panko-Crusted Cod Fillets

**Prep time: 10 minutes | Cook time: 12 minutes | Serves 2**

⅓ cup panko bread crumbs
1 teaspoon vegetable oil
1 small shallot, minced
1 small garlic clove, minced
½ teaspoon minced fresh thyme
Salt and pepper, to taste
1 tablespoon minced fresh parsley
1 tablespoon mayonnaise
1 large egg yolk
¼ teaspoon grated lemon zest, plus lemon wedges for serving
2 (8-ounce / 227-g) skinless cod fillets, 1¼ inches thick
Vegetable oil spray

Preheat the air fryer to 300°F (149°C). Make foil sling for air fryer basket by folding 1 long sheet of aluminum foil so it is 4 inches wide. Lay sheet of foil widthwise across basket, pressing foil into and up sides of basket. Fold excess foil as needed so that edges of foil are flush with top of basket. Lightly spray the foil and basket with vegetable oil spray. Toss the panko with the oil in a bowl until evenly coated. Stir in the shallot, garlic, thyme, ¼ teaspoon salt, and ⅛ teaspoon pepper. Microwave, stirring frequently, until the panko is light golden brown, about 2 minutes. Transfer to a shallow dish and let cool slightly; stir in the parsley. Whisk the mayonnaise, egg yolk, lemon zest, and ⅛ teaspoon pepper together in another bowl. Pat the cod dry with paper towels and season with salt and pepper. Arrange the fillets, skinned-side down, on plate and brush tops evenly with mayonnaise mixture. (Tuck thinner tail ends of fillets under themselves as needed to create uniform pieces.) Working with 1 fillet at a time, dredge the coated side in panko mixture, pressing gently to adhere. Arrange the fillets, crumb-side up, on sling in the prepared basket, spaced evenly apart. When your air fryer displays "READY" (select the cooking preset, and make minor adjustments according to your desired doneness.) and choose a shake reminder. Cook at the corresponding preset mode or Air Fry for 12 to 16 minutes, using a sling to rotate fillets halfway through cooking. Using a sling, carefully remove cod from air fryer. Serve with the lemon wedges.

## Old Bay Tilapia Fillet and Chips

**Prep time: 5 minutes | Cook time: 15 minutes | Serves 3**

Old Bay seasoning
½ cup panko breadcrumbs
1 egg
2 tablespoons almond flour
2 (4- to 6-ounce / 113- to 170-g) tilapia fillets
Frozen crinkle cut fries

Add almond flour to one bowl, beat egg in another bowl, and add panko breadcrumbs to the third bowl, mixed with Old Bay seasoning. Dredge tilapia in flour, then egg, and then breadcrumbs. Place coated fish in air fryer along with fries. When your air fryer displays "READY" (select the cooking preset, and make minor adjustments according to your desired doneness.) and choose a shake reminder. Cook 15 minutes at 390°F (199°C).

## Mustard Calamari

**Prep time: 5 minutes | Cook time: 5 minutes | Serves 4**

2 cups flour
Sea salt and ground black pepper, to taste
1 teaspoon garlic, minced
1 tablespoon mustard
2 tablespoons olive oil
1 pound (454 g) calamari, sliced into rings

In a mixing bowl, thoroughly combine the flour, salt, black pepper, garlic, mustard, and, and olive oil. Mix to combine well. Now, dip your calamari into the flour mixture to coat. When your air fryer displays "READY" (select the cooking preset, and make minor adjustments according to your desired doneness.) and choose a shake reminder. Cook your calamari at 400°F (204°C) for 5 minutes, turning them over halfway through the cooking time. Bon appétit!

## Fried Shrimp with Parsley

**Prep time: 10 minutes | Cook time: 5 minutes | Serves 4**

18 shrimp, shelled and deveined
2 garlic cloves, peeled and minced
2 tablespoons extra-virgin olive oil
2 tablespoons freshly squeezed lemon juice
½ cup fresh parsley, coarsely chopped
1 teaspoon onion powder
1 teaspoon lemon-pepper seasoning
½ teaspoon hot paprika
½ teaspoon salt
¼ teaspoon cumin powder

Toss all the ingredients in a mixing bowl until the shrimp are well coated. Cover and allow to marinate in the refrigerator for 30 minutes. Preheat the air fryer to 400°F (204°C). Arrange the shrimp in the air fryer basket when your air fryer displays "READY" (select the cooking preset, and make minor adjustments according to your desired doneness.) and choose a shake reminder. Cook at the corresponding preset mode or Air Fry for 5 minutes, or until the shrimp are pink on the outside and opaque in the center. Remove from the basket and serve warm.

## Crispy Large Shrimp

**Prep time: 15 minutes | Cook time: 5 minutes | Serves 4**

½ cup self-rising flour
1 teaspoon paprika
1 teaspoon salt
½ teaspoon freshly ground black pepper
1 large egg, beaten
1 cup finely crushed panko bread crumbs
20 frozen large shrimp (about 1-pound / 907-g), peeled and deveined
Cooking spray

In a shallow bowl, whisk the flour, paprika, salt, and pepper until blended. Add the beaten egg to a second shallow bowl and the bread crumbs to a third. One at a time, dip the shrimp into the flour, the egg, and the bread crumbs, coating thoroughly. Preheat the air fryer to 400°F (204°C). Line the air fryer basket with parchment paper. Place the shrimp on the parchment and spritz with oil. When your air fryer displays "READY" (select the cooking preset, and make minor adjustments according to your desired doneness.) and choose a shake reminder. Cook at the corresponding preset mode or Air Fry for 2 minutes. Shake the basket, spritz the shrimp with oil, and air fry for 3 minutes more until lightly browned and crispy. Serve hot.

## Honey Halibut Steaks

**Prep time: 5 minutes | Cook time: 10 minutes | Serves 4**

1 pound (454 g) halibut steaks
¼ cup vegetable oil
2½ tablespoons Worcester sauce
2 tablespoons honey
2 tablespoons vermouth
1 tablespoon freshly squeezed lemon juice
1 tablespoon fresh parsley leaves, coarsely chopped
Salt and pepper, to taste
1 teaspoon dried basil

Preheat the air fryer to 390°F (199°C). Put all the ingredients in a large mixing dish and gently stir until the fish is coated evenly. Transfer the fish to the air fryer basket when your air fryer displays "READY" (select the cooking preset, and make minor adjustments according to your desired doneness.) and choose a shake reminder. Cook at the corresponding preset mode or Air Fry for 10 minutes, flipping the fish halfway through, or until the fish reaches an internal temperature of at least 145°F (63°C) on a meat thermometer. Let the fish cool for 5 minutes and serve.

## Coconut-Crusted Shrimp

**Prep time: 10 minutes | Cook time: 9 minutes | Serves 4**

½ cup whole wheat flour
1 cup coconut, shredded
¼ cup buttermilk
2 tablespoons olive oil
2 garlic cloves, crushed

1 tablespoon fresh lemon juice
Sea salt and red pepper flakes, to taste
1½ pounds (680 g) shrimp, peeled and deveined

Mix the flour, coconut, buttermilk, olive oil, garlic, lemon juice, salt, and red pepper in a mixing bowl. Dip the shrimp in the batter and place them in a well-greased Air Fryer cooking basket. When your air fryer displays "READY" (select the cooking preset, and make minor adjustments according to your desired doneness.) and choose a shake reminder. Cook the shrimp at 400ºF (204ºC) for 9 minutes, tossing the basket halfway through the cooking time. Bon appétit!

## Confetti Salmon Burgers

**Prep time: 10 minutes | Cook time: 12 minutes | Serves 4**

14 ounces (397 g) cooked fresh or canned salmon, flaked with a fork
¼ cup minced scallion, white and light green parts only
¼ cup minced red bell pepper
¼ cup minced celery
2 small lemons

1 teaspoon crab boil seasoning such as Old Bay
½ teaspoon kosher salt
½ teaspoon black pepper
1 egg, beaten
½ cup fresh bread crumbs
Vegetable oil, for spraying

In a large bowl, combine the salmon, vegetables, the zest and juice of 1 of the lemons, crab boil seasoning, salt, and pepper. Add the egg and bread crumbs and stir to combine. Form the mixture into 4 patties weighing approximately 5 ounces (142 g) each. Chill until firm, about 15 minutes. Preheat the air fryer to 400ºF (204ºC). Spray the salmon patties with oil on all sides and spray the air fryer basket to prevent sticking. When your air fryer displays "READY" (select the cooking preset, and make minor adjustments according to your desired doneness.) and choose a shake reminder. Cook at the corresponding preset mode or Air Fry for 12 minutes, flipping halfway through, until the burgers are browned and cooked through. Cut the remaining lemon into 4 wedges and serve with the burgers.

## Parmesan Salmon Patties

**Prep time: 10 minutes | Cook time: 13 minutes | Serves 4**

1 pound (454 g) salmon, chopped into ½-inch pieces
2 tablespoons coconut flour
2 tablespoons grated Parmesan cheese
1½ tablespoons milk
½ white onion, peeled and finely chopped
½ teaspoon butter, at room

temperature
½ teaspoon chipotle powder
½ teaspoon dried parsley flakes
⅓ teaspoon ground black pepper
⅓ teaspoon smoked cayenne pepper
1 teaspoon fine sea salt

Put all the ingredients for the salmon patties in a bowl and stir to combine well. Scoop out 2 tablespoons of the salmon mixture and shape into a patty with your palm, about ½ inch thick. Repeat until all the mixture is used. Transfer to the refrigerator for about 2 hours until firm. Preheat the air fryer to 395ºF (202ºC). Arrange the salmon patties in the basket when your air fryer displays "READY" (select the cooking preset, and make minor adjustments according to your desired doneness.) and choose a shake reminder. Cook at the corresponding preset mode or Air Fry for 13 minutes, flipping them halfway through, or until the patties are golden brown. Cool for 5 minutes before serving.

## Crab Cake Sandwich with Cajun Mayonnaise

**Prep time: 15 minutes | Cook time: 10 minutes | Serves 4**

**Crab Cakes:**
½ cup panko bread crumbs
1 large egg, beaten
1 large egg white
1 tablespoon mayonnaise
1 teaspoon Dijon mustard
¼ cup minced fresh parsley
1 tablespoon fresh lemon juice
½ teaspoon Old Bay seasoning

⅛ teaspoon sweet paprika
⅛ teaspoon kosher salt
Freshly ground black pepper, to taste
10 ounces (283 g) lump crab meat
Cooking spray

**Cajun Mayo:**
¼ cup mayonnaise
1 tablespoon minced dill pickle

1 teaspoon fresh lemon juice
¾ teaspoon Cajun seasoning

**For Serving:**
4 Boston lettuce leaves
4 whole wheat potato buns or

gluten-free buns

For the crab cakes: In a large bowl, combine the panko, whole egg, egg white, mayonnaise, mustard, parsley, lemon juice, Old Bay, paprika, salt, and pepper to taste and mix well. Fold in the crab meat, being careful not to over mix. Gently shape into 4 round patties, about ½ cup each, ¾ inch thick. Spray both sides with oil. Preheat the air fryer to 370ºF (188ºC). Working in batches, place the crab cakes in the air fryer basket. When your air fryer displays "READY" (select the cooking preset, and make minor adjustments according to your desired doneness.) and choose a shake reminder. Cook at the corresponding preset mode or Air Fry for about 10 minutes, flipping halfway, until the edges are golden. Meanwhile, for the Cajun mayo: In a small bowl, combine the mayonnaise, pickle, lemon juice, and Cajun seasoning. To serve: Place a lettuce leaf on each bun bottom and top with a crab cake and a generous tablespoon of Cajun mayonnaise. Add the bun top and serve.

## Lemon Shrimp and Broccoli

**Prep time: 10 minutes | Cook time: 6 minutes | Serves 4**

1 pound (454 g) raw shrimp, peeled and deveined
½ pound (227 g) broccoli florets
1 tablespoon olive oil
1 garlic clove, minced

2 tablespoons freshly squeezed lemon juice
Coarse sea salt and ground black pepper, to taste
1 teaspoon paprika

Toss all ingredients in a lightly greased Air Fryer cooking basket. When your air fryer displays "READY" (select the cooking preset, and make minor adjustments according to your desired doneness.) and choose a shake reminder. Cook the shrimp and broccoli at 400ºF (204ºC) for 6 minutes, tossing the basket halfway through the cooking time. Bon appétit!

## Old Bay Fried Baby Squid

**Prep time: 10 minutes | Cook time: 15 minutes | Serves 6 to 8**

½ teaspoon salt
½ teaspoon Old Bay seasoning
⅓ cup plain cornmeal
½ cup semolina flour

½ cup almond flour
5-6 cups olive oil
1½ pounds (680 g) baby squid

Rinse squid in cold water and slice tentacles, keeping just ¼-inch of the hood in one piece. Combine 1-2 pinches of pepper, salt, Old Bay seasoning, cornmeal, and both flours together. Dredge squid pieces into flour mixture and place into air fryer. Spray liberally with olive oil. When your air fryer displays "READY" (select the cooking preset, and make minor adjustments according to your desired doneness.) and choose a shake reminder. Cook 15 minutes at 345ºF (174ºC) till coating turns a golden brown.

## Oregano Mahi-Mahi Fillet
**Prep time: 10 minutes | Cook time: 14 minutes | Serves 4**

1 pound (454 g) mahi-mahi
fillets
2 tablespoons butter, at room
temperature
2 tablespoons fresh lemon juice
Kosher salt and freshly ground

black pepper, to taste
1 teaspoon smoked paprika
1 teaspoon garlic, minced
1 teaspoon dried basil
1 teaspoon dried oregano

Toss the fish fillets with the remaining ingredients and place them
in a lightly oiled Air Fryer cooking basket. When your air fryer
displays "READY" (select the cooking preset, and make minor
adjustments according to your desired doneness.) and choose a
shake reminder. Cook the fish fillets at 400ºF (204ºC) for about
14 minutes, turning them over halfway through the cooking time.
Bon appétit!

## Greek-Style Monkfish Fillet Pita
**Prep time: 10 minutes | Cook time: 14 minutes | Serves 4**

1 pound (454 g) monkfish fillets
1 tablespoon olive oil
Sea salt and ground black
pepper, to taste
1 teaspoon cayenne pepper
4 tablespoons coleslaw

1 avocado, pitted, peeled and
diced
1 tablespoon fresh parsley,
chopped
4 (6-½ inch) Greek pitas,
warmed

Toss the fish fillets with the olive oil; place them in a lightly oiled
Air Fryer cooking basket. When your air fryer displays "READY"
(select the cooking preset, and make minor adjustments
according to your desired doneness.) and choose a shake
reminder. Cook the fish fillets at 400ºF (204ºC) for about 14
minutes, turning them over halfway through the cooking time.
Assemble your pitas with the chopped fish and remaining
ingredients and serve warm. Bon appétit!

## English Muffin Mozzarella Tuna Melts
**Prep time: 10 minutes | Cook time: 14 minutes | Serves 4**

1 pound (454 g) tuna, boneless
and chopped
½ cup all-purpose flour
½ cup breadcrumbs
2 tablespoons buttermilk
2 eggs, whisked

Kosher salt and ground black
pepper, to taste
½ teaspoon cayenne pepper
1 tablespoon olive oil
4 Mozzarella cheese slices
4 English muffins

Mix all ingredients, except for the cheese and English muffins,
in a bowl. Shape the mixture into four patties and place them
in a lightly oiled Air Fryer cooking basket. When your air fryer
displays "READY" (select the cooking preset, and make minor
adjustments according to your desired doneness.) and choose
a shake reminder. Cook the fish patties at 400ºF (204ºC) for
about 14 minutes, turning them over halfway through the cooking
time. Place the cheese slices on the warm patties and serve on
hamburger buns and enjoy!

## Tangy King Prawn Salad
**Prep time: 10 minutes | Cook time: 6 minutes | Serves 4**

1½ pounds (680 g) king
prawns, peeled and deveined
Coarse sea salt and ground
black pepper, to taste
1 tablespoon fresh lemon juice
1 cup mayonnaise

1 teaspoon Dijon mustard
1 tablespoon fresh parsley,
roughly chopped
1 teaspoon fresh dill, minced
1 shallot, chopped

Toss the prawns with the salt and black pepper in a lightly
greased Air Fryer cooking basket. When your air fryer
displays "READY" (select the cooking preset, and make minor
adjustments according to your desired doneness.) and choose a
shake reminder. Cook the prawns at 400ºF (204ºC) for 6 minutes,
tossing the basket halfway through the cooking time. Add the
prawns to a salad bowl; add in the remaining ingredients and stir
to combine well.
Bon appétit!

## Lemony Tilapia Fillet
**Prep time: 5 minutes | Cook time: 10 to 15 minutes | Serves 4**

1 tablespoon lemon juice
1 tablespoon olive oil
1 teaspoon minced garlic

½ teaspoon chili powder
4 (6-ounce / 170-g) tilapia fillets

Preheat the air fryer to 380ºF (193ºC). Line the air fryer basket
with parchment paper. In a large, shallow bowl, mix together the
lemon juice, olive oil, garlic, and chili powder to make a marinade.
Place the tilapia fillets in the bowl and coat evenly. Place the
fillets in the basket in a single layer, leaving space between each
fillet. You may need to cook in more than one batch. When your
air fryer displays "READY" (select the cooking preset, and make
minor adjustments according to your desired doneness.) and
choose a shake reminder. Cook at the corresponding preset
mode or Air Fry until the fish is cooked and flakes easily with a
fork, 10 to 15 minutes. Serve hot.

## Ritzy Stuffed Shrimp
**Prep time: 15 minutes | Cook time: 24 minutes | Serves 4**

16 tail-on shrimp, peeled and
deveined (last tail section
intact)
**For the Stuffing:**
2 (6-ounce / 170-g) cans lump
crabmeat
2 tablespoons chopped shallots
2 tablespoons chopped green
onions
2 tablespoons chopped celery
2 tablespoons chopped green
bell pepper
½ cup crushed saltine crackers

¾ cup crushed panko
breadcrumbs
Oil for misting or cooking spray

1 teaspoon Old Bay seasoning
1 teaspoon garlic powder
¼ teaspoon ground thyme
2 teaspoons dried parsley
flakes
2 teaspoons fresh lemon juice
2 teaspoons Worcestershire
sauce
1 egg, beaten

Rinse shrimp. Remove tail section (shell) from 4 shrimp, discard,
and chop the meat finely. To prepare the remaining 12 shrimp,
cut a deep slit down the back side so that the meat lies open flat.
Do not cut all the way through. Preheat air fryer to 360ºF (182ºC).
Place chopped shrimp in a large bowl with all of the stuffing
ingredients and stir to combine. Divide stuffing into 12 portions,
about 2 tablespoons each. Place one stuffing portion onto the
back of each shrimp and form into a ball or oblong shape. Press
firmly so that stuffing sticks together and adheres to shrimp.
Gently roll each stuffed shrimp in panko crumbs and mist with oil
or cooking spray. Place 6 shrimp in air fryer basket when your
air fryer displays "READY" (select the cooking preset, and make
minor adjustments according to your desired doneness.) and
choose a shake reminder. Cook at 360ºF (182ºC) for 10 minutes.
Mist with oil or spray and cook 2 minutes longer or until stuffing
cooks through inside and is crispy outside. Repeat step 8 to cook
remaining shrimp.

## Garlicky Cod Fillets

**Prep time: 10 minutes | Cook time: 10 to 12 minutes | Serves 4**

| | |
|---|---|
| 1 teaspoon olive oil | coarsely chopped |
| 4 cod fillets | ½ cup nondairy milk |
| ¼ teaspoon fine sea salt | 1 Italian pepper, chopped |
| ¼ teaspoon ground black | 4 garlic cloves, minced |
| pepper, or more to taste | 1 teaspoon dried basil |
| 1 teaspoon cayenne pepper | ½ teaspoon dried oregano |
| ½ cup fresh Italian parsley, | |

Lightly coat the sides and bottom of a baking dish with the olive oil. Set aside. In a large bowl, sprinkle the fillets with salt, black pepper, and cayenne pepper. In a food processor, pulse the remaining ingredients until smoothly puréed. Add the purée to the bowl of fillets and toss to coat, then transfer to the prepared baking dish. Preheat the air fryer to 380ºF (193ºC). Put the baking dish in the air fryer basket when your air fryer displays "READY" (select the cooking preset, and make minor adjustments according to your desired doneness.) and choose a shake reminder. Cook at the corresponding preset mode or Air Fry for 10 to 12 minutes, or until the fish flakes when pressed lightly with a fork. Remove from the basket and serve warm.

## Pecan-Crusted Catfish Fillet

**Prep time: 5 minutes | Cook time: 12 minutes | Serves 4**

| | |
|---|---|
| ½ cup pecan meal | pepper |
| 1 teaspoon fine sea salt | 4 (4-ounce / 113-g) catfish fillets |
| ¼ teaspoon ground black | Avocado oil spray |
| **For Garnish (Optional):** | |
| Fresh oregano | Pecan halves |

Preheat the air fryer to 375ºF (191ºC). Spray the air fryer basket with avocado oil spray. Combine the pecan meal, sea salt, and black pepper in a large bowl. Dredge each catfish fillet in the meal mixture, turning until well coated. Spritz the fillets with avocado oil spray, then transfer to the air fryer basket. When your air fryer displays "READY" (select the cooking preset, and make minor adjustments according to your desired doneness.) and choose a shake reminder. Cook in the preheated air fryer at the corresponding preset mode or Air Fry for 12 minutes, flipping the fillets halfway through, or until cooked through and no longer translucent. Sprinkle the oregano sprigs and pecan halves on top for garnish, if desired. Serve immediately.

## Simple Scallops

**Prep time: 10 minutes | Cook time: 10 to 15 minutes | Serves 4**

| | |
|---|---|
| 2 teaspoons olive oil | 16 ounces (454 g) small |
| 1 packet dry zesty Italian | scallops, patted dry |
| dressing mix | Cooking spray |
| 1 teaspoon minced garlic | |

Preheat the air fryer to 400ºF (204ºC). Spray the air fryer basket lightly with cooking spray. In a large zip-top plastic bag, combine the olive oil, Italian dressing mix, and garlic. Add the scallops, seal the zip-top bag, and coat the scallops in the seasoning mixture. Place the scallops in the air fryer basket and lightly spray with cooking spray. When your air fryer displays "READY" (select the cooking preset, and make minor adjustments according to your desired doneness.) and choose a shake reminder. Cook at the corresponding preset mode or Air Fry for 5 minutes, shake the basket, and air fry for 5 to 10 more minutes, or until the scallops reach an internal temperature of 120ºF (49ºC). Serve immediately.

## Crab Cakes with Sriracha Mayonnaise

**Prep time: 15 minutes | Cook time: 10 minutes | Serves 4**

**Sriracha Mayonnaise:**

| | |
|---|---|
| 1 cup mayonnaise | 1½ teaspoons freshly squeezed |
| 1 tablespoon sriracha | lemon juice |

**Crab Cakes:**

| | |
|---|---|
| 1 teaspoon extra-virgin olive oil | 1 teaspoon Old Bay seasoning |
| ¼ cup finely diced red bell | 1 egg |
| pepper | 1½ teaspoons freshly squeezed |
| ¼ cup diced onion | lemon juice |
| ¼ cup diced celery | 1¾ cups panko bread crumbs, |
| 1 pound (454 g) lump crab | divided |
| meat | Vegetable oil, for spraying |

Mix the mayonnaise, sriracha, and lemon juice in a small bowl. Place ⅔ cup of the mixture in a separate bowl to form the base of the crab cakes. Cover the remaining sriracha mayonnaise and refrigerate. (This will become dipping sauce for the crab cakes once they are cooked.) Heat the olive oil in a heavy-bottomed, medium skillet over medium-high heat. Add the bell pepper, onion, and celery and sauté for 3 minutes. Transfer the vegetables to the bowl with the reserved ⅔ cup of sriracha mayonnaise. Mix in the crab, Old Bay seasoning, egg, and lemon juice. Add 1 cup of the panko. Form the crab mixture into 8 cakes. Dredge the cakes in the remaining ¾ cup of panko, turning to coat. Place on a baking sheet. Cover and refrigerate for at least 1 hour and up to 8 hours. Preheat the air fryer to 375ºF (191ºC). Spray the air fryer basket with oil. Working in batches as needed so as not to overcrowd the basket, place the chilled crab cakes in a single layer in the basket. Spray the crab cakes with oil. When your air fryer displays "READY" (select the cooking preset, and make minor adjustments according to your desired doneness.) and choose a shake reminder. Cook at the corresponding preset mode or Air Fry until golden brown, 8 to 10 minutes, carefully turning halfway through cooking. Remove to a platter and keep warm. Repeat with the remaining crab cakes as needed. Serve the crab cakes immediately with sriracha mayonnaise dipping sauce.

## Hoisin Tuna with Jasmine Rice

**Prep time: 15 minutes | Cook time: 20 minutes | Serves 4**

| | |
|---|---|
| ½ cup hoisin sauce | ½ small onion, quartered and |
| 2 tablespoons rice wine vinegar | thinly sliced |
| 2 teaspoons sesame oil | 8 ounces (227 g) fresh tuna, cut |
| 2 teaspoons dried lemongrass | into 1-inch cubes |
| 1 teaspoon garlic powder | Cooking spray |
| ¼ teaspoon red pepper flakes | 3 cups cooked jasmine rice |

Preheat the air fryer to 390ºF (199ºC). In a small bowl, whisk together the hoisin sauce, vinegar, sesame oil, lemongrass, garlic powder, and red pepper flakes. Add the sliced onion and tuna cubes and gently toss until the fish is evenly coated. Arrange the coated tuna cubes in the air fryer basket in a single layer. When your air fryer displays "READY" (select the cooking preset, and make minor adjustments according to your desired doneness.) and choose a shake reminder. Cook the fish in batches at the corresponding preset mode or Air Fry for 3 minutes. Flip the fish and cook for another 2 minutes, or until the fish is beginning to flake. Continue cooking for 1 minute, if necessary. Remove from the basket and serve over hot jasmine rice.

## Halibut Burgers

**Prep time: 10 minutes | Cook time: 14 minutes | Serves 4**

1 pound (454 g) halibut, chopped
2 garlic cloves, crushed
4 tablespoons scallions, chopped
Sea salt and ground black

pepper, to taste
1 teaspoon smoked paprika
A pinch of grated nutmeg
1 tablespoon olive oil
4 hamburger buns

Mix all ingredients, except for the hamburger buns, in a bowl. Shape the mixture into four patties and place them in a lightly oiled Air Fryer cooking basket. When your air fryer displays "READY" (select the cooking preset, and make minor adjustments according to your desired doneness.) and choose a shake reminder. Cook the fish patties at 400ºF (204ºC) for about 14 minutes, turning them over halfway through the cooking time. Serve on hamburger buns and enjoy!

## Rosemary Salmon Fillet

**Prep time: 10 minutes | Cook time: 12 minutes | Serves 4**

1½ pounds (680 g) salmon fillets
2 sprigs fresh rosemary
1 tablespoon fresh basil
1 tablespoon fresh thyme
1 tablespoon fresh dill
1 small lemon, juiced

2 tablespoons olive oil
Sea salt and ground black pepper, to taste
1 teaspoon stone-ground mustard
2 cloves garlic, chopped

Toss the salmon with the remaining ingredients; place them in a lightly oiled Air Fryer cooking basket. When your air fryer displays "READY" (select the cooking preset, and make minor adjustments according to your desired doneness.) and choose a shake reminder. Cook the salmon fillets at 380ºF (193ºC) for about 12 minutes, turning them over halfway through the cooking time. Serve immediately and enjoy!

## Scallops with Peas and Beans

**Prep time: 15 minutes | Cook time: 8 to 11 minutes | Serves 4**

1 cup frozen peas
1 cup green beans
1 cup frozen chopped broccoli
2 teaspoons olive oil

½ teaspoon dried oregano
½ teaspoon dried basil
12 ounces (340 g) sea scallops, rinsed and patted dry

Preheat the air fryer to 400ºF (204ºC). Put the peas, green beans, and broccoli in a large bowl. Drizzle with the olive oil and toss to coat well. Transfer the vegetables to the air fryer basket and cook at the corresponding preset mode or Air Fry for 4 to 6 minutes, or until they are fork-tender. Remove the vegetables from the basket to a serving bowl. Scatter with the oregano and basil and set aside. Place the scallops in the air fryer basket when your air fryer displays "READY" (select the cooking preset, and make minor adjustments according to your desired doneness.) and choose a shake reminder. Cook at the corresponding preset mode or Air Fry for 4 to 5 minutes, or until the scallops are firm and just opaque in the center. Transfer the cooked scallops to the bowl of vegetables and toss well. Serve warm.

## Panko Honey Mustard Salmon

**Prep time: 10 minutes | Cook time: 10 minutes | Serves 4**

4 (6-ounce / 170-g) skinless salmon fillets
3 tablespoons honey mustard
½ teaspoon dried thyme

½ teaspoon dried basil
¼ cup panko bread crumbs
⅓ cup crushed potato chips
2 tablespoons olive oil

Place the salmon on a plate. In a small bowl, combine the mustard, thyme, and basil, and spread evenly over the salmon. In another small bowl, combine the bread crumbs and potato chips and mix well. Drizzle in the olive oil and mix until combined. Place the salmon in the air fryer basket and gently but firmly press the bread crumb mixture onto the top of each fillet. When your air fryer displays "READY" (select the cooking preset, and make minor adjustments according to your desired doneness.) and choose a shake reminder. Bake for 9 to 12 minutes or until the salmon reaches at least 145ºF (63ºC) on a meat thermometer and the topping is browned and crisp.

## Italian Squid Tubes

**Prep time: 10 minutes | Cook time: 5 minutes | Serves 4**

1½ pounds (680 g) small squid tubes
2 tablespoons butter, melted
1 chili pepper, chopped
2 garlic cloves, minced
1 teaspoon red pepper flakes
Sea salt and ground black

pepper, to taste
¼ cup dry white wine
2 tablespoons fresh lemon juice
1 teaspoon Mediterranean herb mix
2 tablespoons Parmigiano-Reggiano cheese, grated

Toss all ingredients, except for the Parmigiano-Reggiano cheese, in a lightly greased Air Fryer cooking basket. When your air fryer displays "READY" (select the cooking preset, and make minor adjustments according to your desired doneness.) and choose a shake reminder. Cook your squid at 400ºF (204ºC) for 5 minutes, tossing the basket halfway through the cooking time. Top the warm squid with the cheese. Bon appétit!

## Monkfish Fingers with Cheese

**Prep time: 10 minutes | Cook time: 10 minutes | Serves 4**

½ cup all-purpose flour
Sea salt and ground black pepper, to taste
1 teaspoon cayenne pepper
½ teaspoon onion powder
1 tablespoon Italian parsley, chopped

1 teaspoon garlic powder
1 egg, whisked
½ cup Pecorino Romano cheese, grated
1 pound (454 g) monkfish, sliced into strips

In a shallow bowl, mix the flour, spices, egg, and cheese. Dip the fish strips in the batter until they are well coated on all sides. Arrange the fish strips in the Air Fryer cooking basket. When your air fryer displays "READY" (select the cooking preset, and make minor adjustments according to your desired doneness.) and choose a shake reminder. Cook the fish strips at 400ºF (204ºC) for about 10 minutes, shaking the basket halfway through the cooking time. Bon appétit!

# Chapter 7 Vegetables and Side Dishes

## Tomatoes with Bubbly Cheese Topping
**Prep time: 5 minutes | Cook time: 5 minutes | Serves 4**

½ cup Cheddar cheese, shredded
¼ cup Parmesan cheese, grated
1 teaspoon olive oil

4 tomatoes, cut into ½ inch slices
2 tablespoons parsley, chopped
Salt and black pepper, to taste

Preheat your Air Fryer to 380ºF (193ºC). Lightly salt the tomato slices and put them in the greased fryer basket in a single layer. Top with mozzarella and Parmesan cheeses and sprinkle with black pepper. When your air fryer displays "READY" (select the cooking preset, and make minor adjustments according to your desired doneness.) and choose a shake reminder. AirFry for 5 to 6 minutes until the cheese is melted and bubbly. Serve topped with parsley and enjoy!

## Potato Fries
**Prep time: 5 minutes | Cook time: 20 minutes | Serves 2**

2 potatoes, spiralized
1 tablespoon tomato ketchup
2 tablespoons olive oil

Salt and black pepper, to taste
2 tablespoons coconut oil

Preheat air fryer to 360ºF (182ºC). In a bowl, coat potatoes with coconut oil, salt, and pepper. Place in the frying basket when your air fryer displays "READY" (select the cooking preset, and make minor adjustments according to your desired doneness.) and choose a shake reminder. AirFry for 20 minutes, shaking once halfway through. Serve topped with mango sauce. enjoy!

## Small Parmesan Zucchini
**Prep time: 10 minutes | Cook time: 12 minutes | Serves 4**

4 small zucchinis, cut lengthwise
½ cup Parmesan cheese, grated
½ cup breadcrumbs

¼ cup melted butter
¼ cup fresh parsley, chopped
4 garlic cloves, minced
Salt and black pepper, to taste

Preheat air fryer to 370ºF (188ºC). In a bowl, mix breadcrumbs, Parmesan cheese, garlic, and parsley. Season with salt and pepper and stir in the melted butter. Scoop out the seeds with a spoon. Spoon the mixture into the zucchini. Arrange the zucchini on the greased frying basket when your air fryer displays "READY" (select the cooking preset, and make minor adjustments according to your desired doneness.) and choose a shake reminder. Bake for 12 minutes. Serve. enjoy!

## Broccoli Florets with Parmesan Cheese
**Prep time: 5 minutes | Cook time: 20 minutes | Serves 4**

1 head broccoli, cut into florets
1 tablespoon olive oil
Salt and black pepper, to taste

1 ounce (28 g) Parmesan cheese, grated

Preheat your air fryer to 360ºF (182ºC). In a bowl, mix all the ingredients. Add the mixture to a greased baking dish when your air fryer displays "READY" (select the cooking preset, and make minor adjustments according to your desired doneness.) and choose a shake reminder. Bake in the air fryer for 20 minutes. Serve warm. Enjoy!

## Roasted Balsamic Chopped Veggies
**Prep time: 5 minutes | Cook time: 18 minutes | Serves 4**

2 pounds (907 g) chopped veggies: potatoes, parsnips, zucchini, pumpkin, carrot, leeks
3 tablespoons olive oil

1 tablespoon balsamic vinegar
1 tablespoon agave syrup
Salt and black pepper, to taste

In a bowl, add olive oil, balsamic vinegar, agave syrup, salt, and black pepper; mix well. Arrange the veggies on a baking tray and place them in the frying basket. Drizzle with the dressing and massage with hands until well-coated. When your air fryer displays "READY" (select the cooking preset, and make minor adjustments according to your desired doneness.) and choose a shake reminder. AirFry for 18 to 22 minutes at 360ºF (182ºC), tossing once halfway through. Serve. enjoy!

## Mozzarella Green Cabbage with Blue Cheese
**Prep time: 5 minutes | Cook time: 20 minutes | Serves 4**

1 head green cabbage, cut into wedges
1 cup mozzarella cheese, shredded

4 tablespoons butter, melted
Salt and black pepper, to taste
½ cup blue cheese sauce

Preheat air fryer to 380ºF (193ºC). Brush cabbage wedges with butter and sprinkle with mozzarella. Transfer to a greased baking dish when your air fryer displays "READY" (select the cooking preset, and make minor adjustments according to your desired doneness.) and choose a shake reminder. Bake in the air fryer for 20 minutes. Serve with blue cheese sauce. enjoy!

## Eggplant and Zucchini Chips
**Prep time: 5 minutes | Cook time: 12 minutes | Serves 4**

1 large eggplant, cut into strips
1 zucchini, cut into strips
½ cup cornstarch

3 tablespoons olive oil
Salt to season

Preheat air fryer to 390ºF (199ºC). In a bowl, stir in cornstarch, salt, pepper, olive oil, eggplants, and zucchini. Place the coated veggies in the greased frying basket when your air fryer displays "READY" (select the cooking preset, and make minor adjustments according to your desired doneness.) and choose a shake reminder. AirFry for 12 minutes, shaking once. enjoy!

## Party Nachos
**Prep time: 5 minutes | Cook time: 10 minutes | Serves 2**

1 cup sweet corn
1 cup all-purpose flour
1 tablespoon butter

½ teaspoon chili powder
Salt to taste

Add a small amount of water to the sweet corn and grind until you obtain a very fine paste. In a bowl, mix flour, salt, chili powder, and butter; add corn and stir. Knead with your palm until you obtain a stiff dough. Preheat air fryer to 350ºF (180ºC). On a working surface, dust a little bit of flour and spread the dough with a rolling pin. Make it around ½ inch thick. Cut into tringle-shape. When your air fryer displays "READY" (select the cooking preset, and make minor adjustments according to your desired doneness.) and choose a shake reminder. AirFry in the greased frying basket for around 10 minutes. Serve with guacamole salsa. enjoy!

## Mozzarella Eggplant Schnitzels

**Prep time: 10 minutes | Cook time: 10 minutes | Serves 4**

2 eggplants
½ cup Mozzarella cheese, grated
2 tablespoons milk

1 egg, beaten
2 cups breadcrumbs
2 tomatoes, sliced

Preheat air fryer to 400ºF (205ºC). Cut the eggplants lengthways into ½-in thick slices. In a bowl, mix egg and milk. In another bowl, combine breadcrumbs and mozzarella cheese. Dip eggplant slices in the egg mixture, followed by the crumb mixture. Place in the greased frying basket when your air fryer displays "READY" (select the cooking preset, and make minor adjustments according to your desired doneness.) and choose a shake reminder. AirFry for 10 to 12 minutes, turning once halfway through. Top with tomato slices and serve. enjoy!

## Chili Black Bean and Tomato

**Prep time: 15 minutes | Cook time: 23 minutes | Serves 6**

1 tablespoon olive oil
1 medium onion, diced
3 garlic cloves, minced
1 cup vegetable broth
3 cans black beans, drained and rinsed

2 cans diced tomatoes
2 chipotle peppers, chopped
2 teaspoons cumin
2 teaspoons chili powder
1 teaspoon dried oregano
½ teaspoon salt

Over a medium heat, fry the garlic and onions in the olive oil for 3 minutes. Add the remaining ingredients, stirring constantly and scraping the bottom to prevent sticking. Preheat the air fryer to 400ºF (204ºC). Take a dish and place the mixture inside. Put a sheet of aluminum foil on top. Transfer to the air fryer when your air fryer displays "READY" (select the cooking preset, and make minor adjustments according to your desired doneness.) and choose a shake reminder. Bake for 20 minutes. When ready, plate up and serve immediately.

## Blackened Zucchini with Herb Kimchi Sauce

**Prep time: 10 minutes | Cook time: 20 minutes | Serves 2**

2 (6-ounce / 170-g) medium zucchini, ends trimmed
2 tablespoons olive oil
½ cup kimchi, finely chopped
¼ cup finely chopped fresh cilantro
¼ cup finely chopped fresh flat-leaf parsley, plus more for

garnish
2 tablespoons rice vinegar
2 teaspoons Asian chili-garlic sauce
1 teaspoon grated fresh ginger
Kosher salt and freshly ground black pepper, to taste

Brush the zucchini with half of the olive oil, place in the air fryer when your air fryer displays "READY" (select the cooking preset, and make minor adjustments according to your desired doneness.) and choose a shake reminder. Cook at 400ºF (204ºC), turning halfway through, until lightly charred on the outside and tender, about 15 minutes. Meanwhile, in a small bowl, combine the remaining 1 tablespoon olive oil, the kimchi, cilantro, parsley, vinegar, chili-garlic sauce, and ginger. Once the zucchini is finished cooking, transfer it to a colander and let it cool for 5 minutes. Using your fingers, pinch and break the zucchini into bite-size pieces, letting them fall back into the colander. Season the zucchini with salt and pepper, toss to combine, then let sit a further 5 minutes to allow some of its liquid to drain. Pile the zucchini atop the kimchi sauce on a plate and sprinkle with more parsley to serve.

## Dilled Zucchini Feta Egg Cakes

**Prep time: 5 minutes | Cook time: 13 minutes | Serves 4**

12 ounces (340 g) thawed puff pastry
4 large eggs
1 medium zucchini, sliced
4 ounces (113 g) Feta cheese,

drained and crumbled
2 tablespoons fresh dill, chopped
Salt and black pepper, to taste

Preheat air fryer to 360ºF (182ºC). In a bowl, whisk the eggs with salt and pepper. Stir in zucchini, dill, and Feta cheese. Grease a muffin tin tray with cooking spray. Roll pastry and arrange them to cover the sides of the muffin holes. Divide the egg mixture evenly between the holes. Place the muffin tray in your air fryer when your air fryer displays "READY" (select the cooking preset, and make minor adjustments according to your desired doneness.) and choose a shake reminder. Bake for 13 to 15 minutes, until golden. enjoy!

## Fried Green Tomato

**Prep time: 5 minutes | Cook time: 5 minutes | Serves 2**

1 green tomato, sliced
¼ tablespoon creole seasoning
Salt and black pepper, to taste

¼ cup flour
½ cup buttermilk
1 cup breadcrumbs

Add flour to one bowl and buttermilk to another. Season tomatoes with salt and pepper. Make a mix of creole seasoning and breadcrumbs. Roll tomato slices up in the flour, dip in buttermilk, and then into the breadcrumbs. when your air fryer displays "READY" (select the cooking preset, and make minor adjustments according to your desired doneness.) and choose a shake reminder. AirFry in the greased frying basket for 5 minutes at 400ºF (205ºC), turning once. enjoy!

## Garlicky Brussels Sprouts

**Prep time: 5 minutes | Cook time: 15 minutes | Serves 4**

1 pound (454 g) Brussels sprouts
1 teaspoon garlic powder

2 tablespoons olive oil
Salt and black pepper, to taste

Trim off the outer leaves, keeping only the head of the Brussels sprouts. In a bowl, mix olive oil, garlic powder, salt, and pepper. Add in the sprouts and coat well. Transfer them to the greased frying basket when your air fryer displays "READY" (select the cooking preset, and make minor adjustments according to your desired doneness.) and choose a shake reminder. AirFry for 15 minutes, shaking once halfway through. Serve warm. enjoy!

## Dried Dill Baby Carrots

**Prep time: 5 minutes | Cook time: 12 minutes | Serves 4**

1 pound (454 g) baby carrots
1 teaspoon dried dill
2 tablespoons olive oil

1 tablespoon honey
Salt and black pepper, to taste

Preheat air fryer to 350ºF (180ºC). In a bowl, mix olive oil, carrots, and honey; stir to coat. Season with dill, pepper, and salt. Place coated carrots in the greased frying basket when your air fryer displays "READY" (select the cooking preset, and make minor adjustments according to your desired doneness.) and choose a shake reminder. AirFry for 12 minutes, shaking once. Serve warm or chilled. enjoy!

## Spiced Roasted Cauliflower
**Prep time: 5 minutes | Cook time: 20 minutes | Serves 4**

1 head cauliflower, cut into florets
1 teaspoon garlic powder
1 teaspoon turmeric
1 teaspoon cumin
1 tablespoon olive oil
Salt and black pepper, to taste

Preheat your Air Fryer to 390ºF (199ºC). Thoroughly combine the cauliflower florets, turmeric, cumin, and garlic powder in a mixing bowl; toss to coat the florets well. Add salt and pepper to taste. Add the cauliflower to the greased fryer basket and brush with olive oil. When your air fryer displays "READY" (select the cooking preset, and make minor adjustments according to your desired doneness.) and choose a shake reminder. Air fry until browned and crispy, about 20 minutes. Be sure to shake the basket every 5 minutes or so. Serve hot. enjoy!

## Winter Veggie Delight
**Prep time: 10 minutes | Cook time: 16 minutes | Serves 2**

1 parsnip, sliced
1 cup sliced butternut squash
1 small red onion, cut into wedges
½ celery stalk, chopped
1 tablespoon fresh thyme, chopped
Salt and black pepper, to taste
2 teaspoons olive oil

Preheat air fryer to 380ºF (193ºC). In a bowl, add turnip, squash, onion, celery, thyme, pepper, salt, and olive oil; mix well. Pour the vegetables into the frying basket when your air fryer displays "READY" (select the cooking preset, and make minor adjustments according to your desired doneness.) and choose a shake reminder. AirFry for 16 minutes, tossing once. Serve. enjoy!

## Potato and Onion Patties
**Prep time: 10 minutes | Cook time: 14 minutes | Serves 4**

4 potatoes, shredded
1 onion, chopped
1 egg, beaten
¼ cup milk
2 tablespoons butter
½ teaspoon garlic powder
Salt and black pepper, to taste
3 tablespoons flour

Preheat air fryer to 390ºF (199ºC). In a bowl, add the egg, potatoes, onion, milk, butter, black pepper, flour, garlic powder, and salt and mix well to form a batter. Mold the mixture into four patties. Place the patties in a greased frying basket when your air fryer displays "READY" (select the cooking preset, and make minor adjustments according to your desired doneness.) and choose a shake reminder. AirFry for 14 to 16 minutes, flipping once. Serve warm. enjoy!

## Turmeric Rosemary Chickpeas
**Prep time: 5 minutes | Cook time: 12 minutes | Serves 4**

1 (15 -ounce / 425-g) can chickpeas, rinsed
1 tablespoon butter, melted
½ teaspoon dried rosemary
¼ teaspoon turmeric

Preheat air fryer to 380ºF (193ºC). In a bowl, combine together chickpeas, butter, rosemary, turmeric, and salt; toss to coat. Place the in the greased frying basket when your air fryer displays "READY" (select the cooking preset, and make minor adjustments according to your desired doneness.) and choose a shake reminder. AirFry for 6 minutes. Shake, and cook for 6 more minutes until crispy. enjoy!

## Garlic Cabbage Steaks
**Prep time: 5 minutes | Cook time: 15 minutes | Serves 3**

1 cabbage head
1 tablespoon garlic paste
2 tablespoons olive oil
Salt and black pepper, to taste
2 teaspoons fennel seeds

Preheat air fryer to 350ºF (180ºC). Cut the cabbage into 1½-inch thin slices. In a small bowl, combine all the other ingredients and brush cabbage with the mixture. Arrange the steaks on the greased frying basket when your air fryer displays "READY" (select the cooking preset, and make minor adjustments according to your desired doneness.) and choose a shake reminder. Bake for 15 minutes, flipping once halfway through. Serve warm or chilled. enjoy!

## Indian Masala Fried Okra
**Prep time: 10 minutes | Cook time: 12 minutes | Serves 4**

1 tablespoon chili powder
2 tablespoons garam masala
1 cup cornmeal
¼ cup flour
Salt to taste
½ pound (227 g) okra, trimmed and halved lengthwise
1 egg

Preheat air fryer to 380ºF (193ºC). In a bowl, mix cornmeal, flour, chili powder, garam masala, salt, and pepper. In another bowl, whisk the egg; season with salt and pepper. Dip the okra in the egg and then coat in cornmeal mixture. Spray okra with cooking spray and place in the frying basket. When your air fryer displays "READY" (select the cooking preset, and make minor adjustments according to your desired doneness.) and choose a shake reminder. AirFry for 6 minutes, slide the basket out, shake and cook for another 6 minutes until golden brown. Serve with hot sauce. enjoy!

## Black Sesame Eggplant Toast
**Prep time: 10 minutes | Cook time: 8 minutes | Serves 2**

2 large eggplant slices
1 large spring onion, finely sliced
2 white bread slices
½ cup sweet corn
1 egg white, whisked
1 tablespoon black sesame seeds

In a bowl, place corn, spring onion, egg white, and sesame seeds and mix well. Spread the mixture over the bread slices. Top with eggplants and place in the greased air fryer basket. When your air fryer displays "READY" (select the cooking preset, and make minor adjustments according to your desired doneness.) and choose a shake reminder. Bake for 8 to 10 minutes at 370ºF (188ºC) until golden. Serve enjoy!

## Golden Beetroot Chips
**Prep time: 5 minutes | Cook time: 12 minutes | Serves 2**

2 golden beetroots, thinly sliced
2 tablespoons olive oil
1 tablespoon yeast flakes
1 teaspoon Italian seasoning
Salt to taste

Preheat air fryer to 360ºF (182ºC). In a bowl, add olive oil, beetroot slices, Italian seasoning, and yeast and mix well. Dump the coated chips in the greased frying basket when your air fryer displays "READY" (select the cooking preset, and make minor adjustments according to your desired doneness.) and choose a shake reminder. AirFry for 12 minutes, shaking once. enjoy!

## Shallots and Carrots Bake

**Prep time: 10 minutes | Cook time: 15 minutes | Serves 4**

2 teaspoons olive oil
2 shallots, chopped
3 carrots, sliced
Salt to taste

¼ cup yogurt
2 garlic cloves, minced
2 tablespoons fresh parsley, chopped

Preheat air fryer to 370ºF (188ºC). In a bowl, mix carrots, salt, garlic, shallots, parsley, and yogurt. Drizzle with olive oil. Transfer to a greased baking dish when your air fryer displays "READY" (select the cooking preset, and make minor adjustments according to your desired doneness.) and choose a shake reminder. Bake in the air fryer for 15 minutes, shaking once. enjoy!

## Cauliflower with Parmesan Cheese

**Prep time: 5 minutes | Cook time: 8 minutes | Serves 4**

1 head of cauliflower, cut into florets
2 tablespoons olive oil

4 tablespoons Parmesan cheese, grated
Salt and black pepper, to taste

In a bowl, mix cauliflower, olive oil, salt, and black pepper. Transfer to the greased frying basket when your air fryer displays "READY" (select the cooking preset, and make minor adjustments according to your desired doneness.) and choose a shake reminder. Bake for 8 to 10 minutes at 360ºF (182ºC), shaking once, until crispy. Serve sprinkled with Parmesan cheese. enjoy!

## Turnip and Zucchini Bake

**Prep time: 5 minutes | Cook time: 18 minutes | Serves 4**

1 pound (454 g) turnips, sliced
1 large red onion, cut into rings
1 large zucchini, sliced

Salt and black pepper, to taste
2 cloves garlic, crushed
2 tablespoons olive oil

Preheat air fryer to 330ºF (166ºC). Place turnips, red onion, garlic, and zucchini in a baking pan. Drizzle with olive oil and season with salt and pepper. Place in the frying when your air fryer displays "READY" (select the cooking preset, and make minor adjustments according to your desired doneness.) and choose a shake reminder. Bake for 18 to 20 minutes, turning once. enjoy!

## Creamy-Cheesy Spinach

**Prep time: 10 minutes | Cook time: 15 minutes | Serves 4**

Vegetable oil spray
1 (10-ounce / 283-g) package frozen spinach, thawed and squeezed dry
½ cup chopped onion
2 cloves garlic, minced

4 ounces (113 g) cream cheese, diced
½ teaspoon ground nutmeg
1 teaspoon kosher salt
1 teaspoon black pepper
½ cup grated Parmesan cheese

Preheat the air fryer to 350ºF (177ºC). Spray a heatproof pan with vegetable oil spray. In a medium bowl, combine the spinach, onion, garlic, cream cheese, nutmeg, salt, and pepper. Transfer to the prepared pan. Put the pan in the air fryer basket. Bake for 10 minutes. Open and stir to thoroughly combine the cream cheese and spinach. Sprinkle the Parmesan cheese on top. When your air fryer displays "READY" (select the cooking preset, and make minor adjustments according to your desired doneness.) and choose a shake reminder. Bake for 5 minutes, or until the cheese has melted and browned. Serve hot.

## Butternut Squash with Goat Cheese

**Prep time: 10 minutes | Cook time: 20 minutes | Serves 2**

1 pound (454 g) butternut squash, cut into wedges
½ teaspoon dried rosemary
2 tablespoons olive oil

1 tablespoon maple syrup
1 cup goat cheese, crumbled
Salt to season

Preheat air fryer to 350ºF (180ºC). Brush the squash with olive oil and season with salt and rosemary. Place in the frying basket when your air fryer displays "READY" (select the cooking preset, and make minor adjustments according to your desired doneness.) and choose a shake reminder. Bake for 20 minutes, flipping once halfway through. Top with goat cheese and drizzle with maple syrup. Serve warm. enjoy!

## Blistered Shishito Pepper with Tangy Dipping

**Prep time: 10 minutes | Cook time: 6 minutes | Serves 4**

**Dipping Sauce:**
1 cup sour cream
2 tablespoons fresh lemon juice
1 clove garlic, minced
**Peppers:**
8 ounces (227 g) shishito peppers
1 tablespoon vegetable oil
1 teaspoon toasted sesame oil
Kosher salt and black pepper,

1 green onion (white and green parts), finely chopped

to taste
¼ to ½ teaspoon red pepper flakes
½ teaspoon toasted sesame seeds

In a small bowl, stir all the ingredients for the dipping sauce to combine. Cover and refrigerate until serving time. Preheat the air fryer to 400ºF (204ºC). In a medium bowl, toss the peppers with the vegetable oil. Put the peppers in the air fryer basket. When your air fryer displays "READY" (select the cooking preset, and make minor adjustments according to your desired doneness.) and choose a shake reminder. Air fry for 6 minutes, or until peppers are lightly charred in spots, stirring the peppers halfway through the cooking time. Transfer the peppers to a serving bowl. Drizzle with the sesame oil and toss to coat. Season with salt and pepper. Sprinkle with the red pepper and sesame seeds and toss again. Serve immediately with the dipping sauce.

## Bottom Rice with Currants and Pistachios

**Prep time: 10 minutes | Cook time: 20 minutes | Serves 2**

1 tablespoon olive oil
¼ teaspoon ground turmeric
2 cups cooked white basmati, jasmine, or other long-grain rice
¼ cup dried currants
¼ cup roughly chopped

pistachios
Kosher salt and freshly ground black pepper, to taste
1 tablespoon thinly sliced fresh cilantro

Combine the olive oil and turmeric in the bottom of a 7-inch round cake pan insert, metal cake pan, or foil pan. In a bowl, combine the rice, currants, and pistachios, season with salt and pepper, then spoon the rice over the oil, making sure to not stir the oil up into the rice. Very gently press the rice into an even layer. Place the pan in the air fryer when your air fryer displays "READY" (select the cooking preset, and make minor adjustments according to your desired doneness.) and choose a shake reminder. Cook at 300ºF (149ºC) until the rice is warmed through and the bottom is toasted and crispy, 20 to 25 minutes. Remove the pan from the air fryer and invert onto a serving plate. Break up the crust on the bottom of the rice, sprinkle with the cilantro, and serve warm.

## Cauliflower Tater Tots

**Prep time: 15 minutes | Cook time: 16 minutes | Serves 12**

1 pound (454 g) cauliflower, steamed and chopped
½ cup nutritional yeast
1 tablespoon oats
1 tablespoon desiccated coconuts
3 tablespoons flaxseed meal
3 tablespoons water
1 onion, chopped
1 teaspoon minced garlic
1 teaspoon chopped parsley
1 teaspoon chopped oregano
1 teaspoon chopped chives
Salt and ground black pepper, to taste
½ cup bread crumbs

Preheat the air fryer to 390ºF (199ºC). Drain any excess water out of the cauliflower by wringing it with a paper towel. In a bowl, combine the cauliflower with the remaining ingredients, save the bread crumbs. Using the hands, shape the mixture into several small balls. Coat the balls in the bread crumbs and transfer to the air fryer basket. When your air fryer displays "READY" (select the cooking preset, and make minor adjustments according to your desired doneness.) and choose a shake reminder. Air fry for 6 minutes, then raise the temperature to 400ºF (204ºC) and then air fry for an additional 10 minutes. Serve immediately.

## Fried Brussels Sprouts

**Prep time: 5 minutes | Cook time: 5 minutes | Serves 3**

1 (10-ounce / 283-g) package frozen brussels sprouts, thawed and halved
2 teaspoons olive oil
Salt and pepper, to taste

Toss the brussels sprouts and olive oil together. Place them in the air fryer basket and season to taste with salt and pepper. When your air fryer displays "READY" (select the cooking preset, and make minor adjustments according to your desired doneness.) and choose a shake reminder. Cook at 360ºF (182ºC) for approximately 5 minutes, until the edges begin to brown.

## Dijon Caesar Whole Cauliflower

**Prep time: 10 minutes | Cook time: 30 minutes | Serves 2 to 4**

3 tablespoons olive oil
2 tablespoons red wine vinegar
2 tablespoons Worcestershire sauce
2 tablespoons grated Parmesan cheese
1 tablespoon Dijon mustard
4 garlic cloves, minced
4 oil-packed anchovy fillets, drained and finely minced
Kosher salt and freshly ground black pepper, to taste
1 (1-pound / 454-g) small head cauliflower, green leaves trimmed and stem trimmed flush with the bottom of the head
1 tablespoon roughly chopped fresh flat-leaf parsley (optional)

In a liquid measuring cup, whisk together the olive oil, vinegar, Worcestershire, Parmesan, mustard, garlic, anchovies, and salt and pepper to taste. Place the cauliflower head upside down on a cutting board and use a paring knife to make an "x" through the full length of the core. Transfer the cauliflower head to a large bowl and pour half the dressing over it. Turn the cauliflower head to coat it in the dressing, then let it rest, stem-side up, in the dressing for at least 10 minutes and up to 30 minutes to allow the dressing to seep into all its nooks and crannies. Transfer the cauliflower head, stem-side down, to the air fryer when your air fryer displays "READY" (select the cooking preset, and make minor adjustments according to your desired doneness.) and choose a shake reminder. Cook at 340ºF (171ºC) for 25 minutes. Drizzle the remaining dressing over the cauliflower and cook at 400ºF (204ºC) until the top of the cauliflower is golden brown and the core is tender, about 5 minutes more. Remove the basket from the air fryer and transfer the cauliflower to a large plate. Sprinkle with the parsley, if you like, and serve hot.

## Caribbean-Inspired Yuca Roots Fries

**Prep time: 5 minutes | Cook time: 25 minutes | Serves 4**

3 yuca roots
Vegetable oil for spraying
1 teaspoon kosher salt

Trim the ends off the yuca roots and cut each one into 2 or 3 pieces depending on the length. Have a bowl of water ready. Peel off the rough outer skin with a paring knife or sharp vegetable peeler. Halve each piece of yuca lengthwise. Place the peeled pieces in a bowl of water to prevent them from oxidizing and turning brown. Fill a large pot with water and bring to a boil over high heat. Season well with salt. Add the yuca pieces to the water and cook until they are tender enough to be pierced with a fork, but not falling apart, approximately 12 to 15 minutes. Drain. Some of the yuca pieces will have fibrous string running down the center. Remove it. Cut the yuca into 2 or 3 pieces to resemble thick-cut french fries. Working in batches, arrange the yuca fries in a single layer in the air fryer basket. Spray with oil. When your air fryer displays "READY" (select the cooking preset, and make minor adjustments according to your desired doneness.) and choose a shake reminder. Cook at 400ºF (204ºC) for 10 minutes, turning the fries halfway through, until the outside of the fries is crisp and browned and the inside fluffy. Repeat with the remaining fries. Spray the cooked yuca with oil and toss with 1 teaspoon salt. Serve the yuca fries warm with Toum, Chipotle Ketchup, or Mint Chimichurri.

## Cashew and Basil Stuffed Mushrooms

**Prep time: 10 minutes | Cook time: 15 minutes | Serves 6**

1 cup basil
½ cup cashew, soaked overnight
½ cup nutritional yeast
1 tablespoon lemon juice
2 cloves garlic
1 tablespoon olive oil
Salt, to taste
1 pound (454 g) baby bella mushroom, stems removed

Preheat the air fryer to 400ºF (204ºC). Prepare the pesto. In a food processor, blend the basil, cashew nuts, nutritional yeast, lemon juice, garlic and olive oil to combine well. Sprinkle with salt as desired. Turn the mushrooms cap-side down and spread the pesto on the underside of each cap. Transfer to the air fryer when your air fryer displays "READY" (select the cooking preset, and make minor adjustments according to your desired doneness.) and choose a shake reminder. Air fry for 15 minutes. Serve warm.

## Cheddar Macaroni Balls

**Prep time: 10 minutes | Cook time: 10 minutes | Serves 2**

2 cups leftover macaroni
1 cup shredded Cheddar cheese
½ cup flour
1 cup bread crumbs
3 large eggs
1 cup milk
½ teaspoon salt
¼ teaspoon black pepper

Preheat the air fryer to 365ºF (185ºC). In a bowl, combine the leftover macaroni and shredded cheese. Pour the flour in a separate bowl. Put the bread crumbs in a third bowl. Finally, in a fourth bowl, mix the eggs and milk with a whisk. With an ice-cream scoop, create balls from the macaroni mixture. Coat them the flour, then in the egg mixture, and lastly in the bread crumbs. Arrange the balls in the preheated air fryer when your air fryer displays "READY" (select the cooking preset, and make minor adjustments according to your desired doneness.) and choose a shake reminder. Air fry for about 10 minutes, giving them an occasional stir. Ensure they crisp up nicely. Serve hot.

## Cauliflower, Chickpea, with Bread and Avocado
Prep time: 10 minutes | Cook time: 25 minutes | Serves 4

1 medium head cauliflower, cut
into florets
1 can chickpeas, drained and
rinsed
1 tablespoon extra-virgin olive
oil

2 tablespoons lemon juice
Salt and ground black pepper,
to taste
4 flatbreads, toasted
2 ripe avocados, mashed

Preheat the air fryer to 425ºF (218ºC). In a bowl, mix the
chickpeas, cauliflower, lemon juice and olive oil. Sprinkle salt
and pepper as desired. Put inside the air fryer basket when your
air fryer displays "READY" (select the cooking preset, and make
minor adjustments according to your desired doneness.) and
choose a shake reminder. Air fry for 25 minutes. Spread on top of
the flatbread along with the mashed avocado. Sprinkle with more
pepper and salt and serve.

## Cheddar Green Chile Cornbread
Prep time: 10 minutes | Cook time: 15 minutes | Serves 6

2 large eggs
¼ cup whole milk
1 (8½-ounce / 241-g) package
corn muffin mix
1 cup corn kernels

½ cup grated Cheddar cheese
1 (4-ounce / 113-g) can diced
mild green chiles, undrained
Vegetable oil spray
Parchment paper

In a medium bowl, whisk together the eggs and milk. Add the
muffin mix and stir until the batter is smooth. Stir in the corn,
cheese, and undrained chiles. Spray a 3-cup Bundt pan with
vegetable oil spray. Line the pan with parchment paper. (To do
this, cut a circle of parchment about 1 inch larger in diameter than
the top of the pan. Fold the parchment in half and cut a hole in the
middle to accommodate the center of the Bundt pan. Place the
parchment in the pan; trim any excess parchment from around
the top.) Pour the batter into the prepared pan. Place the pan in
the air fryer basket. When your air fryer displays "READY" (select
the cooking preset, and make minor adjustments according to
your desired doneness.) and choose a shake reminder. Set the
air fryer to 350ºF (177ºC) for 15 minutes. Allow the bread to rest
in the closed air fryer for 10 minutes before serving.

## Creole Spiced Potato Wedges
Prep time: 10 minutes | Cook time: 10 minutes | Serves 3 to 4

1 pound (454 g) medium Yukon
gold potatoes
½ teaspoon cayenne pepper
½ teaspoon thyme
½ teaspoon garlic powder

½ teaspoon salt
½ teaspoon smoked paprika
1 cup dry breadcrumbs
Oil for misting or cooking spray

Wash potatoes, cut into thick wedges, and drop wedges into a
bowl of water to prevent browning. Mix together the cayenne
pepper, thyme, garlic powder, salt, paprika, and breadcrumbs and
spread on a sheet of wax paper. Remove potatoes from water
and, without drying them, roll in the breadcrumb mixture. Spray
air fryer basket with oil or cooking spray and pile potato wedges
into basket. It's okay if they form more than a single layer. When
your air fryer displays "READY" (select the cooking preset, and
make minor adjustments according to your desired doneness.)
and choose a shake reminder. Cook at 390ºF (199ºC) for 8
minutes. Shake basket, then continue cooking for 2 to 7 minutes
longer, until coating is crisp and potato centers are soft. Total
cooking time will vary, depending on thickness of potato wedges.

## Fresh Broccoli Salad
Prep time: 5 minutes | Cook time: 7 minutes | Serves

3 cups fresh broccoli florets
2 tablespoons coconut oil,
melted

¼ cup sliced s
½ medium lemon, juiced

Take a 6-inch baking dish and fill with the broccoli florets. Pour
the melted coconut oil over the broccoli and add in the sliced
s. Toss together. Put the dish in the air fryer when your air fryer
displays "READY" (select the cooking preset, and make minor
adjustments according to your desired doneness.) and choose
a shake reminder. Cook at 380ºF (193ºC) for 7 minutes, stirring
at the halfway point. Place the broccoli in a bowl and drizzle the
lemon juice over it.

## Cauliflower Faux Rice Omelet
Prep time: 15 minutes | Cook time: 40 minutes | Serves 8

1 large head cauliflower, rinsed
and drained, cut into florets
½ lemon, juiced
2 garlic cloves, minced
2 (8-ounce / 227-g) cans
mushrooms
1 (8-ounce / 227-g) can water
chestnuts

¾ cup peas
1 egg, beaten
4 tablespoons soy sauce
1 tablespoon peanut oil
1 tablespoon sesame oil
1 tablespoon minced fresh
ginger
Cooking spray

Preheat the air fryer to 350ºF (177ºC). Mix the peanut oil, soy
sauce, sesame oil, minced ginger, lemon juice, and minced garlic
to combine well. In a food processor, pulse the florets in small
batches to break them down to resemble rice grains. Pour into
the air fryer basket. Drain the chestnuts and roughly chop them.
Pour into the basket. When your air fryer displays "READY" (select
the cooking preset, and make minor adjustments according to
your desired doneness.) and choose a shake reminder. Air fry
for 20 minutes. In the meantime, drain the mushrooms. Add the
mushrooms and the peas to the air fryer and continue to air fry
for another 15 minutes. Lightly spritz a frying pan with cooking
spray. Prepare an omelet with the beaten egg, ensuring it is firm.
Lay on a cutting board and slice it up. When the cauliflower is
ready, throw in the omelet and bake for an additional 5 minutes.
Serve hot.

## Garlic Cauliflower with Tahini Sauce
Prep time: 10 minutes | Cook time: 20 minutes | Serves 4

**For the Cauliflower:**
5 cups cauliflower florets
6 garlic cloves, smashed and
cut into thirds
3 tablespoons vegetable oil

½ teaspoon ground cumin
½ teaspoon ground coriander
½ teaspoon kosher salt

**For the Sauce:**
2 tablespoons tahini (sesame
paste)
2 tablespoons hot water

1 tablespoon fresh lemon juice
1 teaspoon minced garlic
½ teaspoon kosher salt

In a large bowl, combine the cauliflower florets and garlic. Drizzle
with the vegetable oil. Sprinkle with the cumin, coriander, and
salt. Toss until well coated. Place the cauliflower in the air-
fryer basket. When your air fryer displays "READY" (select the
cooking preset, and make minor adjustments according to your
desired doneness.) and choose a shake reminder. Set the air
fryer to 400ºF (204ºC) for 20 minutes, turning the cauliflower
halfway through the cooking time. In a small bowl, combine the
tahini, water, lemon juice, garlic, and salt. (The sauce will appear
curdled at first, but keep stirring until you have a thick, creamy,
smooth mixture.) Transfer the cauliflower to a large serving bowl.
Pour the sauce over and toss gently to coat. Serve immediately.

## Cheddar Cheese-Mushroom Loaf
**Prep time: 5 minutes | Cook time: 15 minutes | Serves 2**

2 cups mushrooms, chopped
½ cups Cheddar cheese, shredded

¾ cup flour
2 tablespoons butter, melted
2 eggs

In a food processor, pulse together the mushrooms, cheese, flour, melted butter, and eggs, along with some salt and pepper if desired, until a uniform consistency is achieved. Transfer into a silicone loaf pan, spreading and levelling with a palette knife. Pre-heat the fryer at 375ºF (190ºC) and put the rack inside. Set the loaf pan on the rack when your air fryer displays "READY" (select the cooking preset, and make minor adjustments according to your desired doneness.) and choose a shake reminder. Cook for 15 minutes. Take care when removing the pan from the fryer and leave it to cool. Then slice and serve.

## Red Potato Pot with Cheese Sauce
**Prep time: 10 minutes | Cook time: 15 minutes | Serves 4**

3 cups cubed red potatoes (unpeeled, cut into ½-inch cubes)
½ teaspoon garlic powder
**For the Sauce:**
2 tablespoons milk
1 tablespoon butter
2 ounces (57 g) sharp Cheddar

Salt and pepper, to taste
1 tablespoon oil
Chopped chives for garnish (optional)

cheese, grated
1 tablespoon sour cream

Place potato cubes in large bowl and sprinkle with garlic, salt, and pepper. Add oil and stir to coat well. When your air fryer displays "READY" (select the cooking preset, and make minor adjustments according to your desired doneness.) and choose a shake reminder. Cook at 390ºF (199ºC) for 13 to 15 minutes or until potatoes are tender. Stir every 4 or 5 minutes during cooking time. While potatoes are cooking, combine milk and butter in a small saucepan. Warm over medium-low heat to melt butter. Add cheese and stir until it melts. The melted cheese will remain separated from the milk mixture. Remove from heat until potatoes are done. When ready to serve, add sour cream to cheese mixture and stir over medium-low heat just until warmed. Place cooked potatoes in serving bowl. Pour sauce over potatoes and stir to combine. Garnish with chives if desired.

## Beer Battered Onion Rings
**Prep time: 5 minutes | Cook time: 12 minutes | Serves 4**

1 large onion
½ cup flour, plus 2 tablespoons
½ teaspoon salt
½ cup beer, plus 2 tablespoons

1 cup crushed panko breadcrumbs
Oil for misting or cooking spray

Peel onion, slice, and separate into rings. In a large bowl, mix together the flour and salt. Add beer and stir until it stops foaming and makes a thick batter. Place onion rings in batter and stir to coat. Place breadcrumbs in a sealable plastic bag or container with lid. Working with a few at a time, remove onion rings from batter, shaking off excess, and drop into breadcrumbs. Shake to coat, then lay out onion rings on cookie sheet or wax paper. When finished, spray onion rings with oil or cooking spray and pile into air fryer basket. When your air fryer displays "READY" (select the cooking preset, and make minor adjustments according to your desired doneness.) and choose a shake reminder. Cook at 390ºF (199ºC) for 5 minutes. Shake basket and mist with oil. Cook 5 minutes and mist again. Cook an additional 2 to 4 minutes, until golden brown and crispy.

## Chermoula Beet Roast
**Prep time: 15 minutes | Cook time: 25 minutes | Serves 4**

**Chermoula:**
1 cup packed fresh cilantro leaves
½ cup packed fresh parsley leaves
6 cloves garlic, peeled
2 teaspoons smoked paprika
2 teaspoons ground cumin
**Beets:**
3 medium beets, trimmed, peeled, and cut into 1-inch chunks
2 tablespoons chopped fresh

1 teaspoon ground coriander
½ to 1 teaspoon cayenne pepper
Pinch of crushed saffron (optional)
½ cup extra-virgin olive oil
Kosher salt, to taste

cilantro
2 tablespoons chopped fresh parsley

In a food processor, combine the cilantro, parsley, garlic, paprika, cumin, coriander, and cayenne. Pulse until coarsely chopped. Add the saffron, if using, and process until combined. With the food processor running, slowly add the olive oil in a steady stream; process until the sauce is uniform. Season with salt. Preheat the air fryer to 375ºF (191ºC). In a large bowl, drizzle the beets with ½ cup of the chermoula to coat. Arrange the beets in the air fryer basket. When your air fryer displays "READY" (select the cooking preset, and make minor adjustments according to your desired doneness.) and choose a shake reminder. Roast for 25 to minutes, or until the beets are tender. Transfer the beets to a serving platter. Sprinkle with the chopped cilantro and parsley and serve.

## Chili Fingerling Potatoes Wedges
**Prep time: 10 minutes | Cook time: 16 minutes | Serves 4**

1 pound (454 g) fingerling potatoes, rinsed and cut into wedges
1 teaspoon olive oil
1 teaspoon salt

1 teaspoon black pepper
1 teaspoon cayenne pepper
1 teaspoon nutritional yeast
½ teaspoon garlic powder

Preheat the air fryer to 400ºF (204ºC). Coat the potatoes with the rest of the ingredients. Transfer to the air fryer basket when your air fryer displays "READY" (select the cooking preset, and make minor adjustments according to your desired doneness.) and choose a shake reminder. Air fry for 16 minutes, shaking the basket at the halfway point. Serve immediately.

## Breaded Brussels Sprouts with Sage
**Prep time: 5 minutes | Cook time: 15 minutes | Serves 4**

1 pound (454 g) Brussels sprouts, halved
1 cup bread crumbs
2 tablespoons grated Grana

Padano cheese
1 tablespoon paprika
2 tablespoons canola oil
1 tablespoon chopped sage

Preheat the air fryer to 400ºF (204ºC). Line the air fryer basket with parchment paper. In a small bowl, thoroughly mix the bread crumbs, cheese, and paprika. In a large bowl, place the Brussels sprouts and drizzle the canola oil over the top. Sprinkle with the bread crumb mixture and toss to coat. Place the Brussels sprouts in the air fryer basket when your air fryer displays "READY" (select the cooking preset, and make minor adjustments according to your desired doneness.) and choose a shake reminder. Roast for 15 minutes, or until the Brussels sprouts are lightly browned and crisp. Shake the basket a few times during cooking to ensure even cooking. Transfer the Brussels sprouts to a plate and sprinkle the sage on top before serving.

## Chinese Five-Spice Butternut Squash

**Prep time: 5 minutes | Cook time: 15 minutes | Serves 4**

4 cups 1-inch-cubed butternut squash
2 tablespoons vegetable oil

1 to 2 tablespoons brown sugar
1 teaspoon Chinese five-spice powder

In a medium bowl, combine the squash, oil, sugar, and five-spice powder. Toss to coat. Place the squash in the air fryer basket. When your air fryer displays "READY" (select the cooking preset, and make minor adjustments according to your desired doneness.) and choose a shake reminder. Set the air fryer to 400ºF (204ºC) for 15 minutes or until tender.

## Lemon Chickpeas

**Prep time: 5 minutes | Cook time: 15 minutes | Serves 4**

1 (15-ounces / 425-g) can chickpeas, drained but not rinsed

2 tablespoons olive oil
1 teaspoon salt
2 tablespoons lemon juice

Preheat the air fryer to 400ºF (204ºC). Add all the ingredients together in a bowl and mix. Transfer this mixture to the air fryer basket. When your air fryer displays "READY" (select the cooking preset, and make minor adjustments according to your desired doneness.) and choose a shake reminder. Air fry for 15 minutes, ensuring the chickpeas become nice and crispy. Serve immediately.

## Breaded Mushrooms with Onion

**Prep time: 10 minutes | Cook time: 10 minutes | Serves 4**

6 small mushrooms
1 tablespoon bread crumbs
1 tablespoon olive oil
1 ounce (28 g) onion, peeled and diced

1 teaspoon parsley
1 teaspoon garlic purée
Salt and ground black pepper, to taste

Preheat the air fryer to 350ºF (177ºC). Combine the bread crumbs, oil, onion, parsley, salt, pepper and garlic in a bowl. Cut out the mushrooms' stalks and stuff each cap with the crumb mixture. When your air fryer displays "READY" (select the cooking preset, and make minor adjustments according to your desired doneness.) and choose a shake reminder. Air fry in the air fryer for 10 minutes. Serve hot.

## Curried Corn Pakodas

**Prep time: 10 minutes | Cook time: 8 minutes | Serves 5**

1 cup flour
¼ teaspoon baking soda
¼ teaspoon salt
½ teaspoon curry powder
½ teaspoon red chili powder

¼ teaspoon turmeric powder
¼ cup water
10 cobs baby corn, blanched
Cooking spray

Preheat the air fryer to 425ºF (218ºC). Cover the air fryer basket with aluminum foil and spritz with the cooking spray. In a bowl, combine all the ingredients, save for the corn. Stir with a whisk until well combined. Coat the corn in the batter and put inside the air fryer. When your air fryer displays "READY" (select the cooking preset, and make minor adjustments according to your desired doneness.) and choose a shake reminder. Air fry for 8 minutes until a golden brown color is achieved. Serve hot.

## Gourmet Chiles Rellenos

**Prep time: 20 minutes | Cook time: 30 minutes | Serves 2**

**For the Peppers:**
2 poblano peppers, rinsed and dried
⅔ cup thawed frozen or drained canned corn kernels
1 scallion, sliced
2 tablespoons chopped fresh

cilantro
½ teaspoon kosher salt
¼ teaspoon black pepper
⅔ cup grated Monterey Jack cheese

**For the Sauce:**
3 tablespoons extra-virgin olive oil
½ cup finely chopped yellow onion
2 teaspoons minced garlic
1 (6-ounce / 170-g) can tomato paste
2 tablespoons ancho chile

powder
1 teaspoon dried oregano
1 teaspoon ground cumin
½ teaspoon kosher salt
2 cups chicken broth
2 tablespoons fresh lemon juice
Mexican crema or sour cream, for serving

Place the peppers in the air-fryer basket. When your air fryer displays "READY" (select the cooking preset, and make minor adjustments according to your desired doneness.) and choose a shake reminder. Set the air fryer to 400ºF (204ºC) for 10 minutes, turning the peppers halfway through the cooking time, until their skins are charred. Transfer the peppers to a resealable plastic bag, seal, and set aside to steam for 5 minutes. Peel the peppers and discard the skins. Cut a slit down the center of each pepper, starting at the stem and continuing to the tip. Remove the seeds, being careful not to tear the chile. In a medium bowl, combine the corn, scallion, cilantro, salt, black pepper, and cheese; set aside. In a large skillet, heat the olive oil over medium-high heat. Add the onion and cook, stirring, until tender, about 5 minutes. Add the garlic and cook, stirring, for 30 seconds. Stir in the tomato paste, chile powder, oregano, and cumin, and salt. Cook, stirring, for 1 minute. Whisk in the broth and lemon juice. Bring to a simmer and cook, stirring occasionally, while the stuffed peppers finish cooking. Cut a slit down the center of each poblano pepper, starting at the stem and continuing to the tip. Remove the seeds, being careful not to tear the chile. Carefully stuff each pepper with half the corn mixture. Place the stuffed peppers in a 7-inch round baking pan with 4-inch sides. Place the pan in the air-fryer basket. Set the air fryer to 400ºF (204ºC) for 10 minutes, or until the cheese has melted. Transfer the stuffed peppers to a serving platter and drizzle with the sauce and some crema.

## Perfect Zucchini Sticks

**Prep time: 5 minutes | Cook time: 14 minutes | Serves 4**

2 small zucchini, cut into 2-inch × ½-inch sticks
3 tablespoons chickpea flour
2 teaspoons arrowroot (or cornstarch)
½ teaspoon garlic granules

¼ teaspoon sea salt
⅛ teaspoon freshly ground black pepper
1 tablespoon water
Cooking spray

Preheat the air fryer to 392ºF (200ºC). Combine the zucchini sticks with the chickpea flour, arrowroot, garlic granules, salt, and pepper in a medium bowl and toss to coat. Add the water and stir to mix well. Spritz the air fryer basket with cooking spray and spread out the zucchini sticks in the basket. Mist the zucchini sticks with cooking spray. When your air fryer displays "READY" (select the cooking preset, and make minor adjustments according to your desired doneness.) and choose a shake reminder. Air fry for 14 minutes, shaking the basket halfway through, or until the zucchini sticks are crispy and nicely browned. Serve warm.

## Classic Corn on the Cob
**Prep time: 5 minutes | Cook time: 12 minutes | Serves 4**

2 large ears fresh corn
Olive oil for misting
Salt (optional)

Shuck corn, remove silks, and wash. Cut or break each ear in half crosswise. Spray corn with olive oil. When your air fryer displays "READY" (select the cooking preset, and make minor adjustments according to your desired doneness.) and choose a shake reminder. Cook at 390ºF (199ºC) for 12 to 15 minutes or until browned as much as you like. Serve plain or with coarsely ground salt.

## Fried Crispy Shallots
**Prep time: 5 minutes | Cook time: 35 minutes | Makes 2 cups fried shallots**

12 ounces (340 g) shallots
Vegetable oil for spraying
1 teaspoon kosher salt

Peel the shallots and slice them as thinly as possible using a sharp knife, a mandoline, or a food processor outfitted with a slicing blade. Place the sliced shallots in the basket of the air fryer. When your air fryer displays "READY" (select the cooking preset, and make minor adjustments according to your desired doneness.) and choose a shake reminder. Cook at 250ºF (121ºC) for 5 minutes then open and shake the basket to toss the shallots. Repeat this process, cooking the shallots at 250ºF (121ºC) and shaking and tossing them every 5 minutes, until they become brown and crispy, approximately 35 to 40 minutes. Halfway through the cooking time, after 15 or 20 minutes, spray the shallots with oil. Once all of the shallots are browned, remove them from the air fryer. Do not allow the shallots to burn or they will become bitter. (Do not be dismayed if the browned shallots are soft immediately upon removal from the air fryer; they will crisp as they cool.) Toss the crispy shallots with salt. If not using right away, transfer the shallots to a covered storage container and store at room temperature until needed.

## Traditional Gobi Manchurian
**Prep time: 15 minutes | Cook time: 20 minutes | Serves 4**

**For the Cauliflower:**
4 cups chopped cauliflower
1 cup chopped yellow onion
1 large bell pepper, chopped
2 tablespoons vegetable oil
2 teaspoons kosher salt
1 teaspoon ground turmeric
**For the Sauce:**
3 tablespoons ketchup
2 tablespoons soy sauce
1 tablespoon rice vinegar
1 teaspoon minced garlic
1 teaspoon minced fresh ginger
1 teaspoon sriracha or other hot sauce

In a large bowl, combine the cauliflower, onion, and bell pepper. Drizzle with the vegetable oil and sprinkle with the salt and turmeric. Stir until the cauliflower is well coated. Place the cauliflower in the air-fryer basket. When your air fryer displays "READY" (select the cooking preset, and make minor adjustments according to your desired doneness.) and choose a shake reminder. Set the air fryer to 400ºF (204ºC) for 20 minutes, stirring the cauliflower halfway through the cooking time. In a small bowl, combine the ketchup, soy sauce, vinegar, garlic, ginger, and sriracha. Transfer the cauliflower to a large bowl. Pour the sauce over and toss well to combine. Serve immediately.

## Small Jicama Fries
**Prep time: 5 minutes | Cook time: 20 minutes | Serves 1**

1 small jicama, peeled
¼ teaspoon onion powder
¾ teaspoon chili powder
¼ teaspoon garlic powder
¼ teaspoon ground black pepper

Preheat the air fryer to 350ºF (177ºC). To make the fries, cut the jicama into matchsticks of the desired thickness. In a bowl, toss them with the onion powder, chili powder, garlic powder, and black pepper to coat. Transfer the fries into the air fryer basket. When your air fryer displays "READY" (select the cooking preset, and make minor adjustments according to your desired doneness.) and choose a shake reminder. Air fry for 20 minutes, giving the basket an occasional shake throughout the cooking process. The fries are ready when they are hot and golden. Serve immediately.

## Potato Croquettes
**Prep time: 15 minutes | Cook time: 15 minutes | Serves 10**

¼ cup nutritional yeast
2 cups boiled potatoes, mashed
1 flax egg
1 tablespoon flour
2 tablespoons chopped chives
Salt and ground black pepper, to taste
2 tablespoons vegetable oil
¼ cup bread crumbs

Preheat the air fryer to 400ºF (204ºC). In a bowl, combine the nutritional yeast, potatoes, flax egg, flour, and chives. Sprinkle with salt and pepper as desired. In a separate bowl, mix the vegetable oil and bread crumbs to achieve a crumbly consistency. Shape the potato mixture into small balls and dip each one into the bread crumb mixture. Put the croquettes inside the air fryer when your air fryer displays "READY" (select the cooking preset, and make minor adjustments according to your desired doneness.) and choose a shake reminder. Air fry for 15 minutes, ensuring the croquettes turn golden brown. Serve immediately.

## Feta Bell Peppers and Nuts Salad
**Prep time: 5 minutes | Cook time: 54 minutes | Serves 4**

4 bell peppers, red, orange, or yellow or a combination thereof
1 tablespoon extra-virgin olive oil plus extra for drizzling
2 tablespoons pine nuts
2 ounces Greek Feta cheese in brine, crumbled
1 teaspoon red wine vinegar
1 sprig basil, leaves removed and cut into ribbons

Simply brush the outside of the peppers with the olive oil and place them in the air fryer basket. You will likely be able to fit 2 or 3 peppers at the most. Roast at 400ºF (204ºC), turning several times, until blackened on all sides, 25 to 30 minutes. Place the cooked peppers in a bowl and cover with a clean towel. Allow the peppers to steam for 10 minutes. While the peppers are steaming, toast the pine nuts. Place the pine nuts in the pizza pan insert for the air fryer. Place the pan in the air fryer basket. When your air fryer displays "READY" (select the cooking preset, and make minor adjustments according to your desired doneness.) and choose a shake reminder. Toast at 325ºF (163ºC) until the pine nuts are lightly browned and smell toasty, 4 to 5 minutes. Check frequently to make sure the pine nuts do not scorch. Remove from the pan and set aside. Once the peppers are cool enough to handle, remove the skin from the peppers and, if necessary, the seeds and core. Tear whole peppers into 3 or 4 pieces. Arrange the peppers on a serving platter. Top with crumbled Feta and toasted pine nuts. Drizzle the peppers with additional olive oil and vinegar. Scatter basil over the peppers. Serve warm or at room temperature.

## Freash Fig, Chickpea, and Arugula Salad

**Prep time: 15 minutes | Cook time: 20 minutes | Serves 4**

8 fresh figs, halved
1½ cups cooked chickpeas
1 teaspoon crushed roasted cumin seeds
4 tablespoons balsamic vinegar
2 tablespoons extra-virgin olive

oil, plus more for greasing
Salt and ground black pepper, to taste
3 cups arugula rocket, washed and dried

Preheat the air fryer to 375ºF (191ºC). Cover the air fryer basket with aluminum foil and grease lightly with oil. Put the figs in the air fryer basket and air fry for 10 minutes. In a bowl, combine the chickpeas and cumin seeds. Remove the air fried figs from the air fryer and replace with the chickpeas. When your air fryer displays "READY" (select the cooking preset, and make minor adjustments according to your desired doneness.) and choose a shake reminder. Air fry for 10 minutes. Leave to cool. In the meantime, prepare the dressing. Mix the balsamic vinegar, olive oil, salt and pepper. In a salad bowl, combine the arugula rocket with the cooled figs and chickpeas. Toss with the sauce and serve.

## French Green Beans with Shallot

**Prep time: 10 minutes | Cook time: 10 minutes | Serves 4**

1½ pounds (680 g) French green beans, stems removed and blanched
1 tablespoon salt
½ pound (227 g) shallots,

peeled and cut into quarters
½ teaspoon ground white pepper
2 tablespoons olive oil

Preheat the air fryer to 400ºF (204ºC). Coat the vegetables with the rest of the ingredients in a bowl. Transfer to the air fryer basket when your air fryer displays "READY" (select the cooking preset, and make minor adjustments according to your desired doneness.) and choose a shake reminder. Air fry for 10 minutes, making sure the green beans achieve a light brown color. Serve hot.

## Buttery Honey Butternut Squash

**Prep time: 10 minutes | Cook time: 15 minutes | Serves 2 to 3**

1 butternut squash, peeled
Olive oil, in a spray bottle
Salt and freshly ground black pepper, to taste
2 tablespoons butter, softened

2 tablespoons honey
Pinch ground cinnamon
Pinch ground nutmeg
Chopped fresh sage

Pre-heat the air fryer to 370ºF (188ºC). Cut the neck of the butternut squash into disks about ½-inch thick. (Use the base of the butternut squash for another use.) Brush or spray the disks with oil and season with salt and freshly ground black pepper. Transfer the butternut disks to the air fryer in one layer (or just ever so slightly overlapping). When your air fryer displays "READY" (select the cooking preset, and make minor adjustments according to your desired doneness.) and choose a shake reminder. Air-fry at 370ºF (188ºC) for 5 minutes. While the butternut squash is cooking, combine the butter, honey, cinnamon and nutmeg in a small bowl. Brush this mixture on the butternut squash, flip the disks over and brush the other side as well. Continue to air-fry at 370ºF (188ºC) for another 5 minutes. Flip the disks once more, brush with more of the honey butter and air-fry for another 5 minutes. The butternut should be browning nicely around the edges. Remove the butternut squash from the air-fryer and repeat with additional batches if necessary. Transfer to a serving platter, sprinkle with the fresh sage and serve.

## Rosemary Green Beans

**Prep time: 5 minutes | Cook time: 5 minutes | Serves 1**

1 tablespoon butter, melted
2 tablespoons rosemary
½ teaspoon salt

3 cloves garlic, minced
¾ cup chopped green beans

Preheat the air fryer to 390ºF (199ºC). Combine the melted butter with the rosemary, salt, and minced garlic. Toss in the green beans, coating them well. When your air fryer displays "READY" (select the cooking preset, and make minor adjustments according to your desired doneness.) and choose a shake reminder. Air fry for 5 minutes. Serve immediately.

## Potatoes with Dried Parsley

**Prep time: 5 minutes | Cook time: 15 minutes | Serves 4**

1 pound (454 g) fingerling potatoes
1 tablespoon light olive oil

½ teaspoon dried parsley
½ teaspoon lemon juice
Coarsely ground sea salt

Cut potatoes in half lengthwise. In a large bowl, combine potatoes, oil, parsley, and lemon juice. Stir well to coat potatoes. Place potatoes in air fryer basket when your air fryer displays "READY" (select the cooking preset, and make minor adjustments according to your desired doneness.) and choose a shake reminder. Cook at 360ºF (182ºC) for 15 to 20 minutes or until lightly browned and tender inside. Sprinkle with sea salt before serving.

## Balsamic Roasted Asparagus

**Prep time: 5 minutes | Cook time: 10 minutes | Serves 4**

1 pound (454 g) asparagus, woody ends trimmed
2 tablespoons olive oil
1 tablespoon balsamic vinegar

2 teaspoons minced garlic
Salt and freshly ground black pepper, to taste

Preheat the air fryer to 400ºF (204ºC). In a large shallow bowl, toss the asparagus with the olive oil, balsamic vinegar, garlic, salt, and pepper until thoroughly coated. Arrange the asparagus in the air fryer basket when your air fryer displays "READY" (select the cooking preset, and make minor adjustments according to your desired doneness.) and choose a shake reminder. Roast for 10 minutes until crispy. Flip the asparagus with tongs halfway through the cooking time. Serve warm.

## Baby Carrot with Sesame Seeds

**Prep time: 5 minutes | Cook time: 16 minutes | Serves 4 to 6**

1 pound (454 g) baby carrots
1 tablespoon sesame oil
½ teaspoon dried dill
Pinch salt

Freshly ground black pepper, to taste
6 cloves garlic, peeled
3 tablespoons sesame seeds

In a medium bowl, drizzle the baby carrots with the sesame oil. Sprinkle with the dill, salt, and pepper and toss to coat well. Place the baby carrots in the air fryer basket when your air fryer displays "READY" (select the cooking preset, and make minor adjustments according to your desired doneness.) and choose a shake reminder. Cook at 380ºF (193ºC) for 8 minutes. Remove the basket and stir in the garlic. Return the basket to the air fryer and cook for another 8 minutes, or until the carrots are lightly browned. Serve sprinkled with the sesame seeds.

## Panko-Crusted Dill Pickles

**Prep time: 10 minutes | Cook time: 15 minutes | Serves 4**

14 dill pickles, sliced
¼ cup flour
⅛ teaspoon baking powder
Pinch of salt
2 tablespoons cornstarch plus 3

tablespoons water
6 tablespoons panko bread
crumbs
½ teaspoon paprika
Cooking spray

Preheat the air fryer to 400ºF (204ºC). Drain any excess moisture out of the dill pickles on a paper towel. In a bowl, combine the flour, baking powder and salt. Throw in the cornstarch and water mixture and combine well with a whisk. Put the panko bread crumbs in a shallow dish along with the paprika. Mix thoroughly. Dip the pickles in the flour batter, before coating in the bread crumbs. Spritz all the pickles with the cooking spray. Transfer to the air fryer basket when your air fryer displays "READY" (select the cooking preset, and make minor adjustments according to your desired doneness.) and choose a shake reminder. Air fry for 15 minutes, or until golden brown. Serve immediately.

## Gorgonzola Mushrooms with Horseradish Mayonnaise

**Prep time: 15 minutes | Cook time: 10 minutes | Serves 5**

½ cup bread crumbs
2 cloves garlic, pressed
2 tablespoons chopped fresh
coriander
⅓ teaspoon kosher salt
½ teaspoon crushed red pepper
flakes
1½ tablespoons olive oil
20 medium mushrooms, stems

removed
½ cup grated Gorgonzola
cheese
¼ cup low-fat mayonnaise
1 teaspoon prepared
horseradish, well-drained
1 tablespoon finely chopped
fresh parsley

Preheat the air fryer to 380ºF (193ºC). Combine the bread crumbs together with the garlic, coriander, salt, red pepper, and olive oil. Take equal-sized amounts of the bread crumb mixture and use them to stuff the mushroom caps. Add the grated Gorgonzola on top of each. Put the mushrooms in a baking pan and transfer to the air fryer. When your air fryer displays "READY" (select the cooking preset, and make minor adjustments according to your desired doneness.) and choose a shake reminder. Air fry for 10 minutes, ensuring the stuffing is warm throughout. In the meantime, prepare the horseradish mayo. Mix the mayonnaise, horseradish and parsley. When the mushrooms are ready, serve with the mayo.

## Air-Fried Green Beans and Bacon

**Prep time: 5 minutes | Cook time: 20 minutes | Serves 4**

3 cups frozen cut green beans
(do not thaw)
1 medium onion, chopped
3 slices bacon, chopped

¼ cup water
Kosher salt and black pepper,
to taste

In a 6 × 3-inch round heatproof pan, combine the frozen green beans, onion, bacon, and water. Toss to combine. Place the pan in the air fryer basket. When your air fryer displays "READY" (select the cooking preset, and make minor adjustments according to your desired doneness.) and choose a shake reminder. Set the air fryer to 375ºF (190ºC) for 15 minutes. Raise the air fryer temperature to 400ºF (204ºC) for 5 minutes. Season the beans with salt and pepper to taste and toss well. Remove the pan from the air fryer basket and cover with foil. Let the beans rest for 5 minutes before serving.

## Mole-Braised Cauliflower with Sesame

**Prep time: 15 minutes | Cook time: 18 minutes | Serves 2**

8 ounces (227 g) medium
cauliflower florets
1 tablespoon vegetable oil
Kosher salt and freshly ground
black pepper, to taste
1½ cups vegetable broth
2 tablespoons New Mexico
chile powder (or regular chili
powder)
2 tablespoons salted roasted

peanuts
1 tablespoon toasted sesame
seeds, plus more for garnish
1 tablespoon finely chopped
golden raisins
1 teaspoon kosher salt
1 teaspoon dark brown sugar
½ teaspoon dried oregano
¼ teaspoon cayenne pepper
⅛ teaspoon ground cinnamon

In a large bowl, toss the cauliflower with the oil and season with salt and black pepper. Transfer to a 7-inch round cake pan insert, metal cake pan, or foil pan. When your air fryer displays "READY" (select the cooking preset, and make minor adjustments according to your desired doneness.) and choose a shake reminder. Place the pan in the preheated air fryer and cook at 375ºF (190ºC) until the cauliflower is tender and lightly browned at the edges, about 10 minutes, stirring halfway through. Meanwhile, in a small blender, combine the broth, chile powder, peanuts, sesame seeds, raisins, salt, brown sugar, oregano, cayenne, and cinnamon and puree until smooth. Pour into a small saucepan or skillet and bring to a simmer over medium heat, then cook until reduced by half, 3 to 5 minutes. Pour the hot mole sauce over the cauliflower in the pan, stir to coat, then cook until the sauce is thickened and lightly charred on the cauliflower, about 5 minutes more. Sprinkle with more sesame seeds and serve warm.

## Panko-Ravioli

**Prep time: 10 minutes | Cook time: 6 minutes | Serves 4**

½ cup panko bread crumbs
2 teaspoons nutritional yeast
1 teaspoon dried basil
1 teaspoon dried oregano
1 teaspoon garlic powder

Salt and ground black pepper,
to taste
¼ cup aquafaba
8 ounces (227 g) ravioli
Cooking spray

Cover the air fryer basket with aluminum foil and coat with a light brushing of oil. Preheat the air fryer to 400ºF (204ºC). Combine the panko bread crumbs, nutritional yeast, basil, oregano, and garlic powder. Sprinkle with salt and pepper to taste. Put the aquafaba in a separate bowl. Dip the ravioli in the aquafaba before coating it in the panko mixture. Spritz with cooking spray and transfer to the air fryer. When your air fryer displays "READY" (select the cooking preset, and make minor adjustments according to your desired doneness.) and choose a shake reminder. Air fry for 6 minutes. Shake the air fryer basket halfway. Serve hot.

## Minty Green Peas

**Prep time: 5 minutes | Cook time: 5 minutes | Serves 4**

1 cup shredded lettuce
1 (10-ounce / 283-g) package
frozen green peas, thawed

1 tablespoon fresh mint,
shredded
1 teaspoon melted butter

Lay the shredded lettuce in the air fryer basket. Toss together the peas, mint, and melted butter and spoon over the lettuce. When your air fryer displays "READY" (select the cooking preset, and make minor adjustments according to your desired doneness.) and choose a shake reminder. Cook at 360ºF (182ºC) for 5 minutes, until peas are warm and lettuce wilts.

## Cornmeal- Crusted Green Tomato with Sriracha Mayo

**Prep time: 15 minutes | Cook time: 13 minutes | Serves 4**

3 green tomatoes
Salt and freshly ground black pepper, to taste
⅓ cup all-purpose flour
2 eggs
½ cup buttermilk
**For the Sriracha Mayo:**
½ cup mayonnaise
1 to 2 tablespoons sriracha hot

1 cup panko breadcrumbs
1 cup cornmeal
Olive oil, in a spray bottle
Fresh thyme sprigs or chopped fresh chives

sauce
1 tablespoon milk

Cut the tomatoes in ¼-inch slices. Pat them dry with a clean kitchen towel and season generously with salt and pepper. Set up a dredging station using three shallow dishes. Place the flour in the first shallow dish, whisk the eggs and buttermilk together in the second dish, and combine the panko breadcrumbs and cornmeal in the third dish. Pre-heat the air fryer to 400ºF (204ºC). Dredge the tomato slices in flour to coat on all sides. Then dip them into the egg mixture and finally press them into the breadcrumbs to coat all sides of the tomato. Spray or brush the air-fryer basket with olive oil. Transfer 3 to 4 tomato slices into the basket and spray the top with olive oil. When your air fryer displays "READY" (select the cooking preset, and make minor adjustments according to your desired doneness.) and choose a shake reminder. Air-fry the tomatoes at 400ºF (204ºC) for 8 minutes. Flip them over, spray the other side with oil and air-fry for an additional 4 minutes until golden brown. While the tomatoes are cooking, make the sriracha mayo. Combine the mayonnaise, 1 tablespoon of the sriracha hot sauce and milk in a small bowl. Stir well until the mixture is smooth. Add more sriracha sauce to taste. When the tomatoes are done, transfer them to a cooling rack or a platter lined with paper towels so the bottom does not get soggy. Before serving, carefully stack the all the tomatoes into air fryer and air-fry at 350ºF (177ºC) for 1 to 2 minutes to heat them back up. Serve the fried green tomatoes hot with the sriracha mayo on the side. Season one last time with salt and freshly ground black pepper and garnish with sprigs of fresh thyme or chopped fresh chives.

## Indian Okra and Red Onion

**Prep time: 15 minutes | Cook time: 15 minutes | Serves 4**

1 pound (454 g) okra, sliced ¼ inch thick
1 cup coarsely chopped red onion
2 tablespoons vegetable oil
1 teaspoon ground turmeric
1 teaspoon kosher salt
1 teaspoon ground cumin

1 teaspoon ground coriander
¼ to ½ teaspoon cayenne pepper
¼ teaspoon amchoor (optional)
½ cup chopped fresh tomato
Juice of 1 lemon
¼ cup chopped fresh cilantro or parsley

In a large bowl, combine the okra and onion. Drizzle with the vegetable oil and sprinkle with the turmeric, salt, cumin, coriander, cayenne, and amchoor (if using). Spread the spiced vegetables over the air-fryer basket, making as even and flat a layer as possible. When your air fryer displays "READY" (select the cooking preset, and make minor adjustments according to your desired doneness.) and choose a shake reminder. Set the air fryer to 375ºF (190ºC) for 15 minutes, stirring halfway through the cooking time. (Don't panic if you see some stickiness to the okra. This will dissipate once it cooks.) After 10 minutes, add the tomato to the basket. Cook for the remaining 5 minutes, until the tomato is wilted and cooked through. Drizzle the vegetables with the lemon juice and toss to combine. Garnish with the cilantro and serve.

## Carrots with Fresh Thyme

**Prep time: 5 minutes | Cook time: 12 minutes | Serves 2**

10 to 12 (1-pound / 454-g) heirloom or rainbow carrots, scrubbed but not peeled
1 teaspoon olive oil
Salt and freshly ground black

pepper, to taste
1 tablespoon butter
1 teaspoon fresh orange zest
1 teaspoon chopped fresh thyme

Pre-heat the air fryer to 400ºF (204ºC). Scrub the carrots and halve them lengthwise. Toss them in the olive oil, season with salt and freshly ground black pepper and transfer to the air fryer. When your air fryer displays "READY" (select the cooking preset, and make minor adjustments according to your desired doneness.) and choose a shake reminder. Air-fry at 400ºF (204ºC) for 12 minutes, shaking the basket every once in a while to rotate the carrots as they cook. As soon as the carrots have finished cooking, add the butter, orange zest and thyme and toss all the ingredients together in the air fryer basket to melt the butter and coat evenly. Serve warm.

## Oregano Radishes

**Prep time: 5 minutes | Cook time: 10 minutes | Serves 2**

1 pound (454 g) radishes
2 tablespoons unsalted butter, melted

¼ teaspoon dried oregano
½ teaspoon dried parsley
½ teaspoon garlic powder

Preheat the air fryer to 350ºF (177ºC). Prepare the radishes by cutting off their tops and bottoms and quartering them. In a bowl, combine the butter, dried oregano, dried parsley, and garlic powder. Toss with the radishes to coat. Transfer the radishes to the air fryer when your air fryer displays "READY" (select the cooking preset, and make minor adjustments according to your desired doneness.) and choose a shake reminder. Air fry for 10 minutes, shaking the basket at the halfway point to ensure the radishes air fry evenly through. The radishes are ready when they turn brown. Serve immediately.

## Cheesy Asparagus Fries

**Prep time: 15 minutes | Cook time: 5 to 7 minutes | Serves 4**

2 egg whites
¼ cup water
¼ cup plus 2 tablespoons grated Parmesan cheese, divided
¾ cup panko bread crumbs

¼ teaspoon salt
12 ounces (340 g) fresh asparagus spears, woody ends trimmed
Cooking spray

Preheat the air fryer to 390ºF (199ºC). In a shallow dish, whisk together the egg whites and water until slightly foamy. In a separate shallow dish, thoroughly combine ¼ cup of Parmesan cheese, bread crumbs, and salt. Dip the asparagus in the egg white, then roll in the cheese mixture to coat well. Place the asparagus in the air fryer basket in a single layer, leaving space between each spear. When your air fryer displays "READY" (select the cooking preset, and make minor adjustments according to your desired doneness.) and choose a shake reminder. You may need to work in batches to avoid overcrowding. Spritz the asparagus with cooking spray and air fry for 5 to 7 minutes until golden brown and crisp. Repeat with the remaining asparagus spears. Sprinkle with the remaining 2 tablespoons of cheese and serve hot.

## Honey-Glazed Roasted Vegetable

**Prep time: 15 minutes | Cook time: 20 minutes | Makes 3 cups**

**Glaze:**

| | |
|---|---|
| 2 tablespoons raw honey | ⅛ teaspoon dried rosemary |
| 2 teaspoons minced garlic | ⅛ teaspoon dried thyme |
| ¼ teaspoon dried marjoram | ½ teaspoon salt |
| ¼ teaspoon dried basil | ¼ teaspoon ground black |
| ¼ teaspoon dried oregano | pepper |
| ⅛ teaspoon dried sage | |

**Veggies:**

| | |
|---|---|
| 3 to 4 medium red potatoes, cut into 1- to 2-inch pieces | rounds |
| 1 small zucchini, cut into 1- to 2-inch pieces | 1 (10.5-ounce / 298-g) package cherry tomatoes, halved |
| 1 small carrot, sliced into ¼-inch | 1 cup sliced mushrooms |
| | 3 tablespoons olive oil |

Preheat the air fryer to 380ºF (193ºC). Combine the honey, garlic, marjoram, basil, oregano, sage, rosemary, thyme, salt, and pepper in a small bowl and stir to mix well. Set aside. Place the red potatoes, zucchini, carrot, cherry tomatoes, and mushroom in a large bowl. Drizzle with the olive oil and toss to coat. Pour the veggies into the air fryer basket when your air fryer displays "READY" (select the cooking preset, and make minor adjustments according to your desired doneness.) and choose a shake reminder. Roast for 15 minutes, shaking the basket halfway through. When ready, transfer the roasted veggies to the large bowl. Pour the honey mixture over the veggies, tossing to coat. Spread out the veggies in a baking pan and place in the air fryer. Increase the temperature to 390ºF (199ºC) and roast for an additional 5 minutes, or until the veggies are tender and glazed. Serve warm.

## Hasselback with Pesto and Sour Cream

**Prep time: 10 minutes | Cook time: 40 minutes | Serves 2**

| | |
|---|---|
| 2 (8- to 10-ounce / 227- to 283-g) medium russet potatoes | leaf parsley leaves |
| 5 tablespoons olive oil | 1 tablespoon chopped walnuts |
| Kosher salt and freshly ground black pepper, to taste | 1 tablespoon grated Parmesan cheese |
| ¼ cup roughly chopped fresh chives | 1 teaspoon fresh lemon juice |
| 2 tablespoons packed fresh flat- | 1 small garlic clove, peeled |
| | ¼ cup sour cream |

Place the potatoes on a cutting board and lay a chopstick or thin-handled wooden spoon to the side of each potato. Thinly slice the potatoes crosswise, letting the chopstick or spoon handle stop the blade of your knife, and stop ½ inch short of each end of the potato. Rub the potatoes with 1 tablespoon of the olive oil and season with salt and pepper. Place the potatoes, cut-side up, in the air fryer when your air fryer displays "READY" (select the cooking preset, and make minor adjustments according to your desired doneness.) and choose a shake reminder. Cook at 375ºF (190ºC) until golden brown and crisp on the outside and tender inside, about 40 minutes, drizzling the insides with 1 tablespoon more olive oil and seasoning with more salt and pepper halfway through. Meanwhile, in a small blender or food processor, combine the remaining 3 tablespoons olive oil, the chives, parsley, walnuts, Parmesan, lemon juice, and garlic and puree until smooth. Season the chive pesto with salt and pepper. Remove the potatoes from the air fryer and transfer to plates. Drizzle the potatoes with the pesto, letting it drip down into the grooves, then dollop each with sour cream and serve hot.

## Baked Tofu the Italian Way

**Prep time: 5 minutes | Cook time: 10 minutes | Serves 2**

| | |
|---|---|
| 1 tablespoon soy sauce | ⅓ teaspoon dried basil |
| 1 tablespoon water | Black pepper, to taste |
| ⅓ teaspoon garlic powder | 6 ounces (170 g) extra firm tofu, |
| ⅓ teaspoon onion powder | pressed and cubed |
| ⅓ teaspoon dried oregano | |

In a large mixing bowl, whisk together the soy sauce, water, garlic powder, onion powder, oregano, basil, and black pepper. Add the tofu cubes, stirring to coat, and let them marinate for 10 minutes. Preheat the air fryer to 390ºF (199ºC). Arrange the tofu in the air fryer basket when your air fryer displays "READY" (select the cooking preset, and make minor adjustments according to your desired doneness.) and choose a shake reminder. Bake for 10 minutes until crisp. Flip the tofu halfway through the cooking time. Remove from the basket to a plate and serve.

## Mozzarella Jalapeño Poppers

**Prep time: 5 minutes | Cook time: 33 minutes | Serves 4**

| | |
|---|---|
| 8 medium jalapeño peppers | ½ teaspoon Italian seasoning |
| 5 ounces (142 g) cream cheese | mix |
| ¼ cup grated Mozzarella cheese | 8 slices bacon |

Preheat the air fryer to 400ºF (204ºC). Cut the jalapeños in half. Use a spoon to scrape out the insides of the peppers. In a bowl, add together the cream cheese, Mozzarella cheese and Italian seasoning. Pack the cream cheese mixture into the jalapeño halves and place the other halves on top. Wrap each pepper in 1 slice of bacon, starting from the bottom and working up. When your air fryer displays "READY" (select the cooking preset, and make minor adjustments according to your desired doneness.) and choose a shake reminder. Bake for 33 minutes. Serve!

## Latkes with Chopped Chives

**Prep time: 10 minutes | Cook time: 12 minutes | Makes 12 latkes**

| | |
|---|---|
| 1 russet potato | taste |
| ¼ onion | Canola or vegetable oil, in a |
| 2 eggs, lightly beaten | spray bottle |
| ⅓ cup flour | Chopped chives, for garnish |
| ½ teaspoon baking powder | Apple sauce |
| 1 teaspoon salt | Sour cream |
| Freshly ground black pepper, to | |

Shred the potato and onion with a coarse box grater or a food processor with the shredding blade. Place the shredded vegetables into a colander or mesh strainer and squeeze or press down firmly to remove the excess water. Transfer the onion and potato to a large bowl and add the eggs, flour, baking powder, salt and black pepper. Mix to combine and then shape the mixture into patties, about ¼-cup of mixture each. Brush or spray both sides of the latkes with oil. Pre-heat the air fryer to 400ºF (204ºC). Air-fry the latkes in batches. Transfer one layer of the latkes to the air fryer basket when your air fryer displays "READY" (select the cooking preset, and make minor adjustments according to your desired doneness.) and choose a shake reminder. Air-fry at 400ºF (204ºC) for 12 to 13 minutes, flipping them over halfway through the cooking time. Transfer the finished latkes to a platter and cover with aluminum foil, or place them in a warm oven to keep warm. Garnish the latkes with chopped chives and serve with sour cream and applesauce.

## Hot Summer Rolls

**Prep time: 15 minutes | Cook time: 15 minutes | Serves 4**

1 cup shiitake mushroom, sliced thinly
1 celery stalk, chopped
1 medium carrot, shredded
½ teaspoon finely chopped ginger
1 teaspoon sugar
1 tablespoon soy sauce
1 teaspoon nutritional yeast
8 spring roll sheets
1 teaspoon corn starch
2 tablespoons water

In a bowl, combine the ginger, soy sauce, nutritional yeast, carrots, celery, mushroom, and sugar. Mix the cornstarch and water to create an adhesive for the spring rolls. Scoop a tablespoonful of the vegetable mixture into the middle of the spring roll sheets. Brush the edges of the sheets with the cornstarch adhesive and enclose around the filling to make spring rolls. Preheat the air fryer to 400ºF (204ºC). When warm, place the rolls inside when your air fryer displays "READY" (select the cooking preset, and make minor adjustments according to your desired doneness.) and choose a shake reminder. Air fry for 15 minutes or until crisp. Serve hot.

## Corn on the Cob with Jerk Rub

**Prep time: 10 minutes | Cook time: 6 minutes | Serves 4**

1 teaspoon ground allspice
1 teaspoon dried thyme
½ teaspoon ground ginger
½ teaspoon ground cinnamon
¼ teaspoon ground nutmeg
⅛ teaspoon ground cayenne pepper
1 teaspoon salt
2 tablespoons butter, melted
4 ears of corn, husked

Pre-heat the air fryer to 380ºF (193ºC). Combine all the spices in a bowl. Brush the corn with the melted butter and then sprinkle the spices generously on all sides of each ear of corn. Transfer the ears of corn to the air fryer basket. It's ok if they are crisscrossed on top of each other. When your air fryer displays "READY" (select the cooking preset, and make minor adjustments according to your desired doneness.) and choose a shake reminder. Air-fry at 380ºF (193ºC) for 6 minutes, rotating the ears as they cook. Brush more butter on at the end and sprinkle with any remaining spice mixture.

## Mascarpone Mushrooms with Pasta

**Prep time: 10 minutes | Cook time: 15 minutes | Serves 4**

Vegetable oil spray
4 cups sliced mushrooms
1 medium yellow onion, chopped
2 cloves garlic, minced
¼ cup heavy whipping cream or half-and-half
8 ounces (227 g) mascarpone
cheese
1 teaspoon dried thyme
1 teaspoon kosher salt
1 teaspoon black pepper
½ teaspoon red pepper flakes
4 cups cooked konjac noodles, for serving
½ cup grated Parmesan cheese

Preheat the air fryer to 350ºF (177ºC). Spray a heatproof pan with vegetable oil spray. In a medium bowl, combine the mushrooms, onion, garlic, cream, mascarpone, thyme, salt, black pepper, and red pepper flakes. Stir to combine. Transfer the mixture to the prepared pan. Put the pan in the air fryer basket. When your air fryer displays "READY" (select the cooking preset, and make minor adjustments according to your desired doneness.) and choose a shake reminder. Bake for 15 minutes, stirring halfway through the baking time. Divide the pasta among four shallow bowls. Spoon the mushroom mixture evenly over the pasta. Sprinkle with Parmesan cheese and serve.

## Lush Veggie Roast

**Prep time: 15 minutes | Cook time: 20 minutes | Serves 6**

1⅓ cups small parsnips, peeled and cubed
1⅓ cups celery
2 red onions, sliced
1⅓ cups small butternut squash, cut in half, deseeded
and cubed
1 tablespoon fresh thyme needles
1 tablespoon olive oil
Salt and ground black pepper, to taste

Preheat the air fryer to 390ºF (199ºC). Combine the cut vegetables with the thyme, olive oil, salt and pepper. Put the vegetables in the basket and transfer the basket to the air fryer. When your air fryer displays "READY" (select the cooking preset, and make minor adjustments according to your desired doneness.) and choose a shake reminder. Roast for 20 minutes, stirring once throughout the roasting time, until the vegetables are nicely browned and cooked through. Serve warm.

## Maple Thyme Cheery Tomatoes

**Prep time: 10 minutes | Cook time: 20 minutes | Serves 2**

10 ounces (283 g) cherry tomatoes, halved
Kosher salt, to taste
2 tablespoons maple syrup
1 tablespoon vegetable oil
2 sprigs fresh thyme, stems removed
1 garlic clove, minced
Freshly ground black pepper, to taste

Place the tomatoes in a colander and sprinkle liberally with salt. Let stand for 10 minutes to drain. Transfer the tomatoes cut-side up to a 7-inch round cake pan insert, metal cake pan, or foil pan, then drizzle with the maple syrup, followed by the oil. Sprinkle with the thyme leaves and garlic and season with pepper. Place the pan in the air fryer when your air fryer displays "READY" (select the cooking preset, and make minor adjustments according to your desired doneness.) and choose a shake reminder. Cook at 325ºF (163ºC) until the tomatoes are soft, collapsed, and lightly caramelized on top, about 20 minutes. Serve straight from the pan or transfer the tomatoes to a plate and drizzle with the juices from the pan to serve.

## Parmesan Artichokes

**Prep time: 5 minutes | Cook time: 10 minutes | Serves 4**

2 medium artichokes, trimmed and quartered, with the centers removed
2 tablespoons coconut oil, melted
1 egg, beaten
½ cup Parmesan cheese, grated
¼ cup blanched, finely ground flour

Place the artichokes in a bowl with the coconut oil and toss to coat, then dip the artichokes into a bowl of beaten egg. In a separate bowl, mix together the Parmesan cheese and the flour. Combine with the pieces of artichoke, making sure to coat each piece well. Transfer the artichoke to the fryer. When your air fryer displays "READY" (select the cooking preset, and make minor adjustments according to your desired doneness.) and choose a shake reminder. Cook at 400ºF (204ºC) for 10 minutes, shaking occasionally throughout the cooking time. Serve hot.

## Pecan Mashed Sweet Potato Tots

**Prep time: 10 minutes | Cook time: 24 minutes | Makes 18–24 tots**

1 cup cooked mashed sweet potatoes
1 egg white, beaten
⅛ teaspoon ground cinnamon
1 dash nutmeg

2 tablespoons chopped pecans
1½ teaspoons honey
Salt, to taste
½ cup panko breadcrumbs
Oil for misting or cooking spray

Preheat air fryer to 390ºF (199ºC). In a large bowl, mix together the potatoes, egg white, cinnamon, nutmeg, pecans, honey, and salt to taste. Place panko crumbs on a sheet of wax paper. For each tot, use about 2 teaspoons of sweet potato mixture. To shape, drop the measure of potato mixture onto panko crumbs and push crumbs up and around potatoes to coat edges. Then turn tot over to coat other side with crumbs. Mist tots with oil or cooking spray and place in air fryer basket in single layer. When your air fryer displays "READY" (select the cooking preset, and make minor adjustments according to your desired doneness.) and choose a shake reminder. Cook at 390ºF (199ºC) for 12 to 13 minutes, until browned and crispy. Repeat steps 5 and 6 to cook remaining tots.

## Mediterranean Baked Eggs with Spinach

**Prep time: 10 minutes | Cook time: 8 to 12 minutes | Serves 2**

2 tablespoons olive oil
4 eggs, whisked
5 ounces (142 g) fresh spinach, chopped
1 medium-sized tomato, chopped

1 teaspoon fresh lemon juice
½ teaspoon ground black pepper
½ teaspoon coarse salt
½ cup roughly chopped fresh basil leaves, for garnish

Preheat the air fryer to 280ºF (137ºC). Generously grease a baking pan with olive oil. Stir together the remaining ingredients except the basil leaves in the greased baking pan until well incorporated. Place the baking pan in the preheated air fryer when your air fryer displays "READY" (select the cooking preset, and make minor adjustments according to your desired doneness.) and choose a shake reminder. Bake for 8 to 12 minutes, or until the eggs are completely set and the vegetables are tender. Serve garnished with the fresh basil leaves.

## Mexican-Style Corn in a Cup

**Prep time: 10 minutes | Cook time: 10 minutes | Serves 4**

4 cups frozen corn kernels (do not thaw)
Vegetable oil spray
2 tablespoons butter
¼ cup sour cream
¼ cup mayonnaise
¼ cup grated Parmesan cheese (or Feta, cotija, or queso fresco)

2 tablespoons fresh lemon or lime juice
1 teaspoon chili powder
Chopped fresh green onion (optional)
Chopped fresh cilantro (optional)

Place the corn in the bottom of the air fryer basket and spray with vegetable oil spray. When your air fryer displays "READY" (select the cooking preset, and make minor adjustments according to your desired doneness.) and choose a shake reminder. Set the air fryer to 350ºF (177ºC) for 10 minutes. Transfer the corn to a serving bowl. Add the butter and stir until melted. Add the sour cream, mayonnaise, cheese, lemon juice, and chili powder; stir until well combined. Serve immediately with green onion and cilantro (if using).

## Breaded Okra

**Prep time: 5 minutes | Cook time: 12 minutes | Serves 4**

to 8-ounce (198- to 227-g) fresh okra
1 egg
1 cup milk

1 cup breadcrumbs
½ teaspoon salt
Oil for misting or cooking spray

Remove stem ends from okra and cut in ½-inch slices. In a medium bowl, beat together egg and milk. Add okra slices and stir to coat. In a sealable plastic bag or container with lid, mix together the breadcrumbs and salt. Remove okra from egg mixture, letting excess drip off, and transfer into bag with breadcrumbs. Shake okra in crumbs to coat well. Place all of the coated okra into the air fryer basket and mist with oil or cooking spray. Okra doesn't need to cook in a single layer, nor is it necessary to spray all sides at this point. A good spritz on top will do. When your air fryer displays "READY" (select the cooking preset, and make minor adjustments according to your desired doneness.) and choose a shake reminder. Cook at 390ºF (199ºC) for 5 minutes. Shake basket to redistribute and give it another spritz as you shake. Cook 5 more minutes. Shake and spray again. Cook for 2 to 5 minutes longer or until golden brown and crispy.

## Panko-Crusted Green Beans

**Prep time: 5 minutes | Cook time: 15 minutes | Serves 4**

½ cup flour
2 eggs
1 cup panko bread crumbs
½ cup grated Parmesan cheese

1 teaspoon cayenne pepper
Salt and black pepper, to taste
1½ pounds (680 g) green beans

Preheat the air fryer to 400ºF (204ºC). In a bowl, place the flour. In a separate bowl, lightly beat the eggs. In a separate shallow bowl, thoroughly combine the bread crumbs, cheese, cayenne pepper, salt, and pepper. Dip the green beans in the flour, then in the beaten eggs, finally in the bread crumb mixture to coat well. Place the green beans in the air fryer basket when your air fryer displays "READY" (select the cooking preset, and make minor adjustments according to your desired doneness.) and choose a shake reminder. Air fry for 15 minutes, shaking the basket halfway through, or until they are cooked to your desired crispiness. Remove from the basket to a bowl and serve.

## Parmesan Broccoli Rice Crust

**Prep time: 5 minutes | Cook time: 28 minutes | Serves 1**

3 cups broccoli rice, steamed
½ cup Parmesan cheese, grated
1 egg

3 tablespoons low-carb Alfredo sauce
½ cup Mozzarella cheese, grated

Drain the broccoli rice and combine with the Parmesan cheese and egg in a bowl, mixing well. Cut a piece of parchment paper roughly the size of the base of the fryer's basket. Spoon four equal-sized amounts of the broccoli mixture onto the paper and press each portion into the shape of a pizza crust. You may have to complete this part in two batches. Transfer the parchment to the fryer. When your air fryer displays "READY" (select the cooking preset, and make minor adjustments according to your desired doneness.) and choose a shake reminder. Cook at 370ºF (188ºC) for 5 minutes. When the crust is firm, flip it over and cook for an additional 2 minutes. Add the Alfredo sauce and Mozzarella cheese on top of the crusts and cook for an additional 7 minutes. The crusts are ready when the sauce and cheese have melted. Serve hot.

# Chapter 8 Rice and Grains

## Air Fried Tofu
**Prep time: 5 minutes | Cook time: 13 minutes | Serves 3**

8 ounces (227 g) firm tofu, pressed and cut into bite-sized cubes
1 tablespoon tamari sauce
1 teaspoon peanut oil
½ teaspoon garlic powder
½ teaspoon onion powder

Toss the tofu cubes with tamari sauce, peanut oil, garlic powder and onion powder. When your air fryer displays "READY" (select the cooking preset, and make minor adjustments according to your desired doneness.) and choose a shake reminder. Cook your tofu in the preheated Air Fryer at 380ºF (193ºC) for about 13 minutes, shaking the basket once or twice to ensure even browning. Enjoy!

## Four-Cheese Pizza
**Prep time: 10 minutes | Cook time: 10 minutes | Serves 4**

1 (11-ounce / 312-g) can refrigerated thin pizza crust
½ cup tomato pasta sauce
2 tablespoons scallions, chopped
¼ cup Parmesan cheese, grated
1 cup Provolone cheese, shredded
1 cup Mozzarella cheese. sliced
4 slices Cheddar cheese
1 tablespoon olive oil

Stretch the dough on a work surface lightly dusted with flour. Spread with a layer of tomato pasta sauce. Top with the scallions and cheese. Place on the baking tray that is previously greased with olive oil. When your air fryer displays "READY" (select the cooking preset, and make minor adjustments according to your desired doneness.) and choose a shake reminder. Bake in the preheated Air Fryer at 390ºF (199ºC) for 5 minutes. Rotate the baking tray and bake for a further 5 minutes. Serve immediately.

## Honey Seeds Granola
**Prep time: 5 minutes | Cook time: 25 minutes | Serves 12**

½ cup rolled oats
1 cup walnuts, chopped
3 tablespoons sunflower seeds
3 tablespoons pumpkin seeds
1 teaspoon coarse sea salt
2 tablespoons honey

Thoroughly combine all ingredients and spread the mixture onto the Air Fryer trays. Spritz with nonstick cooking spray. When your air fryer displays "READY" (select the cooking preset, and make minor adjustments according to your desired doneness.) and choose a shake reminder. Bake at 230ºF (110ºC) for 25 minutes; rotate the trays and bake 10 to 15 minutes more. This granola can be kept in an airtight container for up to 2 weeks. Enjoy!

## Authentic Platanos Slices
**Prep time: 5 minutes | Cook time: 10 minutes | Serves 2**

1 very ripe, sweet plantain
1 teaspoon Caribbean Sorrel
Rum Spice Mix
1 teaspoon coconut oil, melted

Cut your plantain into slices. Toss your plantain with Caribbean Sorrel Rum Spice Mix and coconut oil. When your air fryer displays "READY" (select the cooking preset, and make minor adjustments according to your desired doneness.) and choose a shake reminder. Cook your plantain in the preheated Air Fryer at 400ºF (204ºC) for 10 minutes, shaking the cooking basket halfway through the cooking time. Serve immediately and enjoy!

## Cinnamon Apple Rolls
**Prep time: 5 minutes | Cook time: 13 minutes | Serves 4**

1 (10-ounce / 283-g) can buttermilk biscuits
1 apple, cored and chopped
¼ cup powdered sugar
1 teaspoon cinnamon
1 tablespoon coconut oil, melted

Line the bottom of the Air Fryer cooking basket with a parchment paper. Separate the dough into biscuits and cut each of them into 2 layers. Mix the remaining ingredients in a bowl. Divide the apple/cinnamon mixture between biscuits and roll them up. Brush the biscuits with coconut oil and transfer them to the Air Fryer cooking basket. When your air fryer displays "READY" (select the cooking preset, and make minor adjustments according to your desired doneness.) and choose a shake reminder. Cook the rolls at 330ºF (166ºC) for about 13 minutes, turning them over halfway through the cooking time. Enjoy!

## Aromatic Shrimp Pilaf
**Prep time: 10 minutes | Cook time: 36 minutes | Serves 2**

1 cup jasmine rice
Salt and black pepper, to taste
1 bay leaf
1 small yellow onion, chopped
1 small garlic clove, finely chopped
1 teaspoon butter, melted
4 tablespoons cream of mushroom soup
½ pound (227 g) shrimp, divined and sliced

Bring 2 cups of a lightly salted water to a boil in a medium saucepan over medium-high heat. Add in the jasmine rice, turn to a simmer and cook, covered, for about 18 minutes until water is absorbed. Let the jasmine rice stand covered for 5 to 6 minutes; fluff with a fork and transfer to a lightly greased Air Fryer safe pan. Stir in the salt, black pepper, bay leaf, yellow onion, garlic, butter and cream of mushroom soup; stir until everything is well incorporated. When your air fryer displays "READY" (select the cooking preset, and make minor adjustments according to your desired doneness.) and choose a shake reminder. Cook the rice at 350ºF (177ºC) for about 13 minutes. Stir in the shrimp and continue to cook for a further 5 minutes. Check the rice for softness. If necessary, cook for a few minutes more. Enjoy!

## Shrimp Pilaf with Katsuobushi Flakes
**Prep time: 10 minutes | Cook time: 34 minutes | Serves 3**

1 cup koshihikari rice, rinsed
1 yellow onion, chopped
2 garlic cloves, minced
½ teaspoon fresh ginger, grated
1 tablespoon Shoyu sauce
2 tablespoons rice wine
1 tablespoon sushi seasoning
1 tablespoon caster sugar
½ teaspoon sea salt
5 ounces (142 g) frozen shrimp, thawed
2 tablespoons katsuobushi flakes, for serving

Place the koshihikari rice and 2 cups of water in a large saucepan and bring to a boil. Cover, turn the heat down to low, and continue cooking for 15 minutes more. Set aside for 10 minutes. Mix the rice, onion, garlic, ginger, Shoyu sauce, wine, sushi seasoning, sugar, and salt in a lightly greased baking dish. When your air fryer displays "READY" (select the cooking preset, and make minor adjustments according to your desired doneness.) and choose a shake reminder. Cook in the preheated Air Fryer at 370ºF (188ºC) for 13 to 16 minutes. Add the shrimp to the baking dish and gently stir until everything is well combined. Cook for 6 minutes more. Serve at room temperature, garnished with katsuobushi flakes. Enjoy!

## Black Beans Taquito Casserole

**Prep time: 5 minutes | Cook time: 30 minutes | Serves 4**

½ (15-ounce / 425-g) can black beans, drained and rinsed well
1 tablespoon taco seasoning mix
4 ounces (113 g) mild enchilada sauce
1 cup Mexican cheese blend,
shredded
½ (20-ounce / 567-g) box frozen taquitos (chicken and cheese in tortillas)
2 tablespoons fresh chives, roughly chopped

Start by preheating your Air Fryer to 350ºF (177ºC). Spritz the baking pan with cooking spray. Mix the beans, taco seasoning mix, enchilada sauce and ½ cups of shredded cheese in the baking dish. Top the mixture with taquitos. When your air fryer displays "READY" (select the cooking preset, and make minor adjustments according to your desired doneness.) and choose a shake reminder. Bake for 15 minutes. Top with the remaining ½ cup of shredded cheese and bake for a further 15 minutes. Serve garnished with chopped chives. Enjoy!

## Basic Seeds Granola

**Prep time: 10 minutes | Cook time: 20 minutes | Serves 3**

1 cup rolled oats
A pinch of salt
A pinch of grated nutmeg
¼ teaspoon ground cinnamon
1 tablespoon honey
1 tablespoon coconut oil
¼ cup walnuts, chopped
1 tablespoon sunflower seeds
1 tablespoon pumpkin seeds

In a mixing bowl, thoroughly combine the rolled oats, salt, nutmeg, cinnamon, honey and coconut oil. Spread the mixture into an Air Fryer baking pan when your air fryer displays "READY" (select the cooking preset, and make minor adjustments according to your desired doneness.) and choose a shake reminder. Bake at 330ºF (166ºC) for about 15 minutes. Stir in the walnuts, sunflower seeds and pumpkin seeds. Continue to cook for a further 5 minutes. Store your granola in an airtight container for up to 2 weeks. Enjoy!

## Meaty Taco Bake

**Prep time: 10 minutes | Cook time: 35 minutes | Serves 4**

1 tablespoon olive oil
¼ pound (113 g) ground beef
½ pound (227 g) ground pork
1 shallot, minced
1 garlic, minced
½ cup beef broth
1 bell pepper, seeded and
chopped
1 Mexican chili pepper, seeded and minced
1½ cups tomato sauce
4 flour tortillas for fajitas
1 cup Mexican cheese blend, shredded

Heat the olive oil in a heavy skillet over a moderate flame. Cook the ground meat with the shallots and garlic until no longer pink. Then, add the beef broth, peppers, and tomato sauce to the skillet. Continue to cook on low heat for 3 minutes, stirring continuously. Spritz a baking dish with nonstick cooking spray. Cut the tortillas in half; place 2 tortilla halves in the bottom of the baking dish. Top with half of the meat mixture. Sprinkle with ½ cup of the cheese and the remaining tortilla halves. Top with the remaining meat mixture and cheese. When your air fryer displays "READY" (select the cooking preset, and make minor adjustments according to your desired doneness.) and choose a shake reminder. Cover with a piece of aluminum foil and bake in the preheated Air Fryer at 330ºF (166ºC) for 20 minutes. Remove the foil and bake for a further 12 minutes or until thoroughly heated. Enjoy!

## Tofu-Pearl Onions Bowl

**Prep time: 10 minutes | Cook time: 11 minutes | Serves 4**

16 ounces (454 g) firm tofu, pressed and cut into 1-inch pieces
2 tablespoons vegan Worcestershire sauce
1 tablespoon apple cider vinegar
1 tablespoon maple syrup
½ teaspoon shallot powder
½ teaspoon porcini powder
½ teaspoon garlic powder
2 tablespoons peanut oil
1 cup pearl onions, peeled

Place the tofu, Worcestershire sauce, vinegar, maple syrup, shallot powder, porcini powder, and garlic powder in a ceramic dish. Let it marinate in your refrigerator for 1 hour. Transfer the tofu to the lightly greased Air Fryer basket. Add the peanut oil and pearl onions; toss to combine. When your air fryer displays "READY" (select the cooking preset, and make minor adjustments according to your desired doneness.) and choose a shake reminder. Cook the tofu with the pearl onions in the preheated Air Fryer at 380ºF (193ºC) for 6 minutes; pause and brush with the reserved marinade; cook for a further 5 minutes. Serve immediately. Enjoy!

## Falafel

**Prep time: 10 minutes | Cook time: 10 minutes | Serves 3**

1 cup dry chickpeas, soaked overnight
1 small onion, sliced
2 tablespoons fresh cilantro
2 tablespoons fresh parsley
2 cloves garlic
½ teaspoon cayenne pepper
Sea salt and ground black pepper, to taste
½ teaspoon ground cumin

Drain and rinse your chickpeas and place them in a bowl of a food processor. Add in the remaining ingredients and blitz until the ingredients form a coarse meal. Roll the mixture into small balls with oiled hands. When your air fryer displays "READY" (select the cooking preset, and make minor adjustments according to your desired doneness.) and choose a shake reminder. Cook your falafel in the preheated Air Fryer at 390ºF (199ºC) for 5 minutes; turn them over and cook for another 5 to 6 minutes. Serve and enjoy!

## Mexican Beef Burritos

**Prep time: 10 minutes | Cook time: 20 minutes | Serves 4**

1 tablespoon olive oil
1 cup ground beef
1 teaspoon fresh garlic, minced
2 tablespoons scallions, chopped
1 habanero pepper, seeded and chopped
2 (8-ounce / 227-g) cans
refrigerated crescent dinner rolls
½ cup canned pinto beans, rinsed and drained
1 tablespoon taco seasoning mix
1 cup Colby cheese, shredded

Heat the olive oil in a skillet over medium heat. Now, cook the ground beef, garlic, scallions, and habanero pepper until the beef is no longer pink and the onion is translucent and fragrant. Separate the crescent dinner rolls into 8 rectangles. Divide the beef mixture between rectangles; add the pinto beans and taco seasoning mix; top with the shredded cheese. Roll up and pinch the edge to seal. Place the seam side down on the parchment-lined Air Fryer basket. When your air fryer displays "READY" (select the cooking preset, and make minor adjustments according to your desired doneness.) and choose a shake reminder. Bake in the preheated Air Fryer at 355ºF (179ºC) for 20 minutes. Enjoy!

## Couscous Salad with Goat Cheese
**Prep time: 15 minutes | Cook time: 27 minutes | Serves 4**

½ cup couscous
4 teaspoons olive oil
½ lemon, juiced, zested
1 tablespoon honey
Sea salt and freshly ground
black pepper, to your liking
2 tomatoes, sliced
1 red onion, thinly sliced

½ English cucumber, thinly
sliced
2 ounces (57 g) goat cheese,
crumbled
1 teaspoon ghee
2 tablespoons pine nuts
½ cup loosely packed Italian
parsley, finely chopped

Put the couscous in a bowl; now, pour the boiling water over it. Cover and set aside for 5 to 8 minutes; fluff with a fork. Place the couscous in a cake pan. Transfer the pan to the Air Fryer basket and cook at 360 digress F about 20 minutes. Make sure to stir every 5 minutes to ensure even cooking. Meanwhile, in a small mixing bowl, whisk the olive oil, lemon juice and zest, honey, salt, and black pepper. Toss the couscous with this dressing. Add the tomatoes, red onion, English cucumber, and goat cheese; gently stir to combine. Rub the ghee in the pine nuts, using your hands and place them in the Air Fryer basket. When your air fryer displays "READY" (select the cooking preset, and make minor adjustments according to your desired doneness.) and choose a shake reminder. Roast for 4 minutes; give the nuts a good toss. Put the cooking basket back again and roast for a further 3 to 4 minutes. Scatter the toasted nuts over your salad and garnish with parsley. Enjoy!

## Brussels Sprouts with Sesame Seeds
**Prep time: 10 minutes | Cook time: 15 minutes | Serves 3**

1 pound (454 g) Brussels
sprouts, trimmed and halved
1 teaspoon coconut oil
2 tablespoons Shoyu sauce
1 tablespoon agave syrup
1 teaspoon rice vinegar

½ teaspoon Gochujang paste
1 clove garlic, minced
2 scallion stalks, chopped
1 tablespoon sesame seeds,
toasted

Toss the Brussels sprouts with coconut oil, Shoyu sauce, agave syrup, rice vinegar, Gochujang paste and garlic. When your air fryer displays "READY" (select the cooking preset, and make minor adjustments according to your desired doneness.) and choose a shake reminder. Cook the Brussels sprouts in the preheated Air Fryer at 380ºF (193ºC) for 15 minutes, shaking the basket halfway through the cooking time. Place the roasted Brussels sprouts on a serving platter and garnish with scallions and sesame seeds. Serve immediately!

## Raisins and Nuts Granola
**Prep time: 15 minutes | Cook time: 40 minutes | Serves 8**

2 cups rolled oats
½ cup walnuts, chopped
⅓ cup almonds chopped
¼ cup raisins
¼ cup whole wheat pastry flour
½ teaspoon cinnamon
¼ teaspoon nutmeg, preferably

freshly grated
½ teaspoon salt
⅓ cup coconut oil, melted
⅓ cup agave nectar
½ teaspoon coconut extract
½ teaspoon vanilla extract

Thoroughly combine all ingredients. Then, spread the mixture onto the Air Fryer trays when your air fryer displays "READY" (select the cooking preset, and make minor adjustments according to your desired doneness.) and choose a shake reminder. Spritz with cooking spray. Bake at 230ºF (110ºC) for 25 minutes; rotate the trays and bake 10 to 15 minutes more. This granola can be stored in an airtight container for up to 2 weeks. Enjoy!

## Prosciutto and Basil Bruschetta
**Prep time: 5 minutes | Cook time: 8 minutes | Serves 3**

3 slices sourdough bread
½ cup marinara sauce
3 slices Mozzarella

6 slices prosciutto
6 fresh basil leaves

Using a rolling pin, flatten the bread slightly. Spread the marinara sauce on top of each slice of bread, then, top with Mozzarella and prosciutto. When your air fryer displays "READY" (select the cooking preset, and make minor adjustments according to your desired doneness.) and choose a shake reminder. Now, bake your bruschetta at 360ºF (182ºC) for about 8 minutes until the cheese is melted and golden. Garnish with basil leaves and serve.

## Golden Pretzel Knots with Cumin
**Prep time: 5 minutes | Cook time: 7 minutes | Serves 6**

1 package crescent refrigerator
rolls
2 eggs, whisked with

4 tablespoons of water
1 teaspoon cumin seeds

Roll the dough out into a rectangle. Slice the dough into 6 pieces. Roll each piece into a log and tie each rope into a knot. Cover and let it rest for 10 minutes. Brush the top of the pretzel knots with the egg wash; sprinkle with the cumin seeds. Arrange the pretzel knots in the lightly greased Air Fryer basket when your air fryer displays "READY" (select the cooking preset, and make minor adjustments according to your desired doneness.) and choose a shake reminder. Bake in the preheated Air Fryer at 340ºF (171ºC)or 7 minutes until golden brown. Serve and enjoy!

## Baked Peppery Tortilla Chips
**Prep time: 5 minutes | Cook time: 8 minutes | Serves 3**

6 (6-inch) corn tortillas
1 teaspoon canola oil
1 teaspoon salt
¼ teaspoon ground white

pepper
½ teaspoon ground cumin
½ teaspoon ancho chili powder

Slice the tortillas into quarters. Brush the tortilla pieces with the canola oil until well coated. Toss with the spices and transfer to the Air Fryer basket. When your air fryer displays "READY" (select the cooking preset, and make minor adjustments according to your desired doneness.) and choose a shake reminder. Bake at 360ºF (182ºC) for 8 minutes or until lightly golden. Work in batches. Enjoy!

## Spiced Roasted Almonds
**Prep time: 10 minutes | Cook time: 6 minutes | Serves 6**

1½ cups raw almonds
Sea salt and ground black
pepper, to taste
¼ teaspoon garlic powder

¼ teaspoon mustard powder
½ teaspoon cumin powder
¼ teaspoon smoked paprika
1 tablespoon olive oil

Toss all ingredients in a mixing bowl. Line the Air Fryer basket with baking parchment. Spread out the coated almonds in a single layer in the basket. When your air fryer displays "READY" (select the cooking preset, and make minor adjustments according to your desired doneness.) and choose a shake reminder. Roast at 350ºF (177ºC) for 6 to 8 minutes, shaking the basket once or twice. Work in batches. Enjoy!

## Bacon and Cheese Ciabatta Sandwich
**Prep time: 5 minutes | Cook time: 6 minutes | Serves 2**

2 ciabatta sandwich buns, split
2 tablespoons butter
2 teaspoons Dijon mustard
4 slices Canadian bacon
4 slices Monterey Jack cheese

Place the bottom halves of buns, cut sides up in the parchment lined Air Fryer basket. Spread the butter and mustard on the buns. Top with the bacon and cheese. When your air fryer displays "READY" (select the cooking preset, and make minor adjustments according to your desired doneness.) and choose a shake reminder. Bake in the preheated Air Fryer at 400ºF (204ºC) for 3 minutes. Flip the sandwiches over and cook for 3 minutes longer or until the cheese has melted. Serve with some extra ketchup or salsa sauce. Enjoy!

## Oatmeal with Two Berries
**Prep time: 10 minutes | Cook time: 12 minutes | Serves 4**

1 cup fresh strawberries
½ cup dried cranberries
1½ cups rolled oats
½ teaspoon baking powder
A pinch of sea salt
A pinch of grated nutmeg
½ teaspoon ground cinnamon
½ teaspoon vanilla extract
4 tablespoons agave syrup
1½ cups coconut milk

Spritz a baking pan with cooking spray. Place ½ cup of strawberries on the bottom of the pan; place the cranberries over that. In a mixing bowl, thoroughly combine the rolled oats, baking powder, salt, nutmeg, cinnamon, vanilla, agave syrup, and milk. Pour the oatmeal mixtures over the fruits; allow it to soak for 15 minutes. Top with the remaining fruits. When your air fryer displays "READY" (select the cooking preset, and make minor adjustments according to your desired doneness.) and choose a shake reminder. Bake at 330ºF (166ºC) for 12 minutes. Serve warm or at room temperature. Enjoy!

## Tex-Mex Pasta Bake
**Prep time: 15 minutes | Cook time: 37 minutes | Serves 4**

¾ pound (340 g) pasta noodles
1 tablespoon olive oil
¾ pound (340 g) ground beef
1 medium-sized onion, chopped
1 teaspoon fresh garlic, minced
1 bell pepper, seeded and sliced
1 jalapeno, seeded and minced
Sea salt and cracked black
pepper, to taste
1½ cups enchilada sauce
1 cup Mexican cheese blend, shredded
⅓ cup tomato paste
½ teaspoon Mexican oregano
½ cup nacho chips
2 tablespoons fresh coriander, chopped

Boil the pasta noodles for 3 minutes less than mentioned on the package; drain, rinse and place in the lightly greased casserole dish. In a saucepan, heat the olive oil until sizzling. Add the ground beef and cook for 2 to 3 minutes or until slightly brown. Now, add the onion, garlic, and peppers and continue to cook until tender and fragrant or about 2 minutes. Season with salt and black pepper. Add the enchilada sauce to the casserole dish. Add the beef mixture and ½ cup of the Mexican cheese blend. Gently stir to combine. Add the tomato paste, Mexican oregano, nacho chips, and the remaining ½ cup of cheese blend. Cover with foil. When your air fryer displays "READY" (select the cooking preset, and make minor adjustments according to your desired doneness.) and choose a shake reminder. Bake in the preheated Air Fryer at 350ºF (177ºC) for 20 minutes; remove the foil and bake for a further 10 to 12 minutes. Serve garnished with fresh coriander and enjoy!

## Chocolate Bread Pudding Squares
**Prep time: 10 minutes | Cook time: 15 minutes | Serves 3**

3 thick slices bread, cut into cubes
1 egg
1 cup heavy cream
1 tablespoon agave nectar
¼ teaspoon ground cinnamon
¼ teaspoon ground cloves
2 tablespoons chocolate chips
2 tablespoons icing sugar

Add the bread chunks to a lightly oiled baking dish. In a mixing dish, whisk the egg, heavy cream, agave nectar, cinnamon and cloves. Pour the custard over the bread chunks and press to soak well. Fold in the chocolate chips. When your air fryer displays "READY" (select the cooking preset, and make minor adjustments according to your desired doneness.) and choose a shake reminder. Cook in the preheated Air Fryer at 370ºF (188ºC) for about 13 minutes. Place the bread pudding in the refrigerator until it is chilled completely; cut into 1½-inch squares. Bake the squares at 330ºF (166ºC) for 2 minutes until golden on the top. Dust with icing sugar and serve. Enjoy!

## Special Wasabi Popcorn
**Prep time: 5 minutes | Cook time: 15 minutes | Serves 2**

½ teaspoon brown sugar
1 teaspoon salt
½ teaspoon wasabi powder,
sifted
1 tablespoon avocado oil
3 tablespoons popcorn kernels

Add the dried corn kernels to the Air Fryer basket; toss with the remaining ingredients. When your air fryer displays "READY" (select the cooking preset, and make minor adjustments according to your desired doneness.) and choose a shake reminder. Cook at 390ºF (199ºC) for 15 minutes, shaking the basket every 5 minutes. Work in two batches. Taste, adjust the seasonings and serve immediately. Enjoy!

## New York-Style Cheese Pizza
**Prep time: 5 minutes | Cook time: 10 minutes | Serves 4**

1 pizza dough
1 cup tomato sauce
14 ounces (397 g) Mozzarella
cheese, freshly grated
2 ounces (57 g) Parmesan, freshly grated

Stretch your dough on a pizza peel lightly dusted with flour. Spread with a layer of tomato sauce. Top with cheese. Place on the baking tray when your air fryer displays "READY" (select the cooking preset, and make minor adjustments according to your desired doneness.) and choose a shake reminder. Bake in the preheated Air Fryer at 390ºF (199ºC) for 5 minutes. Rotate the baking tray and bake for a further 5 minutes. Serve immediately.

## Fennel Slices with Mayonnaise
**Prep time: 10 minutes | Cook time: 20 minutes | Serves 3**

1 pound (454 g) fennel bulbs, sliced
1 tablespoon olive oil
½ teaspoon dried basil
½ teaspoon dried marjoram
Sea salt and ground black pepper, to taste
¼ cup vegan mayonnaise

Toss the fennel slices with the olive oil and spices and transfer them to the Air Fryer cooking basket. When your air fryer displays "READY" (select the cooking preset, and make minor adjustments according to your desired doneness.) and choose a shake reminder. Roast the fennel at 370ºF (188ºC) for about 20 minutes, shaking the basket once or twice to promote even cooking. Serve the fennel slice with mayonnaise and enjoy!

## Ciabatta Walnut Bread Pudding

**Prep time: 15 minutes | Cook time: 12 minutes | Serves 4**

4 cups ciabatta bread cubes
2 eggs, slightly beaten
1 cup milk
2 tablespoons butter
4 tablespoons honey
1 teaspoon vanilla extract
½ teaspoon ground cloves
½ teaspoon ground cinnamon
A pinch of salt
A pinch of grated nutmeg
⅓ cup walnuts, chopped

Place the ciabatta bread cubes in a lightly greased baking dish. In a mixing bowl, thoroughly combine the eggs, milk, butter, honey, vanilla, ground cloves, cinnamon, salt, and nutmeg. Pour the custard over the bread cubes. Scatter the chopped walnuts over the top of your bread pudding. Let stand for 30 minutes, occasionally pressing with a wide spatula to submerge. When your air fryer displays "READY" (select the cooking preset, and make minor adjustments according to your desired doneness.) and choose a shake reminder. Cook in the preheated Air Fryer at 370ºF (188ºC) for 7 minutes; check to ensure even cooking and cook an additional 5 to 6 minutes. Serve and enjoy!

## Mom's Cornbread

**Prep time: 10 minutes | Cook time: 25 minutes | Serves 4**

¾ cup cornmeal
1 cup flour
2 teaspoons baking powder
½ tablespoon brown sugar
½ teaspoon salt
5 tablespoons butter, melted
3 eggs, beaten
1 cup full-fat milk

Start by preheating your Air Fryer to 370ºF (188ºC) F. Then, spritz a baking pan with cooking oil. In a mixing bowl, combine the flour, cornmeal, baking powder, brown sugar, and salt. In a separate bowl, mix the butter, eggs, and milk. Pour the egg mixture into the dry cornmeal mixture; mix to combine well. Pour the batter into the baking pan; cover with aluminum foil and poke tiny little holes all over the foil. When your air fryer displays "READY" (select the cooking preset, and make minor adjustments according to your desired doneness.) and choose a shake reminder. Now, bake for 15 minutes. Remove the foil and bake for 10 minutes more. Transfer to a wire rack to cool slightly before cutting and serving. Enjoy!

## Pork and Peppers Wontons

**Prep time: 15 minutes | Cook time: 10 minutes | Serves 3**

1 tablespoon olive oil
¾ pound (340 g) ground pork
1 red bell pepper, seeded and chopped
1 green bell pepper, seeded and chopped
1 habanero pepper, minced
3 tablespoons onion, finely chopped
Salt and ground black pepper, to taste
½ teaspoon dried parsley flakes
1 teaspoon dried thyme
6 wonton wrappers

Heat the olive oil in a heavy skillet over medium heat. Cook the ground pork, peppers, and onion until tender and fragrant or about 4 minutes. Add the seasonings and stir to combine. Lay a piece of the wonton wrapper on your palm; add the filling in the middle of the wrapper. Then, fold it up to form a triangle; pinch the edges to seal tight. Place the folded wontons in the lightly greased cooking basket when your air fryer displays "READY" (select the cooking preset, and make minor adjustments according to your desired doneness.) and choose a shake reminder. Cook at 360ºF (182ºC) for 10 minutes. Work in batches and serve warm. Enjoy!

## Italian Arancini

**Prep time: 10 minutes | Cook time: 30 minutes | Serves 2**

1½ cups chicken broth
½ cup white rice
2 tablespoons Parmesan cheese, grated
Sea salt and cracked black
pepper, to your liking
2 eggs
1 cup fresh bread crumbs
½ teaspoon oregano
1 teaspoon basil

Bring the chicken broth to a boil in a saucepan over medium-high heat. Stir in the rice and reduce the heat to simmer; cook about 20 minutes. Drain the rice and allow it to cool completely. Add the Parmesan, salt, and black pepper. Shape the mixture into bite-sized balls. In a shallow bowl, beat the eggs; in another shallow bowl, mix bread crumbs with oregano and basil. Dip each rice ball into the beaten eggs, then, roll in the breadcrumb mixture, gently pressing to adhere. When your air fryer displays "READY" (select the cooking preset, and make minor adjustments according to your desired doneness.) and choose a shake reminder. Bake in the preheated Air Fryer at 350ºF (177ºC) for 10 to 12 minutes, flipping them halfway through the cooking time. Enjoy!

## Parmesan Cornmeal Crusted Okra

**Prep time: 10 minutes | Cook time: 20 minutes | Serves 2**

¾ cup cornmeal
¼ cup Parmesan cheese, grated
Sea salt and ground black pepper, to taste
1 teaspoon cayenne pepper
1 teaspoon garlic powder
½ teaspoon cumin seeds
½ pound (227 g) of okra, cut into small chunks
2 teaspoons sesame oil

In a mixing bowl, thoroughly combine the cornmeal, Parmesan, salt, black pepper, cayenne pepper, garlic powder, and cumin seeds. Stir well to combine. Roll the okra pods over the cornmeal mixture, pressing to adhere. Drizzle with sesame oil. When your air fryer displays "READY" (select the cooking preset, and make minor adjustments according to your desired doneness.) and choose a shake reminder. Cook in the preheated Air Fryer at 370ºF (188ºC) for 20 minutes, shaking the basket periodically to ensure even cooking. Enjoy!

## Japanese Hibachi Fried Rice

**Prep time: 10 minutes | Cook time: 20 minutes | Serves 2**

1¾ cups leftover jasmine rice
2 teaspoons butter, melted
Sea salt and freshly ground black pepper, to your liking
2 eggs, beaten
2 scallions, white and green
parts separated, chopped
1 cup snow peas
1 tablespoon Shoyu sauce
1 tablespoon sake
2 tablespoons Kewpie Japanese mayonnaise

Thoroughly combine the rice, butter, salt, and pepper in a baking dish when your air fryer displays "READY" (select the cooking preset, and make minor adjustments according to your desired doneness.) and choose a shake reminder. Cook at 340ºF (171ºC) about 13 minutes, stirring halfway through the cooking time. Pour the eggs over the rice and continue to cook about 5 minutes. Next, add the scallions and snow peas and stir to combine. Continue to cook 2 to 3 minutes longer or until everything is heated through. Meanwhile, make the sauce by whisking the Shoyu sauce, sake, and Japanese mayonnaise in a mixing bowl. Divide the fried rice between individual bowls and serve with the prepared sauce. Enjoy!

## French Toast with Neufchâtel Cheese

**Prep time: 10 minutes | Cook time: 4 minutes | Serves 2**

4 slices bread, about 1-inch thick
2 tablespoons butter, softened
1 teaspoon ground cinnamon
2 ounces (57 g) brown sugar

½ teaspoon vanilla paste
A pinch of sea salt
2 ounces (57 g) Neufchâtel cheese, softened

In a mixing dish, combine the butter, cinnamon, brown sugar, vanilla, and salt. Spread the cinnamon butter on both sides of the bread slices. Arrange in the cooking basket when your air fryer displays "READY" (select the cooking preset, and make minor adjustments according to your desired doneness.) and choose a shake reminder. Cook at 390ºF (199ºC) for 2 minutes; turn over and cook an additional 2 minutes. Serve with softened Neufchâtel cheese on individual plates. Serve and enjoy!

## Rum Bread Pudding Squares

**Prep time: 10 minutes | Cook time: 14 minutes | Serves 4**

6 slices bread, cubed
1 cup sugar
2 cups milk
2 large eggs, beaten

½ teaspoon vanilla extract
½ teaspoon ground cinnamon
2 tablespoons dark rum
2 tablespoons icing sugar

Place the bread cubes in a lightly greased baking dish. In a mixing bowl, thoroughly combine the sugar, milk, eggs, vanilla, cinnamon, and rum. Pour the custard over the bread cubes. Let stand for 30 minutes, occasionally pressing with a wide spatula to submerge. Cook in the preheated Air Fryer at 370ºF (188ºC) for 7 minutes; check to ensure even cooking and cook an additional 5 to 6 minutes. Place your bread pudding in the refrigerator to cool completely; cut into 1½-inch squares. When your air fryer displays "READY" (select the cooking preset, and make minor adjustments according to your desired doneness.) and choose a shake reminder. Bake at 330ºF (166ºC) for 2 minutes in the lightly buttered Air Fryer basket. Dust with icing sugar and serve. Enjoy!

## Mexican Brown Rice Cheese Casserole

**Prep time: 15 minutes | Cook time: 48 minutes | Serves 4**

1 tablespoon olive oil
1 shallot, chopped
2 cloves garlic, minced
1 habanero pepper, minced
2 cups brown rice
3 cups chicken broth
1 cup water
2 ripe tomatoes, pureed

Sea salt and ground black pepper, to taste
½ teaspoon dried Mexican oregano
1 teaspoon red pepper flakes
1 cup Mexican Cotija cheese, crumbled

In a nonstick skillet, heat the olive oil over a moderate flame. Once hot, cook the shallot, garlic, and habanero pepper until tender and fragrant; reserve. Heat the brown rice, vegetable broth and water in a pot over high heat. Bring it to a boil; turn the stove down to simmer and cook for 35 minutes. Grease a baking pan with nonstick cooking spray. Spoon the cooked rice into the baking pan. Add the sautéed mixture. Spoon the tomato puree over the sautéed mixture. Sprinkle with salt, black pepper, oregano, and red pepper. When your air fryer displays "READY" (select the cooking preset, and make minor adjustments according to your desired doneness.) and choose a shake reminder. Cook in the preheated Air Fryer at 380ºF (193ºC) for 8 minutes. Top with the Cotija cheese and bake for 5 minutes longer or until cheese is melted. Enjoy!

## Honey Vanilla Muffins

**Prep time: 10 minutes | Cook time: 12 minutes | Serves 3**

2½ ounces (71 g) all-purpose flour
1 teaspoon baking powder
A pinch of ground cloves
A pinch of coarse salt

½ teaspoon vanilla extract
2 tablespoons honey
1 egg
2 ounces (57 g) milk
2 tablespoons butter, melted

In a mixing bowl, combine the ingredients in the order listed above. Spritz a silicone muffin tin with a nonstick cooking spray. Divide the batter between cups. When your air fryer displays "READY" (select the cooking preset, and make minor adjustments according to your desired doneness.) and choose a shake reminder. Bake in the preheated Air Fryer at 330ºF (166ºC) for 12 to 15 minutes. Rotate the muffin tin halfway through the cooking time. Enjoy!

## Famous Paella

**Prep time: 15 minutes | Cook time: 32 minutes | Serves 2**

2 cups water
1 cup white rice, rinsed and drained
1 cube vegetable stock
1 chorizo, sliced
2 cups brown mushrooms, cleaned and sliced
2 cloves garlic, finely chopped
½ teaspoon fresh ginger,

ground
1 long red chili, minced
¼ cup dry white wine
½ cup tomato sauce
1 teaspoon smoked paprika
Kosher salt and ground black pepper, to taste
1 cup green beans

In a medium saucepan, bring the water to a boil. Add the rice and vegetable stock cube. Stir and reduce the heat. Cover and let it simmer for 20 minutes. Then, place the chorizo, mushrooms, garlic, ginger, and red chili in the baking pan. When your air fryer displays "READY" (select the cooking preset, and make minor adjustments according to your desired doneness.) and choose a shake reminder. Cook at 380ºF (193ºC) for 6 minutes, stirring periodically. Add the prepared rice to the casserole dish. Add the remaining ingredients and gently stir to combine. Cook for 6 minutes, checking periodically to ensure even cooking. Serve in individual bowls and enjoy!

## Monkey Bread

**Prep time: 10 minutes | Cook time: 13 minutes | Serves 6**

1 (16-ounce / 454-g) can refrigerated buttermilk biscuits
3 tablespoons olive oil
1 cup Provolone cheese, grated
¼ cup black olives, pitted and

chopped
4 tablespoons basil pesto
¼ cup pine nuts, chopped
1 tablespoon
Mediterranean herb mix

Separate your dough into the biscuits and cut each of them in half; roll them into balls. Dip each ball into the olive oil and begin layering in a nonstick Bundt pan. Cover the bottom of the pan with one layer of dough balls. Prepare the coating mixtures. In a shallow bowl, place the Provolone cheese and olives, add the basil pesto to a second bowl and add the pine nuts to a third bowl. Roll the dough balls in the coating mixtures; then, arrange them in the Bundt pan so the various coatings are alternated. When your air fryer displays "READY" (select the cooking preset, and make minor adjustments according to your desired doneness.) and choose a shake reminder. Top with Mediterranean herb mix Cook the monkey bread in the Air Fryer at 320ºF (160ºC) for 13 to 16 minutes. Serve and enjoy!

## Dad's Favorite Wontons
**Prep time: 10 minutes | Cook time: 16 minutes | Serves 2**

½ pound (227 g) ground turkey
1 teaspoon shallot powder
1 teaspoon instant dashi granules
1 teaspoon fish sauce
1 tablespoon tomato paste

1 teaspoon soy sauce
1 teaspoon sesame oil
Seas salt and ground black pepper, to taste
20 wonton wrappers, defrosted

Brush a nonstick skillet with cooking spray. Once hot, cook the ground turkey until no longer pink, crumbling with a fork. Stir in the other ingredients, except for the wonton wrappers; stir to combine well. Place the wonton wrappers on a clean work surface. Divide the filling between wrappers. Wet the edge of each wrapper with water, fold top half over bottom half and pinch border to seal. When your air fryer displays "READY" (select the cooking preset, and make minor adjustments according to your desired doneness.) and choose a shake reminder. Cook your wontons at 400ºF (204ºC) for 8 minutes; working in batches. Enjoy!

## Sultanas Pancake Cups
**Prep time: 10 minutes | Cook time: 6 minutes | Serves 3**

½ cup all-purpose flour
½ cup coconut flour
⅓ cup carbonated water
⅓ cup coconut milk
1 tablespoon dark rum

2 eggs
½ teaspoon vanilla
¼ teaspoon cardamom
½ cup Sultanas, soaked for 15 minutes

In a mixing bowl, thoroughly combine the dry ingredients; in another bowl, mix the wet ingredients. Then, stir the wet mixture into the dry mixture and stir again to combine well. Let the batter sit for 20 minutes in your refrigerator. Spoon the batter into a greased muffin tin. When your air fryer displays "READY" (select the cooking preset, and make minor adjustments according to your desired doneness.) and choose a shake reminder. Bake the pancake cups in your Air Fryer at 330ºF (166ºC) for 6 to 7 minutes or until golden brown. Repeat with the remaining batter. Enjoy!

## Cornbread Muffins
**Prep time: 10 minutes | Cook time: 25 minutes | Serves 4**

½ cup sorghum flour
½ cup yellow cornmeal
¼ cup white sugar
2 teaspoons baking powder
A pinch of salt

A pinch of grated nutmeg
2 eggs, beaten
½ cup milk
4 tablespoons butter, melted
4 tablespoons honey

Start by preheating your Air Fryer to 370ºF (188ºC) F. Then, line the muffin cups with the paper baking cups. In a mixing bowl, combine the flour, cornmeal, sugar, baking powder, salt, and nutmeg. In a separate bowl, mix the eggs, milk, and butter. Pour the egg mixture into the dry cornmeal mixture; mix to combine well. Pour the batter into the prepared muffin cups. When your air fryer displays "READY" (select the cooking preset, and make minor adjustments according to your desired doneness.) and choose a shake reminder. Bake for 15 minutes. Rotate the pan and bake for 10 minutes more. Transfer to a wire rack to cool slightly before cutting and serving. Serve with honey and enjoy!

## Greek-Style Feta-Spinach Pizza
**Prep time: 10 minutes | Cook time: 10 minutes | Serves 2**

2 ounces (57 g) frozen chopped spinach
Coarse sea salt, to taste
2 personal pizza crusts
1 tablespoon olive oil

¼ cup tomato sauce
2 tablespoons fresh basil, roughly chopped
½ teaspoon dried oregano
½ feta cheese, crumbled

Add the frozen spinach to the saucepan and cook until all the liquid has evaporated, about 6 minutes. Season with sea salt to taste. Preheat the Air Fryer to 390ºF (199ºC). Unroll the pizza dough on the Air Fryer baking tray; brush with olive oil. Spread the tomato sauce over the pizza crust. Add the sautéed spinach, basil, and oregano. Sprinkle the feta cheese, covering the pizza crust to the edges. When your air fryer displays "READY" (select the cooking preset, and make minor adjustments according to your desired doneness.) and choose a shake reminder. Cook for 10 minutes, rotating your pizza halfway through the cooking time. Repeat with another pizza and serve warm.

## Coconut and Seeds Granola
**Prep time: 10 minutes | Cook time: 40 minutes | Serves 12**

2 cups rolled oats
2 tablespoons butter
1 cup honey
½ teaspoon coconut extract

½ teaspoon vanilla extract
¼ cup sesame seeds
¼ cup pumpkin seeds
½ cup coconut flakes

Thoroughly combine all ingredients, except the coconut flakes; mix well. Spread the mixture onto the Air Fryer trays when your air fryer displays "READY" (select the cooking preset, and make minor adjustments according to your desired doneness.) and choose a shake reminder. Spritz with nonstick cooking spray. Bake at 230ºF (110ºC) for 25 minutes; rotate the trays, add the coconut flakes, and bake for a further 10 to 15 minutes. This granola can be stored in an airtight container for up to 3 weeks. Enjoy!

## Mediterranean-Style Pita Pockets
**Prep time: 10 minutes | Cook time: 14 minutes | Serves 4**

1 teaspoon olive oil
1 onion
2 garlic cloves, minced
¾ pound (340 g) ground turkey
Salt and ground black pepper, to taste
½ teaspoon mustard seeds

4 small pitas Tzatziki
½ cup Greek-style yogurt
½ cucumber, peeled
1 clove garlic, minced
2 tablespoons fresh lemon juice
Sea salt, to taste
¼ teaspoon dried oregano

Mix the olive oil, onion, garlic, turkey, salt, black pepper, and mustard seeds; shape the mixture into four patties. Cook in the preheated Air Fryer at 370ºF (188ºC) for 10 minutes, turning them over once or twice. Meanwhile, mix all ingredients for the tzatziki and place in the refrigerator until ready to use. When your air fryer displays "READY" (select the cooking preset, and make minor adjustments according to your desired doneness.) and choose a shake reminder. Warm the pita pockets in the preheated Air Fryer at 360ºF (182ºC) for 4 to 5 minutes or until thoroughly heated. Spread the tzatziki in pita pockets and add the turkey patties. Enjoy!

## Old-Fashioned Turkey Burritos

**Prep time: 10 minutes | Cook time: 14 minutes | Serves 3**

½ pound (227 g) ground turkey
1 teaspoon taco seasoning blend
1 teaspoon deli mustard
8 ounces (227 g) canned black beans
½ red onion, sliced
Sea salt and ground black

pepper, to taste
3 (12-inch) whole-wheat tortillas, warmed
½ cup Cotija cheese, crumbled
1 cup butterhead lettuce, torn into pieces
1 teaspoon olive oil

Cook the ground turkey in a nonstick skillet for about 4 minutes, crumbling with a fork. Stir the taco seasoning blend, mustard, beans, onion, salt and pepper into the skillet. Place the meat mixture in the center of each tortilla. Top with cheese and lettuce. Roll your tortillas to make burritos. Brush each burrito with olive oil and place them in the lightly greased cooking basket when your air fryer displays "READY" (select the cooking preset, and make minor adjustments according to your desired doneness.) and choose a shake reminder. Bake your burritos at 390ºF (199ºC) for 10 minutes, turning them over halfway through the cooking time. Serve immediately with salsa on the side, if desired.

## Ooey-Gooey Blueberry Quesadilla

**Prep time: 10 minutes | Cook time: 20 minutes | Serves 2**

¼ cup blueberries
¼ cup fresh orange juice
½ tablespoon maple syrup
½ cup vegan cream cheese

1 teaspoon vanilla extract
2 (6-inch) tortillas
2 teaspoons coconut oil
¼ cup vegan dark chocolate

Bring the blueberries, orange juice, and maple syrup to a boil in a saucepan. Reduce the heat and let it simmer until the sauce thickens, about 10 minutes. In a mixing dish, combine the cream cheese with the vanilla extract; spread on the tortillas. Add the blueberry filling on top. Fold in half. Place the quesadillas in the greased Air Fryer basket when your air fryer displays "READY" (select the cooking preset, and make minor adjustments according to your desired doneness.) and choose a shake reminder. Cook at 390ºF (199ºC) for 10 minutes, until tortillas are golden brown and filling is melted. Make sure to turn them over halfway through the cooking. Heat the coconut oil in a small pan and add the chocolate; whisk to combine well. Drizzle the chocolate sauce over the quesadilla and serve. Enjoy!

## Homemade Cornbread

**Prep time: 10 minutes | Cook time: 15 minutes | Serves 4**

½ cup self-rising cornmeal mix
A dash of salt
A dash of grated nutmeg
A dash of granulated sugar

1 tablespoon honey
4 tablespoons butter, melted
½ cup full-fat milk

In a mixing bowl, thoroughly combine the dry ingredients. In another bowl, mix the wet ingredients. Then, stir the wet mixture into the dry mixture. Pour the batter into a lightly buttered baking pan. When your air fryer displays "READY" (select the cooking preset, and make minor adjustments according to your desired doneness.) and choose a shake reminder. Now, bake your cornbread at 340ºF (171ºC) for about 15 minutes. Check for doneness and transfer to a wire rack to cool slightly before cutting and serving. Enjoy!

## Savory Colby Cornmeal Biscuits

**Prep time: 15 minutes | Cook time: 17 minutes | Serves 6**

2 cups all-purpose flour
1 teaspoon baking soda
1 teaspoon baking powder
1 teaspoon granulated sugar
¼ teaspoon ground chipotle
Sea salt, to taste
A pinch of grated nutmeg

1 stick butter, cold
6 ounces (170 g) canned whole corn kernels
1 cup Colby cheese, shredded
2 tablespoons sour cream
2 eggs, beaten

In a mixing bowl, combine the flour, baking soda, baking powder, sugar, ground chipotle, salt, and a pinch of nutmeg. Cut in the butter until the mixture resembles coarse crumbs. Stir in the corn, Colby cheese, sour cream, and eggs; stir until everything is well incorporated. Turn the dough out onto a floured surface. Knead the dough with your hands and roll it out to 1-inch thickness. Using 3-inch round cutter, cut out the biscuits. Transfer the cornmeal biscuits to the lightly greased Air Fryer basket when your air fryer displays "READY" (select the cooking preset, and make minor adjustments according to your desired doneness.) and choose a shake reminder. Brush the biscuits with cooking oil. Bake in the preheated Air Fryer at 400ºF (204ºC) for 17 minutes. Continue cooking until all the batter is used. Enjoy!

## Shawarma Chickpeas

**Prep time: 10 minutes | Cook time: 19 minutes | Serves 2**

8 ounces (227 g) canned chickpeas
¼ teaspoon turmeric powder
¼ teaspoon cinnamon
¼ teaspoon allspice

½ teaspoon ground coriander
¼ teaspoon ground ginger
¼ teaspoon smoked paprika
Coarse sea salt and freshly ground black pepper, to taste

Rinse your chickpeas with cold running water and pat it dry using kitchen towels. Place the spices in a plastic bag; add in the chickpeas and shake until all the chickpeas are coated with the spices. Spritz the spiced chickpeas with a nonstick cooking oil and transfer them to the Air Fryer cooking basket. When your air fryer displays "READY" (select the cooking preset, and make minor adjustments according to your desired doneness.) and choose a shake reminder. Cook your chickpeas in the preheated Air Fryer at 390ºF (199ºC) for 13 minutes. Turn your Air Fryer to 350ºF (177ºC) and cook an additional 6 minutes. Enjoy!

## Weekend Potato Fritters

**Prep time: 10 minutes | Cook time: 29 minutes | Serves 3**

1 tablespoon olive oil
½ pound (227 g) potatoes, peeled and cut into chunks
½ cup cashew cream
½ cup chickpea flour
½ teaspoon baking powder

½ onion, chopped
1 garlic clove, minced
Sea salt and ground black pepper, to your liking
1 cup tortilla chips, crushed

Start by preheating your Air Fryer to 400ºF (204ºC). Drizzle the olive oil all over the potatoes. Place the potatoes in the Air Fryer basket and cook approximately 15 minutes, shaking the basket periodically. Lightly crush the potatoes to split; mash the potatoes and combine with the other ingredients. Form the potato mixture into patties. When your air fryer displays "READY" (select the cooking preset, and make minor adjustments according to your desired doneness.) and choose a shake reminder. Bake in the preheated Air Fryer at 380ºF (193ºC) for 14 minutes, flipping them halfway through the cooking time to ensure even cooking. Enjoy!

## Green and Potato Croquettes

**Prep time: 10 minutes | Cook time: 13 minutes | Serves 2**

½ pound (227 g) cup russet potatoes
1 teaspoon olive oil
½ teaspoon garlic, pressed
2 cups loosely packed mixed greens, torn into pieces

2 tablespoons oat milk
Sea salt and ground black pepper, to taste
¼ teaspoon red pepper flakes, crushed

Cook your potatoes for about 30 minutes until they are fork-tender; peel the potatoes and add them to a mixing bowl. Mash your potatoes and stir in the remaining ingredients. Shape the mixture into bite-sized balls and place them in the cooking basket; sprits the balls with a nonstick cooking oil. When your air fryer displays "READY" (select the cooking preset, and make minor adjustments according to your desired doneness.) and choose a shake reminder. Cook the croquettes at 390ºF (199ºC) for about 13 minutes, shaking the cooking basket halfway through the cooking time. Serve with tomato ketchup if desired. Enjoy!

## Banana Oatmeal Cups

**Prep time: 5 minutes | Cook time: 9 minutes | Serves 2**

1 large banana, mashed
1 cup quick-cooking steel cut oats
1 tablespoon agave syrup

1 egg, well beaten
1 cup coconut milk
3 ounces (85 g) mixed berries

In a mixing bowl, thoroughly combine the banana, oats, agave syrup, beaten egg and coconut milk. Spoon the mixture into an Air Fryer safe baking dish when your air fryer displays "READY" (select the cooking preset, and make minor adjustments according to your desired doneness.) and choose a shake reminder. Bake in the preheated Air Fryer at 390ºF (199ºC) for about 7 minutes. Top with berries and continue to bake an additional 2 minutes. Spoon into individual bowls and serve with a splash of coconut milk if desired. Enjoy!

## Baked Corn Tortilla Chips

**Prep time: 5 minutes | Cook time: 10 minutes | Serves 3**

½ (12-ounce /340-g) package corn tortillas
1 tablespoon canola oil

½ teaspoon chili powder
1 teaspoon salt

Cut the tortillas into small rounds using a cookie cutter. Brush the rounds with canola oil. Sprinkle them with chili powder and salt. Transfer to the lightly greased Air Fryer basket when your air fryer displays "READY" (select the cooking preset, and make minor adjustments according to your desired doneness.) and choose a shake reminder. Bake at 360ºF (182ºC) for 5 minutes, shaking the basket halfway through. Bake until the chips are crisp, working in batches. Serve with salsa or guacamole. Enjoy!

## Mexican Oregano Bubble Loaf

**Prep time: 10 minutes | Cook time: 15 minutes | Serves 4**

1 (16-ounce / 454-g) can flaky buttermilk biscuits
4 tablespoons olive oil, melted
½ cup Manchego cheese, grated
½ teaspoon granulated garlic

1 tablespoon fresh cilantro, chopped
½ teaspoon Mexican oregano
1 teaspoon chili pepper flakes
Kosher salt and ground black pepper, to taste

Open a can of biscuits and cut each biscuit into quarters. Brush each piece of biscuit with the olive oil and begin layering in a lightly greased Bundt pan. Cover the bottom of the pan with one layer of biscuits. Next, top the first layer with half of the cheese, spices and granulated garlic. Repeat for another layer. Finish with a third layer of dough. When your air fryer displays "READY" (select the cooking preset, and make minor adjustments according to your desired doneness.) and choose a shake reminder. Cook your bubble loaf in the Air Fryer at 330ºF (166ºC) or about 15 minutes until the cheese is bubbly. Enjoy!

## Honey Cornbread Muffins

**Prep time: 10 minutes | Cook time: 20 minutes | Serves 3**

½ cup cornmeal
½ cup plain flour
1 tablespoon flaxseed meal
1 teaspoon baking powder
3 tablespoons honey
A pinch of coarse sea salt

A pinch of grated nutmeg
½ teaspoon ground cinnamon
1 egg, whisked
¾ cup milk
2 tablespoons butter, melted

In a mixing bowl, thoroughly combine the dry ingredients. In another bowl, mix the wet ingredients. Then, stir the wet mixture into the dry mixture. Pour the batter into a lightly buttered muffin tin. When your air fryer displays "READY" (select the cooking preset, and make minor adjustments according to your desired doneness.) and choose a shake reminder. Now, bake your cornbread muffins at 350ºF (177ºC) for about 20 minutes. Check for doneness with a toothpick and transfer to a wire rack to cool slightly before serving. Enjoy!

## Sweet Raisin French Toast

**Prep time: 10 minutes | Cook time: 4 minutes | Serves 2**

2 eggs
¼ cup full-fat milk
¼ teaspoon ground cloves
½ teaspoon ground cinnamon

4 tablespoons honey
2 tablespoons coconut oil, melted
4 slices sweet raisin bread

Thoroughly combine the eggs, mink, ground cloves, cinnamon, honey and coconut oil. Spread the mixture on both sides of the bread slices. Arrange the bread slices in the cooking basket when your air fryer displays "READY" (select the cooking preset, and make minor adjustments according to your desired doneness.) and choose a shake reminder. Cook them at 390ºF (199ºC) for 2 minutes; flip and cook on the other side for 2 to 3 minutes more. Serve with some extra honey if desired. Enjoy!

## Cranberry Panettone Bread Pudding

**Prep time: 10 minutes | Cook time: 12 minutes | Serves 3**

4 slices of panettone bread, crusts trimmed, bread cut into 1-inch cubes
4 tablespoons dried cranberries
2 tablespoons amaretto liqueur
1 cup coconut milk

½ cup whipping cream
2 eggs
1 tablespoon agave syrup
½ vanilla extract
½ teaspoon ground cloves
½ teaspoon ground cinnamon

Place the panettone bread cubes in a lightly greased baking dish. Scatter the dried cranberry over the top. In a mixing bowl, thoroughly combine the remaining ingredients. Pour the custard over the bread cubes. Let it stand for 30 minutes, occasionally pressing with a wide spatula to submerge. When your air fryer displays "READY" (select the cooking preset, and make minor adjustments according to your desired doneness.) and choose a shake reminder. Cook in the preheated Air Fryer at 370ºF (188ºC) for 7 minutes; check to ensure even cooking and cook an additional 5 to 6 minutes. Serve and enjoy!

### Sesame Kale Chips

**Prep time: 10 minutes | Cook time: 12 minutes | Serves 1**

2 cups loosely packed kale leaves, stems removed
1 teaspoon olive oil
1 tablespoon nutritional yeast flakes
Coarse salt and ground black

pepper, to taste
1 teaspoon sesame seeds, lightly toasted
½ teaspoon poppy seeds, lightly toasted
¼ teaspoon garlic powder

Toss the kale leaves with olive oil, nutritional yeast, salt and black pepper. When your air fryer displays "READY" (select the cooking preset, and make minor adjustments according to your desired doneness.) and choose a shake reminder. Cook your kale at 250ºF (121ºC) for 12 minutes, shaking the basket every 4 minutes to promote even cooking. Place the kale leaves on a platter and sprinkle evenly with sesame seeds, poppy seeds and garlic powder while still hot. Enjoy!

### Mini Monkey Bread

**Prep time: 10 minutes | Cook time: 12 minutes | Serves 3**

6 ounces (170 g) refrigerated crescent rolls
¼ cup ketchup
¼ cup pesto sauce
½ cup Provolone cheese,

shredded
2 cloves garlic, minced
½ teaspoon dried oregano
½ teaspoon dried basil
½ teaspoon dried parsley flakes

Start by preheating your Air Fryer to 350ºF (177ºC). Roll out crescent rolls. Divide the ingredients between crescent rolls and roll them up. Using your fingertips, gently press them to seal the edges. When your air fryer displays "READY" (select the cooking preset, and make minor adjustments according to your desired doneness.) and choose a shake reminder. Bake the mini monkey bread for 12 minutes or until the top is golden brown. Enjoy!

### Fragrant Green Beans with Oyster Mushrooms

**Prep time: 10 minutes | Cook time: 10 minutes | Serves 3**

1 tablespoon extra-virgin olive oil
2 garlic cloves, minced
½ cup scallions, chopped
2 cups oyster mushrooms, sliced

12 ounces (340 g) fresh green beans, trimmed
1 tablespoon soy sauce
Sea salt and ground black pepper, to taste

Start by preheating your Air Fryer to 390ºF (199ºC). Heat the oil and sauté the garlic and scallions until tender and fragrant, about 5 minutes. Add the remaining ingredients and stir to combine well. When your air fryer displays "READY" (select the cooking preset, and make minor adjustments according to your desired doneness.) and choose a shake reminder. Increase the temperature to 400ºF (204ºC) and cook for a further 5 minutes. Serve warm.

### Italian Risi e Bisi

**Prep time: 10 minutes | Cook time: 53 minutes | Serves 4**

2 cups brown rice
4 cups water
½ cup frozen green peas
3 tablespoons soy sauce
1 tablespoon olive oil

1 cup brown mushrooms, sliced
2 garlic cloves, minced
1 small-sized onion, chopped
1 tablespoon fresh parsley, chopped

Heat the brown rice and water in a pot over high heat. Bring it to a boil; turn the stove down to simmer and cook for 35 minutes. Allow your rice to cool completely. Transfer the cold cooked rice to the lightly greased Air Fryer pan. Add the remaining ingredients and stir to combine. When your air fryer displays "READY" (select the cooking preset, and make minor adjustments according to your desired doneness.) and choose a shake reminder. Cook in the preheated Air Fryer at 360ºF (182ºC) for 18 to 22 minutes. Serve warm.

### Smoked Salmon and Rice Rolls

**Prep time: 10 minutes | Cook time: 16 minutes | Serves 3**

1 tablespoon fresh lemon juice
6 slices smoked salmon
1 tablespoon extra-virgin olive oil
½ cup cooked rice
1 tablespoon whole-grain mustard
3 tablespoons shallots,

chopped
1 garlic clove, minced
1 teaspoon capers, rinsed and chopped
Sea salt and ground black pepper, to taste
3 ounces (85 g) sour cream

Drizzle the lemon juice all over the smoked salmon. Then, spread each salmon strip with olive oil. In a mixing bowl, thoroughly combine the cooked rice, mustard, shallots, garlic, and capers. Spread the rice mixture over the olive oil. Roll the slices into individual rollups and secure with a toothpick. Season with salt and black pepper. Place in the lightly greased Air Fryer basket when your air fryer displays "READY" (select the cooking preset, and make minor adjustments according to your desired doneness.) and choose a shake reminder. Bake at 370ºF (188ºC) for 16 minutes, turning them over halfway through the cooking time. Serve with sour cream and enjoy!

### Southwestern Fried Apples Slices

**Prep time: 5 minutes | Cook time: 8 minutes | Serves 3**

2 granny smith apples, peeled, cored and sliced
1 tablespoon coconut oil
1 teaspoon fresh lemon juice

¼ cup brown sugar
1 teaspoon apple pie seasoning mix

Toss the apple slices with the coconut oil, lemon juice, brown sugar and apple pie seasoning mix. Place the apple slices in the Air Fryer cooking basket when your air fryer displays "READY" (select the cooking preset, and make minor adjustments according to your desired doneness.) and choose a shake reminder. Cook them at 360ºF (182ºC) for about 8 minutes, shaking the cooking basket halfway through the cooking time. Serve and enjoy!

### Mascarpone Stuffed French Toast

**Prep time: 10 minutes | Cook time: 4 minutes | Serves 3**

6 slices of challah bread, without crusts
¼ cup Mascarpone cheese
3 tablespoons fig jam
1 egg
4 tablespoons milk

½ teaspoon grated nutmeg
1 teaspoon ground cinnamon
½ teaspoon vanilla paste
¼ cup butter, melted
½ cup brown sugar

Spread the three slices of bread with the Mascarpone cheese, leaving ½-inch border at the edges. Spread the three slices of bread with ½ tablespoon of fig jam; then, invert them onto the slices with the cheese in order to make sandwiches. Mix the egg, milk, nutmeg, cinnamon, and vanilla in a shallow dish. Dip your sandwiches in the egg mixture. When your air fryer displays "READY" (select the cooking preset, and make minor adjustments according to your desired doneness.) and choose a shake reminder. Cook in the preheated Air Fryer at 340ºF (171ºC) for 4 minutes. Dip in the melted butter, then, roll in the brown sugar. Serve warm.

## Pepper Sweet Potato Croquettes

**Prep time: 10 minutes | Cook time: 15 minutes | Serves 3**

½ pound (227 g) sweet
potatoes
¼ cup wheat flour
¼ cup glutinous rice flour
1 teaspoon baking powder

1 tablespoon brown sugar
¼ teaspoon cayenne pepper
A pinch of grated nutmeg
Kosher salt and ground black
pepper, to taste

Mix all ingredients in a bowl; stir until everything is well combined. Transfer the sweet potato balls to the Air Fryer cooking basket and spritz them with a nonstick cooking oil. When your air fryer displays "READY" (select the cooking preset, and make minor adjustments according to your desired doneness.) and choose a shake reminder. Bake the sweet potato balls in the preheated Air Fryer at 360ºF (182ºC) for 15 minutes or until thoroughly cooked and crispy. Enjoy!

## Beef Taco Stuffed Bread

**Prep time: 10 minutes | Cook time: 5 minutes | Serves 4**

1 loaf French bread
½ pound (227 g) ground beef
1 onion, chopped
1 teaspoon garlic, minced
1 package taco seasoning
1½ cups Queso Panela, sliced

Salt and ground black pepper,
to taste
3 tablespoons tomato paste
2 tablespoons fresh cilantro
leaves, chopped

Cut the top off of the loaf of bread; remove some of the bread from the middle creating a well and reserve. In a large skillet, cook the ground beef with the onion and garlic until the beef is no longer pink and the onion is translucent.Add the taco seasoning, cheese, salt, black pepper, and tomato paste. Place the taco mixture into your bread. When your air fryer displays "READY" (select the cooking preset, and make minor adjustments according to your desired doneness.) and choose a shake reminder. Bake in the preheated Air Fryer at 380ºF (193ºC) for 5 minutes. Garnish with fresh cilantro leaves. Enjoy!

## Korean Chili Broccoli

**Prep time: 10 minutes | Cook time: 10 minutes | Serves 2**

½ pound (227 g) broccoli florets
1 tablespoon sesame oil
1 tablespoon soy sauce
¼ teaspoon coriander seeds
½ teaspoon garlic powder

1 tablespoon brown sugar
½ teaspoon gochukaru (Korean
red chili powder)
Sea salt and ground black
pepper, to taste

Toss the broccoli florets with the other ingredients until well coated. When your air fryer displays "READY" (select the cooking preset, and make minor adjustments according to your desired doneness.) and choose a shake reminder. Air fry your broccoli at 390ºF (199ºC) for about 10 minutes, shaking the basket halfway through the cooking time. Serve with your favorite vegan dip. Enjoy!

## Sweet and Sour Tofu

**Prep time: 10 minutes | Cook time: 25 minutes | Serves 3**

2 tablespoons Shoyu sauce
16 ounces (454 g) extra-firm
tofu, drained, pressed and
cubed
½ cup water
¼ cup pineapple juice
2 garlic cloves, minced

½ teaspoon fresh ginger, grated
1 teaspoon cayenne pepper
¼ teaspoon ground black
pepper
½ teaspoon salt
1 teaspoon honey
1 tablespoon arrowroot powder

Drizzle the Shoyu sauce all over the tofu cubes. When your air fryer displays "READY" (select the cooking preset, and make

minor adjustments according to your desired doneness.) and choose a shake reminder. Cook in the preheated Air Fryer at 380ºF (193ºC) for 6 minutes; shake the basket and cook for a further 5 minutes. Meanwhile, cook the remaining ingredients in a heavy skillet over medium heat for 10 minutes, until the sauce has slightly thickened. Stir the fried tofu into the sauce and continue cooking for 4 minutes more or until the tofu is thoroughly heated. Serve warm and enjoy!

## Austrian-Inspired Pancakes

**Prep time: 10 minutes | Cook time: 8 minutes | Serves 4**

½ cup flour
A pinch of salt
A pinch of sugar
½ cup whole milk
3 eggs

1 shot of rum
4 tablespoons raisins
½ cup icing sugar
½ cup stewed plums

Mix the flour, salt, sugar, and milk in a bowl until the batter becomes semi-solid. Fold in the eggs; add the rum and whisk to combine well. Let it stand for 20 minutes. Spritz the Air Fryer baking pan with cooking spray. Pour the batter into the pan using a measuring cup. Scatter the raisins over the top. When your air fryer displays "READY" (select the cooking preset, and make minor adjustments according to your desired doneness.) and choose a shake reminder. Cook at 230ºF (110ºC) for 4 to 5 minutes or until golden brown. Repeat with the remaining batter. Cut the pancake into pieces, sprinkle over the icing sugar, and serve with the stewed plums. Enjoy!

## Fried White Rice

**Prep time: 5 minutes | Cook time: 38 minutes | Serves 2**

1 cup white rice
1 tablespoon sesame oil
Himalayan sea salt and ground
black pepper, to taste

1 teaspoon hot paprika
2 tablespoons vegetable broth
2 tablespoons tamari sauce
1 egg, whisked

Bring 2 cups of a lightly salted water to a boil in a medium saucepan over medium-high heat. Add in the rice, turn to a simmer and cook, covered, for about 18 minutes until water is absorbed. Let your rice stand, covered, for 5 to 7 minutes; fluff with a fork and transfer to a lightly greased Air Fryer safe pan. Stir in the sesame oil, salt, black pepper, paprika and broth; stir until everything is well incorporated. When your air fryer displays "READY" (select the cooking preset, and make minor adjustments according to your desired doneness.) and choose a shake reminder. Cook the rice at 350ºF (177ºC) for about 10 minutes. Stir in the tamari sauce and egg and continue to cook for a further 5 minutes. Serve immediately

## Thai-Style Sweet Potato Balls

**Prep time: 10 minutes | Cook time: 45 minutes | Serves 4**

1 pound (454 g) sweet potatoes
1 cup brown sugar
1 tablespoon orange juice
2 teaspoons orange zest
½ teaspoon ground cinnamon

¼ teaspoon ground cloves
½ cup almond meal
1 teaspoon baking powder
1 cup coconut flakes

Bake the sweet potatoes at 380ºF (193ºC) for 30 to 35 minutes until tender; peel and mash them. Add the brown sugar, orange juice, orange zest, ground cinnamon, cloves, almond meal, and baking powder; mix to combine well. Roll the balls in the coconut flakes. When your air fryer displays "READY" (select the cooking preset, and make minor adjustments according to your desired doneness.) and choose a shake reminder. Bake in the preheated Air Fryer at 360ºF (182ºC) for 15 minutes or until thoroughly cooked and crispy. Repeat the process until you run out of ingredients. Enjoy!

## Colby Cheese Roll-Ups

**Prep time: 5 minutes | Cook time: 8 minutes | Serves 3**

6 slices bread
2 tablespoons butter

6 slices Colby cheese
A pinch of ground black pepper

Flatten the bread slices to ¼ -inch thickness using a rolling pin. Spread the melted butter on top of each slice of bread. Place a cheese slice on top of each slice of bread; sprinkle with black pepper and roll them up tightly. When your air fryer displays "READY" (select the cooking preset, and make minor adjustments according to your desired doneness.) and choose a shake reminder. Bake the cheese roll-ups at 390ºF (199ºC) for about 8 minutes. Enjoy!

## Sultana Muffins

**Prep time: 10 minutes | Cook time: 12 minutes | Serves 4**

1 cup flour
1 teaspoon baking powder
1 tablespoon honey
1 egg
½ teaspoon star anise, ground
1 teaspoon vanilla extract

1 egg
½ cup milk
2 tablespoons melted butter
1 cup dried Sultanas, soaked in
2 tablespoons of rum

Mix all the ingredients until everything is well incorporated. Spritz a silicone muffin tin with cooking spray. Pour the batter into the silicone muffin tin. When your air fryer displays "READY" (select the cooking preset, and make minor adjustments according to your desired doneness.) and choose a shake reminder. Bake in the preheated Air Fryer at 330ºF (166ºC) for 12 to 15 minutes. Rotate the silicone muffin tin halfway through the cooking time to ensure even cooking. Serve and enjoy!

## Honey Potato Flat Bread

**Prep time: 5 minutes | Cook time: 6 minutes | Serves 4**

4 potatoes, medium-sized
1 cup buckwheat flour
½ teaspoon salt

½ teaspoon red chili powder
¼ cup honey

Put the potatoes into a large saucepan; add water to cover by about 1 inch. Bring to a boil. Then, lower the heat, and let your potatoes simmer about 8 minutes until they are fork tender. Mash the potatoes and add the flour, salt, and chili powder. Create 4 balls and flatten them with a rolling pin. When your air fryer displays "READY" (select the cooking preset, and make minor adjustments according to your desired doneness.) and choose a shake reminder. Bake in the preheated Air Fryer at 390ºF (199ºC) for 6 minutes. Serve warm with honey.

## Hungarian Spiced Mushroom Pilaf

**Prep time: 15 minutes | Cook time: 36 minutes | Serves 4**

1½ cups white rice
3 cups vegetable broth
2 tablespoons olive oil
1 pound (454 g) fresh porcini mushrooms, sliced
2 tablespoons olive oil
2 garlic cloves

1 onion, chopped
¼ cup dry vermouth
1 teaspoon dried thyme
½ teaspoon dried tarragon
1 teaspoon sweet Hungarian paprika

Place the rice and broth in a large saucepan, add water; and bring to a boil. Cover, turn the heat down to low, and continue cooking for 16 to 18 minutes more. Set aside for 5 to 10 minutes.

Now, stir the hot cooked rice with the remaining ingredients in a lightly greased baking dish. When your air fryer displays "READY" (select the cooking preset, and make minor adjustments according to your desired doneness.) and choose a shake reminder. Cook in the preheated Air Fryer at 370ºF (188ºC) for 20 minutes, checking periodically to ensure even cooking. Serve in individual bowls. Enjoy!

## Polenta Slices with Prosciutto

**Prep time: 5 minutes | Cook time: 35 minutes | Serves 3**

9 ounces (255 g) pre-cooked polenta roll
1 teaspoon sesame oil
2 ounces (57 g) prosciutto,

chopped
1 teaspoon Italian seasoning blend

Cut the pre-cooked polenta roll into nine equal slices. Brush them with sesame oil on all sides. Then, transfer the polenta slices to the lightly oiled Air Fryer cooking basket. When your air fryer displays "READY" (select the cooking preset, and make minor adjustments according to your desired doneness.) and choose a shake reminder. Cook the polenta slices at 390ºF (199ºC) for about 30 minutes; then, top them with chopped prosciutto and Italian seasoning blend. Continue to cook for another 5 minutes until cooked through. Serve with marinara sauce, if desired. Enjoy!

## Colby Cheese and Herb Biscuits

**Prep time: 10 minutes | Cook time: 15 minutes | Serves 3**

1 cup self-rising flour
½ teaspoon baking powder
½ teaspoon honey
½ stick butter, melted
½ cup Colby cheese, grated

½ cup buttermilk
¼ teaspoon kosher salt
1 teaspoon dried parsley
1 teaspoon dried rosemary

Preheat your Air Fryer to 360ºF (182ºC). Line the cooking basket with a piece of parchment paper. In a mixing bowl, thoroughly combine the flour, baking powder, honey, and butter. Gradually stir in the remaining ingredients. When your air fryer displays "READY" (select the cooking preset, and make minor adjustments according to your desired doneness.) and choose a shake reminder. Bake in the preheated Air Fryer for 15 minutes. Work in batches. Serve at room temperature. Enjoy!

## Brown Rice and Tofu Bake

**Prep time: 10 minutes | Cook time: 50 minutes | Serves 4**

1 cup brown rice
16 ounces (454 g) extra firm
**For the Marinade:**
2 tablespoons sesame oil
½ cup tamari sauce
2 tablespoons maple syrup
1 tablespoon white vinegar

tofu, pressed, drained, and cut into bite-sized cubes

1 teaspoon hot sauce
4 tablespoons cornstarch
Salt and black pepper, to taste

Heat the brown rice and 2½ cups of water in a saucepan over high heat. Bring it to a boil; turn the stove down to simmer and cook for 35 minutes. Place the tofu in a ceramic dish; add the remaining ingredients for the marinade and whisk to combine well. Allow it to marinate for 1 hour in your refrigerator. Grease a baking pan with nonstick cooking spray. Add the hot rice and place the tofu on the top. Stir in the reserved marinade. When your air fryer displays "READY" (select the cooking preset, and make minor adjustments according to your desired doneness.) and choose a shake reminder. Cook at 370ºF (188ºC) for 15 minutes, checking occasionally to ensure even cooking. Enjoy!

# Chapter 9 Snacks and Appetizers

## Italian Romano Tomato Chips
**Prep time: 5 minutes | Cook time: 10 minutes | Serves 2**

2 tomatoes, cut into thick rounds
1 teaspoon extra-virgin olive oil
Sea salt and fresh ground
pepper, to taste
1 teaspoon Italian seasoning mix
¼ cup Romano cheese, grated

Preheat air fryer to 350ºF (180ºC). Toss the tomato sounds with remaining ingredients. Transfer the tomato rounds to the cooking basket without overlapping. When your air fryer displays "READY" (select the cooking preset, and make minor adjustments according to your desired doneness.) and choose a shake reminder. Cook your tomato rounds in the preheated Air Fryer for 5 minutes. Flip them over and cook an additional 5 minutes. Work with batches. Serve warm.

## Parmesan Tomato Crisps
**Prep time: 5 minutes | Cook time: 10 minutes | Serves 4**

4 Roma tomatoes, sliced
2 tablespoons olive oil
Sea salt and white pepper, to taste
1 teaspoon Italian seasoning mix
4 tablespoons Parmesan cheese, grated

Preheat air fryer to 350ºF (180ºC). Generously grease the Air Fryer basket with nonstick cooking oil. Toss the sliced tomatoes with the remaining ingredients. Transfer them to the cooking basket without overlapping. When your air fryer displays "READY" (select the cooking preset, and make minor adjustments according to your desired doneness.) and choose a shake reminder. Cook in the preheated Air Fryer for 5 minutes. Shake the cooking basket and cook an additional 5 minutes. Work in batches. Serve with Mediterranean aioli for dipping, if desired. Enjoy!

## French Fries with Monterey-Jack Cheese
**Prep time: 5 minutes | Cook time: 14 minutes | Serves 2**

8 ounces (227 g) French fries, frozen
½ cup Monterey-Jack cheese,
grated
1 teaspoon paprika Sea salt, to taste

Preheat the air fryer to 400ºF (204ºC). When your air fryer displays "READY" (select the cooking preset, and make minor adjustments according to your desired doneness.) and choose a shake reminder. Cook the French fries in your Air Fryer at 400ºF (204ºC) for about 7 minutes. Shake the basket and continue to cook for a further 6 minutes. Top the French fries with cheese, paprika and salt cheese. Continue to cook for 1 minute more or until the cheese has melted. Serve warm and enjoy!

## Quick Tortilla Chips
**Prep time: 5 minutes | Cook time: 3 minutes | Serves 2**

8 corn tortillas
1 tablespoon olive oil
Salt, to taste

Preheat the air fryer to 390ºF (199ºC). Slice the corn tortillas into triangles. Coat with a light brushing of olive oil. Put the tortilla pieces in the air fryer basket when your air fryer displays "READY" (select the cooking preset, and make minor adjustments according to your desired doneness.) and choose a shake reminder. Air fry for 3 minutes. You may need to do this in batches. Season with salt before serving.

## Cumin Red Beet Chips
**Prep time: 5 minutes | Cook time: 13 minutes | Serves 4**

2 red beets, thinly sliced
1 tablespoon grapeseed oil
1 teaspoon seasoned salt
½ teaspoon ground black
pepper
¼ teaspoon cumin powder
½ cup pizza sauce

Preheat the air fryer to 330ºF (166ºC). Toss the red beets with the oil, salt, black pepper, and cumin powder. Arrange the beet slices in a single layer in the Air Fryer basket. When your air fryer displays "READY" (select the cooking preset, and make minor adjustments according to your desired doneness.) and choose a shake reminder. Cook in the preheated Air Fryer at 330ºF (166ºC) for 13 minutes. Serve with the pizza sauce and enjoy!

## Fried Bacon with Chipotle Dipping
**Prep time: 5 minutes | Cook time: 10 minutes | Serves 3**

6 ounces (170 g) bacon, cut into strips
For the Chipotle Dipping Sauce:
6 tablespoons sour cream
½ teaspoon chipotle chili powder

Preheat the air fryer to 360ºF (182ºC). Place the bacon strips in the Air Fryer cooking basket. When your air fryer displays "READY" (select the cooking preset, and make minor adjustments according to your desired doneness.) and choose a shake reminder. Cook the bacon strips at 360ºF (182ºC) for 5 minutes; turn them over and cook for another 5 minutes. Meanwhile, make the chipotle dipping sauce by whisking the sour cream and chipotle chili powder; reserve. Serve the bacon chips with the chipotle dipping sauce and enjoy!

## Fish Sticks with Mayo Mustard
**Prep time: 5 minutes | Cook time: 10 minutes | Serves 3**

10 ounces (283 g) fish sticks
½ cup mayonnaise
2 teaspoons yellow mustard
2 teaspoons honey

Preheat the air fryer to 400ºF (204ºC). Add the fish sticks to the Air Fryer cooking basket; drizzle the fish sticks with a nonstick cooking spray. When your air fryer displays "READY" (select the cooking preset, and make minor adjustments according to your desired doneness.) and choose a shake reminder. Cook the fish sticks at 400ºF (204ºC) for 5 minutes; turn them over and cook for another 5 minutes. Meanwhile, mix the mayonnaise, yellow mustard and honey until well combined. Serve the fish sticks with the honey mustard sauce for dipping. Enjoy!

## Loaded Tater Tots
**Prep time: 5 minutes | Cook time: 10 minutes | Serves 6**

24 tater tots, frozen
1 cup Swiss cheese, grated
6 tablespoons Canadian bacon,
cooked and chopped
¼ cup Ranch dressing

Preheat the air fryer to 395ºF (202ºC). Spritz the silicone muffin cups with non-stick cooking spray. Now, press the tater tots down into each cup. Divide the cheese, bacon, and Ranch dressing between tater tot cups. When your air fryer displays "READY" (select the cooking preset, and make minor adjustments according to your desired doneness.) and choose a shake reminder. Cook in the preheated Air Fryer at 395ºF (202ºC) for 10 minutes. Serve in paper cake cups. Enjoy!

## Best Party Mix

**Prep time: 5 minutes | Cook time: 9 minutes | Serves 10**

2 cups mini pretzels
1 cup mini crackers
1 cup peanuts

1 tablespoon Creole seasoning
2 tablespoons butter, melted

Preheat the air fryer to 360ºF (182ºC). Toss all ingredients in the Air Fryer basket. When your air fryer displays "READY" (select the cooking preset, and make minor adjustments according to your desired doneness.) and choose a shake reminder. Cook in the preheated Air Fryer at 360ºF (182ºC) approximately 9 minutes until lightly toasted. Shake the basket periodically. Enjoy!

## Deviled Eggs with Peppercorns

**Prep time: 5 minutes | Cook time: 15 minutes | Serves 3**

5 eggs
2 tablespoons mayonnaise
2 tablespoons sweet pickle relish

Sea salt, to taste
½ teaspoon mixed peppercorns, crushed

Preheat the air fryer to 275ºF (135ºC). Place the wire rack in the Air Fryer basket; lower the eggs onto the wire rack. When your air fryer displays "READY" (select the cooking preset, and make minor adjustments according to your desired doneness.) and choose a shake reminder. Cook at 275ºF (135ºC) for 15 minutes. Transfer them to an ice-cold water bath to stop the cooking. Peel the eggs under cold running water; slice them into halves. Mash the egg yolks with the mayo, sweet pickle relish, and salt; spoon yolk mixture into egg whites. Arrange on a nice serving platter and garnish with the mixed peppercorns. Enjoy!

## Bacon and Sea Scallops Kabobs

**Prep time: 5 minutes | Cook time: 6 minutes | Serves 2**

10 sea scallops, frozen
4 ounces (113 g) bacon, diced
1 teaspoon garlic powder

1 teaspoon paprika
Sea salt and ground black pepper, to taste

Preheat the air fryer to 400ºF (204ºC). Assemble the skewers alternating sea scallops and bacon. Sprinkle the garlic powder, paprika, salt and black pepper all over your kabobs. When your air fryer displays "READY" (select the cooking preset, and make minor adjustments according to your desired doneness.) and choose a shake reminder. Bake your kabobs in the preheated Air Fryer at 400ºF (204ºC) for 6 minutes. Serve warm with your favorite sauce for dipping. Enjoy!

## Banana Chips with Coconut Flakes

**Prep time: 5 minutes | Cook time: 8 minutes | Serves 2**

1 large banana, peeled and sliced
1 teaspoon coconut oil

¼ teaspoon ground cinnamon
A pinch of coarse salt
2 tablespoons coconut flakes

Preheat the air fryer to 375ºF (191ºC). Toss the banana slices with the coconut oil, cinnamon and salt. Transfer banana slices to the Air Fryer cooking basket. When your air fryer displays "READY" (select the cooking preset, and make minor adjustments according to your desired doneness.) and choose a shake reminder. Cook the banana slices at 375ºF (191ºC) for about 8 minutes, shaking the basket every 2 minutes. Scatter coconut flakes over the banana slices and let banana chips cool slightly before serving. Enjoy!

## Chili French Fries

**Prep time: 5 minutes | Cook time: 18 minutes | Serves 3**

1 pound (454 g) potatoes, peeled and cut into matchsticks
1 teaspoon olive oil
1 lime, freshly squeezed

1 teaspoon chili powder
Sea salt and ground black pepper, to taste

Preheat the air fryer to 370ºF (188ºC). Toss your potatoes with the remaining ingredients until well coated. Transfer your potatoes to the Air Fryer cooking basket. When your air fryer displays "READY" (select the cooking preset, and make minor adjustments according to your desired doneness.) and choose a shake reminder. Cook the French fries at 370ºF (188ºC) for 9 minutes. Shake the cooking basket and continue to cook for about 9 minutes. Serve immediately. Enjoy!

## Toasted Mixed Nuts

**Prep time: 5 minutes | Cook time: 6 minutes | Serves 4**

½ cup pecans
1 cup almonds
2 tablespoons egg white

1 tablespoon granulated sugar
A pinch of coarse sea salt

Preheat the air fryer to 360ºF (182ºC). Toss the pecans and almonds with the egg white, granulated sugar and salt until well coated. Transfer the pecans and almonds to the Air Fryer cooking basket. When your air fryer displays "READY" (select the cooking preset, and make minor adjustments according to your desired doneness.) and choose a shake reminder. Roast the pecans and almonds at 360ºF (182ºC) for about 6 to 7 minutes, shaking the basket once or twice. Taste and adjust seasonings. Enjoy!

## Cinnamon Pear Slices

**Prep time: 5 minutes | Cook time: 8 minutes | Serves 2**

1 large pear, cored and sliced
1 teaspoon apple pie spice blend

1 teaspoon coconut oil
1 teaspoon honey

Preheat the air fryer to 360ºF (182ºC). Toss the pear slices with the spice blend, coconut oil and honey. Then, place the pear slices in the Air Fryer cooking basket when your air fryer displays "READY" (select the cooking preset, and make minor adjustments according to your desired doneness.) and choose a shake reminder. Cook at 360ºF (182ºC) for about 8 minutes. Shake the basket once or twice to ensure even cooking. Pear chips will crisp up as it cools. Enjoy!

## Cheese Crisps Baked

**Prep time: 5 minutes | Cook time: 6 minutes | Serves 4**

½ cup Parmesan cheese, shredded
1 cup Cheddar cheese,

shredded
1 teaspoon Italian seasoning
½ cup marinara sauce

Start by preheating your Air Fryer to 350ºF (177ºC). Place a piece of parchment paper in the cooking basket. Mix the cheese with the Italian seasoning. Add about 1 tablespoon of the cheese mixture (per crisp) to the basket, making sure they are not touching. When your air fryer displays "READY" (select the cooking preset, and make minor adjustments according to your desired doneness.) and choose a shake reminder. Bake for 6 minutes or until browned to your liking. Work in batches and place them on a large tray to cool slightly. Serve with the marinara sauce. Bon appétit!

## Tasty Pork Crackling with Sriracha Dip

Prep time: 5 minutes | Cook time: 16 minutes | Serves 3

½ pound (227 g) pork rind
Sea salt and ground black pepper, to taste
½ cup tomato sauce

1 teaspoon Sriracha sauce
½ teaspoon stone-ground mustard

Preheat the air fryer to 380ºF (193ºC). Rub sea salt and pepper on the skin side of the pork rind. Allow it to sit for 30 minutes. Then, cut the pork rind into chunks using kitchen scissors. When your air fryer displays "READY" (select the cooking preset, and make minor adjustments according to your desired doneness.) and choose a shake reminder. Roast the pork rind at 380ºF (193ºC) for 8 minutes; turn them over and cook for a further 8 minutes or until blistered. Meanwhile, mix the tomato sauce with the Sriracha sauce and mustard. Serve the pork crackling with the Sriracha dip and enjoy!

## Cheddar Potato Puffs

Prep time: 5 minutes | Cook time: 12 minutes | Serves 4

8 ounces (227 g) potato puffs
1 teaspoon olive oil
4 ounces (113 g) Cheddar cheese, shredded

½ cup tomato sauce
1 teaspoon Dijon mustard
½ teaspoon Italian seasoning mix

Preheat the air fryer to 400ºF (204ºC). Brush the potato puffs with olive oil and transfer them to the Air Fryer cooking basket. When your air fryer displays "READY" (select the cooking preset, and make minor adjustments according to your desired doneness.) and choose a shake reminder. Cook the potato puffs at 400ºF (204ºC) for 10 minutes, shaking the basket occasionally to ensure even browning. Top them with cheese and continue to cook for 2 minutes more until the cheese melts. Meanwhile, whisk the tomato sauce with the mustard and Italian seasoning mix. Serve the warm potato puffs with cocktail sticks and the sauce on the side. Serve warm.

## Beef Steak Sliders with Horseradish Mayonnaise

Prep time: 10 minutes | Cook time: 16 minutes | Makes 8 sliders

1 pound (454 g) top sirloin steaks, about ¾-inch thick
Salt and pepper, to taste
2 large onions, thinly sliced
1 tablespoon extra-light olive oil
8 slider buns
For the Horseradish Mayonnaise:

1 cup light mayonnaise
4 teaspoons prepared horseradish
2 teaspoons Worcestershire sauce
1 teaspoon coarse brown mustard

Place steak in air fryer basket and cook at 390ºF (199ºC) for 6 minutes. Turn and cook 5 to 6 more minutes for medium rare. If you prefer your steak medium, continue cooking for 2 to 3 minutes. While the steak is cooking, prepare the Horseradish Mayonnaise by mixing all ingredients together. When steak is cooked, remove from air fryer, sprinkle with salt and pepper to taste, and set aside to rest. Toss the onion slices with the oil and place in air fryer basket when your air fryer displays "READY" (select the cooking preset, and make minor adjustments according to your desired doneness.) and choose a shake reminder. Cook at 390ºF (199ºC) for 5 to 7 minutes, until onion rings are soft and browned. Slice steak into very thin slices. Spread slider buns with the horseradish mayo and pile on the meat and onions. Serve with remaining horseradish dressing for dipping.

## Asian Rice Logs with Marmalade Dipping

Prep time: 15 minutes | Cook time: 5 minutes | Makes 8 rice logs

1½ cups cooked jasmine or sushi rice
¼ teaspoon salt
2 teaspoons five-spice powder
2 teaspoons diced shallots
1 tablespoon tamari sauce
1 egg, beaten
1 teaspoon sesame oil
2 teaspoons water

⅓ cup plain breadcrumbs
¾ cup panko breadcrumbs
2 tablespoons sesame seeds
For the Orange Marmalade Dipping Sauce:
½ cup all-natural orange marmalade
1 tablespoon soy sauce

Make the rice according to package instructions. While the rice is cooking, make the dipping sauce by combining the marmalade and soy sauce and set aside. Stir together the cooked rice, salt, five-spice powder, shallots, and tamari sauce. Divide rice into 8 equal pieces. With slightly damp hands, mold each piece into a log shape. Chill in freezer for 10 to 15 minutes. Mix the egg, sesame oil, and water together in a shallow bowl. Place the plain breadcrumbs on a sheet of wax paper. Mix the panko breadcrumbs with the sesame seeds and place on another sheet of wax paper. Roll the rice logs in plain breadcrumbs, then dip in egg wash, and then dip in the panko and sesame seeds. When your air fryer displays "READY" (select the cooking preset, and make minor adjustments according to your desired doneness.) and choose a shake reminder. Cook the logs at 390ºF (199ºC) for approximately 5 minutes, until golden brown. Cool slightly before serving with orange marmalade dipping sauce.

## Stuffed Jalapeños with Prosciutto

Prep time: 5 minutes | Cook time: 15 minutes | Serves 2

8 fresh jalapeño peppers, deseeded and cut in half lengthwise
4 ounces (113 g) Ricotta

cheese, at room temperature
¼ teaspoon cayenne pepper
½ teaspoon granulated garlic
8 slices prosciutto, chopped

Preheat the air fryer to 400ºF (204ºC). Place the fresh jalapeño peppers on a clean surface. Mix the remaining ingredients in a bowl; divide the filling between the jalapeño peppers. Transfer the peppers to the Air Fryer cooking basket. When your air fryer displays "READY" (select the cooking preset, and make minor adjustments according to your desired doneness.) and choose a shake reminder. Cook the stuffed peppers at 400ºF (204ºC) for 15 minutes. Serve and enjoy!

## Sticky Glazed Chicken Wings

Prep time: 10 minutes | Cook time: 24 minutes | Serves 2

½ pound (227 g) chicken wings
1 tablespoon sesame oil
2 tablespoons brown sugar
1 tablespoon Worcestershire

sauce
1 tablespoon hot sauce
1 tablespoon balsamic vinegar

Preheat the air fryer to 370ºF (188ºC). Brush the chicken wings with sesame oil and transfer them to the Air Fryer cooking basket. When your air fryer displays "READY" (select the cooking preset, and make minor adjustments according to your desired doneness.) and choose a shake reminder. Cook the chicken wings at 370ºF (188ºC) for 12 minutes; turn them over and cook for a further 10 minutes. Meanwhile, bring the other ingredients to a boil in a saucepan; cook for 2 to 3 minutes or until thoroughly cooked. Toss the warm chicken wings with the sauce and place them on a serving platter. Serve and enjoy!

## Asian-Flavor Chicken Wings

**Prep time: 5 minutes | Cook time: 13 minutes | Serves 4**

2 pounds (907 g) chicken wings
½ cup Asian-style salad dressing

2 tablespoons Chinese five-spice powder

Cut off wing tips and discard or freeze for stock. Cut remaining wing pieces in two at the joint. Place wing pieces in a large sealable plastic bag. Pour in the Asian dressing, seal bag, and massage the marinade into the wings until well coated. Refrigerate for at least an hour. Remove wings from bag, drain off excess marinade, and place wings in air fryer basket when your air fryer displays "READY" (select the cooking preset, and make minor adjustments according to your desired doneness.) and choose a shake reminder. Cook at 360ºF (182ºC) for 13 to 15 minutes or until juices run clear. About halfway through cooking time, shake the basket or stir wings for more even cooking. Transfer cooked wings to plate in a single layer. Sprinkle half of the Chinese five-spice powder on the wings, turn, and sprinkle other side with remaining seasoning.

## Crispy Avocado Chips

**Prep time: 15 minutes | Cook time: 10 minutes | Serves 4**

1 egg
1 tablespoon lime juice
⅛ teaspoon hot sauce
2 tablespoons flour
¾ cup panko bread crumbs

¼ cup cornmeal
¼ teaspoon salt
1 large avocado, pitted, peeled, and cut into ½-inch slices
Cooking spray

Preheat the air fryer to 390ºF (199ºC). Whisk together the egg, lime juice, and hot sauce in a small bowl. On a sheet of wax paper, place the flour. In a separate sheet of wax paper, combine the bread crumbs, cornmeal, and salt. Dredge the avocado slices one at a time in the flour, then in the egg mixture, finally roll them in the bread crumb mixture to coat well. Place the breaded avocado slices in the air fryer basket and mist them with cooking spray when your air fryer displays "READY" (select the cooking preset, and make minor adjustments according to your desired doneness.) and choose a shake reminder. Air fry for 10 minutes, or until the slices are nicely browned and crispy. Transfer the avocado slices to a plate and serve.

## Pita Chips

**Prep time: 5 minutes | Cook time: 6 minutes | Serves 4**

2 pieces whole wheat pita bread
3 tablespoons olive oil
1 teaspoon freshly squeezed

lemon juice
1 teaspoon salt
1 teaspoon dried basil
1 teaspoon garlic powder

Spray the air fryer basket with olive oil. Using a pair of kitchen shears or a pizza cutter, cut the pita bread into small wedges. Place the wedges in a small mixing bowl and add the olive oil, lemon juice, salt, dried basil, and garlic powder. Mix well, coating each wedge. Place the seasoned pita wedges in the greased air fryer basket in a single layer, being careful not to overcrowd them when your air fryer displays "READY" (select the cooking preset, and make minor adjustments according to your desired doneness.) and choose a shake reminder. (You may have to bake the pita chips in more than one batch.) Set the temperature to 350ºF (177ºC). Set the timer and bake for 6 minutes. Every 2 minutes or so, remove the drawer and shake the pita chips so they redistribute in the basket for even cooking. Serve with your choice of dip or alone as a tasty snack.

## Mini Pepper and Bacon Skewers

**Prep time: 10 minutes | Cook time: 6 minutes | Serves 4**

4 ounces (113 g) bacon, diced
2 bell peppers, sliced
¼ cup barbecue sauce
1 teaspoon Ranch seasoning

blend
½ cup tomato sauce
1 teaspoon jalapeno, minced

Preheat the air fryer to 400ºF (204ºC). Assemble the skewers alternating bacon and bell pepper. Toss them with barbecue sauce and Ranch seasoning blend. When your air fryer displays "READY" (select the cooking preset, and make minor adjustments according to your desired doneness.) and choose a shake reminder. Cook the mini skewers in the preheated Air Fryer at 400ºF (204ºC) for 6 minutes. Mix the tomato sauce and minced jalapeno. Bon appétit!

## Apple Chips with Chopped Walnuts

**Prep time: 5 minutes | Cook time: 20 minutes | Serves 2**

2 apples, peeled, cored and sliced
½ teaspoon ground cloves

1 teaspoon cinnamon
¼ cup walnuts

Preheat the air fryer to 360ºF (182ºC). Toss the apple slices with ground cloves and cinnamon. Place the apple slices in the Air Fryer cooking basket when your air fryer displays "READY" (select the cooking preset, and make minor adjustments according to your desired doneness.) and choose a shake reminder. Cook at 360ºF (182ºC) for 10 minutes or until crisp. Reserve. Then, toast the walnuts at 300ºF (149ºC) for 10 minutes; now, shake the basket and cook for another 10 minutes. Chop the walnuts and scatter them over the apple slices and serve.

## Minty Plantain Bites

**Prep time: 5 minutes | Cook time: 10 minutes | Serves 3**

1 pound (454 g) plantains, peeled and cut into rounds
1 teaspoon coconut oil

A pinch of coarse sea salt
1 tablespoon mint leaves, chopped

Preheat the air fryer to 350ºF (177ºC). Start by preheating your Air Fryer to 350ºF (177ºC). Brush the plantain rounds with coconut oil and sprinkle with coarse sea salt. When your air fryer displays "READY" (select the cooking preset, and make minor adjustments according to your desired doneness.) and choose a shake reminder. Cook the plantain rounds in the preheated Air Fryer for 5 minutes; shake the basket and cook for a further 5 minutes or until golden on the top. Garnish with roughly chopped mint and serve. Enjoy!

## Foolproof Popcorn

**Prep time: 5 minutes | Cook time: 15 minutes | Serves 4**

2 tablespoons dried corn kernels
1 teaspoon safflower oil

Kosher salt, to taste
1 teaspoon red pepper flakes, crushed

Preheat the air fryer to 395ºF (202ºC). Add the dried corn kernels to the Air Fryer basket; brush with safflower oil. When your air fryer displays "READY" (select the cooking preset, and make minor adjustments according to your desired doneness.) and choose a shake reminder. Cook at 395ºF (202ºC) for 15 minutes, shaking the basket every 5 minutes. Sprinkle with salt and red pepper flakes. Enjoy!

## Paprika Potato Chips with Ketchup

**Prep time: 5 minutes | Cook time: 15 minutes | Serves 3**

3 potatoes, thinly sliced
1 teaspoon sea salt
1 teaspoon garlic powder

1 teaspoon paprika
¼ cup ketchup

Preheat the air fryer to 400ºF (204ºC). Add the sliced potatoes to a bowl with salted water. Let them soak for 30 minutes. Drain and rinse your potatoes. Pat dry and toss with salt. When your air fryer displays "READY" (select the cooking preset, and make minor adjustments according to your desired doneness.) and choose a shake reminder. Cook in the preheated Air Fryer at 400ºF (204ºC) for 15 minutes, shaking the basket occasionally. Work in batches. Toss with the garlic powder and paprika. Serve with ketchup. Enjoy!

## Thyme-Pepper Sweet Potatoes

**Prep time: 10 minutes | Cook time: 30 minutes | Serves 3**

1 pound (454 g) sweet potatoes, peeled, cut into bite-sized pieces
2 tablespoons olive oil
1 teaspoon sea salt

¼ teaspoon freshly ground black pepper
½ teaspoon cayenne pepper
2 fresh thyme sprigs

Preheat the air fryer to 380ºF (193ºC). Arrange the potato slices in a single layer in the lightly greased cooking basket. Add the olive oil, salt, black pepper, and cayenne pepper; toss to coat. When your air fryer displays "READY" (select the cooking preset, and make minor adjustments according to your desired doneness.) and choose a shake reminder. Bake at 380ºF (193ºC) for 30 minutes, shaking the cooking basket occasionally. Bake until tender and slightly browned, working in batches. Serve warm, garnished with thyme sprigs.

## Panko-Crusted Chicken Wings

**Prep time: 1 hour 20 minutes | Cook time: 17 to 19 minutes | Serves 4**

2 pounds (907 g) chicken wings
**Marinade:**
1 cup buttermilk
½ teaspoon salt
**Coating:**
1 cup flour
1 cup panko bread crumbs
2 tablespoons poultry

½ teaspoon black pepper

seasoning
2 teaspoons salt
Cooking spray

Whisk together all the ingredients for the marinade in a large bowl. Add the chicken wings to the marinade and toss well. Transfer to the refrigerator to marinate for at least an hour. Preheat the air fryer to 360ºF (182ºC). Spritz the air fryer basket with cooking spray. Thoroughly combine all the ingredients for the coating in a shallow bowl. Remove the chicken wings from the marinade and shake off any excess. Roll them in the coating mixture. Place the chicken wings in the air fryer basket in a single layer when your air fryer displays "READY" (select the cooking preset, and make minor adjustments according to your desired doneness.) and choose a shake reminder. You'll need to work in batches to avoid overcrowding. Mist the wings with cooking spray and air fry for 17 to 19 minutes, or until the wings are crisp and golden brown on the outside. Flip the wings halfway through the cooking time. Remove from the basket to a plate and repeat with the remaining wings. Serve hot.

## Panko-Apple Wedges

**Prep time: 10 minutes | Cook time: 8 minutes | Serves 4**

¼ cup panko breadcrumbs
¼ cup pecans
1½ teaspoons cinnamon
1½ teaspoons brown sugar
¼ cup cornstarch

1 egg white
2 teaspoons water
1 medium apple
Oil for misting or cooking spray

In a food processor, combine panko, pecans, cinnamon, and brown sugar. Process to make small crumbs. Place cornstarch in a plastic bag or bowl with lid. In a shallow dish, beat together the egg white and water until slightly foamy. Preheat air fryer to 390ºF (199ºC). Cut apple into small wedges. The thickest edge should be no more than ⅜- to ½-inch thick. Cut away the core, but do not peel. Place apple wedges in cornstarch, reseal bag or bowl, and shake to coat. Dip wedges in egg wash, shake off excess, and roll in crumb mixture. Spray with oil. Place apples in air fryer basket in single layer when your air fryer displays "READY" (select the cooking preset, and make minor adjustments according to your desired doneness.) and choose a shake reminder. Cook for 5 minutes. Shake basket and break apart any apples that have stuck together. Mist lightly with oil and cook 3 to 4 minutes longer, until crispy.

## Bacon-Wrapped Jalapeño Peppers and Cheese

**Prep time: 10 minutes | Cook time: 12 minutes | Serves 12**

12 jalapeño peppers
1 (8-ounce / 227-g) package cream cheese, at room temperature
1 cup shredded Cheddar cheese

1 teaspoon onion powder
1 teaspoon salt
½ teaspoon freshly ground black pepper
12 slices bacon, cut in half

Spray the air fryer basket with olive oil. Cut each pepper in half, then use a spoon to scrape out the veins and seeds. In a small mixing bowl, mix together the cream cheese, Cheddar cheese, onion powder, salt, and pepper. Using a small spoon, fill each pepper half with the cheese mixture. Wrap each stuffed pepper half with a half slice of bacon. Place the bacon-wrapped peppers into the greased air fryer basket in a single layer when your air fryer displays "READY" (select the cooking preset, and make minor adjustments according to your desired doneness.) and choose a shake reminder. (You may have to cook the peppers in more than one batch.) Set the temperature for 320ºF (160ºC). Set the timer and bake for 12 minutes. Using tongs, remove the peppers from the air fryer, place them on a platter, and serve.

## Crisp-Tender Carrot Chips

**Prep time: 15 minutes | Cook time: 8 to 10 minutes | Serves 4**

1 tablespoon olive oil, plus more for greasing the basket
4 to 5 medium carrots, trimmed

and thinly sliced
1 teaspoon seasoned salt

Preheat the air fryer to 390ºF (199ºC). Grease the air fryer basket with the olive oil. Toss the carrot slices with 1 tablespoon of olive oil and salt in a medium bowl until thoroughly coated. Arrange the carrot slices in the greased basket when your air fryer displays "READY" (select the cooking preset, and make minor adjustments according to your desired doneness.) and choose a shake reminder. You may need to work in batches to avoid overcrowding. Air fry for 8 to 10 minutes until the carrot slices are crisp-tender. Shake the basket once during cooking. Transfer the carrot slices to a bowl and repeat with the remaining carrots. Allow to cool for 5 minutes and serve.

## Ricotta-Rosemary Capers with Parmesan

**Prep time: 10 minutes | Cook time: 8 to 10 minutes | Serves 4 to 6**

1½ cups whole milk ricotta cheese
2 tablespoons extra-virgin olive oil
2 tablespoons capers, rinsed
Zest of 1 lemon, plus more for garnish
1 teaspoon finely chopped fresh

rosemary
Pinch crushed red pepper flakes
Salt and freshly ground black pepper, to taste
1 tablespoon grated Parmesan cheese

Preheat the air fryer to 380ºF (193ºC). In a mixing bowl, stir together the ricotta cheese, olive oil, capers, lemon zest, rosemary, red pepper flakes, salt, and pepper until well combined. Spread the mixture evenly in a baking dish and place it in the air fryer basket when your air fryer displays "READY" (select the cooking preset, and make minor adjustments according to your desired doneness.) and choose a shake reminder. Air fry for 8 to 10 minutes until the top is nicely browned. Remove from the basket and top with a sprinkle of grated Parmesan cheese. Garnish with the lemon zest and serve warm.

## Bruschetta with Basil and Tomato

**Prep time: 5 minutes | Cook time: 6 minutes | Serves 6**

4 tomatoes, diced
⅓ cup shredded fresh basil
¼ cup shredded Parmesan cheese
1 tablespoon balsamic vinegar
1 tablespoon minced garlic
1 teaspoon olive oil

1 teaspoon salt
1 teaspoon freshly ground black pepper
1 loaf French bread, cut into 1-inch-thick slices
Cooking spray

Preheat the air fryer to 250ºF (121ºC). Mix together the tomatoes and basil in a medium bowl. Add the cheese, vinegar, garlic, olive oil, salt, and pepper and stir until well incorporated. Set aside. Spritz the air fryer basket with cooking spray. Working in batches, lay the bread slices in the basket in a single layer when your air fryer displays "READY" (select the cooking preset, and make minor adjustments according to your desired doneness.) and choose a shake reminder. Spray the slices with cooking spray. Bake for 3 minutes until golden brown. Remove from the basket to a plate. Repeat with the remaining bread slices. Top each slice with a generous spoonful of the tomato mixture and serve.

## Caramelized Peach Wedges

**Prep time: 10 minutes | Cook time: 10 to 13 minutes | Serves 4**

2 tablespoons sugar
¼ teaspoon ground cinnamon

4 peaches, cut into wedges
Cooking spray

Preheat the air fryer to 350ºF (177ºC). Lightly spray the air fryer basket with cooking spray. Toss the peaches with the sugar and cinnamon in a medium bowl until evenly coated. Arrange the peaches in the air fryer basket in a single layer when your air fryer displays "READY" (select the cooking preset, and make minor adjustments according to your desired doneness.) and choose a shake reminder. You may need to work in batches to avoid overcrowding. Lightly mist the peaches with cooking spray and air fry for 5 minutes. Flip the peaches and air fry for another 5 to 8 minutes, or until the peaches are caramelized. Repeat with the remaining peaches. Let the peaches cool for 5 minutes and serve warm.

## Buffalo Chicken Tenders

**Prep time: 10 minutes | Cook time: 7 minutes | Serves 4**

⅔ cup sour cream
¼ cup creamy blue cheese salad dressing
¼ cup crumbled blue cheese
1 celery stalk, finely chopped
1 pound (454 g) chicken

tenders, cut into thirds crosswise
3 tablespoons Buffalo chicken wing sauce
1 cup panko bread crumbs
2 tablespoons olive oil

In a small bowl, combine the sour cream, salad dressing, blue cheese, and celery, and set aside. In a medium bowl, combine the chicken pieces and Buffalo wing sauce and stir to coat. Let sit while you get the bread crumbs ready. Combine the bread crumbs and olive oil on a plate and mix. Coat the chicken pieces in the bread crumb mixture, patting each piece so the crumbs adhere. When your air fryer displays "READY" (select the cooking preset, and make minor adjustments according to your desired doneness.) and choose a shake reminder. Air-fry in batches for 7 to 9 minutes, shaking the basket once, until the chicken is cooked to 165ºF (74ºC) and is golden brown. Serve with the blue cheese sauce on the side.

## Buffalo Chicken Meatballs

**Prep time: 5 minutes | Cook time: 22 minutes | Makes 16 meatballs**

1 pound (454 g) ground chicken
8 tablespoons buffalo wing sauce

2 ounces (57 g) Gruyère cheese, cut into 16 cubes
1 tablespoon maple syrup

Mix 4 tablespoons buffalo wing sauce into all the ground chicken. Shape chicken into a log and divide into 16 equal portions. With slightly damp hands, mold each chicken portion around a cube of cheese and shape into a firm ball. When you have shaped 8 meatballs, place them in air fryer basket when your air fryer displays "READY" (select the cooking preset, and make minor adjustments according to your desired doneness.) and choose a shake reminder. Cook at 390ºF (199ºC) for approximately 5 minutes. Shake basket, reduce temperature to 360ºF (182ºC), and cook for 5 to 6 minutes longer. While the first batch is cooking, shape remaining chicken and cheese into 8 more meatballs. Repeat step 4 to cook second batch of meatballs. In a medium bowl, mix the remaining 4 tablespoons of buffalo wing sauce with the maple syrup. Add all the cooked meatballs and toss to coat. Place meatballs back into air fryer basket and cook at 390ºF (199ºC) for 2 to 3 minutes to set the glaze. Skewer each with a toothpick and serve.

## Ginger Apple  with Yogurt

**Prep time: 10 minutes | Cook time: 12 minutes | Serves 4**

2 medium apples, cored and sliced into ¼-inch wedges
1 teaspoon canola oil
2 teaspoons peeled and grated

fresh ginger
½ teaspoon ground cinnamon
½ cup low-fat Greek vanilla yogurt, for serving

Preheat air fryer to 360ºF (182ºC). In a large bowl, toss the apple wedges with the canola oil, ginger, and cinnamon until evenly coated. Put the apple wedges in the air fryer basket when your air fryer displays "READY" (select the cooking preset, and make minor adjustments according to your desired doneness.) and choose a shake reminder. Air fry for 12 minutes until crisp-tender. Serve the apple wedges drizzled with the yogurt.

## Cheddar Cheese Wafer Bites

**Prep time: 5 minutes | Cook time: 5 minutes | Makes 4 dozen**

4 ounces (113 g) sharp
Cheddar cheese, grated
¼ cup butter
½ cup flour

¼ teaspoon salt
½ cup crisp rice cereal
Oil for misting or cooking spray

Cream the butter and grated cheese together. You can do it by hand, but using a stand mixer is faster and easier. Sift flour and salt together. Add it to the cheese mixture and mix until well blended. Stir in cereal. Place dough on wax paper and shape into a long roll about 1 inch in diameter. Wrap well with the wax paper and chill for at least 4 hours. When ready to cook, preheat air fryer to 360ºF (182ºC). Cut cheese roll into ¼-inch slices. Spray air fryer basket with oil or cooking spray and place slices in a single layer, close but not touching. When your air fryer displays "READY" (select the cooking preset, and make minor adjustments according to your desired doneness.) and choose a shake reminder. Cook for 5 to 6 minutes or until golden brown. When done, place them on paper towels to cool. Repeat previous step to cook remaining cheese bites.

## Mozzarella Ham Stuffed Baby Bella

**Prep time: 15 minutes | Cook time: 12 minutes | Serves 8**

4 ounces (113 g) Mozzarella
cheese, cut into pieces
½ cup diced ham
2 green onions, chopped
2 tablespoons bread crumbs
½ teaspoon garlic powder

¼ teaspoon ground oregano
¼ teaspoon ground black
pepper
1 to 2 teaspoons olive oil
16 fresh Baby Bella
mushrooms, stemmed removed

Process the cheese, ham, green onions, bread crumbs, garlic powder, oregano, and pepper in a food processor until finely chopped. With the food processor running, slowly drizzle in 1 to 2 teaspoons olive oil until a thick paste has formed. Transfer the mixture to a bowl. Evenly divide the mixture into the mushroom caps and lightly press down the mixture. Preheat the air fryer to 390ºF (199ºC). Lay the mushrooms in the air fryer basket in a single layer when your air fryer displays "READY" (select the cooking preset, and make minor adjustments according to your desired doneness.) and choose a shake reminder. You'll need to work in batches to avoid overcrowding. Roast for 12 minutes until the mushrooms are lightly browned and tender. Remove from the basket to a plate and repeat with the remaining mushrooms. Let the mushrooms cool for 5 minutes and serve warm.

## Curry Chickpeas

**Prep time: 5 minutes | Cook time: 15 minutes | Makes 1 cup**

1 (15-ounce / 425-g) can
chickpeas, drained
2 teaspoons curry powder

¼ teaspoon salt
1 tablespoon olive oil

Drain chickpeas thoroughly and spread in a single layer on paper towels. Cover with another paper towel and press gently to remove extra moisture. Don't press too hard or you'll crush the chickpeas. Mix curry powder and salt together. Place chickpeas in a medium bowl and sprinkle with seasonings. Stir well to coat. Add olive oil and stir again to distribute oil. When your air fryer displays "READY" (select the cooking preset, and make minor adjustments according to your desired doneness.) and choose a shake reminder. Cook at 390ºF (199ºC) for 15 minutes, stopping to shake basket about halfway through cooking time. Cool completely and store in airtight container.

## Cheesy Crab Mwat Toasts

**Prep time: 10 minutes | Cook time: 5 minutes | Makes 15 to 18 toasts**

1 (6-ounce / 170-g) can flaked
crab meat, well drained
3 tablespoons light mayonnaise
¼ cup shredded Parmesan
cheese
¼ cup shredded Cheddar
cheese

1 teaspoon Worcestershire
sauce
½ teaspoon lemon juice
1 loaf artisan bread, French
bread, or baguette, cut into
⅜-inch-thick slices

Preheat the air fryer to 360ºF (182ºC). In a large bowl, stir together all the ingredients except the bread slices. On a clean work surface, lay the bread slices. Spread ½ tablespoon of crab mixture onto each slice of bread. Arrange the bread slices in the air fryer basket in a single layer when your air fryer displays "READY" (select the cooking preset, and make minor adjustments according to your desired doneness.) and choose a shake reminder. You'll need to work in batches to avoid overcrowding. Bake for 5 minutes until the tops are lightly browned. Transfer to a plate and repeat with the remaining bread slices. Serve warm.

## Zucchini Tots with Cheese

**Prep time: 15 minutes | Cook time: 6 minutes | Serves 8**

2 medium zucchini (about 12
ounces / 340 g), shredded
1 large egg, whisked
½ cup grated pecorino romano
cheese

½ cup panko bread crumbs
¼ teaspoon black pepper
1 clove garlic, minced
Cooking spray

Using your hands, squeeze out as much liquid from the zucchini as possible. In a large bowl, mix the zucchini with the remaining ingredients except the oil until well incorporated. Make the zucchini tots: Use a spoon or cookie scoop to place tablespoonfuls of the zucchini mixture onto a lightly floured cutting board and form into 1-inch logs. Preheat air fryer to 375ºF (191ºC). Spritz the air fryer basket with cooking spray. Place the tots in the basket when your air fryer displays "READY" (select the cooking preset, and make minor adjustments according to your desired doneness.) and choose a shake reminder. You may need to cook in batches to avoid overcrowding. Air fry for 6 minutes until golden brown. Remove from the basket to a serving plate and repeat with the remaining zucchini tots. Serve immediately.

## Spicy Chickpeas

**Prep time: 5 minutes | Cook time: 6 to 12 minutes | Makes 1½ cups**

1 can (15-ounce / 425-g)
chickpeas, rinsed and dried
with paper towels
1 tablespoon olive oil
½ teaspoon dried rosemary
½ teaspoon dried parsley

½ teaspoon dried chives
¼ teaspoon mustard powder
¼ teaspoon sweet paprika
¼ teaspoon cayenne pepper
Kosher salt and freshly ground
black pepper, to taste

Preheat the air fryer to 350ºF (177ºC). In a large bowl, combine all the ingredients, except for the kosher salt and black pepper, and toss until the chickpeas are evenly coated in the herbs and spices. Scrape the chickpeas and seasonings into the air fryer when your air fryer displays "READY" (select the cooking preset, and make minor adjustments according to your desired doneness.) and choose a shake reminder. Air fry for 6 to 12 minutes, or until browned and crisp, shaking the basket halfway through. Transfer the crispy chickpeas to a bowl, sprinkle with kosher salt and black pepper, and serve warm.

### Peppery Calamari Rings

**Prep time: 10 minutes | Cook time: 8 minutes | Serves 2**

1 jar (8 ounces) sweet or hot pickled cherry peppers
½ pound calamari bodies and tentacles, bodies cut into ½-inch-wide rings
1 lemon
2 cups all-purpose flour
Kosher salt and freshly ground

black pepper, to taste
3 large eggs, lightly beaten
Cooking spray
½ cup mayonnaise
1 teaspoon finely chopped rosemary
1 garlic clove, minced

Drain the pickled pepper brine into a large bowl and tear the peppers into bite-size strips. Add the pepper strips and calamari to the brine and let stand in the refrigerator for 20 minutes or up to 2 hours. Grate the lemon zest into a large bowl then whisk in the flour and season with salt and pepper. Dip the calamari and pepper strips in the egg, then toss them in the flour mixture until fully coated. Spray the calamari and peppers liberally with cooking spray, then transfer half to the air fryer when your air fryer displays "READY" (select the cooking preset, and make minor adjustments according to your desired doneness.) and choose a shake reminder. Cook at 400ºF (204ºC), shaking the basket halfway into cooking, until the calamari is cooked through and golden brown, about 8 minutes. Transfer to a plate and repeat with the remaining pieces. In a small bowl, whisk together the mayonnaise, rosemary, and garlic. Squeeze half the zested lemon to get 1 tablespoon of juice and stir it into the sauce. Season with salt and pepper. Cut the remaining zested lemon half into 4 small wedges and serve alongside the calamari, peppers, and sauce.

### Greek Feta Hummus Tacos

**Prep time: 5 minutes | Cook time: 3 minutes | Makes 8 small tacos**

8 (4-inch diameter) small flour tortillas
8 tablespoons hummus
4 tablespoons crumbled Feta cheese

4 tablespoons chopped kalamata or other olives (optional)
Olive oil for misting

Place 1 tablespoon of hummus or tapenade in the center of each tortilla. Top with 1 teaspoon of Feta crumbles and 1 teaspoon of chopped olives, if using. Using your finger or a small spoon, moisten the edges of the tortilla all around with water. Fold tortilla over to make a half-moon shape. Press center gently. Then press the edges firmly to seal in the filling. Mist both sides with olive oil. Place in air fryer basket very close but try not to overlap. Cook at 390ºF (199ºC) for 3 minutes, just until lightly browned and crispy.

### Mozzarella Buttered Eggplant Slices

**Prep time: 10 minutes | Cook time: 15 minutes | Serves 4**

1 pound (454 g) eggplant, cut into slices
2 tablespoons butter, melted
½ teaspoon smoked paprika
1 teaspoon Italian seasoning

Sea salt and ground black pepper, to taste
1 cup Mozzarella cheese, shredded

Toss the eggplant with the butter and spices. Arrange the eggplant slices in the Air Fryer basket when your air fryer displays "READY" (select the cooking preset, and make minor adjustments according to your desired doneness.) and choose a shake reminder. Cook the eggplant at 400ºF (204ºC) for about 15 minutes, shaking the basket halfway through the cooking time. Bon appétit!

### Cheddar Corn and Black Bean Salsa

**Prep time: 10 minutes | Cook time: 10 minutes | Serves 4**

½ (15-ounce / 425-g) can corn, drained and rinsed
½ (15-ounce / 425-g) can black beans, drained and rinsed
¼ cup chunky salsa
2 ounces (57 g) reduced-fat cream cheese, softened

¼ cup shredded reduced-fat Cheddar cheese
½ teaspoon paprika
½ teaspoon ground cumin
Salt and freshly ground black pepper, to taste

Preheat the air fryer to 325ºF (163ºC). Combine the corn, black beans, salsa, cream cheese, Cheddar cheese, paprika, and cumin in a medium bowl. Sprinkle with salt and pepper and stir until well blended. Pour the mixture into a baking dish and place in the air fryer basket when your air fryer displays "READY" (select the cooking preset, and make minor adjustments according to your desired doneness.) and choose a shake reminder. Air fry for about 10 minutes until heated through. Rest for 5 minutes and serve warm.

### Panko-Crusted Artichoke Bites

**Prep time: 10 minutes | Cook time: 8 minutes | Serves 4**

14 whole artichoke hearts packed in water
½ cup all-purpose flour
1 egg

⅓ cup panko bread crumbs
1 teaspoon Italian seasoning
Cooking spray

Preheat the air fryer to 375ºF (191ºC). Drain the artichoke hearts and dry thoroughly with paper towels. Place the flour on a plate. Beat the egg in a shallow bowl until frothy. Thoroughly combine the bread crumbs and Italian seasoning in a separate shallow bowl. Dredge the artichoke hearts in the flour, then in the beaten egg, and finally roll in the bread crumb mixture until evenly coated. Place the artichoke hearts in the air fryer basket and mist them with cooking spray when your air fryer displays "READY" (select the cooking preset, and make minor adjustments according to your desired doneness.) and choose a shake reminder. Air fry for 8 minutes, flipping the artichoke hearts halfway through, or until they begin to brown and edges are crispy. Let the artichoke hearts sit for 5 minutes before serving.

### Cuban Pork and Turkey Sandwiches

**Prep time: 20 minutes | Cook time: 8 minutes | Makes 4 sandwiches**

8 slices ciabatta bread, about ¼-inch thick
**Toppings:**
6 to 8 ounces (170 to 227 g) thinly sliced leftover roast pork
4 ounces (113 g) thinly sliced deli turkey

Cooking spray
1 tablespoon brown mustard

⅓ cup bread and butter pickle slices
2 to 3 ounces (57 to 85 g) Pepper Jack cheese slices

Preheat the air fryer to 390ºF (199ºC). On a clean work surface, spray one side of each slice of bread with cooking spray. Spread the other side of each slice of bread evenly with brown mustard. Top 4 of the bread slices with the roast pork, turkey, pickle slices, cheese, and finish with remaining bread slices. Transfer to the air fryer basket when your air fryer displays "READY" (select the cooking preset, and make minor adjustments according to your desired doneness.) and choose a shake reminder. Air fry for about 8 minutes until golden brown. Cool for 5 minutes and serve warm.

## Breaded Cod Fingers

**Prep time: 5 minutes | Cook time: 12 minutes | Serves 4**

2 eggs
2 tablespoons milk
2 cups flour
1 cup cornmeal
1 teaspoon seafood seasoning

Salt and black pepper, to taste
1 cup bread crumbs
1 pound (454 g) cod fillets, cut into 1-inch strips

Preheat air fryer to 400ºF (204ºC). Beat the eggs with the milk in a shallow bowl. In another shallow bowl, combine the flour, cornmeal, seafood seasoning, salt, and pepper. On a plate, place the bread crumbs. Dredge the cod strips, one at a time, in the flour mixture, then in the egg mixture, finally in the bread crumb to coat evenly. Arrange the cod strips in the air fryer basket when your air fryer displays "READY" (select the cooking preset, and make minor adjustments according to your desired doneness.) and choose a shake reminder. Air fry for 12 minutes until crispy. Transfer the cod strips to a paper towel-lined plate and serve warm.

## Green Tomatoes with Horseradish Sauce

**Prep time: 18 minutes | Cook time: 10 to 15 minutes | Serves 4**

2 eggs
¼ cup buttermilk
½ cup bread crumbs
½ cup cornmeal
**Horseradish Sauce:**
¼ cup sour cream
¼ cup mayonnaise
2 teaspoons prepared horseradish

¼ teaspoon salt
1½ pounds (680 g) firm green tomatoes, cut into ¼-inch slices
Cooking spray

½ teaspoon lemon juice
½ teaspoon Worcestershire sauce
⅛ teaspoon black pepper

Preheat air fryer to 390ºF (199ºC). Spritz the air fryer basket with cooking spray. In a small bowl, whisk together all the ingredients for the horseradish sauce until smooth. Set aside. In a shallow dish, beat the eggs and buttermilk. In a separate shallow dish, thoroughly combine the bread crumbs, cornmeal, and salt. Dredge the tomato slices, one at a time, in the egg mixture, then roll in the bread crumb mixture until evenly coated. Working in batches, place the tomato slices in the air fryer basket in a single layer when your air fryer displays "READY" (select the cooking preset, and make minor adjustments according to your desired doneness.) and choose a shake reminder. Spray them with cooking spray. Air fry for 10 to 15 minutes, flipping the slices halfway through, or until the tomato slices are nicely browned and crisp. Remove from the basket to a platter and repeat with the remaining tomato slices. Serve drizzled with the prepared horseradish sauce.

## Paprika Parmesan Zucchini Fries

**Prep time: 110 minutes | Cook time: 20 minutes | Serves 4**

1 pound (454 g) zucchini, cut into sticks
½ cup Parmesan cheese
½ cup almond flour
1 egg, whisked

2 tablespoons olive oil
1 teaspoon hot paprika
Sea salt and ground black pepper, to taste

Start by preheating your Air Fryer to 390ºF (199ºC). Toss the zucchini sticks with the remaining ingredients and arrange them in a single layer in the Air Fryer cooking basket when your air fryer displays "READY" (select the cooking preset, and make minor adjustments according to your desired doneness.) and choose a shake reminder. Cook the zucchini sticks for about 10 minutes at 390ºF (199ºC), shaking the basket halfway through the cooking time. Work in batches. Bon appétit!

## Pear Brie Sandwiches

**Prep time: 10 minutes | Cook time: 5 to 6 minutes | Serves 4 to 8**

8 ounces (227 g) Brie
8 slices oat nut bread
1 large ripe pear, cored and cut

into ½-inch-thick slices
2 tablespoons butter, melted

Preheat the air fryer to 360ºF (182ºC). Make the sandwiches: Spread each of 4 slices of bread with ¼ of the Brie. Top the Brie with the pear slices and remaining 4 bread slices. Brush the melted butter lightly on both sides of each sandwich. Arrange the sandwiches in the air fryer basket when your air fryer displays "READY" (select the cooking preset, and make minor adjustments according to your desired doneness.) and choose a shake reminder. You may need to work in batches to avoid overcrowding. Bake for 5 to 6 minutes until the cheese is melted. Repeat with the remaining sandwiches. Serve warm.

## Chili Chickpeas

**Prep time: 5 minutes | Cook time: 15 to 20 minutes | Serves 4**

½ teaspoon chili powder
½ teaspoon ground cumin
¼ teaspoon cayenne pepper
¼ teaspoon salt

1 (19-ounce / 539-g) can chickpeas, drained and rinsed
Cooking spray

Preheat the air fryer to 390ºF (199ºC). Lightly spritz the air fryer basket with cooking spray. Mix the chili powder, cumin, cayenne pepper, and salt in a small bowl. Place the chickpeas in a medium bowl and lightly mist with cooking spray. Add the spice mixture to the chickpeas and toss until evenly coated. Place the chickpeas in the air fryer basket when your air fryer displays "READY" (select the cooking preset, and make minor adjustments according to your desired doneness.) and choose a shake reminder. Air fry for 15 to 20 minutes, or until the chickpeas are cooked to your preferred crunchiness. Shake the basket three or four times during cooking. Let the chickpeas cool for 5 minutes before serving.

## Muffuletta Sliders with Olive Mix

**Prep time: 10 minutes | Cook time: 5 to 7 minutes | Makes 8 sliders**

¼ pound (113 g) thinly sliced deli ham
¼ pound (113 g) thinly sliced pastrami
4 ounces (113 g) low-fat
**Olive Mix:**
½ cup sliced green olives with pimentos
¼ cup sliced black olives
¼ cup chopped kalamata olives

Mozzarella cheese, grated
8 slider buns, split in half
Cooking spray
1 tablespoon sesame seeds

1 teaspoon red wine vinegar
¼ teaspoon basil
⅛ teaspoon garlic powder

Preheat the air fryer to 360ºF (182ºC). Combine all the ingredients for the olive mix in a small bowl and stir well. Stir together the ham, pastrami, and cheese in a medium bowl and divide the mixture into 8 equal portions. Assemble the sliders: Top each bottom bun with 1 portion of meat and cheese, 2 tablespoons of olive mix, finished by the remaining buns. Lightly spritz the tops with cooking spray. Scatter the sesame seeds on top. Working in batches, arrange the sliders in the air fryer basket when your air fryer displays "READY" (select the cooking preset, and make minor adjustments according to your desired doneness.) and choose a shake reminder. Bake for 5 t0 7 minutes until the cheese melts. Transfer to a large plate and repeat with the remaining sliders. Serve immediately.

## Endive in Curried Yogurt

**Prep time: 5 minutes | Cook time: 10 minutes | Serves 6**

6 heads endive
½ cup plain and fat-free yogurt
3 tablespoons lemon juice
1 teaspoon garlic powder

½ teaspoon curry powder
Salt and ground black pepper, to taste

Wash the endives, and slice them in half lengthwise. In a bowl, mix together the yogurt, lemon juice, garlic powder, curry powder, salt and pepper. Brush the endive halves with the marinade, coating them completely. Allow to sit for at least 30 minutes or up to 24 hours. Preheat the air fryer to 320ºF (160ºC). Put the endives in the air fryer basket when your air fryer displays "READY" (select the cooking preset, and make minor adjustments according to your desired doneness.) and choose a shake reminder. Air fry for 10 minutes. Serve hot.

## Lemony Bosc Pear Chips

**Prep time: 15 minutes | Cook time: 9 to 13 minutes | Serves 4**

2 firm Bosc pears, cut crosswise into ⅛-inch-thick slices
1 tablespoon freshly squeezed

lemon juice
½ teaspoon ground cinnamon
⅛ teaspoon ground cardamom

Preheat the air fryer to 380ºF (193ºC). Separate the smaller stem-end pear rounds from the larger rounds with seeds. Remove the core and seeds from the larger slices. Sprinkle all slices with lemon juice, cinnamon, and cardamom. Put the smaller chips into the air fryer basket when your air fryer displays "READY" (select the cooking preset, and make minor adjustments according to your desired doneness.) and choose a shake reminder. Air fry for 3 to 5 minutes, or until light golden brown, shaking the basket once during cooking. Remove from the air fryer. Repeat with the larger slices, air frying for 6 to 8 minutes, or until light golden brown, shaking the basket once during cooking. Remove the chips from the air fryer. Cool and serve or store in an airtight container at room temperature up for to 2 days.

## Breaded Parmesan Chicken Wings

**Prep time: 15 minutes | Cook time: 13 minutes | Serves 4**

2 pounds (907 g) chicken wings
Oil for misting
**For the Marinade:**
1 cup buttermilk
2 cloves garlic, mashed flat
1 teaspoon Worcestershire
**For the Coating:**
1½ cups grated Parmesan cheese
¾ cup breadcrumbs

Cooking spray

sauce
1 bay leaf

1½ tablespoons garlic powder
½ teaspoon salt

Mix all marinade ingredients together. Remove wing tips (the third joint) and discard or freeze for stock. Cut the remaining wings at the joint and toss them into the marinade, stirring to coat well. Refrigerate for at least an hour but no more than 8 hours. When ready to cook, combine all coating ingredients in a shallow dish. Remove wings from marinade, shaking off excess, and roll in coating mixture. Press coating into wings so that it sticks well. Spray wings with oil. Spray air fryer basket with cooking spray. Place wings in basket in single layer, close but not touching when your air fryer displays "READY" (select the cooking preset, and make minor adjustments according to your desired doneness.) and choose a shake reminder. Cook at 360ºF (182ºC) for 13 to 15 minutes or until chicken is done and juices run clear. Repeat previous step to cook remaining wings.

## Eggplant Fries

**Prep time: 10 minutes | Cook time: 15 minutes | Serves 4**

1 medium eggplant
1 teaspoon ground coriander
1 teaspoon cumin
1 teaspoon garlic powder
½ teaspoon salt

1 cup crushed panko breadcrumbs
1 large egg
2 tablespoons water
Oil for misting or cooking spray

Peel and cut the eggplant into fat fries, ⅜- to ½-inch thick. Preheat air fryer to 390ºF (199ºC). In a small cup, mix together the coriander, cumin, garlic, and salt. Combine 1 teaspoon of the seasoning mix and panko crumbs in a shallow dish. Place eggplant fries in a large bowl, sprinkle with remaining seasoning, and stir well to combine. Beat eggs and water together and pour over eggplant fries. Stir to coat. Remove eggplant from egg wash, shaking off excess, and roll in panko crumbs. Spray with oil. Place half of the fries in air fryer basket when your air fryer displays "READY" (select the cooking preset, and make minor adjustments according to your desired doneness.) and choose a shake reminder. You should have only a single layer, but it's fine if they overlap a little. Cook for 5 minutes. Shake basket, mist lightly with oil, and cook 2 to 3 minutes longer, until browned and crispy. Repeat step 10 to cook remaining eggplant.

## Masala Onion Rings with Minty Mayo

**Prep time: 15 minutes | Cook time: 10 minutes | Serves 2 to 4**

1 (14- to 16-ounce / 397- to 454-g) large red onion
¼ cup garam masala
2 tablespoons sweet paprika
2 tablespoons curry powder
2 tablespoons kosher salt, plus more as needed
2 cups all-purpose flour
6 large eggs, lightly beaten

2 cups panko breadcrumbs
½ cup mayonnaise
2 tablespoons finely chopped fresh mint
2 teaspoons fresh lemon juice
1 scallion, finely chopped
Cooking spray
Ketchup, for serving

Trim the ends from the onion and peel away the papery outer skin. Cut the onion crosswise into ¾- to 1-inch-thick slices, then separate the slices into rings, discarding the feathery skin between the rings. In a small bowl, whisk together the garam masala, paprika, curry powder, and salt. Place the flour, eggs, and breadcrumbs in three separate shallow bowls and season each with one-third (2 tablespoons plus 2½ teaspoons) of the spice mixture. Dip 1 onion ring in the spiced egg, dredge in the flour, then repeat with the egg and flour once more. Dip the ring back into the egg again, then coat in the spiced breadcrumbs. Repeat to coat all the onion rings and arrange them on a wire rack set over a baking sheet. Place the onion rings in the freezer and chill until firm, at least 30 minutes or up to 1 week. Meanwhile, whisk together the mayonnaise, mint, lemon juice, and scallion in a bowl and season with salt. Refrigerate to marry the flavors in the sauce while the onion rings freeze. When ready to fry, spray 5 or 6 of the onion rings liberally with cooking spray and arrange them loosely in the air fryer basket, laying some flat and leaning some against the side of the basket. When your air fryer displays "READY" (select the cooking preset, and make minor adjustments according to your desired doneness.) and choose a shake reminder. Cook at 375ºF (190ºC) until the onion rings are tender and the breading is golden brown and crisp, about 10 minutes. Season with more salt once they come out of the fryer and continue frying as many onion rings as you like. Serve hot with the mint-mayo sauce and ketchup on the side.

## Warm Edamame

**Prep time: 5 minutes | Cook time: 16 to 20 minutes | Serves 4**

2 tablespoon olive oil, divided
1 (16-ounce / 454-g) bag frozen edamame in pods
½ teaspoon garlic salt
½ teaspoon salt
¼ teaspoon freshly ground black pepper
½ teaspoon red pepper flakes (optional)

Preheat the air fryer to 375ºF (191ºC). Grease the air fryer basket with 1 tablespoon of olive oil. Place the edamame in a medium bowl and drizzle the remaining 1 tablespoon of olive oil over the top. Toss to coat well. Stir together the garlic salt, salt, pepper, and red pepper flakes (if desired) in a small bowl. Pour the mixture into the bowl of edamame and toss until the edamame is fully coated. Arrange the edamame in the greased basket. You may need to cook in batches to avoid overcrowding. Air fry for 8 to 10 minutes, shaking the basket halfway through, or until the edamame is crisp. Remove from the basket to a plate and repeat with the remaining edamame. Serve warm.

## Barbecue Sauce Glazed Chicken Wings

**Prep time: 10 minutes | Cook time: 24 minutes | Serves 4**

8 chicken wings
3 tablespoons honey
1 tablespoons lemon juice
1 tablespoon low sodium chicken stock
2 cloves garlic, minced
¼ cup thinly sliced green onion
¾ cup low sodium barbecue sauce
4 stalks celery, cut into pieces

Pat the chicken wings dry. Cut off the small end piece and discard or freeze it to make chicken stock later. Put the wings into the air fryer basket. Air fry for 20 minutes, shaking the basket twice while cooking. Meanwhile, combine the honey, lemon juice, chicken stock, and garlic, and whisk until combined. Remove the wings from the air fryer and put into a 6" x 2" pan. Pour the sauce over the wings and toss gently to coat. Return the pan to the air fryer when your air fryer displays "READY" (select the cooking preset, and make minor adjustments according to your desired doneness.) and choose a shake reminder. Air fry for another 4 to 5 minutes or until the wings are glazed and a food thermometer registers 165ºF (74ºC). Sprinkle with the green onion and serve the wings with the barbecue sauce and celery.

## Healthy Carrot Chips

**Prep time: 5 minutes | Cook time: 6 minutes | Serves 6**

1 pound (454 g) carrots, peeled and sliced ⅛ inch thick
2 tablespoons olive oil
1 teaspoon sea salt

In a large mixing bowl, combine the carrots, olive oil, and salt. Toss them together until the carrot slices are thoroughly coated with oil. Place the carrot chips in the air fryer basket in a single layer when your air fryer displays "READY" (select the cooking preset, and make minor adjustments according to your desired doneness.) and choose a shake reminder. (You may have to bake the carrot chips in more than one batch.) Set the temperature to 360ºF (182ºC). Set the timer and bake for 3 minutes. Remove the air fryer drawer and shake to redistribute the chips for even cooking. Reset the timer and bake for 3 minutes more. Check the carrot chips for doneness. If you like them extra crispy, give the basket another shake and cook them for another 1 to 2 minutes. When the chips are done, release the air fryer basket from the drawer, pour the chips into a bowl, and serve.

## Thyme Pita Chips

**Prep time: 5 minutes | Cook time: 5 to 6 minutes | Serves 4**

¼ teaspoon dried basil
¼ teaspoon marjoram
¼ teaspoon ground oregano
¼ teaspoon garlic powder
¼ teaspoon ground thyme
¼ teaspoon salt
2 whole 6-inch pitas, whole grain or white
Cooking spray

Preheat the air fryer to 330ºF (166ºC). Mix all the seasonings together. Cut each pita half into 4 wedges. Break apart wedges at the fold. Mist one side of pita wedges with oil. Sprinkle with half of seasoning mix. Turn pita wedges over, mist the other side with oil, and sprinkle with remaining seasonings. Place pita wedges in air fryer basket when your air fryer displays "READY" (select the cooking preset, and make minor adjustments according to your desired doneness.) and choose a shake reminder. Bake for 2 minutes. Shake the basket and bake for 2 minutes longer. Shake again, and if needed, bake for 1 or 2 more minutes, or until crisp. Watch carefully because at this point they will cook very quickly. Serve hot.

## BBQ Chicken Sausage Pizza

**Prep time: 5 minutes | Cook time: 8 minutes | Serves 1**

1 piece naan bread
¼ cup Barbecue sauce
¼ cup shredded Monterrey Jack cheese
¼ cup shredded Mozzarella cheese
½ chicken herby sausage,
sliced
2 tablespoons red onion, thinly sliced
Chopped cilantro or parsley, for garnish
Cooking spray

Preheat the air fryer to 400ºF (204ºC). Spritz the bottom of naan bread with cooking spray, then transfer to the air fryer basket when your air fryer displays "READY" (select the cooking preset, and make minor adjustments according to your desired doneness.) and choose a shake reminder. Brush with the Barbecue sauce. Top with the cheeses, sausage, and finish with the red onion. Air fry for 8 minutes until the cheese is melted. Garnish with the chopped cilantro or parsley before slicing to serve.

## Sriracha Hot Chicken Wings

**Prep time: 5 minutes | Cook time: 30 minutes | Serves 4**

1 tablespoon Sriracha hot sauce
1 tablespoon honey
1 garlic clove, minced
½ teaspoon kosher salt
16 chicken wings and drumettes
Cooking spray

Preheat the air fryer to 360ºF (182ºC). In a large bowl, whisk together the Sriracha hot sauce, honey, minced garlic, and kosher salt, then add the chicken and toss to coat. Spray the air fryer basket with cooking spray, then place 8 wings in the basket when your air fryer displays "READY" (select the cooking preset, and make minor adjustments according to your desired doneness.) and choose a shake reminder. Air fry for 15 minutes, turning halfway through. Repeat this process with the remaining wings. Remove the wings and allow to cool on a wire rack for 10 minutes before serving.

## Hot Fried Dill Pickles

**Prep time: 5 minutes | Cook time: 11 minutes | Makes 2 cups**

1 egg
1 tablespoon milk
¼ teaspoon hot sauce
2 cups sliced dill pickles, well

drained
¾ cup breadcrumbs
Oil for misting or cooking spray

Preheat air fryer to 390ºF (199ºC). Beat together egg, milk, and hot sauce in a bowl large enough to hold all the pickles. Add pickles to the egg wash and stir well to coat. Place breadcrumbs in a large plastic bag or container with lid. Drain egg wash from pickles and place them in bag with breadcrumbs. Shake to coat. Pile pickles into air fryer basket and spray with oil when your air fryer displays "READY" (select the cooking preset, and make minor adjustments according to your desired doneness.) and choose a shake reminder. Cook for 5 minutes. Shake basket and spray with oil. Cook 5 more minutes. Shake and spray again. Separate any pickles that have stuck together and mist any spots you've missed. Cook for 1 to 5 minutes longer or until dark golden brown and crispy.

## Lemon Chicken Drumsticks

**Prep time: 5 minutes | Cook time: 30 minutes | Serves 2**

2 teaspoons freshly ground coarse black pepper
1 teaspoon baking powder
½ teaspoon garlic powder

4 chicken drumsticks (4 ounces / 113 g each)
Kosher salt, to taste
1 lemon

In a small bowl, stir together the pepper, baking powder, and garlic powder. Place the drumsticks on a plate and sprinkle evenly with the baking powder mixture, turning the drumsticks so they're well coated. Let the drumsticks stand in the refrigerator for at least 1 hour or up to overnight. Preheat the air fryer to 375ºF (191ºC). Sprinkle the drumsticks with salt, then transfer them to the air fryer, standing them bone-end up and leaning against the wall of the air fryer basket when your air fryer displays "READY" (select the cooking preset, and make minor adjustments according to your desired doneness.) and choose a shake reminder. Air fry for 30 minutes, or until cooked through and crisp on the outside. Transfer the drumsticks to a serving platter and finely grate the zest of the lemon over them while they're hot. Cut the lemon into wedges and serve with the warm drumsticks.

## Air-Fried Mozzarella Arancini

**Prep time: 5 minutes | Cook time: 8 to 11 minutes | Makes 16 arancini**

2 cups cooked rice, cooled
2 eggs, beaten
1½ cups panko bread crumbs, divided
½ cup grated Parmesan cheese

2 tablespoons minced fresh basil
16 ¾-inch cubes Mozzarella cheese
2 tablespoons olive oil

Preheat the air fryer to 400ºF (204ºC). In a medium bowl, combine the rice, eggs, ½ cup of the bread crumbs, Parmesan cheese, and basil. Form this mixture into 16 1½-inch balls. Poke a hole in each of the balls with your finger and insert a Mozzarella cube. Form the rice mixture firmly around the cheese. On a shallow plate, combine the remaining 1 cup of the bread crumbs with the olive oil and mix well. Roll the rice balls in the bread crumbs to coat. When your air fryer displays "READY" (select the cooking preset, and make minor adjustments according to your desired doneness.) and choose a shake reminder. Air fry the arancini in batches for 8 to 11 minutes or until golden brown. Serve hot.

## Seeds Seasoned Sausage Rolls

**Prep time: 10 minutes | Cook time: 10 minutes | Serves 6**

**For the Seasoning:**
2 tablespoons sesame seeds
1½ teaspoons poppy seeds
1½ teaspoons dried minced
**For the Sausages:**
1 (8-ounce / 227-g) package crescent roll dough
1 (12-ounce / 340-g) package

onion
1 teaspoon salt
1 teaspoon dried minced garlic

mini smoked sausages (cocktail franks)

Make the Seasoning In a small bowl, combine the sesame seeds, poppy seeds, onion, salt, and garlic and set aside.
Make the Sausages
Spray the air fryer basket with olive oil. Remove the crescent dough from the package and lay it out on a cutting board. Separate the dough at the perforations. Using a pizza cutter or sharp knife, cut each triangle of dough into fourths. Drain the sausages and pat them dry with a paper towel. Roll each sausage in a piece of dough. Sprinkle seasoning on top of each roll. Place the seasoned sausage rolls into the greased air fryer basket in a single layer when your air fryer displays "READY" (select the cooking preset, and make minor adjustments according to your desired doneness.) and choose a shake reminder. (You will have to bake these in at least 2 batches.) Set the temperature to 330ºF (166ºC). Set the timer for 5 minutes. Using tongs, remove the sausages from the air fryer and place them on a platter. Repeat steps 6 through 8 with the second batch.

## Paprika Potatoes Wedges

**Prep time: 5 minutes | Cook time: 20 minutes | Serves 4**

4 russet potatoes
2 teaspoons salt, divided
1 teaspoon freshly ground black pepper

1 teaspoon paprika
1 to 3 tablespoons olive oil, divided

Cut the potatoes into ½-inch-thick wedges. Try to make the wedges uniform in size, so they cook at an even rate. In a medium mixing bowl, combine the potato wedges with 1 teaspoon of salt, pepper, paprika, and 1 tablespoon of olive oil. Toss until all the potatoes are thoroughly coated with oil. Add additional oil, if needed. Place the potato wedges in the air fryer basket in a single layer when your air fryer displays "READY" (select the cooking preset, and make minor adjustments according to your desired doneness.) and choose a shake reminder. (You may have to roast them in batches.) Set the temperature to 400ºF (204ºC). Set the timer and roast for 5 minutes. After 5 minutes, remove the air fryer drawer and shake the potatoes to keep them from sticking. Reset the timer and roast the potatoes for another 5 minutes, then shake again. Repeat this process until the potatoes have cooked for a total of 20 minutes. Check and see if the potatoes are cooked. If they are not fork-tender, roast for 5 minutes more. Using tongs, remove the potato wedges from the air fryer basket and transfer them to a bowl. Toss with the remaining salt.

## Fried Peach Slices
**Prep time: 10 minutes | Cook time: 6 minutes | Serves 4**

2 egg whites
1 tablespoon water
¼ cup sliced almonds
2 tablespoons brown sugar
½ teaspoon almond extract

1 cup crisp rice cereal
2 medium, very firm peaches, peeled and pitted
¼ cup cornstarch
Oil for misting or cooking spray

Preheat air fryer to 390ºF (199ºC). Beat together egg whites and water in a shallow dish. In a food processor, combine the almonds, brown sugar, and almond extract. Process until ingredients combine well and the nuts are finely chopped. Add cereal and pulse just until cereal crushes. Pour crumb mixture into a shallow dish or onto a plate. Cut each peach into eighths and place in a plastic bag or container with lid. Add cornstarch, seal, and shake to coat. Remove peach slices from bag or container, tapping them hard to shake off the excess cornstarch. Dip in egg wash and roll in crumbs. Spray with oil. Place in air fryer basket when your air fryer displays "READY" (select the cooking preset, and make minor adjustments according to your desired doneness.) and choose a shake reminder. Cook for 5 minutes. Shake basket, separate any that have stuck together, and spritz a little oil on any spots that aren't browning. Cook for 1 to 3 minutes longer, until golden brown and crispy.

## Golden Mozzarella Cheese Sticks
**Prep time: 5 minutes | Cook time: 8 minutes | Serves 6**

1 package Mozzarella sticks
1 (8-ounce / 227-g) package crescent roll dough
3 tablespoons unsalted butter,

melted
¼ cup panko bread crumbs
Marinara sauce, for dipping (optional)

Spray the air fryer basket with olive oil. Cut each cheese stick into thirds. Unroll the crescent roll dough. Using a pizza cutter or sharp knife, cut the dough into 36 even pieces. Wrap each small cheese stick in a piece of dough. Make sure that the dough is wrapped tightly around the cheese. Pinch the dough together at both ends, and pinch along the seam to ensure that the dough is completely sealed. Using tongs, dip the wrapped cheese sticks in the melted butter, then dip the cheese sticks in the panko bread crumbs. Place the cheese sticks in the greased air fryer basket in a single layer when your air fryer displays "READY" (select the cooking preset, and make minor adjustments according to your desired doneness.) and choose a shake reminder. (You may have to cook the cheese sticks in more than one batch.) Set the temperature to 370ºF (188ºC). Set the timer and bake for 5 minutes. After 5 minutes, the tops should be golden brown. Using tongs, flip the cheese sticks and bake for another 3 minutes, or until golden brown on all sides. Repeat until you use all of the dough. Plate, serve with the marinara sauce (if you like), and enjoy!

## Panko-Crusted Parmesan Dill Pickles
**Prep time: 5 minutes | Cook time: 8 minutes | Serves 4**

1 (16-ounce / 454-g) jar sliced dill pickles
⅔ cup panko bread crumbs

⅓ cup grated Parmesan cheese
¼ teaspoon dried dill
2 large eggs

Line a platter with a double thickness of paper towels. Spread the pickles out in a single layer on the paper towels. Let the pickles drain on the towels for 20 minutes. After 20 minutes have passed, pat the pickles again with a clean paper towel to get them as dry as possible before breading. Spray the air fryer basket with olive oil. In a small mixing bowl, combine the panko bread crumbs, Parmesan cheese, and dried dill. Mix well. In a separate small bowl, crack the eggs and beat until frothy. Dip each pickle into the egg mixture, then into the bread crumb mixture. Make sure the pickle is fully coated in breading. Place the breaded pickle slices in the greased air fryer basket in a single layer when your air fryer displays "READY" (select the cooking preset, and make minor adjustments according to your desired doneness.) and choose a shake reminder. (You may have to fry your pickles in more than one batch.) Spray the pickles with a generous amount of olive oil. Set the temperature to 390ºF (199ºC). Set the timer and fry for 4 minutes. Open the air fryer drawer and use tongs to flip the pickles. Spray them again with olive oil. Reset the timer and fry for another 4 minutes. Using tongs, remove the pickles from the drawer. Plate, serve, and enjoy!

## Loaded Potato Skins with Bacon
**Prep time: 10 minutes | Cook time: 12 minutes | Serves 4**

4 medium russet potatoes, baked
Olive oil
Salt, to taste
Freshly ground black pepper, to taste
2 cups shredded Cheddar

cheese
4 slices cooked bacon, chopped
Finely chopped scallions, for topping
Sour cream, for topping
Finely chopped olives, for topping

Spray the air fryer basket with oil. Cut each baked potato in half. Using a large spoon, scoop out the center of each potato half, leaving about 1 inch of the potato flesh around the edges and the bottom. Rub olive oil over the inside of each baked potato half and season with salt and pepper, then place the potato skins in the greased air fryer basket when your air fryer displays "READY" (select the cooking preset, and make minor adjustments according to your desired doneness.) and choose a shake reminder. Set the temperature to 400ºF (204ºC). Set the timer and bake for 10 minutes. After 10 minutes, remove the potato skins and fill them with the shredded Cheddar cheese and bacon, then bake in the air fryer for another 2 minutes, just until the cheese is melted. Garnish the potato skins with the scallions, sour cream, and olives.

# Chapter 10 Desserts

## Cinnamon Baked Pineapples
**Prep time: 5 minutes | Cook time: 10 minutes | Serves 2**

1 teaspoon cinnamon
5 pineapple slices
½ cup brown sugar

1 tablespoon mint, chopped
1 tablespoon honey

Preheat air fryer to 340ºF (171ºC). In a small bowl, mix sugar and cinnamon. Drizzle the sugar mixture over pineapple slices. Place them in the greased frying basket when your air fryer displays "READY" (select the cooking preset, and make minor adjustments according to your desired doneness.) and choose a shake reminder. Bake for 5 minutes. Flip the pineapples and cook for 5 more minutes. Drizzle with honey and sprinkle with fresh mint. Enjoy!

## Dark Spiced Rum Pear Pie
**Prep time: 5 minutes | Cook time: 20 minutes | Serves 4**

1 cup flour
5 tablespoons sugar
3 tablespoons butter, softened

1 tablespoon dark spiced rum
2 pears, sliced

Preheat air fryer to 370ºF (188ºC). In a bowl, place 3 tablespoons of the sugar, butter, and flour and mix to form a batter. Roll out the butter on a floured surface and transfer to the greased baking dish. Arrange the pears slices on top and sprinkle with sugar and dark rum. When your air fryer displays "READY" (select the cooking preset, and make minor adjustments according to your desired doneness.) and choose a shake reminder. Bake in the air fryer for 20 minutes. Serve cooled. Enjoy!s

## Tropical Sesame Pineapple Fritters
**Prep time: 10 minutes | Cook time: 15 minutes | Serves 5**

1½ cups flour
1 pineapple, sliced into rings
3 tablespoons sesame seeds

2 eggs, beaten
1 teaspoon baking powder
½ tablespoon sugar

Preheat air fryer to 350ºF (180ºC). In a bowl, mix salt, sesame seeds, flour, baking powder, eggs, sugar, and 1 cup water. Dip sliced pineapple in the flour mixture and arrange them on the greased frying basket. When your air fryer displays "READY" (select the cooking preset, and make minor adjustments according to your desired doneness.) and choose a shake reminder. AirFryer for 15 minutes, turning once. Enjoy!

## American Moon Pie
**Prep time: 5 minutes | Cook time: 5 minutes | Serves 4**

4 graham cracker sheets, snapped in half
8 large marshmallows

8 squares each of dark, milk, and white chocolate

Preheat air fryer to 340ºF (171ºC). Arrange the crackers on a cutting board. Put 2 marshmallows onto half of the graham cracker halves. Place 2 squares of chocolate on top of the crackers with marshmallows. Put the remaining crackers on top to create 4 sandwiches. Wrap each one in baking paper, so it resembles a parcel. When your air fryer displays "READY" (select the cooking preset, and make minor adjustments according to your desired doneness.) and choose a shake reminder. Bake in the preheated air fryer for 5 minutes at 340ºF (171ºC). Serve at room temperature or chilled. Enjoy!

## Molten Chocolate Cake
**Prep time: 5 minutes | Cook time: 18 minutes | Serves 4**

2 tablespoons butter, melted
3½ tablespoon sugar
1½ tablespoon self-rising flour

3½ ounces (99 g) dark chocolate, melted
2 eggs

Preheat air fryer to 360ºF (182ºC). In a bowl, beat the eggs and sugar until frothy. Stir in butter and chocolate and gently fold in the flour. Divide the mixture between 4 greased ramekins. When your air fryer displays "READY" (select the cooking preset, and make minor adjustments according to your desired doneness.) and choose a shake reminder. Bake in the air fryer for 18 minutes. Let cool for a few minutes before inverting the lava cakes onto serving plates. Enjoy!

## Peach Cake
**Prep time: 10 minutes | Cook time: 25 minutes | Serves 4**

3 tablespoons butter, melted
1 cup peaches, chopped
3 tablespoons sugar
1 cup almond flour

1 cup heavy cream
1 teaspoon vanilla extract
2 eggs, whisked
1 teaspoon baking soda

Preheat air fryer to 360ºF (182ºC). In a bowl, mix all the ingredients and stir well. Pour the mixture into a greased baking dish and insert it in the air fryer basket. When your air fryer displays "READY" (select the cooking preset, and make minor adjustments according to your desired doneness.) and choose a shake reminder. Bake for 25 minutes until golden. Cool, slice, and serve. Enjoy!

## Lemon Curd
**Prep time: 5 minutes | Cook time: 19 minutes | Serves 2**

3 tablespoons butter
3 tablespoons sugar
1 egg

1 egg yolk
¾ lemon, juiced

Preheat air fryer to 220ºF (104ºC). Add sugar and butter to a medium-size ramekin and beat evenly. Slowly whisk in egg and egg yolk until fresh yellow color is obtained. Mix in the lemon juice. Place the ramekin in the preheated air fryer when your air fryer displays "READY" (select the cooking preset, and make minor adjustments according to your desired doneness.) and choose a shake reminder. Bake at 220ºF (104ºC) for 6 minutes. Increase the temperature to 320ºF (160ºC) and cook for 13 to 15 minutes. Remove the ramekin and use a spoon to check for any lumps. Serve chilled. Enjoy!

## Lime-Yogurt Cupcakes
**Prep time: 10 minutes | Cook time: 15 minutes | Serves 4**

2 eggs
1 egg yolk
Juice and zest of 1 lime
1 cup yogurt

¼ cup superfine sugar
8 ounces (227 g) cream cheese
1 teaspoon vanilla extract

Preheat air fryer to 300ºF (149ºC). In a bowl, mix yogurt and cream cheese until uniform. In another bowl, beat eggs, egg yolk, sugar, vanilla, lime juice, and zest. Gently fold the in the cheese mixture. Divide the batter between greased muffin tins. When your air fryer displays "READY" (select the cooking preset, and make minor adjustments according to your desired doneness.) and choose a shake reminder. Bake in the fryer for 15 minutes until golden. Serve chilled.

## Chocolate Glazed Banana Chips
**Prep time: 5 minutes | Cook time: 12 minutes | Serves 2**

2 banana, cut into slices
¼ teaspoon lemon zest
1 tablespoon agave syrup

1 tablespoon cocoa powder
1 tablespoon coconut oil, melted

Preheat air fryer to 370ºF (188ºC). Toss the bananas with the lemon zest and agave syrup. Transfer your bananas to the parchment-lined cooking basket. When your air fryer displays "READY" (select the cooking preset, and make minor adjustments according to your desired doneness.) and choose a shake reminder. Bake in the preheated Air Fryer at 370ºF (188ºC) for 12 minutes, turning them over halfway through the cooking time. In the meantime, melt the coconut oil in your microwave; add the cocoa powder and whisk to combine well. Serve the baked banana chips with a few drizzles of the chocolate glaze. Enjoy!

## Maple Walnut Granola
**Prep time: 10 minutes | Cook time: 23 minutes | Serves 4**

¼ cup walnuts, chopped
½ cup oats
3 tablespoons canola oil
½ cup maple syrup

2 tablespoons muscovado sugar
1 cup fresh blueberries

Preheat air fryer to 380ºF (193ºC). In a bowl, place oil, maple syrup, muscovado sugar, and vanilla and mix. Coat in the oats. Spread out the mixture on a greased baking tray when your air fryer displays "READY" (select the cooking preset, and make minor adjustments according to your desired doneness.) and choose a shake reminder. Bake for 20 to 25 minutes. Sprinkle with blueberries and bake for another 3 minutes. Leave to cool before breaking up and storing in a jar. Enjoy!

## Baked Chocolate Cake
**Prep time: 10 minutes | Cook time: 55 minutes | Serves 4**

Unsalted butter, at room temperature
3 large eggs
1 cup almond flour
⅔ cup sugar
⅓ cup heavy cream

¼ cup coconut oil, melted
¼ cup unsweetened cocoa powder
1 teaspoon baking powder
¼ cup chopped walnuts

Preheat the air fryer to 400ºF (204ºC). Generously butter a round baking pan. Line the bottom of the pan with parchment paper cut to fit. In a large bowl, combine the eggs, almond flour, sugar, cream, coconut oil, cocoa powder, and baking powder. Beat with a hand mixer on medium speed until well blended and fluffy. (This will keep the cake from being too dense, as almond flour cakes can sometimes be.) Fold in the walnuts. Pour the batter into the prepared pan. Cover the pan tightly with aluminum foil. Set the pan in the air fryer basket when your air fryer displays "READY" (select the cooking preset, and make minor adjustments according to your desired doneness.) and choose a shake reminder. Bake for 45 minutes. Remove the foil and bake for 10 to 15 minutes more until a knife (do not use a toothpick) inserted into the center of the cake comes out clean. Let the cake cool in the pan on a wire rack for 10 minutes. Remove the cake from the pan and let cool on the rack for 20 minutes before slicing and serving.

## Fruity Skewers
**Prep time: 10 minutes | Cook time: 6 minutes | Serves 2**

1 cup blueberries
1 banana, sliced
1 mango, peeled and cut into cubes

1 peach, cut into wedges
2 kiwi fruit, peeled and quartered
2 tablespoons caramel sauce

Preheat air fryer to 340ºF (171ºC). Thread the fruit through your skewers. Transfer to the greased frying basket when your air fryer displays "READY" (select the cooking preset, and make minor adjustments according to your desired doneness.) and choose a shake reminder. AirFry for 6 to 8 minutes, turning once until the fruit caramelize slightly. Drizzle with the caramel sauce and serve. Enjoy!

## Chocolate-Coconut Mug Cake
**Prep time: 10 minutes | Cook time: 10 minutes | Serves 2**

½ cup self-rising flour
6 tablespoons brown sugar
5 tablespoons coconut milk
4 tablespoons coconut oil
4 tablespoons unsweetened

cocoa powder
2 eggs
A pinch of grated nutmeg
A pinch of salt

Preheat air fryer to 390ºF (199ºC). Mix all the ingredients together; divide the batter between two mugs. Place the mugs in the Air Fryer cooking basket when your air fryer displays "READY" (select the cooking preset, and make minor adjustments according to your desired doneness.) and choose a shake reminder. Cook at 390ºF (199ºC) for about 10 minutes. Enjoy!

## Chocolate Apple Slices
**Prep time: 5 minutes | Cook time: 10 minutes | Serves 6**

1 large Pink Lady apple, cored and sliced
1 tablespoon light brown sugar

A pinch of kosher salt
2 tablespoons lemon juice
2 teaspoons cocoa powder

Preheat air fryer to 350ºF (177ºC). Toss the apple slices with the other ingredients. When your air fryer displays "READY" (select the cooking preset, and make minor adjustments according to your desired doneness.) and choose a shake reminder. Bake at 350ºF (177ºC) for 5 minutes; shake the basket to ensure even cooking and continue to cook an additional 5 minutes. Enjoy!

## Coconut Pancake
**Prep time: 10 minutes | Cook time: 4 minutes | Serves 4**

½ cup flour
⅓ cup coconut milk
2 eggs
1 tablespoon coconut oil,

melted
1 teaspoon vanilla
A pinch of ground cardamom
½ cup coconut chips

Preheat air fryer to 230ºF (110ºC). Mix the flour, coconut milk, eggs, coconut oil, vanilla, and cardamom in a large bowl. Let it stand for 20 minutes. Spoon the batter into a greased muffin tin. When your air fryer displays "READY" (select the cooking preset, and make minor adjustments according to your desired doneness.) and choose a shake reminder. Cook at 230ºF (110ºC) for 4 to 5 minutes or until golden brown. Repeat with the remaining batter. Decorate your pancakes with coconut chips. Enjoy!

## Cinnamon-Sugar Buttered Peaches

**Prep time: 5 minutes | Cook time: 25 minutes | Serves 2**

2 fresh peaches, pitted and halved
1 tablespoon butter

2 tablespoons caster sugar
¼ teaspoon ground cinnamon

Preheat air fryer to 320ºF (160ºC). Mix the butter, sugar and cinnamon. Spread the butter mixture onto the peaches and transfer them to the Air Fryer cooking basket. When your air fryer displays "READY" (select the cooking preset, and make minor adjustments according to your desired doneness.) and choose a shake reminder. Cook your peaches at 320ºF (160ºC) for about 25 minutes or until the top is golden. Serve with vanilla ice cream, if desired. Enjoy!

## Mini Molten Chocolate Cakes

**Prep time: 10 minutes | Cook time: 10 minutes | Serves 2**

½ cup dark chocolate chunks
3 tablespoons butter
1 egg
1 ounce (28 g) granulated

sugar
1 tablespoon self-rising flour
2 tablespoons almonds, chopped

Preheat air fryer to 370ºF (188ºC). Microwave the chocolate chunks and butter for 30 to 40 seconds until the mixture is smooth. Then, beat the eggs and sugar; stir in the egg mixture into the chocolate mixture. Now, stir in the flour and almonds. Pour the batter into two ramekins. When your air fryer displays "READY" (select the cooking preset, and make minor adjustments according to your desired doneness.) and choose a shake reminder. Bake your cakes at 370ºF (188ºC) for about 10 minutes and serve at room temperature. Enjoy!

## Apple and Golden Raisin Turnovers

**Prep time: 10 minutes | Cook time: 45 minutes | Serves 4**

3½ ounces (99.2 g) dried apples
¼ cup golden raisins
1 tablespoon granulated sugar
1 tablespoon freshly squeezed lemon juice
½ teaspoon cinnamon

1 pound (454 g) frozen puff pastry, defrosted according to package instructions
1 egg beaten with 1 tablespoon water
Turbinado or demerara sugar for sprinkling

Preheat air fryer to 325ºF (163ºC). Place the dried apples in a medium saucepan and cover with about 2 cups of water. Bring the mixture to a boil over medium-high heat, then reduce the heat to low, cover, and simmer until the apples have absorbed most of the liquid, about 20 minutes. Remove the apples from the heat and allow to cool. Add the raisins, sugar, lemon juice, and cinnamon to the rehydrated apples and set aside. On a well-floured board, roll the puff pastry out to a 12-inch square. Cut the square into 4 equal quarters. Divide the filling equally among the 4 squares, mounding it in the middle of each square. Brush the edges of each square with water and fold the pastry diagonally over the apple mixture, creating a triangle. Seal the edges by pressing them with the tines of a fork. Transfer the turnovers to a sheet pan lined with parchment paper when your air fryer displays "READY" (select the cooking preset, and make minor adjustments according to your desired doneness.) and choose a shake reminder. Brush the top of 2 turnovers with egg wash and sprinkle with turbinado sugar. Make 2 small slits in the top of the turnovers for venting and bake at 325ºF (163ºC) for 25 to 30 minutes, until the top is browned and puffed and the pastry is cooked through. Remove the cooked turnovers to a cooling rack and cook the remaining 2 turnovers in the same manner. Serve warm or at room temperature.

## Mom's Sweet Dough

**Prep time: 5 minutes | Cook time: 8 minutes | Serves 4**

8 ounces (227 g) bread dough
2 tablespoons butter, melted

2 ounces (57 g) powdered sugar

Preheat air fryer to 350ºF (177ºC). Cut the dough into strips and twist them together 3 to 4 times. Then, brush the dough twists with melted butter and sprinkle sugar over them. When your air fryer displays "READY" (select the cooking preset, and make minor adjustments according to your desired doneness.) and choose a shake reminder. Cook the dough twists at 350ºF (177ºC) for 8 minutes, tossing the basket halfway through the cooking time. Serve with your favorite dip. Enjoy!

## Chocolate Glazed Banana

**Prep time: 5 minutes | Cook time: 12½ minutes | Serves 2**

2 bananas, peeled and cut in half lengthwise
1 tablespoon coconut oil,

melted
1 tablespoon cocoa powder
1 tablespoon agave syrup

Preheat air fryer to 370ºF (188ºC). When your air fryer displays "READY" (select the cooking preset, and make minor adjustments according to your desired doneness.) and choose a shake reminder. Bake your bananas in the preheated Air Fryer at 370ºF (188ºC) for 12 minutes, turning them over halfway through the cooking time. In the meantime, microwave the coconut oil for 30 seconds; stir in the cocoa powder and agave syrup. Serve the baked bananas with a few drizzles of the chocolate glaze. Enjoy!

## Tasty Strawberry Dessert Dumplings

**Prep time: 5 minutes | Cook time: 8 minutes | Serves 3**

9 wonton wrappers
⅓ strawberry jam

2 ounces (57 g) icing sugar

Start by laying out the wonton wrappers. Divide the strawberry jam between the wonton wrappers. Fold the wonton wrapper over the jam; now, seal the edges with wet fingers. Preheat air fryer to 400ºF (204ºC). When your air fryer displays "READY" (select the cooking preset, and make minor adjustments according to your desired doneness.) and choose a shake reminder. Cook your wontons at 400ºF (204ºC) for 8 minutes; working in batches. Enjoy!

## Baked Sweet Apples

**Prep time: 5 minutes | Cook time: 10 minutes | Serves 4**

4 small apples, cored and cut in half
2 tablespoons salted butter or coconut oil, melted

2 tablespoons sugar
1 teaspoon apple pie spice
Ice cream, heavy cream, or whipped cream, for serving

Preheat the air fryer to 350ºF (177ºC). Put the apples in a large bowl. Drizzle with the melted butter and sprinkle with the sugar and apple pie spice. Use the hands to toss, ensuring the apples are evenly coated. Put the apples in the air fryer basket when your air fryer displays "READY" (select the cooking preset, and make minor adjustments according to your desired doneness.) and choose a shake reminder. Bake for 10 minutes. Pierce the apples with a fork to ensure they are tender. Serve with ice cream, or top with a splash of heavy cream or a spoonful of whipped cream.

## Mixed Berries Crumble

**Prep time: 10 minutes | Cook time: 15 minutes | Serves 4**

**For the Filling:**

2 cups mixed berries
2 tablespoons sugar

1 tablespoon cornstarch
1 tablespoon fresh lemon juice

**For the Topping:**

¼ cup all-purpose flour
¼ cup rolled oats
1 tablespoon sugar
2 tablespoons cold unsalted

butter, cut into small cubes
Whipped cream or ice cream (optional)

Preheat the air fryer to 400ºF (204ºC). For the filling: In a round baking pan, gently mix the berries, sugar, cornstarch, and lemon juice until thoroughly combined. For the topping: In a small bowl, combine the flour, oats, and sugar. Stir the butter into the flour mixture until the mixture has the consistency of bread crumbs. Sprinkle the topping over the berries. Put the pan in the air fryer basket when your air fryer displays "READY" (select the cooking preset, and make minor adjustments according to your desired doneness.) and choose a shake reminder. Air fry for 15 minutes. Let cool for 5 minutes on a wire rack. Serve topped with whipped cream or ice cream, if desired.

## American Cruller Donut

**Prep time: 10 minutes | Cook time: 20 minutes | Serves 4**

¾ cup all-purpose flour
¼ cup butter
¼ cup water
½ cup full-fat milk

¼ teaspoon kosher salt
A pinch of grated nutmeg
3 eggs, beaten

In a mixing bowl, thoroughly combine all ingredients. Place the batter in a piping bag fitted with a large open star tip. Pipe your crullers into circles and lower them onto the greased Air Fryer pan when your air fryer displays "READY" (select the cooking preset, and make minor adjustments according to your desired doneness.) and choose a shake reminder. Cook your crullers in the preheated Air Fryer at 360ºF (182ºC) for 10 minutes, flipping them halfway through the cooking time. Repeat with the remaining batter and serve immediately. Enjoy!

## Bourbon Maple Bread Pudding

**Prep time: 10 minutes | Cook time: 20 minutes | Serves 4**

3 slices whole grain bread, cubed
1 large egg
1 cup whole milk
2 tablespoons bourbon

½ teaspoons vanilla extract
¼ cup maple syrup, divided
½ teaspoons ground cinnamon
2 teaspoons sparkling sugar

Preheat the air fryer to 270ºF (132ºC). Spray a baking pan with nonstick cooking spray, then place the bread cubes in the pan when your air fryer displays "READY" (select the cooking preset, and make minor adjustments according to your desired doneness.) and choose a shake reminder. In a medium bowl, whisk together the egg, milk, bourbon, vanilla extract, 3 tablespoons of maple syrup, and cinnamon. Pour the egg mixture over the bread and press down with a spatula to coat all the bread, then sprinkle the sparkling sugar on top and bake for 20 minutes. Remove the pudding from the air fryer and allow to cool in the pan on a wire rack for 10 minutes. Drizzle the remaining 1 tablespoon of maple syrup on top. Slice and serve warm.

## Indian Donuts (Gulgulas)

**Prep time: 5 minutes | Cook time: 5 minutes | Serves 2**

⅓ cup whole wheat flour
⅓ cup sugar
1 teaspoon ghee

1 tablespoon Indian dahi
1 tablespoon apple juice

Preheat air fryer to 360ºF (182ºC). Mix the ingredients until everything is well incorporated. Drop a spoonful of batter onto the greased Air Fryer pan. When your air fryer displays "READY" (select the cooking preset, and make minor adjustments according to your desired doneness.) and choose a shake reminder. Cook Indian gulgulas at 360ºF (182ºC) for 5 minutes or until golden brown, flipping them halfway through the cooking time. Repeat with the remaining batter. Serve with hot Indian tea and enjoy!

## Fluffy Chocolate Cake

**Prep time: 10 minutes | Cook time: 15 minutes | Serves 6**

½ stick butter, at room temperature
½ cup chocolate chips
2 tablespoons honey

⅔ cup almond flour
A pinch of fine sea salt
1 egg, whisked
½ teaspoon vanilla extract

Begin by preheating your Air Fryer to 330ºF (166ºC). In a microwave-safe bowl, melt the butter, chocolate, and honey. Add the other ingredients to the cooled chocolate mixture; stir to combine well. Scrape the batter into a lightly greased baking pan. When your air fryer displays "READY" (select the cooking preset, and make minor adjustments according to your desired doneness.) and choose a shake reminder. Bake in the preheated Air Fryer for 15 minutes or until the center is springy and a toothpick comes out dry. Enjoy!

## Coconut-Pecan Nuts Cookies

**Prep time: 10 minutes | Cook time: 25 minutes | Serves 10**

1½ cups coconut flour
1½ cups extra-fine almond flour
½ teaspoon baking powder
⅓ teaspoon baking soda
3 eggs plus an egg yolk, beaten
¾ cup coconut oil, at room temperature
1 cup unsalted pecan nuts, roughly chopped

¾ cup monk fruit
¼ teaspoon freshly grated nutmeg
⅓ teaspoon ground cloves
½ teaspoon pure vanilla extract
½ teaspoon pure coconut extract
⅛ teaspoon fine sea salt

Preheat the air fryer to 370ºF (188ºC). Line the air fryer basket with parchment paper. Mix the coconut flour, almond flour, baking powder, and baking soda in a large mixing bowl. In another mixing bowl, stir together the eggs and coconut oil. Add the wet mixture to the dry mixture. Mix in the remaining ingredients and stir until a soft dough forms. Drop about 2 tablespoons of dough on the parchment paper for each cookie and flatten each biscuit until it's 1 inch thick. When your air fryer displays "READY" (select the cooking preset, and make minor adjustments according to your desired doneness.) and choose a shake reminder. Bake for about 25 minutes until the cookies are golden and firm to the touch. Remove from the basket to a plate. Let the cookies cool to room temperature and serve.

## Chocolate Hazelnut Puff Pastry Sticks

**Prep time: 5 minutes | Cook time: 4 minutes | Serves 3**

8 ounces (227 g) frozen puff pastry, thawed, cut into strips
½ stick butter, melted
½ teaspoon ground cinnamon
½ cup chocolate hazelnut spread

Preheat air fryer to 380ºF (193ºC). Brush the strips of the puff pastry with melted butter. Arrange the strips in the Air Fryer cooking basket when your air fryer displays "READY" (select the cooking preset, and make minor adjustments according to your desired doneness.) and choose a shake reminder. Bake them at 380ºF (193ºC) for 2 minutes; flip and cook on the other side for 2 to 3 minutes longer. Top the pastry sticks with cinnamon and chocolate hazelnut spread. Enjoy!

## Summer Fruit Salad

**Prep time: 10 minutes | Cook time: 15 minutes | Serves 2**

1 banana, peeled
1 cooking pear, cored
1 cooking apple, cored
1 tablespoon freshly squeezed lemon juice
½ teaspoon ground star anise
¼ teaspoon ground cinnamon
½ teaspoon granulated ginger
¼ cup brown sugar
1 tablespoon coconut oil, melted

Preheat air fryer to 330ºF (166ºC). Toss your fruits with lemon juice, star anise, cinnamon, ginger, sugar and coconut oil. Transfer the fruits to the Air Fryer cooking basket. When your air fryer displays "READY" (select the cooking preset, and make minor adjustments according to your desired doneness.) and choose a shake reminder. Bake the fruit salad in the preheated Air Fryer at 330ºF (166ºC) for 15 minutes. Serve in individual bowls, garnished with vanilla ice cream. Enjoy!

## Chocolate Banana Crepes

**Prep time: 5 minutes | Cook time: 4 minutes | Serves 2**

1 small ripe banana
⅛ teaspoon baking powder
¼ cup chocolate chips
1 egg, whisked

Preheat air fryer to 230ºF (110ºC). Mix all ingredients until creamy and fluffy. Let it stand for about 20 minutes. Spritz the Air Fryer baking pan with cooking spray. Pour ½ of the batter into the pan using a measuring cup. When your air fryer displays "READY" (select the cooking preset, and make minor adjustments according to your desired doneness.) and choose a shake reminder. Cook at 230ºF (110ºC) for 4 to 5 minutes or until golden brown. Repeat with another crepe. Enjoy!

## Banana-Cinnamon Fritters

**Prep time: 5 minutes | Cook time: 10 minutes | Serves 1**

1 banana, mashed
1 egg, beaten
1 tablespoon coconut oil
¼ teaspoons ground cinnamon
1 tablespoon brown sugar

In a mixing bowl, thoroughly combine all the ingredients. Ladle the batter into a lightly greased Air Fryer pan when your air fryer displays "READY" (select the cooking preset, and make minor adjustments according to your desired doneness.) and choose a shake reminder. Cook the fritter in the preheated Air Fryer at 360ºF (182ºC) for 10 minutes, flipping it halfway through the cooking time. Enjoy!

## Almond-Chocolate Cake

**Prep time: 15 minutes | Cook time: 20 minutes | Serves 6**

1 stick butter, melted
½ cups brown sugar
2 eggs, at room temperature
5 ounces (142 g) chocolate chips
½ teaspoon pure vanilla extract
½ teaspoon pure almond extract
¼ cup cocoa powder
¼ cup all-purpose flour
½ cup almond flour
½ teaspoon baking powder
2 ounces (57 g) almonds, slivered
4 tablespoons coconut milk

Start by preheating your Air Fryer to 340ºF (171ºC). Then, brush the sides and bottom of a baking pan with a nonstick cooking spray. In a mixing bowl, beat the butter and sugar until fluffy. Next, fold in the eggs and beat again until well combined. After that, add in the remaining ingredients. Mix until everything is well combined. When your air fryer displays "READY" (select the cooking preset, and make minor adjustments according to your desired doneness.) and choose a shake reminder. Bake in the preheated Air Fryer for 20 minutes. Enjoy!

## Peanut Butter Chocolate Lava Cupcakes

**Prep time: 10 minutes | Cook time: 10 to 13 minutes | Serves 8**

Nonstick baking spray with flour
1⅓ cups chocolate cake mix
1 egg
1 egg yolk
¼ cup safflower oil
¼ cup hot water
⅓ cup sour cream
3 tablespoons peanut butter
1 tablespoon powdered sugar

Preheat the air fryer to 350ºF (177ºC). Double up 16 foil muffin cups to make 8 cups. Spray each lightly with nonstick spray; set aside. In a medium bowl, combine the cake mix, egg, egg yolk, safflower oil, water, and sour cream, and beat until combined. In a small bowl, combine the peanut butter and powdered sugar and mix well. Form this mixture into 8 balls. Spoon about ¼ cup of the chocolate batter into each muffin cup and top with a peanut butter ball. Spoon remaining batter on top of the peanut butter balls to cover them. Arrange the cups in the air fryer basket, leaving some space between each when your air fryer displays "READY" (select the cooking preset, and make minor adjustments according to your desired doneness.) and choose a shake reminder. Bake for 10 to 13 minutes or until the tops look dry and set. Let the cupcakes cool for about 10 minutes, then serve warm.

## Pineapple Chocolate Cake

**Prep time: 10 minutes | Cook time: 25 minutes | Serves 4**

2 ounces (57 g) dark chocolate, grated
8 ounces (227 g) self-rising flour
4 ounces (113 g) butter
7 ounces (198 g) pineapple
chunks
½ cup pineapple juice
1 egg
2 tablespoons milk
½ cup sugar

Preheat air fryer to 350ºF (180ºC). Place the butter and flour into a bowl and rub the mixture with your fingers until crumbed. Stir in pineapple chunks, sugar, chocolate, and pineapple juice. Beat eggs and milk separately and add to the batter. Transfer the batter to a greased cake pan when your air fryer displays "READY" (select the cooking preset, and make minor adjustments according to your desired doneness.) and choose a shake reminder. Bake in the air fryer for 25 minutes. Let cool for a few minutes before serving. Enjoy!

## Baked Black Forest Pies
**Prep time: 10 minutes | Cook time: 15 minutes | Serves 6**

3 tablespoons milk or dark chocolate chips
2 tablespoons thick, hot fudge sauce
2 tablespoons chopped dried cherries

1 (10-by-15-inch) sheet frozen puff pastry, thawed
1 egg white, beaten
2 tablespoons sugar
½ teaspoon cinnamon

Preheat the air fryer to 350ºF (177ºC). In a small bowl, combine the chocolate chips, fudge sauce, and dried cherries. Roll out the puff pastry on a floured surface. Cut into 6 squares with a sharp knife. Divide the chocolate chip mixture into the center of each puff pastry square. Fold the squares in half to make triangles. Firmly press the edges with the tines of a fork to seal. Brush the triangles on all sides sparingly with the beaten egg white. Sprinkle the tops with sugar and cinnamon. Put in the air fryer basket when your air fryer displays "READY" (select the cooking preset, and make minor adjustments according to your desired doneness.) and choose a shake reminder. Bake for 15 minutes or until the triangles are golden brown. The filling will be hot, so cool for at least 20 minutes before serving.

## Autumn Walnut Pumpkin Pie
**Prep time: 10 minutes | Cook time: 35 minutes | Serves 4**

12 ounces (340 g) refrigerated pie crusts
½ cup pumpkin puree, canned
1 ounce (28 g) walnuts, coarsely chopped

½ cup granulated sugar
1 teaspoon pumpkin pie spice mix
1 teaspoon fresh ginger, peeled and grated

Place the first pie crust in a lightly greased pie plate. In a mixing bowl, thoroughly combine the remaining ingredients to make the filling. Spoon the filling into the prepared pie crust. Unroll the second pie crust and place it on top of the filling. When your air fryer displays "READY" (select the cooking preset, and make minor adjustments according to your desired doneness.) and choose a shake reminder. Bake the pie at 350ºF (177ºC) for 35 minutes or until the top is golden brown. Bon appétit!

## Chickpea Brownies
**Prep time: 10 minutes | Cook time: 20 minutes | Serves 6**

Vegetable oil
1 (15-ounce / 425-g) can chickpeas, drained and rinsed
4 large eggs
⅓ cup coconut oil, melted
⅓ cup honey
3 tablespoons unsweetened

cocoa powder
1 tablespoon espresso powder (optional)
1 teaspoon baking powder
1 teaspoon baking soda
½ cup chocolate chips

Preheat the air fryer to 325ºF (163ºC). Generously grease a baking pan with vegetable oil. In a blender or food processor, combine the chickpeas, eggs, coconut oil, honey, cocoa powder, espresso powder (if using), baking powder, and baking soda. Blend or process until smooth. Transfer to the prepared pan and stir in the chocolate chips by hand. Set the pan in the air fryer baske when your air fryer displays "READY" (select the cooking preset, and make minor adjustments according to your desired doneness.) and choose a shake reminder. Bake for 20 minutes, or until a toothpick inserted into the center comes out clean. Let cool in the pan on a wire rack for 30 minutes before cutting into squares. Serve immediately.

## Cinnamon Apple Pie
**Prep time: 10 minutes | Cook time: 35 minutes | Serves 4**

12 ounces (340 g) refrigerated 2 pie crusts
3 cups apples, peeled and thinly sliced
¼ cup brown sugar

1 tablespoon lemon juice
1 teaspoon pure vanilla extract
½ teaspoon cinnamon
A pinch of ground cardamom
A pinch of kosher salt

Preheat air fryer to 350ºF (177ºC). Place the first pie crust in a lightly greased pie plate. In a mixing bowl, thoroughly combine the remaining ingredients to make the filling. Spoon the filling into the prepared pie crust. Unroll the second pie crust and place it on top of the filling. When your air fryer displays "READY" (select the cooking preset, and make minor adjustments according to your desired doneness.) and choose a shake reminder. Bake the apple pie at 350ºF (177ºC) for 35 minutes or until the top is golden brown. Bon appétit!

## Bubbly Apple, Peach, and Cranberry Crisp
**Prep time: 10 minutes | Cook time: 12 minutes | Serves 8**

1 apple, peeled and chopped
2 peaches, peeled and chopped
⅓ cup dried cranberries
2 tablespoons honey

⅓ cup brown sugar
¼ cup flour
½ cup oatmeal
3 tablespoons softened butter

Preheat the air fryer to 370ºF (188ºC). In a baking pan, combine the apple, peaches, cranberries, and honey, and mix well. In a medium bowl, combine the brown sugar, flour, oatmeal, and butter, and mix until crumbly. Sprinkle this mixture over the fruit in the pan when your air fryer displays "READY" (select the cooking preset, and make minor adjustments according to your desired doneness.) and choose a shake reminder. Bake for 10 to 12 minutes or until the fruit is bubbly and the topping is golden brown. Serve warm.

## Applesauce Brownies
**Prep time: 10 minutes | Cook time: 15 minutes | Serves 8**

¼ cup unsweetened cocoa powder
¼ cup all-purpose flour
¼ teaspoon kosher salt
½ teaspoons baking powder
3 tablespoons unsalted butter, melted

½ cup granulated sugar
1 large egg
3 tablespoons unsweetened applesauce
¼ cup miniature semisweet chocolate chips
Coarse sea salt, to taste

Preheat the air fryer to 300ºF (149ºC). In a large bowl, whisk together the cocoa powder, all-purpose flour, kosher salt, and baking powder. In a separate large bowl, combine the butter, granulated sugar, egg, and applesauce, then use a spatula to fold in the cocoa powder mixture and the chocolate chips until well combined. Spray a baking pan with nonstick cooking spray, then pour the mixture into the pan. Place the pan in the air fryer when your air fryer displays "READY" (select the cooking preset, and make minor adjustments according to your desired doneness.) and choose a shake reminder. Bake for 15 minutes or until a toothpick comes out clean when inserted in the middle. Remove the brownies from the air fryer, sprinkle some coarse sea salt on top, and allow to cool in the pan on a wire rack for 20 minutes before cutting and serving.

## Vanilla Coconut Pancake Cups

**Prep time: 10 minutes | Cook time: 5 minutes | Serves 4**

½ cup flour
2 eggs
⅓ cup coconut milk
1 tablespoon coconut oil,

melted
1 teaspoon vanilla paste
¼ teaspoon ground cinnamon
A pinch of ground cardamom

Mix all the ingredients until well combined. Let the batter stand for 20 minutes. Spoon the batter into a greased muffin tin when your air fryer displays "READY" (select the cooking preset, and make minor adjustments according to your desired doneness.) and choose a shake reminder. Cook at 330ºF (166ºC) for 4 to 5 minutes or until golden brown. Serve with toppings of choice. Bon appétit!

## French Dessert

**Prep time: 10 minutes | Cook time: 7 minutes | Serves 2**

2 eggs
2 tablespoons coconut oil, melted
¼ cup milk

½ teaspoon vanilla extract
¼ teaspoon ground cinnamon
⅛ teaspoon ground nutmeg
4 thick slices baguette

In a mixing bowl, thoroughly combine the eggs, coconut oil, milk, vanilla, cinnamon, and nutmeg. Then, dip each piece of bread into the egg mixture; place the bread slices in a lightly greased baking pan when your air fryer displays "READY" (select the cooking preset, and make minor adjustments according to your desired doneness.) and choose a shake reminder. Air Fryer the bread slices at 330ºF (166ºC) for about 4 minutes; turn them over and cook for a further 3 to 4 minutes. Enjoy!

## Buttery Cinnamon Pears

**Prep time: 5 minutes | Cook time: 17 minutes | Serves 2**

2 pears, peeled, cored, and cut into sticks
2 tablespoons butter
A pinch of grated nutmeg

A pinch of sea salt
½ teaspoon ground cinnamon
1 teaspoon fresh ginger, grated

Preheat air fryer to 340ºF (171ºC). Toss the pears with the remaining ingredients. Pour ¼ cup of water into an Air Fryer safe dish. Place the pears in the dish when your air fryer displays "READY" (select the cooking preset, and make minor adjustments according to your desired doneness.) and choose a shake reminder. Bake the pears at 340ºF (171ºC) for 17 minutes. Serve at room temperature. Bon appétit!

## Walnut-Banana Cake

**Prep time: 10 minutes | Cook time: 25 minutes | Serves 6**

1 pound (454 g) bananas, mashed
8 ounces (227 g) flour
6 ounces (170 g) sugar
3.5 ounces (99 g) walnuts,

chopped
2.5 ounces (71 g) butter, melted
2 eggs, lightly beaten
¼ teaspoon baking soda

Preheat the air fryer to 355ºF (179ºC). In a bowl, combine the sugar, butter, egg, flour, and baking soda with a whisk. Stir in the bananas and walnuts. Transfer the mixture to a greased baking dish. Put the dish in the air fryer when your air fryer displays "READY" (select the cooking preset, and make minor adjustments according to your desired doneness.) and choose a shake reminder. Bake for 10 minutes. Reduce the temperature to 330ºF (166ºC) and bake for another 15 minutes. Serve hot.

## Air-Fried Banana Slices

**Prep time: 5 minutes | Cook time: 13 minutes | Serves 1**

1 banana, peeled and sliced
1 tablespoon coconut oil
2 tablespoons granulated sugar

½ teaspoon ground cloves
½ teaspoon ground cinnamon

Preheat your Air Fryer to 390ºF (199ºC). Toss banana slices with the remaining ingredients. When your air fryer displays "READY" (select the cooking preset, and make minor adjustments according to your desired doneness.) and choose a shake reminder. Bake the prepared banana slices in the preheated Air Fryer approximately 13 minutes, flipping them halfway through the cooking time. Bon appétit!

## Brazilian-Style Pineapple Bake

**Prep time: 5 minutes | Cook time: 16 minutes | Serves 4**

½ cup brown sugar
2 teaspoons ground cinnamon
1 small pineapple, peeled,

cored, and cut into spears
3 tablespoons unsalted butter, melted

Preheat the air fryer to 400ºF (204ºC). In a small bowl, mix the brown sugar and cinnamon until thoroughly combined. Brush the pineapple spears with the melted butter. Sprinkle the cinnamon-sugar over the spears, pressing lightly to ensure it adheres well. Put the spears in the air fryer basket in a single layer when your air fryer displays "READY" (select the cooking preset, and make minor adjustments according to your desired doneness.) and choose a shake reminder. (Depending on the size of the air fryer, you may have to do this in batches.) Bake for 10 minutes for the first batch (6 to 8 minutes for the next batch, as the air fryer will be preheated). Halfway through the cooking time, brush the spears with butter. The pineapple spears are done when they are heated through and the sugar is bubbling. Serve hot.

## Candied Apple Wedges

**Prep time: 5 minutes | Cook time: 17 minutes | Serves 2**

2 apples, peeled, cored, and cut into wedges
2 teaspoons coconut oil
2 tablespoons brown sugar

1 teaspoon pure vanilla extract
1 teaspoon ground cinnamon
¼ cup water

Preheat air fryer to 340ºF (171ºC). Toss the apples with the coconut oil, sugar, vanilla, and cinnamon. Pour ¼ cup of water into an Air Fryer safe dish. Place the apples in the dish when your air fryer displays "READY" (select the cooking preset, and make minor adjustments according to your desired doneness.) and choose a shake reminder. Bake the apples at 340ºF (171ºC) for 17 minutes. Serve at room temperature. Bon appétit!

## Fried Cinnamon Plums

**Prep time: 5 minutes | Cook time: 17 minutes | Serves 4**

1 pound (454 g) plums, halved and pitted
2 tablespoons coconut oil
4 tablespoons brown sugar

4 whole cloves
1 cinnamon stick
4 whole star anise

Toss the plums with the remaining ingredients. Pour ¼ cup of water into an Air Fryer safe dish. Place the plums in the dish when your air fryer displays "READY" (select the cooking preset, and make minor adjustments according to your desired doneness.) and choose a shake reminder. Bake the plums at 340ºF (171ºC) for 17 minutes. Serve at room temperature. Bon appétit!

## Chia Chocolate Cake

**Prep time: 10 minutes | Cook time: 20 minutes | Serves 6**

½ cup coconut oil, room temperature
1 cup brown sugar
2 chia eggs (2 tablespoons ground chia seeds + 4 tablespoons water)
¼ cup all-purpose flour
¼ cup coconut flour
½ cup cocoa powder
½ cup dark chocolate chips
A pinch of grated nutmeg
A pinch of sea salt
2 tablespoons coconut milk

Start by preheating your Air Fryer to 340ºF (171ºC). Now, spritz the sides and bottom of a baking pan with a nonstick cooking spray. In a mixing bowl, beat the coconut oil and brown sugar until fluffy. Next, fold in the chia eggs and beat again until well combined. After that, add in the remaining ingredients. Mix until everything is well incorporated. When your air fryer displays "READY" (select the cooking preset, and make minor adjustments according to your desired doneness.) and choose a shake reminder. Bake in the preheated Air Fryer for 20 minutes. Enjoy!

## Caramelized Peach Shortcakes

**Prep time: 15 minutes | Cook time: 23 minutes | Serves 4**

**For the Shortcakes:**
1 cup self-rising flour
½ cup plus 1 tablespoon heavy
cream
Vegetable oil for spraying
**For the Caramelized Peaches:**
2 peaches, preferably freestone
1 tablespoon unsalted butter, melted
2 teaspoons brown sugar
1 teaspoon cinnamon
**For the Whipped Cream:**
1 cup cold heavy cream
1 tablespoon granulated sugar
½ teaspoon vanilla extract
Zest of 1 lime

Place the flour in a medium bowl and whisk to remove any lumps. Make a well in the center of the flour. While stirring with a fork, slowly pour in ½ cup plus 1 tablespoon of the heavy cream. Continue to stir until the dough has mostly come together. With your hands, gather the dough, incorporating any dry flour, and form into a ball. Place the dough on a lightly floured board and pat into a rectangle that is ½ to ¾ inch thick. Fold in half. Turn and repeat. Pat the dough into a ¾-inch-thick square. Cut dough into 4 equally sized square biscuits. Preheat the air fryer to 325ºF (163ºC). Spray the air fryer basket with oil to prevent sticking. Place the biscuits in the air fryer basket. Cook for 15 to 18 minutes until the tops are browned and the insides fully cooked. (May be done ahead.) Cut the peaches in half and remove the pit. Brush the peach halves with the melted butter and sprinkle ½ teaspoon of the brown sugar and ¼ teaspoon of the cinnamon on each peach half. Arrange the peaches in a single layer in the air fryer basket when your air fryer displays "READY" (select the cooking preset, and make minor adjustments according to your desired doneness.) and choose a shake reminder. Cook at 375ºF (190ºC) for 8 to 10 minutes until the peaches are soft and the tops caramelized. While the peaches are cooking, whip the cream. Pour the cold heavy cream, sugar, and vanilla (if using) into the bowl of a stand mixer or a metal mixing bowl. Beat with the whisk attachment for your stand mixer or a handheld electric mixer on high speed until stiff peaks form, about 1 minute. (If not using the cream right away, cover with plastic wrap and refrigerate until needed.)
To assemble the shortcakes, cut each biscuit in half horizontally. Place a peach on the bottom half of each biscuit and place the top half on top of the peach. Top each shortcake with whipped cream and a sprinkle of lime zest. Serve immediately.

## Vanilla and Cardamom Custard

**Prep time: 5 minutes | Cook time: 25 minutes | Serves 2**

1 cup whole milk
1 large egg
2 tablespoons plus 1 teaspoon sugar
¼ teaspoon vanilla bean paste or pure vanilla extract
¼ teaspoon ground cardamom, plus more for sprinkling

Preheat the air fryer to 350ºF (177ºC). In a medium bowl, beat together the milk, egg, sugar, vanilla, and cardamom. Put two ramekins in the air fryer basket when your air fryer displays "READY" (select the cooking preset, and make minor adjustments according to your desired doneness.) and choose a shake reminder. Divide the mixture between the ramekins. Sprinkle lightly with cardamom. Cover each ramekin tightly with aluminum foil. Bake for 25 minutes, or until a toothpick inserted in the center comes out clean. Let the custards cool on a wire rack for 5 to 10 minutes. Serve warm, or refrigerate until cold and serve chilled.

## Hearty Coconut Brownies

**Prep time: 15 minutes | Cook time: 15 minutes | Serves 8**

½ cup coconut oil
2 ounces (57 g) dark chocolate
1 cup sugar
2½ tablespoons water
4 whisked eggs
¼ teaspoon ground cinnamon
½ teaspoons ground anise star
¼ teaspoon coconut extract
½ teaspoons vanilla extract
1 tablespoon honey
½ cup flour
½ cup desiccated coconut
Sugar, for dusting

Preheat the air fryer to 355ºF (179ºC). Melt the coconut oil and dark chocolate in the microwave. Combine with the sugar, water, eggs, cinnamon, anise, coconut extract, vanilla, and honey in a large bowl. Stir in the flour and desiccated coconut. Incorporate everything well. Lightly grease a baking dish with butter. Transfer the mixture to the dish. Put the dish in the air fryer when your air fryer displays "READY" (select the cooking preset, and make minor adjustments according to your desired doneness.) and choose a shake reminder. Bake for 15 minutes. Remove from the air fryer and allow to cool slightly. Take care when taking it out of the baking dish. Slice it into squares. Dust with sugar before serving.

## Chocolate-Hazelnut Croissants

**Prep time: 5 minutes | Cook time: 24 minutes | Serves 8**

1 sheet frozen puff pastry, thawed
⅓ cup chocolate-hazelnut
spread
1 large egg, beaten

On a lightly floured surface, roll puff pastry into a 14-inch square. Cut pastry into quarters to form 4 squares. Cut each square diagonally to form 8 triangles. Spread 2 teaspoons chocolate-hazelnut spread on each triangle; from wider end, roll up pastry. Brush egg on top of each roll. Preheat the air fryer to 375ºF (191ºC). When your air fryer displays "READY" (select the cooking preset, and make minor adjustments according to your desired doneness.) and choose a shake reminder. Air fry rolls in batches, 3 or 4 at a time, 8 minutes per batch, or until pastry is golden brown. Cool on a wire rack; serve while warm or at room temperature.

## Simple Chocolate Molten Cake

**Prep time: 5 minutes | Cook time: 10 minutes | Serves 4**

3.5 ounces (99 g) butter, melted  melted
3½ tablespoons sugar
3.5 ounces (99 g) chocolate,
1½ tablespoons flour
2 eggs

Preheat the air fryer to 375ºF (191ºC). Grease four ramekins with a little butter. Rigorously combine the eggs, butter, and sugar before stirring in the melted chocolate. Slowly fold in the flour. Spoon an equal amount of the mixture into each ramekin. Put them in the air fryer when your air fryer displays "READY" (select the cooking preset, and make minor adjustments according to your desired doneness.) and choose a shake reminder. Bake for 10 minutes
Put the ramekins upside-down on plates and let the cakes fall out. Serve hot.

## Danish Cinnamon Rolls

**Prep time: 5 minutes | Cook time: 10 minutes | Serves 4**

9 ounces (255 g) refrigerated crescent rolls
1 tablespoon coconut oil
4 tablespoons caster sugar
1 teaspoon ground cinnamon

Separate the dough into rectangles. Mix the remaining ingredients until well combined. Spread each rectangle with the cinnamon mixture; roll them up tightly. Place the rolls in the Air Fryer cooking basket when your air fryer displays "READY" (select the cooking preset, and make minor adjustments according to your desired doneness.) and choose a shake reminder. Bake the rolls at 300ºF (149ºC) for about 5 minutes; turn them over and bake for a further 5 minutes. Bon appétit!

## Cinnamon-Nutmeg Donuts

**Prep time: 5 minutes | Cook time: 20 minutes | Serves 4**

12 ounces (340 g) flaky large biscuits
¼ cup granulated sugar
1 teaspoon ground cinnamon
¼ teaspoon grated nutmeg
2 tablespoons coconut oil

Separate the dough into biscuits and place them in a lightly oiled Air Fryer cooking basket. Mix the sugar, cinnamon, nutmeg, and coconut oil until well combined. Drizzle your donuts with the cinnamon mixture. When your air fryer displays "READY" (select the cooking preset, and make minor adjustments according to your desired doneness.) and choose a shake reminder. Bake your donuts in the preheated Air Fryer at 340ºF (171ºC) for approximately 10 minutes or until golden. Repeat with the remaining donuts. Bon appétit!

## Indian Unnakai Malabar

**Prep time: 5 minutes | Cook time: 13 minutes | Serves 1**

1 plantain, peeled
¼ cup coconut flakes
¼ teaspoon cinnamon powder
¼ teaspoon cardamom powder
1 tablespoon ghee
2 tablespoons brown sugar

Preheat your Air Fryer to 390ºF (199ºC). Toss the plantain with the remaining ingredients. When your air fryer displays "READY" (select the cooking preset, and make minor adjustments according to your desired doneness.) and choose a shake reminder. Bake the prepared plantain in the preheated Air Fryer approximately 13 minutes, flipping it halfway through the cooking time. Bon appétit!

## Cinnamon Almonds Baked

**Prep time: 5 minutes | Cook time: 8 minutes | Serves 4**

1 cup whole almonds
2 tablespoons salted butter, melted
1 tablespoon sugar
½ teaspoon ground cinnamon

Preheat the air fryer to 300ºF (149ºC). In a medium bowl, combine the almonds, butter, sugar, and cinnamon. Mix well to ensure all the almonds are coated with the spiced butter. Transfer the almonds to the air fryer basket and shake so they are in a single layer when your air fryer displays "READY" (select the cooking preset, and make minor adjustments according to your desired doneness.) and choose a shake reminder. Bake for 8 minutes, stirring the almonds halfway through the cooking time. Let cool completely before serving.

## Brownies with a Twist

**Prep time: 10 minutes | Cook time: 20 minutes | Serves 6**

1 stick butter, melted
1 cup brown sugar
2 eggs
¾ cup all-purpose flour
½ teaspoon baking powder
¼ cup cocoa powder
2 tablespoons coconut oil
1 teaspoon coconut extract
A pinch of sea salt

Start by preheating your Air Fryer to 340ºF (171ºC). Now, spritz the sides and bottom of a baking pan with a nonstick cooking spray. In a mixing bowl, beat the melted butter and sugar until fluffy. Next, fold in the eggs and beat again until well combined. After that, add in the remaining ingredients. Mix until everything is well incorporated. When your air fryer displays "READY" (select the cooking preset, and make minor adjustments according to your desired doneness.) and choose a shake reminder. Bake in the preheated Air Fryer for 20 minutes. Enjoy!

## Honey Strawberry Tart

**Prep time: 5 minutes | Cook time: 25 minutes | Serves 2**

1 pound (454 g) strawberries, hulled and thinly sliced
1 tablespoon balsamic vinegar
1 tablespoon honey
1 sprig basil
1 sheet frozen puff pastry, thawed according to package instructions
1 egg beaten with 1 tablespoon water

Place the strawberries in a 7-inch round pizza pan insert for the air fryer and mound them slightly in the center. In a small bowl, whisk together the balsamic vinegar and honey. Drizzle the mixture over the strawberries. Slice the leaves from the sprig of basil into ribbons and sprinkle them over the strawberries. Cut out an 8-inch square from the sheet of puff pastry. Drape the pastry over the strawberries in the pan. Poke holes in the puff pastry with the tines of a fork. Brush the top of the pastry with the egg wash. Place the pan in the basket of the air fryer when your air fryer displays "READY" (select the cooking preset, and make minor adjustments according to your desired doneness.) and choose a shake reminder. Bake at 325ºF (163ºC) for 25 to 30 minutes until the top of the pastry is golden brown and glossy and the underside of the pastry is cooked. Remove the pan from the basket of the air fryer. If desired, cut the pastry in half and divide the dessert among 2 plates. Alternatively, for less mess, two people can enjoy this tart right out of the pan.

## Maple Pecan Pie

**Prep time: 10 minutes | Cook time: 25 minutes | Serves 4**

1 pie dough
½ teaspoons cinnamon
¾ teaspoon vanilla extract
2 eggs
¾ cup maple syrup

⅛ teaspoon nutmeg
3 tablespoons melted butter, divided
2 tablespoons sugar
½ cup chopped pecans

Preheat the air fryer to 370ºF (188ºC). In a small bowl, coat the pecans in 1 tablespoon of melted butter. Transfer the pecans to the air fryer and air fry for about 10 minutes. Put the pie dough in a greased pie pan and add the pecans on top. In a bowl, mix the rest of the ingredients. Pour this over the pecans. Put the pan in the air fryer when your air fryer displays "READY" (select the cooking preset, and make minor adjustments according to your desired doneness.) and choose a shake reminder. Bake for 25 minutes. Serve immediately.

## S'mores

**Prep time: 5 minutes | Cook time: 3 minutes | Serves 12**

12 whole cinnamon graham crackers
2 (1.55-ounce / 44-g) chocolate

bars, broken into 12 pieces
12 marshmallows

Preheat the air fryer to 350ºF (177ºC). Halve each graham cracker into 2 squares. Put 6 graham cracker squares in the air fryer when your air fryer displays "READY" (select the cooking preset, and make minor adjustments according to your desired doneness.) and choose a shake reminder. Do not stack. Put a piece of chocolate into each. Bake for 2 minutes. Open the air fryer and add a marshmallow onto each piece of melted chocolate. Bake for 1 additional minute. Remove the cooked s'mores from the air fryer, then repeat steps 2 and 3 for the remaining 6 s'mores. Top with the remaining graham cracker squares and serve.

## Vanilla Cinnamon French Toast

**Prep time: 10 minutes | Cook time: 7 minutes | Serves 3**

1 egg, whisked
¼ cup coconut milk
2 tablespoons butter, melted
1 teaspoon vanilla paste

½ teaspoon ground cinnamon
A pinch of grated nutmeg
3 slices bread

In a mixing bowl, thoroughly combine the eggs, milk, butter, vanilla, cinnamon, and nutmeg. Then dip each piece of bread into the egg mixture; place the bread slices in a lightly greased baking pan when your air fryer displays "READY" (select the cooking preset, and make minor adjustments according to your desired doneness.) and choose a shake reminder. Air Fryer the bread slices at 330ºF (166ºC) for about 4 minutes; turn them over and cook for a further 3 to 4 minutes. Enjoy!

## Fudgy Cocoa Brownies

**Prep time: 5 minutes | Cook time: 20 to 22 minutes | Serves 8**

1 stick butter, melted
1 cup Swerve
2 eggs
1 cup coconut flour
½ cup unsweetened cocoa powder

2 tablespoons flaxseed meal
1 teaspoon baking powder
1 teaspoon vanilla essence
A pinch of salt
A pinch of ground cardamom
Cooking spray

Preheat the air fryer to 350ºF (177ºC). Spray a baking pan with cooking spray. Beat together the melted butter and Swerve in a large mixing dish until fluffy. Whisk in the eggs. Add the coconut flour, cocoa powder, flaxseed meal, baking powder, vanilla essence, salt, and cardamom and stir with a spatula until well incorporated. Spread the mixture evenly into the prepared baking pan. Place the baking pan in the air fryer basket when your air fryer displays "READY" (select the cooking preset, and make minor adjustments according to your desired doneness.) and choose a shake reminder. Bake for 20 to 22 minutes, or until a toothpick inserted in the center comes out clean. Remove from the basket and place on a wire rack to cool completely. Cut into squares and serve immediately.

## Tropical Fruit Kabab

**Prep time: 10 minutes | Cook time: 10 minutes | Serves 4**

1 cup melon, cut into 1-inch chunks
1 cup pineapple, cut into 1-inch chunks
1 banana, cut into 1-inch

chunks
1 peach, cut into 1-inch chunks
2 tablespoons coconut oil, melted
2 tablespoons honey

Toss your fruits with the coconut oil and honey. Thread the fruits onto skewers and place them in the Air Fryer cooking basket when your air fryer displays "READY" (select the cooking preset, and make minor adjustments according to your desired doneness.) and choose a shake reminder. Then, cook the skewers at 400ºF (204ºC) for approximately 10 minutes, turning them over halfway through the cooking time. Bon appétit!

## Beignets

**Prep time: 10 minutes | Cook time: 10 minutes | Serves 4**

¾ cup all-purpose flour
1 teaspoon baking powder
¼ teaspoon kosher salt
¼ cup yogurt

2 eggs, beaten
¼ cup granulated sugar
2 tablespoons coconut oil, melted

In a mixing bowl, thoroughly combine all the ingredients. Drop a spoonful of batter onto the greased Air Fryer pan when your air fryer displays "READY" (select the cooking preset, and make minor adjustments according to your desired doneness.) and choose a shake reminder. Cook in the preheated Air Fryer at 360ºF (182ºC) for 10 minutes, flipping them halfway through the cooking time. Repeat with the remaining batter and serve warm. Enjoy!

## Almond Shortbread

**Prep time: 5 minutes | Cook time: 12 minutes | Serves 8**

½ cup (1 stick) unsalted butter
½ cup sugar
1 teaspoon pure almond extract
1 cup all-purpose flour

Preheat the air fryer to 375ºF (191ºC). In a bowl of a stand mixer fitted with the paddle attachment, beat the butter and sugar on medium speed until fluffy, 3 to 4 minutes. Add the almond extract and beat until combined, about 30 seconds. Turn the mixer to low. Add the flour a little at a time and beat for about 2 minutes more until well incorporated. Pat the dough into an even layer in a round baking pan when your air fryer displays "READY" (select the cooking preset, and make minor adjustments according to your desired doneness.) and choose a shake reminder. Put the pan in the air fryer basket and bake for 12 minutes. Carefully remove the pan from air fryer basket. While the shortbread is still warm and soft, cut it into 8 wedges. Let cool in the pan on a wire rack for 5 minutes. Remove the wedges from the pan and let cool on the rack before serving.

## Blackberry Cobbler

**Prep time: 15 minutes | Cook time: 25 to 30 minutes | Serves 6**

3 cups fresh or frozen blackberries
1¾ cups sugar, divided
1 teaspoon vanilla extract
8 tablespoons (1 stick) butter, melted
1 cup self-rising flour
Cooking spray

Preheat the air fryer to 350ºF (177ºC). Spritz a baking pan with cooking spray. Mix the blackberries, 1 cup of sugar, and vanilla in a medium bowl and stir to combine. Stir together the melted butter, remaining sugar, and flour in a separate medium bowl. Spread the blackberry mixture evenly in the prepared pan and top with the butter mixture. When your air fryer displays "READY" (select the cooking preset, and make minor adjustments according to your desired doneness.) and choose a shake reminder. Bake in the preheated air fryer for 20 to 25 minutes. Check for doneness and bake for another 5 minutes, if needed. Remove from the air fryer and place on a wire rack to cool to room temperature. Serve immediately.

## Warm Chocolate Donuts

**Prep time: 5 minutes | Cook time: 8 minutes | Serves 8**

1 (8-ounce / 227-g) can jumbo biscuits
Cooking oil
Chocolate sauce, for drizzling

Preheat the air fryer to 375ºF (191ºC)
Separate the biscuit dough into 8 biscuits and place them on a flat work surface. Use a small circle cookie cutter or a biscuit cutter to cut a hole in the center of each biscuit. You can also cut the holes using a knife. Spray the air fryer basket with cooking oil. Put 4 donuts in the air fryer when your air fryer displays "READY" (select the cooking preset, and make minor adjustments according to your desired doneness.) and choose a shake reminder. Do not stack. Spray with cooking oil. Air fry for 4 minutes. Open the air fryer and flip the donuts. Air fry for an additional 4 minutes. Remove the cooked donuts from the air fryer, then repeat steps 3 and 4 for the remaining 4 donuts. Drizzle chocolate sauce over the donuts and enjoy while warm.

## Perfect Fudge Cake

**Prep time: 10 minutes | Cook time: 20 minutes | Serves 5**

½ cup butter, melted
1 cup turbinado sugar
3 eggs
1 teaspoon vanilla extract
¼ teaspoon salt
¼ teaspoon ground cloves
½ teaspoon ground cinnamon
½ cup all-purpose flour
¼ cup almond flour
5 ounces (142 g) chocolate chips

Start by preheating your Air Fryer to 340ºF (171ºC). Now, spritz the sides and bottom of a baking pan with a nonstick cooking spray. In a mixing bowl, beat the butter and sugar until fluffy. Next, fold in the eggs and beat again until well combined. After that, add in the remaining ingredients. Mix until everything is well combined. When your air fryer displays "READY" (select the cooking preset, and make minor adjustments according to your desired doneness.) and choose a shake reminder. Bake in the preheated Air Fryer for 20 minutes. Enjoy!

## Fresh Blueberry Fritters

**Prep time: 10 minutes | Cook time: 10 minutes | Serves 4**

¾ cup all-purpose flour
1 teaspoon baking powder
½ cup coconut milk
2 tablespoons coconut sugar
A pinch of sea salt
1 egg
2 tablespoons melted butter
2 ounces (57 g) fresh blueberries

In a mixing bowl, thoroughly combine all the ingredients. Drop a spoonful of batter onto the greased Air Fryer pan when your air fryer displays "READY" (select the cooking preset, and make minor adjustments according to your desired doneness.) and choose a shake reminder. Cook in the preheated Air Fryer at 360ºF (182ºC) for 10 minutes, flipping them halfway through the cooking time. Repeat with the remaining batter and serve warm. Enjoy!

## Frosted Chocolate Cookie

**Prep time: 10 minutes | Cook time: 8 minutes | Serves 4**

3 tablespoons butter, at room temperature
⅓ cup plus 1 tablespoon brown sugar
1 egg yolk
⅔ cup flour
5 tablespoons peanut butter, divided
¼ teaspoon baking soda
1 teaspoon vanilla
½ cup semisweet chocolate chips

In a medium bowl, beat the butter and brown sugar together until fluffy. Stir in the egg yolk. Add the flour, 3 tablespoons of the peanut butter, the baking soda, and vanilla, and mix well. Line a 6-by-6-by-2-inch baking pan with parchment paper. Spread the batter into the prepared pan, leaving a ½-inch border on all sides when your air fryer displays "READY" (select the cooking preset, and make minor adjustments according to your desired doneness.) and choose a shake reminder. Bake for 7 to 10 minutes or until the cookie is light brown and just barely set. Remove the pan from the air fryer and let cool for 10 minutes. Remove the cookie from the pan, remove the parchment paper, and let cool on a wire rack. In a small heatproof cup, combine the chocolate chips with the remaining 2 tablespoons of peanut butter. Bake for 1 to 2 minutes or until the chips are melted. Stir to combine and spread on the cookie.

## Curry Peach, Pear, and Plum

**Prep time: 5 minutes | Cook time: 5 minutes | Serves 6 to 8**

2 peaches
2 firm pears
2 plums

2 tablespoons melted butter
1 tablespoon honey
2 to 3 teaspoons curry powder

Preheat the air fryer to 325°F (163°C). Cut the peaches in half, remove the pits, and cut each half in half again. Cut the pears in half, core them, and remove the stem. Cut each half in half again. Do the same with the plums. Spread a large sheet of heavy-duty foil on the work surface. Arrange the fruit on the foil and drizzle with the butter and honey. Sprinkle with the curry powder. Wrap the fruit in the foil, making sure to leave some air space in the packet. Put the foil package in the basket when your air fryer displays "READY" (select the cooking preset, and make minor adjustments according to your desired doneness.) and choose a shake reminder. Bake for 5 to 8 minutes, shaking the basket once during the cooking time, until the fruit is soft.
Serve immediately.

## Baked Fudge Pie

**Prep time: 15 minutes | Cook time: 25 to 30 minutes | Serves 8**

1½ cups sugar
½ cup self-rising flour
⅓ cup unsweetened cocoa powder
3 large eggs, beaten
12 tablespoons (1½ sticks)

butter, melted
1½ teaspoons vanilla extract
1 (9-inch) unbaked pie crust
¼ cup confectioners' sugar (optional)

Preheat the air fryer to 350°F (177°C). Thoroughly combine the sugar, flour, and cocoa powder in a medium bowl. Add the beaten eggs and butter and whisk to combine. Stir in the vanilla. Pour the prepared filling into the pie crust and transfer to the air fryer basket when your air fryer displays "READY" (select the cooking preset, and make minor adjustments according to your desired doneness.) and choose a shake reminder. Bake for 25 to 30 minutes until just set. Allow the pie to cool for 5 minutes. Sprinkle with the confectioners' sugar, if desired. Serve warm.

## German-Style Giant Pancake

**Prep time: 10 minutes | Cook time: 13 minutes | Serves 3**

1 small apple, peeled, cored, and sliced
1 tablespoon coconut oil, melted
1 egg, whisked
¼ cup plain flour

¼ teaspoon baking powder
¼ cup full-fat coconut milk
A pinch of granulated sugar
A pinch of kosher salt
½ teaspoon vanilla paste

Drizzle the apple slices with the melted coconut oil; arrange the apple slices in a baking pan. Mix the remaining ingredients to make the batter. Pour the batter over the apples. Transfer the baking pan to the Air Fryer cooking basket when your air fryer displays "READY" (select the cooking preset, and make minor adjustments according to your desired doneness.) and choose a shake reminder. Bake your pancake at 350°F (177°C) for about 13 minutes or until it is golden brown around the edges. Bon appétit!

## Stuffed Pears with Greek Yogurt and Walnut

**Prep time: 10 minutes | Cook time: 17 minutes | Serves 2**

2 pears
¼ teaspoon cloves
⅛ teaspoon grated nutmeg
¼ teaspoon ground cinnamon
2 tablespoons honey

2 tablespoons walnuts, chopped
2 ounces (57 g) Greek-style yogurt

Cut the pears in half and spoon out some of the flesh. In a mixing bowl, thoroughly combine the remaining ingredients. Stuff the pear halves and transfer them to the Air Fryer cooking basket. Pour ¼ cup of water into an Air Fryer safe dish. Place the pears in the dish when your air fryer displays "READY" (select the cooking preset, and make minor adjustments according to your desired doneness.) and choose a shake reminder. Bake the apples at 340°F (171°C) for 17 minutes. Serve at room temperature. Bon appétit!

## Pumpkin Cake

**Prep time: 10 minutes | Cook time: 13 minutes | Serves 3**

4 tablespoons all-purpose flour
4 tablespoons almond flour
1 teaspoon baking powder
4 tablespoons honey
1 teaspoon pumpkin pie spice

blend
A pinch of Himalayan salt
¼ cup milk
¼ cup canned pumpkin
1 egg, beaten

Preheat air fryer to 350°F (177°C). Mix all the ingredients to make the batter. Pour the batter into a lightly oiled baking pan. Place the pan in the Air Fryer cooking basket when your air fryer displays "READY" (select the cooking preset, and make minor adjustments according to your desired doneness.) and choose a shake reminder. Bake your cake at 350°F (177°C) for about 13 minutes or until it is golden brown around the edges. Bon appétit!

## Lemon Raspberry Muffins

**Prep time: 5 minutes | Cook time: 15 minutes | Serves 6**

2 cups almond flour
¾ cup Swerve
1¼ teaspoons baking powder
⅓ teaspoon ground allspice
⅓ teaspoon ground anise star
½ teaspoon grated lemon zest

¼ teaspoon salt
2 eggs
1 cup sour cream
½ cup coconut oil
½ cup raspberries

Preheat the air fryer to 345°F (174°C). Line a muffin pan with 6 paper liners.
In a mixing bowl, mix the almond flour, Swerve, baking powder, allspice, anise, lemon zest, and salt. In another mixing bowl, beat the eggs, sour cream, and coconut oil until well mixed. Add the egg mixture to the flour mixture and stir to combine. Mix in the raspberries. Scrape the batter into the prepared muffin cups, filling each about three-quarters full. When your air fryer displays "READY" (select the cooking preset, and make minor adjustments according to your desired doneness.) and choose a shake reminder. Bake for 15 minutes, or until the tops are golden and a toothpick inserted in the middle comes out clean. Allow the muffins to cool for 10 minutes in the muffin pan before removing and serving.

# Chapter 11 Wraps and Sandwiches

## Ham Sourdough Sandwiches
**Prep time: 5 minutes | Cook time: 12 minutes | Serves 2**

| | |
|---|---|
| 4 slices sourdough bread | 2 lettuce leaves |
| 2 tablespoons mayonnaise | 1 tomato, sliced |
| 2 slices ham | 2 slices Mozzarella chees |

Preheat air fryer to 350ºF (177ºC). On a clean working board, lay the bread slices and spread them with mayonnaise. Top 2 of the slices with ham, lettuce leaves, tomato slices, and Mozzarella. Cover with the remaining bread slices to form two sandwiches. When your air fryer displays "READY" (select the cooking preset, and make minor adjustments according to your desired doneness.) and choose a shake reminder. Air Fryer for 12 minutes, flipping once. Serve hot.

## Bacon and Cheddar Cheese Sandwich
**Prep time: 5 minutes | Cook time: 10 minutes | Serves 1**

| | |
|---|---|
| 2 slices whole-wheat bread | 2 ounces (57 g) bacon, sliced |
| 1 tablespoon ketchup | 1 ounce (28 g) Cheddar |
| ½ teaspoon Dijon mustard | cheese, sliced |

Spread the ketchup and mustard on a slice of bread. Add the bacon and cheese and top with another slice of bread. Place your sandwich in the lightly buttered Air Fryer cooking basket when your air fryer displays "READY" (select the cooking preset, and make minor adjustments according to your desired doneness.) and choose a shake reminder. Now, bake your sandwich at 380ºF (193ºC) for 10 minutes or until the cheese has melted. Make sure to turn it over halfway through the cooking time. Enjoy!

## Prawns in Bacon Wraps
**Prep time: 5 minutes | Cook time: 8 minutes | Serves 4**

8 bacon slices
8 jumbo prawns, peeled and deveined

Wrap each prawn from head to tail with each bacon slice overlapping to keep the bacon in place. Secure the ends with toothpicks. Refrigerate for 15 minutes. Preheat air fryer to 400ºF (204ºC). Arrange the bacon-wrapped prawns on the greased frying basket when your air fryer displays "READY" (select the cooking preset, and make minor adjustments according to your desired doneness.) and choose a shake reminder. Bake for 8 minutes, turning once. Serve hot.

## Pork Sirloin Sandwiches
**Prep time: 5 minutes | Cook time: 50 minutes | Serves 3**

| | |
|---|---|
| 2 teaspoons peanut oil | 1 tablespoon smoked paprika |
| 1½ pounds (680 g) pork sirloin | ¼ cup prepared barbecue |
| Coarse sea salt and ground | sauce |
| black pepper, to taste | 3 hamburger buns, split |

Start by preheating your Air Fryer to 360ºF (182ºC). Drizzle the oil all over the pork sirloin. Sprinkle with salt, black pepper, and paprika. When your air fryer displays "READY" (select the cooking preset, and make minor adjustments according to your desired doneness.) and choose a shake reminder. Cook for 50 minutes in the preheated Air Fryer. Remove the roast from the Air Fryer and shred with two forks. Mix in the barbecue sauce. Serve over hamburger buns. Enjoy!

## Mexican Cheese and Beef Cabbage Wraps
**Prep time: 10 minutes | Cook time: 16 minutes | Serves 4**

| | |
|---|---|
| 1 pound (454 g) ground beef | shredded |
| 8 savoy cabbage leaves | 2 tablespoons olive oil |
| 1 small onion, chopped | Salt and black pepper, to taste |
| 1 teaspoon taco seasoning | 2 garlic cloves, minced |
| 1 tablespoon cilantro-lime rotel | 1 tablespoon fresh cilantro, |
| ⅔ cup Mexican cheese, | chopped |

Preheat the air fryer to 400ºF (204ºC). Heat olive oil in a skillet over medium heat and sauté onion and garlic until fragrant, about 3 minutes. Add in ground beef, salt, black pepper, and taco seasoning. Cook until the beef browns while breaking it with a vessel as it cooks. Add cilantro rotel and stir to combine. Lay 4 savoy cabbage leaves on a flat surface and scoop ¼ of the beef mixture in the center; sprinkle with Mexican cheese. Wrap diagonally and double wrap with the remaining cabbage leaves. Arrange the rolls on the greased air fryer basket when your air fryer displays "READY" (select the cooking preset, and make minor adjustments according to your desired doneness.) and choose a shake reminder. Bake for 8 minutes. Flip the rolls and cook for 5 more minutes. Remove to a plate, garnish with cilantro, and let cool before serving.

## Perfect Pork Loin Wraps
**Prep time: 15 minutes | Cook time: 51 minutes | Serves 2**

| | |
|---|---|
| ½ pound (227 g) pork loin | ½ teaspoon marjoram |
| 1 teaspoon butter, melted | ½ teaspoon hot paprika |
| Salt and black pepper, to | 2 tortillas |
| season | |
| **For the Sauce:** | |
| 2 tablespoons tahini | 1 teaspoon fresh ginger, peeled |
| 1 tablespoon sesame oil | and grated |
| 2 tablespoons soy sauce | 2 garlic cloves, pressed |
| 1 tablespoon lime juice | 1 teaspoon honey |
| 1 tablespoon white vinegar | |

Preheat the air fryer to 360ºF (182ºC). Rub the pork with melted butter and season with salt, pepper, marjoram and hot paprika. Place in the cooking basket when your air fryer displays "READY" (select the cooking preset, and make minor adjustments according to your desired doneness.) and choose a shake reminder. Cook at 360ºF (182ºC) for 25 minutes. Turn the meat over and cook an additional 20 minutes. Place the roasted pork loin on a cutting board. Slice the roasted pork loin into strips using a sharp kitchen knife. In the meantime, mix the sauce ingredients with a wire whisk. Turn the temperature to 390ºF (199ºC). Spoon the pork strips and sauce onto each tortilla; wrap them tightly. Drizzle with a nonstick cooking spray and bake about 6 minutes. Serve warm. Enjoy!

## Egg and Bacon Tortilla Wraps
**Prep time: 5 minutes | Cook time: 10 minutes | Serves 3**

| | |
|---|---|
| 3 flour tortillas | 3 tablespoons cream cheese |
| 2 eggs, scrambled | 1 cup Pepper Jack cheese, |
| 3 slices bacon, cut into strips | grated |
| 3 tablespoons salsa | |

Preheat air fryer to 390ºF (199ºC). Spread the cream cheese on the tortillas. Add the eggs and bacon and top with salsa. Scatter over the grated cheese and roll up tightly. Place in the fryer's basket when your air fryer displays "READY" (select the cooking preset, and make minor adjustments according to your desired doneness.) and choose a shake reminder. Air Fryer for 10 minutes or until golden. Cut in half and serve warm.

## Pork, Bacon, and Cheddar Sandwiches

**Prep time: 10 minutes | Cook time: 26 minutes | Serves 2**

½ pound (227 g) pork steak
1 teaspoon steak seasoning
Salt and black pepper, to taste
5 thick bacon slices

½ cup Cheddar cheese, grated
½ tablespoon Worcestershire sauce
2 burger buns, halved

Preheat air fryer to 400ºF (204ºC). Season the pork steak with black pepper, salt, and steak seasoning. Place in the air fryer when your air fryer displays "READY" (select the cooking preset, and make minor adjustments according to your desired doneness.) and choose a shake reminder. Bake for 15 minutes, turn, and continue cooking for 6 minutes. Remove the steak to a chopping board, let cool slightly, and using two forks, shred into small pieces. Place the bacon in the frying basket and Air Fryer at 370ºF (188ºC) for 5 to 8 minutes. Chop the bacon and transfer to a bowl. Mix in the pulled pork, Worcestershire sauce, and cheddar cheese. Adjust the seasoning and spoon the mixture into the halved buns to serve.

## Beef Sausage and Veggie Sandwiches

**Prep time: 10 minutes | Cook time: 30 minutes | Serves 4**

4 bell peppers
2 tablespoons canola oil
4 medium-sized tomatoes, halved

4 spring onions
4 beef sausages
4 hot dog buns
1 tablespoon mustard

Start by preheating your Air Fryer to 400ºF (204ºC). Add the bell peppers to the cooking basket. Drizzle 1 tablespoon of canola oil all over the bell peppers. Cook for 5 minutes. Turn the temperature down to 350ºF (177ºC). Add the tomatoes and spring onions to the cooking basket and cook an additional 10 minutes. Reserve your vegetables. Then, add the sausages to the cooking basket when your air fryer displays "READY" (select the cooking preset, and make minor adjustments according to your desired doneness.) and choose a shake reminder. Drizzle with the remaining tablespoon of canola oil. Cook in the preheated Air Fryer at 380ºF (193ºC) for 15 minutes, flipping them halfway through the cooking time. Add the sausage to a hot dog bun; top with the air-fried vegetables and mustard; serve. Enjoy!

## Avocado and Slaw Tacos with Sour Cream

**Prep time: 15 minutes | Cook time: 6 minutes | Serves 4**

¼ cup all-purpose flour
¼ teaspoon salt, plus more as needed
¼ teaspoon ground black pepper
2 large egg whites
1¼ cups panko breadcrumbs
2 tablespoons olive oil
2 avocados, peeled and halved, cut into ½-inch-thick slices
½ small red cabbage, thinly

sliced
1 deseeded jalapeño, thinly sliced
2 green onions, thinly sliced
½ cup cilantro leaves
¼ cup mayonnaise
Juice and zest of 1 lime
4 corn tortillas, warmed
½ cup sour cream
Cooking spray

Preheat the air fryer to 400ºF (204ºC). Spritz the air fryer basket with cooking spray. Pour the flour in a large bowl and sprinkle with salt and black pepper, then stir to mix well. Whisk the egg whites in a separate bowl. Combine the panko with olive oil on a shallow dish. Dredge the avocado slices in the bowl of flour, then into the egg to coat. Shake the excess off, then roll the slices over the panko. Arrange the avocado slices in a single layer in the basket and spritz the cooking spray when your air fryer displays "READY" (select the cooking preset, and make minor adjustments according to your desired doneness.) and choose

a shake reminder. Air fry for 6 minutes or until tender and lightly browned. Flip the slices halfway through with tongs. Combine the cabbage, jalapeño, onions, cilantro leaves, mayo, lime juice and zest, and a touch of salt in a separate large bowl. Toss to mix well. Unfold the tortillas on a clean work surface, then spread with cabbage slaw and air fried avocados. Top with sour cream and serve.

## Smoky Paprika Chicken Sandwich

**Prep time: 10 minutes | Cook time: 11 minutes | Serves 2**

2 boneless, skinless chicken breasts (8 ounces / 227 g each), sliced horizontally in half and separated into 4 thinner cutlets
Kosher salt and freshly ground black pepper, to taste
½ cup all-purpose flour
3 large eggs, lightly beaten

½ cup dried bread crumbs
1 tablespoon smoked paprika
Cooking spray
½ cup marinara sauce
6 ounces (170 g) smoked Mozzarella cheese, grated
2 store-bought soft, sesame-seed hamburger or Italian buns, split

Preheat the air fryer to 350ºF (177ºC). Season the chicken cutlets all over with salt and pepper. Set up three shallow bowls: Place the flour in the first bowl, the eggs in the second, and stir together the bread crumbs and smoked paprika in the third. Coat the chicken pieces in the flour, then dip fully in the egg. Dredge in the paprika bread crumbs, then transfer to a wire rack set over a baking sheet and spray both sides liberally with cooking spray. Transfer 2 of the chicken cutlets to the air fryer when your air fryer displays "READY" (select the cooking preset, and make minor adjustments according to your desired doneness.) and choose a shake reminder. Air fry for 6 minutes, or until beginning to brown. Spread each cutlet with 2 tablespoons of the marinara sauce and sprinkle with one-quarter of the smoked Mozzarella. Increase the temperature to 400ºF (204ºC) and air fry for 5 minutes more, or until the chicken is cooked through and crisp and the cheese is melted and golden brown. Transfer the cutlets to a plate, stack on top of each other, and place inside a bun. Repeat with the remaining chicken cutlets, marinara, smoked Mozzarella, and bun. Serve the sandwiches warm.

## Crab Meat and Cream Cheese Wontons

**Prep time: 10 minutes | Cook time: 10 minutes per batch | Serves 6 to 8**

24 wonton wrappers, thawed if frozen
**For the Filling:**
5 ounces (142 g) lump crabmeat, drained and patted dry
4 ounces (113 g) cream cheese, at room temperature
2 scallions, sliced

Cooking spray

1½ teaspoons toasted sesame oil
1 teaspoon Worcestershire sauce
Kosher salt and ground black pepper, to taste

Preheat the air fryer to 350ºF (177ºC). Spritz the air fryer basket with cooking spray. In a medium-size bowl, place all the ingredients for the filling and stir until well mixed. Prepare a small bowl of water alongside. On a clean work surface, lay the wonton wrappers. Scoop 1 teaspoon of the filling in the center of each wrapper. Wet the edges with a touch of water. Fold each wonton wrapper diagonally in half over the filling to form a triangle. Arrange the wontons in the air fryer basket when your air fryer displays "READY" (select the cooking preset, and make minor adjustments according to your desired doneness.) and choose a shake reminder. Spritz the wontons with cooking spray. Work in batches, 6 to 8 at a time. Air fry for 10 minutes, or until crispy and golden brown. Flip once halfway through. Serve immediately.

## Philly Cheese Steaks Sandwich Rolls

**Prep time: 20 minutes | Cook time: 20 minutes | Serves 2**

12 ounces (340 g) boneless rib-eye steak, sliced thinly
½ teaspoon Worcestershire sauce
½ teaspoon soy sauce
Kosher salt and ground black pepper, to taste
½ green bell pepper, stemmed, deseeded, and thinly sliced

½ small onion, halved and thinly sliced
1 tablespoon vegetable oil
2 soft hoagie rolls, split three-fourths of the way through
1 tablespoon butter, softened
2 slices provolone cheese, halved

Preheat the air fryer to 400ºF (204ºC). Combine the steak, Worcestershire sauce, soy sauce, salt, and ground black pepper in a large bowl. Toss to coat well. Set aside. Combine the bell pepper, onion, salt, ground black pepper, and vegetable oil in a separate bowl. Toss to coat the vegetables well. Pour the steak and vegetables in the preheated air fryer when your air fryer displays "READY" (select the cooking preset, and make minor adjustments according to your desired doneness.) and choose a shake reminder. Air fry for 15 minutes or until the steak is browned and vegetables are tender. Transfer them on a plate. Set aside. Brush the hoagie rolls with butter, then place in the air fryer to toast for 3 minutes or until lightly browned. Transfer the rolls on a clean work surface and divide the steak and vegetable mix in between the rolls. Spread with cheese. Arrange the rolls in the air fryer and air fry for 2 minutes or until the cheese melts. Serve immediately.

## Cheddar Cheese Sandwich

**Prep time: 5 minutes | Cook time: 6 minutes | Serves 1**

2 slices artisan bread
1 tablespoon butter, softened
1 tablespoon tomato ketchup

½ teaspoon dried oregano
2 slices Cheddar cheese

Preheat the air fryer to 360ºF (182ºC). Brush one side of each slice of the bread with melted butter. Add the tomato ketchup, oregano, and cheese. Arrange the sandwich in the air fryer when your air fryer displays "READY" (select the cooking preset, and make minor adjustments according to your desired doneness.) and choose a shake reminder. Bake at 360ºF (182ºC) for 9 minutes or until cheese is melted. Enjoy!

## Baja Fish Tacos with Salsa

**Prep time: 15 minutes | Cook time: 17 minutes | Makes 6 tacos**

1 egg
5 ounces (142 g) Mexican beer
¾ cup all-purpose flour
¾ cup cornstarch
¼ teaspoon chili powder
**For the Salsa:**
1 mango, peeled and diced
¼ red bell pepper, diced
½ small jalapeño, diced
¼ red onion, minced
Juice of half a lime

½ teaspoon ground cumin
½ pound (227 g) cod, cut into large pieces
6 corn tortillas
Cooking spray

Pinch chopped fresh cilantro
¼ teaspoon salt
¼ teaspoon ground black pepper

Preheat the air fryer to 380ºF (193ºC). Spritz the air fryer basket with cooking spray. Whisk the egg with beer in a bowl. Combine the flour, cornstarch, chili powder, and cumin in a separate bowl. Dredge the cod in the egg mixture first, then in the flour mixture to coat well. Shake the excess off. Arrange the cod in the preheated air fryer and spritz with cooking spray when your air fryer displays "READY" (select the cooking preset, and make minor adjustments according to your desired doneness.) and

choose a shake reminder. Air fry for 17 minutes or until golden brown and crunchy. Flip the cod halfway through. Meanwhile, combine the ingredients for the salsa in a small bowl. Stir to mix well. Unfold the tortillas on a clean work surface, then divide the fish on the tortillas and spread the salsa on top. Fold to serve.

## Vegan Nugget and Veggie Taco Wraps

**Prep time: 5 minutes | Cook time: 15 minutes | Serves 4**

1 tablespoon water
4 pieces commercial vegan nuggets, chopped
1 small yellow onion, diced
1 small red bell pepper,

chopped
2 cobs grilled corn kernels
4 large corn tortillas
Mixed greens, for garnish

Preheat the air fryer to 400ºF (204ºC). Over a medium heat, sauté the nuggets in the water with the onion, corn kernels and bell pepper in a skillet, then remove from the heat. Fill the tortillas with the nuggets and vegetables and fold them up. Transfer to the inside of the fryer when your air fryer displays "READY" (select the cooking preset, and make minor adjustments according to your desired doneness.) and choose a shake reminder. Air fry for 15 minutes. Once crispy, serve immediately, garnished with the mixed greens.

## Light Tuna Muffin Sandwich

**Prep time: 8 minutes | Cook time: 4 to 8 minutes | Serves 4**

1 (6-ounce / 170-g) can chunk light tuna, drained
¼ cup mayonnaise
2 tablespoons mustard
1 tablespoon lemon juice
2 green onions, minced

3 English muffins, split with a fork
3 tablespoons softened butter
6 thin slices Provolone or Muenster cheese

Preheat the air fryer to 390ºF (199ºC). In a small bowl, combine the tuna, mayonnaise, mustard, lemon juice, and green onions. Set aside. Butter the cut side of the English muffins. Bake, butter-side up, in the air fryer for 2 to 4 minutes, or until light golden brown. Remove the muffins from the air fryer basket. Top each muffin with one slice of cheese and return to the air fryer when your air fryer displays "READY" (select the cooking preset, and make minor adjustments according to your desired doneness.) and choose a shake reminder. Bake for 2 to 4 minutes or until the cheese melts and starts to brown. Remove the muffins from the air fryer, top with the tuna mixture, and serve.

## Crispy Cream Cheese Wontons

**Prep time: 5 minutes | Cook time: 6 minutes | Serves 4**

2 ounces (57 g) cream cheese, softened
1 tablespoon sugar

16 square wonton wrappers
Cooking spray

Preheat the air fryer to 350ºF (177ºC). Spritz the air fryer basket with cooking spray. In a mixing bowl, stir together the cream cheese and sugar until well mixed. Prepare a small bowl of water alongside. On a clean work surface, lay the wonton wrappers. Scoop ¼ teaspoon of cream cheese in the center of each wonton wrapper. Dab the water over the wrapper edges. Fold each wonton wrapper diagonally in half over the filling to form a triangle. Arrange the wontons in the air fryer basket when your air fryer displays "READY" (select the cooking preset, and make minor adjustments according to your desired doneness.) and choose a shake reminder. Spritz the wontons with cooking spray. Air fry for 6 minutes, or until golden brown and crispy. Flip once halfway through to ensure even cooking. Divide the wontons among four plates. Let rest for 5 minutes before serving.

## Cabbage, Carrot, and Mushroom Spring Rolls

Prep time: 20 minutes | Cook time: 35 minutes | Makes 14 spring rolls

2 tablespoons vegetable oil
4 cups sliced Napa cabbage
5 ounces (142 g) shiitake mushrooms, diced
3 carrots, cut into thin matchsticks
1 tablespoon minced fresh ginger
1 tablespoon minced garlic
1 bunch scallions, white and

light green parts only, sliced
2 tablespoons soy sauce
1 (4-ounce / 113-g) package cellophane noodles
¼ teaspoon cornstarch
1 (12-ounce / 340-g) package frozen spring roll wrappers, thawed
Cooking spray

Heat the olive oil in a nonstick skillet over medium-high heat until shimmering. Add the cabbage, mushrooms, and carrots and sauté for 3 minutes or until tender. Add the ginger, garlic, and scallions and sauté for 1 minutes or until fragrant. Mix in the soy sauce and turn off the heat. Discard any liquid remains in the skillet and allow to cool for a few minutes. Bring a pot of water to a boil, then turn off the heat and pour in the noodles. Let sit for 10 minutes or until the noodles are al dente. Transfer 1 cup of the noodles in the skillet and toss with the cooked vegetables. Reserve the remaining noodles for other use. Dissolve the cornstarch in a small dish of water, then place the wrappers on a clean work surface. Dab the edges of the wrappers with cornstarch. Scoop up 3 tablespoons of filling in the center of each wrapper, then fold the corner in front of you over the filling. Tuck the wrapper under the filling, then fold the corners on both sides into the center. Keep rolling to seal the wrapper. Repeat with remaining wrappers. Preheat the air fryer to 400ºF (204ºC) and spritz with cooking spray. Arrange the wrappers in the preheated air fryer and spritz with cooking spray when your air fryer displays "READY" (select the cooking preset, and make minor adjustments according to your desired doneness.) and choose a shake reminder. Air fry in batches for 10 minutes or until golden brown. Flip the wrappers halfway through. Serve immediately.

## Pork and Cabbage Gyoza

Prep time: 10 minutes | Cook time: 10 minutes per batch | Makes 48 gyozas

1 pound (454 g) ground pork
1 small head Napa cabbage (about 1 pound / 454 g), sliced thinly and minced
½ cup minced scallions
1 teaspoon minced fresh chives
1 teaspoon soy sauce

1 teaspoon minced fresh ginger
1 tablespoon minced garlic
1 teaspoon granulated sugar
2 teaspoons kosher salt
48 to 50 wonton or dumpling wrappers
Cooking spray

Make the filling: Combine all the ingredients, except for the wrappers in a large bowl. Stir to mix well. Unfold a wrapper on a clean work surface, then dab the edges with a little water. Scoop up 2 teaspoons of the filling mixture in the center. Make the gyoza: Fold the wrapper over to filling and press the edges to seal. Pleat the edges if desired. Repeat with remaining wrappers and fillings. Preheat the air fryer to 360ºF (182ºC) and spritz with cooking spray. Arrange the gyozas in the preheated air fryer and spritz with cooking spray when your air fryer displays "READY" (select the cooking preset, and make minor adjustments according to your desired doneness.) and choose a shake reminder. Air fry for 10 minutes or until golden brown. Flip the gyozas halfway through. Work in batches to avoid overcrowding. Serve immediately.

## Bacon and Egg Cheese Wraps

Prep time: 15 minutes | Cook time: 20 minutes | Serves 3

3 corn tortillas
3 slices bacon, cut into strips
2 scrambled eggs
3 tablespoons salsa
1 cup grated Pepper Jack

cheese
3 tablespoons cream cheese, divided
Cooking spray

Preheat the air fryer to 390ºF (199ºC). Spritz the air fryer basket with cooking spray. Unfold the tortillas on a clean work surface, divide the bacon and eggs in the middle of the tortillas, then spread with salsa and scatter with cheeses. Fold the tortillas over. Work in batches, arrange the tortillas in the preheated air fryer when your air fryer displays "READY" (select the cooking preset, and make minor adjustments according to your desired doneness.) and choose a shake reminder. Air fry for 10 minutes or until the cheeses melt and the tortillas are lightly browned. Flip the tortillas halfway through. Repeat with remaining tortillas. Serve immediately.

## Mexican Cheese Potato Taquitos

Prep time: 5 minutes | Cook time: 6 minutes per batch | Makes 12 taquitos

2 cups mashed potatoes
½ cup shredded Mexican cheese

12 corn tortillas
Cooking spray

Preheat the air fryer to 400ºF (204ºC). Line the baking pan with parchment paper. In a bowl, combine the potatoes and cheese until well mixed. Microwave the tortillas on high heat for 30 seconds, or until softened. Add some water to another bowl and set alongside. On a clean work surface, lay the tortillas. Scoop 3 tablespoons of the potato mixture in the center of each tortilla. Roll up tightly and secure with toothpicks if necessary. Arrange the filled tortillas, seam side down, in the prepared baking pan when your air fryer displays "READY" (select the cooking preset, and make minor adjustments according to your desired doneness.) and choose a shake reminder. Spritz the tortillas with cooking spray. Air fry for 6 minutes, or until crispy and golden brown, flipping once halfway through the cooking time. You may need to work in batches to avoid overcrowding. Serve hot.

## Vegetable Pita Sandwich

Prep time: 10 minutes | Cook time: 9 to 12 minutes | Serves 4

1 baby eggplant, peeled and chopped
1 red bell pepper, sliced
½ cup diced red onion
½ cup shredded carrot

1 teaspoon olive oil
⅓ cup low-fat Greek yogurt
½ teaspoon dried tarragon
2 low-sodium whole-wheat pita breads, halved crosswise

Preheat the air fryer to 390ºF (199ºC). In a baking pan, stir together the eggplant, red bell pepper, red onion, carrot, and olive oil. Put the vegetable mixture into the air fryer basket and roast for 7 to 9 minutes, stirring once, until the vegetables are tender. Drain if necessary. In a small bowl, thoroughly mix the yogurt and tarragon until well combined. Stir the yogurt mixture into the vegetables. Stuff one-fourth of this mixture into each pita pocket. Place the sandwiches in the air fryer when your air fryer displays "READY" (select the cooking preset, and make minor adjustments according to your desired doneness.) and choose a shake reminder. Bake for 2 to 3 minutes, or until the bread is toasted. Serve immediately.

## Lettuce Fajita Beef Meatball Wraps

**Prep time: 10 minutes | Cook time: 10 minutes | Serves 4**

1 pound (454 g) 85% lean ground beef
½ cup salsa, plus more for serving
¼ cup chopped onions
¼ cup diced green or red bell peppers
**For Serving:**
8 leaves Boston lettuce
Pico de gallo or salsa

1 large egg, beaten
1 teaspoon fine sea salt
½ teaspoon chili powder
½ teaspoon ground cumin
1 clove garlic, minced
Cooking spray

Lime slices

Preheat the air fryer to 350ºF (177ºC). Spray the air fryer basket with cooking spray. In a large bowl, mix together all the ingredients until well combined. Shape the meat mixture into eight 1-inch balls. Place the meatballs in the air fryer basket, leaving a little space between them when your air fryer displays "READY" (select the cooking preset, and make minor adjustments according to your desired doneness.) and choose a shake reminder. Air fry for 10 minutes, or until cooked through and no longer pink inside and the internal temperature reaches 145ºF (63ºC). Serve each meatball on a lettuce leaf, topped with pico de gallo or salsa. Serve with lime slices.

## Tomato and Avocado Egg Rolls

**Prep time: 10 minutes | Cook time: 5 minutes per batch | Serves 5**

10 egg roll wrappers
3 avocados, peeled and pitted
1 tomato, diced

Salt and ground black pepper, to taste
Cooking spray

Preheat the air fryer to 350ºF (177ºC) and spritz with cooking spray. Pu the tomato and avocados in a food processor. Sprinkle with salt and ground black pepper. Pulse to mix and coarsely mash until smooth. Unfold the wrappers on a clean work surface, then divide the mixture in the center of each wrapper. Roll the wrapper up and press to seal. Transfer the rolls in the preheated air fryer and spritz with cooking spray when your air fryer displays "READY" (select the cooking preset, and make minor adjustments according to your desired doneness.) and choose a shake reminder. Air fry for 5 minutes or until golden brown. Flip the rolls halfway through. Work in batches to avoid overcrowding. Serve immediately.

## Tuna Steak and Lettuce Wraps

**Prep time: 10 minutes | Cook time: 4 to 7 minutes | Serves 4**

1 pound (454 g) fresh tuna steak, cut into 1-inch cubes
1 tablespoon grated fresh ginger
2 garlic cloves, minced
½ teaspoon toasted sesame oil

4 low-sodium whole-wheat tortillas
¼ cup low-fat mayonnaise
2 cups shredded romaine lettuce
1 red bell pepper, thinly sliced

Preheat the air fryer to 390ºF (199ºC). In a medium bowl, mix the tuna, ginger, garlic, and sesame oil. Let it stand for 10 minutes. When your air fryer displays "READY" (select the cooking preset, and make minor adjustments according to your desired doneness.) and choose a shake reminder. Air fry the tuna in the air fryer basket for 4 to 7 minutes, or until lightly browned. Make the wraps with the tuna, tortillas, mayonnaise, lettuce, and bell pepper. Serve immediately.

## Crispy Spring Rolls

**Prep time: 10 minutes | Cook time: 18 minutes | Serves 4**

4 spring roll wrappers
½ cup cooked vermicelli noodles
1 teaspoon sesame oil
1 tablespoon freshly minced ginger
1 tablespoon soy sauce

1 clove garlic, minced
½ red bell pepper, deseeded and chopped
½ cup chopped carrot
½ cup chopped mushrooms
¼ cup chopped scallions
Cooking spray

Preheat the air fryer to 340ºF (171ºC). Spritz the air fryer basket with cooking spray and set aside. Heat the sesame oil in a saucepan on medium heat. Sauté the ginger and garlic in the sesame oil for 1 minute, or until fragrant. Add soy sauce, red bell pepper, carrot, mushrooms and scallions. Sauté for 5 minutes or until the vegetables become tender. Mix in vermicelli noodles. Turn off the heat and remove them from the saucepan. Allow to cool for 10 minutes. Lay out one spring roll wrapper with a corner pointed toward you. Scoop the noodle mixture on spring roll wrapper and fold corner up over the mixture. Fold left and right corners toward the center and continue to roll to make firmly sealed rolls. Arrange the spring rolls on the prepared air fryer basket and spritz with cooking spray when your air fryer displays "READY" (select the cooking preset, and make minor adjustments according to your desired doneness.) and choose a shake reminder. Air fryer the spring rolls for 6 minutes, then flip the spring rolls and air fry for 6 more minutes or until golden brown and crispy. Serve warm.

## Mozzarella Veggie Salsa Wraps

**Prep time: 5 minutes | Cook time: 7 minutes | Serves 4**

1 cup red onion, sliced
1 zucchini, chopped
1 poblano pepper, deseeded and finely chopped

1 head lettuce
½ cup salsa
8 ounces (227 g) Mozzarella cheese

Preheat the air fryer to 390ºF (199ºC). Place the red onion, zucchini, and poblano pepper in the air fryer basket when your air fryer displays "READY" (select the cooking preset, and make minor adjustments according to your desired doneness.) and choose a shake reminder. Air fry for 7 minutes, or until they are tender and fragrant. Divide the veggie mixture among the lettuce leaves and spoon the salsa over the top. Finish off with Mozzarella cheese. Wrap the lettuce leaves around the filling. Serve immediately.

## Chicken and Yogurt Taquitos

**Prep time: 15 minutes | Cook time: 12 minutes | Serves 4**

1 cup cooked chicken, shredded
¼ cup Greek yogurt
¼ cup salsa
1 cup shredded Mozzarella

cheese
Salt and ground black pepper, to taste
4 flour tortillas
Cooking spray

Preheat the air fryer to 380ºF (193ºC) and spritz with cooking spray. Combine all the ingredients, except for the tortillas, in a large bowl. Stir to mix well. Make the taquitos: Unfold the tortillas on a clean work surface, then scoop up 2 tablespoons of the chicken mixture in the middle of each tortilla. Roll the tortillas up to wrap the filling. Arrange the taquitos in the preheated air fryer and spritz with cooking spray when your air fryer displays "READY" (select the cooking preset, and make minor adjustments according to your desired doneness.) and choose a shake reminder. Air fry for 12 minutes or until golden brown and the cheese melts. Flip the taquitos halfway through. Serve immediately.

## Chicken and Veggie Egg Rolls

**Prep time: 10 minutes | Cook time: 23 to 24 minutes | Serves 4**

1 pound (454 g) ground chicken
2 teaspoons olive oil
2 garlic cloves, minced
1 teaspoon grated fresh ginger
2 cups white cabbage, shredded
1 onion, chopped
¼ cup soy sauce
8 egg roll wrappers
1 egg, beaten
Cooking spray

Preheat the air fryer to 370ºF (188ºC). Spritz the air fryer basket with cooking spray. Heat olive oil in a saucepan over medium heat. Sauté the garlic and ginger in the olive oil for 1 minute, or until fragrant. Add the ground chicken to the saucepan. Sauté for 5 minutes, or until the chicken is cooked through. Add the cabbage, onion and soy sauce and sauté for 5 to 6 minutes, or until the vegetables become soft. Remove the saucepan from the heat. Unfold the egg roll wrappers on a clean work surface. Divide the chicken mixture among the wrappers and brush the edges of the wrappers with the beaten egg. Tightly roll up the egg rolls, enclosing the filling. Arrange the rolls in the prepared air fryer basket when your air fryer displays "READY" (select the cooking preset, and make minor adjustments according to your desired doneness.) and choose a shake reminder. Air fry for 12 minutes, or until crispy and golden brown. Turn halfway through the cooking time to ensure even cooking. Transfer to a platter and let cool for 5 minutes before serving.

## Steak and Bell Pepper Fajitas

**Prep time: 15 minutes | Cook time: 10 minutes | Serves 4**

1 pound (454 g) beef sirloin steak, cut into strips
2 shallots, sliced
1 orange bell pepper, sliced
1 red bell pepper, sliced
2 garlic cloves, minced
2 tablespoons Cajun seasoning
1 tablespoon paprika
Salt and ground black pepper, to taste
4 corn tortillas
½ cup shredded Cheddar cheese
Cooking spray

Preheat the air fryer to 360ºF (182ºC) and spritz with cooking spray. Combine all the ingredients, except for the tortillas and cheese, in a large bowl. Toss to coat well. Pour the beef and vegetables in the preheated air fryer and spritz with cooking spray when your air fryer displays "READY" (select the cooking preset, and make minor adjustments according to your desired doneness.) and choose a shake reminder. Air fry for 10 minutes or until the meat is browned and the vegetables are soft and lightly wilted. Shake the basket halfway through. Unfold the tortillas on a clean work surface and spread the cooked beef and vegetables on top. Scatter with cheese and fold to serve.

## Bulgogi Burgers with Korean Mayo

**Prep time: 15 minutes | Cook time: 10 minutes | Serves 4**

**For the Burgers:**
1 pound (454 g) 85% lean ground beef
2 tablespoons gochujang
¼ cup chopped scallions
2 teaspoons minced garlic
2 teaspoons minced fresh ginger
**For the Korean Mayo:**
1 tablespoon gochujang
¼ cup mayonnaise
2 teaspoons sesame seeds
1 tablespoon soy sauce
1 tablespoon toasted sesame oil
2 teaspoons sugar
½ teaspoon kosher salt
4 hamburger buns
Cooking spray

¼ cup chopped scallions
1 tablespoon toasted sesame oil

Combine the ingredients for the burgers, except for the buns, in a large bowl. Stir to mix well, then wrap the bowl in plastic and refrigerate to marinate for at least an hour. Preheat the air fryer to 350ºF (177ºC) and spritz with cooking spray. Divide the meat mixture into four portions and form into four balls. Bash the balls into patties. Arrange the patties in the preheated air fryer and spritz with cooking spray when your air fryer displays "READY" (select the cooking preset, and make minor adjustments according to your desired doneness.) and choose a shake reminder. Air fry for 10 minutes or until golden brown. Flip the patties halfway through. Meanwhile, combine the ingredients for the Korean mayo in a small bowl. Stir to mix well. Remove the patties from the air fryer and assemble with the buns, then spread the Korean mayo over the patties to make the burgers. Serve immediately.

## Ricotta Spring Chicken Wraps

**Prep time: 30 minutes | Cook time: 5 minutes per batch | Serves 12**

2 large-sized chicken breasts, cooked and shredded
2 spring onions, chopped
10 ounces (284 g) Ricotta cheese
1 tablespoon rice vinegar
1 tablespoon molasses
1 teaspoon grated fresh ginger
¼ cup soy sauce
⅓ teaspoon sea salt
¼ teaspoon ground black pepper, or more to taste
48 wonton wrappers
Cooking spray

Preheat the air fryer to 375ºF (191ºC) and spritz with cooking spray. Combine all the ingredients, except for the wrappers in a large bowl. Toss to mix well. Unfold the wrappers on a clean work surface, then divide and spoon the mixture in the middle of the wrappers. Dab a little water on the edges of the wrappers, then fold the edge close to you over the filling. Tuck the edge under the filling and roll up to seal. Arrange the wraps in the preheated air fryer when your air fryer displays "READY" (select the cooking preset, and make minor adjustments according to your desired doneness.) and choose a shake reminder. Air fry in batches for 5 minutes or until lightly browned. Flip the wraps halfway through. Serve immediately.

## Cheesy Vegetable Wraps

**Prep time: 15 minutes | Cook time: 8 to 10 minutes per batch | Serves 4**

8 ounces (227 g) green beans
2 portobello mushroom caps, sliced
1 large red pepper, sliced
2 tablespoons olive oil, divided
¼ teaspoon salt
1 (15-ounce / 425-g) can chickpeas, drained
3 tablespoons lemon juice
¼ teaspoon ground black pepper
4 (6-inch) whole-grain wraps
4 ounces (113 g) fresh herb or garlic Goat cheese, crumbled
1 lemon, cut into wedges

Preheat the air fryer to 400ºF (204ºC). Add the green beans, mushrooms, red pepper to a large bowl. Drizzle with 1 tablespoon olive oil and season with salt. Toss until well coated. Transfer the vegetable mixture to a baking pan when your air fryer displays "READY" (select the cooking preset, and make minor adjustments according to your desired doneness.) and choose a shake reminder. Air fry in the preheated air fryer in 2 batches, 8 to 10 minutes per batch, stirring constantly during cooking. Meanwhile, mash the chickpeas with lemon juice, pepper and the remaining 1 tablespoon oil until well blended
Unfold the wraps on a clean work surface. Spoon the chickpea mash on the wraps and spread all over. Divide the cooked veggies among wraps. Sprinkle 1 ounce crumbled goat cheese on top of each wrap. Fold to wrap. Squeeze the lemon wedges on top and serve.

# Chapter 12 Holiday Specials

## French Ratatouille
**Prep time: 10 minutes | Cook time: 15 minutes | Serves 2**

2 tablespoons olive oil
2 Roma tomatoes, thinly sliced
2 garlic cloves, minced
1 zucchini, thinly sliced
2 yellow bell peppers, sliced

1 tablespoon vinegar
2 tablespoons herbs de Provence
Salt and black pepper, to taste

Preheat air fryer to 390ºF (199ºC). Place all ingredients in a bowl. Season with salt and pepper and stir to coat. Arrange them on a baking dish and place them inside the air fryer when your air fryer displays "READY" (select the cooking preset, and make minor adjustments according to your desired doneness.) and choose a shake reminder. Bake for 15 minutes. Serve warm. enjoy!

## Chinese Pork Dumplings
**Prep time: 15 minutes | Cook time: 8 minutes | Serves 3**

½ pound (227 g) ground pork
1 cup Napa cabbage, shredded
2 scallion stalks, chopped
1 ounce (28 g) bamboo shoots, shredded
**For the Sauce:**
2 tablespoons rice vinegar
¼ cup soy sauce
1 tablespoon ketchup
1 teaspoon deli mustard

½ teaspoon garlic paste
1 teaspoon fresh ginger, peeled and grated
8 ounces (227 g) round wheat dumpling

1 teaspoon honey
1 teaspoon sesame seeds, lightly toasted

Cook the pork in a wok that is preheated over medium-high heat; cook until no longer pink and stir in the Napa cabbage, scallions, bamboo shoots, garlic paste and ginger; salt to taste and stir to combine well. Divide the pork mixture between dumplings. Moisten the edge of each dumpling with water, fold the top half over the bottom half and press together firmly. Place your dumplings in the Air Fryer cooking basket and spritz them with cooking spray when your air fryer displays "READY" (select the cooking preset, and make minor adjustments according to your desired doneness.) and choose a shake reminder. Cook your dumplings at 400ºF (204ºC) for 8 minutes. Work with batches. While your dumplings are cooking, whisk the sauce ingredients. Serve the warm dumplings with the sauce for dipping. Enjoy!

## Traditional Pakora
**Prep time: 10 minutes | Cook time: 12 minutes | Serves 2**

1 large zucchini, grated
½ cup besan flour
½ teaspoon baking powder
2 scallion stalks, chopped
½ teaspoon paprika

¼ teaspoon curry powder
¼ teaspoon ginger-garlic paste
Sea salt and ground black pepper, to taste
1 teaspoon olive oil

Preheat the air fryer to 380ºF (193ºC). Sprinkle the salt over the grated zucchini and leave it for 20 minutes. Then, squeeze the zucchini and drain off the excess liquid. Mix the grated zucchini with the flour, baking powder, scallions, paprika, curry powder and ginger-garlic paste. Salt and pepper to taste. Shape the mixture into patties and transfer them to the Air Fryer cooking basket when your air fryer displays "READY" (select the cooking preset, and make minor adjustments according to your desired doneness.) and choose a shake reminder. Brush the zucchini patties with 1 teaspoon of olive oil. Cook the pakora at 380ºF (193ºC) for about 12 minutes, flipping them halfway through the cooking time. Serve on dinner rolls and enjoy!

## Rizzi Bizzi Rice
**Prep time: 5 minutes | Cook time: 43 minutes | Serves 2**

1 cup long-grain brown rice, soaked overnight
1 carrot, grated
1 cup green peas, fresh or

thawed
¼ cup Shoyu sauce
1 teaspoon sesame oil

Preheat the air fryer to 340ºF (171ºC). Add the brown rice and 2 cups of water to a saucepan. Bring to a boil. Cover and reduce the heat to a slow simmer. Cook your rice for 30 minutes, then, fluff it with a fork. Combine your rice with the remaining ingredients and transfer it to the cooking basket when your air fryer displays "READY" (select the cooking preset, and make minor adjustments according to your desired doneness.) and choose a shake reminder. Cook your rizzi bizzi at 340ºF (171ºC) for about 13 minutes, stirring halfway through the cooking time. Serve immediately!

## Crunchy Party Mix
**Prep time: 15 minutes | Cook time: 13 minutes | Serves 8**

1 cup whole-grain Rice Chex
2 cups cheese squares
1 cup pistachios
½ cup almonds
1 cup cheddar-flavored mini pretzel twists

2 tablespoons butter, melted
¼ cup poppy seeds
½ cup sunflower seeds
1 tablespoon coarse sea salt
1 tablespoon garlic powder
1 tablespoon paprika

Preheat the air fryer to 310ºF (154ºC). Mix all ingredients in a large bowl. Toss to combine well. Place in a single layer in the parchment-lined cooking basket when your air fryer displays "READY" (select the cooking preset, and make minor adjustments according to your desired doneness.) and choose a shake reminder. Bake in the preheated Air Fryer at 310ºF (154ºC) for 13 to 16 minutes. Allow it to cool completely before serving. Store in an airtight container for up to 3 months. Enjoy!

## Traditional Churros
**Prep time: 35 minutes | Cook time: 10 minutes per batch | Makes 12 churros**

4 tablespoons butter
¼ teaspoon salt
½ cup water
½ cup all-purpose flour

2 large eggs
2 teaspoons ground cinnamon
¼ cup granulated white sugar
Cooking spray

Put the butter, salt, and water in a saucepan. Bring to a boil until the butter is melted on high heat. Keep stirring. Reduce the heat to medium and fold in the flour to form a dough. Keep cooking and stirring until the dough is dried out and coat the pan with a crust. Turn off the heat and scrape the dough in a large bowl. Allow to cool for 15 minutes. Break and whisk the eggs into the dough with a hand mixer until the dough is sanity and firm enough to shape. Scoop up 1 tablespoon of the dough and roll it into a ½-inch-diameter and 2-inch-long cylinder. Repeat with remaining dough to make 12 cylinders in total. Combine the cinnamon and sugar in a large bowl and dunk the cylinders into the cinnamon mix to coat. Arrange the cylinders on a plate and refrigerate for 20 minutes. Preheat the air fryer to 375ºF (191ºC). Spritz the air fryer basket with cooking spray. Place the cylinders in batches in the air fryer basket and spritz with cooking spray when your air fryer displays "READY" (select the cooking preset, and make minor adjustments according to your desired doneness.) and choose a shake reminder. Air fry for 10 minutes or until golden brown and fluffy. Flip them halfway through. Serve immediately.

## Coconut-Chocolate Macaroons

Prep time: 10 minutes | Cook time: 8 minutes per batch |Makes 24 macaroons

| | |
|---|---|
| 3 large egg whites, at room temperature | 4½ tablespoons unsweetened cocoa powder |
| ¼ teaspoon salt | 2¼ cups unsweetened shredded coconut |
| ¾ cup granulated white sugar | |

Preheat the air fryer to 375ºF (191ºC). Line the air fryer basket with parchment paper. Whisk the egg whites with salt in a large bowl with a hand mixer on high speed until stiff peaks form. Whisk in the sugar with the hand mixer on high speed until the mixture is thick. Mix in the cocoa powder and coconut. Scoop 2 tablespoons of the mixture and shape the mixture in a ball. Repeat with remaining mixture to make 24 balls in total. Arrange the balls in a single layer in the preheated air fryer and leave a little space between each two balls when your air fryer displays "READY" (select the cooking preset, and make minor adjustments according to your desired doneness.) and choose a shake reminder. You need to work in batches to avoid overcrowding. Air fry for 8 minutes or until the balls are golden brown. Serve immediately.

## Famous Western Cheddar Eggs

Prep time: 10 minutes | Cook time: 12 minutes | Serves 6

| | |
|---|---|
| 6 eggs | ¼ teaspoon paprika |
| ¾ cup milk | 6 ounces (170 g) cooked ham, diced |
| 1 ounce (28 g) cream cheese, softened Sea salt, to your liking | 1 onion, chopped |
| ¼ teaspoon ground black pepper | ⅓ cup Cheddar cheese, shredded |

Begin by preheating the Air Fryer to 360ºF (182ºC). Spritz the sides and bottom of a baking pan with cooking oil. In a mixing dish, whisk the eggs, milk, and cream cheese until pale. Add the spices, ham, and onion; stir until everything is well incorporated. Pour the mixture into the baking pan; top with the cheddar cheese. When your air fryer displays "READY" (select the cooking preset, and make minor adjustments according to your desired doneness.), choose a shake reminder. Bake in the preheated Air Fryer for 12 minutes. Serve warm and enjoy!

## Party Fruity Pancake Kabobs

Prep time: 15 minutes | Cook time: 4 minutes | Serves 4

**For the Pancakes:**

| | |
|---|---|
| 1 cup all-purpose flour | ½ cup milk |
| 1 teaspoon baking powder | ½ teaspoon vanilla extract |
| 1 tablespoon sugar | 2 tablespoons unsalted butter, melted |
| ¼ teaspoon salt | |
| 1 large egg, beaten | |

**For the Kabobs:**

| | |
|---|---|
| 1 banana, diced | ¼ cup maple syrup, for serving |
| 1 Granny Smith apples, diced | |

Preheat the air fryer to 230ºF (110ºC). Mix all ingredients for the pancakes until creamy and fluffy. Let it stand for 20 minutes. Spritz the Air Fryer baking pan with cooking spray. Drop the pancake batter on the pan with a small spoon. When your air fryer displays "READY" (select the cooking preset, and make minor adjustments according to your desired doneness.) and choose a shake reminder. Cook at 230ºF (110ºC) for 4 minutes or until golden brown. Repeat with the remaining batter. Tread the mini pancakes and the fruit onto bamboo skewers, alternating between the mini pancakes and fruit. Drizzle maple syrup all over the kabobs and serve immediately. Enjoy!

## Spanish-Inspired Bolitas de Queso

Prep time: 10 minutes | Cook time: 8 minutes | Serves 3

| | |
|---|---|
| ½ cup plain flour | crushed |
| 2 tablespoons cornstarch | ½ teaspoon pimentón |
| 2 eggs | 6 ounces (170 g) goat cheese, shredded |
| 1 garlic clove minced | 1 cup tortilla chips, crushed |
| ½ teaspoon red pepper flakes, | |

Preheat the air fryer to 390ºF (199ºC). In a mixing bowl, thoroughly combine all ingredients, except for the crushed tortilla chips. Shape the mixture into bite-sized balls. Roll your balls into the crushed tortilla chips and transfer them to a lightly greased cooking basket when your air fryer displays "READY" (select the cooking preset, and make minor adjustments according to your desired doneness.) and choose a shake reminder. Cook the balls at 390ºF (199ºC) for about 8 minutes, shaking the basket halfway through the cooking time to promote even cooking. Enjoy!

## Homemade Jacket Potatoes

Prep time: 5 minutes | Cook time: 23 minutes | Serves 4

| | |
|---|---|
| 1 pound (454 g) potatoes | 1 teaspoon dried rosemary |
| 2 garlic cloves, minced | 2 teaspoons butter, melted |
| Salt and black pepper, to taste | |

Preheat air fryer to 360ºF (182ºC). Prick the potatoes with a fork. Place them in the greased frying basket when your air fryer displays "READY" (select the cooking preset, and make minor adjustments according to your desired doneness.) and choose a shake reminder. Bake for 23 to 25 minutes, turning once halfway through. Remove and cut in half. Drizzle with melted butter and season with salt and black pepper. Sprinkle with rosemary and serve enjoy!.

## Hearty Whole Chicken Roast

Prep time: 10 minutes | Cook time: 1 hour | Serves 6

| | |
|---|---|
| 1 teaspoon salt | ½ teaspoon onion powder |
| 1 teaspoon Italian seasoning | 2 tablespoons olive oil, plus more as needed |
| ½ teaspoon freshly ground black pepper | 1 (4-pound / 1.8-kg) fryer chicken |
| ½ teaspoon paprika | |
| ½ teaspoon garlic powder | |

Preheat the air fryer to 360ºF (182ºC). Grease the air fryer basket lightly with olive oil. In a small bowl, mix the salt, Italian seasoning, pepper, paprika, garlic powder, and onion powder. Remove any giblets from the chicken. Pat the chicken dry thoroughly with paper towels, including the cavity. Brush the chicken all over with the olive oil and rub it with the seasoning mixture. Truss the chicken or tie the legs with butcher's twine. This will make it easier to flip the chicken during cooking. Put the chicken in the air fryer basket, breast-side down when your air fryer displays "READY" (select the cooking preset, and make minor adjustments according to your desired doneness.) and choose a shake reminder. Air fry for 30 minutes. Flip the chicken over and baste it with any drippings collected in the bottom drawer of the air fryer. Lightly brush the chicken with olive oil. Air fry for 20 minutes. Flip the chicken over one last time and air fry until a thermometer inserted into the thickest part of the thigh reaches at least 165ºF (74ºC) and it's crispy and golden, 10 more minutes. Continue to cook, checking every 5 minutes until the chicken reaches the correct internal temperature. Let the chicken rest for 10 minutes before carving and serving.

## Chili Onion Bhaji

**Prep time: 10 minutes | Cook time: 20 minutes | Serves 3**

1 egg, beaten
2 tablespoons olive oil
2 onions, sliced
1 green chili, deseeded and finely chopped

2 ounces (57 g) chickpea flour
1 ounce (28 g) all-purpose flour
Salt and black pepper, to taste
1 teaspoon cumin seeds
½ teaspoon ground turmeric

Preheat air fryer to 370ºF (188ºC). Place all ingredients, except for the onions, in a mixing dish; mix to combine well, adding a little water to the mixture. Once you've got a thick batter, add the onions; stir to coat well. When your air fryer displays "READY" (select the cooking preset, and make minor adjustments according to your desired doneness.) and choose a shake reminder. Cook in the preheated Air Fryer at 370ºF (188ºC) for 20 minutes flipping them halfway through the cooking time. Work in batches and transfer to a serving platter. Enjoy!

## Blistered Cherry Tomatoes

**Prep time: 5 minutes | Cook time: 10 minutes | Serves 4 to 6**

2 pounds (907 g) cherry tomatoes
2 tablespoons olive oil
2 teaspoons balsamic vinegar

½ teaspoon salt
½ teaspoon ground black pepper

Preheat the air fryer with a cake pan to 400ºF (204ºC). Toss the cherry tomatoes with olive oil in a large bowl to coat well. Pour the tomatoes in the cake pan when your air fryer displays "READY" (select the cooking preset, and make minor adjustments according to your desired doneness.) and choose a shake reminder. Air fry the cherry tomatoes for 10 minutes or until the tomatoes are blistered and lightly wilted. Shake the basket halfway through. Transfer the blistered tomatoes to a large bowl and toss with balsamic vinegar, salt, and black pepper before serving.

## Arancini Balls

**Prep time: 5 minutes | Cook time: 30 minutes | Makes 10 arancini**

⅔ cup raw white Arborio rice
2 teaspoons butter
½ teaspoon salt
1⅓ cups water
2 large eggs, well beaten

1¼ cups seasoned Italian-style dried breadcrumbs
10 ¾-inch semi-firm Mozzarella cubes
Cooking spray

Pour the rice, butter, salt, and water in a pot. Stir to mix well and bring a boil over medium-high heat. Keep stirring. Reduce the heat to low and cover the pot. Simmer for 20 minutes or until the rice is tender. Turn off the heat and let sit, covered, for 10 minutes, then open the lid and fluffy the rice with a fork. Allow to cool for 10 more minutes. Preheat the air fryer to 375ºF (191ºC). Pour the beaten eggs in a bowl, then pour the breadcrumbs in a separate bowl. Scoop 2 tablespoons of the cooked rice up and form it into a ball, then press the Mozzarella into the ball and wrap. Dredge the ball in the eggs first, then shake the excess off the dunk the ball in the breadcrumbs. Roll to coat evenly. Repeat to make 10 balls in total with remaining rice. Transfer the balls in the preheated air fryer and spritz with cooking spray when your air fryer displays "READY" (select the cooking preset, and make minor adjustments according to your desired doneness.) and choose a shake reminder. You need to work in batches to avoid overcrowding. Air fry for 10 minutes or until the balls are lightly browned and crispy. Remove the balls from the air fryer and allow to cool before serving.

## Banana Buttermilk Cake

**Prep time: 25 minutes | Cook time: 20 minutes | Serves 8**

1 cup plus 1 tablespoon all-purpose flour
¼ teaspoon baking soda
¾ teaspoon baking powder
¼ teaspoon salt
9½ tablespoons granulated white sugar

5 tablespoons butter, at room temperature
2½ small ripe bananas, peeled
2 large eggs
5 tablespoons buttermilk
1 teaspoon vanilla extract
Cooking spray

Preheat the air fryer to 325ºF (163ºC). Spritz a cake pan with cooking spray. Combine the flour, baking soda, baking powder, and salt in a large bowl. Stir to mix well. Beat the sugar and butter in a separate bowl with a hand mixer on medium speed for 3 minutes. Beat in the bananas, eggs, buttermilk, and vanilla extract into the sugar and butter mix with a hand mixer. Pour in the flour mixture and whip with hand mixer until sanity and smooth. Scrape the batter into the cake pan and level the batter with a spatula. Place the cake pan in the preheated air fryer when your air fryer displays "READY" (select the cooking preset, and make minor adjustments according to your desired doneness.) and choose a shake reminder. Bake for 20 minutes or until a toothpick inserted in the center comes out clean. Check the doneness during the last 5 minutes of the baking. Invert the cake on a cooling rack and allow to cool for 15 minutes before slicing to serve.

## Ritzy Honey Yeast Rolls

**Prep time: 10 minutes | Cook time: 20 minutes | Makes 8 rolls**

¼ cup whole milk, heated to 115ºF (46ºC) in the microwave
½ teaspoon active dry yeast
1 tablespoon honey
⅔ cup all-purpose flour, plus more for dusting

½ teaspoon kosher salt
2 tablespoons unsalted butter, at room temperature, plus more for greasing
Flaky sea salt, to taste

In a large bowl, whisk together the milk, yeast, and honey and let stand until foamy, about 10 minutes. Stir in the flour and salt until just combined. Stir in the butter until absorbed. Scrape the dough onto a lightly floured work surface and knead until smooth, about 6 minutes. Transfer the dough to a lightly greased bowl, cover loosely with a sheet of plastic wrap or a kitchen towel, and let sit until nearly doubled in size, about 1 hour. Uncover the dough, lightly press it down to expel the bubbles, then portion it into 8 equal pieces. Prep the work surface by wiping it clean with a damp paper towel (if there is flour on the work surface, it will prevent the dough from sticking lightly to the surface, which helps it form a ball). Roll each piece into a ball by cupping the palm of the hand around the dough against the work surface and moving the heel of the hand in a circular motion while using the thumb to contain the dough and tighten it into a perfectly round ball. Once all the balls are formed, nestle them side by side in the air fryer basket. Cover the rolls loosely with a kitchen towel or a sheet of plastic wrap and let sit until lightly risen and puffed, 20 to 30 minutes. Preheat the air fryer to 270ºF (132ºC). Uncover the rolls and gently brush with more butter, being careful not to press the rolls too hard. When your air fryer displays "READY" (select the cooking preset, and make minor adjustments according to your desired doneness.) and choose a shake reminder. Air fry until the rolls are light golden brown and fluffy, about 12 minutes. Remove the rolls from the air fryer and brush liberally with more butter, if you like, and sprinkle each roll with a pinch of sea salt. Serve warm.

## Holiday Smoked Beef Roast
**Prep time: 10 minutes | Cook time: 45 minutes | Serves 8**

2 pounds (907 g) roast beef, at room temperature
2 tablespoons extra-virgin olive oil
1 teaspoon sea salt flakes
1 teaspoon black pepper,
preferably freshly ground
1 teaspoon smoked paprika
A few dashes of liquid smoke
2 jalapeño peppers, thinly sliced

Preheat the air fryer to 330ºF (166ºC). Pat the roast dry using kitchen towels. Rub with extra-virgin olive oil and all seasonings along with liquid smoke. When your air fryer displays "READY" (select the cooking preset, and make minor adjustments according to your desired doneness.) and choose a shake reminder. Roast for 30 minutes in the preheated air fryer. Turn the roast over and roast for additional 15 minutes. Check for doneness using a meat thermometer and serve sprinkled with sliced jalapeños. Bon appétit!

## Yummy Snack Mix
**Prep time: 10 minutes | Cook time: 10 minutes | Serves 10**

½ cup honey
3 tablespoons butter, melted
1 teaspoon salt
2 cups sesame sticks
2 cup pumpkin seeds
2 cups granola
1 cup cashews
2 cups crispy corn puff cereal
2 cup mini pretzel crisps

In a bowl, combine the honey, butter, and salt. In another bowl, mix the sesame sticks, pumpkin seeds, granola, cashews, corn puff cereal, and pretzel crisps. Combine the contents of the two bowls. Preheat the air fryer to 370ºF (188ºC). Put the mixture in the air fryer basket when your air fryer displays "READY" (select the cooking preset, and make minor adjustments according to your desired doneness.) and choose a shake reminder. Air fry for 10 to 12 minutes to toast the snack mixture, shaking the basket frequently. Do this in two batches. Put the snack mix on a cookie sheet and allow it to cool fully. Serve immediately.

## Mushroom, Green Bean, and Onion Casserole
**Prep time: 10 minutes | Cook time: 15 minutes | Serves 4**

4 tablespoons unsalted butter
¼ cup diced yellow onion
½ cup chopped white mushrooms
½ cup heavy whipping cream
1 ounce (28 g) full-fat cream cheese
½ cup chicken broth
¼ teaspoon xanthan gum
1 pound (454 g) fresh green beans, edges trimmed
½ ounce (14 g) pork rinds, finely ground

In a medium skillet over medium heat, melt the butter. Sauté the onion and mushrooms until they become soft and fragrant, about 3 to 5 minutes. Add the heavy whipping cream, cream cheese, and broth to the pan. Whisk until smooth. Bring to a boil and then reduce to a simmer. Sprinkle the xanthan gum into the pan and remove from heat. Preheat the air fryer to 320ºF (160ºC). Chop the green beans into 2-inch pieces and place into a baking dish. Pour the sauce mixture over them and stir until coated. Top the dish with ground pork rinds. Put into the air fryer basket when your air fryer displays "READY" (select the cooking preset, and make minor adjustments according to your desired doneness.) and choose a shake reminder. Bake for 15 minutes. Top will be golden and green beans fork-tender when fully cooked. Serve warm.

## Dill Pickles with Buttermilk Dressing
**Prep time: 45 minutes | Cook time: 8 minutes | Serves 6 to 8**

**Buttermilk Dressing:**
¼ cup buttermilk
¼ cup chopped scallions
¾ cup mayonnaise
½ cup sour cream
½ teaspoon cayenne pepper
½ teaspoon onion powder
½ teaspoon garlic powder
1 tablespoon chopped chives
2 tablespoons chopped fresh dill
Kosher salt and ground black pepper, to taste
**Fried Dill Pickles:**
¾ cup all-purpose flour
1 (2-pound / 907-g) jar kosher dill pickles, cut into 4 spears, drained
2½ cups panko breadcrumbs
2 eggs, beaten with 2 tablespoons water
Kosher salt and ground black pepper, to taste
Cooking spray

Preheat the air fryer to 400ºF (204ºC). Combine the ingredients for the dressing in a bowl. Stir to mix well. Wrap the bowl in plastic and refrigerate for 30 minutes or until ready to serve. Pour the flour in a bowl and sprinkle with salt and ground black pepper. Stir to mix well. Put the breadcrumbs in a separate bowl. Pour the beaten eggs in a third bowl. Dredge the pickle spears in the flour, then into the eggs, and then into the panko to coat well. Shake the excess off. Arrange the pickle spears in a single layer in the preheated air fryer and spritz with cooking spray when your air fryer displays "READY" (select the cooking preset, and make minor adjustments according to your desired doneness.) and choose a shake reminder. Air fry for 8 minutes. Flip the pickle spears halfway through. Serve the pickle spears with buttermilk dressing.

## Cinnamon-Brown Sugar Rolls with Cream Glaze
**Prep time: 15 minutes | Cook time: 10 minutes | Serves 8**

1 pound (454 g) frozen bread dough, thawed
2 tablespoons melted butter
**Cream Glaze:**
4 ounces (113 g) softened cream cheese
½ teaspoon vanilla extract
1½ tablespoons cinnamon
¾ cup brown sugar
Cooking spray
2 tablespoons melted butter
1¼ cups powdered erythritol

Place the bread dough on a clean work surface, then roll the dough out into a rectangle with a rolling pin. Brush the top of the dough with melted butter and leave 1-inch edges uncovered. Combine the cinnamon and sugar in a small bowl, then sprinkle the dough with the cinnamon mixture. Roll the dough over tightly, then cut the dough log into 8 portions. Wrap the portions in plastic, better separately, and let sit to rise for 1 or 2 hours. Meanwhile, combine the ingredients for the glaze in a separate small bowl. Stir to mix well. Preheat the air fryer to 350ºF (177ºC). Spritz the air fryer basket with cooking spray. Transfer the risen rolls to the preheated air fryer when your air fryer displays "READY" (select the cooking preset, and make minor adjustments according to your desired doneness.) and choose a shake reminder. You may need to work in batches to avoid overcrowding. Air fry for 5 minutes or until golden brown. Flip the rolls halfway through. Serve the rolls with the glaze.

## Pork and Veggie Egg Rolls

**Prep time: 40 minutes | Cook time: 1 hour 30 minutes | Makes 25 egg rolls**

**For the Egg Rolls:**

| | |
|---|---|
| 1 tablespoon mirin | 4 cups shredded Napa cabbage |
| 3 tablespoons soy sauce, divided | ¼ cup sliced scallions |
| 1 pound (454 g) ground pork | 1 teaspoon grated fresh ginger |
| 3 tablespoons vegetable oil, plus more for brushing | 1 clove garlic, minced |
| 5 ounces (142 g) shiitake mushrooms, minced | ¼ teaspoon cornstarch |
| | 1 (1-pound / 454-g) package frozen egg roll wrappers, thawed |

**For the Dipping Sauce:**

| | |
|---|---|
| 1 scallion, white and light green parts only, sliced | Pinch sesame seeds |
| ¼ cup rice vinegar | Pinch red pepper flakes |
| ¼ cup soy sauce | 1 teaspoon granulated sugar |

Combine the mirin and 1 tablespoon of soy sauce in a large bowl. Stir to mix well. Dunk the ground pork in the mixture and stir to mix well. Wrap the bowl in plastic and marinate in the refrigerator for at least 10 minutes. Heat the vegetable oil in a nonstick skillet over medium-high heat until shimmering. Add the mushrooms, cabbage, and scallions and sauté for 5 minutes or until tender. Add the marinated meat, ginger, garlic, and remaining 2 tablespoons of soy sauce. Sauté for 3 minutes or until the pork is lightly browned. Turn off the heat and allow to cool until ready to use. Preheat the air fryer to 400ºF (204ºC). Line a baking pan with parchment paper. Put the cornstarch in a small bowl and pour in enough water to dissolve the cornstarch. Put the bowl alongside a clean work surface. Put the egg roll wrappers in the preheated air fryer when your air fryer displays "READY" (select the cooking preset, and make minor adjustments according to your desired doneness.) and choose a shake reminder. Air fry in batches for 15 minutes or until golden brown. Flip the wrappers halfway through the cooking time. Remove the egg roll wrappers from the air fryer and allow to cool for 10 minutes or until you can handle them with your hands. Lay out one egg roll wrapper on the work surface with a corner pointed toward you. Place 2 tablespoons of the pork mixture on the egg roll wrapper and fold corner up over the mixture. Fold left and right corners toward the center and continue to roll. Brush a bit of the dissolved cornstarch on the last corner to help seal the egg wrapper. Arrange the rolls on the baking pan when making the remaining rolls, then brush the rolls with more vegetable oil. Arrange the rolls in the air fryer. Air fry in batches for 10 minutes or until the rolls are well browned and crispy. Meanwhile, combine the ingredients for the dipping sauce in a small bowl. Stir to mix well. Serve the rolls with the dipping sauce immediately.

## Chocolate Glazed Custard Donut Holes

**Prep time: 1 hour 50 minutes | Cook time: 4 minutes per batch | Makes 24 donut holes**

**Dough:**

| | |
|---|---|
| 1½ cups bread flour | 2 tablespoons butter, melted |
| 2 egg yolks | 1 tablespoon sugar |
| 1 teaspoon active dry yeast | ¼ teaspoon salt |
| ½ cup warm milk | Cooking spray |
| ½ teaspoon pure vanilla extract | |

**Custard Filling:**

| | |
|---|---|
| 1 (3.4-ounce / 96-g) box French vanilla instant pudding mix | Chocolate Glaze: |
| ¼ cup heavy cream | ⅓ cup heavy cream |
| ¾ cup whole milk | 1 cup chocolate chips |

**Special Equipment:**
A pastry bag with a long tip

Combine the ingredients for the dough in a food processor, then pulse until a satiny dough ball forms. Transfer the dough on a lightly floured work surface, then knead for 2 minutes by hand and shape the dough back to a ball. Spritz a large bowl with cooking spray, then transfer the dough ball into the bowl. Wrap the bowl in plastic and let it rise for 1½ hours or until it doubled in size. Transfer the risen dough on a floured work surface, then shape it into a 24-inch long log. Cut the log into 24 parts and shape each part into a ball. Transfer the balls on two or three baking sheets and let sit to rise for 30 more minutes. Preheat the air fryer to 400ºF (204ºC). Arrange the baking sheets in the air fryer when your air fryer displays "READY" (select the cooking preset, and make minor adjustments according to your desired doneness.) and choose a shake reminder. You need to work in batches to avoid overcrowding. Spritz the balls with cooking spray. Bake for 4 minutes or until golden brown. Flip the balls halfway through. Meanwhile, combine the ingredients for the filling in a large bowl and whisk for 2 minutes with a hand mixer until well combined. Pour the heavy cream in a saucepan, then bring to a boil. Put the chocolate chips in a small bowl and pour in the boiled heavy cream immediately. Mix until the chocolate chips are melted and the mixture is smooth. Transfer the baked donut holes to a large plate, then pierce a hole into each donut hole and lightly hollow them. Pour the filling in a pastry bag with a long tip and gently squeeze the filling into the donut holes. Then top the donut holes with chocolate glaze. Allow to sit for 10 minutes, then serve.

## Chocolate Cake

**Prep time: 20 minutes | Cook time: 20 minutes | Serves 8**

| | |
|---|---|
| 1 cup all-purpose flour | ⅔ cup buttermilk |
| ⅔ cup granulated white sugar | 2 tablespoons plus 2 teaspoons vegetable oil |
| ¼ cup unsweetened cocoa powder | 1 teaspoon vanilla extract |
| ¾ teaspoon baking soda | Cooking spray |
| ¼ teaspoon salt | |

Preheat the air fryer to 325ºF (163ºC). Spritz a cake pan with cooking spray. Combine the flour, cocoa powder, baking soda, sugar, and salt in a large bowl. Stir to mix well. Mix in the buttermilk, vanilla, and vegetable oil. Keep stirring until it forms a grainy and thick dough. Scrape the chocolate batter from the bowl and transfer to the cake pan, level the batter in an even layer with a spatula. Place the cake pan in the preheated air fryer when your air fryer displays "READY" (select the cooking preset, and make minor adjustments according to your desired doneness.) and choose a shake reminder. Bake for 20 minutes or until a toothpick inserted in the center comes out clean. Check the doneness during the last 5 minutes of the baking. Invert the cake on a cooling rack and allow to cool for 15 minutes before slicing to serve.

# Chapter 13 Fast and Easy Everyday Favorites

## Farmer's Deviled Eggs

**Prep time: 10 minutes | Cook time: 21 minutes | Serves 3**

6 eggs
6 slices bacon
2 tablespoons mayonnaise
1 teaspoon hot sauce
½ teaspoon Worcestershire sauce

2 tablespoons green onions, chopped
1 tablespoon pickle relish
Salt and ground black pepper, to taste
1 teaspoon smoked paprika

Preheat the air fryer to 270ºF (132ºC). Place the wire rack in the Air Fryer basket; lower the eggs onto the wire rack when your air fryer displays "READY" (select the cooking preset, and make minor adjustments according to your desired doneness.) and choose a shake reminder. Cook at 270ºF (132ºC) for 15 minutes. Transfer them to an ice-cold water bath to stop the cooking. Peel the eggs under cold running water; slice them into halves. Cook the bacon at 400ºF (204ºC) for 3 minutes; flip the bacon over and cook an additional 3 minutes; chop the bacon and reserve. Mash the egg yolks with the mayo, hot sauce, Worcestershire sauce, green onions, pickle relish, salt, and black pepper; add the reserved bacon and spoon the yolk mixture into the egg whites. Garnish with smoked paprika. Enjoy!

## Butternut Squash with Hazelnuts

**Prep time: 10 minutes | Cook time: 20 minutes | Makes 3 cups**

2 tablespoons whole hazelnuts
3 cups butternut squash, peeled, deseeded, and cubed
¼ teaspoon kosher salt

¼ teaspoon freshly ground black pepper
2 teaspoons olive oil
Cooking spray

Preheat the air fryer to 300ºF (149ºC). Spritz the air fryer basket with cooking spray. Arrange the hazelnuts in the preheated air fryer. Air fry for 3 minutes or until soft. Chopped the hazelnuts roughly and transfer to a small bowl. Set aside. Set the air fryer temperature to 360ºF (182ºC). Spritz with cooking spray. Put the butternut squash in a large bowl, then sprinkle with salt and pepper and drizzle with olive oil. Toss to coat well. Transfer the squash in the air fryer when your air fryer displays "READY" (select the cooking preset, and make minor adjustments according to your desired doneness.) and choose a shake reminder. Air fry for 20 minutes or until the squash is soft. Shake the basket halfway through the frying time. When the frying is complete, transfer the squash onto a plate and sprinkle with chopped hazelnuts before serving.

## Speedy Air Fried Shishito Peppers

**Prep time: 5 minutes | Cook time: 5 minutes | Serves 4**

½ pound (227 g) shishito peppers (about 24)
1 tablespoon olive oil

Coarse sea salt, to taste
Lemon wedges, for serving
Cooking spray

Preheat the air fryer to 400ºF (204ºC). Spritz the air fryer basket with cooking spray. Toss the peppers with olive oil in a large bowl to coat well. Arrange the peppers in the preheated air fryer when your air fryer displays "READY" (select the cooking preset, and make minor adjustments according to your desired doneness.) and choose a shake reminder. Air fryer for 5 minutes or until blistered and lightly charred. Shake the basket and sprinkle the peppers with salt halfway through the cooking time. Transfer the peppers onto a plate and squeeze the lemon wedges on top before serving.

## Corn Tortilla Chips

**Prep time: 5 minutes | Cook time: 10 minutes | Serves 4**

4 six-inch corn tortillas, cut in half and slice into thirds
1 tablespoon canola oil

¼ teaspoon kosher salt
Cooking spray

Preheat the air fryer to 360ºF (182ºC). Spritz the air fryer basket with cooking spray. On a clean work surface, brush the tortilla chips with canola oil, then transfer the chips in the preheated air fryer when your air fryer displays "READY" (select the cooking preset, and make minor adjustments according to your desired doneness.) and choose a shake reminder. Air fry for 10 minutes or until crunchy and lightly browned. Shake the basket and sprinkle with salt halfway through the cooking time. Transfer the chips onto a plate lined with paper towels. Serve immediately.

## Air-Fried Zucchini

**Prep time: 5 minutes | Cook time: 20 minutes | Serves 4**

1 medium zucchini, cut into 48 sticks
¼ cup seasoned breadcrumbs

1 tablespoon melted buttery spread
Cooking spray

Preheat the air fryer to 360ºF (182ºC). Spritz the air fryer basket with cooking spray and set aside. In 2 different shallow bowls, add the seasoned breadcrumbs and the buttery spread. One by one, dredge the zucchini sticks into the buttery spread, then roll in the breadcrumbs to coat evenly. Arrange the crusted sticks on a plate. Place the zucchini sticks in the prepared air fryer basket when your air fryer displays "READY" (select the cooking preset, and make minor adjustments according to your desired doneness.) and choose a shake reminder. Work in two batches to avoid overcrowding. Air fry for 10 minutes, or until golden brown and crispy. Shake the basket halfway through to cook evenly. When the cooking time is over, transfer the fries to a wire rack. Rest for 5 minutes and serve warm.

## Lime Avocado Wedge Fries

**Prep time: 10 minutes | Cook time: 8 minutes | Makes 12 fries**

1 cup all-purpose flour
3 tablespoons lime juice
¾ cup orange juice
1¼ cups plain dried breadcrumbs
1 cup yellow cornmeal

1½ tablespoons chile powder
2 large Hass avocados, peeled, pitted, and cut into wedges
Coarse sea salt, to taste
Cooking spray

Preheat the air fryer to 400ºF (204ºC). Spritz the air fryer basket with cooking spray. Pour the flour in a bowl. Mix the lime juice with orange juice in a second bowl. Combine the breadcrumbs, cornmeal, and chile powder in a third bowl. Dip the avocado wedges in the bowl of flour to coat well, then dredge the wedges into the bowl of juice mixture, and then dunk the wedges in the breadcrumbs mixture. Shake the excess off. Transfer the well-coat avocado wedges in a single layer in the preheated air fryer when your air fryer displays "READY" (select the cooking preset, and make minor adjustments according to your desired doneness.) and choose a shake reminder. Spritz with cooking spray. Air fry for 8 minutes or until the avocado wedges are tender and crispy. Shake the basket and sprinkle the avocado with salt halfway through the cooking time. Serve immediately.

## Beer Battered Onion Rings

**Prep time: 10 minutes | Cook time: 16 minutes | Serves 2 to 4**

⅔ cup all-purpose flour
1 teaspoon paprika
½ teaspoon baking soda
1 teaspoon salt
½ teaspoon freshly ground
black pepper
1 egg, beaten

¾ cup beer
1½ cups breadcrumbs
1 tablespoons olive oil
1 large Vidalia onion, peeled
and sliced into ½-inch rings
Cooking spray

Preheat the air fryer to 360ºF (182ºC). Spritz the air fryer basket with cooking spray. Combine the flour, paprika, baking soda, salt, and ground black pepper in a bowl. Stir to mix well. Combine the egg and beer in a separate bowl. Stir to mix well. Make a well in the center of the flour mixture, then pour the egg mixture in the well. Stir to mix everything well. Pour the breadcrumbs and olive oil in a shallow plate. Stir to mix well. Dredge the onion rings gently into the flour and egg mixture, then shake the excess off and put into the plate of breadcrumbs. Flip to coat the both sides well. Arrange the onion rings in the preheated air fryer when your air fryer displays "READY" (select the cooking preset, and make minor adjustments according to your desired doneness.) and choose a shake reminder. Air fry in batches for 16 minutes or until golden brown and crunchy. Flip the rings and put the bottom rings to the top halfway through. Serve immediately.

## Panko-Crusted Corn on the Cob

**Prep time: 10 minutes | Cook time: 10 minutes | Serves 4**

2 tablespoons mayonnaise
2 teaspoons minced garlic
½ teaspoon sea salt
1 cup panko breadcrumbs

4 (4-inch length) ears corn on
the cob, husk and silk removed
Cooking spray

Preheat the air fryer to 400ºF (204ºC). Spritz the air fryer basket with cooking spray. Combine the mayo, garlic, and salt in a bowl. Stir to mix well. Pour the panko on a plate. Brush the corn on the cob with mayo mixture, then roll the cob in the breadcrumbs and press to coat well. Transfer the corn on the cob in the preheated air fryer and spritz with cooking spray when your air fryer displays "READY" (select the cooking preset, and make minor adjustments according to your desired doneness.) and choose a shake reminder. Air fry for 10 minutes or until the corn kernels on the cob are almost browned. Flip the corn on the cob at least three times during the cooking. Serve immediately.

## Candied Cumin Pecans

**Prep time: 5 minutes | Cook time: 10 minutes | Makes 4 cups**

2 egg whites
1 tablespoon cumin
2 teaspoons smoked paprika
½ cup brown sugar

2 teaspoons kosher salt
1 pound (454 g) pecan halves
Cooking spray

Preheat the air fryer to 300ºF (149ºC). Spritz the air fryer basket with cooking spray. Combine the egg whites, cumin, paprika, sugar, and salt in a large bowl. Stir to mix well. Add the pecans to the bowl and toss to coat well. Transfer the pecans into the preheated air fryer when your air fryer displays "READY" (select the cooking preset, and make minor adjustments according to your desired doneness.) and choose a shake reminder. Air fry in batches for 10 minutes or until the pecans are lightly caramelized. Shake the basket at least two times during the cooking. Serve immediately.

## Cauliflower Parmesan and Chives Fritters

**Prep time: 10 minutes | Cook time: 20 minutes | Serves 6**

2 cups cooked cauliflower
1 cup panko breadcrumbs
1 large egg, beaten
½ cup grated Parmesan cheese

1 tablespoon chopped fresh
chives
Cooking spray

Preheat the air fryer to 390ºF (199ºC). Spritz the air fryer basket with cooking spray. Put the cauliflower, panko breadcrumbs, egg, Parmesan, and chives in a food processor, then pulse to lightly mash and combine the mixture until chunky and thick. Shape the mixture into 6 flat patties, then arrange 3 of them in the preheated air fryer and spritz with cooking spray. When your air fryer displays "READY" (select the cooking preset, and make minor adjustments according to your desired doneness.) and choose a shake reminder. Air fry for 8 minutes or until the patties are crispy and golden brown. Flip the patties halfway through the cooking time. Repeat with the remaining patties. When the air frying is complete, serve the fritters immediately.

## Cheddar Jalapeño Cornbread

**Prep time: 10 minutes | Cook time: 20 minutes | Serves 8**

⅔ cup cornmeal
⅓ cup all-purpose flour
¾ teaspoon baking powder
2 tablespoons buttery spread,
melted
½ teaspoon kosher salt
1 tablespoon granulated sugar

¾ cup whole milk
1 large egg, beaten
1 jalapeño pepper, thinly sliced
⅓ cup shredded sharp Cheddar
cheese
Cooking spray

Preheat the air fryer to 300ºF (149ºC). Spritz the air fryer basket with cooking spray. Combine all the ingredients in a large bowl. Stir to mix well. Pour the mixture in a baking pan. Arrange the pan in the preheated air fryer when your air fryer displays "READY" (select the cooking preset, and make minor adjustments according to your desired doneness.) and choose a shake reminder. Bake for 20 minutes or until a toothpick inserted in the center of the bread comes out clean. When the cooking is complete, remove the baking pan from the air fryer and allow the bread to cool for a few minutes before slicing to serve.

## Maple Bacon Pinwheels

**Prep time: 10 minutes | Cook time: 10 minutes | Makes 8 pinwheels**

1 sheet puff pastry
2 tablespoons maple syrup
¼ cup brown sugar

8 slices bacon
Ground black pepper, to taste
Cooking spray

Preheat the air fryer to 360ºF (182ºC). Spritz the air fryer basket with cooking spray. Roll the puff pastry into a 10-inch square with a rolling pin on a clean work surface, then cut the pastry into 8 strips. Brush the strips with maple syrup and sprinkle with sugar, leaving a 1-inch far end uncovered. Arrange each slice of bacon on each strip, leaving a ⅛-inch length of bacon hang over the end close to you. Sprinkle with black pepper. From the end close to you, roll the strips into pinwheels, then dab the uncovered end with water and seal the rolls. Arrange the pinwheels in the preheated air fryer and spritz with cooking spray when your air fryer displays "READY" (select the cooking preset, and make minor adjustments according to your desired doneness.) and choose a shake reminder. Air fry for 10 minutes or until golden brown. Flip the pinwheels halfway through. Serve immediately.

## Golden Latkes

**Prep time: 15 minutes | Cook time: 10 minutes | Makes 4 latkes**

1 egg
2 tablespoons all-purpose flour
2 medium potatoes, peeled and shredded, rinsed and drained
¼ teaspoon granulated garlic
½ teaspoon salt
Cooking spray

Preheat the air fryer to 380ºF (193ºC). Spritz the air fryer basket with cooking spray. Whisk together the egg, flour, potatoes, garlic, and salt in a large bowl. Stir to mix well. Divide the mixture into four parts, then flatten them into four circles. Arrange the circles into the preheated air fryer when your air fryer displays "READY" (select the cooking preset, and make minor adjustments according to your desired doneness.) and choose a shake reminder. Spritz the circles with cooking spray, then air fry for 10 minutes or until golden brown and crispy. Flip the latkes halfway through. Serve immediately.

## Mexican Street Corn with Cheese

**Prep time: 5 minutes | Cook time: 7 minutes | Serves 4**

4 medium ears corn, husked
Cooking spray
2 tablespoons mayonnaise
1 tablespoon fresh lime juice
½ teaspoon ancho chile powder
¼ teaspoon kosher salt
2 ounces (57 g) crumbled Cotija or feta cheese
2 tablespoons chopped fresh cilantro

Preheat the air fryer to 375ºF (191ºC). Spritz the corn with cooking spray. Working in batches, arrange the ears of corn in the air fryer basket in a single layer when your air fryer displays "READY" (select the cooking preset, and make minor adjustments according to your desired doneness.) and choose a shake reminder. Air fry for about 7 minutes, flipping halfway, until the kernels are tender when pierced with a paring knife. When cool enough to handle, cut the corn kernels off the cob. In a large bowl, mix together mayonnaise, lime juice, ancho powder, and salt. Add the corn kernels and mix to combine. Transfer to a serving dish and top with the Cotija and cilantro. Serve immediately.

## Rosemary Purple Potato Chips

**Prep time: 10 minutes | Cook time: 9 to 14 minutes | Serves 6**

1 cup Greek yogurt
2 chipotle chiles, minced
2 tablespoons adobo sauce
1 teaspoon paprika
1 tablespoon lemon juice
10 purple fingerling potatoes
1 teaspoon olive oil
2 teaspoons minced fresh rosemary leaves
⅛ teaspoon cayenne pepper
¼ teaspoon coarse sea salt

Preheat the air fryer to 400ºF (204ºC). In a medium bowl, combine the yogurt, minced chiles, adobo sauce, paprika, and lemon juice. Mix well and refrigerate. Wash the potatoes and dry them with paper towels. Slice the potatoes lengthwise, as thinly as possible. You can use a mandoline, a vegetable peeler, or a very sharp knife. Combine the potato slices in a medium bowl and drizzle with the olive oil; toss to coat. When your air fryer displays "READY" (select the cooking preset, and make minor adjustments according to your desired doneness.) and choose a shake reminder. Air fry the chips, in batches, in the air fryer basket, for 9 to 14 minutes. Use tongs to gently rearrange the chips halfway during cooking time. Sprinkle the chips with the rosemary, cayenne pepper, and sea salt. Serve with the chipotle sauce for dipping.

## Famous Poutine

**Prep time: 15 minutes | Cook time: 25 minutes | Serves 2**

2 russet potatoes, scrubbed and cut into ½-inch sticks
2 teaspoons vegetable oil
2 tablespoons butter
¼ onion, minced
¼ teaspoon dried thyme
1 clove garlic, smashed
3 tablespoons all-purpose flour
1 teaspoon tomato paste
1½ cups beef stock
2 teaspoons Worcestershire sauce
Salt and freshly ground black pepper, to taste
⅔ cup chopped string cheese

Bring a pot of water to a boil, then put in the potato sticks and blanch for 4 minutes. Preheat the air fryer to 400ºF (204ºC). Drain the potato sticks and rinse under running cold water, then pat dry with paper towels. Transfer the sticks in a large bowl and drizzle with vegetable oil. Toss to coat well. Place the potato sticks in the preheated air fryer when your air fryer displays "READY" (select the cooking preset, and make minor adjustments according to your desired doneness.) and choose a shake reminder. Air fry for 25 minutes or until the sticks are golden brown. Shake the basket at least three times during the frying. Meanwhile, make the gravy: Heat the butter in a saucepan over medium heat until melted. Add the onion, thyme, and garlic and sauté for 5 minutes or until the onion is translucent. Add the flour and sauté for an additional 2 minutes. Pour in the tomato paste and beef stock and cook for 1 more minute or until lightly thickened. Drizzle the gravy with Worcestershire sauce and sprinkle with salt and ground black pepper. Reduce the heat to low to keep the gravy warm until ready to serve. Transfer the fried potato sticks onto a plate, then sprinkle with salt and ground black pepper. Scatter with string cheese and pour the gravy over. Serve warm.

## Corn-Buttermilk Fritters

**Prep time: 15 minutes | Cook time: 8 minutes | Serves 6**

1 cup self-rising flour
1 tablespoon sugar
1 teaspoon salt
1 large egg, lightly beaten
¼ cup buttermilk
¾ cup corn kernels
¼ cup minced onion
Cooking spray

Preheat the air fryer to 350ºF (177ºC). Line the air fryer basket with parchment paper. In a medium bowl, whisk the flour, sugar, and salt until blended. Stir in the egg and buttermilk. Add the corn and minced onion. Mix well. Shape the corn fritter batter into 12 balls. Place the fritters on the parchment and spritz with oil when your air fryer displays "READY" (select the cooking preset, and make minor adjustments according to your desired doneness.) and choose a shake reminder. Bake for 4 minutes. Flip the fritters, spritz them with oil, and bake for 4 minutes more until firm and lightly browned. Serve immediately.

## Cinnamon Chickpeas

**Prep time: 10 minutes | Cook time: 10 minutes | Serves 2**

1 tablespoon cinnamon
1 tablespoon sugar
1 cup chickpeas, soaked in
water overnight, rinsed and drained

Preheat air fryer to 390ºF (199ºC). Combine the cinnamon and sugar in a bowl. Stir to mix well. Add the chickpeas to the bowl, then toss to coat well. Pour the chickpeas in the preheated air fryer when your air fryer displays "READY" (select the cooking preset, and make minor adjustments according to your desired doneness.) and choose a shake reminder. Air fry for 10 minutes or until golden brown and crispy. Shake the basket periodically. Serve immediately.

## Panko-Crusted Green Tomatoes Slices

**Prep time: 10 minutes | Cook time: 8 minutes | Makes 12 slices**

½ cup all-purpose flour
1 egg
½ cup buttermilk
1 cup cornmeal
1 cup panko
2 green tomatoes, cut into

¼-inch-thick slices, patted dry
½ teaspoon salt
½ teaspoon ground black pepper
Cooking spray

Preheat the air fryer to 400ºF (204ºC). Line the air fryer basket with parchment paper. Pour the flour in a bowl. Whisk the egg and buttermilk in a second bowl. Combine the cornmeal and panko in a third bowl. Dredge the tomato slices in the bowl of flour first, then into the egg mixture, and then dunk the slices into the cornmeal mixture. Shake the excess off. Transfer the well-coated tomato slices in the preheated air fryer and sprinkle with salt and ground black pepper when your air fryer displays "READY" (select the cooking preset, and make minor adjustments according to your desired doneness.) and choose a shake reminder. Spritz the tomato slices with cooking spray. Air fry for 8 minutes or until crispy and lightly browned. Flip the slices halfway through the cooking time. Serve immediately.

## Kale Chips

**Prep time: 5 minutes | Cook time: 5 minutes | Serves 2**

4 medium kale leaves, about 1 ounce (28 g) each, stems removed, tear the leaves in

thirds
2 teaspoons soy sauce
2 teaspoons olive oil

Preheat the air fryer to 400ºF (204ºC). Toss the kale leaves with soy sauce and olive oil in a large bowl to coat well. Place the leaves in the preheated air fryer when your air fryer displays "READY" (select the cooking preset, and make minor adjustments according to your desired doneness.) and choose a shake reminder. Air fry for 5 minutes or until the kale leaves are crispy. Flip the leaves with tongs gently halfway through. Serve immediately.

## Potato Chips with Tangy Lemony Cream

**Prep time: 20 minutes | Cook time: 15 minutes | Serves 2 to 4**

2 large russet potatoes, sliced into ⅛-inch slices, rinsed
Sea salt and freshly ground
**Lemony Cream Dip:**
½ cup sour cream
¼ teaspoon lemon juice
2 scallions, white part only, minced

black pepper, to taste
Cooking spray

1 tablespoon olive oil
¼ teaspoon salt
Freshly ground black pepper, to taste

Soak the potato slices in water for 10 minutes, then pat dry with paper towels. Preheat the air fryer to 300ºF (149ºC). Transfer the potato slices in the preheated air fryer when your air fryer displays "READY" (select the cooking preset, and make minor adjustments according to your desired doneness.) and choose a shake reminder. Spritz the slices with cooking spray. You may need to work in batches to avoid overcrowding. Air fry for 15 minutes or until crispy and golden brown. Shake the basket periodically. Sprinkle with salt and ground black pepper in the last minute. Meanwhile, combine the ingredients for the dip in a small bowl. Stir to mix well. Serve the potato chips immediately with the dip.

## Crunchy Okra Slices

**Prep time: 5 minutes | Cook time: 8 to 10 minutes | Serves 4**

1 cup self-rising yellow cornmeal
1 teaspoon Italian-style seasoning
1 teaspoon paprika
1 teaspoon salt

½ teaspoon freshly ground black pepper
2 large eggs, beaten
2 cups okra slices
Cooking spray

Preheat the air fryer to 400ºF (204ºC). Line the air fryer basket with parchment paper. In a shallow bowl, whisk the cornmeal, Italian-style seasoning, paprika, salt, and pepper until blended. Place the beaten eggs in a second shallow bowl. Add the okra to the beaten egg and stir to coat. Add the egg and okra mixture to the cornmeal mixture and stir until coated. Place the okra on the parchment and spritz it with oil when your air fryer displays "READY" (select the cooking preset, and make minor adjustments according to your desired doneness.) and choose a shake reminder. Air fry for 4 minutes. Shake the basket, spritz the okra with oil, and air fry for 4 to 6 minutes more until lightly browned and crispy. Serve immediately.

## Air-Fried Edamame

**Prep time: 5 minutes | Cook time: 7 minutes | Serves 6**

1½ pounds (680 g) unshelled edamame

2 tablespoons olive oil
1 teaspoon sea salt

Preheat the air fryer to 400ºF (204ºC). Place the edamame in a large bowl, then drizzle with olive oil. Toss to coat well. Transfer the edamame to the preheated air fryer when your air fryer displays "READY" (select the cooking preset, and make minor adjustments according to your desired doneness.) and choose a shake reminder. Cook for 7 minutes or until tender and warmed through. Shake the basket at least three times during the cooking. Transfer the cooked edamame onto a plate and sprinkle with salt. Toss to combine well and set aside for 3 minutes to infuse before serving.

## Avocado Fries with Pomegranate Molasses

**Prep time: 5 minutes | Cook time: 7 to 8 minutes | Serves 4**

1 cup panko bread crumbs
1 teaspoon kosher salt, plus more for sprinkling
1 teaspoon garlic powder
½ teaspoon cayenne pepper
2 ripe but firm avocados

1 egg, beaten with 1 tablespoon water
Cooking spray
Pomegranate molasses, for serving

Preheat the air fryer to 375ºF (191ºC). Whisk together the panko, salt, and spices on a plate. Cut each avocado in half and remove the pit. Cut each avocado half into 4 slices and scoop the slices out with a large spoon, taking care to keep the slices intact. Dip each avocado slice in the egg wash and then dredge it in the panko. Place the breaded avocado slices on a plate. Working in 2 batches, arrange half of the avocado slices in a single layer in the air fryer basket when your air fryer displays "READY" (select the cooking preset, and make minor adjustments according to your desired doneness.) and choose a shake reminder. Spray lightly with oil. Bake the slices for 7 to 8 minutes, turning once halfway through. Remove the cooked slices to a platter and repeat with the remaining avocado slices. Sprinkle the warm avocado slices with salt and drizzle with pomegranate molasses. Serve immediately.

## Cinnamon Toast

**Prep time: 5 minutes | Cook time: 20 minutes | Serves 6**

1½ teaspoons cinnamon
1½ teaspoons vanilla extract
½ cup sugar
2 teaspoons ground black

pepper
2 tablespoons melted coconut oil
12 slices whole wheat bread

Preheat the air fryer to 400ºF (204ºC). Combine all the ingredients, except for the bread, in a large bowl. Stir to mix well. Dunk the bread in the bowl of mixture gently to coat and infuse well. Shake the excess off. Arrange the bread slices in the preheated air fryer when your air fryer displays "READY" (select the cooking preset, and make minor adjustments according to your desired doneness.) and choose a shake reminder. Air fry for 5 minutes or until golden brown. Flip the bread halfway through. You may need to cook in batches to avoid overcrowding. Remove the bread slices from the air fryer and slice to serve.

## Queso Fundido with Chorizo

**Prep time: 10 minutes | Cook time: 25 minutes | Serves 4**

4 ounces (113 g) fresh Mexican chorizo, casings removed
1 medium onion, chopped
3 cloves garlic, minced
1 cup chopped tomato
2 jalapeños, deseeded and diced

2 teaspoons ground cumin
2 cups shredded Oaxaca or Mozzarella cheese
½ cup half-and-half
Celery sticks or tortilla chips, for serving

Preheat the air fryer to 400ºF (204ºC). In a baking pan, combine the chorizo, onion, garlic, tomato, jalapeños, and cumin. Stir to combine. Place the pan in the air fryer basket when your air fryer displays "READY" (select the cooking preset, and make minor adjustments according to your desired doneness.) and choose a shake reminder. Air fry for 15 minutes, or until the sausage is cooked, stirring halfway through the cooking time to break up the sausage. Add the cheese and half-and-half; stir to combine. Air fry for 10 minutes, or until the cheese has melted. Serve with celery sticks or tortilla chips.

## Indian Seasoned Sweet Potato Fries

**Prep time: 5 minutes | Cook time: 8 minutes | Makes 20 fries**

**Seasoning Mixture:**
¾ teaspoon ground coriander
½ teaspoon garam masala
½ teaspoon garlic powder
**Fries:**
2 large sweet potatoes, peeled

½ teaspoon ground cumin
¼ teaspoon ground cayenne pepper

2 teaspoons olive oil

Preheat the air fryer to 400ºF (204ºC). In a small bowl, combine the coriander, garam masala, garlic powder, cumin, and cayenne pepper. Slice the sweet potatoes into ¼-inch-thick fries. In a large bowl, toss the sliced sweet potatoes with the olive oil and the seasoning mixture. Transfer the seasoned sweet potatoes to the air fryer basket when your air fryer displays "READY" (select the cooking preset, and make minor adjustments according to your desired doneness.) and choose a shake reminder. Air fry for 8 minutes, until crispy. Serve warm.

## Devils on Horseback

**Prep time: 5 minutes | Cook time: 7 minutes | Serves 12**

24 petite pitted prunes (4½ ounces / 128 g)
¼ cup crumbled blue cheese,

divided
8 slices center-cut bacon, cut crosswise into thirds

Preheat the air fryer to 400ºF (204ºC). Halve the prunes lengthwise, but don't cut them all the way through. Place ½ teaspoon of cheese in the center of each prune. Wrap a piece of bacon around each prune and secure the bacon with a toothpick. Working in batches, arrange a single layer of the prunes in the air fryer basket when your air fryer displays "READY" (select the cooking preset, and make minor adjustments according to your desired doneness.) and choose a shake reminder. Air fry for about 7 minutes, flipping halfway, until the bacon is cooked through and crisp. Let cool slightly and serve warm.

## Fast Roasted Asparagus

**Prep time: 5 minutes | Cook time: 6 minutes | Serves 4**

1 pound (454 g) asparagus, trimmed and halved crosswise
1 teaspoon extra-virgin olive oil

Salt and pepper, to taste
Lemon wedges, for serving

Preheat the air fryer to 400ºF (204ºC). Toss the asparagus with the oil, ⅛ teaspoon salt, and ⅛ teaspoon pepper in bowl. Transfer to air fryer basket. Place the basket in air fryer when your air fryer displays "READY" (select the cooking preset, and make minor adjustments according to your desired doneness.) and choose a shake reminder. Roast for 6 to 8 minutes, or until tender and bright green, tossing halfway through cooking. Season with salt and pepper and serve with lemon wedges.

## Air-Fried French Fries

**Prep time: 10 minutes | Cook time: 25 minutes | Serves 2**

2 russet potatoes, peeled and cut into ½-inch sticks
2 teaspoons olive oil

Salt, to taste
¼ cup ketchup, for serving

Bring a pot of salted water to a boil. Put the potato sticks into the pot and blanch for 4 minutes. Preheat the air fryer to 400ºF (204ºC). Rinse the potatoes under running cold water and pat dry with paper towels. Put the potato sticks in a large bowl and drizzle with olive oil. Toss to coat well. Transfer the potato sticks to the preheated air fryer when your air fryer displays "READY" (select the cooking preset, and make minor adjustments according to your desired doneness.) and choose a shake reminder. Air fry for 25 minutes or until crispy and golden brown. Shake the basket periodically to fry the potato sticks evenly. Sprinkle them with salt halfway through. Remove the French fries from the air fryer and serve with ketchup.

## Herb-Roasted Vegetable

**Prep time: 10 minutes | Cook time: 14 to 18 minutes | Serves 4**

1 red bell pepper, sliced
1 (8-ounce / 227-g) package sliced mushrooms
1 cup green beans, cut into 2-inch pieces
⅓ cup diced red onion
3 garlic cloves, sliced
1 teaspoon olive oil
½ teaspoon dried basil
½ teaspoon dried tarragon

Preheat the air fryer to 350ºF (177ºC). In a medium bowl, mix the red bell pepper, mushrooms, green beans, red onion, and garlic. Drizzle with the olive oil. Toss to coat. Add the herbs and toss again. Place the vegetables in the air fryer basket when your air fryer displays "READY" (select the cooking preset, and make minor adjustments according to your desired doneness.) and choose a shake reminder. Roast for 14 to 18 minutes, or until tender. Serve immediately.

## Indian Masala Omelet

**Prep time: 10 minutes | Cook time: 12 minutes | Serves 2**

4 large eggs
½ cup diced onion
½ cup diced tomato
¼ cup chopped fresh cilantro
1 jalapeño, deseeded and finely
chopped
½ teaspoon ground turmeric
½ teaspoon kosher salt
½ teaspoon cayenne pepper
Olive oil, for greasing the pan

Preheat the air fryer to 250ºF (121ºC). Generously grease a 3-cup Bundt pan. In a large bowl, beat the eggs. Stir in the onion, tomato, cilantro, jalapeño, turmeric, salt, and cayenne. Pour the egg mixture into the prepared pan. Place the pan in the air fryer basket when your air fryer displays "READY" (select the cooking preset, and make minor adjustments according to your desired doneness.) and choose a shake reminder. Bake for 12 minutes, or until the eggs are cooked through. Carefully unmold and cut the omelet into four pieces. Serve immediately.

## Brown Rice and Carrot Fritters

**Prep time: 10 minutes | Cook time: 8 to 10 minutes | Serves 4**

1 (10-ounce / 284-g) bag frozen cooked brown rice, thawed
1 egg
3 tablespoons brown rice flour
⅓ cup finely grated carrots
⅓ cup minced red bell pepper
2 tablespoons minced fresh basil
3 tablespoons grated Parmesan cheese
2 teaspoons olive oil

Preheat the air fryer to 380ºF (193ºC). In a small bowl, combine the thawed rice, egg, and flour and mix to blend. Stir in the carrots, bell pepper, basil, and Parmesan cheese. Form the mixture into 8 fritters and drizzle with the olive oil. Put the fritters carefully into the air fryer basket when your air fryer displays "READY" (select the cooking preset, and make minor adjustments according to your desired doneness.) and choose a shake reminder. Air fry for 8 to 10 minutes, or until the fritters are golden brown and cooked through. Serve immediately.

## Tangy Rosemary Roasted Chickpeas

**Prep time: 5 minutes | Cook time: 10 to 12 minutes | Makes 4 cups**

4 cups cooked chickpeas
2 tablespoons vegetable oil
1 teaspoon kosher salt
1 teaspoon cumin
1 teaspoon paprika
Zest of 1 orange
1 tablespoon chopped fresh rosemary

Preheat the air fryer to 400ºF (204ºC). Make sure the chickpeas are completely dry prior to roasting. In a medium bowl, toss the chickpeas with oil, salt, cumin, and paprika. Working in batches, spread the chickpeas in a single layer in the air fryer basket when your air fryer displays "READY" (select the cooking preset, and make minor adjustments according to your desired doneness.) and choose a shake reminder. Air fry for 10 to 12 minutes until crisp, shaking once halfway through. Return the warm chickpeas to the bowl and toss with the orange zest and rosemary. Allow to cool completely. Serve.

## Scalloped Vegetables Mix

**Prep time: 10 minutes | Cook time: 15 minutes | Serves 4**

1 Yukon Gold potato, thinly sliced
1 small sweet potato, peeled and thinly sliced
1 medium carrot, thinly sliced
¼ cup minced onion
3 garlic cloves, minced
¾ cup 2 percent milk
2 tablespoons cornstarch
½ teaspoon dried thyme

Preheat the air fryer to 380ºF (193ºC). In a baking pan, layer the potato, sweet potato, carrot, onion, and garlic. In a small bowl, whisk the milk, cornstarch, and thyme until blended. Pour the milk mixture evenly over the vegetables in the pan when your air fryer displays "READY" (select the cooking preset, and make minor adjustments according to your desired doneness.) and choose a shake reminder. Bake for 15 minutes. Check the casserole—it should be golden brown on top, and the vegetables should be tender. Serve immediately.

## Delicious Croutons

**Prep time: 5 minutes | Cook time: 8 minutes | Serves 4**

2 slices friendly bread
1 tablespoon olive oil
Hot soup, for serving

Preheat the air fryer to 390ºF (199ºC). Cut the slices of bread into medium-size chunks. Brush the air fryer basket with the oil. Place the chunks inside when your air fryer displays "READY" (select the cooking preset, and make minor adjustments according to your desired doneness.) and choose a shake reminder. Air fry for at least 8 minutes. Serve with hot soup.

## Pea Delight Baked

**Prep time: 5 minutes | Cook time: 15 minutes | Serves 2 to 4**

1 cup flour
1 teaspoon baking powder
3 eggs
1 cup coconut milk
1 cup cream cheese

3 tablespoons pea protein
½ cup chicken or turkey strips
Pinch of sea salt
1 cup Mozzarella cheese

Preheat the air fryer to 390ºF (199ºC). In a large bowl, mix all ingredients together using a large wooden spoon. Spoon equal amounts of the mixture into muffin cups. Arrange the muffin cups to the air fryer when your air fryer displays "READY" (select the cooking preset, and make minor adjustments according to your desired doneness.) and choose a shake reminder. Bake for 15 minutes. Serve immediately.

## Buttery Sweet Potato Soufflé

**Prep time: 10 minutes | Cook time: 30 minutes | Serves 4**

1 sweet potato, baked and mashed
2 tablespoons unsalted butter, divided

1 large egg, separated
¼ cup whole milk
½ teaspoon kosher salt

Preheat the air fryer to 330ºF (166ºC). In a medium bowl, combine the sweet potato, 1 tablespoon of melted butter, egg yolk, milk, and salt. Set aside. In a separate medium bowl, whisk the egg white until stiff peaks form. Using a spatula, gently fold the egg white into the sweet potato mixture. Coat the inside of four 3-inch ramekins with the remaining 1 tablespoon of butter, then fill each ramekin halfway full. Place 2 ramekins in the air fryer basket when your air fryer displays "READY" (select the cooking preset, and make minor adjustments according to your desired doneness.) and choose a shake reminder. Bake for 15 minutes. Repeat this process with the remaining ramekins. Remove the ramekins from the air fryer and allow to cool on a wire rack for 10 minutes before serving

## Garlicky Spinach and Carrot Balls

**Prep time: 10 minutes | Cook time: 10 minutes | Serves 4**

2 slices toasted bread
1 carrot, peeled and grated
1 package fresh spinach, blanched and chopped
½ onion, chopped
1 egg, beaten

½ teaspoon garlic powder
1 teaspoon minced garlic
1 teaspoon salt
½ teaspoon black pepper
1 tablespoon nutritional yeast
1 tablespoon flour

Preheat the air fryer to 390ºF (199ºC). In a food processor, pulse the toasted bread to form bread crumbs. Transfer into a shallow dish or bowl. In a bowl, mix together all the other ingredients. Use your hands to shape the mixture into small-sized balls. Roll the balls in the bread crumbs, ensuring to cover them well. Put in the air fryer basket when your air fryer displays "READY" (select the cooking preset, and make minor adjustments according to your desired doneness.) and choose a shake reminder. Air fry for 10 minutes.
Serve immediately.

## Carrot and Sweet Corn Fritters

**Prep time: 10 minutes | Cook time: 8 to 11 minutes | Serves 4**

1 medium-sized carrot, grated
1 yellow onion, finely chopped
4 ounces (113 g) canned sweet corn kernels, drained
1 teaspoon sea salt flakes
1 tablespoon chopped fresh cilantro

1 medium-sized egg, whisked
2 tablespoons plain milk
1 cup grated Parmesan cheese
¼ cup flour
⅓ teaspoon baking powder
⅓ teaspoon sugar
Cooking spray

Preheat the air fryer to 350ºF (177ºC). Place the grated carrot in a colander and press down to squeeze out any excess moisture. Dry it with a paper towel. Combine the carrots with the remaining ingredients. Mold 1 tablespoon of the mixture into a ball and press it down with your hand or a spoon to flatten it. Repeat until the rest of the mixture is used up. Spritz the balls with cooking spray. Arrange in the air fryer basket, taking care not to overlap any balls when your air fryer displays "READY" (select the cooking preset, and make minor adjustments according to your desired doneness.) and choose a shake reminder. Bake for 8 to 11 minutes, or until they're firm. Serve warm.

# Chapter 14 Casseroles, Frittatas, and Quiches

## Breakfast Cheddar Scramble Casserole
**Prep time: 10 minutes | Cook time: 13 minutes | Serves 4**

6 slices bacon
6 eggs
Salt, to taste
Pepper, to taste
Cooking oil
½ cup chopped red bell pepper

½ cup chopped green bell pepper
½ cup chopped onion
¾ cup shredded Cheddar cheese

In a skillet over medium-high heat, cook the bacon, 5 to 7 minutes, flipping to evenly crisp. Drain on paper towels, crumble, and set aside. In a medium bowl, whisk the eggs. Add salt and pepper to taste. Spray a barrel pan with cooking oil. Make sure to cover the bottom and sides of the pan. Add the beaten eggs, crumbled bacon, red bell pepper, green bell pepper, and onion to the pan. Place the pan in the air fryer. When your air fryer displays "READY" (select the cooking preset, and make minor adjustments according to your desired doneness.) and choose a shake reminder. Cook for 6 minutes. Open the air fryer and sprinkle the cheese over the casserole. Cook for an additional 2 minutes. Cool before serving.

## Cheddar Sausage and Cauliflower Casserole
**Prep time: 5 minutes | Cook time: 45 minutes | Serves 4**

1 pound (454 g) sausage, cooked and crumbled
2 cups heavy whipping cream
1 head cauliflower, chopped
1 cup grated Cheddar cheese,

plus more for topping
8 eggs, beaten
Salt and ground black pepper, to taste

Preheat the air fryer to 350ºF (177ºC). In a large bowl, mix the sausage, heavy whipping cream, chopped cauliflower, cheese and eggs. Sprinkle with salt and ground black pepper. Pour the mixture into a greased casserole dish. When your air fryer displays "READY" (select the cooking preset, and make minor adjustments according to your desired doneness.) and choose a shake reminder. Bake in the preheated air fryer for 45 minutes or until firm. Top with more Cheddar cheese and serve.

## Asparagus and Goat Cheese Frittata
**Prep time: 10 minutes | Cook time: 25 minutes | Serves 2 to 4**

1 cup asparagus spears, cut into 1-inch pieces
1 teaspoon vegetable oil
6 eggs
1 tablespoon milk

2 ounces (57 g) goat cheese
1 tablespoon minced chives (optional)
Kosher salt and pepper, to taste

Toss the asparagus pieces with the vegetable oil in a small bowl. Place the asparagus in a 7-inch round air fryer cake pan insert and place the pan in the air fryer. When your air fryer displays "READY" (select the cooking preset, and make minor adjustments according to your desired doneness.) and choose a shake reminder. Cook at 400ºF (204ºC) for 5 minutes until the asparagus is softened and slightly wrinkled. Remove the pan. Whisk together the eggs and milk and pour the mixture over the asparagus in the pan. Crumble the goat cheese over the top of the eggs and add the chives, if using. Season with a pinch of salt and pepper. Return the pan to the air fryer and bake at 320ºF (160ºC) for 20 minutes, until the eggs are set and cooked through. Serve immediately.

## Greek Vegetable Frittata
**Prep time: 10 minutes | Cook time: 17 minutes | Serves 4**

5 eggs
1 cup baby spinach
½ cup grape tomatoes, halved
½ cup Feta cheese, crumbled

10 Kalamata olives, sliced
Salt and black pepper, to taste
2 tablespoons fresh parsley, chopped

Preheat air fryer to 360ºF (182ºC). Beat the eggs, salt, and pepper in a bowl, combining well before adding the spinach and stirring until all is mixed. Pour half the mixture into a greased baking pan. On top of the mixture, add half of the tomatoes, olives, and Feta. Cover the pan with foil, making sure to close it tightly around the edges, then place the pan in the air fryer. When your air fryer displays "READY" (select the cooking preset, and make minor adjustments according to your desired doneness.) and choose a shake reminder. Cook for 12 minutes. Remove the foil and cook for an additional 5 to 7 minutes, until the eggs are fully cooked. Place the finished frittata on a serving plate and repeat the above instructions for the remainder of the ingredients. Decorate with parsley and cut into wedges. Serve hot or at room temperature.

## Spanish Chorizo and Corn Frittata
**Prep time: 10 minutes | Cook time: 12 minutes | Serves 2**

4 eggs
1 large potato, boiled and cubed
½ cup sweet corn
½ cup Feta cheese, crumbled

1 tablespoon parsley, chopped
1 chorizo sausage, sliced
2 tablespoons olive oil
Salt and black pepper, to taste

Preheat air fryer to 330ºF (166ºC). Heat olive oil in a skillet over medium heat and cook the chorizo until slightly browned, about 4 minutes; set aside. In a bowl, beat the eggs with salt and black pepper. Stir in all of the remaining ingredients, except for the parsley. Grease a baking pan that fits your air fryer with the chorizo fat and pour in the egg mixture. Insert into the air fryer when your air fryer displays "READY" (select the cooking preset, and make minor adjustments according to your desired doneness.) and choose a shake reminder. Bake for 8 to 10 minutes until golden. Serve topped with parsley. Enjoy!

## Mediterranean Cheesy Quiche
**Prep time: 10 minutes | Cook time: 30 minutes | Serves 2**

4 eggs
½ cup tomatoes, chopped
1 cup Feta cheese, crumbled
½ tablespoon fresh basil, chopped
½ tablespoon fresh oregano,

chopped
¼ cup Kalamata olives, sliced
¼ cup onions, chopped
½ cup milk
Salt and black pepper, to taste

Preheat air fryer to 340ºF (171ºC). Beat the eggs along with the milk, salt, and pepper. Stir in all the remaining ingredients. Pour the egg mixture into a greased baking pan that fits in your air fryer and place in the fryer. When your air fryer displays "READY" (select the cooking preset, and make minor adjustments according to your desired doneness.) and choose a shake reminder. Bake for 30 minutes or until lightly golden. Serve warm with a green salad.

## Rice, Shrimp, and Baby Spinach Frittata

**Prep time: 15 minutes | Cook time: 14 to 18 minutes | Serves 4**

4 eggs
Pinch salt
½ cup cooked rice
½ cup chopped cooked shrimp
½ cup baby spinach
½ cup grated Monterey Jack or Cojack cheese
Nonstick cooking spray

Preheat the air fryer to 320ºF (160ºC). Spritz a baking pan with nonstick cooking spray. Whisk the eggs and salt in a small bowl until frothy. Place the cooked rice, shrimp, and baby spinach in the baking pan when your air fryer displays "READY" (select the cooking preset, and make minor adjustments according to your desired doneness.) and choose a shake reminder. Pour in the whisked eggs and scatter the cheese on top. Bake in the preheated air fryer for 14 to 18 minutes, or until the frittata is golden and puffy. Let the frittata cool for 5 minutes before slicing to serve.

## Ricotta Butternut Squash-Sage Frittata

**Prep time: 10 minutes | Cook time: 13 minutes | Serves 2**

1 cup cubed (½-inch) butternut squash
2 tablespoons olive oil
Kosher salt and freshly ground black pepper, to taste
4 fresh sage leaves, thinly sliced
6 large eggs, lightly beaten
½ cup Ricotta cheese
Cayenne pepper, for garnish

Preheat the air fryer to 400ºF (204ºC). In a bowl, toss the squash with the olive oil and season with salt and black pepper until evenly coated. Sprinkle the sage on the bottom of a 7-inch round cake pan insert, metal cake pan, or foil pan and place the squash on top. Place the pan in the air fryer when your air fryer displays "READY" (select the cooking preset, and make minor adjustments according to your desired doneness.) and choose a shake reminder. Cook at 400ºF (204ºC) for 10 minutes. Stir to incorporate the sage, then cook until the squash is tender and lightly caramelized at the edges, about 3 minutes more. Pour the eggs over the squash, dollop the ricotta all over, and sprinkle with cayenne. Cook at 300ºF (149ºC) until the eggs are set and the frittata is golden brown on top, about 20 minutes. Remove the pan from the air fryer and cut the frittata into wedges to serve.

## Lush Sherry Seafood Casserole

**Prep time: 8 minutes | Cook time: 22 minutes | Serves 2**

1 tablespoon olive oil
1 small yellow onion, chopped
2 garlic cloves, minced
4 ounces (113 g) tilapia pieces
4 ounces (113 g) rockfish pieces
½ teaspoon dried basil
Salt and ground white pepper, to taste
4 eggs, lightly beaten
1 tablespoon dry sherry
4 tablespoons cheese, shredded

Preheat the air fryer to 360ºF (182ºC). Heat the olive oil in a nonstick skillet over medium-high heat until shimmering. Add the onion and garlic and sauté for 2 minutes or until fragrant. Add the tilapia, rockfish, basil, salt, and white pepper to the skillet. Sauté to combine well and transfer them on a baking pan. Combine the eggs, sherry and cheese in a large bowl. Stir to mix well. Pour the mixture in the baking pan over the fish mixture. Place the baking pan in the preheated air fryer when your air fryer displays "READY" (select the cooking preset, and make minor adjustments according to your desired doneness.) and choose a shake reminder. Bake for 20 minutes or until the eggs are set and the edges are lightly browned. Serve immediately.

## Salmon, Spinach, and Brown Rice Frittata

**Prep time: 10 minutes | Cook time: 15 minutes | Serves 4**

Olive oil, for greasing the pan
1 egg
4 egg whites
½ teaspoon dried thyme
½ cup cooked brown rice
½ cup cooked, flaked salmon
½ cup fresh baby spinach
¼ cup chopped red bell pepper
1 tablespoon grated Parmesan cheese

Rub a 6-by-2-inch pan with a bit of olive oil and set aside. In a small bowl, beat the egg, egg whites, and thyme until well mixed. In the prepared pan, stir together the brown rice, salmon, spinach, and red bell pepper. Pour the egg mixture over the rice mixture and sprinkle with the Parmesan cheese. Bake for about 15 minutes, or until the frittata is puffed and golden brown. Serve.

## Breakfast Sausage and Cheddar Cheese Quiche

**Prep time: 5 minutes | Cook time: 25 minutes | Serves 4**

12 large eggs
1 cup heavy cream
Salt and black pepper, to taste
12 ounces (340 g) sugar-free
breakfast sausage
2 cups shredded Cheddar cheese
Cooking spray

Preheat the air fryer to 375ºF (191ºC). Coat a casserole dish with cooking spray. Beat together the eggs, heavy cream, salt and pepper in a large bowl until creamy. Stir in the breakfast sausage and Cheddar cheese. Pour the sausage mixture into the prepared casserole dish when your air fryer displays "READY" (select the cooking preset, and make minor adjustments according to your desired doneness.) and choose a shake reminder. Bake for 25 minutes, or until the top of the quiche is golden brown and the eggs are set. Remove from the air fryer and let sit for 5 to 10 minutes before serving.

## Keto Cheese Quiche Baked

**Prep time: 20 minutes | Cook time: 1 hour | Serves 8**

**Crust:**
1¼ cups blanched almond flour
1 large egg, beaten
1¼ cups grated Parmesan
**Filling:**
4 ounces (113 g) cream cheese
1 cup shredded Swiss cheese
⅓ cup minced leeks
4 large eggs, beaten
½ cup chicken broth
⅛ teaspoon cayenne pepper
cheese
¼ teaspoon fine sea salt
¾ teaspoon fine sea salt
1 tablespoon unsalted butter, melted
Chopped green onions, for garnish
Cooking spray

Preheat the air fryer to 325ºF (163ºC). Spritz a pie pan basket with cooking spray. Combine the flour, egg, Parmesan, and salt in a large bowl. Stir to mix until a satiny and firm dough forms. Arrange the dough between two grease parchment papers, then roll the dough into a ¹⁄₁₆ -inch thick circle. Make the crust: Transfer the dough into the prepared pie pan and press to coat the bottom, then arrange the pie pan in the preheated air fryer when your air fryer displays "READY" (select the cooking preset, and make minor adjustments according to your desired doneness.) and choose a shake reminder. Bake for 12 minutes or until the edges of the crust are lightly browned. Meanwhile, combine the ingredient for the filling, except for the green onions in a large bowl. Pour the filling over the cooked crust and cover the edges of the crust with aluminum foil. Bake for 15 more minutes, then reduce the heat to 300ºF (149ºC) and bake for another 30 minutes or until a toothpick inserted in the center comes out clean. Remove the pie pan from the air fryer and allow to cool for 10 minutes before serving.

## Cheddar Bacon Quiche

**Prep time: 15 minutes | Cook time: 20 minutes | Serves 4**

1 tablespoon olive oil
1 shortcrust pastry
3 tablespoons Greek yogurt
½ cup grated Cheddar cheese
3 ounces (85 g) chopped bacon
4 eggs, beaten
¼ teaspoon garlic powder
Pinch of black pepper
¼ teaspoon onion powder
¼ teaspoon sea salt
Flour, for sprinkling

Preheat the air fryer to 330ºF (166ºC). Take 8 ramekins and grease with olive oil. Coat with a sprinkling of flour, tapping to remove any excess. Cut the shortcrust pastry in 8 and place each piece at the bottom of each ramekin. Put all the other ingredients in a bowl and combine well. Spoon equal amounts of the filling into each piece of pastry. When your air fryer displays "READY" (select the cooking preset, and make minor adjustments according to your desired doneness.) and choose a shake reminder. Bake the ramekins in the air fryer for 20 minutes. Serve warm.

## Curry Chicken and Mushroom Casserole

**Prep time: 15 minutes | Cook time: 20 minutes | Serves 4**

4 chicken breasts
1 tablespoon curry powder
1 cup coconut milk
Salt, to taste
1 broccoli, cut into florets
1 cup mushrooms
½ cup shredded Parmesan cheese
Cooking spray

Preheat the air fryer to 350ºF (177ºC). Spritz a casserole dish with cooking spray. Cube the chicken breasts and combine with curry powder and coconut milk in a bowl. Season with salt. Add the broccoli and mushroom and mix well. Pour the mixture into the casserole dish. Top with the cheese. Transfer to the air fryer when your air fryer displays "READY" (select the cooking preset, and make minor adjustments according to your desired doneness.) and choose a shake reminder. Bake for about 20 minutes. Serve warm.

## Chicken Breast and Vegetable Casserole

**Prep time: 15 minutes | Cook time: 15 minutes | Serves 4**

4 boneless and skinless chicken breasts, cut into cubes
2 carrots, sliced
1 yellow bell pepper, cut into strips
1 red bell pepper, cut into strips
**Sauce:**
1 teaspoon Sriracha
3 tablespoons soy sauce
2 tablespoons oyster sauce
1 tablespoon rice wine vinegar
1 teaspoon cornstarch
15 ounces (425 g) broccoli florets
1 cup snow peas
1 scallion, sliced
Cooking spray

1 tablespoon grated ginger
2 garlic cloves, minced
1 teaspoon sesame oil
1 tablespoon brown sugar

Preheat the air fryer to 370ºF (188ºC). Spritz a baking pan with cooking spray. Combine the chicken, carrot, and bell peppers in a large bowl. Stir to mix well. Combine the ingredients for the sauce in a separate bowl. Stir to mix well. Pour the chicken mixture into the baking pan, then pour the sauce over when your air fryer displays "READY" (select the cooking preset, and make minor adjustments according to your desired doneness.) and choose a shake reminder. Stir to coat well. Bake in the preheated air fryer for 5 minutes, then add the broccoli and snow peas to the pan and cook for 8 more minutes or until the vegetables are tender. Remove the casserole from the air fryer and sprinkle with sliced scallion before serving.

## Creamy Parmesan Tomato Casserole

**Prep time: 5 minutes | Cook time: 30 minutes | Serves 4**

5 eggs
2 tablespoons heavy cream
3 tablespoons chunky tomato
sauce
2 tablespoons grated Parmesan cheese, plus more for topping

Preheat the air fryer to 350ºF (177ºC). Combine the eggs and cream in a bowl. Mix in the tomato sauce and add the cheese. Spread into a glass baking dish when your air fryer displays "READY" (select the cooking preset, and make minor adjustments according to your desired doneness.) and choose a shake reminder. Bake in the preheated air fryer for 30 minutes. Top with extra cheese and serve.

## Mini Sausage Quiche Cups

**Prep time: 15 minutes | Cook time: 16 minutes | Makes 10 quiche cups**

4 ounces (113 g) ground pork sausage
3 eggs
¾ cup milk
Cooking spray
4 ounces (113 g) sharp Cheddar cheese, grated

**Special Equipment:**
20 foil muffin cups

Preheat the air fryer to 390ºF (199ºC). Spritz the air fryer basket with cooking spray. Divide sausage into 3 portions and shape each into a thin patty. Put patties in air fryer basket when your air fryer displays "READY" (select the cooking preset, and make minor adjustments according to your desired doneness.) and choose a shake reminder. Air fry for 6 minutes. While sausage is cooking, prepare the egg mixture. Combine the eggs and milk in a large bowl and whisk until well blended. Set aside. When sausage has cooked fully, remove patties from the basket, drain well, and use a fork to crumble the meat into small pieces. Double the foil cups into 10 sets. Remove paper liners from the top muffin cups and spray the foil cups lightly with cooking spray. Divide crumbled sausage among the 10 muffin cup sets. Top each with grated cheese, divided evenly among the cups. Put 5 cups in air fryer basket. Pour egg mixture into each cup, filling until each cup is at least ⅔ full. Bake for 8 minutes and test for doneness. A knife inserted into the center shouldn't have any raw egg on it when removed. Repeat steps 8 through 11 for the remaining quiches. Serve warm.

## Feta Kale Frittata

**Prep time: 5 minutes | Cook time: 11 minutes | Serves 2**

1 cup kale, chopped
1 teaspoon olive oil
4 large eggs, beaten
Kosher salt, to taste
2 tablespoons water
3 tablespoons crumbled Feta
Cooking spray

Preheat the air fryer to 360ºF (182ºC). Spritz an air fryer baking pan with cooking spray. Add the kale to the baking pan and drizzle with olive oil. Arrange the pan in the preheated air fryer when your air fryer displays "READY" (select the cooking preset, and make minor adjustments according to your desired doneness.) and choose a shake reminder. Broil for 3 minutes. Meanwhile, combine the eggs with salt and water in a large bowl. Stir to mix well. Make the frittata: When the broiling time is complete, pour the eggs into the baking pan and spread with feta cheese. Reduce the temperature to 300ºF (149ºC). Bake for 8 minutes or until the eggs are set and the cheese melts. Remove the baking pan from the air fryer and serve the frittata immediately.

## Mediterranean Olives Quiche

**Prep time: 10 minutes | Cook time: 30 minutes | Serves 4**

4 eggs
¼ cup chopped Kalamata olives
½ cup chopped tomatoes
¼ cup chopped onion
½ cup milk
1 cup crumbled Feta cheese

½ tablespoon chopped oregano
½ tablespoon chopped basil
Salt and ground black pepper, to taste
Cooking spray

Preheat air fryer to 340ºF (171ºC). Spritz a baking pan with cooking spray. Whisk the eggs with remaining ingredients in a large bowl. Stir to mix well. Pour the mixture into the prepared baking pan, then place the pan in the preheated air fryer when your air fryer displays "READY" (select the cooking preset, and make minor adjustments according to your desired doneness.) and choose a shake reminder. Bake for 30 minutes or until the eggs are set and a toothpick inserted in the center comes out clean. Check the doneness of the quiche during the last 10 minutes of baking. Serve immediately.

## Pastrami Cheese Casserole

**Prep time: 10 minutes | Cook time: 8 minutes | Serves 2**

1 cup pastrami, sliced
1 bell pepper, chopped
¼ cup Greek yogurt
2 spring onions, chopped
½ cup Cheddar cheese, grated

4 eggs
¼ teaspoon ground black pepper
Sea salt, to taste
Cooking spray

Preheat the air fryer to 330ºF (166ºC). Spritz a baking pan with cooking spray. Whisk together all the ingredients in a large bowl. Stir to mix well. Pour the mixture into the baking pan. Place the baking pan in the preheated air fryer when your air fryer displays "READY" (select the cooking preset, and make minor adjustments according to your desired doneness.) and choose a shake reminder. Bake for 8 minutes or until the eggs are set and the edges are lightly browned. Check the doneness during the last 2 minutes of the baking. Remove the baking pan from the air fryer and allow to cool for 10 minutes before serving.

## Cheddar Sausage and Colorful Peppers Casserole

**Prep time: 15 minutes | Cook time: 25 minutes | Serves 6**

1 pound (454 g) minced breakfast sausage
1 yellow pepper, diced
1 red pepper, diced
1 green pepper, diced
1 sweet onion, diced

2 cups Cheddar cheese, shredded
6 eggs
Salt and freshly ground black pepper, to taste
Fresh parsley, for garnish

Cook the sausage in a nonstick skillet over medium heat for 10 minutes or until well browned. Stir constantly. Preheat the air fryer to 360ºF (182ºC). When the cooking is finished, transfer the cooked sausage to a baking pan and add the peppers and onion. Scatter with Cheddar cheese. Whisk the eggs with salt and ground black pepper in a large bowl, then pour the mixture into the baking pan. Arrange the pan in the preheated air fryer when your air fryer displays "READY" (select the cooking preset, and make minor adjustments according to your desired doneness.) and choose a shake reminder. Bake for 15 minutes or until the egg is set and the edges are lightly browned. Remove the baking pan from the air fryer and top with fresh parsley before serving.

## Riced Cauliflower-Okra Casserole

**Prep time: 8 minutes | Cook time: 12 minutes | Serves 4**

1 head cauliflower, cut into florets
1 cup okra, chopped
1 yellow bell pepper, chopped
2 eggs, beaten

½ cup chopped onion
1 tablespoon soy sauce
2 tablespoons olive oil
Salt and ground black pepper, to taste

Preheat air fryer to 380ºF (193ºC). Spritz a baking pan with cooking spray. Put the cauliflower in a food processor and pulse to rice the cauliflower. Pour the cauliflower rice in the baking pan and add the remaining ingredients. Stir to mix well. Arrange the baking pan in the preheated air fryer when your air fryer displays "READY" (select the cooking preset, and make minor adjustments according to your desired doneness.) and choose a shake reminder. Bake for 12 minutes or until the eggs are set. Remove the baking pan from the air fryer and serve immediately.

## Turkey, Pimento, and Almond Casserole

**Prep time: 5 minutes | Cook time: 32 minutes | Serves 4**

1 pound (454 g) turkey breasts
1 tablespoon olive oil
2 boiled eggs, chopped
2 tablespoons chopped pimentos
¼ cup slivered almonds, chopped
¼ cup mayonnaise

½ cup diced celery
2 tablespoons chopped green onion
¼ cup cream of chicken soup
¼ cup breadcrumbs
Salt and ground black pepper, to taste

Preheat air fryer to 390ºF (199ºC). Put the turkey breasts in a large bowl. Sprinkle with salt and ground black pepper and drizzle with olive oil. Toss to coat well. Transfer the turkey in the preheated air fryer when your air fryer displays "READY" (select the cooking preset, and make minor adjustments according to your desired doneness.) and choose a shake reminder. Air fry for 12 minutes or until well browned. Flip the turkey halfway through. Remove the turkey breasts from the air fryer and cut into cubes, then combine the chicken cubes with eggs, pimentos, almonds, mayo, celery, green onions, and chicken soup in a large bowl. Stir to mix. Pour the mixture into a baking pan, then spread with breadcrumbs. Arrange the pan in the preheated air fryer. Bake for 20 minutes or until the eggs are set. Remove the baking pan from the air fryer and serve immediately.

## Shrimp and Baby Spinach Frittata

**Prep time: 6 minutes | Cook time: 14 minutes | Serves 4**

4 whole eggs
1 teaspoon dried basil
½ cup shrimp, cooked and chopped
½ cup baby spinach

½ cup rice, cooked
½ cup Monterey Jack cheese, grated
Salt, to taste
Cooking spray

Preheat the air fryer to 360ºF (182ºC). Spritz a baking pan with cooking spray. Whisk the eggs with basil and salt in a large bowl until bubbly, then mix in the shrimp, spinach, rice, and cheese. Pour the mixture into the baking pan, then place the pan in the preheated air fryer when your air fryer displays "READY" (select the cooking preset, and make minor adjustments according to your desired doneness.) and choose a shake reminder. Bake for 14 minutes or until the eggs are set and the frittata is golden brown. Slice to serve.

## Trout and Crème Fraiche Frittata

**Prep time: 8 minutes | Cook time: 17 minutes | Serves 4**

2 tablespoons olive oil
1 onion, sliced
1 egg, beaten
½ tablespoon horseradish sauce
6 tablespoons crème fraiche
1 cup diced smoked trout
2 tablespoons chopped fresh dill
Cooking spray

Preheat the air fryer to 350ºF (177ºC). Spritz a baking pan with cooking spray. Heat the olive oil in a nonstick skillet over medium heat until shimmering. Add the onion and sauté for 3 minutes or until translucent. Combine the egg, horseradish sauce, and crème fraiche in a large bowl. Stir to mix well, then mix in the sautéed onion, smoked trout, and dill. Pour the mixture in the prepared baking pan, then set the pan in the preheated air fryer when your air fryer displays "READY" (select the cooking preset, and make minor adjustments according to your desired doneness.) and choose a shake reminder. Bake for 14 minutes or until the egg is set and the edges are lightly browned. Serve immediately.

## Spinach, Tomato, and Chickpea Casserole

**Prep time: 10 minutes | Cook time: 21 to 22 minutes | Serves 4**

2 tablespoons olive oil
2 garlic cloves, minced
1 tablespoon ginger, minced
1 onion, chopped
1 chili pepper, minced
Salt and ground black pepper,
to taste
1 pound (454 g) spinach
1 can coconut milk
½ cup dried tomatoes, chopped
1 (14-ounce / 397-g) can chickpeas, drained

Preheat the air fryer to 370ºF (188ºC). Heat the olive oil in a saucepan over medium heat. Sauté the garlic and ginger in the olive oil for 1 minute, or until fragrant. Add the onion, chili pepper, salt and pepper to the saucepan. Sauté for 3 minutes. Mix in the spinach and sauté for 3 to 4 minutes or until the vegetables become soft. Remove from heat. Pour the vegetable mixture into a baking pan. Stir in coconut milk, dried tomatoes and chickpeas until well blended. Put the baking pan in the air fryer when your air fryer displays "READY" (select the cooking preset, and make minor adjustments according to your desired doneness.) and choose a shake reminder. Bake for 15 minutes, stirring constantly to ensure even cooking. Transfer to a serving dish. Let cool for 5 minutes before serving.

## Taco Beef and Green Chile Casserole

**Prep time: 10 minutes | Cook time: 15 minutes | Serves 4**

1 pound (454 g) 85% lean ground beef
1 tablespoon taco seasoning
1 (7-ounce / 198-g) can diced mild green chiles
½ cup milk
2 large eggs
1 cup shredded Mexican cheese blend
2 tablespoons all-purpose flour
½ teaspoon kosher salt
Cooking spray

Preheat the air fryer to 350ºF (177ºC). Spritz a baking pan with cooking spray. Toss the ground beef with taco seasoning in a large bowl to mix well. Pour the seasoned ground beef in the prepared baking pan. Combing the remaining ingredients in a medium bowl. Whisk to mix well, then pour the mixture over the ground beef. Arrange the pan in the air fryer when your air fryer displays "READY" (select the cooking preset, and make minor adjustments according to your desired doneness.) and choose a shake reminder. Bake for 15 minutes or until a toothpick inserted in the center comes out clean. Remove the casserole from the air fryer and allow to cool for 5 minutes, then slice to serve.

## Beef and Cannellini Bean Chili Casserole

**Prep time: 15 minutes | Cook time: 31 minutes | Serves 4**

1 tablespoon olive oil
½ cup finely chopped bell pepper
½ cup chopped celery
1 onion, chopped
2 garlic cloves, minced
1 pound (454 g) ground beef
1 can diced tomatoes
½ teaspoon parsley
½ tablespoon chili powder
1 teaspoon chopped cilantro
1½ cups vegetable broth
1 (8-ounce / 227-g) can cannellini beans
Salt and ground black pepper, to taste

Preheat the air fryer to 350ºF (177ºC). Heat the olive oil in a nonstick skillet over medium heat until shimmering. Add the bell pepper, celery, onion, and garlic to the skillet and sauté for 5 minutes or until the onion is translucent. Add the ground beef and sauté for an additional 6 minutes or until lightly browned. Mix in the tomatoes, parsley, chili powder, cilantro and vegetable broth, then cook for 10 more minutes. Stir constantly. Pour them in a baking pan, then mix in the beans and sprinkle with salt and ground black pepper. Transfer the pan in the preheated air fryer when your air fryer displays "READY" (select the cooking preset, and make minor adjustments according to your desired doneness.) and choose a shake reminder. Bake for 10 minutes or until the vegetables are tender and the beef is well browned. Remove the baking pan from the air fryer and serve immediately.

## Lush Vegetable Frittata

**Prep time: 15 minutes | Cook time: 20 minutes | Serves 2**

4 eggs
⅓ cup milk
2 teaspoons olive oil
1 large zucchini, sliced
2 asparagus, sliced thinly
⅓ cup sliced mushrooms
1 cup baby spinach
1 small red onion, sliced
⅓ cup crumbled Feta cheese
⅓ cup grated Cheddar cheese
¼ cup chopped chives
Salt and ground black pepper, to taste

Preheat the air fryer to 380ºF (193ºC). Line a baking pan basket with parchment paper. Whisk together the eggs, milk, salt, and ground black pepper in a large bowl. Set aside. Heat the olive oil in a nonstick skillet over medium heat until shimmering. Add the zucchini, asparagus, mushrooms, spinach, and onion to the skillet and sauté for 5 minutes or until tender. Pour the sautéed vegetables into the prepared baking pan, then spread the egg mixture over and scatter with cheeses. Place the baking pan in the preheated air fryer when your air fryer displays "READY" (select the cooking preset, and make minor adjustments according to your desired doneness.) and choose a shake reminder. Bake for 15 minutes or until the eggs are set the edges are lightly browned. Remove the frittata from the air fryer and sprinkle with chives before serving.

# Appendix 1 Measurement Conversion Chart

## VOLUME EQUIVALENTS(DRY)

| US STANDARD | METRIC (APPROXIMATE) |
|---|---|
| 1/8 teaspoon | 0.5 mL |
| 1/4 teaspoon | 1 mL |
| 1/2 teaspoon | 2 mL |
| 3/4 teaspoon | 4 mL |
| 1 teaspoon | 5 mL |
| 1 tablespoon | 15 mL |
| 1/4 cup | 59 mL |
| 1/2 cup | 118 mL |
| 3/4 cup | 177 mL |
| 1 cup | 235 mL |
| 2 cups | 475 mL |
| 3 cups | 700 mL |
| 4 cups | 1 L |

## VOLUME EQUIVALENTS(LIQUID)

| US STANDARD | US STANDARD (OUNCES) | METRIC (APPROXIMATE) |
|---|---|---|
| 2 tablespoons | 1 fl.oz. | 30 mL |
| 1/4 cup | 2 fl.oz. | 60 mL |
| 1/2 cup | 4 fl.oz. | 120 mL |
| 1 cup | 8 fl.oz. | 240 mL |
| 1 1/2 cup | 12 fl.oz. | 355 mL |
| 2 cups or 1 pint | 16 fl.oz. | 475 mL |
| 4 cups or 1 quart | 32 fl.oz. | 1 L |
| 1 gallon | 128 fl.oz. | 4 L |

## TEMPERATURES EQUIVALENTS

| FAHRENHEIT(F) | CELSIUS(C) (APPROXIMATE) |
|---|---|
| 225 °F | 107 °C |
| 250 °F | 120 °C |
| 275 °F | 135 °C |
| 300 °F | 150 °C |
| 325 °F | 160 °C |
| 350 °F | 180 °C |
| 375 °F | 190 °C |
| 400 °F | 205 °C |
| 425 °F | 220 °C |
| 450 °F | 235 °C |
| 475 °F | 245 °C |
| 500 °F | 260 °C |

## WEIGHT EQUIVALENTS

| US STANDARD | METRIC (APPROXIMATE) |
|---|---|
| 1 ounce | 28 g |
| 2 ounces | 57 g |
| 5 ounces | 142 g |
| 10 ounces | 284 g |
| 15 ounces | 425 g |
| 16 ounces (1 pound) | 455 g |
| 1.5 pounds | 680 g |
| 2 pounds | 907 g |

# Appendix 2 Air Fryer Cooking Chart

## Beef

| Item | Temp (°F) | Time (mins) | Item | Temp (°F) | Time (mins) |
|---|---|---|---|---|---|
| Beef Eye Round Roast (4 lbs.) | 400 °F | 45 to 55 | Meatballs (1-inch) | 370 °F | 7 |
| Burger Patty (4 oz.) | 370 °F | 16 to 20 | Meatballs (3-inch) | 380 °F | 10 |
| Filet Mignon (8 oz.) | 400 °F | 18 | Ribeye, bone-in (1-inch, 8 oz) | 400 °F | 10 to 15 |
| Flank Steak (1.5 lbs.) | 400 °F | 12 | Sirloin steaks (1-inch, 12 oz) | 400 °F | 9 to 14 |
| Flank Steak (2 lbs.) | 400 °F | 20 to 28 | | | |

## Chicken

| Item | Temp (°F) | Time (mins) | Item | Temp (°F) | Time (mins) |
|---|---|---|---|---|---|
| Breasts, bone in (1 ¼ lb.) | 370 °F | 25 | Legs, bone-in (1 ¾ lb.) | 380 °F | 30 |
| Breasts, boneless (4 oz) | 380 °F | 12 | Thighs, boneless (1 ½ lb.) | 380 °F | 18 to 20 |
| Drumsticks (2 ½ lb.) | 370 °F | 20 | Wings (2 lb.) | 400 °F | 12 |
| Game Hen (halved 2 lb.) | 390 °F | 20 | Whole Chicken | 360 °F | 75 |
| Thighs, bone-in (2 lb.) | 380 °F | 22 | Tenders | 360 °F | 8 to 10 |

## Pork & Lamb

| Item | Temp (°F) | Time (mins) | Item | Temp (°F) | Time (mins) |
|---|---|---|---|---|---|
| Bacon (regular) | 400 °F | 5 to 7 | Pork Tenderloin | 370 °F | 15 |
| Bacon (thick cut) | 400 °F | 6 to 10 | Sausages | 380 °F | 15 |
| Pork Loin (2 lb.) | 360 °F | 55 | Lamb Loin Chops (1-inch thick) | 400 °F | 8 to 12 |
| Pork Chops, bone in (1-inch, 6.5 oz) | 400 °F | 12 | Rack of Lamb (1.5 – 2 lb.) | 380 °F | 22 |

## Fish & Seafood

| Item | Temp (°F) | Time (mins) | Item | Temp (°F) | Time (mins) |
|---|---|---|---|---|---|
| Calamari (8 oz) | 400 °F | 4 | Tuna Steak | 400 °F | 7 to 10 |
| Fish Fillet (1-inch, 8 oz) | 400 °F | 10 | Scallops | 400 °F | 5 to 7 |
| Salmon, fillet (6 oz) | 380 °F | 12 | Shrimp | 400 °F | 5 |
| Swordfish steak | 400 °F | 10 | | | |

| Vegetables | | | | | |
|---|---|---|---|---|---|
| INGREDIENT | AMOUNT | PREPARATION | OIL | TEMP | COOK TIME |
| **Asparagus** | 2 bunches | Cut in half, trim stems | 2 Tbsp | 420°F | 12-15 mins |
| **Beets** | 1½ lbs | Peel, cut in ½-inch cubes | 1Tbsp | 390°F | 28-30 mins |
| **Bell peppers (for roasting)** | 4 peppers | Cut in quarters, remove seeds | 1Tbsp | 400°F | 15-20 mins |
| **Broccoli** | 1 large head | Cut in 1-2-inch florets | 1Tbsp | 400°F | 15-20 mins |
| **Brussels sprouts** | 1lb | Cut in half, remove stems | 1Tbsp | 425°F | 15-20 mins |
| **Carrots** | 1lb | Peel, cut in ¼-inch rounds | 1 Tbsp | 425°F | 10-15 mins |
| **Cauliflower** | 1 head | Cut in 1-2-inch florets | 2 Tbsp | 400°F | 20-22 mins |
| **Corn on the cob** | 7 ears | Whole ears, remove husks | 1 Tbps | 400°F | 14-17 mins |
| **Green beans** | 1 bag (12 oz) | Trim | 1 Tbps | 420°F | 18-20 mins |
| **Kale (for chips)** | 4 oz | Tear into pieces,remove stems | None | 325°F | 5-8 mins |
| **Mushrooms** | 16 oz | Rinse, slice thinly | 1 Tbps | 390°F | 25-30 mins |
| **Potatoes, russet** | 1½ lbs | Cut in 1-inch wedges | 1 Tbps | 390°F | 25-30 mins |
| **Potatoes, russet** | 1lb | Hand-cut fries, soak 30 mins in cold water, then pat dry | ½ -3 Tbps | 400°F | 25-28 mins |
| **Potatoes, sweet** | 1lb | Hand-cut fries, soak 30 mins in cold water, then pat dry | 1 Tbps | 400°F | 25-28 mins |
| **Zucchini** | 1lb | Cut in eighths lengthwise, then cut in half | 1 Tbps | 400°F | 15-20 mins |

# Appendix 3 Index